Dreamweaver MX/ Fireworks MX

Dreamweaver® MX/ Fireworks® MX

CHRISTIAN CRUMLISH

SAN FRANCISCO | LONDON

SYBEX®

Associate Publisher: DAN BRODNITZ
Acquisitions and Developmental Editor: WILLEM KNIBBE
Editor: REBECCA RIDER
Production Editor: LIZ BURKE
Technical Editor: SCOTT ONSTOTT
Production Manager: AMY CHANGAR
Cover and Interior Designer: CARYL GORSKA
Technical Illustrator: CARYL GORSKA
Icon Illustrator: TINA HEALEY ILLUSTRATIONS
Compositors: MAUREEN FORYS, KATE KAMINSKI, HAPPENSTANCE TYPE-O-RAMA
Proofreaders: EMILY HSUAN, DAVE NASH, LAURIE O'CONNELL, NANCY RIDDIOUGH, NELSON KIM
Indexer: TED LAUX
CD Coordinator: DAN MUMMERT
CD Technician: KEVIN LY
Cover Photographer: MONTY FRESCO, HULTON ARCHIVE

Dear Reader,

Thank you for choosing *Dreamweaver MX / Fireworks MX Savvy*. This book is part of a new line of Sybex web publishing and graphics books that features beautiful designs, great quality throughout, and above all, outstanding authors who really know their stuff. Christian Crumlish and a team of experts deliver one of the most comprehensive and truly useful Dreamweaver books ever published, continuing the trend for top-notch quality established with our *Flash MX Savvy* and *Photoshop 7 Savvy* books.

With each book, we're working hard to set a new standard, both for the industry and for ourselves. From the quality of the contents to the paper it's printed on, from the cover to the interior design, our goal is to publish the best graphics and Web design books available.

I hope you see all that reflected in this book. I'd be very interested in hearing your feedback on how we're doing. To let us know what you think about *Dreamweaver MX / Fireworks MX Savvy*, please visit us at www.sybex.com. Once there, go to the book's page, click Submit a Review, and fill out the questionnaire. Your input is greatly appreciated.

Best regards,

Daniel A. Brodnitz
Associate Publisher
Sybex Inc.

Software License Agreement: Terms and Conditions

About the Authors

Born in a log cabin on the Missouri river… no wait, wrong bio. Born and raised on the mean streets of New York City, Christian Crumlish matriculated at the school of hard knocks (OK, and Princeton) and has since pursued a number of exciting career options, including typist, gopher, editor, and small-business owner. Since the early '90s Christian has been writing about technology, music, popular culture, and the media. He co-founded a webzine, *Enterzone*, in 1994, and a web-solutions consultancy in 1996. He has registered far too many domain names, most of which will probably never see the light of day. Christian has packaged books and e-books, consulted on matters of information architecture and content-management strategy with Fortune 500 companies, represented other authors as a literary agent, and written nearly 20 books on technology, the Internet, and web development. He maintains the website for this book at `http://dreamweaversavvy.com/`.

Christian is the lead author of *Dreamweaver MX/Fireworks MX Savvy* and he recruited the other writers (collectively known as the "Dream Team") to contribute their specialized expertise and help make this book as well-rounded and packed with useful information as possible.

The Dream Team

The writers who've contributed to this book all have a great deal of experience with Dreamweaver and/or Fireworks and the Web, as well as hands-on experience and thriving training or consulting practices. As the lead author, Christian tried to maintain a consistent voice throughout the book, not to smother the individual voices of the contributors, but to make the experience for you, the reader, as seamless as possible. Some of the chapters were written outright by the contributor while others contain incorporated examples, suggestions, or sections prepared by the contributors.

Joyce J. Evans Joyce J. Evans has over 10 years of experience in educational teaching, tutorial development, and web design. For additional tutorials and updated information, visit `http://www.JoyceJEvans.com`. She has received Editors Choice Awards for her *Fireworks 4 f/x & Design* book (Coriolis Group, 2001), and has authored numerous graphic design titles including *Dreamweaver MX Complete Course* (Hungry Minds, Inc., 2002). She has also contributed to several books, such as *Dreamweaver MX Magic* (New Riders Publishing,

2002), *Fireworks MX Magic* (New Riders Publishing, 2002), and *Dreamweaver 4: The Complete Reference* (Osborne McGraw-Hill, 2001). Joyce actively writes reviews and articles for several graphic design magazines.

Lucinda Dykes Lucinda Dykes has been writing code and developing websites since 1994, and she teaches web-related classes at Santa Fe Community College in Santa Fe, New Mexico. Her students claim her most-used phrase is "Show me the code!" She is the coauthor of *XML Schemas* (Sybex, 2002) and *Mastering XHTML* (Sybex, 2002).

Heather Williamson Heather Williamson manages a small Internet and Web Design consulting firm in northeast Oregon, where she uses Dreamweaver and Fireworks every day in the process of completing her client's requests. She has written numerous books on Internet technology, and she was the compilation editor for *XHTML Complete* (Sybex, 2002).

Greg Holden Greg Holden has written about Dreamweaver and other web software in the course of producing 16 books on computer- and Internet-related subjects. He's also the author of *Literary Chicago: A Book Lover's Tour of the Windy City* (`http://www.literarychicago.com`), which includes walking and driving tours of the city where he lives with his two daughters and an assortment of fish.

Guy Rish Guy Rish is an independent consultant specializing in Web technologies and object-oriented design. He holds instructor certifications from Rational Software and Macromedia and has taught both in corporate and academic settings. Guy has recently contributed work to books from Sybex and New Riders on ColdFusion MX, Flash MX, and Dreamweaver MX.

Michele Davis Michele Davis is a technical consultant for companies implementing new documentation for `.pdf` manuals, websites, marketing brochures, training, and online help. She is savvy in Oracle, Retek, as well as numerous other applications, and she has written and coauthored several trade publications and works of fiction. She can be found on the Web at `http://www.krautgrrl.com`.

Rita Lewis Rita helped me develop the original outline for this book and helped with some early drafts of the chapters in Part I. Rita's website is `http://lewiswrite.com/`.

Rick Tracewell Rick writes an excellent Dreamweaver column for *Mac Design Magazine* and helped with the development of Chapters 13 and 18.

Acknowledgments

Writing a book this long, this detailed, and this timely is a labor of many hands and minds. I'd like to try to thank and acknowledge the contributions of those who helped in many different ways. If I have forgotten to mention any names, please forgive me.

First, I have to thank Briggs Nisbet for her forbearance during a very difficult and challenging writing schedule. Without her love and support, none of this would have been possible.

Next, I would like to acknowledge the work of Macromedia's developers, especially those involved in running the beta test, which was a model of how you'd like beta tests to work. I'm not allowed to go into much detail about that, but I think it's safe to say that they endeavored mightily to address and accommodate the assiduous suggestions made by the dedicated (sometimes to the point of being fanatic) beta testers.

I'd like to thank Jacques Vigeant of Enterpulse, whose timely loan of a mostly functioning Dell enabled me to test the Windows version of Dreamweaver MX and capture the lion's share of the screenshots in this book.

This book would not have been at all possible in its present form without the contributions of my "Dream Team" of other writers who stepped in to cover some of the more specialized and tricky features of web development for me, enabling me to put together a better book than I could have done by myself, and on a shorter timeline. Please see the introduction for a full listing about each writer's contribution.

I'd also like to thank contributors to the book's CD, namely Alien Skin, Rabi S. Raj, David G. Miles, and Nathan Pitman. For more information about these contributors please see the Introduction.

Richard Frankel and Scot Hacker are always available to me with advice and suggestions, and I've benefited from their greater experience countless times. Thanks, guys!

Since I am not myself a graphic designer, no matter how hard I try, I'd like to thank Sarah Murgel, Josh Rose, and Dan Shearer, who've taught me a lot about how to read and understand design, and how to solve problems with design. I'd recommend their work to anybody.

I'd like to thank people on the Antiweb mailing list who encouraged me and who are always ready with advice when web conundra present themselves. Speaking of mailing lists, I'd also like to thank the Merry Punsters who helped keep my spirits up when the hours were ticking by faster than the pages. Similarly, I'd like to thank the members of the Web

For Smee

conference on the Well, whose lively debates informed a number of the insights I've passed off here in this book as my own!

People I don't know personally but whose work and ideas have inspired me include Jeffrey Zeldman and Eric Costello.

At Sybex, I'd like to thank Associate Publisher Dan Brodnitz and Acquisitions and Developmental Editor Willem Knibbe, who convinced me to do this book. Willem's developmental editing evoked a much better book from me than I had any right to produce. Production Editor Liz Burke handled a nearly impossible schedule with aplomb, juggling like mad and still somehow keeping the trains running (mostly) on time. Copyeditor Rebecca Rider read each line with an attentive eye, posing well informed queries and bringing about a degree of consistency I find unattainable on my own. Scott Onstott, the technical editor for this book, gently corrected my wildly unsustainable assertions and added real gold from time to time where additional nuance was welcome. Caryl Gorska created the beautiful book design. Rarely does an author of technical books get to see his or her work looking this good in print. Maureen Forys and Kate Kaminski of Happenstance Type-O-Rama did the actual page makeup, which is tricky in a design as complicated and yet elegant as this book's—I appreciate their skillful work. A lot of other people at Sybex helped on this project without interacting with me directly, and I'd like to acknowledge their contributions (most are listed on the copyright page) as well. Thank you all!

I'd like to thank my agent, Danielle Jatlow of Waterside Productions, Inc., for dealing with the paperwork, and Maureen Maloney, also of Waterside, for processing my checks so efficiently.

I learned a lot doing web consulting with the now defunct Groundswell. The Groundswell 'hogs went through a lot together, in the trenches of the dotcom boom-and-bust, and I know I'll be working with people I met there on and off for the rest of my life. Before Groundswell, I knew how to throw together a one-person site, but from my colleagues there, I learned how to collaborate on large-scale production-ready sites. It was quite thrilling. Thanks also to clients at Sprint, Visa USA, Executive Greetings, and All Charities, whose real-world projects gave me all kinds of work to sink my teeth into. Similarly, I'd like to thank the people I've worked with at Enterpulse (another consultancy) which has survived the worst part of the crash and will probably be around for a long time. Lastly, I'd like to thank the people at Open Publishing, for supporting all of my writing work.

CONTENTS AT A GLANCE

Introduction ■ **xxvii**

PART I ■ **PLANNING YOUR PROJECT AND SETTING UP DREAMWEAVER 1**

Chapter 1 ■ Planning and Preparing for a Web Project 3

Chapter 2 ■ Web Pages Deconstructed 11

Chapter 3 ■ Setting Up Your Workspace and Your Site 21

Chapter 4 ■ Saving Labor with Templates and Libraries 45

PART II ■ **USING FIREWORKS 67**

Chapter 5 ■ Getting into Fireworks 69

Chapter 6 ■ Adding Strokes, Fills, and Live Effects 85

Chapter 7 ■ Working With Vectors 121

Chapter 8 ■ Working with Bitmaps 147

Chapter 9 ■ Designing Navigation Objects 171

Chapter 10 ■ Slicing, Optimizing, and Exporting Images 189

PART III ■ **BUILDING A WEB PAGE 225**

Chapter 11 ■ Page Layout with Tables and Layers 227

Chapter 12 ■ Inserting and Formatting Text Content 251

Chapter 13 ■ Working with Graphics 275

Chapter 14 ■ Interactivity with Framesets and Frames 285

Chapter 15 ■ Cascading Style Sheets 307

Chapter 16 ■ Making and Maintaining Hyperlinks 319

PART IV ■ **INSERTING DYNAMIC CONTENT 335**

Chapter 17 ■ Adding Multimedia 337

Chapter 18 ■ Rollovers, Navigation Bars, and Jump Menus 355

Chapter 19 ■ Behavioral Science 369

Chapter 20 ■ Going Interactive with Forms 399

Chapter 21 ■ Building an E-Commerce Site 421

PART V ■ **DEVELOPING WEB APPLICATIONS 439**

Chapter 22 ■ Building Web Applications 441

Chapter 23 ■ Handcrafting Your Code 447

Chapter 24 ■ Database Connectivity 465

Chapter 25 ■ Working with ColdFusion 493

Chapter 26 ■ Working with XML and XHTML 509

Chapter 27 ■ Working with Emerging Technologies—Web Services and .NET 531

PART VI ■ **SITE ADMINISTRATION FROM START TO FINISH 543**

Chapter 28 ■ Setting Up Administration Behind a Site 545

Chapter 29 ■ Checking Browser Compatibility 557

Chapter 30 ■ Going Live or Delivering the Site 567

Chapter 31 ■ Administering the Site 575

Chapter 32 ■ Customizing and Extending Dreamweaver 593

PART VII ■ **APPENDICES 619**

Appendix A ■ Online Resources 621

Appendix B ■ Dreamweaver MX Keyboard Shortcuts 625

Index ■ **633**

Contents

Introduction   xxvii

PART I ▪ PLANNING YOUR PROJECT AND SETTING UP DREAMWEAVER   **1**

Chapter 1 ▪ Planning and Preparing for a Web Project   **3**

When to Use Dreamweaver and Fireworks   4

Getting Your Process Squared Away   5

Gathering Requirements   6

Getting the Information Architecture Right   7

Ready, Set, Rumble!   10

Chapter 2 ▪ Web Pages Deconstructed   **11**

The Elements of a Web Page   12

Working with Content   13

Designing for the Web   14

Setting Up a Navigation Scheme   18

The Whole Enchilada   20

Chapter 3 ▪ Setting Up Your Workspace and Your Site   **21**

The Integrated Workspace versus the Floating Layout   22

Getting Oriented   25

Customizing Your Workspace   36

Setting Up Your Site   38

Importing an Existing Site   43

Turning On Accessibility Reminders   44

Look-and-Feel Standards   44

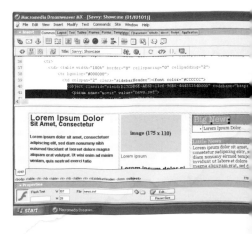

Chapter 4 ■ **Saving Labor with Templates
and Libraries**   **45**

What Is a Template?   46

Fitting Templates into Your
Development Process   48

Making Templates   48

Configuring a Template   52

Applying a Template   56

Modifying Template-Based Pages   58

Using Your Old Dreamweaver 4 Templates   59

Managing Your Other Assets   59

Building a Library   62

Using Server Side Includes (SSIs) as
Repeating Elements   65

Taking a Jump Backward   66

PART II ■ **USING FIREWORKS**   **67**

Chapter 5 ■ **Getting into Fireworks**   **69**

Workspace Overview   70

The Fireworks Menu Bar and Toolbars   71

A Look at Fireworks Panels   77

Working with Layers   79

Setting Preferences   81

Hands On: Setting Up a Document and
Importing an Image   82

Stroke, Fill, or Enliven…   84

Chapter 6 ■ **Adding Strokes, Fills, and
Live Effects**   **85**

Adding Strokes   86

Adding Fills   96

Filling with Patterns and Textures   97

Adding Borders to Bitmap Images   99

Using Gradient Fills   100

Adding Live Effects   103

Web Dithering   107

Customizing the Swatches Panel   109

Fireworks MX Commands   110

Hands On: Batch Processing   116

From Effects to Vectors   119

Chapter 7 ■ Working With Vectors   **121**

Vector Tools   122

Using Vector Shape Tools   122

Becoming Familiar with Drawing Tools   126

Editing Vectors   127

Reshaping Paths Using Path Operations   133

Miscellaneous Actions   135

Transformations   136

Using the Crop Tool   137

Aligning Objects   137

Working with the Text Tool   138

Hands On: Making a Navigational Element   143

From Vectors to Pixel Power   145

Chapter 8 ■ Working with Bitmaps   **147**

Understanding Bitmaps   148

Working with Selection Tools   149

Working with the Select Menu   151

Touch-Up Tools   153

Using the Rubber Stamp Tool   156

Masking Images   157

The Filters Menu   163

Hands On: Using a Third Party Plugin   166

Putting It All Together   169

Chapter 9 ■ Designing Navigation Objects   **171**

Using Symbols, Instances, and Libraries   172

Using the Button Editor   174

Adding Rollover Behaviors   177

Making Image Maps   181

Pop-Up Menus   181

Exporting the Pop-Up Menu   185

Hands On: Making a Nav Bar   185

Opt for Speed   187

**Chapter 10 ■ Slicing, Optimizing, and
Exporting Images**   **189**

Slicing a Web Page Layout or an Image   190

Slice Options   193

Image File Formats for the Web   196

Optimization Methods   198

Optimizing for GIF Compression   200

Optimizing Options for JPEG Compression   206

Optimizing a JPEG Image   208

Selective JPEG Compression   209

Exporting with Fireworks   211

Hands On: Slicing, Optimizing, and
Exporting a Web Page   221

From Pictures to Pages   224

PART III ■ BUILDING A WEB PAGE   **225**

**Chapter 11 ■ Page Layout with
Tables and Layers**   **227**

Selecting a Predesigned Layout   228

Creating a New Table   231

Finessing Table Properties   234

Designing in Layers   240

Finessing Layer Variables   242

Working with Complex Page Layouts   244

Hands On: Design a Page with Tables
   and Layers   247

Filling the News Hole   249

**Chapter 12 ■ Inserting and Formatting
Text Content**   **251**

Getting Copy onto the Page   252

Editing Text   259

Formatting Text   262

Working with Raw HTML   270

Layout, Words, … Pictures!   273

Chapter 13 ■ Working with Graphics   **275**

Inserting a Graphic   276

Designing with Image Placeholders
   (When the Art Isn't Ready Yet)   281

Modifying a Graphic Using Fireworks   282

Can You Imagine?   284

**Chapter 14 ■ Interactivity with Framesets
and Frames**   **285**

Creating a New Frameset   286

Modifying Frames and Framesets   295

Adding Navigation Elements to Frames   299

Creating NoFrames Content   301

Hands On: Design a Frames-Based Page   302

One Holy Grail   306

Chapter 15 ■ Cascading Style Sheets   **307**

Why Use Style Sheets?   308

What to Use Style Sheets For   308

How Styles Are Applied   309

Types of Style Sheets   310

For Further Reading on CSS   310

CSS Tools in Dreamweaver 311

Working with Styles 312

Working with Style Sheets 315

Previewing Styled Pages 317

Get Hip to Hyper 318

**Chapter 16 ■ Making and Maintaining
Hyperlinks** **319**

Some Fundamental Concepts About Links 320

Inserting Links 322

Building Image Maps 327

Avoiding or Fixing Broken Links 329

Put the Multi in Multimedia 332

PART IV ■ INSERTING DYNAMIC CONTENT **335**

Chapter 17 ■ Adding Multimedia **337**

Deciding to Include Multimedia 338

Understanding Web Audio and Video Formats 339

Using Multimedia Players 340

Adding Sound and Movies 341

Adding Media Elements 346

Using Dreamweaver Behaviors to Control
Media Elements 351

Hands On: Launching and Editing Flash MX
Files from Dreamweaver MX 352

To Add Multimedia or Not to
Add Multimedia… 354

**Chapter 18 ■ Rollovers, Navigation Bars,
and Jump Menus** **355**

Gathering Your Graphic Assets 356

Making a Rollover 356

Making a Navigation Bar 357

Using Dreamweaver's Flash Buttons
(and When Not To) 358

Making a Jump Menu 362

Keeping It Simple 368

Chapter 19 ■ Behavioral Science **369**

Introducing Dreamweaver's Built-in
Behaviors 370

Using Behaviors with Layers and Timelines 390

Using Flash Objects 393

Hands On: Creating an Animation
Using Layers, Timelines, and Behaviors 396

That's All, Folks! 398

Chapter 20 ■ Going Interactive with Forms **399**

Exploring Form Elements 400

Enhancing Forms with Hidden Tags 410

Implementing Jump Menus 411

Working with CGI Scripts 412

Editing a CGI Script 415

Creating Target Pages 416

Hands On: Build a Search Form 417

From Forms to Transactions 419

Chapter 21 ■ Building an E-Commerce Site **421**

Creating an Identity for an Online Store 422

Marketing Your Site 426

Processing Transactions 428

Hands On: Create a Shopping Cart 435

Putting the e- In Everything 437

PART V ■ DEVELOPING WEB APPLICATIONS **439**

Chapter 22 ■ Building Web Applications **441**

Designing and Testing Web Applications 442

Choosing a Supported Server Model 442

Setting Up Your Web Server 442

Setting Up Your Application Server   443

Setting Up Your Web Application as a
    Dreamweaver Site   443

Connecting to the Database   446

Delving into the Code   446

Chapter 23 ■ Handcrafting Your Code   **447**

The Ergonomics of Coding   448

Writing Code   454

Debugging Your Code   460

Coding an Application   463

Chapter 24 ■ Database Connectivity   **465**

The Basics of Dreamweaver MX   466

The Birthing of a Dynamic Page   466

Defining a Data Source   470

Dreamweaver MX Window Components   473

Adding Dynamic Content to Your Page   474

Defining a Search and Result Page Set   476

Designing Your Database Schema   478

Exploring SQL   480

Manipulating Database Records   484

Navigating Recordsets   487

Troubleshooting   489

Hands On: Rapid Development of a
    Master Detail Page Set   490

Dynamic Sites with ColdFusion   492

Chapter 25 ■ Working with ColdFusion   **493**

Important Features for ColdFusion Developers 494

Setting Up a Dreamweaver Site for ColdFusion 496

Connecting to ColdFusion Data Sources   496

Setting Up Bindings   498

Using Server Behaviors   499

Continuing Work   507

To the Bleeding Edge   508

Chapter 26 ■ Working with XML and XHTML   509

XML Concepts   510

Importing and Exporting XML with
  XML Templates   514

Third-Party Tags: Creating Custom
  Tags Using XML   517

Supporting XHTML in Dreamweaver   520

Validating XML and XHTML Documents   522

XML Behind the Scenes: Dreamweaver Menus   523

Hands On: Modifying Your
  Dreamweaver Menus   525

Why Should You Care About XML?   529

**Chapter 27 ■ Working with Emerging
              Technologies—Web
              Services and .NET   531**

Understanding Web Services   532

Accessing Web Services   532

Adding a Web Service to a Page   534

Understanding .NET   537

Using ASP.NET   538

Emerging Technologies   541

**PART VI ■ SITE ADMINISTRATION FROM
           START TO FINISH   543**

**Chapter 28 ■ Setting Up Administration
              Behind a Site   545**

Developing User Administration   546

Login Pages and Processes   550

Page Access Restriction   552

Developing a Portal   553

Testing, 1, 2 …   556

Personal

The Personal W
publish your per
right from your

Dreamweaver MX

Chapter 29 ■ **Checking Browser Compatibility**   **557**

Defining the Target Audience   558

Evaluating Browsers   558

Testing Browser Compatibility in Dreamweaver   559

Avoiding Common Problems   564

Getting Ready to Launch   566

Chapter 30 ■ **Going Live or Delivering the Site**   **567**

Quality Assurance and Final Testing   568

Meeting Section 508 Accessibility Standards   569

From Staging to Production   570

Turnover (At Last!)   571

Teach Them to Fish: Knowledge Transfer   574

The Long Haul   574

Chapter 31 ■ **Administering the Site**   **575**

Managing Content   576

Workflow   582

Journaling and Rollback   585

Hands On: Updating an Existing Website   589

Extend Your Reach   592

Chapter 32 ■ **Customizing and Extending Dreamweaver**   **593**

Using the Extension Manager   594

Creating Custom Shortcut Keys   600

Changing the Default Document Template   602

Creating Dreamweaver Commands   603

Creating Custom Menus   605

Adding Objects to the Insert Bar   610

Updating Dreamweaver Dialog Boxes   612

Hands On 1: Using the Advanced Random Images Extension   614

Hands On 2: Add Custom Characters
    to the Insert Bar   616

Ready, Set, Go!   618

PART VII ▪ APPENDICES   **619**

Appendix A ▪ Online Resources   **621**

Starting Points   622

Dreamweaver Software   622

Tutorials and Instruction   623

Newsgroups and Mailing Lists   624

Appendix B ▪ Dreamweaver MX
                     Keyboard Shortcuts   **625**

Index   633

Introduction

In the old days, we made websites by typing one tag at a time, uphill both ways, in the snow, against the wind. You've heard this story before haven't you? Well, we've come a long way baby, and Macromedia's Dreamweaver MX and Fireworks MX now make the process of developing robust, production-ready websites almost easy. This is a book by and for professionals working in any of the fields now affected by the Web, which is to say, the entire global economy. You can work your way through this book from Chapter 1 to Chapter 32, or you might find it more productive to jump around, especially if you are already experienced with web development, or with earlier versions of Dreamweaver or Fireworks.

Who Needs This Book

Most early users of Dreamweaver (and Fireworks) were designers. Interactive designers, perhaps, but still graphic or visual designers trained at art schools and used to working in the agency model (based on the structure of advertising agencies). Today, designers are one of many different job types and backgrounds involved in the development of sites. To get the benefits of working with Dreamweaver, you don't necessarily have to be a designer (although it helps). Other specialties that might make up a collaborative team that could use Dreamweaver and Fireworks as a common development environment include the following:

- Graphic designers
- Information architects
- Database architects
- Interface designers
- Usability experts
- Developers
- Coders
- Producers

- Project managers
- Artists
- Writers
- Managers
- Agencies
- Consultancies
- Website owners
- Students

All should get something of value from this book.

Conventions Used in This Book

In a technical book such as this one, we try to make it as easy as possible for you to pick out the information you need. (Even our parents don't read these books from cover to cover.) To help you find your way through the book as effectively as possible, we've incorporated a number of design elements to call out material that may (or may not) be of interest to you.

New features in Dreamweaver or Fireworks MX are marked with this margin icon.

References to the book's website are singled out with this icon. We didn't use this one too often, but we hope you will visit the site (`http://dreamweaversavvy.com`). We think you'll find it a useful complement to the book and a valuable resource as you learn Dreamweaver and Fireworks.

References to the accompanying CD are indicated with this margin icon.

In addition, many procedures are broken down into numbered steps, and many chapters also include tutorials that enable you to try out what you've learned with a specific project.

> Tips, comments, and warnings that are not necessarily part of the procedural flow are called out as Notes.

SIDEBARS

Occasionally, interesting bits of information that may not be essential to your understanding of Dreamweaver or Fireworks will be boxed as standalone sidebars, like so. These are usually much longer than notes and you can feel free to skip over them if you are in a hurry to get to the next paragraph.

Because there are many different ways of working on the Web and you may not need to make use of every possible feature of Dreamweaver, you should feel free to skip around from chapter to chapter as necessary. To minimize redundancy and pack as much fresh information as possible into this book, we've liberally included cross-references throughout to suggest when you might profit from looking at another chapter.

How This Book Is Organized

This book has six parts composed of 32 chapters and one appendix. Here's a quick rundown of what you'll find inside:

Part I ■ Planning Your Project and Setting Up Dreamweaver

This part is all about getting your project started and your site set up to optimize the development process. Chapter 1 covers what to do before you even take Dreamweaver out of the box, including the essentials of website planning and preparation. Chapter 2 breaks down web pages into their component parts, based on how Dreamweaver works with HTML files and other web documents. Chapter 3 shows you how to get the Dreamweaver workspace set up for efficiency and comfort, and how to set up a website for the first time. Chapter 4 explains how to use sitewide components—templates, assets, and library items—to save effort and maintain consistency.

Part II ■ Using Fireworks

This part is all about helping you get your graphical design work done with Fireworks. Chapter 5 gets you started with Fireworks. Chapter 6 covers the elements of a Fireworks file (strokes, fills, and live effects). Chapters 7 and 8 cover vector and bitmap images and tools; Fireworks enables you to use both types of effects together. Chapter 9 shows you how to design menu bars and other navigation objects. Chapter 10 explains how to prepare images for exporting into Dreamweaver by cutting them into slices (when necessary) and how to optimize them for rapid download. (Joyce J. Evans handled this entire part.)

Part III ■ Building a Web Page

This part is the heart of the matter: how to assemble the essential elements needed to construct a web page. Chapter 11 covers layout with tables or layers. Chapter 12 is all about working with text. Chapter 13 shows you how to apply what you learned in Part II by adding graphics to your pages in Dreamweaver. Chapter 14 explains how to set up framesets and work with frames. Chapter 15 discusses how to use Dreamweaver's CSS 2.0 (Cascading Style Sheets) features to develop cutting-edge standards-compliant designs. Chapter 16 covers how to insert local and external hyperlinks into your pages. (Greg Holden did the heavy lifting for Chapters 11 and 14.)

Part IV ▪ **Inserting Dynamic Content**

This part takes you a step beyond flat, static web pages and shows you how to add movement and interactivity to your pages. Chapter 17 discusses adding multimedia objects to your pages. Chapter 18 shows you how to incorporate "rollovers," dynamic navigation bars, and jump menus. Chapter 19 introduces Dreamweaver's behaviors—pre-made JavaScript routines you can add to your pages without learning how to code. Chapter 20 covers everything you need to know about web forms. Chapter 21 is a little bonus that walks you through developing an e-commerce site. (Lucinda Dykes handled Chapters 17 and 19, Michele Davis contributed to Chapter 18, Heather Williamson put together Chapter 20, and Greg Holden wrote Chapter 21.)

Part V ▪ **Developing Web Applications**

This part takes you into the world of dynamic, database-backed websites, also known as web applications. At this point, you are developing software that happens to run over web protocols. Chapter 22 gets you started setting up web applications with Dreamweaver. Chapter 23 helps you customize your coding environment. Chapter 24 is a crash course in database development for the Web. Chapter 25 shows you how to use Dreamweaver with ColdFusion sites. Chapters 26 and 27 get you up to speed with some of the most recently emerged web standards: using XML, XHTML, .NET, and the concept of web services in general. (Michele Davis did Chapter 24, Guy Rish pinch-hit for Chapter 25, and Lucinda Dykes stepped in to handle Chapters 26 and 27.)

Part VI ▪ **Site Administration from Start to Finish**

This part is about wrapping up your development project and handing over a site that doesn't just look cool but actually works! Chapter 28 explains how to set up administration modules for managing a new site. Chapter 29 shows how to verify browser compatibility before going live. Chapter 30 discusses the issues involved with launching a site or turning it over to a client. Chapter 31 covers maintaining a site long after the hoopla of opening day has passed. And Chapter 32 is a bonus, explaining how to customize and extend Dreamweaver to get the maximum use out of it as your primary web development tool. (Michele Davis put together Chapter 28, Lucinda Dykes handled Chapter 29, Greg Holden composed Chapter 31, and Heather Williamson took care of Chapter 32.)

Appendices ▪ **Web Resources**

The Appendix includes a set of useful Dreamweaver resources that are available on the Web. We'll update this information and add to it from time to time at the book's website (see "Visit

Our Website," later in this introduction). Appendix B includes a comprehensive list of keyboard shortcuts for Dreamweaver MX.

Note to Macintosh (and PC) Users

I wish we could have done two editions of this book, one just for Windows users and one just for Mac users. Although I work on both systems myself, out of necessity, my "home base" computer is a titanium PowerBook G4 (a "tiBook"), running OS X, and that should tell you where my aesthetic preferences lie. Unfortunately for me, the majority of users of Dreamweaver and Fireworks are, and the majority of readers of this book will turn out to be, Windows users, and so most of the illustrations in this book show either Windows XP or Windows NT screens.

Rest assured, though, this book is perfectly designed for use with a Mac. I've personally tested every command sequence on my PowerBook, and where necessary, I've included separate instructions or screen shots to illustrate when the Macintosh version of Dreamweaver looks or functions differently in some way from the PC version. As a nod to the cutting-edge nature of many Mac designers and developers, I've also done all the screen shots in Chapter 15 ("Cascading Style Sheets") on the Mac. For PC users, this chapter again is perfectly serviceable, but the minor inconvenience of viewing the look-and-feel of another OS is on the other foot this time.

About the CD

The accompanying CD includes demos, extensions, tutorial files, and example files:

Demos We've included demo versions of the MX Studio programs, including Dreamweaver MX, Fireworks MX, Flash MX, and ColdFusion MX, so that you can try out any of the programs you don't currently own. We've also included Alien Skin's Splat! Demo, which is referred to in Part II. An all-new, user-requested, Photoshop filter set, Splat! delivers frames, textures, edges, borders, mosaics, and more in Eye Candy's easy-to-use interface. Add impact to your images with Splat!

Extensions As a bonus, we've included some extensions for both Dreamweaver and Fireworks. Chapter 32 explains how to install extensions. In most of these cases, we've also included links to the developers' websites, so that you can find updated and additional new extensions online.

Extension contributors include

Rabi S. Raj (`http://www.dreamweaver-extensions.com`), David G. Miles, (`http://www.z3roadster.net`), and Nathan Pitman (`http://www.dovelop.com`).

Rabi Raj says, "I created all these extensions during my free time at home. My intention is to help creative people who do not have programming background and web designers who want to save time on routine coding."

David Miles is a web developer based in the United Kingdom. In addition to a passion for web application development and for Dreamweaver, David is often found to be helping others on the Macromedia Newsgroups. In his spare time fast cars and developing his own web site are high on the list of priorities. David has produced a number of frequently downloaded and used extensions.

Four years of training in 3-dimensional design equipped Nathan Pitman for a career in new media. After diving in at the deep end with his first commercial project; the official Virgin Global Challenger web site, he's not looked back. Nathan is currently working as a Creative Developer for a UK-based agency and investing much of his spare time in developing extensions for Dreamweaver and Fireworks.

Tutorials Most of the tutorials in this book require the use of files supplied on this CD (and on the book's website). To try out a tutorial, copy the files from the appropriate chapter to a new folder on your own computer or network and then follow the steps of the tutorial.

Visit Our Website

This book has a website that can be reached at `http://dreamweaverfireworkssavvy.com/` or `http://dreamweaversavvy.com/`. (I suggested that we register both the long form and the shortened domain name, not to leave out Fireworks users but just to save us all some typing!) The site includes copies of the tutorial and example files; news and developments about Dreamweaver, Fireworks, web design, and information architecture; corrections and updates for the book; and a way to suggest improvements for the next edition.

Join the Discussion

There's a Yahoo!Groups discussion list for this book. Any reader of the book is welcome to join in on the discussion. To visit the group's web page, go to `http://groups.yahoo.com/group/dreamweaversavvy/`. (To join the list, go directly to `http://groups.yahoo.com/group/dreamweaversavvy/join/`—you'll need to set up a Yahoo! ID to participate.)

Contact the Author

To contact the author directly by e-mail, you can send me mail at `<comment@fireweaver.com>`. I will respond when possible.

## PART I

Planning Your Project and Setting Up Dreamweaver

Although it might *be more exhilarating to start designing web pages on the first day of your project, experience has taught us that a successful web development project starts with some strategy. First you want to take a step back and look at the big picture. What is your site or application going to do? Who's going to use it? How does it have to work? How should it be organized?*

Next, to make the most of Dreamweaver, take a little time to understand how the software creates, interprets, and displays web pages. Get the software set up in a way that suits your workflow, and then finally start developing your site.

Even then, before you get into the process of building actual pages, you're going to need to spend some time setting up your site in Dreamweaver, and creating the shared templates, library items, and other assets that will enable a rapid, efficient development process.

CHAPTER 1 ■ Planning and Preparing for a Web Project

CHAPTER 2 ■ Web Pages Deconstructed

CHAPTER 3 ■ Setting Up Your Workspace and Your Site

CHAPTER 4 ■ Saving Labor with Templates and Libraries

Planning and Preparing for a Web Project

Dreamweaver and Fireworks can help your project run more smoothly whether you are building a website from scratch all by yourself for yourself, collaborating with a multidisciplinary team to deliver a web application for a client, or anything in between. Regardless of the scope of your project, take some time in advance to think through the *architecture* of your site (fundamentally, its site map), develop a look-and-feel (graphic design and interface); and gather the content. When this preliminary work is done, you can plunge into the development, staging, launching, and maintenance of the site.

This chapter assists you in sorting through the elements of your preferred methodology before you get down to brass tacks with Dreamweaver and Fireworks. Topics addressed in this chapter include:

- **When to use Dreamweaver and Fireworks**

- **Nailing down your process**

- **Gathering requirements for your web project**

- **Designing the project's information architecture**

When to Use Dreamweaver and Fireworks

When we're grandparents, the little kids are going to roll their eyes whenever we start reminiscing about "the dawn of the Web" when we had to hand-code our websites. We'll say, "That's right, kids, we typed all those little angle brackets into text processors with no validation or nothing! We didn't have these fancy-schmancy what-you-see-is-what-you-get, self-correcting, self-updating, automated whatchamacallits." And they'll be right to roll their eyes. Who cares about how these things used to be done? It was ridiculous that we ever had to work that way. "Why, if we moved one page, we had to find all the links referring to that page and then manually change them. Why, one time...."

OK, there we go again. Anyway, the point is, Dreamweaver is a really cool way to keep an entire web project in the palm of your hand (or at least on the hard drive of your laptop), and Fireworks is a unique tool expressly designed for the development and optimization of web graphics. Dreamweaver goes beyond enabling you to design web pages visually—it helps you manage your entire site from the top down. Best of all, it enables a team of people to work together on the same project without accidentally munging each other's work.

> *Munging* means over-writing or otherwise erasing or corrupting an existing file. Use this around your techy-er colleagues and they'll give you a jot more respect.

If you are working with collaborators, chances are not everyone is going to do their work in Dreamweaver. That's OK. Dreamweaver produces clean code that even the most hardcore code jockey can't complain about. From the point of view of programmers and technical architects, you're working on the front end of the site, or the presentation layer (not to be confused with other kinds of layers, which we'll get to later). Sure, if you've got UltraDev, you may be delving into all kinds of database calls and scripted routines, but chances are you'll be handing off your front-end design to someone doing the back-end work somewhere along the way.

With Dreamweaver, though, you can keep your part of the project all in one place, and there's no reason not to do all of your work inside the application (at least after you're done doodling on cocktail napkins).

Fireworks is where you'll develop and refine the graphical look-and-feel for the site—the site's logo, the graphical elements, the navigational hoo-ha's, and so on. The entire site won't live inside Fireworks the way it will in Dreamweaver, but because they're both Macromedia products designed to work together, any graphics you develop or import into Fireworks will flow easily into your site templates and pages over on the Dreamweaver side.

WHEN TO USE FLASH AND SHOCKWAVE

Other web-oriented Macromedia products that play well with Dreamweaver and Fireworks include Flash and Shockwave. Both of these products are descendents of Macromedia Director, an application used to design interactive, well, applications. Chances are, last time you stuck a CD in your drive and watched a little promo or clicked on a bulbous shiny set of interface buttons, they were developed in Director. When the Web came along, Macromedia rolled out Shockwave as a way of adapting Director-like material to the vicissitudes of the Web (bandwidth limitations, mainly, as well as the nasty habit of web users who click away when you want them to sit still—something people developing for CD-ROM never had to worry about).

But Flash is every designer's favorite tool for developing interactive movies, animations, and every other kind of beast that slithers, crawls, runs, or flies across your screen. Optimized for streaming over the Web, and widely accepted as a format, Flash is the first choice when you need that level of production values, or when you want your users to be able to, say, play a video game at your website. Artists love Flash too (see http://www.snarg.net/ for a hypnotic example of what we're talking about).

And clients love Flash too, or at least they usually do when you demo the little bugger for them running on your laptop. They don't necessarily love it quite so much when users decide that the site is too slow or too Flash-y and fail to stick around to register for the great bargain or stock their shopping cart with whatever widgets your client is trying to e-commercially sell.

So, having sung the praises of Flash, let us now warn you to use it sparingly and when it is called for by the project's requirements, and not just because you finished a course on interactive design and need something "rilly kewl" for your portfolio.

Needless to say, Shockwave and Flash are sold separately, but also play well with Dreamweaver. See Chapter 20 for more on such dynamic, animatronic, interactive magic.

Getting Your Process Squared Away

Before you fire up the software and start cranking out web pages, take a step back to sort out your process (ur, methodology). Nowadays, most web design and development projects are collaborative and require a lot of coordination among team members. Yes, if you're running a one-person project or shop, you don't have to answer to anybody, you don't have to use anyone else's lingo, you don't have to adhere to anyone's deadlines, and no one is going to second-guess your work. But even then you're going to have to figure out what to do first, what part of the project depends on other parts being completed first (sometimes referred to, for short, as *dependencies*), and what your timeline and milestones are going to need to be...unless maybe you're building a website for your cat and there's no deadline.

In most situations, you've got a "someone" to answer to, whether it's your boss, your client, or simply your audience. That's right, web design requires you to anticipate and meet your audience's needs; that is, if you expect them to come to your site, use your interactive application, register with your enterprise, or come back again after the first visit. As the bard once said, "You're gonna have to serve somebody." Furthermore, in most commercial projects, you're going to have to collaborate with somebody, or with a whole team of somebodies. There might be a branding expert, a writer (perhaps called a content developer), some developers (technical architects, front-end scripters, back-end coders, middleware specialists, and so on), and possibly a project manager. Oh, yes, and a visual designer or graphic designer. But maybe that's you?

You may be working with people who cut their teeth in the field of professional services, interactive or advertising agencies, publishing, and software development. You're going to discover that everyone has a different name for the same thing (is it a *storyboard* or a *wireframe*, a *site map* or *thumbnail series*, *use cases* or *process flows*?), and most people see the project revolving around their discipline. In any collaborative project, some time—at least an hour—should be spent up front hashing out the division of labor, the dependencies (such as, "I can't develop the content inventory until you finish the site map"), the points of handoff or turnover, and the milestones and deliverables expected by the client (even if the client is just your boss).

For more ideas and discussion about various web-development methodologies (and there are a number of equally valid approaches), check out the author-created website for this book, at `http://dreamweaversavvy.com/`.

Gathering Requirements

How are you going to know what to put into your site or application unless you spend some time and effort learning the needs of your website's or application's eventual users? (Consultants call this stage of a project *discovery*—not to be confused with lawyers pawing through your files.) This discovery phase should involve interviewing representatives of every audience type or anyone else with a stake in the usefulness and success of the site. This means not just your boss or client, your client's boss or team members, and other obvious stakeholders, but also, if at all possible, some potential users of the site—often customers, partners, or vendors. Find out what they want. Your client may not always know what their users want as well as they think they do. Also, it makes a killer argument when the client has gotten attached to some horrible idea to be able to say, "But your site's users don't want that. See, here in these interview notes, they say they'd never come back if you had *that* as part of your site."

This leads to the first commandment of web design (perhaps the only commandment, we're not sure).

Know Thy Audience

What if they built a web site and nobody came? They did. And nobody did. It was called the dotcom bubble. Maybe you missed it? Just because you can sell your boss, or your client, or a venture capitalist (VC) on an idea doesn't mean that people are going to come and pay you to keep executing that idea. Understand your audience. Go meet them if possible. Interview them, but also watch them as they work. Study what they like and dislike. Learn as much as you can about usability. If your ultimate product isn't usable, guess what? People won't use it. If your site doesn't meet a need, then no one will need it. This sounds simple, but a lot of VC money went down the drain because people wearing the right shade of blue shirts who knew consultantspeak put together some really hep-looking Powerpoints and 10-page business plans with no revenue model.

OK, that's not really fair. When tulips are the rage, everybody buys tulips. But don't end up like the dotcommers taking their one-way U-Hauls back out of the San Francisco Bay Area even as we type this. Think about the needs and desires of your audience. Understand them. What are they reaching out for? How can you satisfy those needs? Get that straight and the rest of the project will practically take care of itself.

Getting the Information Architecture Right

Information architecture is a $10 word that means how your site's information is organized. What do people see first when they come in the front door? How many levels down is certain information buried? How many clicks does it take to get to crucial information? What is the structure of the navigation? Dreamweaver won't figure any of this out for you. (And Fireworks? Fuggedaboudit). Sure, once you've sorted it out, Dreamweaver is an awesome tool for maintaining the site map, navigation links, and so on. But you have to do the hard thinking first.

ENSURING THAT YOUR SITE IS ACCESSIBLE

One of the most important changes to the specifications for HTML in Version 4.0 is the inclusion of requirements that your site be accessible to people with disabilities. This means that your work can be used and appreciated by the estimated 10 percent of the world's population with some sort of physical disability that makes it difficult to access most websites. The World Wide Web Consortium (W3C) has set up a special organization and website that provides helpful checklists, guidelines, and ideas in support of the Web Accessibility Initiative (WAI). Check out http://www.w3.org/WAI/ to find out how to insert accessibility into your website relatively painlessly. Another very useful site that serves as both an example of a well designed, accessible website and as a tutorial is the Web Accessibility In Mind (WebAIM) site (http://www.webaim.org/).

Fortunately, because Dreamweaver is so flexible and easy to use, you can make mistakes when you start and still correct them later on in the project. That's right, no matter how carefully you gather your requirements, know thy audience, or massage your client, guess what? New requirements will emerge at the 11th hour. Projects you've never heard of will suddenly demand to be integrated into your pristine site map. Entire divisions will be defunded and no longer entitled to that valuable real estate on the home page. Never fear, with a few points and clicks, subsections can be promoted to top-level categories, and entire site areas can be snipped out and placed in limbo. I'd like to see a "real" architect try to rearrange a real building once the contractors are in the house!

Still, just because things are inevitably going to change, that's no excuse for not trying to get it right at first. (That's what our editor told us when we said we didn't need to do an outline for this book. "It's all going to change!" we whined. He was having none of it....) In fact, getting your architecture clarified at the beginning makes it that much easier to *track the changes* as they emerge. Think about it. It's a lot easier to see what's changed if you know what it changed from!

Also, remember those other people on the team (or your cat). They need to know where you're planning on putting stuff. They may be writing scripts and have to know what directory (a.k.a. folder) a certain piece of content is going to live in. They may need to know how many levels down their funky little application is going to be running. Sorting out the site's architecture is step one of designing any substantial web project.

Developing a Site Map (or Thumbnails, or Process Flows)

A great way to get an overview of a website at a glance is to create and maintain a site map. Ultimately, Dreamweaver can generate or show you a site-map type view of your site, but that's once you've actually created all the pages. When you're just getting started, you can literally just draw it by hand or use any illustration software to put it together. A site map looks something like a family tree (except without the male and female figures). Pages are represented as boxes and labeled. You can indicate the name of a page or—if you really want to get into it at this stage—what the page will contain. Navigational links are represented as lines between boxes. Then, like a family tree, child and sibling pages all stem from a parent page, and you can take this organization down as many levels as you like. Some people make the boxes smaller as they go down in levels. Often the third level of links is represented as a simple text list. The level of detail depends on your own needs or those of your client.

Figure 1.1 shows a scrawny little site map we just whipped up for an imaginary vanity site for a cat named Fraidy.

Site maps are also sometimes referred to as *thumbnails* because they represent each page of the site (or each major page) as a tiny thumbnail version of the actual page. (If your bosses are fans of *Spinal Tap,* they may wonder if you are actually going to deliver teeny-Stonehenge-sized pages. Reassure them that this will not be so.)

When you are developing an interactive application (as opposed to a series of static, linked pages), the site map might be referred to as a *process flow*, because it shows how the user might flow through the various pages or screens to accomplish some task. (For example, let's say you developed a new search engine for a site, and they already had a site map. You could create a process-flow diagram showing how users can go from the basic search box to the advanced search page or to the search tips, and then ultimately to the search results.)

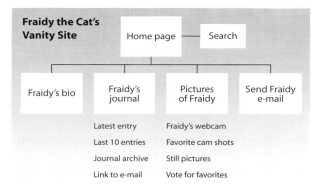

You can create whatever codes or symbols you'd like to indicate different types of pages. Use dotted lines for dynamic pages (pages that are created from a database), or use rounded edges for new pages. Have fun with it. This is information design without that tedious "making it work" part.

Figure 1.1

Fraidy's site has a main page with a search link (off to the side as part of the persistent navigation at the site) and four subpages reached from the home page's side navigation. Two of those subpages have subsubpages of their own.

Creating Wireframes (or Storyboards, or Process Flows)

At least as useful as a site map is a set of *wireframes* for your project. Wireframes are analogous to what people in the movie, television, and advertising business call *storyboards*. Except storyboards usually show pictures of people saying stuff and indicate a flow of action. Wireframes indicate a desired progression through the website's pages. You can think of them as being drilled down to one further level of detail from the site map.

> Wireframes are usually done without color. They don't show the actual design of the pages, and in fact, they are presented denuded of as many design elements as possible so that your client doesn't get the idea that you are presenting the actual, final design. Instead, you are just showing the functional elements and content areas for each page and trying to get some signoff on that so that you can go ahead and develop a real look-and-feel.

Each page in your site map can be represented as a wireframe, usually a full page showing roughly where the navigation, content areas, and any interactive elements (such as forms or image maps) will go. The exact placement of these elements is not the point. The point is that the wireframes indicate a list of the elements that will eventually populate each page. They should also indicate where any of the links will lead so that anyone reviewing the wireframes can easily see how the user would step through the site. This is much easier to do with barebones wireframes than with a complete site mockup—if you use one of these, you risk having to listen to the marketing department representative ask, "Why did you put that purple color under the logo?"

Figure 1.2 shows a mocked up wireframe page showing one step in a content-management process (gleefully adapted from the brilliant work of designer and information architect Dan Shearer of New York, New York).

Ready, Set, Rumble!

This chapter explained some of the planning and organizational work you'll need to do before you launch a serious web-development project. This includes determining when it's appropriate to use Dreamweaver, Fireworks, and other Macromedia products during this development process; hashing out a process or methodology for developing your site or application; figuring out how to collaborate with other team members (if necessary); gathering requirements for your site; and developing an information architecture.

This information is useful no matter what tools you were going to use to assist you as a web designer. Don't ignore these steps because they involve thought processes and decisions that your software applications can't do for you. Once you know how you're going to design your project, what you're going to do it with, how and when you are going to use your tools, who the product is for, and how the information at the site will be organized, you're ready to start cranking away in Dreamweaver and Fireworks. The next chapter will take you through the elements of a web page and a website and will even show you some actual Dreamweaver screens! Remember, have fun.

Figure 1.2

Without looking like an actual web page, this wireframe shows that the interface will include a logo; tabs at the top; options along the left side; text boxes; and buttons for publishing the content or canceling the process.

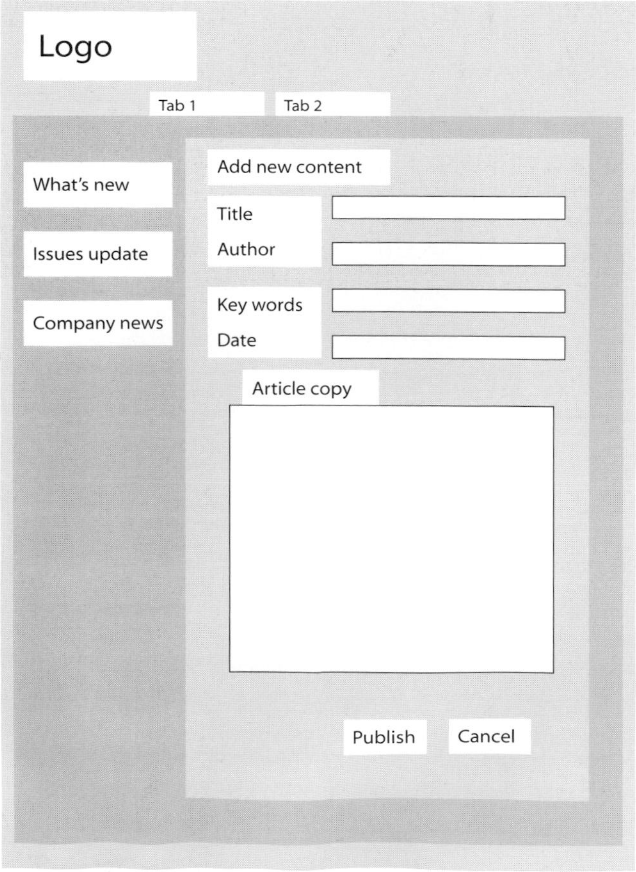

## CHAPTER 2

Web Pages Deconstructed

As you know, the basic unit of display on the Web is commonly called a page. Like all metaphors in the electronic world, this one only partly conveys the idea. In a book, the pages are all the same length. On the Web, a page can be any length. In a book or magazine, the elements on each page are static (unchanging). On the Web, the elements of a page may be dynamic (changeable). In this chapter we discuss the components of a typical web page and explain how you'll use Dreamweaver to manage these different types of web page elements. Web pages consisting of content, design, and navigation.

- **Text, graphical, and other content**
- **Design, layout, and style sheets**
- **Navigation elements**

The Elements of a Web Page

From a human point of view, a web page consists of *content* (information in all its forms), *design* (how the content is displayed), and *navigation* (how users move around the site).

Of course, from the point of view of server and browser software, web pages consist of text and code, which is made up of HTML tags and other coding that represents embedded files and scripting elements. So *content* can be text, data, images, and other forms of information. *Text* is also called writing, copy, or just content. Other types of content appear on web pages in the form of embedded graphics files or other media.

The *design* of a page is the way text formatting, graphical elements, and other style standards are used to produce the site's look-and-feel. *Navigation,* is the system of interactive elements that lets the user move from page to page. Navigation can be in the form of text, though it is usually handled with graphical elements and sometimes script objects that enable actions (as with a *rollover*, an animation activated by the mouse hovering over an available navigation graphic).

From Dreamweaver's point of view, everything on a web page is either *text* or *objects*. Text and objects are integrated on the page by *code* (tags, mostly). Sure, you can view or touch code directly, but Dreamweaver's metaphor, at least in Design view, is of pages comprising text and objects. Text is written material, as always. Objects are everything else. Figure 2.1 shows how Dreamweaver displays text and objects held together by tags. Manipulating text and objects is web design in a nutshell.

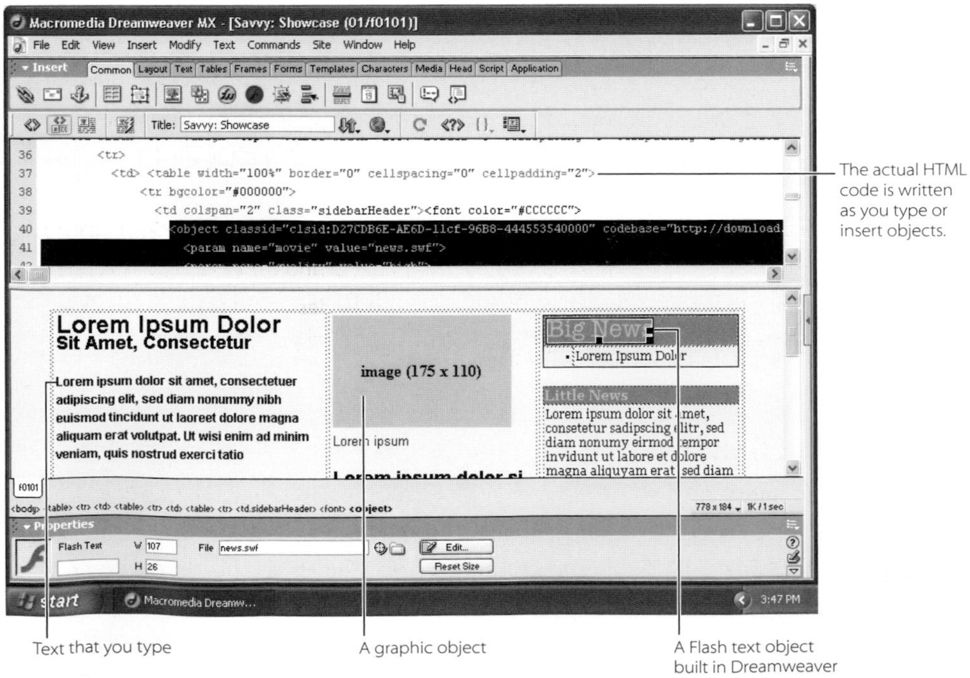

Figure 2.1

Dreamweaver enables you to manipulate text and objects on a web page.

The actual HTML code is written as you type or insert objects.

Text that you type

A graphic object

A Flash text object built in Dreamweaver

Working with Content

Before you can construct your web pages from the basic elements Dreamweaver recognizes (text and objects), you'll need to collect *assets*, meaning any prepared material or "ingredients" needed to build your pages. For example, you will insert the text on your web pages either by importing it from a word processing program or by typing it directly onto the page—either way, you need the text to be ready when the time comes to build the page.

You'll need to have your artwork ready, and you may also need to collect Java applets or scripts as well as Macromedia extensions to include any interactivity you wish to incorporate into the site.

Before you begin to work, you need to do one other thing: set up your directories or folders to receive the assets you collect. Chapter 3 discusses how to set up the structure of your site on your computer or on a local network and how to manage files using the Site panel.

STAYING ON THE RIGHT SIDE OF COPYRIGHT LAW

Make sure you have the right to use any written content you intend to include at your site. The general rule of thumb about copying material from another person's website, by the way, is *don't do it* without proper permission. For more information, visit the Friends of Active Copyright Education (FA©E) website (`http://www.law.duke.edu/copyright/face/softint/index.htm`).

Working With Text

Once you have your text assets prepared (the word processing files, or copy, as interactive designers usually call it), cutting and pasting them into Dreamweaver is a snap. Formatting the text is a little more complicated, but we'll go into that in detail in Chapter 12.

There are many websites that discuss web design theory. One of the best is The Site Wizard at `http://www.thesitewizard.com`. These materials are practical and extremely easy to understand and implement. Another classic site for insight into web design theory and human interface design is Jakob Nielsen's `http://www.useit.com`.

Working with Graphics

How are web graphics different from any other electronic images (computer graphics)? They have to make it over your user's Internet connection, whether it is a "fat" broadband connection such as a T1, cable, or DSL link, or a connection with much less bandwidth, such as a dial-up modem. In every case, an optimized graphic (one that has been compressed in size as much as possible without sacrificing too much quality) is preferable. Similarly, unless you can be sure that your readers have monitors that display a sufficiently large number of colors, you're safer off using graphics with only 256 colors (or, really, the 216 web-safe colors out of the standard 256).

The standard web file formats are JPEG (JPG), GIF, and PNG, which combines the best features of the other two formats. PNG is Fireworks' native format, but not all browsers currently handle PNG files, so you'll probably have to stick to JPEGs and GIFs for most projects.

> Use the JPEG file format for images with smooth gradations of color, such as most photographs. Use the GIF file format for images that use large patterns of single colors. (You also use the GIF89a format for a type of animated graphical file.)

Designing for the Web

When you are designing for the Web, you must be cognizant not only of your local computer and software restraints, but your viewer's constraints as well (which, as you remember, you usually don't know). You can guess at what your viewers will be using to visit your website and base your designs on these suppositions. Your guess must address several factors.

You must design for the computer screen and not for the printed page. This means that you do not necessarily know the size of a page on your visitor's computer or the quality of the color displayed there, and you don't even have control over where on that screen the image is placed. For example, some people view web pages using a portable computer with a very small monitor that supports only 256 colors. In fact, monitors can get even more limited. Nowadays, portable digital assistants (PDAs), such as the Palm Connected Organizer and its competitors, are often used to view websites, and they have itty-bitty screens. Others might view your pages using a 21-inch super VGA monitor that supports millions of colors.

Not all monitors display colors the same way. One of the most important factors to control when you are designing web graphics is the quality of the images. Quality comes down to how color is managed by the software drivers used to control the monitors. Color calibration, color bit-depth, and resolution all affect how graphics are displayed. You must learn to use colors that can work on many different monitors at the same time. For example, an image must display effectively on both 8-bit monitors, which support only the basic 256 colors on 640×480-pixel screens, and 24- or 32-bit monitors, which support 16 million colors on 1024×768-pixel screens.

People do not use the same tools to view the Web. The software used to view websites is called the browser. There are currently several browsers on the market. The "big guys" are Microsoft Internet Explorer and AOL's Netscape Communicator (though some say that an independent browser, Opera, may eclipse Netscape in users soon). There are alternative browsers available. For example, Mac users may be using a new beta browser called iCab that cannot currently support JavaScript. Others who wish to avoid mainstream products prefer Opera. Linux users also have their own browsers.

There are many different versions of each of these browsers still being used, each with its own support of a selection of the entire HTML standard as well as proprietary HTML tags not supported on other browsers. Each browser displays web pages differently. Also, the web medium is constantly "oozing" onto new devices, such as Web TV boxes, handheld organizers such as Palms, cell phones, and who knows what will be next? Our game-loving editor sez "Oooh, ooh, I do, I do: videogame consoles, digital TV recorders.…" Usually these newer devices have severe limitations on what they can display. For example, the Wireless Application Protocol (WAP) format, used for wireless devices like cell phones, displays only text and links—no graphics.

Not everyone has a fat pipe. Your web graphics (and page sizes) must be made very small so that users connecting to the Internet at speeds as slow as 2400 bits per second (and less) can access your information quickly. To support users with slow connections, web images are compressed (using the three file formats we just discussed: GIF, JPEG, and PNG). Compression can mean degradation of the image, so you must design your graphics to work with this loss of detail.

Not everyone is using the same operating system. Designers most often have Macs, but their users are more often running Windows on a PC. Some people use a flavor of Unix, such as Linux. Different operating platforms display graphics differently. In fact, even the same operating system running on different hardware configurations of video cards, audio cards, or drivers displays graphics differently. For example, a Sun running Solaris will display an image completely differently than a Silicon Graphics computer running Irix. Macs and PCs use completely different color management methods to display images, as well. You must be aware of these differences and test your graphics on as many platforms as you can to ensure their quality translates as well as possible across computer platforms.

Having considered some of the cross-platform and accessibility issues involved in planning a web project, you'll then also need to think about some of the specific design approaches available to you in the web medium, such as text-based design, use of style sheets, and methods of page layout based on the use of tables or layers.

Designing with Text

Text is the simplest element of a web page, but it is also the least controllable of your variables when you are laying out a page. Unless you can assume that your users have a specific font installed or a certain type of setup (as you sometimes can on, say, an intranet), stick to the most popular fonts, such as Times New Roman, Arial, MS Sans Serif, or Courier. Better yet, use Cascading Style Sheets (described next) to gain better control over the presentation of text in the body of your pages.

To overcome this constraint on the types of fonts, designers tend to rely on objects, in this case graphical files, to display more sophisticated treatments of text. For instance, if they wish to use more typographically interesting fonts, they often create graphical text in Fireworks and import it into Dreamweaver as an object.

This practice is especially useful when you need complete control of the appearance of text. Any text that you wish to format with other fonts, colors, graphics, and so forth (as you would with banners, logos, navigation buttons, and headlines), should be inserted as an object onto your page. In this case, the object is a graphic.

Here is where Fireworks fits into the scheme of things. Note that Fireworks is described in detail in Part II.

Cascading Style Sheets

As shown in Figure 2.2, there is another way to format—by using Cascading Style Sheets (CSS). Recently accepted into the HTML 4.0 standard, Cascading Style Sheets originated with Internet Explorer 4.5 and are now also supported by Netscape Communicator 4.*x* and above. *Style sheets* allow you to define how you want page elements that you define, such as paragraphs, table cells, text boxes, and headings, to appear every time you use them. You just associate one or more formatting attributes with a style and give that style a name. All such style definitions can be stored in a single style sheet file. Once you associate that style sheet with a page, you can use any defined style by applying the name to the element. Best of all, if you revise your design specifications, you can make the change in one place (in the style sheet), instead of hunting through every page and making the change over and over and over.

Laying Out Pages with Tables or Layers

Because the web medium is less flexible than most print-design applications, laying out a web page usually requires a laborious process of manually situating objects in table cells that are nested within other table cells to give the illusion of columns, side-by-side graphics, or grids. Dreamweaver's layout mode enables you to lay out pages visually without having to manage the coding of the nested table cells. Figure 2.3 presents a table and its HTML code. Tables are discussed in Chapter 11.

Figure 2.2

Text formatting can be managed using Cascading Style Sheets.

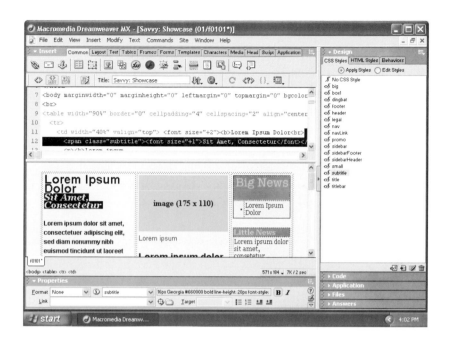

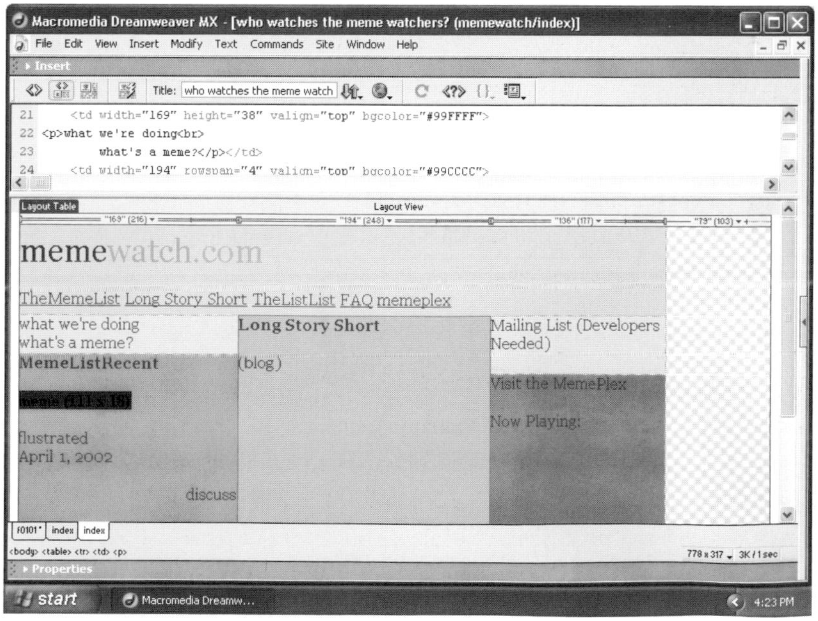

Figure 2.3

Dreamweaver supports the use of tables for achieving traditional page-layout effects.

In addition, the most current version of HTML (Version 4.0) offers a new way to create side-by-side and overlapping layouts through the use of layers. *Layers* are transparent areas that can be hidden, overlapped, or displayed at will. (You can use layers instead of tables if you know that your readers will be using up-to-date browsers that can parse layers. Dreamweaver can also convert a page designed with a table-based layout to one with a layer-based layout, and vice versa.)

Dreamweaver supports the use of layers in a way that makes web layout more natural and more like desktop publishing. You can use your mouse to size and place any layer to fit your requirements directly on the worksheet. The downside of layers is that no browsers older than Version 4.0 can interpret them. Layers and their uses are discussed in more detail in Chapter 11.

You can also use a concept called *frames* to allow portions of your page to serve as the repository for other pages pulled into your page based on navigation buttons you create (see Chapter 14).

Along with Cascading Style Sheets, layers let you control the placement of content, the look-and-feel, and the navigation throughout a site.

Setting Up a Navigation Scheme

One factor that distinguishes the Web from traditional print media is interactivity. Users experience this when they navigate from one page to another through a variety of means. In order to help your users understand their web experience and your website, you must provide them with an easy-to-grasp navigation scheme.

Organizing a Site

Sites are usually organized hierarchically, with a series of top-level pages that have their own subhierarchies. A good navigation scheme should make it clear what level the user is on and what related pages are available. We'll explore navigation objects thoroughly in Chapter 9 and the chapters of Part IV.)

Designing Navigation with Hypertext

Before you can design an appropriate scheme, you need to understand how hypertext works. Here is a little background for you.

The original purpose of the World Wide Web, as devised by Tim Berners-Lee, was to enable the visual linking of disparate types of information. This concept was revolutionized with the development of the *Hypertext Transfer Protocol (HTTP)*. HTTP enabled information to be presented graphically and allowed links to other information to be created using graphics.

Without hypertext there would be no Web. The more links you can build into your site, the more useful it becomes to your readers. The Web grows from these serendipitous interconnections that are built into each web page. Sometimes the most difficult part of designing a site is locating possible links to build into your site. You should always think ahead to possible places you can take your readers (but always build ways to return to your site, of course).

Hypertext Links and Hotspots

There are two ways to link information on web pages: by using hypertext links, or by using hot spots.

Hypertext Links

The easiest way to create a connection between two pieces of information is by using a *hypertext link*. For example, if you wished to place a link to a page called `contactus.html` from a selection of text, your HTML code might look like this: `<a href="contactus.html">Contact Us</a>`. (We see a lot of references to this "Contactus" fellow in URLs—must have been an important ancient Roman.) By the way, Dreamweaver automatically generates this type of code when you select the graphic or text and type the target address into the Link text box or point to the target file from the Property Inspector, but we'll get to that in Chapter 16.

Hotspots

Another very powerful way of linking areas of your page to related information elsewhere is by identifying an area of a graphic as a *hotspot* and then creating a link from this area. Hotspots are areas of an image on a browser screen that, if clicked, jump the viewer to another Universal Resource Locator (URL) on the Internet. Hotspots can be created by slicing up a graphic image in Fireworks and then designating certain areas of the image as linkable; slices are discussed in more detail in the next section. (Also see Chapter 9 for a discussion of slicing and linking hotspots in Fireworks.)

Graphics with hotspots are called *client-side image maps* because what you are really doing is mapping the location of every pixel of a graphic to identify those areas where links exist. The reason this list of links is called a "client-side" image map is that the list resides with the graphic image. *Server-side image maps* are an older way of creating graphical links; they require special software, called the Common Gateway Interface (CGI), to initiate the connection between the hotspot and the list of locations. You can also create hotspots in Dreamweaver by drawing the spots onto the designated graphic using the Map tool in the Property Inspector. Chapters 9 and 16 describe how to create linked graphics and how to build links in Dreamweaver.

Graphical Menus

Though pages can be hyperlinked together with a perfectly adequate navigation scheme using only text links (we'll explain how to create and insert these links in Chapter 16), the most elegant navigation interfaces use graphical menus. For these, you need to first use a graphics program, such as Fireworks, to develop the images to be used in the menus (as described in Chapter 9).

> Graphical menus may work using either hyperlinks or hotspots. If each of the menu options is a separate image, then each one will be a hyperlink as well. If the entire menu bar is a single image, then the options will all be hotspots.

Fireworks automates the difficult process of using graphics to create multiple hypertext links through the use of *slices* and *behaviors*. Slices are cut-up pieces of a graphic, with each piece functioning as a hotspot. Behaviors are scripted actions that can be triggered by pointing to or clicking part of a graphic. They can be as simple as blinking text or as complex as pulling in pictures for a slide show.

With slices and behaviors, images may appear to change shape or appearance when you roll over or click them with your mouse.

Jump Menus and Hierarchical Menus

There are several other specialized ways to navigate. Dreamweaver, for instance, can assist you in building a pop-up menu (also called a jump menu) containing linked items. This functions like the typical drop-down menus of choices that you see in dialog boxes in most common applications.

Another type of navigation tool is the *hierarchical menu*. These menus use JavaScript and layers to display and hide hotspots, and they also give the user the experience of pulling down a menu and selecting an item. Although hierarchical menus are difficult to build, they can add a professional sheen to your site. See Chapter 18 for instructions on how to construct these types of menus.

The Whole Enchilada

OK, now that you have an overview of how a single page is assembled, we're going to zoom out a little, conceptually, and look at an entire site (or application, or project). Usually, a site consists of many pages, at least from the browser's point of view. To work with an entire site in Dreamweaver, you need to first set up the site's structure or "architecture." That's what we'll explain in the following chapter.

## CHAPTER 3

Setting Up Your Workspace and Your Site

So, you've worked out a site development plan and thought about what you're going to be putting on your pages. This must mean you're ready to actually work in Dreamweaver! In this chapter, we're going to start by giving you the cook's tour of the Dreamweaver workspace because you need to understand what assumptions the software makes about your development process. Most of the time the primary focus of your workspace will be a page, but tools for working at the site level, with files, links, styles, templates, assets, and so on, are never out of reach. When you're moderately comfortable with the interface, we'll show you how to set up a new site, telling Dreamweaver where to store the local files and where to publish the remote files.

Here are some of the topics that will be addressed:

- **Choosing a workspace style**
- **Understanding the Dreamweaver workspace**
- **Customizing your workspace**
- **Setting up a new site**
- **Importing an existing site**
- **Planning ahead for accessibility**

The Integrated Workspace versus the Floating Layout

Previous versions of Dreamweaver on both Windows and Macintosh platforms featured a "floating palette" not unlike other design software. For this version, Macromedia has developed an integrated workspace (they call it the Dreamweaver MX Workspace, to differentiate it from the Dreamweaver 4 Workspace), but only for Windows users. The integrated style is how most Windows applications (such as the exemplars in the Office suite) work now. The issue has always been how to organize all the floating panels used to provide shortcuts and efficient workflows. With either style, Dreamweaver now offers a Hide Panels command that instantly removes most of the clutter from the workspace.

For Windows users, the first time you run Dreamweaver, you will be asked to choose a default workspace style (see Figure 3.1). If you are not the first person to run this installation of Dreamweaver, then the decision already will have been made, but you can change the workspace style at will, as explained later in this chapter.

> Macintosh users don't have the same workspace choice (yet), and the new interface for Mac users is similar to that of earlier versions, although the Insert bar (formerly the Objects Palette) is now by default docked horizontally below the Mac's title bar instead of vertically along the left edge of the screen. More on the Insert bar momentarily.

Dreamweaver MX's New Integrated Workspace

The new workspace is designed to ease clutter while retaining the availability of numerous shortcuts (see Figure 3.2).

What's different:

- Everything's docked. It's the Windows style (Word) versus the Mac style (Photoshop).

- The old Site window is now the first tab in the Files panel.

- Macromedia says this style is not as good for some accessibility features, meaning that if you use tools to assist you in reading or navigating the screen, then you should probably use the floating layout.

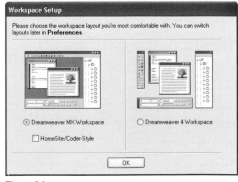

Figure 3.1

Quick, choose… a-la-cartridge or floating free?

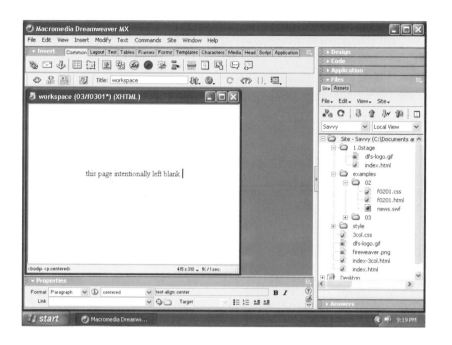

Figure 3.2

Dreamweaver recommends this all-in-one format (for Windows users only).

The Homesite/Coder Alternative Integrated Style

In Figure 3.1, you may have noticed that there's a check box on the integrated side of the divide for something called the HomeSite/Coder Style layout. This choice exists primarily to offer compatibility to former HomeSite users or other hand-coders who are migrating to Dreamweaver. Besides putting the panels on the left side of the screen, this style also defaults to a code-only view of the page (I'll explain about Design and Code views in the next section). Figure 3.3 shows a new page in the HomeSite/Coder style for a dynamic site. See Chapter 23 for more about setting up your coding environment.

The Classic Floating Layout

Macromedia recommends the MX layout but doesn't insist upon it (yet), giving you the option of choosing the Dreamweaver 4 Workspace… more or less. This is the only choice of workspace for Macintosh users (see Figure 3.4). These panels do now dock with each other easily and can all be hidden with a single command (F4), as in the other workspaces, but there is no multiple-document window, and the Site panel floats freely and does not dock with the other panels.

Figure 3.3

For former HomeSite users and other coders who like their panels on the left side, Dreamweaver offers this variant (also Windows only).

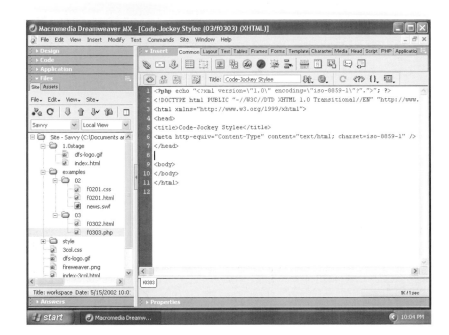

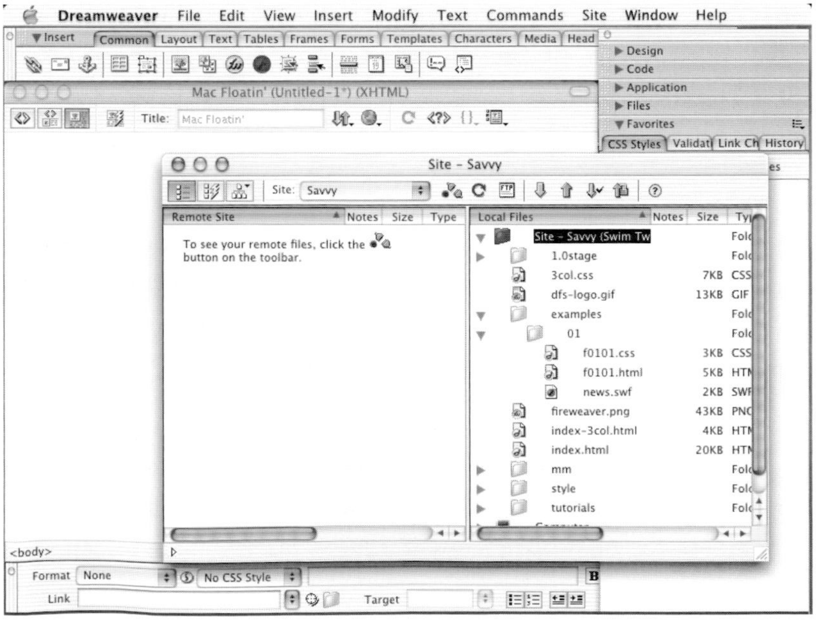

Figure 3.4

The "classic" look, and the only choice for Macintosh users

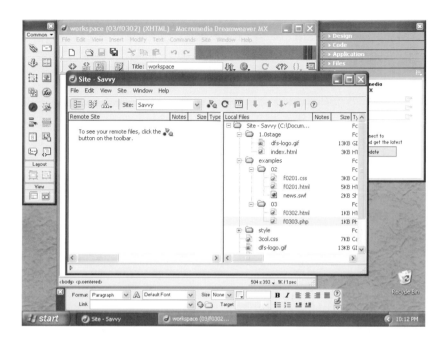

Figure 3.5

The floating look for Windows users, primarily those who've used earlier versions of Dreamweaver and prefer the old ways

The Windows version of the Dreamweaver 4 Workspace is a little different. The Insert bar reverts to the old position of the Objects Palette (along the left side of the screen) and can't easily be dragged into the other position. Also, in Windows, each open window gets a button on the Windows Taskbar. As with the Mac, the Site panel does not function as a dockable panel in this workspace (see Figure 3.5).

Getting Oriented

At first sight, Dreamweaver's working environment may seem cluttered and overwhelming. As shown in Figure 3.6, Dreamweaver offers numerous tabbed panels, a toolbar for switching among three working modes, and much information about the contents of whatever web page you've got open. Let's first sort out what is important on the Dreamweaver desktop.

> Because Dreamweaver relies so heavily on panels to control the behavior of whatever is in the Document window (for example, creating links using the Site panel, formatting using the Property Inspector, or selecting objects from the Assets Manager), run Dreamweaver with the largest monitor you have available (at least 17 inches is nice).

Figure 3.6

**The Dreamweaver
desktop**

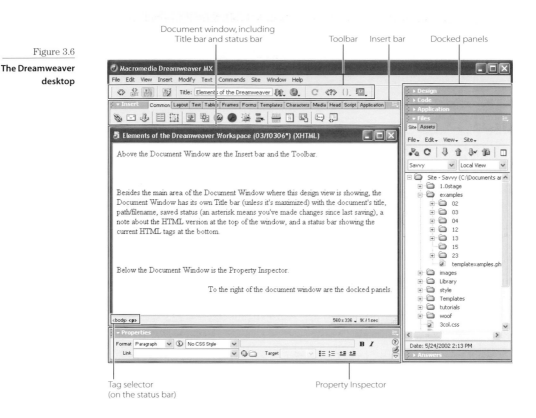

The Document window, including
Title bar and status bar · Toolbar · Insert bar · Docked panels

Tag selector
(on the status bar) · Property Inspector

The Document Window

The main focus of your attention in Dreamweaver will almost always be the Document window, and thus most of the compromises in the interface deal with making room for the Document window (or failing to).

The Document window has three parts: a small Title bar at the top, a large-ish area for viewing the contents of the document in the middle, and a status bar at the bottom. Nearby (actually in the same window on the Mac side) is a toolbar for the Document window. The rest of the interface consists of panels (and in the Dreamweaver 4 workspace, the Site panel) that all have the ability to affect the contents of the Document window.

The Document's Title Bar

The document's own title bar (as opposed to the Title bar of the Dreamweaver application, although both appear together in Windows when the document is maximized) displays three pieces of information: the page title as it will appear in a browser's title bar, the filename of the document, and the saved file status (an asterisk means you've made changes since last saving). Dreamweaver will also indicate up there if the file is in XHTML format instead of older versions of HTML (see Chapter 26 for more on XHTML and XML).

Before you can create links *to* a page, you must save it as a file at least once (or else how is Dreamweaver supposed to know where to point the link?).

The View Area

The main area of the Document window shows you the contents of the current document. For web pages, you can choose to see just the Design view (a visual representation of how the page will be rendered in a browser with click-and-drag shortcuts for manipulating the design), Code view (the literal HTML and script code that makes up the web page), or Code and Design view (a split view showing both views in two different panes). For some other file formats, such as script and style sheet files, you can only use Code view. We'll show you how to change the view in "The Toolbar" section.

Most of what you'll do in the Document window is insert, paste, and enter text and objects, and then manipulate them mostly using the panels and other shortcuts.

The Status Bar

The status bar of the Document window features a tag selector. Wherever the insertion point is in a document, the status bar will show any of the tags that currently have a bearing on that spot in the document (in HTML files, the `<body>` tag is in effect in much of the document). Clicking a tag selects the tag and lets you to edit it. (See Chapter 12 for more on using the tag selector and Chapter 23 for more on tags in general.)

The Toolbar

The Toolbar provides quick and easy access to most of Dreamweaver's essential tools—tools that let you switch between viewing modes, debug your HTML, preview your site in a browser of your choice, refresh the page, and locate a file with the Site panel. Consider the Toolbar your chief navigational aid because its buttons and pop-up menus provide access to just about every area of the program. They also let you reach outside the program and grab information you may need to build your site.

THE LAUNCHER

A feature older users may wonder about is the launcher, a set of icons that open specific panels. The Launcher still exists as a feature of the Document window's status bar, but it is turned off by default. To turn it on, go to the Panels category of the Preferences dialog box, and click the check box that says Show Icons in Panels and Launcher. (Then click OK.)

Let's take a look at the objects on the toolbar, one at a time.

Three Views: Code, Design, or Both

As I mentioned earlier, Dreamweaver offers three different ways of viewing your work; you can access all three through the Toolbar:

Design view This is the standard view used for doing layout. It lets you place objects visually with the Insert bar. Design view itself has two modes: *layout mode* and *standard mode*. Layout mode is used for adding new objects, such as tables, layers, and so forth. Standard mode is for editing existing objects.

Code view This view shows the raw HTML tags and scripts that are generated by Dreamweaver to reflect your choices in the Design view. You can edit tags directly and cut, copy, and paste HTML.

Code and Design view This view uses a split screen, enabling you to work in the Design view mode and check the resulting HTML code in the Code view at the same time. Select HTML from the Code view to jump to an area of the Design view and vice versa. The split screen can also be useful for controlling the placement of imported code, such as Java scripts or applets.

By the way, you might prefer to see the code peeking out at the bottom of the Design view instead of at the top (sometimes I do). You can switch them easily, just click the View Options button at the right side of the toolbar and select Design View on Top. To see more design than code, drag the divider toward the bottom of the Document window.

> If you're developing database-backed web applications, then you'll have a fourth button for selecting the Live Data view. See Part VI of this book for more on web applications.

> The toolbar is customizable. See Chapter 32 for details.

The Title Field

The Title field shows you your document's current title (by default, it will be something like "untitled3" or "Untitled Document"). You can alter the way the name of your page will be displayed in a browser's Title bar by typing it in the Title field. All you need to do to change the name is highlight the text, type a new name, and hit Enter. The Title bar immediately changes to show the new name. Note that giving the page a name does not automatically save the document to a file! You must also use the Save command (File → Save) to name the file. (For experienced HTML users, you'll realize that this Title field is merely supplying the contents of the `<title>` tag in the `<head>` section of the document.)

The File Management Pop-Up Menu

You will use the File Management pop-up menu to upload and download files. You can perform updates by quickly swapping files between the remote and local sites using the Get and Put or Check In and Check Out commands on the File Management pop-up menu.

> We'll explain more about your local site versus your remote site soon. The basic idea is that the real site (or the production or staging version of the site) is "out there" on a remote server, but you keep a copy of the entire site on your own computer or on a local file server as well. You do most of your work "back here" on the local site and eventually put finished stuff "out there" on the remote site.

You may also prefer the keyboards shortcuts:

COMMAND	WINDOWS SHORTCUT	MAC SHORTCUT	HOW TO REMEMBER IT
Get	Shift + Ctrl + D	Shift + Cmd + D	Think "download"
Put	Shift + Ctrl + U	Shift + Cmd + U	Think "upload"
Check Out	Alt + Shift + Ctrl + D	Option + Shift + Cmd + D	Think "fancy download"
Check In	Alt + Shift + Ctrl + U	Option + Shift + Cmd + U	Think "fancy upload"

Check In and Check Out are used to facilitate collaboration and prevent people from accidentally overwriting their colleagues' work.

- When you check a file out, Dreamweaver marks the remote file (so that no one else can change it) and copies it to your local site.

- When you check a file in, Dreamweaver replaces the file on the remote site and unmarks it (so others are free to alter it again).

Checking in or out will ensure that no other collaborator will be able to get the file while you are making your changes. This feature also records such changes so that you can trace who is working on which file either remotely or locally

If you are working alone (without collaborators), you don't need to worry about checking pages in and out. Just use the Get and Put commands.

The File Management pop-up menu also lets you open the Design Notes dialog box (where you can document changes you make to files as you work) and quickly locate the current page in the Site panel (explained later in this chapter) with the Locate In Site command (Site → Locate In Site).

The Preview/Debug Pop-Up Menu

When Tim Berners-Lee invented the Hypertext Transfer Protocol (HTTP) and its attendant Hypertext Markup Language (HTML) as the underpinnings of the World Wide Web, he intended that any browser should be able to display web pages identically as long as they follow HTML standards. Sadly, over the years, browser support for standard HTML has begun to vary greatly. Both Microsoft and Netscape have often invented their own tags to "enhance" HTML, thus introducing different approaches to everything from how to indicate paragraph breaks to how to implement Cascading Style Sheets. As a result, today, individual browsers may not display your pages in exactly the same way.

In addition, Macintosh computers use a different default monitor resolution (72 dots per inch) than Windows machines (96 dots per inch); this results in drastic differences in the size of text displayed on the two machines. In addition, color support varies between the two platforms. Add in the fact that many people use Unix-based platforms, such as Sun Solaris or Linux, to view the Web and you have a virtual Tower of Babel when it comes to displaying pages.

One more variable is the age of the browser used to view the Web. For example, schools generally use older browsers, as do many individuals who can't be bothered with constantly upgrading to the latest version of their software. These older browsers generally cannot display newer, nonstandard tags, such as those adopted in version 4 of HTML (and supported by Dreamweaver and Fireworks).

All this information leads us to the use of the Preview/Debug pop-up menu; using this menu, you test your site's appearance and performance. When you are designing a website, you must test it in as many browsers as you possibly can (depending, of course, on how much you know about the browsers your audience will or might be using), and on as many different computer platforms as possible to ensure that it displays correctly. Dreamweaver helps you with this process by providing access to an unlimited number of browsers via this portion of the Toolbar menu. You can also access Microsoft Internet Explorer's JavaScript debugger and Netscape Communicator's JavaScript console from your Dreamweaver desktop by choosing commands from the Preview/Debug pop-up menu.

DESIGNING FOR MULTIPLE BROWSER TYPES

If you decide to design your website so that it may be viewed in all or most types of platforms and browsers (and you should do this unless you are developing for a clearly defined audience, as on some intranets), then you may want to plan on creating various versions of your site and giving your viewers links to the different site versions. Dreamweaver provides Java scripts that automatically check for a browser type and make the switch to a separate site based on the results of its check. (See Chapter 29 for a description of how to use this script.) Dreamweaver also makes alternate page designing easier to view by providing the user with tools that can convert layers to tables and remove Cascading Style Sheets. (Chapter 29 explains these features as well.)

The Refresh Button and the Reference Panel

If you are working in the Code view or the Code and Design view, you can edit your HTML directly. If you do so, however, changes will *not* be automatically reflected in the Design view until you refresh it. To do so, you can click the Refresh Design View button on the Reference panel, select View → Refresh Design View, or press F5.

The Code Navigation Pop-Up Menu

OK, it may be a little premature to start talking about JavaScript. So let's just skip this one and save it for Chapter 23, where we can get as geeky as we want to be.

The View Options Pop-Up Menu

As hinted at when we were talking about swapping the Design and Code view panes, you use the View Options pop-up menu to turn off and on hidden tags and other visual aids. This menu is contextual—meaning that what is shown on the menu depends on which view you are using (Design, Code, or Code and Design).

The Insert Bar

The most important panel in your Dreamweaver arsenal is the Insert bar, formerly referred to as the Objects palette or Objects panel (see Figure 3.7). The Insert bar contains almost every tool you need to insert, edit, and manage components on your web page. You'll have at least twelve different tabs in the Insert bar, including the following: Common, Layout, Text, Tables, Frames, Forms, Characters, Media, Head, Script, and Application. Each tab is customizable to suit your needs (and Dreamweaver will automatically populate a tab with the appropriate objects depending on the file format and server model you're using for your site).

JAVA AND JAVASCRIPT

Java is a programming language developed by Sun Microsystems intended to be platform independent. Java programs run in a virtual Java engine typically supplied by either the browser or, as in the case of Macintosh computers, by the operating system. Java is used extensively in Internet programming to create interactivity in websites. Java programs are self-contained and can be inserted into your web page designs like any other object. Such objects are called *applets* (meaning little applications). *JavaScript* is a scripting language that uses Java-like routines but is embedded directly in your HTML code. When you apply a behavior in Dreamweaver, you are really inserting a piece of JavaScript into your code.

If the Insert bar is not visible when you start up Dreamweaver, choose Window → Insert or press the keyboard combination Ctrl + F2 (Command + F2 Mac). (This command toggles the Insert bar on or off.)

Table 3.1 describes the contents most of the tabs on the Insert bar. (Remember that some tabs will appear only when needed).

Table 3.1

The Insert Bar

TAB NAME	CONTENTS	DESCRIPTION
Common	Insert Hyperlink, Insert Email Link, Insert Link Anchor, Insert Table, Draw Layer, Insert Image, Insert Image Placeholder, Fireworks HTML, Flash, Rollover Image, Navigation Bar, Horizontal Rule, Date, Tabular Data, Comment, Tag Chooser	These are the most common objects you will use in Dreamweaver. These objects are described as they are encountered throughout the book.
Layout	Insert Table, Draw Layer, Standard View, Layout View, Draw Layout Table, Draw Layout Cell	All the commands you need to rough out layouts and designs using tables or layers.
Text	Font Tag Editor, Bold, Italics, Strong Emphasis, Paragraph, Block Quote, Preformatted Text, Heading 1, Heading 2, Heading 3, Unordered List, Ordered List, List Item, Definition List, Definition Term, Definition Description, Abbreviation, Acronym	These are the standard HTML formatting options. They all correspond to well-accepted HTML tags. For tags with further attributes to select, a dialog box pops up to collect that information from you.
Tables	Insert Table, Table Tag, Table Row, Table Header, Table Data, Table Caption	When working on actual tables (as opposed to using tables to hack the layout), these are the commands you need most often.
Frames	Left Frame, Right Frame, Top Frame, Bottom Frame, Bottom and Nested Left Frame, Bottom and Nested Right Frame, Left and Nested Bottom Frame, Right and Nested Bottom Frame, Top and Bottom Frames, Left and Nested Top Frame, Right and Nested Top Frame, Top and Nested Left Frame, Top and Nested Bottom Frame, Frameset, Frame, Floating Frame, No Frames	Frames are a way to call outside web pages into your web page while still reserving portions of the page for static information. Chapter 14 discusses frames.
Forms	Form, Text Field, Hidden Field, Text Area, Check Box, Radio Button, Radio Group, List/Menu, Jump Menu, Image Field, File Field, Button, Label, Fieldset.	Forms are specialized areas of your Document window that are linked to an external program called a Common Gateway Interface (CGI). This tab lets you rapidly insert Form object types and their variables. See Chapter 20 for more about Forms.
Templates	Make Template, Make Nested Template, Editable Region, Optional Region, Repeating Region, Editable Optional Region, Repeating Table	Use templates to establish and easily maintain design and page-layout standards for an entire site. See Chapter 4 for more about templates.
Characters	Line Break, Non-breaking space, Left Quote, Right Quote, Em Dash, Pound, Euro, Yen, Copyright, Registered Trademark, Trademark, Other Characters	HTML requires the use of ASCII character entity codes to insert special symbols. Dreamweaver writes the unique numbers or names (for example — for an em dash) into HTML for you and then inserts the represented symbol into the Design view.

TAB NAME	CONTENTS	DESCRIPTION
Media		Here is an assortment of shortcuts for inserting various media types, including those developed using Macromedia products (such as the Flash and Shockwave options) and those not (such as ActiveX). See Chapter 19 for more on inserting multimedia into your pages.
Head	Meta, Keywords, Description, Refresh, Base, Link	Head Objects are those that appear within the <head> tag. This category contains objects that install additions to the <head> tag.
Scripts, Applications, other Script-specific tabs	The options offered depend on the context.	You'll only have these if you're developing a database backed site.

You can reshape the Insert bar to fit your monitor by clicking any edge of the panel. When the cursor turns into a two-headed arrow, drag your mouse. In addition, you can create a rectangular panel for placing at the bottom or top of your screen by dragging any corner (in Windows) or the bottom-right corner (in Macintosh).

The Insert bar's tabs reflect folders in the Objects folder, and you can actually customize the Insert bar further by modifying the contents of these folders, as discussed in Chapter 32.

The Property Inspector

Every object in Dreamweaver can be modified by adjusting its attributes (such as foreground color, background color, location relative to the monitor screen, and so forth). The place where you can make these adjustments without resorting to menu commands is called the *Property Inspector* (see Figure 3.8).

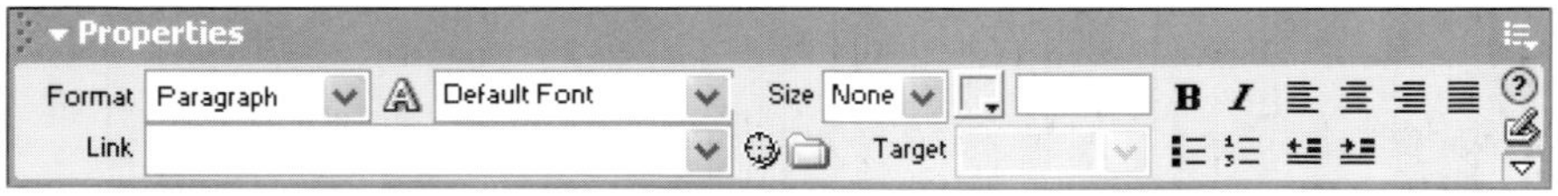

Figure 3.8

The Property Inspector

The Property Inspector is context sensitive, meaning that its contents change based upon which object you select in the Document window. In addition, the Property Inspector expands to include more options, such as opening a linked Fireworks file if you select a graphic element that you wish to edit. Also, tables can be extensively edited using the expanded Property Inspector. Toggle the arrow at the bottom right of the Property Inspector to open or close this expanded view.

The Property Inspector lets you change attributes by either typing new information into text boxes (such as the size of a font) or by using pop-up menus that open related panels. One of the most powerful uses of the Property Inspector is to create links from an object to either a site-based file or an external website simply by dragging the pointer on the Property Inspector to the target file in the Site Manager. The full path of the link is entered into the Link text box.

> We'll be referring to the Property Inspector throughout the book, offering tips and tricks to enhance your efficiency with Dreamweaver through its use.

The Panels

The Insert bar and the Property Inspector are both technically panels, but they tend to dock at the top and bottom of the screen respectively, while the rest of the panels hang out at the side of the screen. All panels have a small triangle button at their left edge for opening or closing the view of the panel. They also all have a textured "Gripper" area for dragging the panel around the screen or for docking it with the rest of the panels. When panels are closed, they take up very little space.

If you open just one panel, it will get all the space available. If you open more, they have to share the space.

Most panels contain several tabs, each of which can be selected to bring its contents to the fore.

Let's take a quick walk through the available panels.

The Answers Panel This is a new feature that connects your application to the online Dreamweaver knowledge base and, if necessary, live technical support.

The Design Panel This panel features three subpanels and is geared toward page layout and composition:

> **CSS Styles** For designing with Cascading Style Sheets (see Chapter 15).
>
> **HTML Styles** For designing with old-school HTML formatting (see Chapter 12).
>
> **Behaviors** For working with standard interactive behaviors (see Chapter 19).

The Code Panel This panel features three subpanels and is geared toward working directly with code (see Chapter 23):

> **Tag Inspector** Enables you to walk through all the tags in your document in hierarchical presentation format.
>
> **Snippets** Used to store useful bits of code, and comes with a pretty cool starter set.

Reference Contains hyperlinked versions of references for various markup and scripting languages.

The Application Panel This panel features four subpanels, all geared toward web application development (see Part V):

Databases Used to connect to your data source.

Bindings Helps make data available.

Server Behaviors Takes advantage of server-side features.

Components Used for introspection into the properties and methods of a component such as a JavaBeans. Now, aren't you glad you asked?

The Files Panel This panel features two subpanels in the MX workspace and just one in the floating layout. It gives you easy access to the files (both documents and assets) used in your site:

Site (only in MX workspace) Takes the place of the old Site window. You can drag this panel out of the Files panel if you want to expand it. It also now offers direct access to your local computer's or network's files through an explorer-type icon in the list view.

Assets Functions as a repository where you keep all your objects handy. More on this in Chapter 4.

The Results Panel This panel is not shown by default, but like all panels, you can bring it up by choosing any of its subpanels from the Windows menu. When you display this panel, it appears like the Property Inspector, docked to the bottom of the screen. Here are its subpanels:

Search Shows search results.

Validation Checks your code (see Chapter 23).

Target Browser Check Checks for browser compatibility (see Chapter 29).

Link Checker Check links sitewide (see Chapter 16).

Site Reports Generate statistics about your site.

FTP Log Tracks FTP "GETs" and "PUTs."

Server Debug Debug scripts code.

Other Panels As in all systems, there are a few miscellaneous panels:

History Shows the undoable history of commands you have used.

Various others Includes the Code Inspector (which is like a floating code view), Layers and Frames panels, a horizontal Timelines panel for interactive behaviors, and a Site-spring panel to use in case you're using Macromedia's project management application as part of your development process.

Customizing Your Workspace

As you begin working with Dreamweaver, you'll find your own preferred style of working with the interface. You may find some layouts easier to work with in specific circumstances, and you may therefore find yourself jumping back and forth or changing things around as you go. Dreamweaver makes it pretty easy to set up the workspace the way you want it.

Changing Your Workspace Style (Windows Users Only)

As mentioned earlier in this chapter, Windows users are asked to choose a workspace layout when they first start running the program—Mac users don't have any such choice. Windows users can also change the preferred workspace at any point from the Preferences dialog box (Edit → Preferences, or Ctrl + U). In the General category, click the Change Workspace button. This brings up the Workspace Setup dialog box shown earlier in Figure 3.1. Choose a new workspace and click OK to switch. Dreamweaver will inform you that the change will take place the next time you start the program.

Hide Panels

One quick way to maximize the screen space available for your Document window is to instantly hide all the panels with the Hide Panel command (F4, or View → Hide Panels); the result of this action is shown in Figure 3.9 for the integrated MX workspace.

Figure 3.10 shows the result of hiding panels in the Dreamweaver 4 workspace. Because the Site panel is not functioning as a panel in this layout, it remains visible (if open) after panels have been hidden.

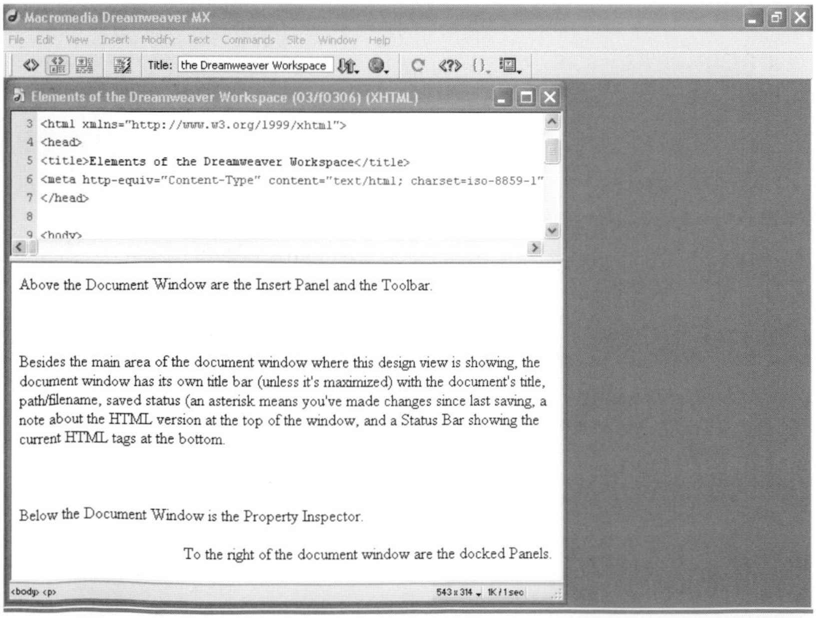

Figure 3.9

The Hide Panels command has been used to maximize the workspace for your document

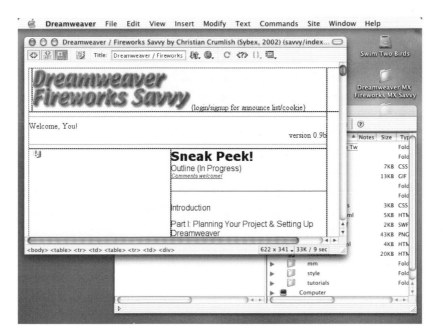

Figure 3.10

Hiding panels in the Dreamweaver 4 Workspace leaves an additional window lying around

In the integrated workspace, you can also click-and-drag the little handle in the middle of the left (inner) edge of the panels docked on the right side. (These directions are reversed, of course, in the HomeSite/Coder style layout.) Double-clicking the handle hides those panels all at once. Click it once to restore the panels docked along the right side.

Docking and Undocking Panels

To undock a panel, drag it from where it's docked until it floats free.

To dock a panel, drag it by its Gripper (the textured area to the left of the panel's name) into the panel area. A black outline will appear to show where the panel will be docked when you release the mouse button.

A floating undocked panel will have a close button on it like any other window (this is true in both Windows and Mac operating systems). You can hide the panel by clicking the close button. To bring it back (docked or undocked), select any of the panel's tabs by name from the Windows menu.

Because of an Adobe lawsuit, you can no longer drag tabs from one panel to another or to clear space to create a new panel group. Now when you grab the tab, you'll be prompted to use the Group...With command.

Setting Up Your Site

OK, enough of the grand tour. Let's get down to business! As you probably know, a website is a conglomeration of web pages grouped together via associated hypertext links. Dreamweaver works with entire websites, not just individual pages, so the first thing you have to do to begin designing is designate a group of folders on your computer or local network as a "site."

As soon as you designate a group of folders as a site in Dreamweaver, you can start to take advantage of Dreamweaver's site management tools. Dreamweaver keeps track of every link on every web page within a site, inserting the source and link information for each page into that page's properties; it also ties the same information into the site's folders. This tracking capability enables you to move around files within the site while maintaining their links. You can also rename files and folders without disturbing these links.

> Remember, the links essentially *are* the website. Do not move any folder or rename a file manually (outside of Dreamweaver). That way you won't accidentally disturb the integrity of your website.

Setting Up Local Site Folders

Setting up your website in Dreamweaver is a two-part process:

1. First, you create your folders on your hard drive or local network.
2. Then you designate those folders as a site in Dreamweaver.

It is very important to plan out your folder hierarchy before you actually create the folders. A good rule of thumb is to designate a folder for documents or web pages, a folder for graphics, and a folder for assets such as style sheets, CGIs, extensions, and other files. The front page or first page of your site should always be stored at the site's root level and is nearly always named `index.html`.

Here are some general guidelines for naming your folders.

Create a master location. Create a master location on your hard disk or file server to hold all your websites. Then store all of your sites in this folder.

Create a folder for the specific site. Create a folder for the specific site you are setting up and give it a descriptive name without any spaces or special characters. This will become the name of the site in Dreamweaver. (For example, the site for Fraidy the Cat (introduced in Chapter 1) was stored in a folder called `fraidysite`.) This folder is also called the *root* level of your site.

Keep subfolder names simple. Keep the names of your subfolders simple so that they are easy to navigate in the Property Inspector and Site panel. For example, a good name for your graphics folder is "images" or "media." The simpler the name, the shorter the pathname you have to remember (at some point, you may be required to edit the pathname by hand or you may have to type it into the Property Inspector).

Don't use spaces or special characters. Make sure that your folder names do not contain spaces or special characters. It is also a good idea to use only lowercase letters without any spaces because some server software, such as the ubiquitous Apache Server, is based on Unix, and thus requires case-sensitive and spaceless naming.

Once you have created the folders that will contain your site, you are ready to designate these folders in Dreamweaver as your local site.

Using the Site Setup Wizard

To define a new site, select Site → New Site to bring up the Site Definition dialog box. To make site setup easier, Dreamweaver now provides a Site Setup Wizard as the basic option in this dialog box (see Figure 3.11). Experienced users will probably prefer the Advanced options (discussed in the next section), and can skip the Wizard by choosing the Advanced tab at the top of the Site Definition dialog box.

Then follow these steps:

1. Type a name for your site and click the Next button.

2. For now, leave "No, I do not want to use a server technology" selected (unless you know for a fact that you do, in which case, see Chapter 22 for further details), and click Next.

3. If you plan to edit your local site on your own computer, leave the first option selected. If your local files are on a network, choose "Edit directly on server using local network," and if you are working on a remote server (if, for instance, you're building the site directly in a staging area) accessible via FTP or RDS, choose the third option, "Edit directly on server using FTP or RDS." Even then you'll still be prompted for a local folder where Dreamweaver can mirror the remote site.

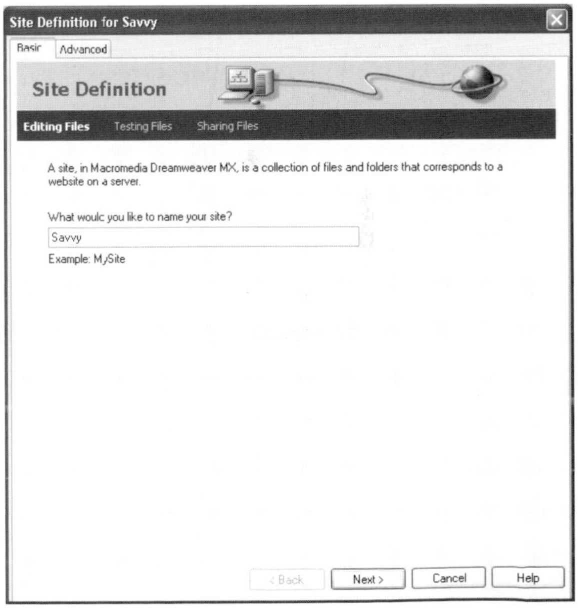

Figure 3.11

The Wizard starts simple by asking you to name your new site.

- If you choose to work with local copies (or if you choose the third option), type or browse to a root folder where the site will be stored on your computer.

- If you choose to work on files over a network, type or browse to the network folder you'll be using as your root.

Either way, after indicating your local root folder, click the Next button (see Figure 3.12).

Unless you chose a server technology in step 2 (in which case you've moved on to Chapter 23, right?), the wizard won't ask you anything about where your testing server can be found. Instead, you'll be asked about the remote site—the public site or staging area where the site is actually being built, as opposed to the local site where your working files are kept conveniently available for you at all times without any risk of compromising the integrity of the public site... phew). The most common choice here is FTP, but Dreamweaver also supports other ways of connecting to remote sites, such as via a standard network connection with Remote Data Services (RDS), or by using code-integrity database/authentication tools such as SourceSafe or Web-based Distributed Authoring and Versioning (WebDAV), which is an extension to the HTTP protocol.

To set up your remote connection, follow these steps:

1. Choose a connection method, and then either add your FTP remote hostname, folder, and login info (see Figure 3.13), browse to the remote network location, or for any of the other options, click the Settings button and enter the connection information. Then click Next.

If you're not sure about your FTP information yet, you can choose None from the drop-down list at this step and add the information when you have it available.

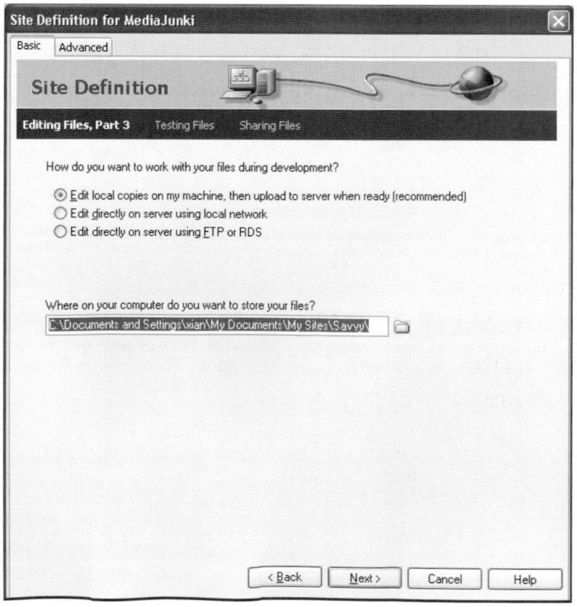

Figure 3.12

Dreamweaver is flexible about where you store and how you access both local and remote files.

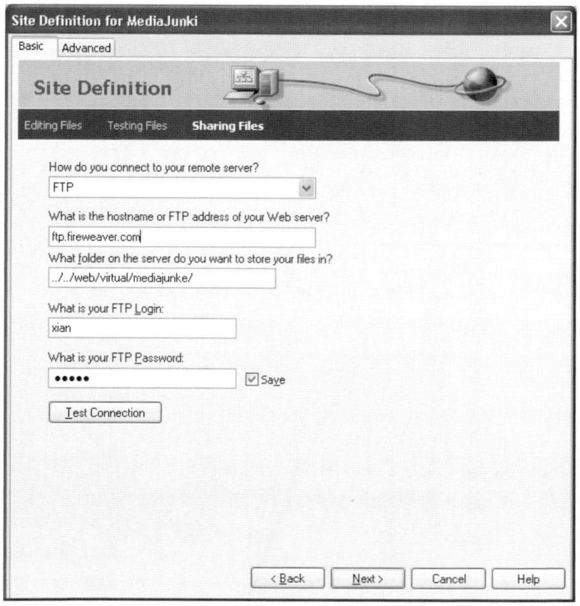

Figure 3.13

Dreamweaver now offers a Test Connection button that helps ensure your FTP (or other access method) information is correct before you move on.

2. If you chose any of the secure connection methods, then file Check In/Check Out is enabled by definition. For FTP or network connections, you can choose whether or not to turn on Check In/Check Out. (A good rule of thumb is that you do want it on unless you are working alone.) To turn it on, leave "Yes, enable check in and check out" selected. (To decline to use Check In/Check Out, select "No, do not enable check in and check out," then click the Next button, and then skip to step 6.)

3. Leave "Dreamweaver should check it out" selected as the answer to the next question, unless you want to shadow the project by viewing read-only files and preventing any opportunity for accidentally munging (overwriting) files.

4. Type your name or a unique, recognize moniker in the next box.

5. Type your e-mail address in the last box so that other collaborators can send you e-mail based on your check-out name, and then click the Next button.

6. Review the information you have entered and then click the Done button.

Whenever a file is checked out, Dreamweaver places a small text file with a .1ck (lock) extension on both the server and remote site. The LCK file stores the Check Out name of the person who has the file as well as their e-mail address. Do not delete this LCK file from the server or the status of the checked out file will be lost.

SETTING UP FOR COLLABORATION

In today's world, few commercial sites are built by a single person anymore. (Did I ever tell you about the old days...?) The more common practice is to assemble a team with different specialties and divvy out responsibilities for different portions of the site. In order to manage this potentially chaotic situation, Dreamweaver supports collaborative web design via the secure connection methods mentioned in this section, as well as by Check In/Check Out management, which is available even over an ordinary FTP connection.

You can manage who checks files in or out of the server during the design process by using Dreamweaver's Check In and Check Out commands (instead of just Put and Get). This prevents collaborators from accidentally overwriting someone else's work because only one person can have access to a file at any one time. Ever had someone upload an old version of a file over one you've just spent hours fine-tuning? It's not pretty.

Advanced Site Setup

If you don't need or want to use Dreamweaver's Site Setup Wizard, click the Advanced tab at the top of the Site Definition dialog box and then just work your way through the categories (Local Info, Remote Info, Testing Server, Cloaking—which means hiding files so they don't get uploaded to the site, Design Notes, Site Map Layout, and File View Columns). Most of the information covered is the same as in the Basic approach, but the presentation is more like a series of forms and less like a conversation (see Figure 3.14).

Here are some of the issues to consider:

- The Local Root folder identifies where you do your work locally, as opposed to the server where your site will ultimately be stored for serving over the Internet.

- If you know the URL (the domain name) of the server where your site will ultimately reside, type its address in the HTTP Address text box.

- Leave Enable Cache checked as long as you want Dreamweaver to track all the links at your site and update them automatically when you rearrange the furniture.

Setting Up Your Remote Site Server

In the Remote Info category, enter your access method and authentication information. For FTP or network-type connections, also indicate the path of the root folder on the remote server.

Figure 3.14

Advanced Setup doesn't hold your hand, but it can be faster for experienced users.

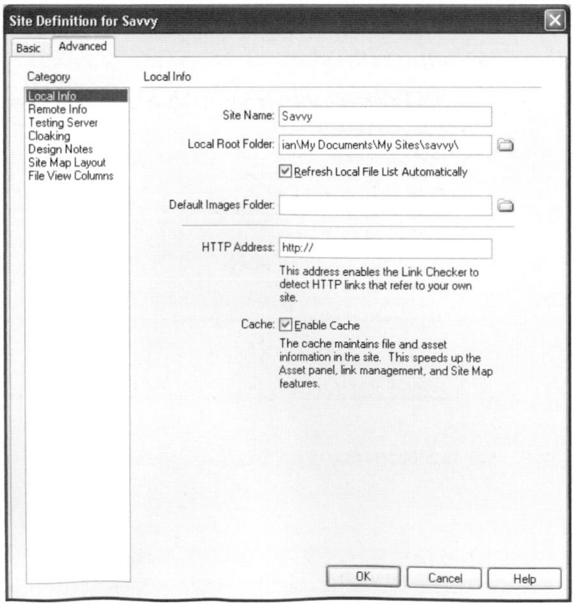

To set up a testing server for a database-backed web application project, choose the Testing Server category and enter the connection information required there. (See Chapter 22 for more on setting up web applications).

The Cloaking category enables you to shield files with specific extensions from upload or download. Dreamweaver suggests, for example, that you cloak .png files, which are Fireworks working files, because they cannot be displayed by all browsers—they are generally used as source files for .jpg or .gif files.

The Design Notes category enables you to turn on a collaborative feature for sharing comments about specific pages among the members of the design team.

Initializing a Site Map

Dreamweaver uses the Site Map portion of the Site panel to display file associations for your site. To set up your site map, you need to designate a file as the home page. If the page does not yet exist, Dreamweaver will create it as a blank document. This home page is generally the first page a reader will see when surfing to your site. (You can call this file anything, but `index.html` is the standard name on most web servers. Microsoft server software uses `default.htm` (or `default.asp` for dynamic pages, but that's another story) instead because Microsoft likes to be different.)

To initialize your site map, follow these steps:

1. Choose the Site Map Layout category from the Advanced tab of the Site Definition dialog box.

2. Type the filename of the home page or browse to it in the file hierarchy if it already exists.

3. Click OK.

Dreamweaver will then collect the folders, any contents such as presaved graphics and so forth, and build its cache, effectively indexing the website such as it is so far.

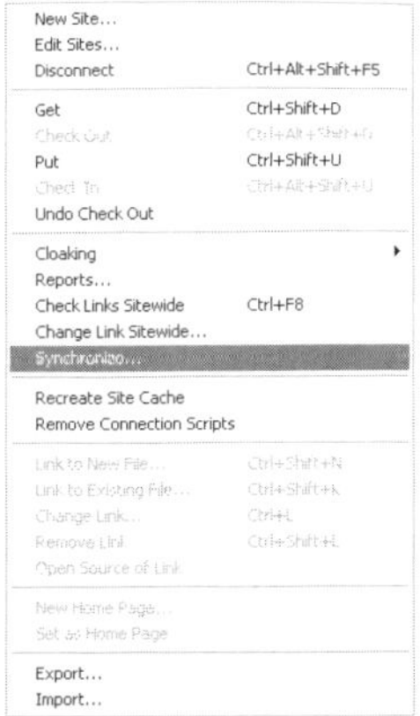

Importing an Existing Site

You will not always be fortunate enough to be there at the start of a new site or project. Often, you will be inheriting someone else's partially completed site, working on a site upgrade or revision, or even converting a site to Dreamweaver that you started with some other software or method.

To import a site, follow these steps.

1. First use the Site Definition Wizard or Advanced mode to set up your remote site and your local site (this was described in the previous sections).

2. Then, with the Site panel open, connect to the remote site by selecting Site → Connect or by clicking the Connect button.

3. Then select Site → Synchronize (see Figure 3.15).

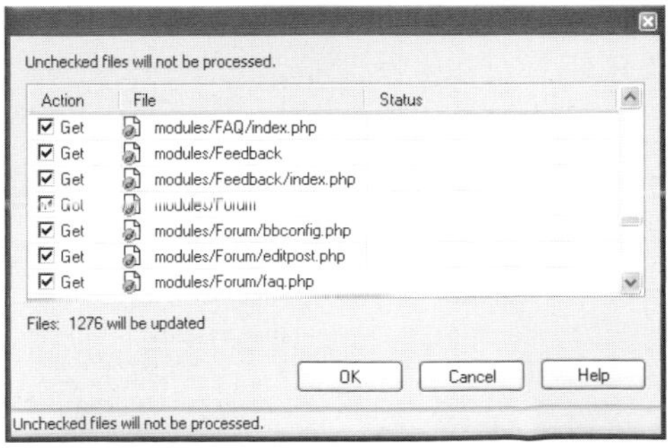

> On the Mac, you can use the main Site menu, but on the PC you must use the Site menu on the Site panel to select the Synchronize command.

4. From the resulting Synchronize Files dialog box, choose Entire '*Name Of Your Site*' Site in the first drop-down list menu and Get Newer Files from Remote in the second one.

Figure 3.15

Use the Synchronize command to import an entire remote site when you first set up, and then use it subsequently to keep the remote and local versions of the site in sync.

Figure 3.16

You can uncheck any files you, on reflection, decide not to synchronize, but if you want to download the entire remote site, just click OK.

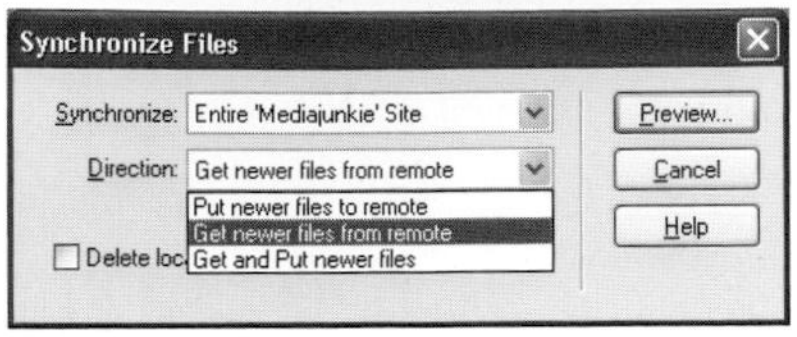

5. Then click the Preview button. Dreamweaver will review the selected files, and it will show you which ones it plans to download in the Synchronize dialog box that pops up (see Figure 3.16).

6. Click OK to begin the synchronization process. When you're done, you should have an entire mirror of the remote site at your local location.

Turning On Accessibility Reminders

One last thing you might want to consider doing before plunging with both feet into your web development schedule is to turn on reminders that help you develop a more accessible website (one that can be read by people with different abilities using special browsers, for example). Accessibility is a worthy topic unto itself, and in fact, in Chapter 30 we'll show you how to check your site's accessibility features before you go live, but for now let us show you how to turn on the reminders, and then you can decide on your own design criteria.

Figure 3.17

Tell Dreamweaver here that you want to be reminded about accessibility practices when inserting objects.

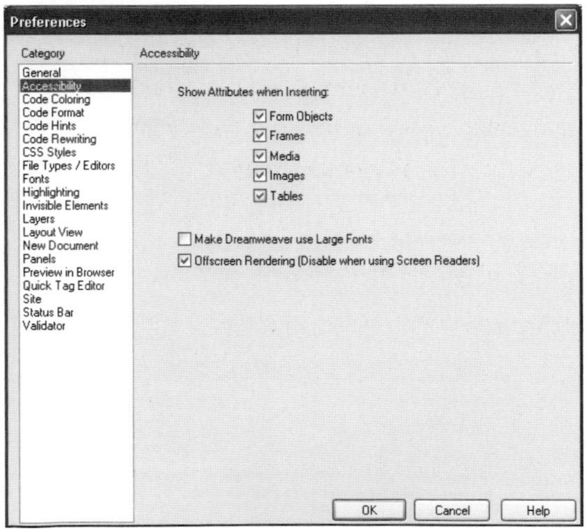

To turn on accessibility reminders, go the Preferences dialog box (Edit → Preferences) and choose the Accessibility category (see Figure 3.17).

Check the first five check boxes (Form Objects, Frames, Media, Images, Tables) to turn on the reminders. These reminders will take the form of a prompt, for example, one that prompts you to supply alternative text for images when inserting them.

The last two check boxes have more to do with making Dreamweaver itself more accessible. Use them to force the use of large fonts or to enable screen readers for those who cannot read from the screen directly.

Click OK.

As for Dreamweaver's accessibility as an application itself, Macromedia recommends using the Dreamweaver 4 (floating layout style) Workspace if you are using a screen reader; probably because this makes it easier for the reader to parse out the various elements on the screen if they are each in their own boxes.

Look-and-Feel Standards

Admittedly, this chapter is somewhat dry. It's that necessary housekeeping you have to do, at least once, so that Dreamweaver can count the beans for you and perform all of its automated tasks neatly, without error or complaint. In the next chapter, you get to work on the more interesting part of setting up a site: establishing design templates and using other tools to impose a consistent look-and-feel sitewide, with efficient use of repeating elements.

## CHAPTER 4

Saving Labor with Templates and Libraries

With a team in place, a plan on the easel, and your site folders assigned, one last aspect of sitewide setup remains: establishing a consistent look-and-feel for your site using Dreamweaver's powerful template feature. When you update a template, every page using that template is updated automatically. Beyond templates, you can also build up a collection of reusable objects and store them in something called the Library to make them available for any page. You'll access your templates, library items, and other reusable page elements through the Assets Manager. If you take the time to arrange your toolkit of resources before building pages, you can save a lot of time and effort during the development process, especially when changes are required or the work is shared among members of a collaborative team.

This chapter discusses the following items:

- ■ **Creating templates from example pages and from scratch**
- ■ **Nesting templates within other templates**
- ■ **Updating Dreamweaver 4 templates**
- ■ **Developing pages with a template**
- ■ **Editing a template's contents**
- ■ **The Assets Manager and the Library**
- ■ **Server-side includes (SSIs)**

What Is a Template?

The concept of a template comes to us from crafts and manufacturing: a *template* is a model used to replicate a design, as with a sewing pattern used to make clothing or a stencil used to guide a design in woodworking. Today, most applications that produce documents offer some sort of template that helps enforce a master design. In word-processing applications, templates are collections of content, styles, and page-formatting selections that can be used to create new documents with consistent design elements.

Dreamweaver's templates enable you to lock down some layout elements while allowing other content to be customized; this enables you to enforce consistency across a website. When you create a new page from a template, the page is linked to the template, so changes to the template update the linked page.

As shown in Figure 4.1, templates can have four different types of regions:

- Locked (noneditable regions)
- Editable regions
- Repeating regions
- Optional regions

Figure 4.1

A template can have locked, editable, repeating, and optional regions

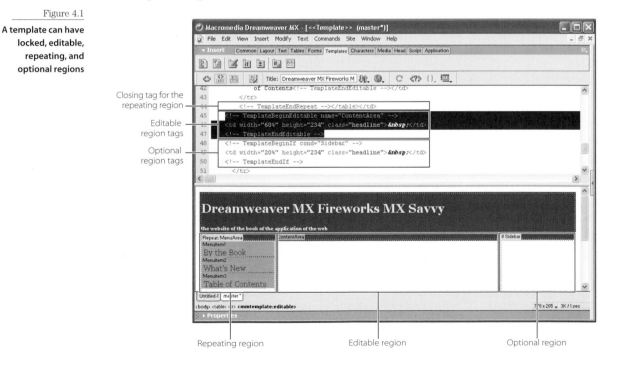

By default, all regions of a new template are locked. You must make specific regions editable (or repeating or optional). (Templates can also make tag attributes editable, which means that the tag will be required, but some of its attributes may be up to the individual page designer.)

Templates can help speed up the development of pages for a site. Without such a method for enforcing consistency, a team of collaborators will inevitably produce slightly inconsistent pages, requiring a reconciliation phase or an unprofessional-looking result. With templates, a large team can confidently build numerous pages rapidly, and as a result, updating a site becomes easier. This is a real plus in today's extremely competitive web environment where the more quickly new information is uploaded, the more visitors will gravitate to your site.

Templates are wonderful prototyping tools because any changes you make to a template will be replicated on all of its attached pages. You can build and edit a prototype page until all the elements are finalized, and then you can make the page a template and apply it to existing pages, automatically updating them to the new design.

Templates can contain not only text and HTML tags (encoding formatting, links, and multimedia), but also pre-programmed Java scripts that can do such things as

- Display current dates and times.
- Compare browsers for compatibility.
- Download snippets of HTML (called *server-side includes*) from databases or outside files (discussed at the end of this chapter).

Templates can also include any objects in your Library items directory (accessible via the Assets Manager, both discussed later in this chapter.) The more detail you include in your template, the quicker your team can turn around a project.

ECONOMIES OF SCALE IN WEB DEVELOPMENT

Many of the tools that have evolved to help web developers function in one way or another—by abstracting content and layout information from the individual page level and by sharing this information among multiple pages—speed development and make updating easier. Templates offer a Dreamweaver-specific method of doing this. Server-side includes (SSIs), discussed at the end of this chapter, represent another way to share page elements, and Cascading Style Sheets (CSS), discussed in Chapter 15, offer a web standards–compliant way of abstracting and sharing design information.

Fitting Templates into Your Development Process

Templates and pages represent a bit of a chicken-and-egg paradox. An efficient development process requires templates to make page production quick and accurate, but templates have to come from somewhere. Whether you create a template from scratch or convert an existing page into a template (we'll explain both methods soon), you must know a thing or two about page development to do so. The truth, therefore, is that the process is usually a bit iterative (or even recursive)—something like this:

1. Plan templates based on page content and navigation and site information architecture.

2. Develop sample pages for various parts of the site, including a sample home page, subordinate pages, and navigation dummies (pages with navigation but no content).

3. Turn reviewed and finalized samples into templates.

4. Develop actual site pages from templates.

5. Launch site and hand over templates to whoever will be administering and maintaining the site.

This means you also have some choices about how to navigate this book. Because making templates is a key part of setting up a site for development, we have chosen to include this chapter here in the first part of the book. But as we just alluded to, making templates depends on some skills related to page development, so you will probably have to read this chapter for informational purposes and then work on Parts II and III of this book to learn how to construct web pages. Eventually, you may want to come back to this chapter to turn those pages into templates.

Making Templates

There are two ways to prepare a template: by creating a blank page and saving it as a template (and then adding the design elements), or by opening an existing page and saving it as a template. Both approaches are appropriate in different situations. When you have the formatting ideas specified first, you can create the template from a blank page, implement the design on the blank template, and then create pages attached to that template. If you decide to use the design of an existing page as a template for other pages, then use the latter approach (open the model page and save it as a template).

Making a Template Page from Scratch

Build your template from scratch if you've planned out your layout carefully—you've measured the height and width of the areas where you wish to place graphics, text, links, multimedia, and so forth. Then lay out "dummy" elements to fill those specified spaces and inform your collaborators where their data should be placed. To create a new page, choose File → New, make sure the General tab is selected, as well as the Basic Page category and the HTML type basic page, and then click the Create button. A blank page is displayed on the desktop. Use the Insert bar to add layers, tables, images, and so forth.

You can also construct an actual page first, with all of its links, title bars, and so forth in place, and then identify where new content should be inserted.

> When creating a master page, before turning it into a template, use Modify → Page Properties
> (Ctrl/Cmd + J) to set up text, links, background colors, margins, and other page-design stan-
> dards for all the pages that will be based on the template. Or, you may alternatively want
> to attach a style sheet to the template to control these same sort of page-layout features.
> (See Chapter 15 for more on style sheets).

To make a template from your master page, choose File → Save as Template (or click the Make Template button on the Templates tab of the Insert bar). Dreamweaver displays the Save As Template dialog box (Figure 4.2). Indicate which site the template is for with the Site pop-up menu, and give the template a descriptive name.

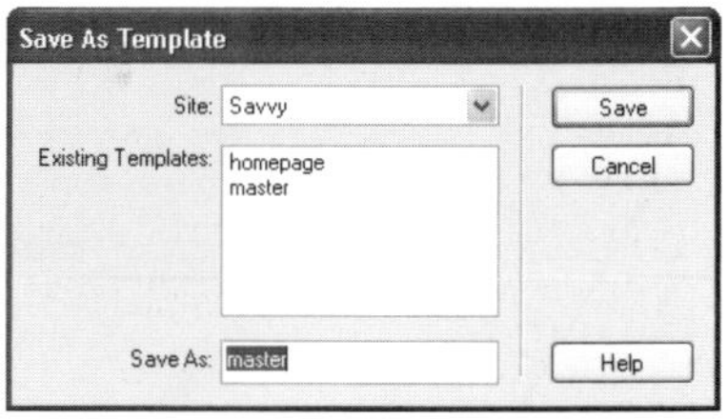

Figure 4.2

Templates can be applied to more than one site. Use this dialog box to assign a new template to a site and give the template a name.

Another Way to Create a Template from Scratch

Instead of making a page and then saving it as a template, you can also make a new blank template and then insert the locked and edited regions you need. You can make a new template using the New Template button in the Templates area of the *Assets Manager*, a tool that collects all of your site objects together in one handy panel from which you can drag and drop objects onto pages. The Assets Manager is in the File panel.

> In the floating layout, the only workspace available to Mac users, the Asset Manager is the
> only tab in the File panel.

Icons identifying the various objects available for use on a website are displayed down the left side. To create a new template, first click the Templates icon to show the Templates category of the Assets Manager (see Figure 4.3).

> On the bottom of every panel in Dreamweaver and Fireworks you will see a series of small
> icons. These buttons let you quickly perform four functions: refresh, create a new item, edit
> an item, or delete an item.

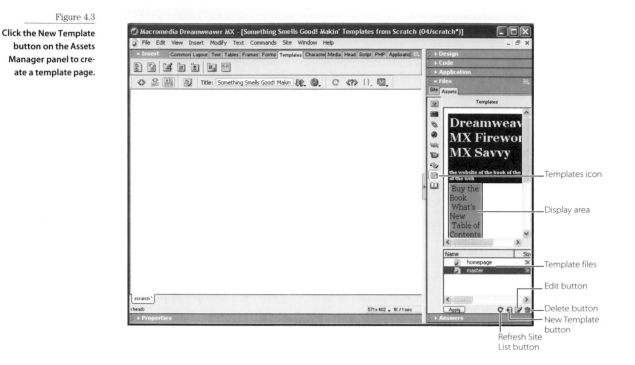

Now, to create a new template once you have this Templates category showing, click the New Template button on the bottom panel (it looks like a piece of paper with a plus sign). Dreamweaver adds a new template with a text box in which you type a name for the new page. You are also given instructions (that appear in the display area located above the file list) on how to create the template from the resulting blank page.

The default name for a new template (or any page for that matter) is "untitled." Type a new name for the embryonic template and hit Enter. The page is added to the template file list, but there is nothing *on* the page as of yet.

Select the new template page from the Templates category and click the Edit button (it looks like a pencil and paper). The blank page is displayed and ready for you to add content.

Save your new content but do not close the page yet because you need to unlock areas to allow editing.

Making a Template from an Existing Page

There are times when you will have a page already designed and you'll realize you want to turn it into a template (or, more properly, create a new template based on the existing page). For example, if your job is to take over or refresh an existing site, some of the current pages may make good models for a template.

Making a new template from an existing web page is very easy. Just double-click the page in the Site panel, or choose File → Open and choose the page from the resulting Open dialog box. Then, after you have made any changes to the page, choose File → Save as Template. Be sure to keep the resulting template page open so that you can define editable areas.

Tips for Creating Templates

You will make it easier on your collaborators if you follow these "best practices":

- Document your design.
- Finalize as much material on the page as possible.
- Set up underlying parameters.
- Include `<meta>` tag information.
- Add your Dreamweaver extensions and their behaviors to the template.

Documenting Your Design

Document your design so that your collaborators understand the types of materials they will need to add to each editable region. The easiest way to communicate your wishes is to add dummy text or graphics to the editable areas of your template that indicate the types of information that should be inserted. For example, if your page is a "contact us" page, add a dummy e-mail address table in the space provided. Your coworkers then simply have to replace the dummy with the real thing. Another trick is to make the dummy a Library item. In this way, your collaborators simply have to edit the object and Dreamweaver automatically updates any page using that element via the template. See the "Building a Library" section below for further discussion on how to update Library items.

Finalizing Content

The more structure you provide to the page, the faster it is completed. For this reason, you should finalize as much material on the page as possible, without compromising the ability of your team to diversify pages as required. For example, if you have a masthead, advertising banner, navigation bar with links or rollover buttons, copyright blurb, and web ring links on every page, add these objects to the template. Also add a table or layer to indicate any block where new content is to be placed.

Setting Up Parameters

Set up underlying parameters for areas where a graphic or multimedia object is to be placed, such as borders, cell height and width, background color, and so forth, so that any new object inserted will inherit and thereby comply with the layout requirements of the page. Use the Property Inspector to preset parameters.

Including *<meta>* Tag Information

Search engines use keywords coded into the `<meta>` tag area of the `<head>` tag to find sites. It is a good idea to precode these keywords, or any other type of information you wish to document to browsers in the template, so that they appear on every page of your site. Choose Insert → Head Tags → Meta to display the Meta dialog box as shown in Figure 4.5. In the resulting dialog box, type "Keywords" in the Value text box. Enter your keywords separated by spaces (and bound with quotation marks for multiword phrases) in the Contents text box. See Chapter 25 for further discussion of advertising your site and the use of `<meta>` tag data.

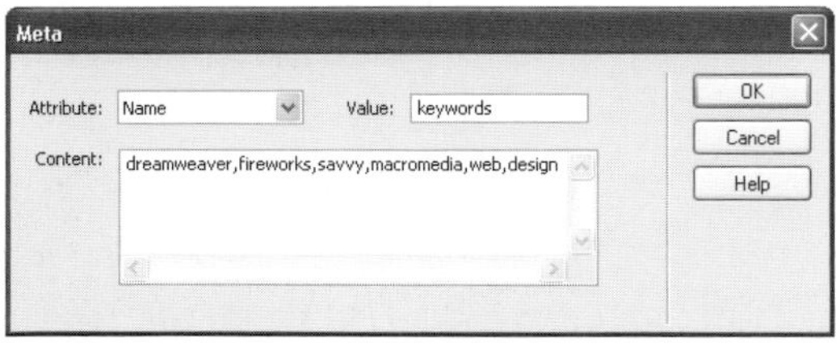

Figure 4.4

Use this dialog box to add <meta> **keywords to your** <head> **area to allow successful retrieval of your site by search engines.**

Adding Extensions and Behaviors

Add all your Dreamweaver extensions and their attendant behaviors into the template. Also attach the Cascading Style Sheet (CSS) to the template and prebuild all of the styles you wish to use. The problem with using a template is that the `<head>` area (where most behavior code is stored) is automatically locked and cannot be defined as an editable region in a template. Therefore, all information, including Java scripts, that is included in the `<head>` area must be in place prior to saving a page as a template. Don't get scared yet, we'll walk you through how to use CSS and behaviors in later chapters in the book. Just be aware that templates should contain this information because it cannot be later hard-coded into separate pages.

When you create a template page, Dreamweaver saves the file with a special extension, `.dwt`, in the Templates folder that is created for each defined site. Dreamweaver adds the word `<Template>` to the file title whenever you save a page as a template to indicate its special purpose. All of the contents of the Templates folder are reflected in the Templates category of the Assets Manager.

Configuring a Template

At this point, you have a template, but it is not usable by anyone because by default, all of its elements are locked and cannot be changed.

To unlock areas for editing, you need to define editable regions. There are two ways to do this:

- You can assign an existing layout element as editable.
- You can add new editable areas.

Give each editable area a unique descriptive name. Anybody building a page for your site from the template can press the Tab key to jump through the editable areas, skipping the locked areas.

Assigning an Editable Area

To choose a layout element (usually a table cell or layer) and make it editable, do the following:

1. Select the element with your mouse or, in the status bar, select the `<td>` (table cell) tag for tables or the `<div>` (page division) tag for layers.

2. Click the Editable Region button on the Templates tab of the Insert bar (or choose Insert → Template Objects → Editable Region). You can also use the keyboard combination Ctrl + Alt + V (Cmd + Option + V on the Mac) to do the same thing.

3. In the New Editable Region dialog box, type a name for the editable area (see Figure 4.5) and click OK.

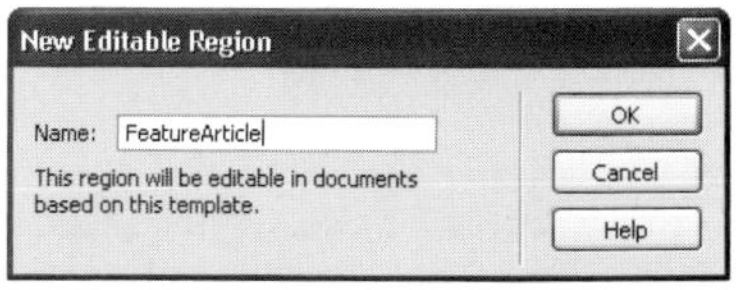

Figure 4.5

Give the new editable region a name identifying its purpose.

> Template names can contain spaces (although it is not recommended). When naming your template, do not use the following characters: ampersand (&), double quotation mark ("), single quotation mark ('), or the left or right angle brackets (</>). This rule is a general naming convention for all filenames within Dreamweaver.

4. Dreamweaver puts a blue outline around the editable region and displays its name.

Creating a New Editable Region

You can also just insert blank editable regions anywhere with the New Editable Region command. To do so, click your mouse where you wish to add the region and click the Editable Region button. Give the region a name that identifies the type of content to be entered into the space.

> You can edit the region label by selecting the text inside the brackets in either the Document window or in Code view and typing a new message. Anything appearing within the brackets is hidden and will not appear on the published page.

Repeating Regions and Optional Regions

You insert the other types of regions the same way you do editable regions. Actually, the terminology can be a little confusing. For example, repeating regions are themselves editable. Optional regions can be editable or not. Also, there are really two types of repeating regions: one type is called simply repeating regions, and the other is called repeating tables. Repeating tables are still repeating regions, but they include table tags automatically, since tables are the most common type of repeating page element.

The Insert bar is the most useful tool for inserting the other types of regions. Just select the area you want to designate and click the Repeating Region, Optional Region, Editable Optional Region, or Repeating Table button. If you insert an optional region, you'll be prompted to describe the conditions (such as variables that can be set and checked) that will determine whether the optional region should appear. You can also leave the conditions unspecified to allow individual page designers discretion about whether to include or exclude the optional template region in their page.

Relocking Regions

To lock a region so that it is no longer editable, chose Modify → Templates → Remove Template Markup. Dreamweaver unmarks the area, relocking it from use. When you save the template, Dreamweaver updates all of its associated pages.

TIPS AND TRICKS FOR EDITABLE REGIONS

Here are some important tips to remember when assigning editable regions.

Always select a complete tag pair (for example, an entire table begins with the `<table>` tag and concludes with the `</table>` tag). Note that HTML uses pairs of tags to indicate the beginning of a formatting selection and its ending. Everything between the opening tag and the closing tag uses the specified formatting. This has very important ramifications for tables because it precludes you from selecting multiple rows or columns and it allows you only to select an entire table or a single cell (indicated by the `<td>`/`</td>` tag pair). The easiest way to ensure that you have selected an entire tag pair is to choose the tag label from the status bar. Dreamweaver will indicate on the Document window the extent of your selection.

Be sure to include the `<p>` tag in your editable region, if you want to use paragraph returns within an edited area. If you don't include the `<p>`/`</p>` tag pair, you will be limited to the use of the less powerful soft-return `<br>` option between paragraphs, and subsequently, you will have formatting issues to deal with because the `<br>` tag does not complete a formatting instruction in the same way that the `<p>` tag does. To ensure that you include a least one hard return within a selection, choose the `<p>` tag in the Tag Selector in the status bar.

Be sure to apply all text formatting. You should apply all text formatting including any CSS styles, before you define an editable region because you will want to carry your formats across pages via the template's editable regions.

Open the Code and Design view. A good technique when creating editable regions is to open the Code and Design view so that you can watch the code as you define editable areas. This way you can ensure that you pick up the entire tag pair.

Adding Links to a Template

You must be careful when you add links to a template because making those links work correctly on attached pages is a tricky business. If you wish to anticipate links in the template to pages that have not yet been created, their (prospective) filenames must be typed by hand.

For example, in our sample template, we have a link to a file called `employment.html`. Because the page does not yet exist, Dreamweaver places a blank placeholder page in the Templates folder called `employment.html` (with a pathname of …/`Templates/employment.html`). The potential problem is that if the referred-to file is moved later in the process, the link will fail (just as embedded objects would fail to display if moved).

The best solution is not to hand-type links, but to pre-create all pages that will exist in the site (at least set up files with formal filenames in a proper folder) prior to creating the template. Then, use the pointer or folder icon link and the Property Inspector and let Dreamweaver manage file names and locations. Never manually type in hypertext links if you can help it.

> Templates must be saved in the Templates folder on the root level of the site. Do not move the Templates folder or its contents or you will detach the template from the site, and it will be inaccessible (although it will still show up in the Templates category).

Closing and Reopening Templates

To close a template you're working on, just close its window, as you would with any other kind of document. After closing a template, you can open it again in several ways. The easiest way is to select its name from the Template category of the Assets Manager and click the Edit button on the bottom of the Assets Manager panel.

You can also double-click the template name in the Template category or choose File → Open (keyboard combination Ctrl + O, or Cmd + O on the Mac) and choose the template straight from the Template folder inside your site folder. One further way to open the template is to locate it in the Site window and double-click it.

Basing Templates on Other Templates

With Dreamweaver MX, you can now base a new template on an existing template. Such templates are referred to as *nested templates*. The nested template inherits the design and editable regions from the parent template, but you can define further locked and editable regions in the nested template.

Why would you want to do this? Well, let's say that all the pages at your site are going to have the same banner and universal navigation at the top, but that different site sections will have different subnavigation, say, down the left side of each page below the banner. Well, then, an easy way to control this standard and its variations would be to create a master template that defines the top area of the page. Then templates for each subsection of the site could be based on (nested from) the master template, with different subnavigation defined for each. Changes to the master template would trickle down to all pages based on these subtemplates, but changes to the side navigation on a nested template would change only the pages in that section (that is, those based on the nested template).

To make a nested template, first make a new document based on the master template (as explained in the next section), and then click the Make Nested Template button on the Templates tab of the Insert bar (or select File → Save as Template), and save the new document as a template.

> You can nest as many templates as you like, although if you get too creative it can get pretty confusing!

Applying a Template

There are several ways to apply your template to pages in the site. The most typical way is to create a new page from the template and then work on it. The benefit of this method is that you do not have to deal with existing information on the page; instead, you can start fresh using the template as a layout guide. Most of the time, this is the tactic you'll take in collaboration scenarios.

An alternative way of using the template is to apply the template to an existing page. This method is best implemented when you wish to update existing pages and use a new template. This happens when sites are radically altered. Applying the template to an existing page is fraught with peril.

Let's look at these two options more closely.

Creating a New Page from a Template

The cleanest and easiest way to use a template is to create a new page from it. There are two ways to do this.

- Right-click (Ctrl-click on the Mac) the template name in the Assets Manager and choose New from Template.

- Click File → New, and choose the Templates tab, choose your site in the Templates For box, and then choose the template you want to base your new page on from the Site section (see Figure 4.6).

Applying the Template to an Existing Page

Templates are easily applied to existing pages, but the resulting confusion between new information and existing information can be difficult to manage.

To associate a template with an existing page, open the page in question from either the Site panel or by using the File → Open command. Then, drag the template from the Asset Manager onto the open page window. You can also choose Modify → Templates → Apply Template to Page and choose the template that you wish to attach to the page from the resulting dialog box. In both cases, if there's any existing content on the page, you have to assign it a region of the template, using the Inconsistent Region Names dialog box (see Figure 4.7).

Remember that templates contain locked and editable spaces. Dreamweaver's template assumes that all areas of the page that are to be attached are locked until you associate them with existing editable areas. The only option Dreamweaver offers is to dump the entire contents of the existing page into one of the editable regions of the templated page. Yech. The best option is to delete everything on the existing page by selecting the Nowhere option from the dialog box. If you wish to keep information from the original page, choose an editable region and dump the material in it. You then must manually delete those pieces that you do not wish to retain.

One of the most frustrating things about creating template-based web pages is the fact that when you are building the template, you must take into account the largest size block required by every page so that you can make allowances should you wish to add a repeating object, such as a copyright notice, beneath the block. If you don't calculate the height and width of a table or layer in advance, then you run the risk of overlapping the locked item lying below the editable region with the contents of the editable region, and you have no way to fix the problem without detaching the template from the page with the error. To avoid this problem, specify the maximum size of an editable region and size your content accordingly.

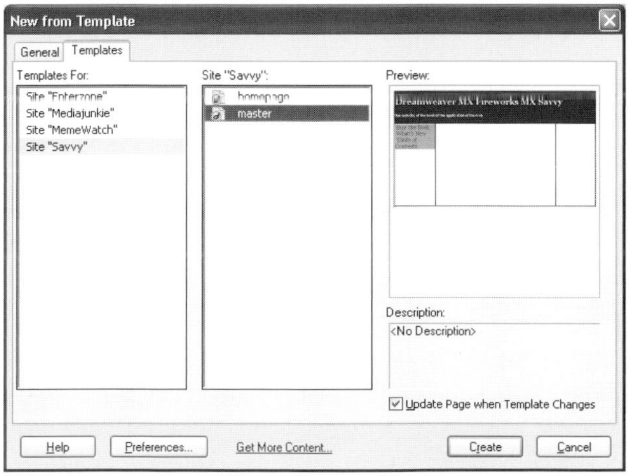

Figure 4.6

You can use a template from any site by using the New From Template command.

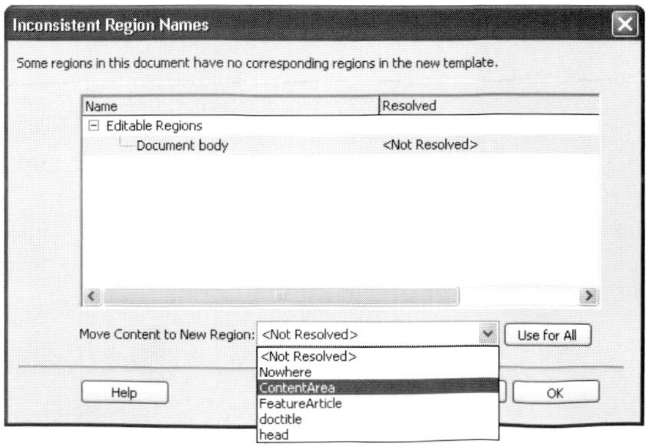

Figure 4.7

When you attach a template to an existing page, you must select where you wish existing content to be placed.

Modifying Template-Based Pages

When you attach a template to a page, you carry across every item that exists on the template to the attached page. This is both good and bad. The good part is that you don't have to reproduce difficult Java scripts or replace graphics because they already will be available from the template. *The bad part is that you cannot add behaviors to individual pages that use templates because the <head> tag region is always locked.* There are three solutions to this problem:

- Add the template, detach it from the page (by doing this you'll get the formatting and layout but you'll be unlocking every element, thus losing one of the more useful features of a template), and then add the behavior to the page.

- Add the behavior to the template, or add a special code in the <head> area to hold the place where you can later add code as required.

- Add the material to the template in the first place. This is the best solution.

Detaching a Template

To detach an attached template from a page, choose Modify → Templates → Detach From Template. Don't reapply the template again later once you've changed the page, though, because if you do, any changes you have made to the detached page will be lost.

Editing a Template from an Associated Page

If you have permission to work on the template, you can edit the template from an associated page. From the linked page, choose Modify → Templates → Open Attached Template. Make the changes to the template and update only the page you are working on by choosing Modify → Templates → Update Current Page. Of course any changes you make to the template will be reflected ultimately on every other page on the site, so think carefully before editing the template.

Adding Behaviors Code to a Template

To set up a template so that you can enable unique behaviors to be added later to attached pages, do the following.

1. Open the template by selecting its name from the Template category and clicking the Edit button on the Asset Manager.

2. Use the Code and Design view and scroll in the Code view area to the </head> tag. A quick way to jump to the right area in the code is to select the <body> tag in the Tag Selector. The </head> tag is right above the <body> tag.

3. Type the following code above the `</head>` tag:

```
<mm:editable>
<script>
</script>
</mm:editable>

<mm:editable>
<!--Dummy comment, to be deleted by Dreamweaver -->
</mm:editable>
```

4. Save the template and update the pages.

Dreamweaver removes the dummy comment but keeps the editable region containing the `<script>` tag pair. In the attached pages, you can then copy and paste your script between these tags.

> See Chapter 26 for information on importing and exporting XML in Dreamweaver using templates.

Updating Pages Linked to Templates

Whenever you make or edit a template, you have to save it before Dreamweaver will update any pages linked to it. To save the template, choose File → Save (or press the keyboard combination Ctrl + S or Command + S on the Mac). Dreamweaver instantly updates any linked files.

Using Your Old Dreamweaver 4 Templates

If you are an experienced Dreamweaver user and have created templates with the previous version of the software, then your work is reusable. It's true that Macromedia has changed the syntax used in the custom codes Dreamweaver inserts in templates and template-based documents to control and track the locked and editable regions, but Dreamweaver MX understands the older syntax and, perhaps more importantly, will not change or update the syntax to the MX style.

However, if you are working with a Dreamweaver 4 template in Dreamweaver MX and you insert a new region into the document, the syntax of the tags used to create the new region will be the newer style, and this will make the template unreadable in older versions of Dreamweaver.

Managing Your Other Assets

The Assets Manager is the collection point for all of the objects and elements you use in your site. As you build the site, the Assets Manager grows. All colors, external and internal links, images, Flash files, templates, Java scripts, Library items, and snippets of HTML are available via the Assets Manager for dragging and dropping into a page. In this way, you have at your fingertips all of the things you may need to efficiently build a consistent site.

As mentioned earlier, the Assets Manager is in the Files panel (see Figure 4.3), and you can open it by choosing Window → Assets if it's not already visible.

The Assets Manager consists of nine category buttons, a file list section, and a display section along with the ubiquitous pop-up menu and bottom icons. Table 4.1 lists the contents of each category and how it is used.

One of the shortcomings of the Assets Manager panel is the way it lists files: alphabetically. This makes it especially difficult to locate specific files. Take for example the images category. As you will see later on in this book, rollovers often have arcane names based on the location of the image on the page and their rollover type (see Chapter 18 for more on rollovers). These multiple images are included in the list as is every iteration of a graphic ever saved in your local site.

In addition, all of these files are listed without folders in a linear fashion. The only saving grace of this system is that when you select a file, its contents are displayed in the Contents window above the file list. But you definitely cannot browse quickly through the list depending upon filenames alone to find your way.

Dreamweaver does include a Favorites view for each category in which you can save favorite objects for quick access. In this view, you can give your files names that help organize them alphabetically, preceding common elements with the same prefix (such as movie-, flash-, graphic-, and so on).

To jump to a file (if you know its name) type the first letter of its name.

Table 4.1

The Assets Manager Categories

CATEGORY	CONTENTS
Images	All of the graphics contained in every page along with any other graphics saved under the Images folder in the Site folder.
Colors	All of the actual colors used in the site. This color palette is a subset of the web-safe palette. In addition, any colors extracted from a graphic with the Eyedropper tool are also included. Drag colors from the palette to color layers, table cells, and so forth.
URLs	The Uniform Resource Locator (URL) addresses, both external and internal to the site, are listed. All hypertext links to e-mail addresses, external graphics, Java scripts, server-side includes, or Internet addresses are listed. Drag an address on to an object to create a new link.
Flash	The Shockwave Flash files (identified by the `.swf` extension) that you used in the site are saved here. See Chapter 17 for a discussion of these.
Shockwave	Macromedia Shockwave files are listed in this category. See Chapter 17 for a discussion of multimedia plugins.
Movies	QuickTime movies and MPEG video files are listed in this category. See Chapter 17 for a discussion of multimedia plugins.
Scripts	This category lists the independent script files that are called by Dreamweaver. These include Java scripts, VBScripts, SSI scripts, or other applets used by the site. See Chapter 19 for information about applying behaviors to the site.
Templates	Templates used by the site are listed here. But you know all about these already, right?
Library	This is a special category that holds objects used on multiple pages. When you change a Library item, it is updated throughout the site. These objects can be scraps of text, graphics, tables, and more. You can pre-create Library items and repeat their use throughout the site. See the discussion in "Building a Library," later in this chapter for a description of how this works.

Working with the Assets Manager

To use an asset from the Assets Manger, click a category button and then select a file name from the resulting list. To use the element, drag it on to the page. The Assets Manager has several other interesting features that you can access through the following tabs: Favorites, Renaming, Editing, and Updating.

Using the Favorites Tab

When you start to use Dreamweaver and its Assets Manager, you will quickly notice how fast objects build up in its categories. It becomes very time consuming to browse down the file list trying to locate the one file you need to complete a page. The solution is to switch from the Site view to the Favorites view within the Assets panel. Click the Favorites radio button to switch views. The Favorites view provides the same nine categories, but you get to select what is included in the file list in each category.

To add an item to its Favorites view, select the filename and click the Favorites button (it looks like a little purple ribbon with a plus sign) on the bottom of the Assets panel. You can also use the Shortcuts menu by right-clicking and choosing Add To Favorites (you Mac users will need to press Ctrl-click and open the pop-up menu and then do the same thing). You can also use the pop-up menu on the Assets panel to select Add To Favorites.

ADDING COLORS TO THE FAVORITES VIEW

One of the strongest uses for the Favorites view is using it to copy colors from any source. When you collect colors on the Favorites view, you can quickly add them to other objects by dragging and dropping them from the Assets' Color category onto an object. To copy a color, do the following.

1. Click the Favorites radio button to switch to Favorites view.

2. Click the Color category button.

3. Click the New Color button on the bottom of the Assets panel (it looks like a piece of paper with a plus sign).

4. In the resulting color palette shown here, use the Eyedropper to either choose a color from the palette or click anywhere on the Document window to pick up that color.

5. The color is added to the Favorites file list along with its hexadecimal value. As you see, the color's name reflects this value. Because it is difficult to identify a color by its numerical value, give the color a nickname by right-clicking the color. In the resulting shortcut menu, choose Edit Nickname. Type a new name in the resulting text box. (Mac users, you should Ctrl-click to reveal the pop-up menu and do the same thing.)

The colors you add to the Favorites list won't appear on the Site panel until you use them on a page.

> Add an URL to the Favorites view by selecting the URL category and clicking the Add To Favorites button on the bottom of the Assets panel. In the resulting dialog box, type the URL's address and a nickname by which to remember the link. The URL is added to the Favorites view. Use the URL in another page to add it to your Site Assets.

Inserting an Asset on a Page

There are two ways to insert assets: you can drag and drop them or you can insert them using the Insert button. Dragging and dropping an object is the easiest way of applying it to a page. To do this, simply select the object and drag it onto the Document window. Dragging and dropping works well for images, applets, multimedia files and such, but it does not work well for certain applications, such as colors or URLs. For these objects, you need to use the Insert button on the bottom of the Assets panel or from the Assets pop-up menu. (Note that depending on the object you are inserting, the command may say "Apply" rather than "Insert," but it means the same thing.)

> When you use the Insert button to change the color of text, the color will apply only to any text you type from the point forward from your current cursor position. To change the color of existing text, always select it first before you drag and drop the color or use the Insert button.

Building a Library

One of the most tedious and laborious things you have to do when you are maintaining a website is update every page when one tidbit of information changes. Dreamweaver has conquered this tedium by providing you with a way to edit a repeating item once and then have its appearance updated on every subsequent page where it is used. The magical device that performs this service is the Library.

Before the advent of the Library in Dreamweaver 4, the only way to include repeating information was through an arcane piece of scripting called the server-side include (SSI). SSIs are bits of HTML (which lack the `<head>` tag pair) that can be inserted into documents by the server on delivery. SSIs are most useful when they are used for shared content, such as standard navigation elements. SSIs have their uses—such as when you wish to create a dynamically changing piece of content (a query report from a database or a real-time news report, for example). In fact, we'll show you how to insert SSIs in the next section of this chapter, but repeatedly sucking in objects from outside HTML files (which is what SSIs do) is a very processing-intense, I/O-intense drain on the web server. For this reason, many ISPs and IP organizations do not allow the use of SSIs.

The Library is also accessed from the Assets Manager panel (it's the last category button).

Library items are saved in the Library folder at the root level of your site directory and given the file extension .lbi. Do not move items from the Library folder or rename the folder; if you do, the links to and from the Library items will be lost.

Adding Content to the Library

You can create Library items before you begin building your website, or you can select existing items on a page and add them to the Library. There are of course, a couple methods available for building up the Library's contents.

- Use the New Library Item button on the Assets panel.

  To do this, select the text, graphic, or other object on the web page and click the New Library Item button on the bottom of the Assets panel or from the Assets panel's pop-up menu. As shown in Figure 4.8, your item is added to the file list, displayed in the Contents screen, and given the name "untitled." Give the item a name that you will remember. The selected object is also highlighted in yellow on the web page to indicate that it is a Library item.

- Drag and drop the object into the Library category.

  To do this, select the item from your web page and drag it on to the File List section of the Library panel. The result is the same as what happened when you used the New Library Item command.

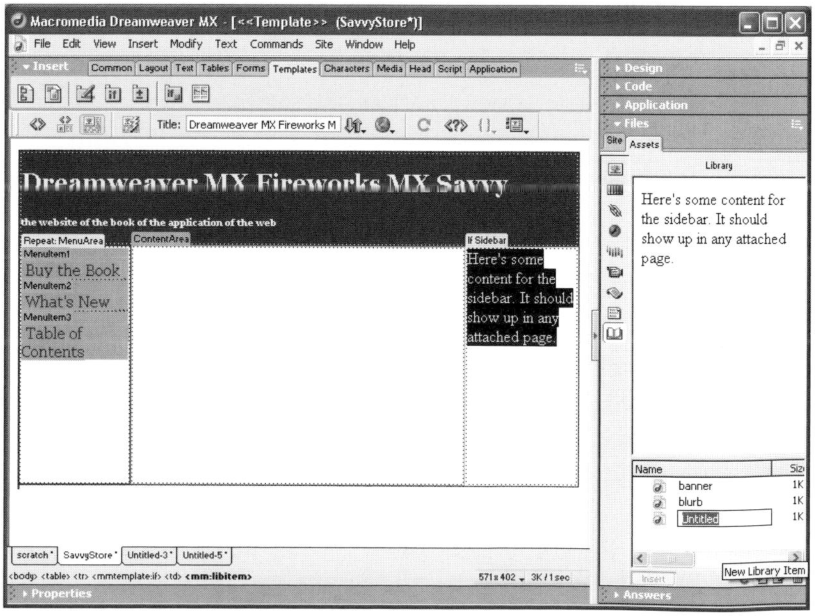

Figure 4.8

When you create a new Library item from an existing object, the object is highlighted on the page, indicating that it is now a reusable element.

When you create a Library item from text that has been styled using a Cascading Style Sheet, be aware that the style sheet does not transfer with the Library item—thus, the formatting will not appear the same on a page that uses a different style sheet than the one attached to the page that the element came from.

Inserting a Library Item on a Page

The easiest way to insert a Library item on a page is to drag it from the Library category on to the page. You can also select the filename of the Library item and click the Insert button. The element is placed where you clicked your cursor on the page.

Editing a Library Item

Library items are useful because they can be edited once and updated on every page on which they are used on the site. The element can be edited either in the special Library Editing window (in the case of text or a combination element) or via its originating program. To edit a Library item, select its filename and click the Edit button on the bottom of the Assets panel. Make your changes in the resulting Library Item window, which, for objects Dreamweaver can edit, is just like an ordinary document window.

To edit Library items that originated in another application (such as Fireworks), click the small arrow to expand the Property Inspector's panel and then click the Edit button.

You can also edit a Library item by selecting it directly on the page and then clicking the Open button on the resulting Library Inspector window (see Figure 4.9).

Figure 4.9

The Library Inspector enables you to open, re-create, or detach Library items from a page.

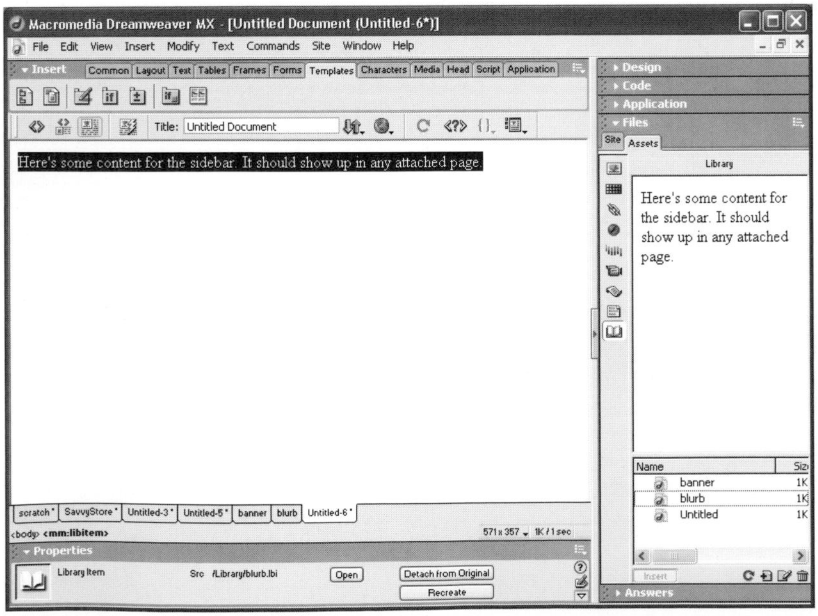

Updating the Website When Library Items Change

Whenever you make changes to a Library item or add a new one to a page, you must save the page and update the site so that Dreamweaver can propagate the change to pages that incorporate the Library item. To update the Library, choose Modify → Library → Update Pages. In the dialog box that appears, choose Entire Site and then click the Start button (see Figure 4.10).

You can also update the current page (with Modify → Library → Update Current Page) to reflect changes and see how they work before applying the change or addition to the every page that uses the element.

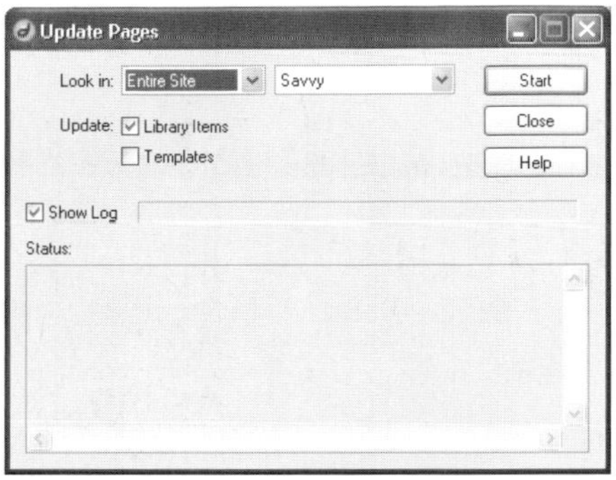

Figure 4.10

Updating a site after changing a Library item.

Deleting a Library Item

If you no longer wish to use a Library item, you can delete it from the Assets panel. Actually deleting it from a page takes a second step that requires you to detach the library item from the page, thus breaking the link. The element is now fully editable in the document.

To delete an element, select it from the file list in the Library category and click the Delete button on the bottom of the Assets Manager (the little trash can). You can also delete an item by selecting it and choosing Delete from either the shortcut menu (contextual menu for you Mac fans) or the pop-up menu on the Assets panel.

To detach the deleted Library item from the actual element on the page (and thus release it from bondage), select the element and click the Detach From Original button on the Library Inspector.

> Should you accidentally delete a Library item from the Library category, you can retrieve it if you still have a web page that uses the element. Open that web page and select the element. In the Library Inspector, click Recreate. Dreamweaver re-creates the Library, thus restoring the element. Whew, no harm done.

Using Server Side Includes (SSIs) as Repeating Elements

As discussed in the previous section, some site developers like to use server-side includes (SSIs) to store a piece of reusable content in a single file and let the web server include that content when pages containing a SSI referring to that file are served up. Dreamweaver makes it very easy to insert SSIs and even shows you how the included content will appear in Design view.

> The use of SSIs, and CGI for that matter, is being superseded by more sophisticated server-side scripting languages, such as PHP (supposedly it stands for PHP: Hypertext Preprocessor).

By the way, to use SSIs, you'll have to make sure that your web server has enabled server-side includes. If you don't know how to do this, talk to your host or your system administrator and let them know what you're planning to do.

Inserting an SSI

To insert an SSI, select Insert → Script Object → Server-Side Include. In the Select File dialog box that appears, browse to a local file, choose a data source, or indicate a URL (see Figure 4.11). For included scripts, you can select parameters as well.

Dreamweaver inserts the include.

Editing an SSI

Although Dreamweaver will display the contents of an included file in Design view, you can't edit the included file directly from the including page. You can however, right-click (Ctrl-click for Mac users) the include and select Edit from the pop-up menu to edit the SSI. Dreamweaver will open the included file in a new window. After you edit and save the file, its display will be updated on the page in which it is included.

Taking a Jump Backward

In this chapter, we took a big jump forward to discuss the use of collaborative tools. Templates, assets, and Library items are used to maintain the consistency of your web pages throughout a site. Your problem is that you now know how to apply templates and their contents, but you still don't know how to build a page. The next couple of chapters explore the contents of web pages and how to produce them using Fireworks, Macromedia's image-processing/web development program. When you have the ability to build graphic images, rollovers, and buttons, you'll be ready to construct a web page. Chapter 5 introduces Fireworks and its graphic tools. To continue working with Dreamweaver, skip ahead to Chapter 11 or any of the other chapters in Part III.

Figure 4.11

Use the Select File dialog box for SSIs to pick a local file, a data source, or a URL.

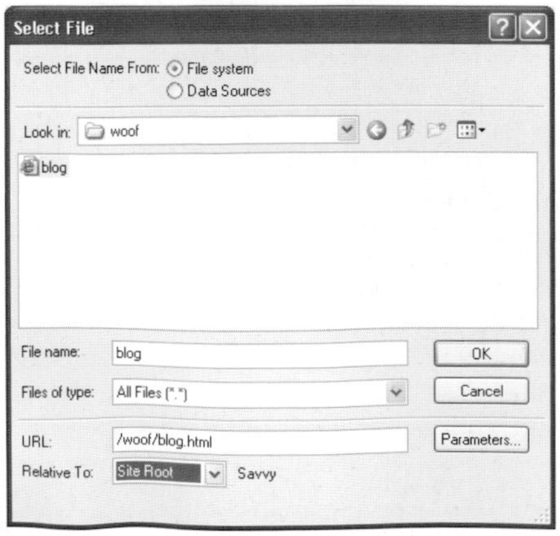

## PART II

Using Fireworks

The development *of any serious website or application is going to require sophisticated images, whether for the purposes of illustration and design or for more utilitarian purposes, such as navigation objects or labels. Part II of this book is a concentrated dose of Fireworks savvy penned by Fireworks expert Joyce J. Evans.*

Joyce offers more resources for people working with Fireworks at her website `http://www.JoyceJEvans.com`, *and she can be reached for comments or questions at this address:* `Joyce@JoyceJevans.com`.

CHAPTER 5 ■ Getting into Fireworks

CHAPTER 6 ■ Adding Strokes, Fills, and Live Effects

CHAPTER 7 ■ Working with Vectors

CHAPTER 8 ■ Working with Bitmaps

CHAPTER 9 ■ Designing Navigation Objects

CHAPTER 10 ■ Slicing, Optimizing, and Exporting Images

Getting into Fireworks

Just as Dreamweaver has taken the drudgery out of building web pages and managing websites, Fireworks was specifically designed for producing web-ready graphic art. This includes not just logos, menu items, and other images, but also entire web page layouts that can be "cut up" and converted to HTML for direct insertion into Dreamweaver websites. The integration of Dreamweaver and Fireworks is very smooth, and as a result, any time you need to work on—or create—a graphic, you can just pop into Fireworks to do so. In this chapter, you will learn how to get around in Fireworks and how to find the tools and panels of tool options that you need. For experienced users, you will find the Property Inspector and the docked panel groups new to Fireworks MX. In general, we'll point out any tools and menus that have been moved or replaced, as well as new tools and features to Fireworks MX.

Some of the topics covered in this chapter are as follows:

- **Exploring the Fireworks Menu bar and toolbars**
- **Examining Fireworks' panels**
- **Working with layers**
- **Opening and saving a new document**

Workspace Overview

First, we'll look at the different components of the Fireworks workspace, and then we'll look at each area in more depth. Figure 5.1 shows the Fireworks new document workspace when you first begin to use the program.

Figure 5.1

The Fireworks work-space with a new document open

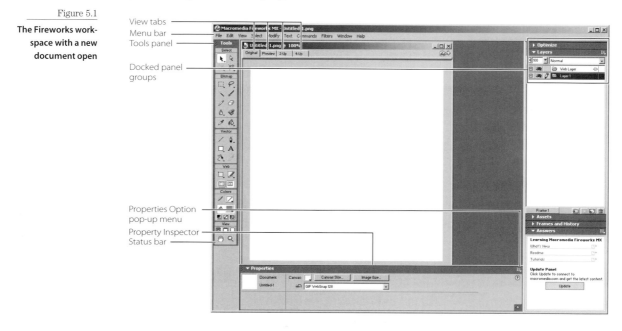

The look of the docked panel group area is new to Fireworks MX; in addition, there are some names and terms you'll need to be familiar with prior to reading the examples in the rest of this Fireworks portion of this book. Figure 5.2 shows some of the areas that are common to many of the panels. To open each of the panels, just click the white triangle arrow (expander arrow) that points to the right. When you click it, the arrow will point down.

You can customize how the panels are grouped together by clicking the Options pop-up menu of any panel. For instance, if you wanted to group Frames with Layers, you would click the Frame panel, click the Options pop-up menu, and choose Group Frames With → Layers.

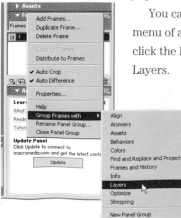

That is it! Now Frames is grouped with Layers. Notice that the panel name changes from Layers to Layers and Frames, and the History and Frames panel group name is now changed to History. You can also rename the panel groups if you want. Or, if you want to add a new panel group, just select New Panel Group from the Options pop-up menu.

Although you can't undock a specific panel, you can in effect achieve the same result if you want a panel that floats. To do so, select the panel and choose New Panel Group from the Options pop-up menu. The panel is now floating. To move the panel back into the docked panel group area, click and drag into the docked area until you see a blue line. This line indicates not only when it can be docked but also where it will be docked.

Gripper
Title bar
Layers Option pop-up menu

Figure 5.2

The Layers panel, showing new names and features of all panels in Fireworks.

The Fireworks Menu Bar and Toolbars

In this section, you will get a quick overview of the different areas of the Fireworks environment. If you need more information, the help menu found within Fireworks (Window → Using Fireworks) does a good job of explaining each tool in-depth. The individual panels and tools are also covered in more detail throughout the Fireworks portion of this book as each tool or panel is taught and used.

Blue line

Figure 5.3

The blue line, which is visible when a panel is about to be docked.

Title Bar

When you first open a new document or an existing one, you will notice that the name Fireworks and the title of your document appear at the top of the Fireworks workspace, in the bar referred to as the Title bar. If it's a new document, the default title is `Untitled-1.png`. Note that Fireworks now places an asterisk by the title to signify that the document has not yet been saved—just like Dreamweaver does (this is new to Fireworks MX). The magnification percentage is also noted in this title area.

Reviewing Menu Bar Details

Below the Title bar is the Menu bar. The Menu bar contains 10 different categories. If you are a previous user of Fireworks, please take the time to review this section because some things have changed. For instance, the Insert menu has been removed and its contents are now in the Edit menu. In addition, a new Select menu, which contains many of the bitmap selection options, has been added. Also, the Xtras menu has been renamed and is now referred to as the Filters menu. You'll now briefly take a look at each of the menus in the Menu bar and learn some of their options.

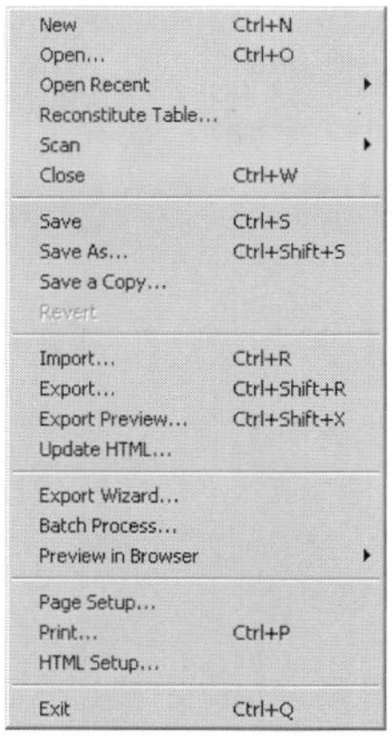

Figure 5.4

The contents of the File menu

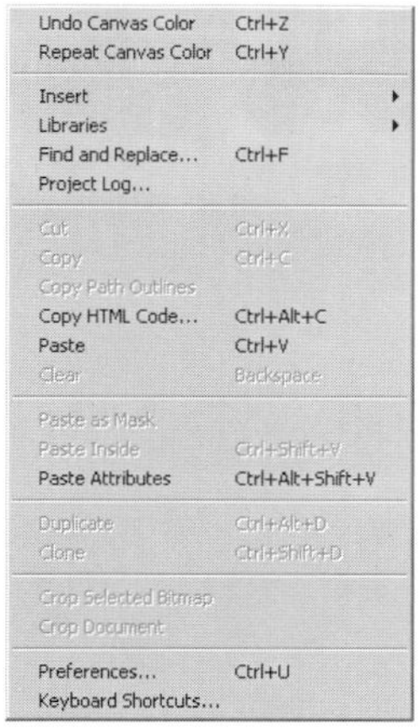

Figure 5.5

The Edit menu and its contents

Figure 5.6

The Insert option and its pop-up menu

The File Menu

The most notable change to the File menu (shown in Figure 5.4) is the addition of the Reconstitute Table feature. You can now open an HTML document and reconstitute the images and HTML code in a Fireworks document even if you don't have the original PNG file.

The Edit Menu

There are a lot of new features in the Edit menu (shown in Figure 5.5). You can do the normal things, such as copy, cut, copy and paste, and so on. In addition, you can perform all of the options on the Insert pop-up (see Figure 5.6); these options were formerly available from the Insert menu, which has been removed.

There are a few other new options or name changes, but their names pretty much say it all. And if you are looking for the Select All and other options that were formerly in the Edit menu, they have moved to the Select menu.

The View Menu

The View menu can be seen in Figure 5.7. The only notable change here is the addition of the 66, 150, and 300 percent Magnification options. You can always return to 100 percent by double-clicking the Zoom tool in the Tools panel.

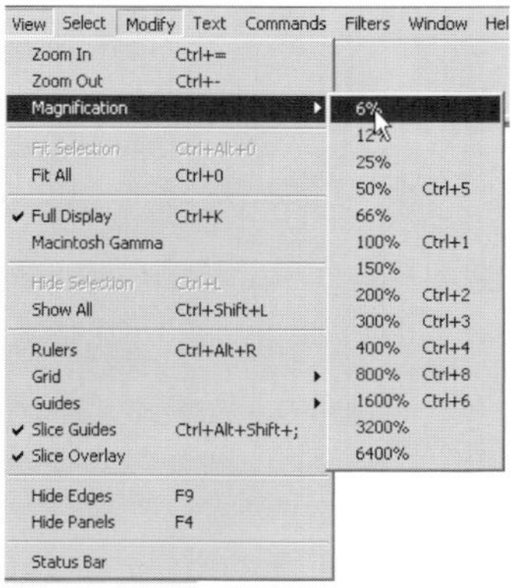

Figure 5.7

The View menu showing the Magnification options

The Select Menu

The Select menu is new to Fireworks MX; Figure 5.8 shows its options. Some of the options used to be part of the Edit menu, but most came from the Modify menu.

One of the most interesting changes is that you can now modify your bitmap selections from the Select menu and you can also save one selection per document. Having a separate selection menu makes it easier to find and access the various commands. In earlier versions, because you were in the Modify menu it was more difficult to find the options quickly.

Figure 5.8

The Select menu options

> If you are a Photoshop user, you'll be used to the fact that a selection(s) can be saved to a channel. But, in Fireworks, the saved selection does not get saved to a separate channel or location that you can see. It's just saved with each document and it can be restored for that document only.

The Modify Menu

There are several changes to the Modify menu. First of all, the Canvas option now has a pop-up that includes all the options pertaining to the canvas (they used to be listed on the Modify menu itself) as seen in Figure 5.9.

In addition, you'll notice that the Pop-up Menu options are now in this menu (they were formerly in the Insert menu). There is also a new capability that has been added to Fireworks MX: Merge Down. You can now select vector and or bitmap objects and merge them into one bitmap object. The objects you choose to merge into one bitmap can be from different layers. The objects will be merged into the bitmap, which is below the lowest selection in the Layers panel. Any vector objects you merge into a bitmap will loose their editability because they are now part of a bitmap.

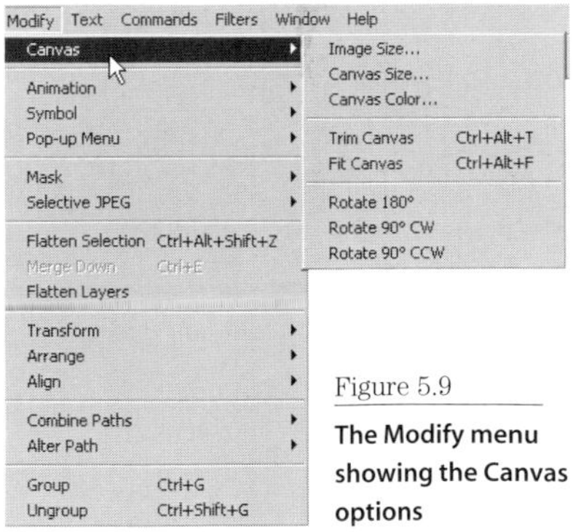

The Convert to Bitmap option has been removed, but it was replaced with Flatten Selection. Flatten Selection works like Convert to Bitmap, which converts a vector object or a selection of vector objects into a flattened bitmap image.

Figure 5.9

The Modify menu showing the Canvas options

> There is also a new Align panel, which can be opened from the Window menu. If you end up using alignment options often, you may want to dock this panel (as discussed earlier).

Because you'll be making buttons, nav bars, and all kinds of images and transformations, you'll be using the options in the Modify menu frequently throughout this Fireworks portion of this book.

Figure 5.10

The Text menu

The Text Menu

The Text menu (Figure 5.10) contains various options for working with text, such as attaching your text to a path, making font changes, and more. You can access the Text Editor from this menu as well as by right-clicking any text in your document.

> In previous versions of Fireworks, the use of the Text tool automatically opened the Text Editor. In Fireworks MX, text is placed in the document directly and the editing is done via the Property Inspector.

The Commands Menu

This menu has changed quite a bit from previous versions of Fireworks. The first option is Manage Saved Commands; this is for commands you have made yourself or ones you have added from others. Using this command and the Command menu is discussed in greater detail in Chapter 6. The next option is Manage Extensions, that's right—Extensions. Fireworks now has extension capabilities and you'll be able to obtain third-party extensions like you can for Dreamweaver.

As you can see in Figure 5.11, there is also a new Arrowhead command, which adds a variety of arrow shapes to one or both ends of a path.

You should also pay particular attention to some of the neat things in the Creative pop-up menu (see Figure 5.11). Wait until you try the new Fade Image command. It makes masking possible in one step! The Add Picture Frame option has also been greatly improved. You'll explore many of these options in Chapter 6.

The DashedLine command you see in Figure 5.11 is one I made. If you'd like, you can find it on the accompanying CD.

The Filters Menu

The Filters menu was formerly named Xtras. The middle portion of this menu (see Figure 5.12) shows the filters that ship with Fireworks MX and are also available in the Effects pop-up menu located in the Property Inspector. The difference between these and the ones in the Effects pop-up menu is that when a filter is applied from the Filters menu, any vector object will be converted into a bitmap and the filter will not be editable (except for undo). The same filter applied through the Effects pop-up menu is a Live Effect and is editable.

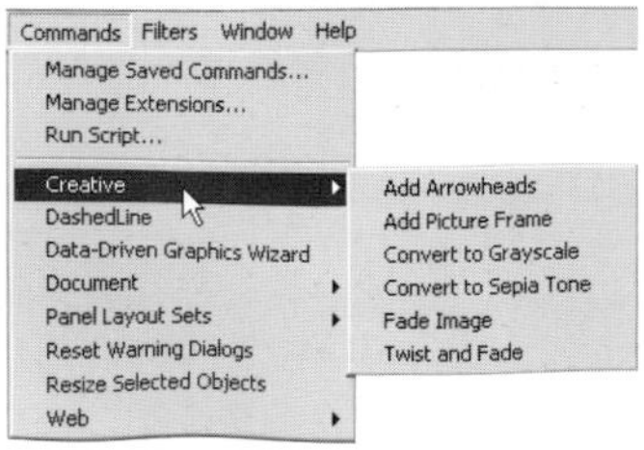

Figure 5.11

The Commands menu showing the Creative options

Fireworks MX also ships with one effect of the full version of Splat!. The rest of your third party demos will be listed beneath Splat!. You can find some demos or trials of plugins such as Splat! on this book's accompanying CD.

> The trial version of Splat! included on this book's CD is fully functional for 30 days. The version in Fireworks only includes Edges.

Figure 5.12

The Filters menu

The Window Menu

The Window menu (shown in Figure 5.13) gives you access to the panels in Fireworks. Many of the panels shown are already in the panel group area of your workspace. For instance, the Styles, URL, and Library panels are all in the Assets panel group set.

Figure 5.13

The Window menu

Fireworks Toolbars

There are two toolbars in Fireworks, the Main toolbar (which isn't open by default) and the Modify toolbar, which docks by default just below the Property Inspector when you choose it from Windows → Toolbars → Modify. These toolbars provide instant access to numerous functions.

Main Toolbar

The Main toolbar displays the most commonly accessed menu functions. To open the Main toolbar, choose Window → Toolbars → Main. When the toolbar opens, it docks below the main menus (Figure 5.14) for easy access.

Modify Toolbar

The Modify toolbar allows you to quickly group, arrange, align, and rotate objects. If you use Modify tools often, you may want this toolbar open in your work area. To open it, choose Window → Toolbars → Modify; it is docked by default under the Property Inspector (Figure 5.15). You can, of course, move it where you'd like it.

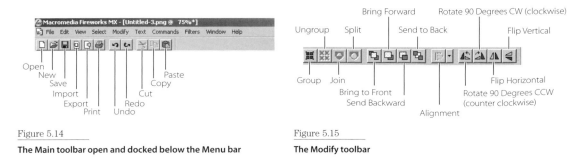

Figure 5.14

The Main toolbar open and docked below the Menu bar

Figure 5.15

The Modify toolbar

Tools Panel

All of Fireworks drawing and editing tools can be accessed from the Tools panel. Figure 5.16 shows the many tools that are available. Notice how the Bitmap and Vector tools are separated—this is new to Fireworks MX. There is also a section for the tools that can be used with both vector and bitmap images.

The Property Inspector

Every object in Fireworks can be modified by adjusting its attributes. The place where you can make these adjustments is in the Property Inspector. Figure 5.17 shows the Property Inspector fully extended. Instructions in this Fireworks section and the tutorials in the Fireworks help files assume you have it fully extended, as seen in Figure 5.17. Figure 5.18 shows the Property Inspector when it is not extended.

The Property Inspector is context sensitive, meaning that its contents change based upon which object you select in the Document window.

The Property Inspector lets you change attributes by either typing new information into text boxes (such as the size of a font), or by using a slider. If you use the slider, you can see the changes on-screen right away. If you type in values, you have to press Enter (Return for a Mac) to accept the settings.

Figure 5.16

The Tools panel

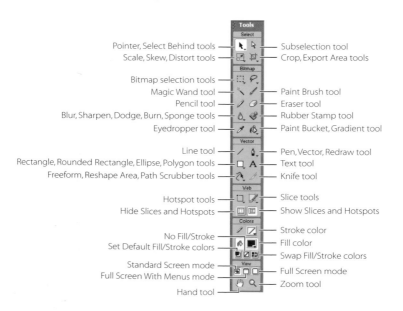

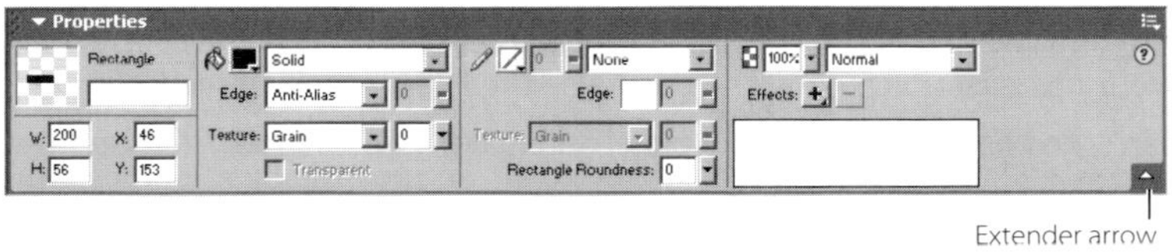

Figure 5.17

The Property Inspector fully extended

Extender arrow

Figure 5.17

The Property Inspector fully extended

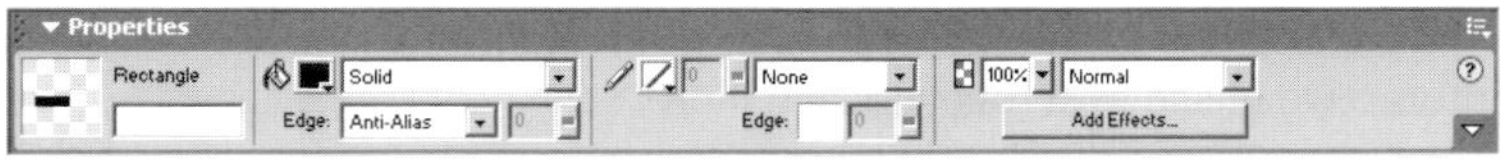

Figure 5.18

The Property Inspector not fully extended.

The Status Bar

The status bar on the bottom of every document window provides information about your document size and magnification. It also contains VCR-like controls that you can use when you are making animations. The red circle with an X is to Exit Bitmap mode. As far as we can tell, there is no real reason to use it in Fireworks MX because you no longer have to change between vector and bitmap modes—it changes automatically depending on the tool or object you select.

A Look at Fireworks Panels

Fireworks functionality is accessed not only through the menus but also through the docked panel groups. When you open the Window menu, you will see the panels listed—they are arranged in the Window menu by type.

How you arrange your panels and which ones you have available on your desktop will depend on your work habits and type of projects you deal with. If you find you use certain panels more than others, you may want to leave them docked for easy access. You can also save your panel arrangement by choosing Commands → Panel Layouts; when the JavaScript window opens, name the panel configuration and click OK. It will now be available in the Commands menu.

There is one menu that is in all the panels—a menu that we refer you to often in the Fireworks section. It's the Options pop-up menu and it is referred to by the panels name; for instance, if you are using the Layers panel it is called the "Layers Options pop-up menu." Figure 5.19 shows you where the Options pop-up menu is located.

Now, you will briefly look at what most of the panels are and how they function. If the following panels aren't in your panel groups in the docked area, then they can be accessed by choosing Window → *the panel's name*.

Figure 5.19

Layers Options pop-up menu

Layers Options pop-up menu

such as a rollover, a pop-up menu, or maybe a pop-up window. Slices are also used to define the cutting areas where Fireworks needs to cut an image for exporting.

Adding Layers

There are several ways to add new layers. The easiest method by far is by using the New Duplicate Layer icon—the yellow folder located at the bottom of the Layers panel in Figure 5.20.

Click on the yellow folder to add a new layer. A new layer will be added above the layer that is currently selected. You can also add a layer by choosing Edit → Insert → Layer, or by accessing the Layers Options pop-up menu and choosing New Layer.

Duplicate Layers

Figure 5.21

The Duplicate Layer dialog box

Duplicating layers couldn't be easier; with the layer selected that you want to duplicate, simply access the Layers Options pop-up menu and select Duplicate layer. A window will open, as seen in Figure 5.21, giving you options of where to add the duplicate layer—to the top, bottom, before the current selection or after—as well as how many duplicates you'd like to add.

Delete a Layer

Deleting layers can be done in three different ways: by highlighting the layer you want to delete and using the delete key on the keyboard, by clicking and dragging the layer on top of the trash can icon in the Layers panel, or, the easiest way, by selecting the layer (to select multiple layers or objects use Shift + click), and clicking the trash can icon.

Opacity Settings

In Figure 5.20, near the top-left corner, there is a gray and white check icon with the number 100 (grayed out) next to it—this is the opacity setting. You can adjust the opacity not only for each individual layer, but also for each individual object or image on a layer independently. To change the opacity, select the layer (or object), and either type in the opacity number you want or use, or use the slider to adjust the opacity amount.

Showing/Hiding Layers

To show or hide whole layers (or objects), click the eye icon (shown to the left in Figure 5.20) of any layer or object. If the eye is on, the layer or object is visible in your document, if you click it again, it will toggle the visibility off.

Lock Layers

To lock a layer, click the box to the left of the layers name. Look at Figure 5.20; the padlock indicates that the layer is locked. Once a layer is locked, you can't alter anything in that layer, you can't even select it. To lock or unlock all the layers, click the right pointing arrow in the Layers panel and choose the appropriate action.

Name a Layer

To name a layer or an object, double-click the layer or object name and rename it in the dialog box that pops up. If you use the Layers Options pop-up menu and you choose New Layer, a dialog box opens in which you name the layer.

Single Layer Editing

If you want to work on one layer only in Fireworks, you need to lock all the layers or choose the Single Layer Editing mode. To use this mode, access the Layers Options pop-up menu, and select Single Layer Editing. Now you can only select or edit objects on the current layer. Even though the other layers are visible, you can't alter them.

Share a Selected Layer

Share a Selected Layer comes in handy when you are producing animations and when you are making navigation bars (see Chapter 9). If you have repeating elements on a layer that you want on all layers, then all you have to do is to select the layer, access the Layers Options pop-up menu, and choose Share This Layer.

Setting Preferences

There are many preferences you can choose to set and/or change in Fireworks. Figure 5.22 shows the Preferences dialog box where you'll notice all the different tabs. Take the time to familiarize yourself with the various options. For instance, the Folders tab is where you set up the location to find your plugin folder. Another important preference is in the Edit folder. If you want your cropped images to be really cropped—in other words the cropped area to be gone—check the Delete Objects When Cropping option. Otherwise the bounding box for the object is the same size as it was prior to the cropping.

Figure 5.22

The Preferences dialog box

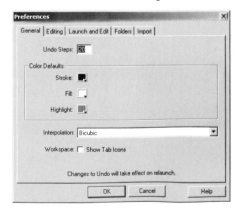

Hands On: Setting Up a Document and Importing an Image

In this tutorial, you will learn how to use a few of the option in the File menu. You'll open a new document and save it, and you'll also import a Photoshop file into Fireworks. You will then learn how to use rulers and add guides to your document.

Opening and Saving a Document

To begin, follow these steps.

1. Choose File → New. Figure 5.23 shows the New Document dialog box that opens.

2. Enter a Width amount of 400.

3. Enter a Height amount of 400.

> The resolution is 72 by default, which is what you use for web pages, but it can be changed.

4. Select your canvas color. Choose white for this example.

5. Click OK.

> If you copy an object or image, and then choose File → New, the Width and Height will be automatically set to the exact size needed to paste the copied object.

Importing a Photoshop File

You can now import an image into your document by following these steps.

1. Choose File → Import, which opens the Import dialog box.

2. Navigate to the Chapter 5 folder on the accompanying CD, select `Sunset.psd`, and click Open. Your cursor will turn into a corner icon.

3. Click the canvas to place the image.

   Figure 5.24 shows the image from the Photoshop file as it appears imported into Fireworks. Don't be alarmed with how the image looks right now. Figure 5.26 shows how it is supposed to look. Because this is a Photoshop file, the texture did not get placed inside the text. This is easy enough to fix.

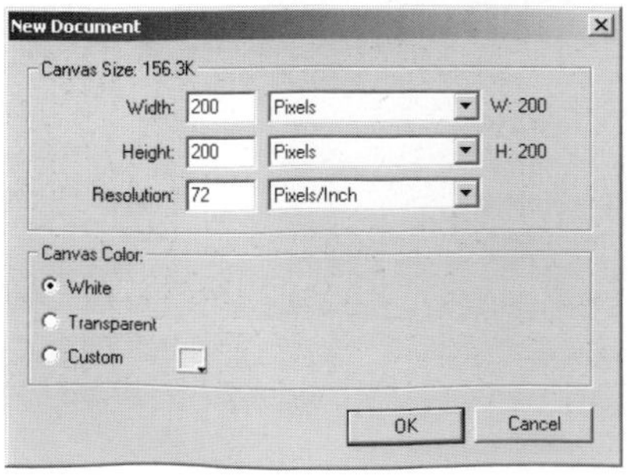

Figure 5.23

The New Document dialog box

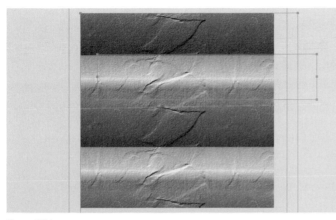

Figure 5.24

A Photoshop file imported into Fireworks. It needs a bit of work to correct it.

Figure 5.25

The text placed over a portion of the texture that we wanted to see in the text

4. In the Layers panel, click and drag the pattern image (Bitmap 1) below the text layer (Sunset).

5. Click the text, Sunset; in the Property Inspector change the size and font to one that will fit your canvas. For this tutorial, let's use Arial Black and keep the size it imported as 60.

6. Place the text over an area of the background texture that you'd like to show in the text. Figure 5.25 shows where we placed the text.

7. Select the colorful texture and choose Edit → Cut.

8. Select the text and choose Edit → Paste Inside.

Figure 5.26

The imported Photoshop file fixed with the texture pasted inside the text.

Wasn't that easy? The color area that you positioned below the text is now inside the text. Your canvas now looks like Figure 5.26 showing the background image of the sunset.

Setting Up Rulers and Guides

If you wanted to measure something in your document, you'd need to have the rulers visible (you also need rulers visible to place guides).

1. Choose View → Rulers. Notice the rulers added to the top and left side of the Document window (Figure 5.27).

Figure 5.27

Rulers visible in the document window.

Figure 5.27

Rulers visible in the document window.

Many times you'll need guides to help position elements on a page. The next two steps show you how to view and place them.

2. Choose View → Guides → Show Guides. A check mark indicates that it's selected. Notice that Snap to Guides is selected by default. Always leave this as the default because it is especially helpful when you are using guides for slices.

3. Place your cursor in the top horizontal ruler.

4. Click and drag into your document.

5. As you enter the active canvas area, you will see a green line. Use the rulers to help position the guide where you want it.

6. Repeat for the vertical guides by clicking and dragging from the vertical ruler.

7. Choose File → Save As and navigate to the location you'd like to save your file.

8. Name the file and click Save.

Stroke, Fill, or Enliven...

We realize that getting comfortable with a program's interface is probably the most boring aspect of learning a new program. But as you probably know, it's also vital to the learning process. Now that you have familiarized yourself with the Fireworks environment and its panels, you are ready for the really fun stuff—adding fills, strokes, and effects to your objects and images for that professional gloss.

## CHAPTER 6

Adding Strokes, Fills, and Live Effects

A lot of the power (and the fun!) of using Fireworks is in applying its amazing array of strokes, fills, and effects. Strokes define the width, quality, texture, and color of the paths they overlay. Fills define the interior texture, color, and quality within these paths. Effects, called *Live Effects* in Fireworks, are applied over strokes and fills to add three-dimensionality and oomph to your vector images. If you gain control of strokes, fills, and effects, you have mastered the intricacies of Fireworks. This chapter covers the following topics related to this subject:

- **Adding strokes to your objects and bitmaps**

- **Adding texture to strokes**

- **Adding fills**

- **Filling with patterns and textures**

- **Adding effects**

- **Using the Styles panel**

- **Commands and batch process**

Adding Strokes

When you draw a path (at least two points, yielding a line segment), the stroke is what allows you to see it. If you have the Stroke option turned off, then the path is still there, it just is not visible. Adding a stroke is more than just adding a color; you can add a special stroke shape, alter the width and softness of the stroke, and even alter the tip size and shape. When you use a pressure sensitive tablet, even the speed, direction, and pressure you draw with alter the appearance of the stroke.

The Stroke Options

The Stroke area of the Property Inspector is one that you will find yourself returning to again and again. Figure 6.1 shows the Stroke area in the Property Inspector.

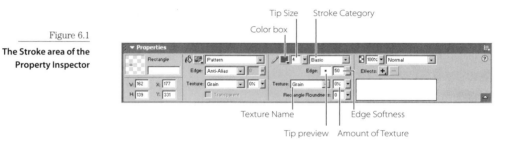

Figure 6.1

The Stroke area of the Property Inspector

Here are some brief descriptions of the stroke properties found in the Property Inspector.

Color box You access the color swatches to make color changes (click in the square of color) through the color box. If your fill is a gradient, then the gradient editor will open when you click in the color box.

Tip Size This is where you choose the size of a stroke by using the slider or typing in a value.

Stroke Category pop-up menu From this pop-up menu, you choose the type of stroke you want and then you choose the stroke property from the little submenu for each stroke category.

Texture Name From this pop-up, you choose the type of texture you want; you can even choose Other to use custom textures.

Amount of Texture This slider is used to adjust the opacity of the texture or the amount you want to use. You can also type in a value and then press Enter (Return for a Mac).

Figure 6.2

Stroke categories

Edge Softness The softness of an edge is automatically set depending on the Stroke category and property you select. But you can adjust the softness of an edge manually at any time. The higher the number, the softer the edge.

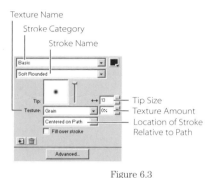

Figure 6.2 shows the options in the Stroke Category pop-up menu. As you pass your cursor over each stroke name, you will see various other options that are available for each stroke type.

The Stroke Category pop-up menu has 48 built-in strokes, but you can produce an infinite number of variations of these. For instance, options such as color, strokes, patterns, textures, width, edge, softness, and so on, can change the text effect slightly or drastically. All you need to do to apply a stroke, or a variant of one, is select the object to which you want to apply the stroke, and then choose a stroke selection from the Stroke Category pop-up menu.

Figure 6.3

The Stroke Options pop-up menu

The selections you make for a stroke, such as fill, color, and so on, remain the default for the next time you use the Pen tool or the Shape tool. But if you use the Pencil tool, no matter what the previous stroke settings were, the default of Pencil, 1-Pixel Hard is in effect.

Also notice that there is a Stroke Options button at the bottom of the Stroke Category pop-up menu. Figure 6.3 shows the pop-up menu that results when this button is pressed.

You'll notice in the Stroke Options pop-up that there is an Advanced button. Figure 6.4 shows the Edit Stroke dialog box that appears when this button is clicked. You will be using this menu later in this chapter in the "Making a Custom Stroke for a Dashed Line" section. Figure 6.5 shows the color pop-up you get when you click in the color box (the square with color in it).

Figure 6.4

The Edit Stroke dialog box of the Stroke Options pop-up

Adding a Stroke to an Object

You can add strokes to newly drawn objects or existing objects. When you add a stroke in the Property Inspector by choosing a Stroke Category, Tip Size, color, and the type of edge you want, you can see the results in real time on the canvas.

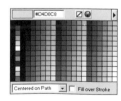

Figure 6.5

The color swatches accessed from the color box

> If you type in hex (hexadecimal) numbers for colors, percentage numbers, or tip size numbers, you will need to press the Enter (Return for the Mac) key to activate the change. On the other hand, if you use the eyedropper to select a color, or you use the sliders to select the texture amount and tip size, the change is automatically visible on your canvas. The bottom line is: if you type it, press Enter (Return for Mac).

Stroke properties are added from the Property Inspector's Stroke area. The options in the Property Inspector are visible only when an object is selected (not a bitmap image) because strokes can only be added to vector objects or when one of the Vector tools is selected.

> You will learn more about vectors and bitmaps in Chapters 7 and 8, but basically, a vector is comprised of paths, which are lines with at least two points. The tools in the vector section of the Tools panel are what can be used for strokes or for drawing objects that can have a stroke.

To add a stroke, follow these steps:

1. Open a new document (File → New) with a white canvas and a size of 300 × 300.
2. Select the Rectangle tool from the Tools panel and draw a rectangle on your canvas; it can be of any size and any color.
3. Access the Stroke area in the Property Inspector and then click the Stroke Category icon to access its pop-up menu.
4. From the Stroke Category choose Basic, and from the Basic flyout choose Hard Line.

> There are several ways you can remove a stroke. One way is by clicking in the color box next to the Pencil icon in either the Tools panel or the Property Inspector. You can then click the white square with the diagonal red line through it. To see this icon, look just below the Fill icon in the Tools panel, you will see that the middle icon is the white square with red diagonal line through it.

5. Choose a variation of a stroke from the Stroke Name area, which is in the Stroke Category pop-up.
6. To alter how the edge of the stroke looks, you can adjust the Edge Softness using the slider control. (0 is a hard edge and 100 is a very soft edge. Some of the Stroke options have edge options, but most do not.)
7. Click in the Stroke Color box in the Property Inspector to select the color you'd like to use.
8. Then adjust the Tip Size by using the slider or by typing in a number. Remember that if you type in a number, you must press Enter (Return for the Mac) to accept the change. You have just finished adding a stroke to an object.

Using Preset Strokes

We'll now take a look at a few samples of the different strokes so that you can get an idea of how presets work and some of the differences between them.

Figure 6.6 shows a Basic stroke, with a Hard Line attribute applied to it. In this example, we are using a curved line so that you can better see the jagged edges. Though using the Basic stroke and a Hard Line are good choices when you want a sharp crisp edge (as you would on a rectangle or straight line), if you use these options on a rounded or curved edge as shown here, it will appear jagged. You can, however, soften the edge by adjusting the Edge Softness option (the slider next to the Edge preview area in the Property Inspector). In Figure 6.6, the edge softness of 100 was added to the bottom stroke.

Basic stroke, Hard Line

Basic stroke, Hard Line, Edge Softness 100

Figure 6.6

A curved line with a Basic stroke, Hard Line attribute to demonstrate the jagged edges. The bottom line demonstrates how altering the edge softness smoothes out the jaggedness.

This next example is similar to the previous one. Like Figure 6.6, Figure 6.7 shows a Basic stroke, and a Hard Line attribute being applied. But in this figure, a Hatch 1 Texture with the Amount of Texture set to 100 percent has been added (more on textures later in this chapter in the "Adding Textures" section.). As you can see, this application really changes the appearance by adding a texture. The second line shows the Basic stroke, and a Hard Rounded line attribute being applied. Though the ends of this second line are rounded, the edge is still jagged. The third line in this example shows the Basic stroke, and a Soft Rounded line. This line is the smoothest because its ends are also rounded and it has an Anti-Alias edge so that the edge won't appear jagged.

Figure 6.8 shows some of the other stroke types that are available.

When you explore these different types of strokes, pay particular attention to the Unnatural category because it has some really interesting effects. Because you can see what the stroke looks like in the workspace, it's easy to experiment until you get the look you want.

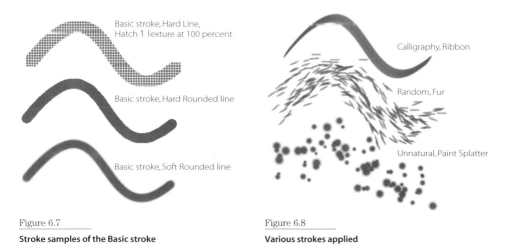

Basic stroke, Hard Line, Hatch 1 texture at 100 percent

Basic stroke, Hard Rounded line

Basic stroke, Soft Rounded line

Calligraphy, Ribbon

Random, Fur

Unnatural, Paint Splatter

Figure 6.7

Stroke samples of the Basic stroke

Figure 6.8

Various strokes applied

STROKE TIP MODIFICATIONS

Before we leave the Strokes discussion, let's take a look at some of the tip options. To see these, click Stroke Options from the Stroke Category pop-up menu; then from the Stroke Options dialog box, click the Advanced button to access the Edit Stroke pop-up. You'll see three tabs: Options, Shape, and Sensitivity.

The first image shows the Edit Stroke dialog box with the Options tab selected. This is where you set the ink amount, the spacing, and the flow rate, as well as the texture options. If you change the number of tips you'd like to paint with to more than one, the variations and spacing options become available also. The preview of the changes you've made will appear right at the bottom of this dialog box—what a timesaver! When you get the settings the way you like them, click Apply, and then OK.

You'll also see the contents of the Shape tab. In this tab, you can assert a lot of control over the shape of the stroke by altering the tip shape, and the size, edge, aspect, and angle of your stroke. When you get the shape just right, click Apply and then click OK.

The last image you will see is the Sensitivity tab; here you can choose a stroke property such as Size, Ink Amount, or Saturation from the drop-down menu of the Stroke Property option. In the Affected By option, you can choose the degree to which sensitivity data affects your current stroke. Preview in the panel window and click Apply and OK when you are satisfied.

Strokes can produce some pretty interesting effects as well. Figure 6.9 shows text with the selections of 3D and Size 6 from the Unnatural category being applied. The second example shows text that has had both Calligraphy and Ribbon applied to it. Interesting effect isn't it? The Calligraphy and Ribbon effects look totally different on text than they did on a line.

Now that you know how simple it is to apply strokes and vary their look with different textures, go ahead and experiment. Beware, however, it may be addicting!

Unnatural, 3D

Calligraphy, Ribbon

Figure 6.9

Two different strokes applied to text

Making a Custom Stroke for a Dashed Line

Designers frequently need dashed lines, especially if they happen to draw maps and need roads or railroad images. For instance, you may find yourself in need of a coupon for an ad—dashed lines are perfect for this sort of thing. Of course, there are many other uses for a dashed line—a button outline, for instance.

> You can make a simple dashed or dotted line using the Text tool. Type out a line of dots or dashes. Because it's text, you can also apply it to a path, such as a box, or a curve, and so on. The problem that you'll run into with this method arises when you try to use it on a rectangle. The dashes in the corners won't space properly.

In this exercise, you will make a dashed line and save it as a command to use again. To do so, follow these steps:

1. Open a new document (File → New) with a size of 300 × 400 and a white canvas.

2. Click the Line tool in the Tools panel and draw a line that is about two inches long. Just before you release the mouse, press the Ctrl key (Option on a Mac) to constrain the line to a straight line. (Don't press the Ctrl/Option key while you are drawing.) In the following illustrations, the tip size has been set to 10 so that you can see this effect better.

3. In the Stroke area of the Property Inspector, access the Stroke Category pop-up, and choose Random, Dots. Figure 6.10 shows the result so far.

4. In the Stroke Category pop-up, click the Stroke Options button, and then click the click the Advanced button to access the Edit Stroke dialog box.

5. The first tab on the Edit Stroke dialog box is Options (see Figure 6.11); use these settings in this tab:

   Ink Amount: 100%

   Spacing: 250%

   Tips: 1

Figure 6.10

A Random, Dots stroke applied to a line with a tip size of 10

6. Then click the Shape tab (see Figure 6.12), and use these settings:

> Size: 30
>
> Edge: 8
>
> Aspect: 20
>
> Angle: 360

Also check the Square option, unless you want to make a dotted line instead of a dashed line.

7. Then click the Sensitivity tab and use these settings (as shown in Figure 6.13):

> Stroke Property: **Saturation**
>
> Pressure: **0**
>
> Speed: **0**
>
> Horizontal: **0**
>
> Vertical: **0**
>
> Random: **0**

Continue to use the setting of 0 for every option in the Stroke Property drop-down menu (Size, Angle, Ink Amount, Scatter, Hue, and Lightness). When you are finished click OK. You will see these choices applied in Figure 6.14.

8. If you want a different look or size, go back to the Edit Strokes panel (by clicking the Advanced button from Stroke Options) and change the spacing and/or the size of the dash.

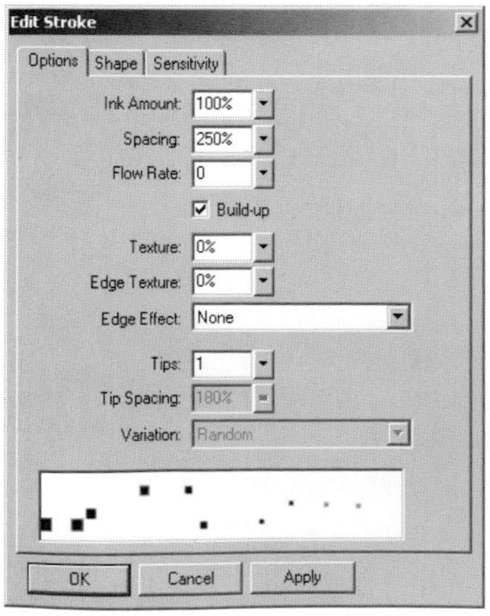

Figure 6.11

The changes made in the Options tab

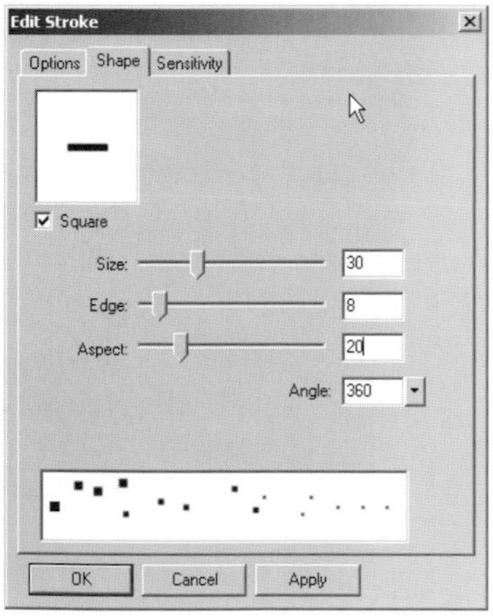

Figure 6.12

The settings used for the options in the Shape tab

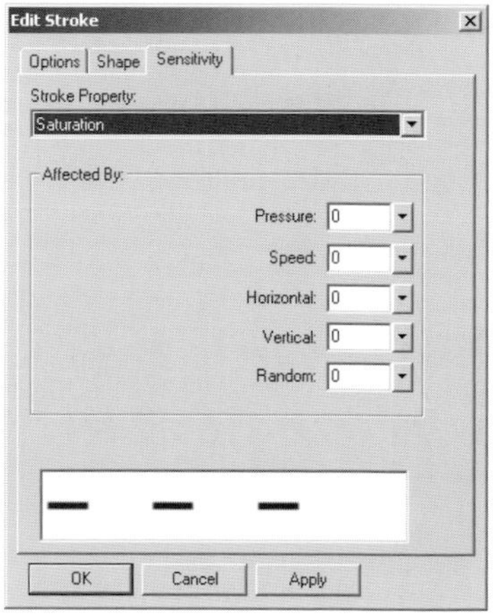

Figure 6.13

The settings used for all the Stroke properties in the Sensitivity tab

These next two steps are optional; use them if you want to make a command that will auto-mate the process of making a dashed or dotted line. To do this, you would first make all of your settings and then make a command. If you need more information on making com-mands, refer to "Installing Commands" section later in this chapter.

9. Open the History panel (docked with the Frames panel by default), and click the History tab. Select the very last step called Stroke. This step includes all the previous steps you've done.

10. From the History Options pop-up menu, choose Save As a Command. Give it a name that you will recognize—we named ours DashedLine. A copy of this command (also one for a dotted line and a shorter dash) is included on the companion CD. The command is automatically available for use from the Commands menu.

The Apply button will apply your settings to your stroke before you click OK to accept the changes.

Saving Strokes as Styles

You have probably experimented with strokes and come up with some unique ones you'd like to use again. Once you have completed your stroke and any effects or fills you add, it can be saved as a style, which you can then apply from the Style panel with just a click. To make this work, follow these steps:

1. Open the Style panel (docked in the Asset panel group) and from the Styles Options pop-up menu (down pointing arrow in the top-right corner), choose New Style.

2. Check the features you would like saved for the style. For instance, when you are work-ing with text, you may not want to save the font style, so just uncheck that option. If you check font, then when the style is applied, it will also use the font information. If it is unchecked, only the stroke, fill, and effects will be applied to any text or object.

When you choose to save the font information, the style will work on computers that have the font installed; otherwise just the effects, stroke, and fill will be applied.

3. Enter a name and click OK.

That's all there is to it. The new style will be added to the bottom of your Style panel for use on any object.

Figure 6.14

The custom stroke applied to the original line drawn in step 2

Adding Texture to Strokes

When you add texture to a stroke, you can really make an object pop out from the page. Fireworks MX ships with a large list of textures. There are grids and horizontal and vertical lines, which are all very useful. The lines are great for the TV screen effect so many people like. In addition, you can quickly add a grid to a design. Of course there are plenty of other options. To see some, click the down arrow in the Texture pane of the Stroke area of the Property Inspector, which will allow you to access the preset Textures. In Figure 6.15, you'll notice part of the list and the preview pane. The preview sure makes it easy to make a decision.

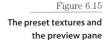

Figure 6.15

The preset textures and the preview pane

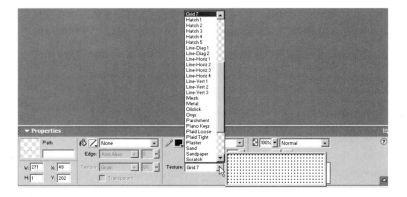

To add a stroke with texture, follow these steps:

1. Select the object to which you want to add a stroke. From the Stroke Category pop-up menu, select a stroke type and style.

2. Adjust the Tip Size to make it larger; a larger stroke will yield a better texture effect—size 20 or larger should work nicely. Adjust the size by typing in a new number or using the slider.

3. From the Texture pop-up menu, choose one of the textures listed, then set the opacity of the texture by typing in a percentage or choosing it with the slider. If you type in a percentage, press the Enter key (or the Return key on a Mac).

> You can also add your own textures by choosing, "Other" at the bottom of the list. You can then browse to any image on your hard drive or CD and use it as a texture.

4. Choose File → Save As to save your work, or you can choose New Style from the Styles Options pop-up menu to save as a style.

The texture you select as Other is document-specific. In other words, when you close and open a new document, the "Other" that you added will no longer be on the list. However, you can add textures to the list permanently by coping the image file to the Textures folder in the Fireworks MX program file folders.

Enhance an Image with a Unique Stroke

In this exercise, we are going to add special strokes around an image. Strokes can't be applied to an image, only to paths (vector objects and text), so we need to make an adjustment to our image here. If you want to apply this effect to text, then skip steps one through four.

1. We have supplied a photo for you to practice on. Open `photo.png` from the Chapter 6 folder on the accompanying CD. Choose Modify → Canvas Size and change the dimensions to 400 × 400.

2. We need to add a path around the image. Since it's an ellipse, you can use the Ellipse tool to do this. First, be sure you have a stroke style selected from the Stroke Category—Basic, Soft Rounded, and 1 Pixel will work fine.

3. For this example, you want a path only, no fill. From the Tools panel, select the Fill tool and change the fill to None (the circle with the line through it). Draw an ellipse around the photo. Get very close to the edge—you may even want to even go into the image a bit depending on the effect you want. Draw the ellipse the best you can.

4. Select the Subselection tool, and select the ellipse. You'll see the points on the ellipse now. Click and drag the points to the proper location, as seen in Figure 6.16. Now you have a path and can still see the image below.

Figure 6.16

The ellipse being fitted to the photo using the Subselection tool

If you have an irregular shape, use the Pen tool in the Tools panel. The Pen tool is discussed in detail in Chapter 7.

5. In Figure 6.16, the color of the canvas was modified to compliment the image. To do this, from the menu bar, select Modify → Canvas Color. Click the color box and take a sample with the eyedropper from the green shirt.

We are changing the canvas color now so that as you continue to add a stroke, you can see the effect against the new background color.

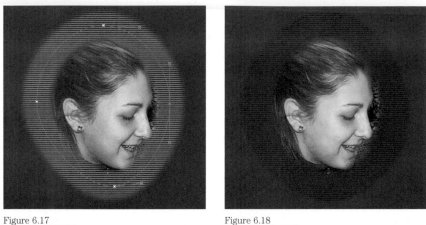

Figure 6.17

The points pulled out, expanding the path

Figure 6.18

The completed image with scan lines applied

6. In the Stroke area of the Property Inspector, change the Tip Size to 70. From the Texture pop-up list, select Line-Horiz-3, and a percentage of 100%.

7. As you can see, the lines go too far into the image. To fix this, click the Subselection tool from the Tools panel and pull each point out until the lines are on the outside of the image. See Figure 6.17 to see the new placement of the points.

8. If you used the default stroke color of black, the lines may be too dark for this effect. To alter them, select the path and go to the Layers panel. Click the down arrow next to the opacity number and choose 50 percent. In the Mode box (it probably says Normal right now), select Tint (this is a blend mode). Now you will see (Figure 6.18) that the effect is much more subtle. A better view can be seen in the color insert for this book.

Adding Fills

The Fill area in the Property Inspector works very much like the Stroke area. From it, you select the type of fill you want, the color, the type of edge, and a texture, if you want one. Figure 6.19 shows the Fill panel of the Property Inspector.

Figure 6.19

The Fill area of the Property Inspector

Color box   Fill Category

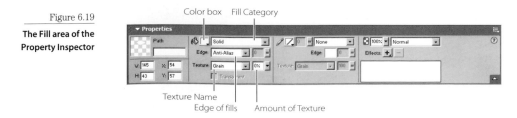

Texture Name

Edge of fills   Amount of Texture

Everything in the Property Inspector is context sensitive. In order to see the Fill area, you'll need a to select a vector object, or you'll need to select the Pen tool, the Shape tool, or the Paint Bucket (for bitmap objects).

Figure 6.20 shows a list of the available fill options from the Fill Category. To fill an object, text, or path, follow these simple steps:

1. Select a shape tool or a drawing tool and draw something that needs a fill. Whatever the current fill color is will be applied to your selection.

2. In the Property Inspector, access the Fill Category options pop-up by clicking the down arrow, and selecting Solid.

3. From the Edge area in the Property Inspector, click the drop-down list and make a selection. Anti-Alias is the default—it helps smooth the edges. A Hard edge will give you a sharp edge, but it will be jagged on any curves that it has; you can use the Feather option to soften these edges a great deal, depending on the amount of feather you use. When the Feather option is selected, the Amount of Feather option becomes available.

4. If you want a texture, click the arrow next to Texture Name to access the Textures pop-up, and choose a texture from the list. (Notice the Other menu option; this option will be discussed in the upcoming "Filling with Patterns and Textures" section.) If you select a texture, you have to increase the opacity so that you can see the texture. As soon as you increase the texture amount, a Transparent option becomes available. If you click Transparent to select it, the objects or image below (assuming there is something below your object) will show through.

None
Solid
Web Dither
Pattern

Linear
Radial
Ellipse
Rectangle
Cone
Starburst
Bars
Ripples
Waves
Satin
Folds

Fill Options...

Figure 6.20

The fill options available in the Fill Category pop-up

A word on transparency. The Transparent option does not represent a true transparency; it will only appear transparent over the object you are using in Fireworks. In other words, you can't export the object alone and expect it to be transparent in the browser. At this time, only a PNG32 file will do this, but unfortunately, this format is not supported by all browsers.

Filling with Patterns and Textures

Filling with patterns and textures is a technique that is commonly used to add depth and interest to objects. Fireworks MX ships with some preset patterns and textures, but the real diversity comes from your ability to use almost any pattern or texture that you have available.

Adding Textures

Textures can be added to any fill or stroke. Also, you can use your own textures in addition to the ones that ship with Fireworks MX. To add texture to a fill, follow these steps:

1. Select any object that contains any fill.

2. From the Fill area of the Property Inspector, click the Texture Name down arrow to access the Texture pop-up, and choose one of the included texture files. Or, click Other to access an image on your hard drive or a CD for use in this document only.

3. Adjust the percentage of the Amount of Texture by adjusting the amount with the slider, which will determine the percentage of the texture that you see.

Texture files use the grayscale value of an image; you can use any PNG, GIF, JPEG, BMP, TIF, or PICT file as a texture. To add your own texture files to the pop-up menu for use in other documents, simply place the image file in the Fireworks MX Textures folder.

Working with Patterns

By using a pattern in a vector object, you will increase your designing flexibility. Fireworks MX ships with a small selection of 14 patterns. The Other option in the Fill area opens the door to limitless other patterns. You are limited only by what you can hold on your hard drive or on CD-ROMs. As long as an image is a 32-bit image in a file format of BMP, PNG, GIF, JPEG, TIFF, or PICT (for the Macintosh), then you can use it as a pattern. To use a pattern, follow these steps:

1. Select the object you want to fill.

2. From the Fill area in the Property Inspector, choose Pattern, and then choose the pattern of your choice.

3. Alternatively you can choose Other. Once you do, browse to an image file, select it, and click Open.

Patterns can be altered in the same way as gradients (more on gradients later in this chapter in the "Working with Gradients" section)—by moving the handles and the rotation symbol. Another similarity between textures and patterns is that any alterations you make cannot be saved for use in another document. If you really like the adjustments you've made to a pattern and think you would like to have it available for another use, then you must save it as a style.

Sometimes patterns will tile in (repeat itself) an image that you fill with your own pattern. If this happens, just click the center circle (visible if the object is selected) and drag it to the bottom-right corner of the canvas or object.

If you use a custom texture or pattern in a style and you want to share your style, you don't have to send a separate texture or pattern file. The information is embedded in the style.

Adding Borders to Bitmap Images

There are several different ways to add a border to your bitmap image. You've seen one example already—the textured stroke added around a photo. You may not have realized that this same technique will add a border to your photo. Follow these steps to do this:

1. Open the `flowers.png` file from the Chapter 6 folder on the accompanying CD.

2. Using the Rectangle tool, draw a rectangle around the photo.

3. In the Tools panel, select the Fill icon and click the No Stroke or Fill icon.

4. Add a stroke in the width, color, and style you like. The following settings were used for the example shown in Figure 6.21:

   Color: **Black**

   Stroke Category: **Basic, Hard Line**

   Roundness: **0%**

5. For a variation, change the Roundness to 30% (see Figure 6.22). Notice how you can see the corners of the photo, and how jagged the corners are.

6. To fix this jagged look, change the stroke to Basic, Hard Rounded.

7. Now you will want to fix the corners of the image. Do so by selecting the photo, not the border.

8. Then choose Edit → Cut.

Figure 6.21

A black border added to an image

Figure 6.22

The photo edges expand beyond the new frame border.

9. Now select just the border, and choose Edit → Paste Inside. Isn't that great! What you did was fill the border with the image. Take a look at Figure 6.23 to see the results.

Figure 6.23

The corners of the image removed by placing the image inside the border

The Paste Inside command is great for placing something in a specific area of an object. Just position the image beneath the object exactly where you want it to appear. For instance, if you are using text and you want a specific object to show in a specific place, you'd place that object where you want it. Then when you Cut it and use the Paste Inside command, it will be in the same place. You can also click on the cloverleaf icon to adjust the image position within the object.

Using Gradient Fills

A *gradient* is a blend of two or more colors. Gradients are often used to produce lighting effects to give the illusion of depth. They are also used to form terrific backgrounds and as a fill for transparency masks when you are working with bitmaps (see Chapter 8). In addition to these common uses, a new feature in Fireworks MX has been added to gradients—the ability to add transparency.

Filling with Gradients

You can add unique colorization to a graphic with the use of a gradient fill. Fireworks MX ships with 11 gradient patterns and 13 preset gradient color sets. The best way to describe these is to show you a small sample of

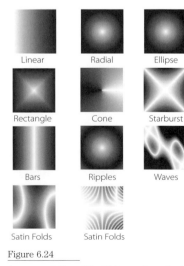

Figure 6.24

A representation of the 11 types of gradients in Fireworks MX

each. Figure 6.24 shows a representation of each gradient pattern and Figure 6.25 shows you the 13 color sets.

To fill using a gradient, follow these steps:

1. Select an object you want to fill with a gradient.

2. In the Fill area of the Property Inspector, choose one of the gradient options from the Fill Category pop-up.

3. Depending on what you want to do and the choices you have to make, you can access the gradient options in two different ways. You can choose Fill Options from the Fill Category, which gives you the opportunity to change the gradient type and see real time what it looks like (edge, texture, and color presets can all be accessed from this pop-up). Or you can click the color box next to the Fill icon in the Tools panel. Doing this gives you the Edit pop-up and a button to access the Fill Options pop-up.

4. After you have selected the gradient options you want to use using one of the above methods, choose the color combination you like from the preset gradient color sets, or use the gradient that is the default. (The default is a combination of whatever color your stroke is and the current color of the Fill tool.)

5. You can now adjust the Edge attributes in the Fill Options pop-up; the choices are Anti-Alias, Hard, or Feather. If you choose Feather, you have the option of typing in how many pixels wide you want the feather at the edge of your gradient to be.

> If your object is selected, it is automatically filled with the gradient.

6. Once you have the gradient you like, you can either save the file or make a style out of it. The next section will show you how to edit your gradients colors.

Editing Gradient Colors

Existing colors in a gradient can be changed, deleted, and moved around, and new colors can be added with ease. To change the colors of a Preset gradient or even a custom gradient, follow these steps:

1. Draw a rectangle, and from the Fill Category in the Property Inspector choose Radial.

2. Click the color box to access the Edit pop-up (as shown in Figure 6.26).

    You will see color markers below the gradient representation as well as above. There will be color markers for each color in the gradient and at the position that each color begins.

3. To change any of the colors, simply click the color marker you want to change and choose another color. (Transparency will be discussed in the next section.)

Figure 6.25

The 13 preset color sets for gradients

Figure 6.26

The Edit pop-up

4. To add another color, place your cursor anywhere in the row containing the current color markers where you want another color added. As you pass your cursor over the area you want a new color to appear, you will see a plus sign (+) next to your cursor. Simply click to add a new marker.

5. Select the color you want to add by clicking the new color marker to access the color swatches, and then choose a color.

6. To move the position of any of the colors, click and drag the color marker to the new location.

7. To delete a color, click and drag the color marker toward the bottom of the panel.

8. To close the Gradient Edit pop-up, just click the canvas. You are now finished editing the colors of the gradient.

As you can see, you have a lot of control when it comes to gradient colors. In addition to the options mentioned here, you can produce some interesting color combinations by sampling colors from other images with the Eyedropper tool. If you have an image that you really like the color composition of, you can make a custom gradient from it by sampling colors in this manner.

Adding Transparency

The ability to add transparency to your gradients is new to Fireworks MX. But before you get too excited, remember that this "transparency" is only transparent in your document—you can see through to objects below. When you export the slice with the object below, it will appear transparent. But if you export just the transparent object and you expect to see through it to the web page background, you are in for a surprise—that isn't going to happen. Only the PNG32 file format has this capability. You can use this format, but not all browsers support it yet.

To adjust the transparency of a gradient, follow these steps:

1. Fill an object with a gradient of any color and style.

2. Click the color box to access the same Edit pop-up you can access from the Fill Options dialog box's Edit button. Refer back to Figure 6.26 to see the label for the transparency markers.

3. Click the marker to access the Opacity pop-up.

4. Move the slider to the desired position. You can do the same thing to the transparency marker on the right as well.

5. Add additional transparency markers by simply clicking over the area in which you want to add one, and then click again to set the Opacity for each one you add.

6. Click the canvas area to exit the gradient Edit pop-up.

Altering Gradients

The real power of the Gradient tool becomes evident when you experiment with altering gradients. You can customize such gradients by adjusting the pattern's center, width, and skew. Here is an example of the steps you would follow to alter a gradient's position:

Figure 6.27

The gradient handles are visible when the object is selected.

1. Follow the preceding steps for filling with a gradient.

2. Then, to alter the gradients position, select the Pointer tool and click the object to make it active; when you do so, the gradient handles will appear (as shown in Figure 6.27).

3. To change the position of the gradient, drag the handles to adjust the gradient's starting point. In this example, we want the linear gradient to be horizontal instead of vertical.

Figure 6.28

The direction of the linear gradient reversed

4. Drag the square handle (right side) to the bottom center of the rectangle, and drag the circle handle to the top center. The results are shown in Figure 6.28.

5. You can now save your file.

> It is very difficult to change the gradient handles for a perfectly straight line. If you need to do this, you can select the Gradient tool (from the bitmap area of the Tools panel) and click and drag in your object. To constrain the line to a perfect horizontal, vertical, or 45 degree diagonal, press the Shift key (Enter on the Mac) as you drag.

> A gradient's control handles do not have to be constrained within the object. You can drag the round or square handles outside of the object area to achieve the desired effect; in fact, you can drag both handles completely off the object.

Adding Live Effects

The Effects pop-up menu in the Property Inspector can be accessed by clicking the plus sign next to the word Effects when the Property Inspector is at its full height, or by clicking the Add/Edit Effects button when the Property Inspector is not fully open. The Effects pop-up menu contains a list of Live Effects, such as Bevel and Emboss, and Shadows and Glows, as well as some third-party plugin filters.

> You may have noticed that the Filters menu has the same options as the Effects list. What's the difference? The difference is that when used, the options on the Filters menu are not Live Effects. This means that you can't alter any of the settings after you've added them as you can with Live Effects. The Filters menu is also usually used on bitmap images rather than vector objects (a vector object is converted to a bitmap before the plugin is applied). There are also some filters or plugins that do not have Live Effects. In this case, the only way to apply them would be through the Filters menu.

Adding Bevel and Emboss

The Bevel and Emboss effects have several options and they are also Live Effects and therefore editable. However, they can only be applied to vector images or objects. The Bevel and Emboss options are shown in Figure 6.29 with their default settings.

> You can add Bevel and Emboss and Shadows and Glows to a bitmap image if you select it as an object. You'll know it's selected as an object when you see its blue outline. You can double-click the bitmap to edit it as a bitmap. If you are not sure of what mode Fireworks is currently working in (vector or bitmap) check the History panel in the Assets panel group.

To apply one of the Bevel and Emboss effects, simply follow these steps:

1. Select an object and click the plus sign in the Property Inspector to access the Effects pop-up menu.

2. Then choose the appropriate Bevel and Emboss option.

3. When you do, a little pop-up with additional options for customization will pop up.

4. Choose the additional options that you want to apply and click the canvas (or anywhere away from the open dialog box) to accept the changes.

> You can apply multiple effects to the same object.

Shadows and Glows

Shadows and Glows are also Live Effects, meaning that once they are applied, they can be edited. The Shadow and Glow effect also changes as the object changes. For instance, if you have an interface that you drew with a drop shadow applied and you punch a hole in it, the hole will automatically obtain the same shadow. Remember that Live Effects can only be applied to a vector object or image (unless you have a bitmap image selected with a blue outline around it). The Shadow and Glow options are shown in Figure 6.30 using their default settings.

Applying Blurs

The Blur filters in the Effect pop-up menu can be applied to vector objects (as well as bitmaps), are Live Effects, and are editable. The Blur filter adds a bit of blur; the More Blur filter, adds a bit more. The problem with both of these filters is that they offer no control because they are automatic filters. Because it can be altered, the most useful filter is the Gaussian Blur filter. To add a Gaussian Blur follow these steps:

1. Select the object to which you would like to add a blur.

> For a bitmap image, you can use the Selection tools to make a selection. Then the blur filter will be applied only to the selection area.

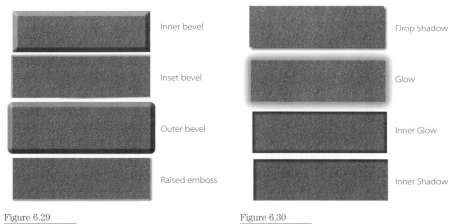

Figure 6.29

The Bevel and Emboss effects

Figure 6.30

The Shadow and Glow options using the default settings

2. From the Effects list, choose Blur → Gaussian Blur. A window will open in which you will choose how much blur you want to add.

3. If you adjust the amount of blur using the slider; you will see the results in real time on the canvas. If you type in the amount, you will need to click OK to view.

4. When you have made your blur amount selection, click OK to apply the filter.

Editing Effects

If you ever want to edit a file that contains a Live Effect, all you do is open your PNG file and follow these steps:

1. Click the object that contains the effect you would like to view or alter.

2. Once the object is selected, look in the Property Inspector, below the word Effects. You will see a list of effects added with a check mark next to them.

3. To view what the object would look like without a certain effect, uncheck that effect.

4. If you decide you don't want a particular effect, select it and click the minus sign to delete it.

5. To view the specific settings of any effect and make alterations, choose the Edit and Arrange Effect icon (little I) to the left of the effect name.

6. Once the alterations or the exploration is complete, click outside the pop-up to accept the changes and close the pop-up.

The ability to see the effects applied to any object can really be a timesaver, especially if you have an effect and you forgot how you produced it. Not only can you edit via the Effects list, you can deconstruct using it as well.

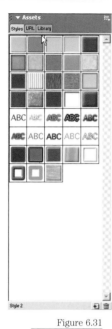

Figure 6.31

The Styles panel

Using the Styles Panel

Fireworks ships with a number of styles. Styles are presets that you can apply to an object with the click of a button. The preset styles can be edited so that you can make your own. The Styles panel is shown in Figure 6.31.

To apply a style to an object, follow these steps:

1. Select the object to receive the style.

2. Open the Styles panel (Window → Styles).

3. Scroll through the list of styles and click one. When you do, the style will be automatically applied to your object.

That's all there is to it!

Modifying Styles

After you apply a style, you may want to change it. Even if you open a previously saved object with a style applied, you can still change it. To modify or edit a style follow these steps:

1. Select the object with a style attached.

2. In the Property Inspector, you can see if there are any effects on the object shown in the Effects list (many styles contain effects). If there are Live Effects applied, they will show up here. If there are effects that are applied, click the Edit and Arrange Effects icon, to alter the settings to your liking.

3. If you want to see what the object would look like without a particular effect, you can turn off the view of the effect by clicking the ⓘ icon next to the effect. When you do this, only the view is turned off, the effect is still there. To turn it back on, just click the ⓘ icon again.

4. If you want to delete an effect, just click it and then click the minus (–) sign.

5. After you have looked for effects, check to see whether there are any fills applied; these will also show up in the Property Inspector. Edit the fills as you would any other fill.

6. Finally, check to see if there are any strokes applied; they will show up in the Property Inspector as well. Edit them just like any other stroke.

7. When you are finished with your edits and changes, remember to save your file. You can also make it into a style if you'd like. You'll see how to save styles in the next section.

Saving Styles

If you have an object to which you have applied a custom fill and special effects that you'd like to keep and maybe use again on another object, then you can save it as a style. The styles you save, as well as those in the Style panel, can also be used for the Pop-Up Menus

that Fireworks can make. See Chapter 9 for more on making instant Pop-Up Menus. To save
a style, follow these steps:

1. Select the object whose effects you want to save as a style.

2. Access the Styles Option pop-up menu (upper-right corner of the Styles panel), choose
    New Style, and give your style a name.

3. In the New Style dialog box that opens, select the options you want to save as a style.
    Remember, if the style is attached to a font, you don't have to choose Font. If you
    do choose Font, then the same font will be applied when you apply the style. If you
    don't choose Font, then the style effects will be added to whatever text to which you
    are adding the style.

4. Click OK in the New Style dialog box.

Importing and Exporting Styles

When you make new styles, you can export just one of them or you can make several and
export them as a set. To import or export styles, follow these steps:

1. Open the Styles panel (Window → Styles).

2. Access the Styles Options pop-up menu, and from there choose either Import Styles or
    Export Styles.

3. A window will open. Here you can either locate and choose the file to import or choose
    where to save the export.

4. Click Open or Save depending on whether you are performing an import or an export.

Web Dithering

Web-safe colors are the 216 colors that display consistently on monitors that can only utilize
256 colors, across multiple platforms. Many designers today are not as concerned about this
problem as they were a few years ago because more and more people are upgrading to
better system monitors with better video cards that support millions of colors. However,
many designers still want to use web-safe colors because of the global reach of the Internet.
The choice of whether to use web-safe colors or not is up to you. Of course, if you know that
your audience doesn't include people from other countries or new users, then you can skip
this section.

Web dithering will expand your color palette greatly and it will still be web-safe. Dithering
was originally used when all that was available was the GIF format, and photographs with
millions of colors were being used for the Web and being viewed with monitors using only
256 colors.

The process of *dithering* involves taking two or more pixels of different colors and positioning them close to one another in such a way that they produce a pattern. This pattern

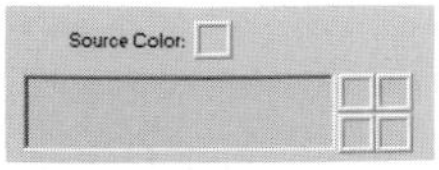

Figure 6.32

The Web Dither pop-up

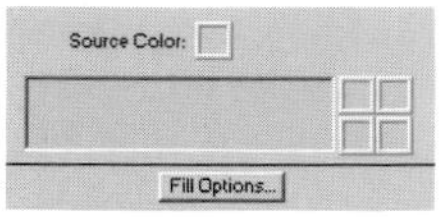

Figure 6.33

The Web Dither window that opens from the Fill color box in the Tools panel

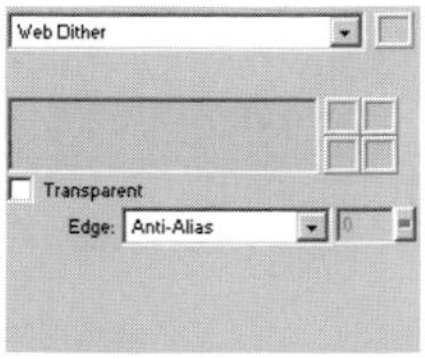

Figure 6.34

The Fill Options pop-up that opens when the Fill Options button is clicked

tricks the eye into seeing a different color. This technique works great with simple GIFs, but when you use it on photographs, you lose a lot of detail because many colors blend. The best path to take is to use the JPEG format for photographs and the GIF format for vectors and images containing few colors. Chapter 10 goes into great detail on the differences between the GIF and the JPEG formats.

Web Dither contains two web safe colors in an alternating 2 pixel-by-2 pixel pattern that produces a third color. With this technique, Fireworks makes it so that you now have 46,656 web-safe "designer" colors. Don't worry, Fireworks provides you with a simple-to-use interface (the Web Dither dialog box) from which you can choose the colors you want to dither or from which you can simply view the automatic selection that Fireworks makes when you select a non–web-safe color you want to dither. The best way to understand how this dithering works in Fireworks is to try it out.

To use the web dithering feature, follow these steps:

1. Choose Web Dither from the Fill Category drop-down list in the Properties Inspector.

2. Click the color box and you'll see the Web Dither pop-up shown in Figure 6.32.

3. Click the color box from the Fill area in the Tools panel for more options. Figure 6.33 shows the Dither pop-up that opens and Figure 6.34 shows the Fill Options pop-up that opens when you click the Fill Options button.

4. In the Dither pop-up, the first color box on the top represents the current fill color. To convert a non–web-safe color into a web safe one, click this color box to choose a non–web-safe color, type a Hexadecimal number, or select a color with the eyedropper.

   Once you select the non–web-safe color you'll notice that the four color boxes in the center of the pop-up have alternating colors. The center preview is a representation of the new color that is a combination of the two that Fireworks has chosen to best match the color you chose in the top color box.

5. Click outside the Dither pop-up to close it and have the color applied to your selected object.

With the eyedropper, you can sample outside of your document—from the menus in Fireworks, or from another document.

The color you see in the large color area of the Dither pop-up is the color that will be applied to your object by default. Fireworks automatically selects the best web-safe colors to mix to obtain the color closest to the one you choose. However, you can click in either color box on the right and choose a different color.

Customizing the Swatches Panel

Fireworks' default Swatches panel is the web-safe 216 color Hexadecimal panel. You can add to the Swatches panel by mixing your own custom colors in the Color Mixer (Windows → Color Mixer) or by using the Eyedropper tool to sample a color.

The Swatches panel can be accessed by choosing Window → Swatches. This panel (shown in Figure 6.35) is grouped with Mixer in a panel group named Color. There are a number of activities you can perform that you start from the Swatches Options pop-up menu (accessed from the icon in the top-right corner of the panel).

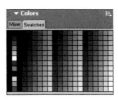

Figure 6.35

The Swatches panel in the Color panel group

Export the Current Export Palette

You may have an image that uses colors that you'd like to use throughout a website design. Perhaps you work others and want to be sure they use the same color palette. You can save a palette of the colors in your current GIF image. To do so, just follow these steps.

1. In the Swatches panel, access the Swatches Options pop-up menu (click the icon in the top-right corner).

2. From the Swatches Options pop-up menu, select Current Export Palette. You'll see the current colors in the Swatches panel.

3. Open Swatches Options pop-up menu and select Save Swatches. Save to any folder on your hard drive that you'd like, there is no specific place you have to save to. Fireworks saves in the ACT (Active Color Table) format.

> If the Current Export Palette option is grayed out and you have an Export File Format of GIF, Animated GIF, WBMP, PNG 8, TIFF8, or BMP8, then click the Rebuild button to show the colors in your image. The Current Export Palette option will now be available.

Loading Saved Color Palettes

If you have a custom color palette you would like to add to your Swatches panel, be sure that it is a GIF file or an ACT file (ACO files can be loaded as well, refer to the note below). To add your custom color palette, open the Swatches options pop-up menu from the Swatches panel and choose Add Swatches. Then select the appropriate file (a saved ACT or GIF file) and click OK.

> You can force Fireworks to use Photoshop ACO files as well. To do this, choose Add or Replace Swatches from the right arrow in the Swatches panel. When the dialog box opens so that you can locate your file, go to the folder on your hard drive where you know a Photoshop ACO file resides. In the File box, type ***.aco** and press the Enter/Return key. You can now see your ACO files. Choose the one you want and click Open.

Adding swatches in this manner extends the existing palette. If you just want to use a saved palette, then choose Replace Swatches. If you simply want to add a few additional color swatches, then choose Add Swatches from the Swatches Options pop-up menu. The additional swatches will be added to the bottom of the current Swatches panel.

Explore the Swatches panel by clicking some of the other options to see what changes are made. One such option allows you to load just the Windows palette or just the Macintosh palette.

Fireworks MX Commands

Fireworks MX ships with a good selection of *commands*—recorded actions that produce an automatic effect. If you are a Photoshop user (or ever have been) then commands in Fireworks are similar to actions in Photoshop. Fireworks commands are closely tied in with the History panel, which shows a list of each action you can take. These actions can then be saved as a command. You will learn how to make your own commands in the "Making Your Own Commands" section, later in this chapter.

Commands can be accessed through the Commands menu. If you are a previous Fireworks user, you will notice a few new items in the Commands menu. The first new option is Manage Saved Commands. When you click this option, the Manage Saved Command dialog box opens; in it, you can rename or delete your commands. Just click OK when you are finished.

The Manage Saved Commands option is only for working with commands that you make and save, or for ones that someone gives you that you have added to the Commands folder of the Fireworks MX program. Everything below the line you see in the Command menu is in the Commands menu can be managed with the Manage Saved Commands option.

Another notable addition is the Manage Extensions option. Although Dreamweaver has had extensions for a long time, this is the first version of Fireworks that supports extensions.

The new Data-Driven Graphics Wizard (shown here) lets you insert variables into a PNG file and replace the variables with data from an XML file. Using this wizard you can split out a series of images with different text or images. This wizard is a huge step forward for Fireworks working together with Dreamweaver.

Creative Options

There is a nice collection of commands available in the Creative menu pop-up (Commands →
Creative): Add Arrowheads, Add Picture Frame, Convert to Grayscale, Convert to Sepia
Tone, Image Fader, and Twist and Fade. Each of these choices will be discussed in the following sections. The Add Arrowheads, Add Picture Frame, Image Fader, and Twist and Fade
are new commands made by using the new SWF extension capabilities of Fireworks.

Add Arrowheads

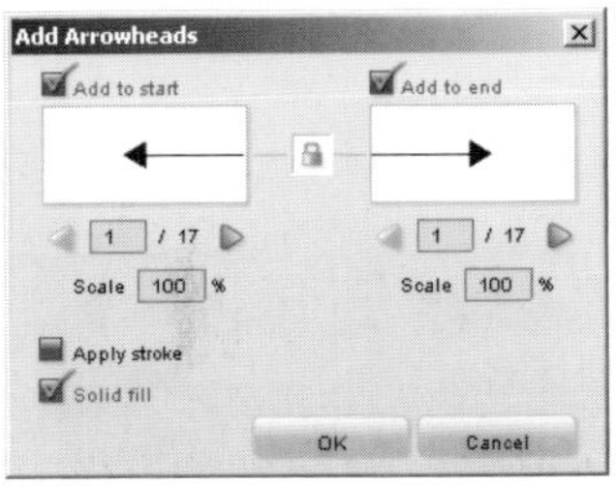

This is the first version of Fireworks that has given you the option of adding an arrowhead to a path (or line). When you select an open path and choose Commands →
Creative → Add Arrowheads you can make several different decisions on which end
(or both) ends of the path to attach an arrowhead as well as determine the size, the
stroke, and/or fill.

Add Picture Frame

The Add Picture Frame command is an improvement over the Create Picture Frame command from Fireworks 4, which only allowed you to choose the size of the frame. The Add
Picture Frame command allows you to choose from 46 different patterns in addition to allowing you to pick the size that you'd like (see Figure 6.36).

Once you choose the pattern and size you want, click OK. The frame is added to your canvas, not a selected object. Even if you select an image, the frame will still be applied to the
edge of the canvas. You can also apply more than one frame per image.

To use the Add Picture Frame command, follow these steps:

1. Open the `flowers.png` file from the Chapter 6 folder on the accompanying CD. You will
   add a frame to this image.

2. Choose Commands → Creative → Add Picture Frame. The Add Picture Frame dialog box
   will open. For now, just accept the defaults of this dialog box and click OK. In your canvas, notice how the frame is placed on the edge of the canvas?

3. Then choose Edit → Undo to get the photo back and remove the frame you just
   applied. You will now add a frame to just the image of the flowers.

4. Choose Modify → Canvas → Trim Canvas. This removes the extra canvas and
   leaves just the photo. Now a frame will be applied to the edge of the photo.

5. Now choose Commands → Creative → Add Picture Frame. Pick a style and size
   and click OK; the frame now surrounds your photo.

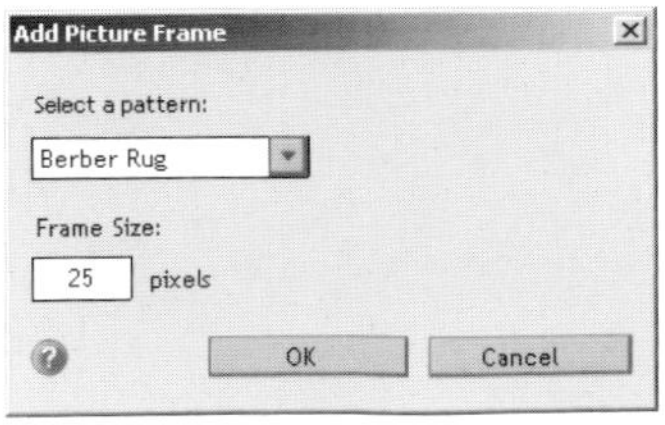

You can add more than one frame per image if you'd like. Figure 6.37 shows three frames
added. Though you may not be able to come up with a practical use for this exercise now,
you may find it useful sometime in the future.

Figure 6.36

**The dialog box for the
Add Picture Frame
command**

Figure 6.37

**Three frames added to
the image using the
Add Picture Frame
command**

Convert to Grayscale

If you want to get rid of all color and end up with a grayscale image, use this option because it is quick and easy. To convert an image or object to grayscale, simply select it and choose Commands → Creative → Convert to Grayscale. This is an automatic command, no dialog opens because there is nothing for you to choose.

> Alternatively, you can choose Adjust Color → Hue and Saturation from the Effects list, and then you can move the Hue and Saturation sliders to 0.

Convert to Sepia

Sepia gives the appearance of an old fashioned image, the tones are brownish instead of gray. To convert an image or object to sepia, choose Commands → Creative → Convert to Sepia.

> If you want an image to be two colors, similar to sepia, but a different color, you can also choose, Filters → Adjust Color → Hue and Saturation. Check the Colorize box and choose the color you want.

Fade Image

This is another new command for Fireworks MX. If you are new to Fireworks, you'll love this one! This command allows you to make an image fade into the background. There are eight different options for how the image will fade into the background. To use the Image Fade command, simply select an image, choose Commands → Creative → Fade Image. Select the icon of the fade you want and click OK (below left). That's all there is to it. This is the same result you'd get if you made a mask for the image (described in Chapter 8).

Twist and Fade

The Twist and Fade command has a lot of options to choose from. The best way to get used to this command is to play with the controls and see what you can do. Here is a picture of the Twist and Fade dialog box (below right) showing the many options you have.

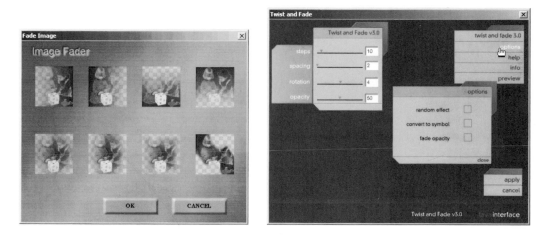

Here is an example to give you an idea of how this works. On the left side of this image is a nautilus shell image that we made. We opened it and applied the Twist and Fade command, accepting the default settings.

Making Your Own Commands

As mentioned earlier, commands are similar to actions in other applications. To make your own commands follow these steps:

1. Perform the steps involved in a task that you think you might want to repeat again in another document or to another object.

2. Then open the History panel (docked panel set of Frames and History).

3. Select the last step in the History list—this step contains all of the previous ones.

4. Finally, access the History Options pop-up menu, choose Save as Command, and then type a name for your command in the appropriate text box.

> Sometimes the last step in the History list doesn't work as a command. If this happens, try again by Shift + Selecting all the steps and saving again. Be sure to test your command.

That is all there is to making a simple command in Fireworks. When you are looking at the History panel, you will see that it shows the steps or actions you've taken. As you perform actions you will notice in the History panel a list with a little scroll icon to the left. The list has a thin line below it. If at any time an action shows below the line in the History panel, it may not record properly. If this happens to you, you may need to repeat some steps or perform your action in a different way so that you will be able to record it and save it properly as a command.

> When you save a command that has actions below the line you will get a warning that says some of your actions may not work, just click OK and try it anyway. Most of the time they seem to work.

You can also make commands by writing your own JavaScript. The major functions in Fireworks are JavaScript-based, therefore they can be changed according to the way you work if you can write JavaScript code. This topic is beyond the scope of this book, but you can find out more about writing your own JavaScript commands at the Macromedia website (`http://www.macromedia.com`). Commands with an SWF interface are new to Fireworks MX, you can also find directions for making your own at Macromedia. The Twist and Fade command is a SWF as well as the Align panel.

Using Free Commands

You can find additional commands that other Fireworks users have made at various websites
that are listed at the end of this section. For instance, the SWF commands are new to Fireworks
MX and there are many Fireworks users and developers who are making new ones. We have
included a light version of a Gel button on this book's accompanying CD-ROM as an example of
this. In addition, extensions like those that are available for Dreamweaver are now available for
Fireworks too; just check Macromedia's website for a list (`http://www.macromedia.com`).

Once you find a command that you think sounds useful, you will need to place it in your
Fireworks MX Commands folder. Once commands are placed in this folder, you can use them
without restarting Fireworks. If the file that contains the command is zipped, you will need
to unzip it before you can use it.

> The Manage Extension command (Commands → Manage Extensions) is a new feature of Fire-
> works MX that you can use to install and uninstall commands. You can also manage the SWF
> commands that ship with Fireworks MX as well as ones you find at private websites.

Any command that you make and save in Fireworks will automatically be saved to the correct folder and be immediately available in the Commands menu.

Third Party Commands

This is a small list of sites that currently have commands available for you to download free
of charge. At the time this book was being written, the SWF and Extension capabilities were
still new. There will soon be many more resources available—not only free commands, but
for extensions as well. Be sure to check the Macromedia website and the Macromedia Fireworks forum (look for `http://forums.macromedia.com` in your news reader).

Fireworks support Support and extensibility docs can be found here `http://www.macromedia`
`.com/support/fireworks/extensibility.html`.

JoyceJEvans.com Find free commands and tutorials at `http://www.JoyceJEvans.com`.

Massimo Foti This site contains Fireworks commands. In addition, it also has helpful information about Dreamweaver and UltraDev: `http://www.massimocorner.com`.

Project Fireworks An archive of downloadable commands, patterns, textures, and symbols
can be found at `http://www.projectfireworks.com`.

Ultraweaver A growing Fireworks source for PNG files and commands can be found at
`http://www.ultraweaver.com`.

Hands On: Batch Processing

In this tutorial, you'll learn how to process a batch of images, but you will also be applying some of the things you've learned throughout this chapter. We have put together a collection of images taken with our digital camera. They are not anything special, but we wanted to give you something to practice on. You can find them in the Images folder inside the Chapter 6 folder on the accompanying CD. Save them to your hard drive before you start the exercises below.

We'll be showing you how to use a command within a batch process, so you'll need to make the command. After you have made your command, you'll need to decide what you want to do with your images. You'll need to do these three things to all the images: resize the images, add a border, and add a drop shadow.

Make a Command

As you may have noticed, all of the images that you copied from the CD are 896 × 592 pixels in size. In this section, you will take the appropriate steps to add a border and a drop shadow to one of these images. That way, you can use the History panel to make a command that can be used on the rest of the images in the Chapter 6 folder on the CD using a batch process. Because the batch command will do the resizing, it doesn't need to be part of the command you make, so we saved a smaller version (the size the batch process will use) of one image named makecommand.png.

Open makecommand.png now, but do not select the image. Instead, open the History panel (Frames and History panel set). As in the earlier example, all the steps that you take will be recorded in this panel, and this is what you'll be using to make your command.

This makecommand.png image is an example of what your images would look like if you ran a batch process just to resize. But we want to do more than just resize during our batch process. In addition to resizing, you will add a border and a drop shadow all in one batch process. But to do so, you will need additional canvas space for the extra effects. As a result, your command will start with the steps needed to do this, as shown in the following steps.

1. First, choose Modify → Canvas → Canvas Size and use 350 for the width and 250 for the height; then click OK.

2. Next, select the rectangle tool and cover the image as well as you can. In the Property Inspector, change the width to 300 and the height to 198 if there are any different numbers.

> Remember, whenever you enter values you have to press Enter (Return for Mac) for the setting to be applied.

3. You'll want your rectangle to be in the exact same position as the photo so that the borders are equal. Because you can't see the photo (covered with the rectangle) to check its x and y coordinates, select it (photo) in the Layers panel (see Figure 6.38), and then write down the x and y coordinates (probably something like $x:25$ $y:26$). Now select the rectangle again, and be sure that its x and y coordinates are the same as in the photo.

4. Choose Modify → Arrange → Send to Back.

If you don't send the rectangle to the back, the command you are making won't work.

5. Click the No Stroke/Fill icon in the Tools panel, and then click the Stroke icon and choose Black.

6. In the Property Inspector, change the Tip Size to 6, and the Stroke Category to Pencil, 1-Pixel Hard.

7. Click the plus (+) sign to access the Effects pop-up menu and choose Shadow and Glow → Drop Shadow. Change the Distance to 12 and the Softness to 8, and then click away from the pop-up.

8. Look at the History panel where you should see all the steps you've taken (as shown in Figure 6.39).

9. Finally, Shift + Select all the steps you took starting with the Crop Document to Set Effects step. From the History Options pop-up menu, choose Save Command, name it BorderShadow, and click OK. A warning will open (see Figure 6.40) saying that some of the effects may not work. Click OK because they will work in this case.

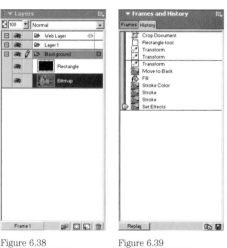

Figure 6.38

The Layers panel showing the image and the rectangle

Figure 6.39

The contents of the History panel after you are done making the command

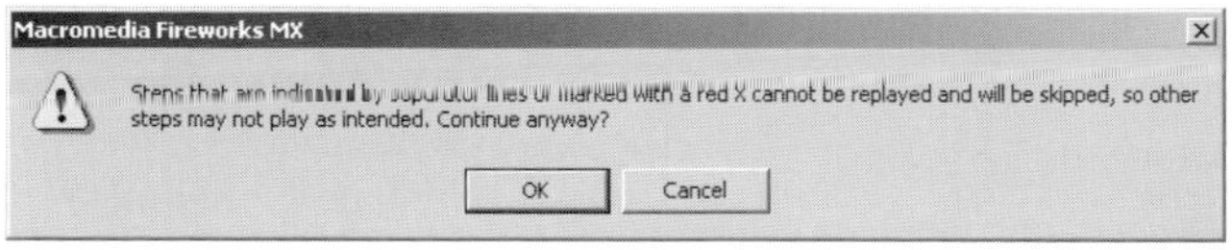

Figure 6.40

The warning that opens because some of the steps may not record

Perform the Batch Process

Now comes the easy part. Now that all the work has been done one time, you can process any number of images quickly.

1. Choose File → Batch Process.

2. Change the Files of Type to All Files and navigate to where you saved the images folder. If you didn't save it, that's OK, just navigate to the Chapter 6 folder on the accompanying CD and double-click to open the images folder.

3. Click Add All (Figure 8.41), and then click Next (see Figure 6.42).

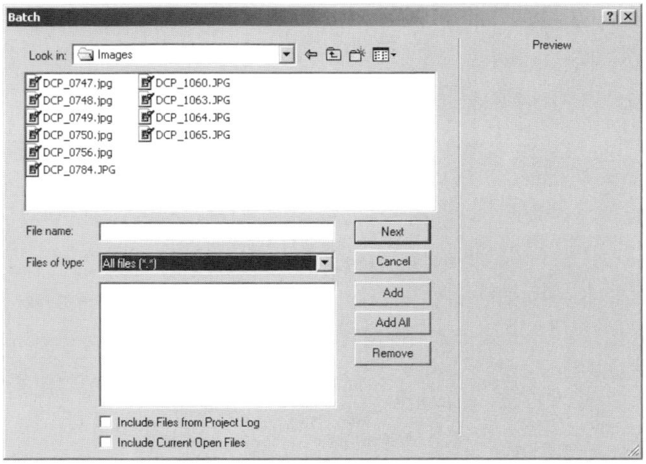

Figure 6.41

The Batch dialog box

[Figure 6.41: The Batch dialog box]

4. Figure 6.42 shows the Batch Process dialog box. In the Scale area of the Batch Process dialog box, choose Scale to Size and type in 300 for the width and 198 for the height.

> Because all the images are the same size, you choose Scale to Size. If you had images of different sizes you could choose Scale to Fit Area. You would then type in a Max Width and a Max Height. This option will retain the images' proportions, yet it will keep them inside a width and height range.

5. To add the command you made to the Batch Process, click the plus (+) sign next to the word Commands. Then scroll down to ShadowBorder (or whatever you named it) and select it. Click the Add button (see Figure 6.43), and then click Next.

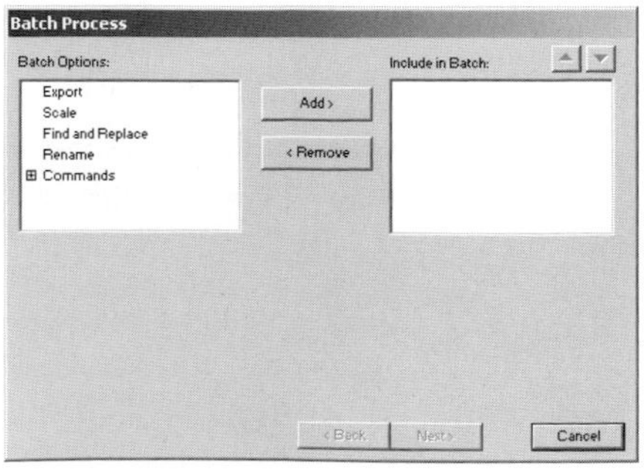

Figure 6.42

The Batch Process dialog box

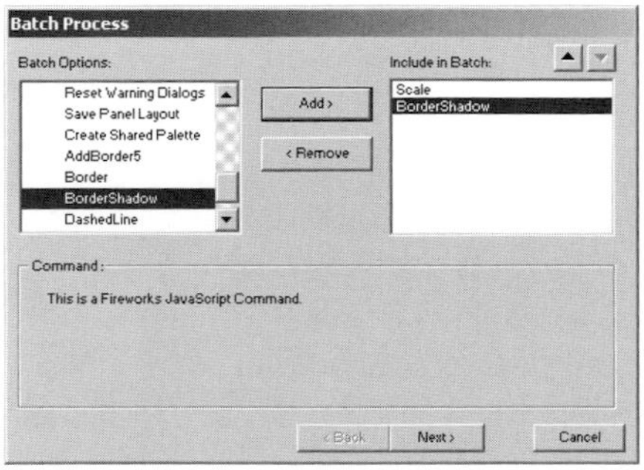

Figure 6.43

The Batch Process dialog box with our commands and effects added

6. In the Saving Files area, choose Custom Location and browse to select a folder. You should follow this step so that you don't overwrite anything. If you think you may want to use this batch process on anything else, you can save the script by clicking the Save Script button (see Figure 6.44) and choosing where to save it and what to name it.

7. Finally, Click Batch, and then when the process is finished, click OK.

8. Now open an image and see if you got what you wanted. The two images in Figure 6.45 show the starting image and the image after the batch process. What a tremendous time savings!

Figure 6.44

The last dialog box of the Batch Process

Figure 6.45

The before and after images

From Effects to Vectors

Fireworks has supplied you with great tools, and now that you know how to effectively use them, you'll be able to tackle a multitude of projects. The different fills, patterns, and textures really expand your ability to get innovative. Not only did you learn how to use different fills and strokes, but you also learned how to save them as styles so that they could be used in other documents. If that wasn't enough, you also discovered that you could automate many tasks by making commands and even applying these commands to a batch process. In addition, you saw how to manage and work with colors, from subjects like web dithering to gradients.

In the next chapter, you'll learn to work with vector images in Fireworks, and in Chapter 8 we'll look at bitmap images.

## CHAPTER 7

Working With Vectors

In this chapter, you will be exploring the world of vectors. A vector is just a line pointing in one direction (students of film may remember the line, "What's the vector, Victor?" from the movie *Airplane*—great, now I'm showing my age). Vector images are composed of paths. This contrasts with bitmaps, which are composed of pixels. The path is stored as mathematical information whereas bitmap images are stored as pixel-by-pixel color assignments (something like a mosaic or a pointillist painting). In Fireworks, an object is called a path or a vector graphic.

Because of the mathematical nature of vectors, they are very flexible. A vector object can be stretched to a larger size, both in height and in width, and still maintain its image integrity. This is because as the object increases in size, your computer recalculates the math necessary to render a great-looking image. It's this quality that makes vector objects so popular for use in animations and web page graphics.

In the following pages, you will learn how to use the vector tools, and then you will learn how to draw and manipulate vector graphics into different shapes suitable for web navigation, logos, and buttons. These are the topics covered in this chapter:

- **Editing vector shapes**
- **Manipulating Bézier curves**
- **Using path operations**
- **Transformations and numeric transformations**
- **Cutting text out of an image**
- **Make a navigational element**

Vector Tools

The Tools panel groups all the vector tools together and all the bitmap tools together, as you can see in Figure 7.1. Then there are two tools between the bitmap and vector sections of the Tools panel—the Eyedropper tool and the Paint Bucket/Gradient Fill. These tools can be used for both vector and bitmap images.

In previous versions of Fireworks, you needed to switch between vector and bitmap mode, but now this switching happens automatically. When you open a vector image you are automatically in vector mode, and if you select a bitmap tool, it may or may not work depending on what you have on the canvas. For instance, if you draw a rectangle (vector) and click the selection tools, they won't work because there is no bitmap present for them to select. But if you select the Brush tool (bitmap), you can paint because the mode is switched automatically to bitmap, allowing you to paint.

To see how the mode automatically changes, open the History panel (docked in a panel group). You'll see the Edit Bitmap icon when you selected the Brush tool. Then, if you select another vector tool, you'll see Exit Bitmap in the History panel. This shows that Fireworks has automatically changed modes; this will save you all the time you used to spend switching between modes.

Using Vector Shape Tools

The vector shape tools are some of the easiest to use. Every object drawn with a vector shape tool always contains a starting point and an ending point, which are used to plot the path of a line. With the vector shape tools, these points are automatically placed.

Shape Tools have several common characteristics. First, to constrain the shape of an entire vector, press the Alt + Shift (Option + Shift for Mac) key combination while dragging to draw. Another way that all shape tools can be used in a similar fashion is if you want to draw from the center out; to do so, you would press the Alt key (Option for a Mac) and drag to draw. Similarly, to resize an object and constrain the shape, you would press the Shift key as you drag the corner handle in or out.

Most of the shape tools also have a number of properties to set. After you select a specific tool, you can find its properties or options in the Property Inspector.

Pen tool
Line tool
Rectangle tool
Text tool
Freeform tool
Knife tool

Figure 7.1

The Tools panel showing the vector tools and their various pop-up menus

Rectangle Tool

The Rectangle tool will probably be the vector shape tool that you use the most. You'll use it for buttons, layout designs, headers, banners, and the list goes on. To draw a rectangle, follow these steps:

1. Select the Rectangle tool from the Tools panel.

2. Click and drag a rectangle on your canvas.

3. If you want to set a specific size for your rectangle, enter in the specific height and width measurements in the boxes provided in the Property Inspector (the lower-left corner). That's all there is to drawing a rectangle. Now let's look at editing it.

4. To edit the shape, select the object with the Subselection tool. The blue points in each corner of the object will now look like hollow squares, and they will be editable (as shown in Figure 7.2).

5. Click and drag out the point in the lower-right corner. An error dialog box will open stating, "To edit a rectangle's points, it must first be ungrouped, click OK to ungroup the rectangle and turn it into a vector?" Click OK.

> A rectangle in Fireworks is a group of four points, which is why you receive this error—in order for the rectangle to be recognized as a path object, it must first be ungrouped. Once it's ungrouped, you will be able to manipulate each point separately from the other three. The second half of the error message may lead you to think that you are not in Vector mode, but you are.

6. Now use the Subselection tool to click and drag any of the points to alter the shape of the rectangle.

7. Save your work if you desire to do so at this time.

Rounded Rectangle Tool

When you select the Rounded Rectangle tool from the Rectangle tool pop-up, you can see its properties in the Property Inspector. The roundness of the corners is 30 degrees by default. Using the Rounded Rectangle tool is actually quite easy to do. Let's make a few tab shapes.

1. Open a new document that is 400 × 200 and has a white canvas.

2. Select the Rounded Rectangle tool from the pop-up.

Figure 7.2

The rectangle selected with the Subselection tool, which makes the points editable

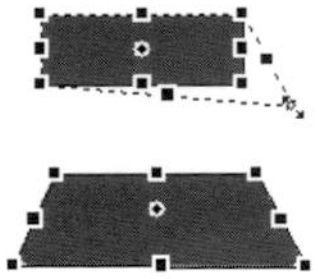

Figure 7.3

The shape being distorted from the right, and then on both sides

3. Drag a shape on the canvas.

4. Set its size in the Property Inspector. Change the Width (W) to 100 and the Height (H) to 35. The roundness is already set to 30 and that's fine. If you want to change it, though, you'd just move the slider near the roundness field to the desired amount.

That's all there is to making a shape with the Rounded Rectangle. But now let's make this a better-looking tab.

1. Choose Modify → Transform → Distort.

2. Pull out the right corner (as shown in Figure 7.3), and then pull out on the left corner until the shape looks like the bottom shape in Figure 7.3.

3. Double-click to accept this transformation.

4. Make two copies (using the Edit → Copy command) or press the Alt (Option on a Mac) key and drag a copy two times.

5. Line the copies up end to end.

6. With the Rounded Rectangle tool, add a small rectangle to cover the bottom of all the tabs to make it look like a folder (as shown in Figure 7.4).

Figure 7.4

The tab duplicated twice and a rectangle added underneath so that it resembles a folder

According to a study made by Jakob Nielson (http://www.useit.com) the use of a tabbed interface along the top of a web page is equal to the left margin usage for navigation. You just learned how easy it is to make the images for a tabbed navigational interface.

Ellipse Tool

An ellipse that you draw will have four points added to it automatically, like the rectangles you just drew. The difference is that these points are not grouped, so when you go to edit them, you will not have to ungroup them first. If you use the Subselection tool to alter a point, you will notice "handles" that appear on the points of the ellipse. These are Bézier control handles. To learn more about using these handles see the "Manipulating Bézier Curves with the Control Handles" section of this chapter.

To draw an ellipse, follow these steps:

1. Select the Ellipse tool from the Tools panel.

2. Click and drag an ellipse on your canvas. Press the Shift key as you drag to make a perfect circle.

3. If you want to set a specific size for your ellipse, enter the dimensions in the Property Inspector.

4. Add any strokes, fills, or effects you'd like.

Polygon Tool

In Fireworks, you can draw any equilateral polygon—from a triangle with three sides to a polygon with 360 sides. To make a polygon, follow these steps:

1. Select the Polygon tool to access its tool options in the Property Inspector. Figure 7.5 show these options.

2. Select either Polygon or Star from the Property Inspector.

   If the Star shape is selected, an Angle option is also available. If you choose the Automatic option, Angle varies according to how many sides you have. The closer to 0 Angle is, the thinner the point is. The closer to 100 Angle is, the thicker the point is. Choose the settings you'd like to use.

3. Drag and draw a star or a polygon on your canvas. If you try to change the settings now, you will see that they do not change the current shape; you would have to draw a new shape to use new settings.

The Polygon tool always draws from the center out. If you want to constrain the shape to a 45-degree angle, hold down the Shift key and drag the shape.

4. Click anywhere on the canvas to deselect your new object. You can now change its Fill and/or Stroke properties or add effects to it (refer to Chapter 6). You can save your work if you'd like.

Line Tool

The Line tool only draws a straight line with two points (either horizontal or vertical). If you want to constrain the line to a 45-degree angle, hold down the Shift key and drag the shape.

To use the Line tool, follow these steps:

1. Select the Line tool from the Tools panel.

2. Drag a diagonal line on the canvas by holding down the Shift key and dragging.

3. To alter the lines properties, change the settings in the Property Inspector after you've selected the line you want to alter.

4. Save if you'd like.

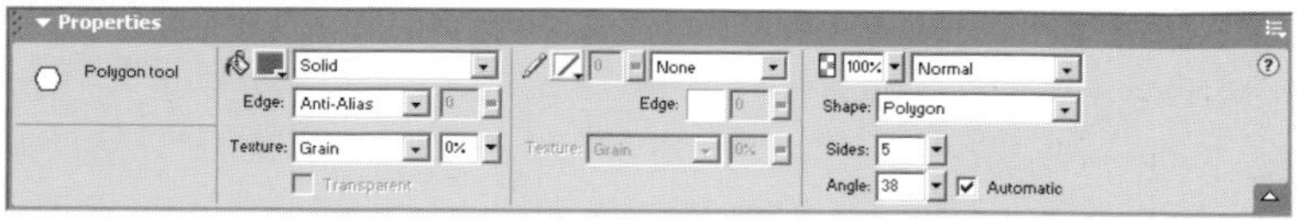

Figure 7.5

The Property Inspector after the Polygon tool has been selected

Becoming Familiar with Drawing Tools

The freeform drawing tools enable you to draw any shape you want. If you have a digital drawing tablet, now would be the time to use it. It's much easier to draw freeform lines with a drawing pen than it is with a mouse. Of course, you can still draw quite well even with a mouse in Fireworks.

Vector Path Tool

The Vector Path tool is like a paintbrush, but the result is still a path containing points. Instead of placing points like you do with the Pen tool; you draw like you would with a pencil or a brush. The lines you draw with the Vector Path tool can be edited like any other path and you can use strokes, fills, and effects. To draw with the Vector Path tool, follow these steps:

1. Select the Vector Path tool from the Pen tool pop-up.

2. Click and drag to draw.

3. If you want an open path, release the mouse when you are done drawing.

4. If you want a closed path, finish drawing at the beginning of the line you drew and release the mouse.

Pen Tool

With the Pen tool, you don't actually draw the line, you just define the points that make up the line—plot out the points, if you will. This process is similar to drawing a dot-to-dot picture. Each time you click, you put down a point (dot); the next place you click adds another point. The line is automatically added between the points, thereby completing a line segment.

The Pen tool has two kinds of points: a Corner point, which has at least one straight segment, and a Curve point, which has at least one curved segment. To see first-hand the difference between these two types of points, follow these steps:

1. Open a new document (File → New) and use a size of 300 pixels × 300 pixels.

2. Select the Pen tool; check to be sure you have a stroke color set. (Do this by choosing a color from the color well next to the Pencil icon in the Property Inspector.)

3. Click somewhere on the left side of the canvas; go straight across the page a few inches and click again. A line connects the two points you added. Continue clicking anywhere on the canvas. No matter where you click, the lines keep connecting the "dots."

4. Close your first practice document and open a new one (File → New); any size is fine. Select the Pen tool and click the left side of the canvas; click again a few inches away, and then go down the page a bit and click and drag. See what happens as you drag? The line is curved.

   As you click and drag, you are adding a Bézier curve, which you will learn to manipulate using the control handles in the next section.

Editing Vectors

Fireworks has several editing tools you can use on vector objects; you will explore them in this section. You can easily alter vector shapes by using Bézier curves or by pushing a new shape with the Reshape Area tool.

Manipulating Bézier Curves with the Control Handles

A Bézier curve, pronounced Bezz-ey-ay, is based on mathematical calculations. The name comes from Pierre Bézier, who, in the 1970s, formulated the principles on which most vector objects are now based. This theory says that all shapes are composed of segments and points. A *segment* can be straight, curved, or a combination of both straight and curved. When you have a combination of two or more points that are joined by a line or a curve, it is referred to as a *path*.

You learned how to add Bézier curves in the previous section (click and drag while placing a point), now you will learn how to edit and alter them.

Working with the control handles is done by using the Subselection tool and clicking a point on the path to first select it. When the cursor is near a point, it (the cursor) changes to a white arrowhead, which indicates that the point can be selected. When you click a point, the hollow square turns into a solid square. Bézier handles are usually visible when you select a point that has a Bézier curve.

> If you press the Alt key (Option on a Mac) and drag and the whole point moves, it's because you didn't select it first (using Subselection tool). Make sure to do this first, and then press the Alt or Option key and drag.

To practice manipulating Bézier curves using Bézier control handles, follow these steps:

1. Select the Pen tool and click three points in a row, double-click the ending point of the path (Figure 7.6).

2. Select the Subselection tool. Click any point; no handles appear because this is a straight line.

3. Select a point—it will turn solid blue when selected—and then press and hold the Alt key (Option for the Mac) and drag the middle point down. As you drag, a control handle will be visible, as seen in Figure 7.7.

4. Now press the Alt key (Option for the Mac) on the same point (not the handle, the point) and drag straight up; you can see what happens in Figure 7.8. Another curve has been added and another Bézier control handle is added as well.

Figure 7.6

A path with three points made using the Pen tool

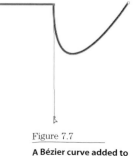

Figure 7.7

A Bézier curve added to the center point

5. Practice pulling the Bézier control handles by clicking and dragging to the right and down. You can move the handles up, down, and all around. The more you practice, the better the feel you'll get for how the curves function. Figure 7.9 shows the control handle on the bottom being moved. Notice the blue outline—this is where the current curve will be redrawn once the mouse button is released.

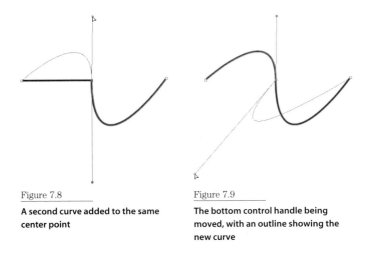

Figure 7.8

A second curve added to the same center point

Figure 7.9

The bottom control handle being moved, with an outline showing the new curve

Editing with the Pen Tool

If you have several separate paths that you want to join together, break apart, or continue drawing, you do all of this using the Pen tool. The following sections will show you how to alter your paths using the Pen tool.

Closing a Path

If you try to fill a path object and nothing happens, or the fill doesn't go just inside the path and produces very strange results, your path most likely is not closed. If this happens, you will need to close the path, or close multiple paths. To close a path, follow these steps:

1. With the Pointer tool, select the path you want to close.

2. Select the Pen tool, move your cursor over one of the end points of the path (when you are near the end point a little inverted v will appear in the lower-right corner of the cursor), and click the end point once.

If you've changed your Edit preferences (in the Editing tab) to use a Precise cursor, you won't see the Smart Cursor icons such as the inverted v and the o.

3. Move your cursor to the ending point (the first point of the path). There will be a little *o* near the cursor; click it once. The path is now closed. If you need additional points before you reach the end to which you want to connect, you can add points before you click the ending point.

Continue a Path

You can easily add to a previously drawn path. This technique is similar to closing a path, except you don't have to close a path to add on to it. If you want to add on to a previous path, follow these steps:

1. With the Pointer tool, select the path you want to add on to.

2. Select the Pen tool, move your cursor over one of the end points of the path, and click the end point once (a little inverted *v* indicates that you can continue adding additional points).

3. Move your cursor to the next location at which you want to add a point and click once. Continuing clicking to add points until you have the path you want.

Joining Paths

Joining paths may sound similar to closing paths. It is almost the same, but the difference is that you don't have to close the paths; you can just connect multiple paths together. To join paths together follow these steps:

1. With the Pointer tool, select the path you want to join.

2. Select the Pen tool, and move your cursor over one of the end points of the path; then click the end point once.

3. Move your cursor to the end point of the path to which you are connecting and click once. Continue as many times as needed.

Add and Delete Points

If you have a straight path and want to suddenly change direction, you will need to add points to the path. To add points to an existing path follow these steps:

1. With the Pointer tool, select the path to which you want to add points.

2. Select the Pen tool, and click once on the path's line to add one point. A little plus (+) sign will show up in the right corner of your cursor when you can add a point. Basically, anywhere on a path that there isn't already a point, you can add one. If you want a curved point with Bézier control handles, click and drag as described earlier.

3. Repeat this process for as many points as you need. When you are done, select any other tool to end adding points.

If your path has more points than necessary to maintain the design's shape, or you want to delete points to alter the shape, follow these steps:

1. With the Pointer tool, select the path from which you want to delete points.

2. Select the Pen tool. As your cursor passes over a point, you will see a minus (–) sign on the right corner of the cursor. Select the point you want to delete by clicking it once.

Another way to remove unwanted points is by choosing Modify → Alter Path → Simplify. But if you do this, you will have to type in a value. Though this option doesn't give you precise control, it is a fast way to make simple changes.

The number portion of the Simplify dialog box can be quite difficult to understand because it doesn't represent a point amount or a percentage. This is because the Simplify operation looks at more than just the number of points. It will get rid of points that are on top of each other and redraw the path with a similar curvature. For example, a simple half-circle requires only two points, but if you drew it with the Vector Path tool, you'll have many points. You can use Simplify to get it to two points. The larger the number you add to the Simplify amount, the fewer points your path will have. If you go too low, the resulting path's shape may be altered.

Editing Paths with Vector Freeform Editing Tools

A couple of the vector editing tools allow you to push and pull points visually without editing separate points. You can also cut the paths with the Knife tool.

Redraw Path Tool

The Redraw Path tool is in the same pop-up menu as the Pen tool. This tool allows you to alter a path by redrawing a portion of it. To use the Redraw Path tool, follow these steps:

1. Draw any shape path you'd like. We're using a rectangle, which we've ungrouped for this exercise.

> Be sure to have a stroke applied to the object or the Redraw Path tool won't work.

2. Select the Redraw Path tool from the Pen tool pop-up.

3. Select the path to alter, place the cursor (a circle) over the path's line, and click and drag to reshape it. Figure 7.10 shows the cursor right on the path near the right corner.

4. Draw the new path; be sure you start on the path line and end on another path line (as shown in Figure 7.11). The results of reshaping the path can be seen in Figure 7.12.

5. If you try to reshape the path and you overlap the previous path, as shown in Figure 7.13, the results will be totally different, as seen in Figure 7.14.

Figure 7.10

The cursor on the path ready to draw

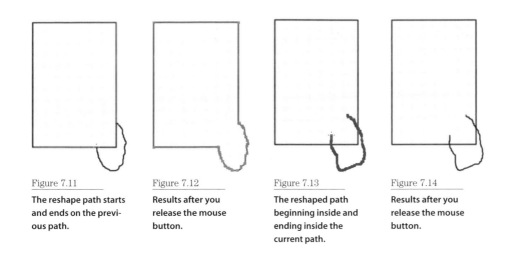

Figure 7.11

The reshape path starts and ends on the previous path.

Figure 7.12

Results after you release the mouse button.

Figure 7.13

The reshaped path beginning inside and ending inside the current path.

Figure 7.14

Results after you release the mouse button.

Freeform Tool

The Freeform tool enables you to push or pull points to adjust the shape of a path. The biggest difference between using this tool and using the Subselection tool to move points is that the Freeform tool automatically adds points as you push or pull a new shape.

When you select the Freeform tool, you have several options in the Property Inspector (see Figure 7.15). You can choose the size of the tool and the pressure amount. Preview is checked by default.

Figure 7.15

The Property Inspector when the Freeform tool is selected

You can push with the Freeform tool from inside the object or from the outside. If you place the tool inside and press the mouse, you'll see a red circle in the size you selected.

If you place your cursor anywhere inside an object, the little *s* next to the cursor is visible indicating that you can use the Freeform tool. If you place the cursor outside the object, the *s* isn't visible until you pass the cursor over the path.

To use the Freeform tool, follow these steps:

1. Open a new document (File → New) which is 300 × 300 pixels and a white canvas.

2. Select the Rectangle tool, draw a rectangle, and ungroup it (Modify → Ungroup).

3. Select the Freeform tool. In the Property Inspector you can set the Amount to Reshape (we're using 72), and whether or not Pressure will apply (Pressure is if you are using a pressure sensitive tablet such as a Wacom tablet).

4. Move the cursor toward the bottom of the rectangle to push in on it (Figure 7.16).

Figure 7.16

The Freeform tool at a size of 72 when it is being pushed in from outside the object

Figure 7.17

The Freeform tool with a size of 72 when it is being pushed out from inside the object

5. Choose Edit → Undo. This time, place the cursor inside the rectangle and push down and out, as seen in Figure 7.17. There is a big difference in the result depending on whether you use the tool inside or outside of the object.

Reshape Area Tool

The Reshape Area tool works much like the Freeform tool. The only difference is that the Reshape Area tool can be used to warp an entire image. By setting the size of the circle in the Tool Options dialog box so that it is larger than the path you want to alter, you can get some pretty interesting warped effects.

When you select the Reshape Area tool, you'll see its properties in the Property Inspector (as shown in Figure 7.18). You can set the Strength, which is the amount of the gravitational pull, and the Size of the stroke you want to use. Pressure can be selected if you are using a drawing tablet. When you place your cursor inside the object and press the mouse, you will see a double circle. Notice in Figure 7.19 that the shape doesn't begin to change until the edge is between the two circles. The area between the two circles is where your strength setting affects the strength of the pull or push you make.

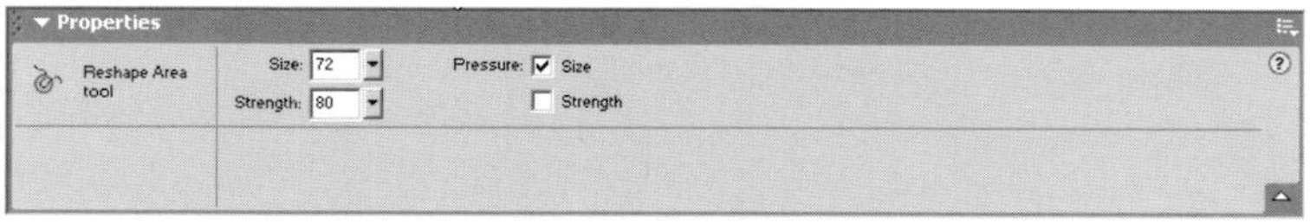

Figure 7.18

The Property Inspector when the Reshape Area tool is selected

Path Scrubber Tool

The Path Scrubber tool alters the stroke of a path after it has been drawn by adding to the stroke or subtracting from it. By changing the settings in the Property Inspector, you can alter the state of a path. The best way to explain this tool is to demonstrate its use. To use the Path Scrubber tool, follow these steps:

1. Open a new document (File → New) with a size of 300×300 pixels. Click Custom and choose black for the background.

2. Select the Line tool and draw a line on the canvas.

3. In the Stroke panel of the Property Inspector, choose Air Brush, Basic, a color of white, an Edge of 100, and a large Tip Size of 70 for easy viewing.

4. Select the Path Scrubber Tool-Subtractive from the pop-up to see the Path Scrubber Tool Options in the Property Inspector (see Figure 7.20).

Figure 7.19

The Reshape Area tool, with a Tip Size of 72 and a Strength of 80, pushing out on the shape

5. Leave the Pressure and the Speed checked and set the Rate to 80.

The tool options for the Path Scrubber Tool-Additive are the same as they are for the Tool-Subtractive.

Figure 7.20

The tool options for the Path Scrubber tool

6. Place your cursor outside of the end of the stroke (see Figure 7.21) before you click. Click once and the result is seen in Figure 7.22. You have subtracted from the path.

   Choose Edit → Undo if you want to try a different effect. Then place the cursor over the top part of the path and click. You can get some pretty interesting results. Experiment with the tool to see the possibilities available to you.

Figure 7.21

The placement of the Path Scrubber tool

Figure 7.22

The results of using the Path Scrubber tool

Knife Tool

The Knife tool works only on paths, not on bitmaps. You can use the Knife tool to cut an open path into pieces or to cut a closed path apart. The Knife tool has no tool options in the Property Inspector.

To use the Knife tool, follow these steps:

1. Open a new document (File → New) with a size of 300 × 300 pixels and a white canvas.

2. Select the Rectangle tool and draw a rectangle. Fill it with any color you'd like.

3. To cut a closed path, select the Knife tool and click and drag it through the rectangle. Start at the top and drag all the way through. The slice won't be apparent when you are done.

4. Select the Pointer tool and click anywhere other than the rectangle to deselect the rectangle. Then, click one side of the rectangle and drag. This will separate the piece you just cut.

> You can use guides to help you cut a straight line.

Reshaping Paths Using Path Operations

Combining, joining, intersecting, and punching holes in paths are all functions you will probably find yourself using often. The options necessary to perform these actions can be found by choosing Modify → Combine; they include Union, Join, Intersect, Crop, Punch, and Split.

Union

Figure 7.23

Four rectangles over-lapping each other

The Union option is used when you want to merge two or more objects. This operation combines all of the shapes into the shape of all the shapes' outside edges as demonstrated in Figure 7.23 and Figure 7.24, and it removes any overlapping areas. In Figure 7.23 you will see four different rectangles that have been drawn so that they overlap.

Figure 7.24

The new shape filled with the color of the first object drawn

When you using the Union command, all that will remain is the outline of all the rectangles. Shift + Select all the rectangles (order doesn't matter) and choose Modify → Combine Paths → Union. The resulting shape will be filled with the color of the object that was drawn first. You can check the Layers panel to see which one is on the bottom of the stack; this is the color that will be used to fill the new shape (see Figure 7.24).

Join

Figure 7.25

Join applied to the same rectangles used in the Union section

To use the Join option, take the example used in the previous section, and use Edit → Undo to return to the overlapping rectangles. This time, Shift + Select all the rectangles and choose Modify → Combine Paths → Join. Figure 7.25 shows the result, which is quite different from what happened when you used Union.

If you don't like any of the Path operations, you can choose Modify → Combine Paths → Split to break apart the Combine Path operation you applied. Doing this is not quite the same as using Edit → Undo. With Edit → Undo, you return to the colored rectangles; with Split, you have individual objects but they are all the color of the joined object.

Intersect

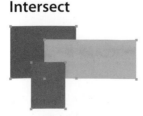

Figure 7.26

The objects are all selected and ready for the Intersect command.

The Intersect operation is the opposite of Union. Where Union throws away the overlapping area, Intersect keeps these and throws away the rest. If you were to select all the rectangles in the Union example and use the Intersect command, there would only be a little rectangle left. To make it a bit more interesting and to better demonstrate what Intersect does, we have rearranged the rectangles a bit (see Figure 7.26) to cause more overlapping.

Select all the shapes, as seen in Figure 7.26, and choose Modify → Combine → Intersect. Figure 7.27 shows just the little area where all the shapes intersect.

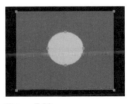

Figure 7.27

The results of intersecting all of the rectangle shapes.

> The Crop command has the same results as Intersect, so I won't demonstrate it.

Punch

Punch is one of our favorites; we love to punch holes that you can see through. With this option, you can punch objects or text. The example used here is a rectangle with a circle on top. To use the Punch operation, follow these steps:

1. With the Pointer tool, Shift + Select the object you want to punch a hole through and the object you are using as the "cookie cutter." In this case, use the rectangle and the circle (as shown in Figure 7.28).

2. Choose Modify → Combine → Punch—the results are shown in Figure 7.29. Notice how you can see the background through the hole.

3. In this example, we changed the background to white so that you could see the effect of adding a drop shadow to the punched object. In the Property Inspector, access the Effects pop-up menu by clicking the plus (+) sign. Choose Shadow and Glow → Drop Shadow and accept the defaults. Figure 7.30 shows the results. Notice that the cut out area gets the shadow as well as the outside object.

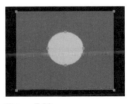
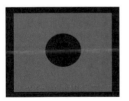

Figure 7.28

A rectangle and a circle, both selected

Figure 7.29

The circle punched out of the rectangle. The background shows through.

Figure 7.30

The punched object with a drop shadow added

Miscellaneous Actions

There are miscellaneous commands and tools you can use when using objects. We have detailed some of them here.

Make a selection within a group You have already used the Group and Ungroup command. Once you have a group, you may want to select just one object of that group. You don't have to ungroup to do it. Just select the Subselection tool to select any one of the objects.

Select an object behind other objects There may be times when you have many objects on a page and you want to select something that exists under the other objects. You can do this in one of two ways: either select the object from the Layers panel, or select the Select Behind tool from the Pointer tool pop-up. You can then select an object behind other objects.

Choosing between duplicating and cloning In the Edit menu, you can choose to duplicate or clone an object. The difference is that a clone is copied and placed directly on top of the object, while with Duplicate a copy is made and pasted in an offset position. You get the same result as Clone by using the keyboard shortcuts of Ctrl + C and Ctrl + V (Cmd + C and Cmd + V for Macs), which is copy and paste.

> You can also make a copy of an object by pressing the Alt key (Option key for the Mac) and dragging.

Transformations

After an object is drawn, you can transform it by using the Transform commands in the Modify menu. One of the commands is Free Transform, which allows you to scale and rotate freely. Try it out:

1. Draw a rectangle and choose Modify → Transform → Free Transform, or press Q on the keyboard.

2. Pull in on the corners or side points and you'll see a double arrow. If you want to scale proportionately, press the Shift key as you drag a corner point in or out.

3. Hover your cursor just outside the selected object and you'll see the rotate cursor (curved arrow). Click and drag to rotate (as shown in Figure 7.31).

4. Double-click to accept the transformation.

The other transformation tools are Skew and Distort. Skew allows you to pull the points out or in as seen in Figure 7.32.

Distort allows you much more freedom in the movement of the points. Figure 7.33 shows the top-right point being moved over the bottom-left point.

> You can access the Scale, Rotate, Skew, and Distort tools via the Modify menu or the Tools panel. The easiest way, however, is to select the object and press Q on the keyboard. If you press Q again, you go to the Skew tool, and if you press it a third time you get the Distort tool.

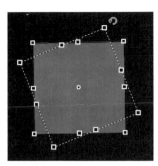

Figure 7.31

The object being rotated

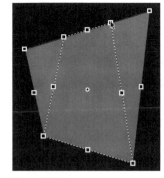

Figure 7.32

The Skew tool being used

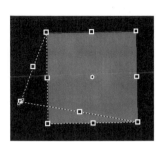

Figure 7.33

The Distort tool being used

You can also scale, resize, or rotate an object by enter-ing specific values and percentages for the size or amount of change you want to occur into the Numeric Transform dialog box, as seen in Figure 7.34.

Using the Crop Tool

As you would expect, you can crop an image in Fireworks. To do so, select the Crop tool from the Tools panel and click and drag a selection around the area you want to crop. You can pull the points in or out on the sides and top to adjust the selection area. When it's where you want it, double-click to accept.

Figure 7.34

The Numeric Transform dialog box

Another function of the Crop tool that you may not be aware of is that you can crop to make the canvas larger. To do so, you drag a selection, and then pull the selection outside the canvas area. When you double-click, the canvas size changes to include your selection.

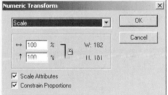

You can also crop a document to fit the objects in it exactly by choosing Modify ⟩ Trim Canvas. Or, If you have things that overlap the canvas edges, you can choose Modify → Fit Canvas and the canvas will enlarge.

Aligning Objects

You can align objects using the Modify → Align menu as you did in previous versions of Fire-works, with the exception of the Center in Document command. This command used to be a in the Command folder but has since been removed. The alignment options (including Cen-ter to the Canvas) are now also included in a new Align panel. This new panel was made by using the SWF extensibility of Fireworks MX.

This new extensibility feature allows third-party developers to make these great exten-sions for our use. The Align panel is packaged with Fireworks MX, but there are others avail-able at the Fireworks Support site (http://www.macromedia.com/support/fireworks).

If you find that you use Align options often, you can open the Align panel by choosing Window → Align and docking it with your other panels. To dock a panel, click the little dots (also referred to as the Gripper) on the left of the gray top (also referred to as the Title bar), and drag into the docked area. When you see a colored line appear, release your mouse and the Align panel will dock.

Figure 7.35 shows the new Align panel. You can choose to align your objects to the canvas by clicking To Canvas (it turns orange when it is selected), or to anchors by selecting Anchors.

Figure 7.35

The Align panel

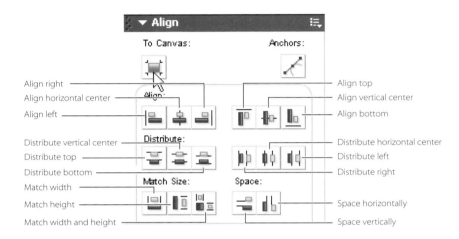

Working with the Text Tool

You may be wondering why we are discussing text in the vector chapter—because text in Fireworks is a vector object and it is quite flexible.

You'll probably use the Text tool pretty frequently in Fireworks, especially for adding text to buttons and making logos and banners. It's one of the easiest tools to use and has a lot of flexibility to boot. The great thing about text in Fireworks is that it remains editable—even after you've added strokes, fills, styles, patterns, effects, and whatever else!

If you convert text into a path, the effects are editable but the text is not.

You can edit text and its effects even if someone shares a native Fireworks file or a Photoshop PSD file that has effects added—you can open them and deconstruct them quite easily.

In the Property Inspector, if a selected object has an effect, you will be able to see the effect name in the Effects list. If you click the Edit and Arrange Effect icon (the little I in a circle) you will have access to the options for that effect, which you can then change or just study.

Using the Text Tool and the Property Inspector

The way you work with text in Fireworks has totally changed. In previous versions, after you selected the Type tool and clicked the canvas, the Text Editor would open. This Text Editor contained the various choices you had for the font style and alignment. In Fireworks MX, text is now handled right in your open document, and the text options are now found on the Property Inspector instead of in the Text Editor (as seen in Figure 7.36).

> You can still use the Text Editor if you prefer by right-clicking (Ctrl-click on a Mac) on the text and choosing Editor.

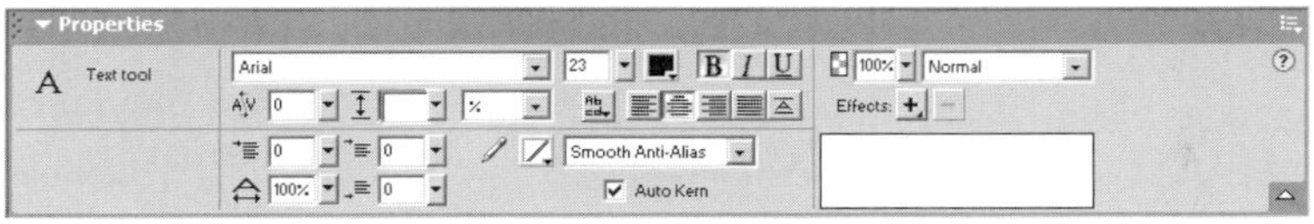

There are a few special text-handling techniques, such as attaching text to a path or reversing the direction of the text on the path, which are found in Text menu rather than on the Property Inspector. Something else you can now find in the Text menu is a Spell Checker.

Adding text is now as easy as clicking the canvas and typing. To change the text, highlight it with the Text tool or select it with the Pointer tool.

If you've used any image-editing program before, nothing in this editor should look foreign. The top row is the area where you select the font you want to use, and it is where you set the size, color, and attributes, such as bold, italic, or underlined.

The next row is where you set the Kerning or Range Kerning (how much space is between two characters), the Leading (how much space is between lines), and the alignment settings. The alignment—Left, Right, Center, and so on—are familiar, I'm sure.

The Horizontal Text and the Vertical Text options are pretty handy. In some programs, you would have to rotate the text to get the special alignments. To the left of the alignment options, you will also notice that you can set the direction in which the text will flow.

The third line of options is where you set the Horizontal Scale, the Baseline Shift and the Anti-Aliasing (smoothing out jagged edges) Levels. The choices for Anti-Aliasing are No Anti-Aliasing, Crisp Anti-Aliasing, and Strong Anti-Aliasing Smooth Anti-Aliasing.

Converting Text to a Path

Why would you want to convert text to a path and what is its purpose once you do? Your text object is one object and all changes that you apply to it must be applied to the whole unit, but if you convert this text to a path, you can apply effects to just one letter at a time. Once the

Figure 7.36

The Property Inspector showing the various text options

Figure 7.37

Text converted to a path, then one letter selected with the Subselection tool

text is converted to a path, you will see the individual nodes that make up the path of each letter. To see the actual nodes, you'll have to select the text and choose Modify → Ungroup (see Figure 7.37). You can now use the Subselection tool to move and alter any of the individual points.

Inset Path

There are other reasons to convert text into a path. For instance, you can expand or contract the size of your text by using the Inset Path command if the text is a path (which you'll do in a moment). This process is different from scaling. If you scale text, it gets larger or smaller, but not by a certain pixel amount all around. For example, if you have a bitmap selection and you choose to expand that selection by 3 pixels, 3 pixels will be added to the selection. The problem with this is that the selection tools only work for bitmap images and are not editable or scalable like a vector object. Scaling a vector object does not add an incremental amount of pixels to the selected object.

To see how to use the Inset Path command, on the other hand, you have to first convert the text to paths; therefore, you may as well make something useful while you are at it. In this exercise, you will make a custom bevel for your text.

Figure 7.38

The visibility turned off of the original text

1. Type the word **Elegance** on your canvas. Make it large enough so that you can see it and work with it. We used Arial, a size of 64, and made the text black.

2. Choose Text → Convert to Paths. Don't touch it yet.

3. Now choose Modify → Ungroup.

4. Then choose Modify → Combine Paths → Union. You now have one path, which is your word.

> What you did was convert the text to paths but when you did, the letters were grouped together. Because we can't alter a grouped path, you had to ungroup it and then combine all the letters into one shape. Although this object is still a vector, you can no longer edit the text as text.

5. Choose Edit → Clone. This cloned text will be used to make a custom bevel and add dimension to your text.

6. In the Layers panel, hide the visibility of the original text (click the eye icon off). See Figure 7.38.

7. Choose Modify → Alter Path → Inset Path. The Inset Path dialog box will appear (see Figure 7.39).

8. Choose Inside, and enter a value of 3 to increase the size of the text by 3 pixels. If you choose Outside, the text will become smaller by the amount of pixels you choose.

9. Then click OK.

10. Drag the larger text below the original text and change the fill to a gold color with a 1-pixel orange stroke.

11. Turn the visibility back on for the original text see Figure 7.40).

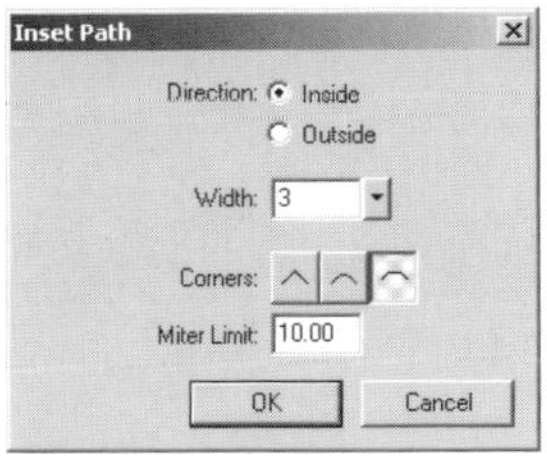

Figure 7.39

The Inset Path dialog box

Try making a duplicate of the text and then try scaling it larger so that you can experience the difference between scaling and using Inset Path firsthand. As you will see, Inset Path does exactly what's needed when you want to increase or decrease the text proportionately.

Cutting Text Out of an Image

You can convert text to a path, ungroup it, and then use the Modify → Combine Paths → Union command to make it into one vector shape. This is very useful when you want to cut text from another image or object.

After text is converted into a path, it can be used just like a cookie cutter. By placing the converted text on top of another path object, you can punch it out, leaving a see-through hole. You can produce some pretty neat effects with this process. In this exercise, you will punch a hole through an image and see the image that has been placed below it.

1. Open `water.png` from the Chapter 7 folder on the accompanying CD.

2. Select the Rectangle tool and draw a rectangle to cover the entire canvas.

3. In the Property Inspector, select "Pattern" from the Fill Category pop-up menu.

4. Click the color box and choose Other from the Pattern Name pop-up. Then navigate to the Chapter 7 folder on the accompanying CD and select `starfish.png`. The canvas will be filled with the shell background.

5. The image will be tiled, so click and drag the circle in the center to the far-right corner to fill the rectangle with one image (see Figure 7.41).

Figure 7.40

The larger text moved below the original and the color changed to gold.

Figure 7.41

The rectangle filled with the starfish image

6. Type the text you want to use as a cookie cutter. As shown in Figure 7.42, the text and settings used in this exercise are

   Text: **Starfish**

   Font: **Splash**

   Point Size: **120**

   Color: **Black**

   Edge: **Smooth Anti-Alias**

7. To make the text into a punch or cookie cutter, select the text and choose these commands in the following order:

   • Text ➜ Convert to Paths

   • Modify ➜ Ungroup

   • Modify ➜ Combine Paths ➜ Union

8. Shift + Select the text and the rectangle with the starfish. From the menu bar choose Modify ➜ Combine Paths ➜ Punch.

9. The hole is punched through the seashell object, and the water below is visible through the cutout.

10. Normally we'd add a drop shadow at this point, but in this case, it would make the text look raised instead of cutout, so we added a 2-pixel dark gray stroke instead. The finished image is seen in Figure 7.43.

Figure 7.42

The text added to the starfish image

Figure 7.43

The text cutout and a stroke added

Hands On: Making a Navigational Element

The inverted L shape is a popular element used for headers and navigation in web pages. Here, you'll learn how to make one, plus you'll develop a rounded curve at the inside corner of the inverted L.

1. Open a new canvas (File → New) that is 800 × 600 and is white.

2. Select the Rectangle tool and draw a rectangle.

3. In the Property Inspector, set Width to 700 and Height to 130 and then press Enter (Return for a Mac).

4. Draw a second rectangle and change Width to 130 and Height to 500.

5. Position the rectangles together at the left corner (as shown in Figure 7.44).

Figure 7.44

The rectangles placed together

Figure 7.45

The bottom of the left side being reshaped

6. Shift + Select both rectangles and choose Modify → Combine Paths → Union. They are now one shape.

7. In the Property Inspector, change the fill to a color of a nice blue. We used #003366.

8. Select the Reshape Area tool.

9. In the Property Inspector, change the size to 125 and push the bottom corner, as seen in Figure 7.45.

10. Select the Subselection tool and move the bottom-left point up a tad (Figure 7.46).

Figure 7.46

**The bottom left
point moved up**

Figure 7.47

**The star moved onto
the reshaped area**

11. Select the Polygon shape tool, and in the Property Inspector, choose Star for the Shape, 8 Sides, and an Angle of 30.

12. Draw the star and make the size 100 × 100 pixels. You may want to change the color temporarily because this will be placed on the navigation shape.

13. Move the star to the reshaped area (Figure 7.47).

14. Select the star and the blue bar and choose Modify → Combine Paths → Punch.

15. To curve the top-right end, draw an ellipse; make the size 90 × 130 and place it over the end.

16. Shift + Select the ellipse and the navigation shape and choose Modify → Combine Paths → Union (as shown in Figure 7.48).

17. Punch a rounded rectangle from the current shape to get a curve at the inside junction and perform these steps:

    1. Draw a rounded rectangle with a roundness of 30.

    2. In the Property Inspector, make the new rounded rectangle a size of 670 wide × 275 high.

    3. Lower the opacity of the rounded rectangle to 30 (in the Layers panel or the Property Inspector) so that you can see through it.

    4. Place the top-left curve of the new shape into the intersection of the navigation shape (as shown in Figure 7.49). Make sure that the curves on the other edges don't interfere with your current shape.

18. Once you have your shape in place, choose Modify → Combine Paths → Punch. If it isn't quite right, choose Edit → Undo, reposition, and try again.

Figure 7.48

**A curve shape added to
the top-right end**

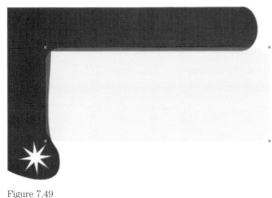

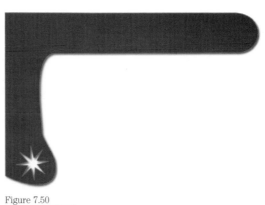

Figure 7.49

The rounded rectangle in place to punch a new shape.

Figure 7.50

The nav shape completed

19. If the lines aren't quite as smooth as you'd like, try Modify → Alter Paths → Simplify with a value of 10. This should smooth the bottom curve a bit and make the transition of the punched shape better as well.

20. Add a drop shadow with the default settings and perhaps a 2-pixel gray stroke. The results are shown in Figure 7.50. You will add the buttons to this shape in Chapter 9.

From Vectors to Pixel Power

You have learned a lot about working with the vector tools and making various shapes. In addition, you've seen how to edit and transform not only shapes but also text. Armed with the power of Fireworks vector tools, you are now ready to tackle any design situation that comes up.

In Chapter 8, you will learn how to work with bitmaps or raster images. These images are pixel based, normally in the form of a photo. You will learn how to make compositions and how to edit your photos.

## CHAPTER 8

Working with Bitmaps

Bitmap images are pixel-based—made up of a lot of dots of color—similar to a mosaic. Fireworks MX has a variety of tools devoted just to working with bitmaps.

The first set of tools you will learn how to use are the selection tools. With these tools, you will define areas that you want to work on.

You will also discover many ways that you can alter your image; these activities include changing its colors, masking out a portion of it, making selections from it, applying a multitude of effects to it, and a lot more. Because photographs are bitmap images, you will find that the functions that Fireworks has are extremely useful because websites are filled with photographs. You can retouch sections to cover flaws or simply remove them. If you want, you can even copy elements from one image to another.

In addition to all of this, Fireworks gives you the ability to add shadows, glows, bevels, and many other effects to your images. What you can do is really unlimited, especially when you realize that most of the third-party Photoshop compatible plugins also work in Fireworks.

Topics addressed in this chapter include the following:

- **Understanding bitmaps**
- **Using selection tools**
- **Using touch-up tools**
- **Masking images**
- **Exploring the Filters menu**

Understanding Bitmaps

In case you are coming from a vector-only world, here is a quick course in pixel-based images. Photographs are comprised of *pixels*, the smallest component of a bitmapped image—also known as a *raster image* in some programs, or as an *image object* in Fireworks. Pixels are little squares of color reminiscent of a mosaic composition. Editing pixels involves adding, removing, or coloring individual pixels.

The pixels are what distinguish a bitmapped image from a *vector image*—an image that consists of paths, which are made up of a line with at least two points. Because vector objects (called *objects* in Fireworks) are made up of a series of lines, they are fully scalable. Pixel images, on the other hand, lose detail as they are scaled up because each image contains a set number of pixels. When you scale a bitmapped image up, Fireworks has to guess at which pixels need to be resampled so that it can "fake" the detail in the increased space. This stretching of pixels results in what is known as a *pixelated image*. You can identify pixelated images by the obvious squares that can be seen or by the blurring of detail. The more the image is stretched, the worse it will look.

Resolution is a word that comes up often when working with bitmap images. The *resolution* is what determines how many pixels there are per inch. The resolution in an image is determined when you scan it, or if you use a digital camera, you decide on the resolution when you take the picture. The higher the resolution, the more pixels there will be per inch, and therefore the image can be larger without degradation. Because Fireworks specializes in producing graphics for the Web, the resolution of 82dpi is sufficient because that is the resolution of monitor screens. Just for comparison, print resolutions are usually about 300dpi. Fireworks is also not suitable for print because it is an RGB-only environment. This means that only the red, green, and blue channels are used (as in a monitor or a television) whereas when printing an image, a commercial printer uses CMYK—cyan, magenta, yellow, and black. An inkjet printer, however, does use RGB.

Automatic Switching between Modes

In former versions of Fireworks, you needed to be aware of which mode you were working in—vector or bitmap—and at times, you needed to manually make a change. In Fireworks MX, there is no changing of modes; everything is automatic. In this new version, the Tools panel is divided up into sections, and the top portion contains the bitmap tools. Fireworks is smart enough to know when you have opened a bitmap image, and when you select a vector tool, the mode changes by itself.

Figure 8.1

The History panel shows the switch between bitmap mode and vector mode.

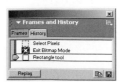

To see this illustrated, try this: open a bitmap image, and then open the History panel. Select the Marquee Selection tool and draw a shape. Now click the vector Rectangle tool and draw a rectangle. Figure 8.1 shows the History panel. See where it says Exit Bitmap Mode? The mode change is automatic. Other than that, you'd never know the switch even happened.

The New Tools Panel

Before you start digging deeper into the bitmap capabilities of Fireworks, let's take a look at the new Tools panel. In Figure 8.2, you'll see the pointer in the bitmap section of the Tools panel. Then notice the thin line below the Rubber Stamp tool. This line places the Eyedropper and Paint Bucket/Gradient tools into their own mini section. These tools are usable in both bitmap and vector modes.

In the next section, you will learn how to work with the various selection tools.

Working with Selection Tools

The selection tools are only available when you are editing bitmap images. The bitmap selection tools include the Marquee tool, the Oval Marquee, the Lasso tool, the Polygon Lasso tool, and the Magic Wand tool.

The selection tools are used whether it's to isolate problem areas or to select a specific portion to edit or add effects to. Selections can also be copied and pasted elsewhere on the same document or to a separate file. By using the selection tools, you can also assure yourself that any changes that you make while the selection is active will occur only to the selected portion, thereby protecting other portions of an image.

> If you make a selection and then you add a layer, you loose your selection. So if you want to preserve the original, make the selection, and then copy and paste it into the new layer.

Using the Marquee Tools

The Marquee tool and the Oval Marquee tool make selections according to their respective shapes. Click the tool of your choice and drag the cursor over an area of the image. To constrain the action performed by the tool to a square or a circle hold the Alt key (Option for Mac) and drag. To draw from the center out, hold the Shift key and draw.

The Marquee tools have properties that can be set by selecting the Marquee tool of choice, and making selections in the Property Inspector. Figure 8.3 shows the properties for the Marquee tools.

There are three styles of marquees you can choose from: Normal, Fixed Ratio, and Fixed Size. When you choose Fixed Ratio or Fixed Size, you can enter your values. You also have three choices for the edge: Hard, Anti-alias, and Feather. When you choose Feather, you

Figure 8.2

The Tools panel showing the placement of the Bitmap tools

Figure 8.3

The properties for the Marquee tools

enter the number of pixels you want to feather. In addition to the style and edge choices, you also have to choose your Blend Mode options and specify the Height, and Width. Notice that you can also see the coordinate area of your project, which comes in handy for specific place-ment of elements. Figure 8.4 shows the Property Inspector with the pop-ups open for the Style and Edge options. Of course, only one of these would be open at a time, this is for illustration only.

Figure 8.4

The pop-ups for Style and Edge options are open.

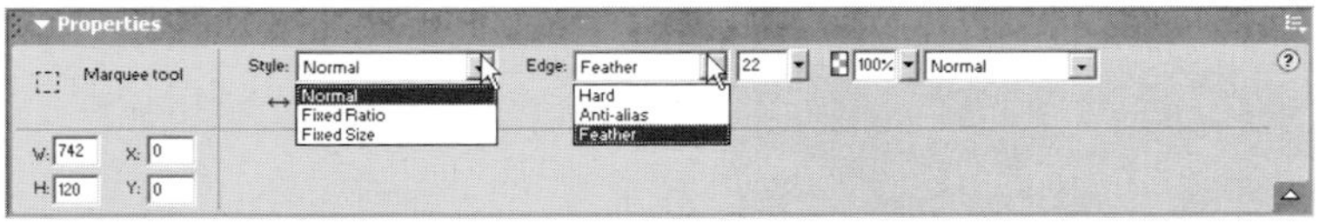

When using Feather to feather your edge as you draw, you must choose the feather amount *prior* to drawing the selection. If you decide after the selection is made that you want a feather, add it through the Select menu.

> The Fixed Ratio style can be very helpful in making a specific selection, especially if you need a very small selection of perhaps, 2 pixels wide by 100 pixels high. There is no way to easily draw a selection this precisely or so narrow, so by choosing a fixed size and entering in the dimensions, you can do it very easily.

Once you make a selection, it will be surrounded by a moving dotted line, referred to as "marching ants." It is in this area that any changes you make will occur. Within this bound-ary, you can do a number of things, such as add blur, use plugin filters, change colors, adjust hue and saturation, use the Rubber Stamp tool, and much more.

For instance, if you make a selection and want to fill it, select the Paint Bucket tool and be sure to check the Fill Selection option in the Property Inspector (Figure 8.5).

You can add or subtract from a selection you've made by understanding these processes.

Adding to a selection Once you've made your selection, you may decide that there are addi-tional areas that you would like to add to the selection. To add to the selection, put your cursor just inside the selected area and hold the Shift key while you drag with one of the Selection tools to enclose the new area, ending inside the current selection. To add a totally new selec-tion in a different area, simply press the Shift key and make the selection. You can use the Marquee tools or the Lasso tools to define the area or areas you want to add to the selection.

Figure 8.5

The Property Inspector showing the Paint Bucket tool properties and the Fill Selection option.

Subtracting from a selection Subtracting from a selection works the same way as adding except that you press the Alt (Option for a Mac) key to subtract. You can use the Marquee tools or the Lasso tools to define the area to subtract.

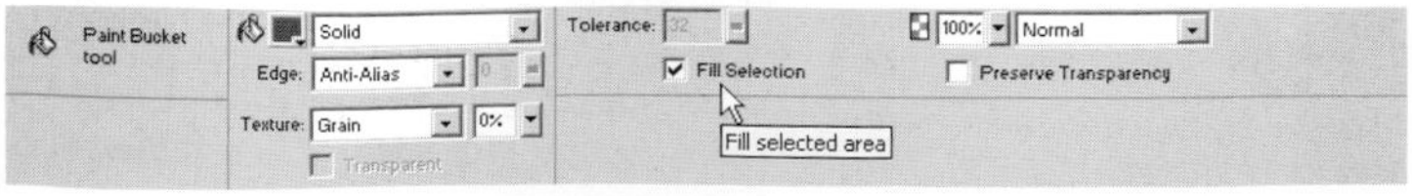

The Magic Wand and the Polygon Lasso tool are both a bit different than the other marquee selections tools, as you can see here.

Using the Magic Wand The Magic Wand tool works differently than all the other selection tools. The Magic Wand tool makes selections based on color. You determine the range of color in the selection by setting the tolerance. To do so, select the Magic Wand tool, and then in the Property Inspector adjust the tolerance value. The higher the tolerance value, the more colors will be added to the selection.

Figure 8.6

The dialog box that opens for Border Marquee. A similar window opens for the Modify and Contract Marquee—in which you enter a value for each.

Using the Polygon Lasso tool The Polygon Lasso tool is used for making precise selections of irregular shaped areas. To use the Polygon Lasso tool, select it and click where you want to begin the selection. You will see a blue line representing where the selection will be made. Keep clicking each time you need to change direction, until the selection is complete. Double-click at the starting point to close the selection.

Working with the Select Menu

There are several different options in the Select menu for altering your selection. After you have made a selection, you can expand it, contract it, or modify its border. A dialog box, such as the one for expanding the border (Figure 8.6), opens, and in it you enter the value you want. Figure 8.7 shows the border option with a value of 10. The illustration is filled to make it easier to see what Border Marquee does.

Another menu item you'll probably use frequently is the Select Inverse. After you've made a selection, you choose Select → Select Inverse to select everything except the selection you just made. This is a good way to remove background or to recolor, blur, or alter areas other than the focal selection.

Adding a Feathered Edge to a Photo

To practice using a Marquee tool (the Oval Marquee in this case) and the tool options, try this short but useful exercise:

1. Open the DCP_0784.jpg file from the Chapter 6 folder on the accompanying CD; this image contains orange flowers. In Chapter 6, we added the images folder, so with all those images just sitting there, you may as well practice on one.

2. Select the Oval Marquee tool, and in the Property Inspector, change the Edge to Feather.

3. Enter a value of 20 or so. The amount you enter will depend on how large the selected area is and how much blend you want on the edges. Choosing the value amount will get easier as you practice using the Feather tool.

4. Draw an ellipse over the part of the photo you'd like cut out. Figure 8.8 shows my selection.

Figure 8.7

A value of 10 is entered for the Border Marquee. The resulting border is filled in.

Figure 8.8

A selection made of a portion of the image

5. Once you've made your selection (you can drag the center of the selection to move it), choose Select → Select Inverse.

6. Then press the delete key. Figure 8.9 shows the cropped end result.

> You can also copy (Ctrl + C/Cmd + C) and paste (Ctrl + V/Cmd + V) a selection into a new document.

7. If you'd like a softer edge, deselect your selection by pressing Ctrl + D (Cmd + D for Mac), select the Oval Marquee tool, change the Feather value to 35, and draw a new selection around the flower.

8. Repeat Step 5. The result is seen in Figure 8.10.

Figure 8.9

The selection has been inverted and deleted, leaving the selected area with a feathered edge.

Figure 8.10

A larger feather value has been selected prior to making the selection.

Although many people make their vignettes this way, it is not the best choice. When this method is used, you lose all the unused pixels of your image, and there is little control if you want to edit the selection area. The only thing you can do is to add to or subtract from a marquee selection. The best way to make vignettes is to use a vector mask, discussed later in this chapter, which gives you much more precise control over the shape of your selection (or mask).

Touch-Up Tools

There is a new set of tools in Fireworks MX. You'll notice that they all have similar properties, but some have additional values you can enter. These tools are wonderful when you are looking for a quick fix for specific problem areas. These are useful for small changes, but there are similar tools available in the Filters menu for larger repairs (see the section called "The Filters Menu"). You'll see a few uses for the touch-up tools in this section.

The Blur Tool

When you select the Blur tool from the Tools panel, you'll notice its properties in the Property Inspector. The properties are much like those that apply to any painting or drawing tool. From the Property Inspector (Figure 8.11), you can choose the size, the softness of the edge, the shape (round or square), and the intensity of the blur—the higher the intensity, the more blur there is; even at a value of 100, the blur is pretty gentle.

So what can you do with this tool? You can blur areas around something that you want to pop or stand out from the page. For instance, how about blurring sensitive subject matter that you don't want to appear on your site?

Figure 8.11

The properties available for the Blur tools once those tools are selected

The Blur, Blur More, and Gaussian Blur from the Filters menu or the Effects pop-up menu would do a better job for a large area.

The Sharpen Tool

The Sharpen tool adds clarity to an edge. More details on Sharpen follow later in this chapter because Sharpen is also one of the Live Effects found in the Effects pop-up menu, and it is also a filter for just bitmaps found in the Filters menu, where it is used on a grander scale for larger areas. In this context, however, this tool is great for smaller areas or for sharpening an edge.

So you can see this tool demonstrated, try blurring some text on a button you've made. Now go over the blurred area with the Sharpen tool. Much of the blur is removed as a result. But be careful, over sharpening begins to leave odd colors around the edges. Practice with the settings of the properties for this tool (Figure 8.12) to get a feel for how they work and how much intensity you need to use for a specific effect.

Figure 8.12

The properties that are available for the Sharpen tool once this tool is selected

The Dodge Tool

The Dodge tool has no counterpart in the Filters menu or in the Effects pop-up menu. It is a brand new tool for Fireworks MX, and you will probably be as glad to see it as we are. If you use the Dodge tool carefully, you can gently lighten an area. In a traditional darkroom, "dodging" decreases the amount of light hitting the photosensitive paper, thus making the resulting image brighter. The Dodge tool in Fireworks desaturates an area based on the values you enter in the Property Inspector. Figure 8.13 shows the properties available for the Dodge tool. Notice the Range pop-up menu. By using the options in this menu, you can adjust the Shadows, Midtones, or Highlights. Try each to see their effects.

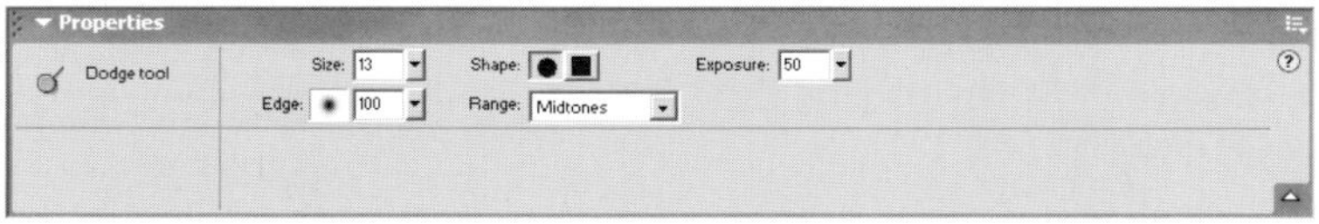

Figure 8.13

The properties available for the Dodge tool once the tool is selected

To practice using the Dodge tool, use the dark image named `dodge.png` (shown in Figure 8.14) that you will find in this chapter's folder on the accompanying CD.

To bring more of this image's background detail out, you will use the Dodge tool to lighten, or desaturate, the image.

1. Open `dodge.png`.

2. Select the Dodge tool, and in the Property Inspector, use these settings:

    Size: **100**

    Edge: **100**

    Shape: **Round** or **Square** (it makes no difference)

    Exposure: **50**

3. Drag the tool over the entire image. Notice how much brighter and more detailed the image has become (see Figure 8.15)?

4. Close `dodge.png` without saving it and open it again.

5. This time, use the large size of 100 just for the top two-thirds of the file, just to the bottom edge of the carousel above where the foliage begins.

6. Decrease the size to about 25, and select Highlights.

7. Click over the white area of the top umbrella, and over the lights. As you go over the lights, you will see that it's just like turning them on. Also click over some of the white flowers—several times for the front ones to increase the three dimensional effect.

8. Now change the Range to Shadows. To do so, go into the dark areas of the foliage and click, but be careful not to remove too much of the dark, or it will look washed out. Figure 8.16 shows the results. To better see the results, refer to this book's color insert.

An alternative to this process is using Midtones for the bottom third of the figure to see whether you like this effect better.

Figure 8.14

A very dark image with little background detail

Figure 8.15

This shows the results of using the Dodge tool on the image when an Intensity value of 50 was selected for the Mid-tones option.

Figure 8.16

The image with more dodge applied in spe-cific areas, especially the highlights

The Dodge tool works great when you are trying to repair areas that are slightly too dark. For instance, I've used it to lighten dark circles under a model's eyes.

The Burn Tool

The Burn tool (properties shown in Figure 8.17) is another tool that has no counterpart in the Filters menu or the Effects pop-up menu. When used as a touch-up tool, Burn works the opposite way that Dodge does—it adds darkness. When you burn photographic paper in a darkroom, it darkens. In a traditional darkroom, burning an image means you increase the amount of light reaching the photographic paper, thus darkening the image.

Figure 8.17

The properties avail-able for the Burn tool once the tool is selected

The Smudge Tool

The Smudge tool (properties shown in Figure 8.18), smears colors around. This tool, like Blur, can also be used effectively for blocking out sensitive parts of images. For those of you who paint, you may find that this tool simulates what you can do with natural media most closely; you can paint several colors in Fireworks and then smear them together just as you would with paints on your palette or your canvas.

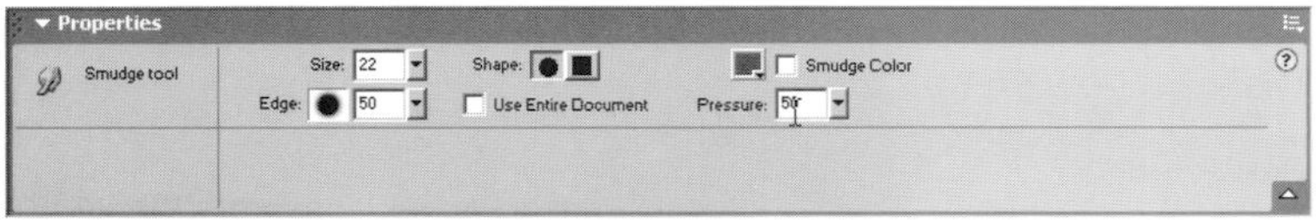

Figure 8.18

The properties available for the Smudge tool once the tool is selected

Using the Rubber Stamp Tool

If you do a lot of image repair, then you'll use this handy tool often. The Rubber Stamp tool works by copying one area of an image onto another area. It's a convenient tool for making both small and large repairs. For instance, you may want to add a person to a photo or cut one out. An old boyfriend or girlfriend, perhaps? Remove them! Not only is it easy, but also it's oh so satisfying. On a more serious note, you can also use this tool to remove utility wires, a car, or other undesirable elements from a scenic photo.

The Rubber Stamp tool is indispensable for those of you who often work with bitmap images. To get a feel for how the Rubber Stamp works, do the following:

1. Open any bitmap image.

2. Select the Rubber Stamp tool from the Tools panel. Figure 8.19 shows the options that are available from the Property Inspector after you select the Rubber Stamp tool.

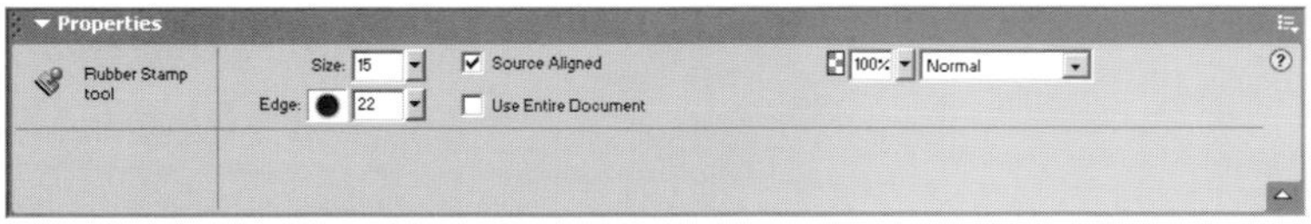

Figure 8.19

The Rubber Stamp properties as seen in the Property Inspector

3. Set the size of the area you are sampling from; this is done in the Size box in the Property Inspector.

4. Adjust the Edge softness. The higher the setting, the softer the edge will be.

5. Select the Use Entire Document option if you have objects stacked on top of each other or you have multiple layers and you want to sample from the composite.

6. After you have chosen the settings for the sampling area, set the sampling point. To do this, press the Alt (Option on a Mac) key and click in the area you want to sample.

7. Choose either the Source Aligned or Fixed option before you begin to stamp.

The Aligned option means that the sampling spot is aligned with the Rubber Stamp tool—as the Rubber Stamp tool moves, so does the sampling point. The Fixed option has a sampling point that stays in the same spot when you move the Rubber Stamp tool.

8. To control the amount of paint you are copying, set the Opacity slider.

This is especially important when you are working on textures or patterned areas, or on skin. It's a good idea to lower the opacity and make repairs in a multipass process.

9. Click the area you want to cover with the sampling area to begin stamping.

10. Drag to paint the sampled area over a new location.

Masking Images

If you make collages, or montages—image compositions—then you'll use the masking features of Fireworks frequently. Using a mask is quite easy once you understand the concept. A *mask* blocks off portions of an image, using one shape to block another one. Often masks are used to blend one image into another, to isolate an area to be removed from an image, or simply to add special effects, as you'll see later in this chapter.

Bitmap masks in Fireworks are similar to Layer Masks in Photoshop. Photoshop Layer Clipping paths are similar to Fireworks' vector masks.

In Fireworks, a *mask object* is what you apply a mask to. The mask object resides above the image to be masked; in other words, a mask isn't applied directly to the image. You will understand this statement a bit better when you follow the steps in "Using a Bitmap Image as a Mask" momentarily. A mask object contains a fill, which affects the pixels of the image or the object that is being masked. The fill color or texture determines how much of an image will show through the mask. In the areas of a mask that are white, the underlying area will be totally visible. Where such areas are solid black, the image will be totally invisible. The varying degrees of gray determine the amount of transparency.

If you have used previous versions of Fireworks, the white and black are reversed from what they used to be. In Fireworks 4, white was invisible and black was visible.

Making a Bitmap Mask

There are two types of masks in Fireworks, bitmap masks and vector masks. You'll start with the bitmap mask first. In the following example, you will select part of an image to cut out from the background of a photo, and then you will make the selection into a mask. You will then learn how to save the mask as a bitmap image to use as a mask in other photos. If you are new to masking, then it may seem intimidating, so we will break down the process into bite size pieces, starting with making a selection.

Making the Selection

The first thing you will do is make a selection of the portion of an image that you want to remove from the rest of the image.

1. Open the `cats.png` file in the Chapter 8 folder on the accompanying CD. Bet you were surprised when you opened it—not real cats at all, more like a couple of clowns!

2. Select the Oval Marquee tool and draw an ellipse around the little girl, as shown in Figure 8.20.

3. Choose Select → Feather and enter a value of 30, to add a feather to the edge. You can also select the Feather amount from the Property Inspector prior to drawing the selection. If you decide that you want to add a feather after the selection is drawn, use the Select menu to add it.

Figure 8.20

A marquee selection is made.

You are now ready to turn your selection into a bitmap mask.

MAKING PRECISE SELECTIONS

You can make the selection described here using any of the selection tools. You can also make a precise selection around the girls to cut them out specifically. Because vector masks do a better job of precise selections (in our opinion), you'll do that in the "Using Vector Masks" section.

Precise selections can take a long time to make, and if you make a mistake, you may end up having to start over. If this happens to you, you can save these selections (only one per document) by choosing Select → Save Bitmap Selection. To restore the selection, choose Select → Restore Bitmap Selection. Saved selections are stored with the document. You can restore them even after a document has been closed and reopened.

Adding a Mask

You will now add the mask to your selection by following these steps:

1. In the Layers panel, click the Add Mask icon. Notice the mask (black and white) is grouped with the image (Figure 8.21). Also take note that the white center is where the image shows through (see Figure 8.22).

Figure 8.21

The Layers panel showing the Add Mask tool tip and the grouping of the mask with bitmap

Figure 8.22

The image with the mask applied

Figure 8.23

The bitmap image selected in the Layers panel and the cloverleaf icon, which is now visible

Figure 8.24

The image moved within the mask.

2. Then select the bitmap icon in the Layers panel. Figure 8.23 is zoomed in so that you can see the cloverleaf after the selection of the bitmap icon. The cloverleaf shows that there is an image inside the mask.

3. Click and drag the cloverleaf to move the image (as shown in Figure 8.24).

4. Save the mask.

Saving A Mask as a Bitmap Image

It is especially important to save the mask if you are working on a precise or custom mask that you spent a lot of time making and you might want to use in other images. In a little bit, you will see that you can use bitmap images as masks. To make the mask you just made into a bitmap image, follow these steps.

1. Click the mask icon (black and white) in the Layers panel.

2. Drag the icon below the image (or another layer).

3. As you drag you will see a slight flicker at the edge of the layer. When you do, release the mouse button.

    Figure 8.25 may be difficult to see since it's white but this is what the mask looks like as a bitmap image.

4. Save your mask. You may want to make a special folder for saved masks if you frequently use saved masks.

Figure 8.25

The mask converted into a bitmap image

Using a Bitmap Image as a Mask

Any image or shape can be used as a mask. Just remember, that the light and dark values determine what shows through. In this example, you will use a black and white bitmap image and then quickly apply a color image as a mask.

1. Open the `cats.png` file.

2. Choose File → Import and navigate to the Chapter 8 folder on the accompanying CD and open the `bitmapmask.png` file.

3. Place the corner cursor shape in the document window, and click the image to place the imported mask image.

4. Arrange the bitmap cat (which is being used as a mask) over the photo and use Shift + Select to select the cat image and the photo.

5. Then choose Modify → Mask → Group as Mask (Figure 8.26) to mask the photo in the shape of the cat image used as a mask.

Figure 8.26

A bitmap image used as a mask

6. If you want to move the image within the mask, click the Photo icon in the Layers panel and move the cloverleaf.

7. Save using a different name and close or just close the document.

Masking with a Color Image

Now let's try a full color image. If your color image has a lot of light values in it, you won't have to lighten it as was done with this photo.

1. Open the `cats.png` image again.

2. Choose File → Import and select the `dodge.png` image. This image is so dark that if you selected the two images and grouped as a mask you wouldn't see much.

3. Because of this, just select the carousel portion of the image (check the Layers panel to be sure only the carousel is selected).

4. Choose Filters → Adjust Color → Curves.

5. Click and drag the center of the line to the top, as seen in Figure 8.27. Or you could type in the Input of 31 and Output of 208. Don't worry about how to use Curves, just know for now that as you pull up the curve it gets lighter.

6. Click OK.

7. Shift + Select the cat's image and the bitmap image.

8. Then choose Modify → Mask → Group as Mask (see Figure 8.28). Isn't that an interesting result?

Using Vector Masks

Vector masks are often the best masks to use because of their flexibility. Because the mask is a vector object, it has points, which can be manipulated into a perfect fit. Plus, if you make a mistake, you don't lose all of your selection like you would with a Selection tool.

Because a vector mask is an object, you can add varying degrees of black and white using gradients to adjust the transparency. Now that Fireworks MX also has gradient transparency, you have even more options. To make a vector mask and then apply it to a photo, follow these steps:

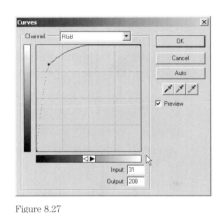

Figure 8.27

The Curves dialog box showing the adjusted curve

Figure 8.28

A colored image lightened and used as a mask

1. Open `cats.png` again.

2. Select the Pen tool (Basic, Soft Rounded, no fill) and make a selection around the girls.

3. Use the Subselection tool to edit the individual points that need it (refer to Chapter 7 for detailed instructions on using the Pen tool). You can see the selection in Figure 8.29.

4. Because you want everything in the selection to be visible, select a solid fill and a color of white (as shown in Figure 8.30).

Figure 8.29

The selection made

Figure 8.30

The vector selection filled with white

5. In the Fill area of the Property Inspector, change the Edge to Feather with a value of 3. Doing this will make the edges nice and smooth without blurring them.

6. Shift + Select the vector object and the image, and then choose Modify → Mask → Group as Mask. In Figure 8.31 you can see the results—a white background was added so that you could see the effect. Leave this image open for use in the next exercise.

Figure 8.31

The result of using a vector object to mask the image.

Using Gradients for Transparency

To see how gradients work to fade images, which is a technique used to blend images together, follow these steps using the vector mask you just made.

1. Select the mask group in the Layers panel and choose Modify → Ungroup. You now are back to the step prior to masking, which is your photo and the vector mask object.

2. Select the white vector object, and change the fill to Linear.

3. Click the color box and choose white/black from the Gradient Preset pop-up.

4. Move the gradient handles so that the right edge of the image is black and the left is white. Figure 8.32 shows the position we used in this example.

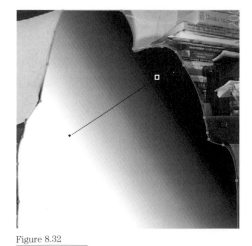

Figure 8.32

The gradient position used to blend in the right edge with the background

Figure 8.33

The image blended on the right side into the background

5. Shift + Select the image and vector mask and choose Modify → Mask → Group as Mask; the result can be seen in Figure 8.33.

6. Look in the Layers panel. You should be able to see a pen icon in the mask, which indicates that it is a vector mask. Click the pen icon to make the gradient handles visible, which allows you to adjust the gradient without ungrouping the mask.

The Filters Menu

The options in the Filters menu are applied to bitmap images. If you are trying to use an effect from the Filters menu on a vector object, the vector will be converted to a bitmap object prior to using the filter. You will take a look at a few of the filters in this section. The plugins and filters in the Filters menu are also in the Effects pop-up menu (see Chapter 6).

> The difference between using the Filters menu and the Effects pop-up menu is that the Effects pop-up menu uses *Live Effects*, which remain editable, whereas the Filters menu converts everything to a bitmap that is not editable.

Using the Blur Filters

The Blur filters are helpful in many retouching situations. There are three types of Blur filters in the Filters menu and they should be used for large repairs. For very small areas or for a really quick fix, you can use the Blur tool from the Tools panel. The Blur filters are more powerful than the Blur tool found in the Tools panel. Blurring can be applied to an image that looks scratchy, speckled, or one that seems a bit dirty.

> Before you start blurring an image that you are repairing, make a duplicate layer; you can always delete it later if you don't need it.

Be forewarned, the Blur and More Blur filters give you no control at all—you get what they are preset to and that's that. The most useful blur filter is the Gaussian Blur. With this filter, you can set just how much blur to add. If you use the slider to adjust the amount, you will see the effect in your document. If you type in an amount, you'll have to accept the changes to preview it.

> A popular effect is motion blur. Fireworks doesn't have one but it ships with a light version of Eye Candy 4000, which includes Motion Blur. If you want a horizontal motion, set the taper to 0 and the direction to 90 percent.

Using the Sharpen Filters

The Sharpen and the Sharpen More filters are automatically adjusted and have no choices available. What the sharpening filters do, especially the Unsharp Mask filter, is increase the clarity of an image by using contrast. The contrast is emphasized in an image based on the selections you make in the Unsharp Mask dialog box. There are three selections to enter:

Sharpen Amount Specifies the intensity—how much effect neighboring pixels have on one another. The Sharpen Amount is affected by the Radius and Threshold amount as well, so you may have to adjust this setting. The best settings for the Sharpen Amount are between 50 percent and 100 percent.

Pixel Radius Determines how many pixels are evaluated—similar to a feather. The larger the number you select, the more pronounced the contrast will be. The Pixel Radius settings range should be between .5 percent and 1.5 percent of the dpi of the image. So for a 72dpi image, the Pixel Radius should be in the range of between .35 and 1 pixel. If your image is busy and has low contrast, use the high end of the Pixel Radius settings. If the image is not so busy and has high contrast, use the low end of the settings range.

Threshold Determines which pixels are affected. This is based on the number of levels of difference in the surrounding pixels. If the number of levels is greater than the threshold, sharpening will be applied based on the settings for the Pixel Radius and the Sharpen Amount. The higher the Threshold number, the fewer pixels are affected. The Threshold is based on how the pixels work against each other, which is based on their differences. For instance, a Threshold of 0 allows neighboring pixels to affect one another, while a high threshold of 255 prevents pixels from affecting each other.

> The Threshold setting is normally between 0 to 5 (up to 255 is available), but most often 0 is the best choice. If you have an image with a lot of noise, a Threshold of 1 or 2 is the better choice because it will prevent the noise from being sharpened. The noisier the image, the higher the Threshold setting should be. Settings above 5 are used only when you want to emphasize contrast of image elements.

To use Unsharp Mask follow these steps:

1. Select an image or make a selection of a portion of an image.
2. Choose Filters → Sharpen → Unsharp Mask. If your image or object isn't a bitmap, this window opens telling you it will be converted to a bitmap; click OK.
3. When the Unsharp Mask window opens. Enter the settings for the Sharpen Amount, the Pixel Radius, and the Threshold.
4. Click OK.

Adjusting Color

Many of the Adjust Color options are more advanced and beyond the scope of this book. If you do a lot of image color correction, you may want to get one of the many Photoshop books available. Why Photoshop books? Because serious image retouchers use Photoshop. Fireworks is for web work; if you plan on doing a lot of print work, then Photoshop is the better choice. The levels and curves functions of Photoshop and Fireworks are very similar, so you can learn a lot from Photoshop books that focus on these features.

We will now look briefly at each option in the Adjust Color menu, and then some instructions will be given for some of the easier and very useful options.

Auto Levels Auto Levels can adjust the tonal range of an image. If detail isn't visible, levels can often bring it out. Auto Levels is like most automatic tools, you have no control. But if you don't know how to make adjustments to the levels manually, you may want to try this filter to see if the correction it makes is acceptable.

Brightness and Contrast Use the Brightness and Contrast option to adjust an image's appearance quickly. To use Brightness and Contrast, select an image, and then choose Filters → Adjust Color → Brightness and Contrast. By moving the sliders to the left or right, you can view the changes that will be made in real-time on the canvas. When you get it the way you want, click OK.

Curves Curves is another advanced feature of Fireworks; this option is used to adjust the different levels of individual colors. You can adjust the level of one color, such as green, without affecting the balance of light in the image.

In the Curves dialog box, you can make color adjustments to the entire image or to separate channels. For instance, if you want to change the contrast of just the red channel, you can select the red channel and make alterations.

Hue and Saturation Use the Hue and Saturation option to change the color of an image. Let's say you have a button you really like, and you would like to use it, but it's red and you need a blue one. All you need to do is select the object, and then choose Filters → Adjust Color → Hue and Saturation.

In the resulting dialog box, you can move the sliders provided and you will see the color change. You can also add contrast, or lightness, or color. If you click the Colorize option, you can change an RGB image into a two-tone image, or you can add color to a grayscale image. Be sure to check the Preview option so that you can see the effect of your choices on the canvas as you move the sliders. When you get the color you want, click OK.

Invert The Invert filter can add a funky look to an image, or if you use it on a button with a gradient fill, it can be quite stunning. What the Invert filter does is change each color in an object or image to its inverse on the RGB color wheel. For example, if you apply Invert to a red image it changes the color to light blue. To use the Invert filter select an object, choose Filters → Adjust Color → Invert.

Levels Levels is one of the options that requires more explanation than this book can cover. Levels are used to make tonal corrections in images. They adjust the ranges of light in an image—the shadows, midtones, and highlights. The Auto Levels option isn't a bad one to try until you learn how use the Shadow Points and the Histogram of levels.

Plugins

Plugins come in handy for special effects and quick fixes. Fireworks MX is compatible with most third party, Photoshop compatible plugins, but it is not compatible with Photoshop 6 or 7 native plugins. In Fireworks 4, even non-compatible Photoshop 6 filters would show up in your Xtras menu and Effects panel. To avoid this in the current version, Fireworks MX will not list any plugin found in the Photoshop 6 Plug-Ins folder. If you are using Photoshop and want to use your third-party plugins, just install them in a separate folder.

To tell Fireworks where to find the plugins, choose Edit → Preferences and click the Folders tab. Check Photoshop Plug-Ins and Browse to the folder in which you have the plugins installed.

You can use Photoshop 5.5 and earlier native plug-ins. So if you have an older version, you can install your plugins in the Photoshop Plug-Ins folder.

Hands On: Using a Third Party Plugin

In this tutorial, you will use a new plugin by Alien Skin called Splat! You won't use all of the filters, but you will apply multiple filters to the same image. A demo of Splat! can be found on this book's accompanying CD. To use the Splat! plugin to add a matte and a picture frame, follow these steps:

1. On the accompanying CD locate the Splat! Plugin; there is a demo for both Windows and Mac. Double-click it to install. When you get to the Select Host window, choose Fireworks MX as the application to use.

   You can also click the Choose Location button seen in Figure 8.34 to choose another folder. If you select Fireworks MX, the installer will automatically install to the Fireworks folder.

2. After you are finished installing, choose Edit → Preferences and click the Folder tab (shown in Figure 8.35). Check the Photoshop Plug-Ins option and then click the Browse button to select the folder you installed your plugin to, and then click OK.

3. Close Fireworks and then reopen it. Your plugin will now show in the Filters menu and the Effects pop-up menu.

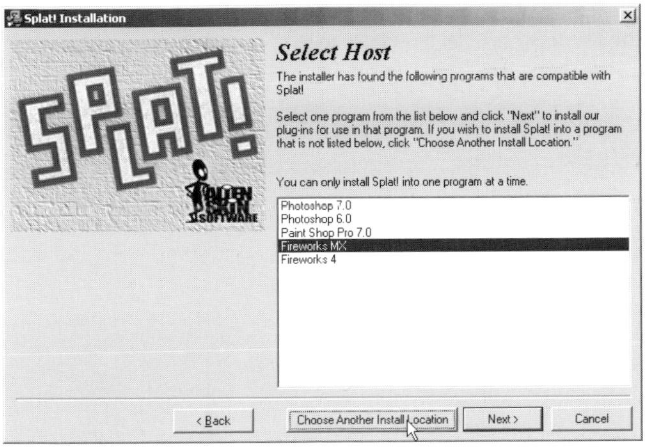

Figure 8.34

The Select Host window of the Splat! installer showing the Choose Another Install Location option.

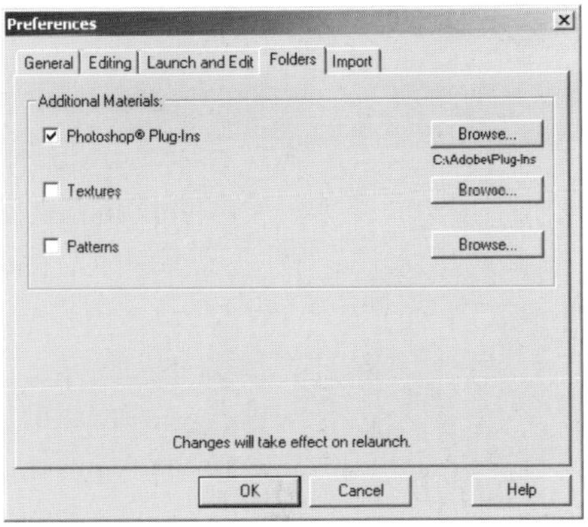

Figure 8.35

The Folders tab of the Preferences dialog box

4. Open the `flower.png` file from the Chapter 8 folder on the book's CD.

This image was supplied by Fred Showker of `http://www.graphic-design.com` for your use. It was scaled down and placed on a complementary colored background.

5. Select the flower photo.

6. Choose Filters → Splat → Frame. The Frame dialog box will open as seen in Figure 8.36. What you see in the preview will depend on the last frame you've used.

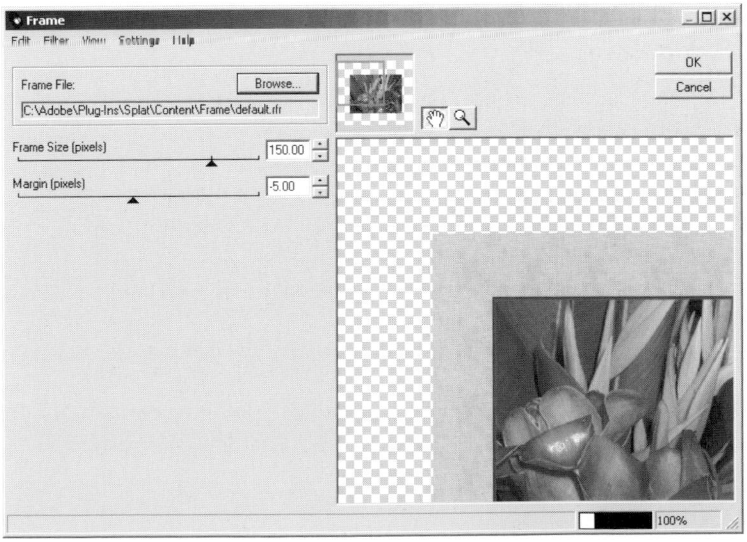

Figure 8.36

The Frame dialog box of Splat!

7. In the Frame File area, click the Browse button. Double-click the Matte folder and select `matte 009 beige.rfr`.

8. Set the Margin pixels to –8.50 by moving the slider or typing in the value.

> We found it easiest to adjust the margin until a bit of the photo's edge showed, then move the slider back up a small amount until the background wasn't visible. We also found it more effective to adjust the margin than the Frame size.

9. Set the Frame Size to 57.23. Of course, these values all depend on the look you are going for. We are simply supplying the values we used.

10. Click OK. Figure 8.37 shows the photo so far with a matte applied.

Figure 8.37

A matte applied to the photo.

Customizing the Matte

Now you will add texture to the matte and change its color by following these steps:

1. Select the Magic Wand tool, and in the Property Inspector, set the Tolerance to 32 and the Edge to Anti-alias.

2. Click the matte to select it.

3. Choose Filters → Splat → Resurface, and then press the Browse button and choose `default.jpg` if it hasn't already been chosen. Click OK.

4. While the selection is still active, choose Filters → Adjust Color → Hue/Saturation.

5. In the Hue/Saturation dialog box, enter a value of 24 for Hue, 9 for Saturation, and 0 for Lightness. Press OK.

6. Deselect the selection (Ctrl + D for PC and Cmd + D for Mac). Now you will add another frame to the image.

7. Select the image and choose Filters → Splat → Frame. Press the Browse button and open the Dover folder. Select `Art Nouveau 024.rfr`.

8. Change the Margin to –23.01, the Frame Size to 85.11, and click OK. Figure 8.38 shows the result.

For more information about Splat! go to `http://www.alienskin.com`. What we like about this plugin is that it's extendable. You can make your own frames, mattes, and border images to use with Splat!

You can apply every setting used in this tutorial using the Effects pop-up menu and the effects will be Live Effects and editable. The reason we used the Filters menu instead is because of the preview capabilities of Splat!. In the Filters menu, you can see the matte or the first filter applied in the preview when you apply a second effect such as another frame. The preview for the Effects pop-up menu does not show the first matte while you are applying the second frame.

Putting It All Together

In this chapter, you really covered a lot of ground with bitmaps. In fact, there are so many options that you may feel overwhelmed. Just take it a section at a time and practice on the many images we've supplied you with on the accompanying CD. No one becomes an expert overnight, and believe us when we say that bitmap manipulation can be a real art.

You also learned how to use masks to utilize portions of an image, as well as how to cut out, blend, and feather the edges. If you make collages, you'll certainly be using the skills you've obtained here. Lastly, you've gotten a quick overview of what some of the Filters menu commands will do and how to access your plugins.

In Chapter 9, you will learn all about navigation elements for your web pages.

Figure 8.38

The flower image matted and framed using the Splat! plugin and the Fireworks Hue/Saturation filter.

## CHAPTER 9

Designing Navigation Objects

The most important part of a web page is the navigational controls, which guide the user to the information they are looking for. You will learn to make rollovers for navigation as well as instant pop-up menus. You will also discover how easy it is to design disjoint or remote rollovers (sometimes called arrays) using Fireworks' new drag-and-drop feature.

In this chapter, you will use symbols, instances, and the Library panel extensively. You'll be importing symbols from one document into another and making a navigational element with multiple buttons into one symbol. With a click of a button, you can add a nav bar complete with buttons and links.

These are the topics you'll delve into in this chapter:

- **Learning to use symbols, instances, and libraries**

- **Using the Button editor**

- **Making simple and disjoint rollovers**

- **Making a pop-up menu**

- **Designing a navigational symbol**

Using Symbols, Instances, and Libraries

A large part of Fireworks' efficiency lies in the fact that you can automate many processes. Since symbols, instances, and libraries are used extensively when you are designing effective navigation, you'll learn a bit about each before you learn how to make different navigational systems.

Whenever you can utilize the same piece of artwork or the same object multiple times, it helps you cut your production time, not to mention the download time for a web page. Fireworks uses symbols to allow you to use the same object multiple times. The symbols that you generate are stored in libraries and instances and are present in the document.

Symbols

You can convert any object into a symbol. For example, if you have designed a custom button, you can make it a symbol, which can then be used over and over again. You can also make buttons into symbols using the Button editor, as you'll see later in this chapter. In addition to adding new symbols, you can convert any button or object that has already been produced to a symbol.

They're three types of symbols in Fireworks.

Graphic symbols These are basically any object or image that you'd like to use multiple times. Graphic symbols are static, meaning they have no behaviors, such as rollovers, attached to them.

Button symbols These usually contain multiple frames, which contain the different states of a button or a simple swap image. Button symbols are generated in the Button editor, which also automatically applies a slice.

Animation symbols These contain all the frames and timing of your animation. A completed animation, including its links, is contained in the symbol.

To make any existing object or an animation into a symbol, follow these steps:

1. Draw any object you'd like, or open an existing object you've made.

2. Select the Pointer tool and select an object, choose Modify → Symbol → Convert to Symbol. The Symbol Properties dialog box will open as seen in Figure 9.1.

3. Name your new symbol and choose the type of symbol you want it to be (Graphic, Button, or Animation) by clicking the appropriate option.

4. Click OK when you are finished.

Symbols are also editable. As soon as you make a symbol, it is automatically stored in the Library panel (in the Assets panel group) and an instance is placed on the canvas.

When you double-click the instance, a dialog box will open. Which dialog box opens will depend on the type of symbol you are editing: a Graphic symbol will open the Symbol Properties dialog box, a Button symbol will open the Button editor, and an Animation symbol will open the Animate dialog box. When you edit the master symbol the changes will be made globally to all instances of that symbol.

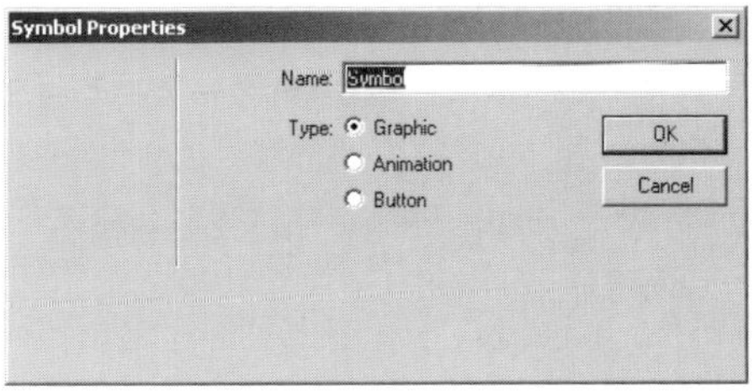

Figure 9.1

The Symbol Properties dialog box

Instances

Once you have a symbol, you can drag additional instances from the Library (in the docked Assets panel group) onto your canvas—but when you do, you should be aware that it's not the actual symbol you see, it's an *instance* of the symbol, a copy.

An instance maintains a link to the parent symbol. You can always tell when there is an instance on the canvas because there is a dotted box and an arrow in the corner. For Windows users, the symbol resembles a shortcut icon.

As you know, editing a symbol opens the appropriate dialog box and changes are made globally to all instances, but there are a couple of things you can do to an individual instance that don't affect all the others: you can use the transform tools and alter the opacity on individual instances, and you can add effects to an instance, which can be edited instance by instance.

The editing of the effects becomes especially important when you are tweening instances you want to use in an animation. For example, in order for you to use two symbols and tween them, the symbols have to be the same in Fireworks. If they each contain an effect, they are considered the same, even if you alter one of the effects.

Libraries

Symbols are the "master copies" and are stored in a library; they are never present on your canvas. When you make a symbol, you don't have to put it into the Library—it is automatically added to the current document's library and is saved with that document file.

If you have symbols in your current document that you think you may want to use in another document, you can export them. To export symbols, follow these easy steps:

1. Open the Assets panel group and select the Library tab to access the Library panel.

2. Click the down pointing arrow (top-right corner of the Assets panel) to access the Library Options pop-up menu.

3. Choose Export Symbols.

4. Select the symbols you want to export—if you want them all, choose Select All; if you want several in a row, Shift-click; and if you want to pick and choose, Ctrl-click (Option-click on the Mac) the desired symbols. When you are done, click Export.

5. Then name your library and choose where you want to save it and click Save.

> Save or move libraries you think you may use often to the Fireworks Library folder, which is in Macromedia\Fireworks MX\Configurations\Libraries (this path is for Windows 2000, your location may vary. For instance, for OS X it is HD/Users/<username>/Library/Application-tion Support/Macromedia/Fireworks MX/Styles). By placing your file here, you can access it by choosing Edit → Libraries. Any new libraries you export into the Libraries folder will be available the next time you start Fireworks.

> Fireworks MX ships with several libraries: Bullets, Animations, Buttons, Nav Bars, and Themes. You can open the source PNG files for each and add your own symbols to these libraries if you'd like.

If you want to use a library you have currently saved, you will need to import it. To import a saved library, follow these steps:

1. Open the Library panel.

2. Access the Library Options pop-up menu and choose Import Symbols.

3. Locate your saved library and choose Open.

4. The Import Symbols dialog box opens with the list of symbols in the library you selected to save. Choose one or all of those that you want and click Import.

Using the Button Editor

The Button editor enables you to make multiple rollover states. You can use this editor to help streamline your workflow because you can apply up to four different states for the same button as well as add links and a slice. All the JavaScript code for the different rollovers gets exported with the button. Figure 9.2 shows the Button editor.

The following are the four different states of a button:

Up The default appearance of the button as first seen by the user.

Over The way the button looks when the user passes the mouse pointer over it. The Over state alerts users that this button is "hot," meaning that it leads to another page when clicked.

Down The appearance of the button after it has been clicked; often it appears as if it has been pressed down. In Fireworks, you can set the Down state to be active when the page it links to opens, to designate the button as the current page (it's the default setting).

Over While Down The appearance of the Down state button when the mouse pointer moves over it.

Making a Button Symbol

You can make a button directly in the Button editor or you can convert an existing button into a Button symbol and edit it in the Button editor. A Button symbol encapsulates up to four different button states. Instead of spending a lot of time reproducing similar buttons, you simply have to place an instance of a symbol onto your canvas and edit the text and link. To use the Button editor, follow these steps:

Figure 9.2

The Button editor dialog box

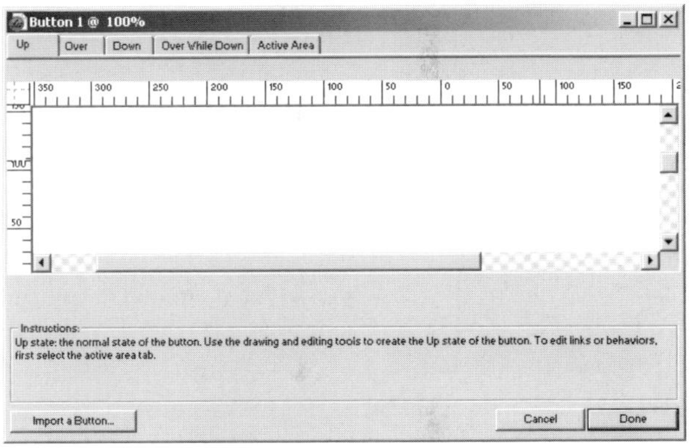

1. Choose Edit → Insert → New Symbol. When the Symbol Properties dialog box opens, enter the name **Green Button** and choose Button for the Type. Click OK.

2. The Button editor will open with the Up state tab active. Select the Rectangle tool and draw a rectangle with the following properties (which you should set in the Property Inspector):

    Size: 130×25

    Fill: **Linear**, # 66FF00 (**green**) is the color we used for the left side of the gradient, and # 003366 (**blue**) was used on the right.

    Fill Texture: **Parchment, 50%**

    Stroke: **Pencil 2, dark gray**

    Effects: **Inner Bevel, Frame 2, Width 4**

3. Center the button by using the Align panel. Select the To Canvas icon (should be orange) and the center icon in each group of three in the Align section (center horizontally, center vertically).

4. We wanted the gradient to be a bit bluer, so we moved the square handle in toward the center (to do this, make sure the button is selected), as seen in this illustration. Your button will look like this in the Up state.

5. Select the Text tool and type the text you want on the button (for this exercise type **Home**). Remember that the text is fully editable and can easily be changed later. Use any font and size that looks good on your button. We used blue text in our example.

6. To center this text, use the Align panel. Select the To Canvas icon (should be orange) and the center icon in each group of three in the Align section (center horizontally, center vertically).

> You can use the Center Text function, but be aware that the text is only centered in its text box, not to the object.

> In previous versions of Fireworks, adding text at this stage would mean that a new symbol would be generated every time you altered the text—not so anymore. This is a great enhancement for Fireworks MX.

7. Click the Over tab and click the Copy Up Graphic button to put a copy of the Up state in the Over state's editing box.

8. Select the button and change the stroke color to yellow and the text color to gold. Leave the Include Nav Bar Down State option checked.

> If you leave the Include Nav Bar Down State checked, at export, you will have the option of exporting multiple HTML documents. If you choose this option at export, the Down state will be active when the corresponding page loads.

9. Click the Down tab and then click the Copy Over Graphic button.

10. Change the stroke color to gray and click the + sign in the Property Inspector to access the Effects list.

11. Then choose Bevel and Emboss → Inset Emboss and accept the default settings. In this example, we also made the text gray with a 1-pixel stroke of blue.

12. Click the Active Area tab; you will see a slice added to your document automatically. The Active Area is set to Automatic by default and generates a slice large enough to cover all the button states. There is one slice for all four button states; you can change the size of the slice by unchecking the automatic option and dragging the slice points.

> If you want to add links to your buttons, you can easily do it in the Property Inspector instead of using the Link wizard that was here in the Button editor in previous versions of Fireworks. It's now much easier to add links and Alt text in the Property Inspector. When you add it to the Up state, all the states are updated automatically.

13. Click the Done button when you are finished with all the states of the button. An instance of the button is automatically placed in your document, indicated by the little arrow in the corner, and the symbol is automatically added to the Library panel.

14. To add more buttons to your document, drag them from the Library panel (in the Asset panel group) by clicking and dragging either the Button symbol or the name of the symbol onto your document. Figure 9.3 shows the symbol in the Library panel.

15. To preview the button, click the Preview tab in your document window, pass your mouse over the button, and click the button to see the different states.

Editing Button Symbols

With the addition of the Property Inspector in Fireworks MX, editing the buttons you have made is easier than ever. The following is a list of the different portions of your buttons and the steps for editing each portion:

Text Select the text you want to edit. In the Property Inspector you can change the Text, add a Link, and add Alt text as well if you need to. This works only if the button symbol has text on it.

Button characteristics Double-click to open the Button editor, click the tab for the state or states you'd like to alter, and make your changes. Close the Button editor when you are done.

Imported symbols When you edit an instance of a button, which you imported, it doesn't affect any documents containing the original symbol. But if you choose to Update (Library Options pop-up menu), the symbol will return to its original state. If you truly want to break the link between the original imported symbol and your new document, make a duplicate through the Library Options pop-up menu. Then drag an instance of this button onto your document (the copy won't say Import).

Active area If you want to change the active area of the button slice, you can now do it right in your document. Click and drag the red slice lines to adjust the active area.

Adding Rollover Behaviors

Rollovers are very popular in web pages. They add interactivity and are quite easy to implement. JavaScript rollovers all work the same way—when a cursor passes over one graphic, it triggers the display of another graphic. The trigger is always a hotspot or a slice, which trigger events and perform actions.

Figure 9.3

The button symbol added to the Library panel

Simple Rollovers

A simple rollover has only two states, usually an Up state and an Over state, or a swapped image. A *swapped image* occurs when a mouse cursor passes over the trigger image (the slice containing rollover behaviors) and an image from Frame 2 is swapped, giving the appearance of the original image changing.

> Both images must be the same size in simple rollovers. For instance, if you add a stroke to the Over state to add a glow, the image will be a bit larger. The first image will need its canvas size expanded a bit to match the size of the second image. Things will go more quickly if you have your images prepared and sized before you start implementing the rollovers.

To make a simple two-state rollover, follow these steps:

1. Select, draw, or import the image you want as the trigger image or the Up state—the button that the visitor sees when they enter your site.

2. Place the image or button where you want it, right-click to access the contextual menu (Ctrl-click on a Mac), and choose Insert Slice.

3. In the Frames panel, add one more frame by clicking the New/Duplicate Frame icon.

4. Select Frame 2, open or draw the second image (the same size as the first), and place it over the first image in your document.

> Here is an easy way to get an image to be the same size and in the correct location in Frame 2. First, return to the Layers panel, and select the object (not the slice). Then, choose Edit → Clone, then Edit → Copy, and Select Frame 2. Finally, choose Edit → Paste, and then make alterations to the clone.

> You do not need another slice for a new frame; you only need one slice for the target object, and it is in the Web layer for every frame automatically.

5. On the canvas (or the Web layer in the Layers panel), select the slice you added.

6. Open the Behaviors panel, choose Window → Behaviors, click the + sign, and choose Simple Rollover. In Figure 9.4 you can see that the onMouseOver Simple Rollover behavior has been added in the Behaviors panel.

Figure 9.4

The Simple Rollover behavior added to the Behaviors panel

Making a Disjoint Rollover

A *disjoint rollover* is frequently called an array or a remote rollover. It occurs when you hover the mouse cursor over an image and an image or text is displayed in a different location on the web page. To produce a disjoint rollover utilizing Fireworks drag-and-drop functionality, follow these steps:

1. Select the object that will be your trigger—the object that gets the behavior attached to it. Let's practice on a real image. Open the `disjointstarter.png` file from the Chapter 9 folder on the accompanying CD.

> You can use a fully functional button with rollover states as the trigger of a disjoint rollover.

2. You can skip this step for this exercise because we are using a Button symbol. In case you are using a static image to do this in the future, however, follow these steps:

   • Select the button/object and choose Edit → Insert → Slice if your object isn't a Button symbol.

   • In the Property Inspector, name your button (in the far left corner of the Property Inspector).

3. In the Frames panel (Window → Frames), access the Frames Options pop-up menu and choose Duplicate Frame; then choose the After Current Frame option.

4. Open the image you want to be displayed when the mouse hovers over the target image. For this exercise, open `parrots.png` from the Chapter 9 folder on the accompanying CD. With Frame 2 selected, place this image where you want it to appear on your canvas (Figure 9.5).

Figure 9.5

The image placed where it will appear in Frame 2

5. To check what you just did, click Frame 1 (Figure 9.6 shows what is on Frame 1), and then click Frame 2 (Figure 9.7 shows what is on Frame 2).

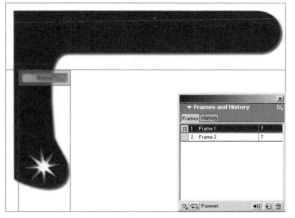

Figure 9.6

The contents in Frame 1

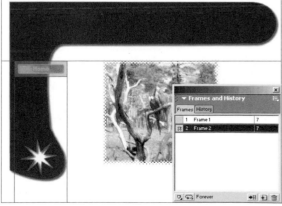

Figure 9.7

The contents in Frame 2

Figure 9.8

**The cursor changes to a fist when you press the mouse
button over the center circle of the slice.**

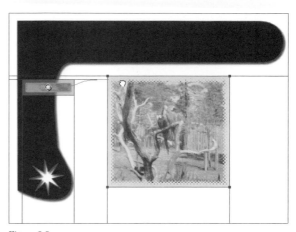

Figure 9.9

**There is a line connecting the button slice to the large
disjoint areas slice.**

6. Select the rollover image and choose Edit → Insert → Slice.

7. Now set up a Swap Image behavior for a disjoint rollover. To do so, select the slice over
   the button (the one placed in step 2). In the center of the button is a white circle—the
   pointer turns into a hand as you get near. Click and hold the mouse button down, and
   the pointer turns into a fist (Figure 9.8). Drag to the slice covering the image you want
   to change with your fist (Figure 9.9).

8. When you release the mouse button, a dialog box
   pops up and asks you which frame to swap the image
   from. Your image is on Frame 2, so that is what you
   type in, although it will probably already say Frame 2
   (Figure 9.10).

Figure 9.10

The Swap Image dialog box

9. Choose File → Preview in Browser to see your new disjoint
   rollover. As you mouse over, you will see the parrots, and as
   you move your mouse away you won't.

If you press the More Options button, you will see the names of all your frames, in case you
are using multiple disjoint rollovers. This is why it's important to name your slices—it makes it
easier to identify for the Swap Image behavior.

Making Image Maps

An image map is a single image with multiple hotspots —spots that are clickable. You can make an image map either in Dreamweaver or in Fireworks, whichever is more comfortable.

1. Open imagemap.png from the Chapter 9 images folder on the accompanying CD.
2. Select the Rectangle Hotspot tool. If you click and hold the corner of the tool icon, you'll see that there is a Circle and a Polygon shape available as well.

> When you make a Polygon shape, the shape area is the hotspot, although it will still be sliced as a rectangle.

3. Draw a rectangle over the Home word as seen in Figure 9.11. It will have a blue overlay when the hotspot is drawn.
4. In the Property Inspector, add the link name and the Alt tag, as seen in Figure 9.12.
5. Repeat Steps 2–4 for each word.

Figure 9.11

A hotspot is added to the word Home.

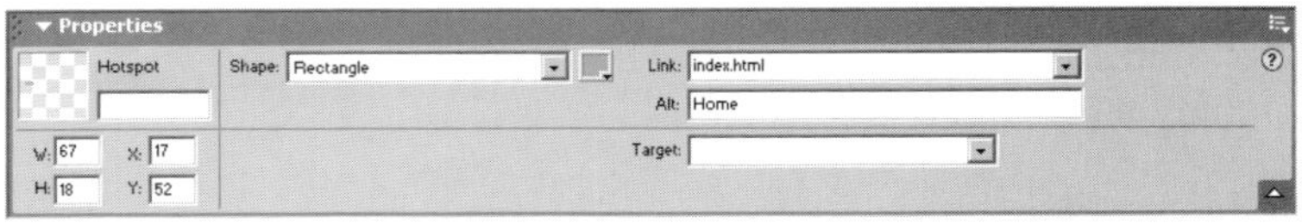

Figure 9.12

The Property Inspector showing the Link and the Alt tag added

Pop-Up Menus

Pop-up menus are very popular on the Web right now. You can make them in Dreamweaver using layers, or you can build them instantly in Fireworks. You have more flexibility in Dreamweaver, but if you are in a hurry or are still learning how to use Dreamweaver (or another professional HTML editor) then these instant pop-ups (because you don't have to write any code) may be just what you need.

> Dreamweaver MX has added the same pop-up menu behavior that Fireworks uses. It is accessed differently (by selecting an object and choosing Show Pop-Up Menu from the Behaviors panel), but these Fireworks instructions work in Dreamweaver once the Pop-Up Editor dialog box is opened.

To build a pop-up menu follow these steps:

1. Open the `imagemap.png` file from the Chapter 9 folder on the accompanying CD.

2. To insert the Pop-Up Menu behavior, add or select a hotspot or slice to attach a pop-up menu to. For this example, draw a hotspot over the Products name.

3. Choose Modify → Pop-Up Menu → Add Pop-Up Menu. On a PC you can right-click (Ctrl-click on a Mac) and choose Add Pop-Up Menu. For this example, we add a pop-up menu to the Products hotspot.

4. The Pop-Up Menu Editor dialog box opens (Figure 9.13). In the Text box, double-click in the text area and type the name of a menu entry (Small Appliances). If you want a link, type one in the Link box (no link for this example). Then click the plus (+) sign at the top left of the Editor to add the menu item (Figure 9.14).

5. Select the next text area (highlighted in dark blue when selected); double-click here to add a submenu item. Type in **Coffee Pots** and `coffeepot.htm` for the link. Click the + sign to add the menu item.

> The next item doesn't have to be a submenu item; instead, you can add as many menu items as you'd like and as many submenu items as you'd like. Just be sure to add the submenu items under the menu item they go with.

6. The second item you added (in step 4) has been added to the menu, but you want it to be a submenu item. Select the second entry (Coffee Pots) and click the Indent Menu icon. (Figure 9.15 has an arrow pointing to the this icon.)

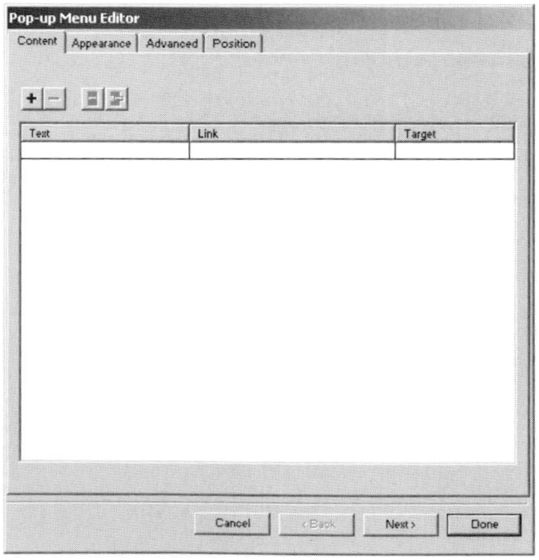

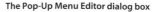

Figure 9.13

The Pop-Up Menu Editor dialog box

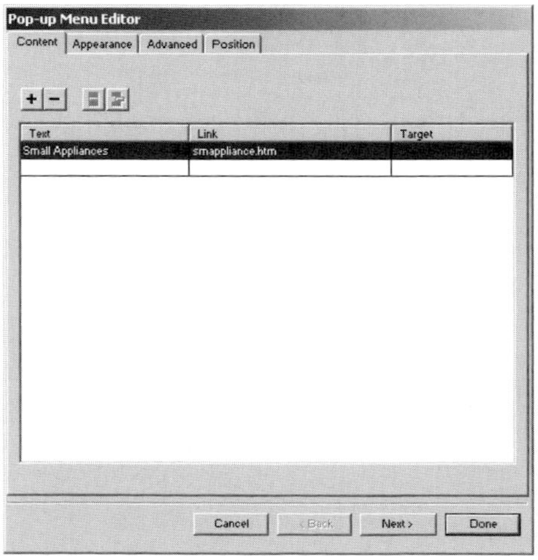

Figure 9.14

The first menu entry being added by clicking the plus sign

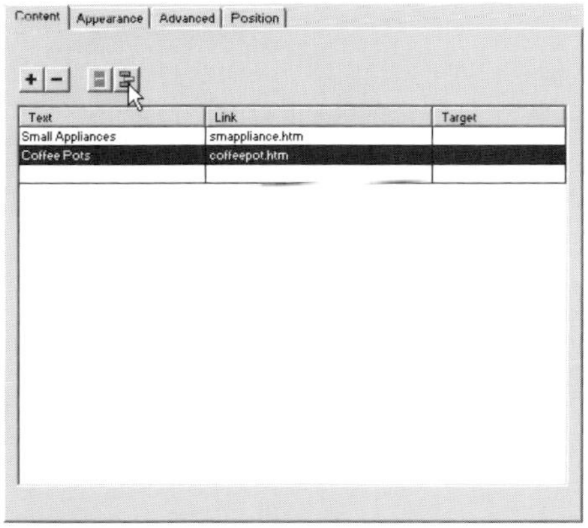

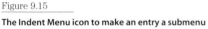

Figure 9.15

The Indent Menu icon to make an entry a submenu

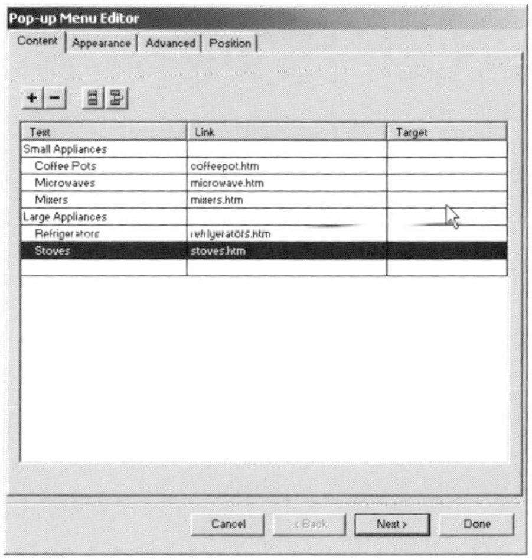

Figure 9.16

Additional menu and submenu items were added. Indented submenus are shown.

7. Continue adding menu and submenu entries. Figure 9.16 shows the additional menu items that were added to the example. Each indented entry is a submenu item. Click the Next button when you are finished.

> Menu items are not indented; when you want a submenu, click the Indent Menu icon, which denotes an entry as a submenu. When you want an item that appears indented to be a menu item, click the Outdent Menu icon.

8. The Appearance tab in which you set the appearance of your menus is now active (see Figure 9.17). In this tab, you can choose to make the cells HTML or Image; we'll use HTML for this example.

   You can see a preview of how the menu will look at the bottom of the dialog box. For each of the following options what we used in this example is in parenthesis.

   - Font (Verdana…)
   - Point size (12)
   - Up state text (black) and cell color (sample from the image background)
   - Over state text (red) and cell color (green sampled from the document)

   Experiment a bit here until you get the look that you like. Also choose the alignment of the pop-up menu to either a Vertical Menu or a Horizontal Menu; we chose Vertical.

When the Image option is selected, that means that a graphic is used instead of HTML code. The graphic used is a style; you can place any of your own custom styles in the Nav Bar folder of the Fireworks MX program files.

The fonts included in the Pop-Up Menu Editor are the ones most likely to be on everyone's computer. If you are using the Image option, only the graphic is exported, not the text; the browser renders the HTML text.

9. Click Next. The Advanced tab dialog box should appear (see Figure 9.18). This tab is totally new to Fireworks MX. On it, you can change the Cell Height and/or Width from the Automatic settings for the button size by choosing Pixels and entering an amount. You can also choose to indent the text or pad the cells. We used a value of 5 for the cell padding to separate the link text just a bit. In addition, you can change border color or eliminate the border altogether. You can also add additional spaces between your buttons. When you have the look you want, click Next.

10. You will now see the Position dialog box (shown in Figure 9.19). For this example, we also chose to have our menu appear on the bottom of the slice (second icon from the left) and we chose to have the submenu appear to the right of the menu (center icon). When you have chosen your settings, click Done.

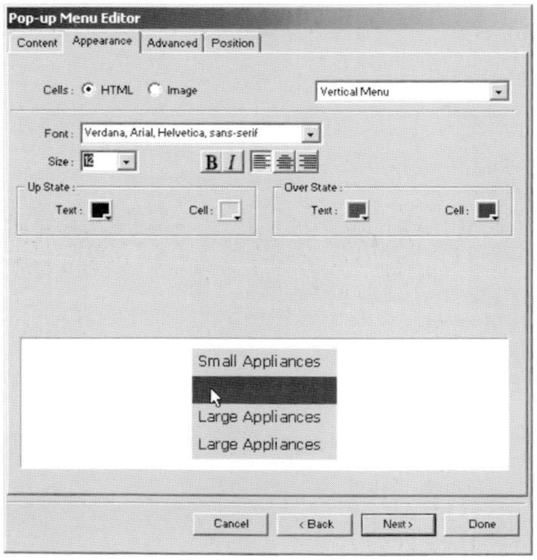

Figure 9.17

The Appearance options available for the pop-up menus.

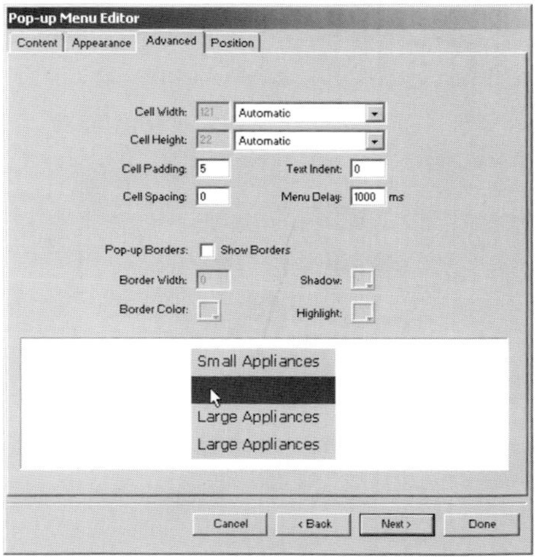

Figure 9.18

The Advanced tab showing the options available

11. In your document, all you will now see is a blue outline indicating the pop-up menu. If you'd like, you can move this outline around to position it by clicking and dragging it into position. You can't preview a pop-up menu with the Preview tab in the document window; instead, you have to preview it in a browser (an example of this is shown in Figure 9.20).

12. To edit the menu, double-click the blue outline in the document window to open the Pop-Up Menu editor. Click the appropriate tab for the change you want to make and make your changes.

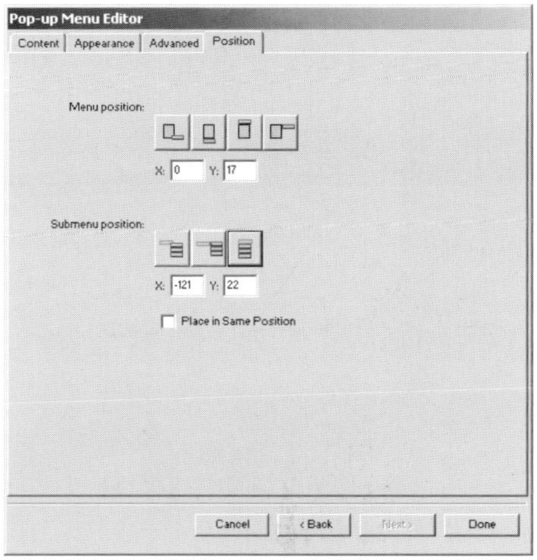

Exporting the Pop-Up Menu

Once your pop-up menu is done, it's time to export it. Do this like you would for any other document. Choose File → Export and export as HTML and Images.

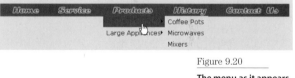

Figure 9.19

The Position tab options

The difference between exporting files and exporting pop-up menus and other slices is that Fireworks will generate all the JavaScript for the menu in a file called `fw_menu.js`, which is placed in the same folder as the HTML file. If you place the `fw_menu.js` file in a folder other than the folder the HTML file is in, you will need to change all the links that reference the `fw_menu.js` file.

Be sure to upload the `fw_menu.js` file to your server or your menus won't work. There is only one `fw_menu.js` file no matter how many menus are included. If you have submenus, then an `Arrow.gif` image file is produced as well.

Hands On: Making a Nav Bar

In this tutorial, you will turn the buttons you made in Chapter 7 into a navigation bar that can be added with the click of a button to any document you want to use it in.

1. Open the `navelement.png` file from the Chapter 9 folder on the accompanying CD. This nav shape will eventually be sliced and placed in a table.

2. We want to make a navigational symbol using the center part of the vertical shape as the background for the buttons. To do this, crop the document as seen in Figure 9.21. Figure 9.22 shows the cropped shape.

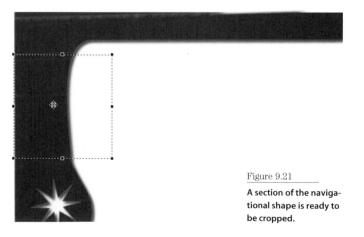

Figure 9.20

The menu as it appears in a browser

Figure 9.21

A section of the navigational shape is ready to be cropped.

Figure 9.22

The cropped shape

A copy of the nav section is saved in the Chapter 9 folder; it is named `navsection.png`.

3. Select the shape and choose Modify → Symbol → Convert to Symbol. Name the symbol NavSymbol, and choose a Type of Graphic; then click OK.

4. Notice that in the Library panel you now have a Graphic symbol. Double-click the instance in the document window to open the Symbol editor.

5. Select the shape, and in the Layers panel, access the Layers Option pop-up menu and choose Share This Layer.

If you ever make a navigational symbol and you see white around your buttons, it's because you forgot to share the layer.

Figure 9.23

The button instances added to the nav shape

6. In the Library panel, access the Library Options pop-up menu (top-right corner) and choose, Import Symbol.

7. Navigate to the Chapter 9 folder on the accompanying CD and select `GreenButton.png`.

8. Then, select Open, select the button from the list, and click Import.

9. Now drag an instance of the button from the Library onto the document. Press the Alt key (Option for a Mac), drag three more copies, and place them as seen in Figure 9.23.

10. Click the Home button in the Property Inspector, and add a link and an Alt tag.

11. Click the next button, and in the Text area, change the name to Products; then add a link and Alt tag.

12. Click the third button, name it Services, and add a link and Alt tag.

13. Select the last button, name it Contact Us, and add an e-mail link as seen in Figure 9.24.

Figure 9.24

An e-mail link added to the Contact Us button

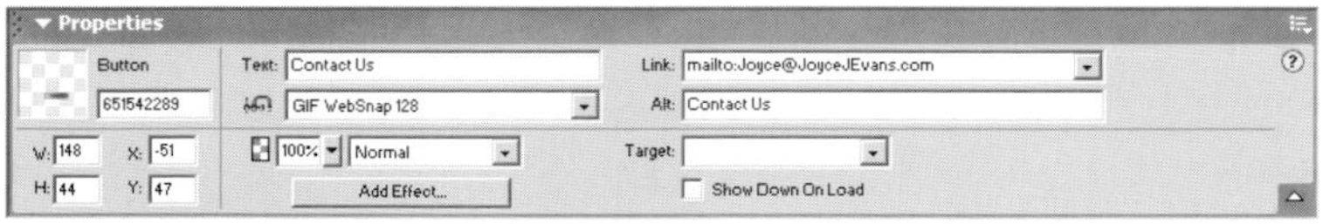

14. Close the Symbol editor. Figure 9.25 shows the completed navigation in the Symbol editor, and Figure 9.26 shows it in the document window.

15. Click the Preview tab. If you are satisfied, save your symbol as `NavSymbol.png`. If not, double-click the instance to open the Symbol editor and edit it.

Opt for Speed

In this chapter, you learned many ways to make navigational buttons, bars, and menus for your web pages. Now, you can even add an entire navigational element with multiple buttons all by simply dragging one instance onto your document. You've also learned how to make disjoint rollovers and pop-up menus that don't require any code writing at all.

In the next chapter, you will learn to optimize your graphics. Optimization is what determines how large your file sizes will be, and these file sizes in turn determine how fast your web page will load in a browser.

Figure 9.25

The navigation symbol as seen in the Symbol editor

Figure 9.26

The finished navigation symbol as seen in the document window

## CHAPTER 10

Slicing, Optimizing, and Exporting Images

Images on web pages can be mere eye candy or they can be an integral part of the user interface. They can also be a distraction if used inappropriately. For example, if they are too large and take forever to load they can drive users away. Therefore, in order to build fast-loading web pages, you should learn early on which format to use when you are exporting your images.

After you decide which format is needed for each image, you will need to determine if your images need slicing or not. Then—sliced or not—you will need to optimize each image or slice to obtain the smallest possible file size while still maintaining acceptable quality. This file size is what determines how fast your new graphics will load and be seen in a browser.

You'll learn how to slice, optimize, and export your images in this chapter. These are the main topics that will be discussed:

- **When to slice and how to use Slice tools**
- **Optimizing images**
- **Using selective JPEG**
- **Exporting options**

Slicing a Web Page Layout or an Image

In this section, you will learn when to slice a document or an image and how to slice it. In addition, you will see how to use rulers and guides to help you make the perfect slice using the various slice tools.

To Slice or Not to Slice

Slicing a web page layout is one of the most important things you will do in Fireworks. You also have the issue of dealing with individual images: to slice or not to slice? This decision will determine how your web page is viewed or perceived. Slicing actually does improve overall load time on large images. TCP/IP is more efficient transmitting packets in multiple threads, rather than waiting on one large image to download in a single thread.

What slicing does do is give the user the perception that the page is loading faster because parts of the image can be seen as it loads. This is an important perception; it sure beats having your user look at a blank screen for an extended period of time. Face it, Internet users are an impatient lot—if it takes longer than a few seconds to see something, it's too long and they are apt to move on.

When you are preparing your web page layout or individual images, you'll need to decide whether you need to slice individual objects into more than one piece. There are many reasons to slice an image. For instance, if the image is over 20KB, it needs to be sliced to give the perception that it's loading faster. Or, if you need to export some slices in the JPEG format, some in the GIF format, and some as GIF animations within the same document, you'll need slices. In addition, if you want to attach JavaScript behaviors to a portion of the image, it needs to be sliced.

An advantage of using slices is that it is easier to update one section or slice than it is to redo a whole image. For instance, if you have a complicated navigation bar that is optimized, sliced, exported, and incorporated into every page on a large site and you discover that one of the major links is spelled wrong, all you need to do is fix the one image (or two if it's a rollover) and then optimize, export, upload, and replace just the problem slice(s).

Using Ruler Guides for Slicing

Fireworks gives you the option of using guides to assist in alignment. If you want to use guides, you'll need to be sure that the option that allows you to view them is turned on. To check if they are set to be visible, choose View → Show Guides. If there is a check mark, they are turned on to be visible, if not, click the option and a check will be added.

Once you can view the guides, it's helpful to set them up so that they help you make your slice selection. Using them is also an efficient way of defining your slices because you also choose from the View → Guides → Snap to Guides option, which will snap your slices to the guides. This helps prevent overlapping slices. You won't actually see guides in your document until you place them. To place guides, follow these steps:

1. To enable guides, the rulers have to be visible. From the Menu bar, choose View → Rulers.

2. Then Choose View → Guides → Snap to Guides.

> You can set you own preference for how the Snap to Guides responds. To do so, choose Edit → Preferences and click the Editing tab. In the Snap Distance box, enter the amount of distance, in pixels, before your object will be snapped to the guide.

3. To place guides, click a horizontal or a vertical ruler and then drag a guide into your document.

4. The guide will not be visible until you begin to pull it onto the canvas area; when you do, you will see a green line, which is the default color.

5. Place the guide where you want it. You can use the ruler for more precise positioning.

The guides can be used when you are ready to export your document. More details on exporting are in the "Exporting with Fireworks" section.

When selected, one of the Fireworks Exporting options slices along the guides. For instance, if this option is chosen, you could export your whole image right after you finished placing the guides, and Fireworks would automatically slice it for you along those guides. To do this, go to the Menu bar and choose File → Export. Under the Slices option, choose Slice along Guides. (Refer to the "Exporting with Fireworks" section for details on exporting.) But if you want to just export using the guides, you can click Save and be done with the export.

There is a downside to using guides as a slicing method, however; you can't attach behaviors to a slice made this way. In order to attach a behavior to the slice, you have to define it; you will see how to do so in the following section.

Using the Rectangle Slice Tool

You can find the Slice tool in the Web section of the Tools panel. It's the green icon with the knife. If you press and hold the corner triangle on this icon, a pop-up will appear. This is where the Slice tool and Polygon Slice tool reside; select the rectangle that is labeled Slice tool. This Slice tool works the same way as the Rectangle drawing tool does. Just follow these steps.

1. Select the Slice tool from the Tools panel.

2. Following the guides you set up in the previous section (or following the new ones that you place now), drag a rectangular selection around the area you want to be a slice.

A green overlay will appear when a slice is drawn. You can toggle this view on and off using the icons below the Slice tool.

3. Repeat step 2 for the rest of the slices you want to define in your image.

Notice that red lines will appear after you define your first slice. These are just there to show you where Fireworks will automatically slice on Export if you choose to have Fireworks slice the remainder of the image. If you want to define more slices, just continue, and the red lines will adjust after each slice is defined. This process can be viewed in Figure 10.1, where two slices have been defined. A slice has been added to Services and Contact Us.

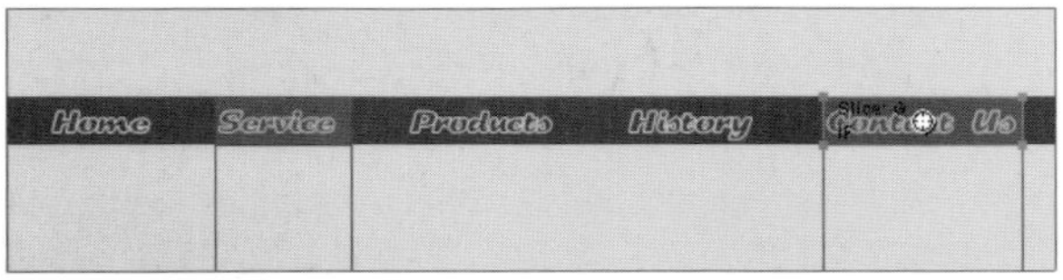

4. Once the slicing is complete, save your file (File → Save As).

Figure 10.1

Two slices defined. The lines that Fireworks generates automatically indicate potential slices.

Using the Polygon Slice Tool

To access the Polygon Slice tool, click and hold the rectangle in the right corner of the Slice tool to access the pop-up. Then select the Polygon Slice tool option. Drawing with the Polygon Slice tool is very similar to the process involved in using the Polygon shape tool. Just click a starting point and then continue clicking to add points to define a shape.

It's important to note that though you are able to define a polygonal shape with the Polygon Slice tool, the shape cannot be exported as a polygonal shape. All slices are rectangular—period. What happens is rectangular slices are automatically generated when the polygonal shape is cut up as you defined.

Since you can't export a polygonal shape, then why would you bother doing this? The answer is that there may be instances in which you need to define a polygonal shape, such as a complex shape that you want to divide up so that different behaviors can be attached to each section.

The one drawback with polygonal shapes is that many smaller rectangles are automatically generated to make all slices rectangular, which usually results in an excessive amount of slices. As a result, you should only use this tool if you absolutely have to.

Figure 10.2 shows a round object with four polygonal shapes defined for illustrative purposes. Notice all the small rectangles generated to make each shape a rectangle.

Figure 10.2

Here you see defined polygon shapes and the automatic slicing lines that are generated showing what the actual slices will look like.

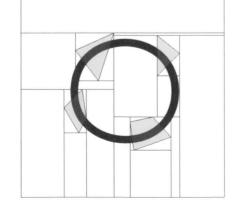

Making Slices from Objects

The easiest way to make a slice is to add it automatically. If you use an object that has already been drawn, you can access the contextual menu by right-clicking an object (Ctrl-clicking for a Mac) and choosing Insert Slice (or by choosing Edit → Insert → Insert Slice). If you have several objects that you'd like to slice together, you can group them and then add the slice via the Edit menu or the contextual menu.

In Figure 10.3 we drew several shapes. We then Shift + Selected them all and then grouped them (Modify → Group). Then we chose Edit → Insert→ Insert Slice. Notice how there is only one slice covering all the shapes.

Viewing Slices

Seeing the slices is helpful when you need to slice your image or optimize it, but during the design process or when you are just looking at an image's preview screen, they get in the way. It's easy enough to turn off the view, though; here are two different methods:

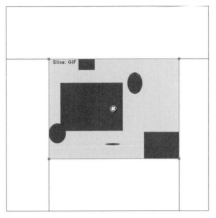

Figure 10.3

Shapes that were selected and grouped, and then one slice was added

- Click the eye icon in the Web Layer of the Layers panel.

- Click the Show/Hide Web Layer icons in the View section of the Tools panel.

You can also choose to hide or view the slice guides by choosing View → Slice Guides.

> In the "Optimization Methods" section of this chapter, you will see that when you optimize a slice or a group of slices, the selected slices in the preview tab of the Document window preview without the slice overlay. The unselected slices don't have the green overlay either, but the objects are muted or paler than the ones that are selected.

Slice Options

There are several values you can change for each slice or for multiple slices. The options are found in the Property Inspector. Figure 10.4 shows the Property Inspector when a slice is selected.

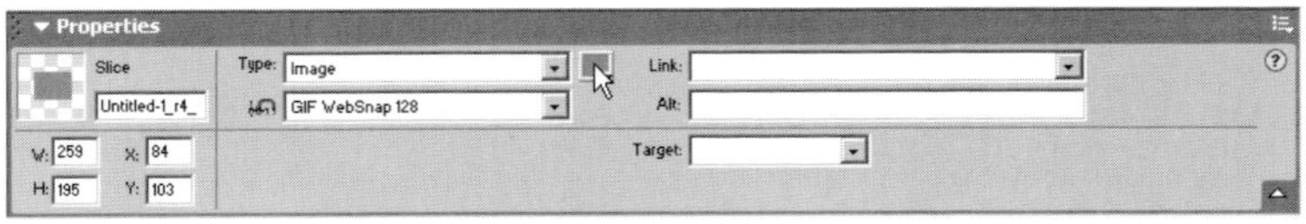

Figure 10.4

The Property Inspector showing the properties of a selected slice

Slice Overlay Color

You can change the color of the slice by clicking the color box (the cursor arrow is pointing to it in Figure 10.4) and selecting a new color. This is particularly important if the image you are working on is already green (the default slice color).

Naming Slices

The naming of slices is also done in the Property Inspector. When you add a slice, it autonames slices. Autonaming uses the root name of your document plus the row number and column number. The row and column number are determined by the slices in your document or image.

> If your document hasn't been saved and named, then the name of the slices will be untitled-1_r4_03 (as seen in Figure 10.4). r4 is row 4 and 03 is column 3.

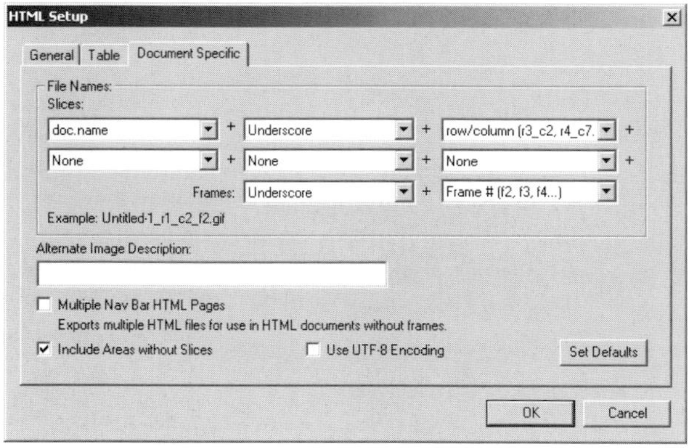

Figure 10.5

The HTML Setup dialog box with the Document Specific tab selected

If you want to change the name to something descriptive, highlight the name in the Property Inspector and type in a new one without the file extension.

You can customize the autonaming function. To do so, Select File → HTML Setup, and click the Document Specific tab. Figure 10.5 shows the options on this tab with their current default settings. You can set these defaults to anything you want. The down arrows give you some alternative naming options to choose from. When you are done, click the Set Defaults button to save.

Notice the Multiple Nav Bar HTML Pages check box. If you check this box, a new HTML page will be generated for each link in a nav bar. Just before you are ready to export a nav bar, choose this option if you want to automatically generate the HTML pages for each link. When you made the buttons for the nav bar, there was an option to include the nav bar down state for each button. That option, in combination with the Multiple Nav Bar HTML Pages option, will generate a separate HTML page for each button with the down state of the button showing when the page loads.

> For more information on making nav bars, see Chapter 9.

The Include Areas without Slices option is checked by default. You may want to uncheck that one and save the Default settings if you export only selected slices. But decide what works best for you and how you work.

In the Alternate Image Description text box, you can type in alternative text. This text is not for individual slices but for the entire image when there are no slices or the slices are undefined.

Adding URLs and Alt Tags

Many designers believe that every image with a link should contain an Alt (alternative text) tag. You should include alternate text on logo images with or without a link so that while the image is loading, the user can see what is coming, or if they have images turned off, they can read a description of what is there. What you put in the alternate text area is what the user sees before the image loads when the mouse is placed over the image. Providing this text may also expedite browsing, because the user may find the link they want via the Alt tag before the page finishes loading the images.

> Alternate text also makes your site more user-friendly for the visually impaired, since the Alt text is what the reader reads.

To add alternative text or URLs to your images, follow these steps:

1. Click the slice of the object to which you want to add a URL or alternate text.

2. Type your URL into the Link field on the Property Inspector or select a URL from the pop-up menu. This list contains any URLs you have added to the URL panel (Window → URL).

3. Fill in your target choices (optional). The Target field is used if you are developing a framed site. The targets choices are as follows:

   _blank Loads the linked document in a new, unnamed browser window.

   _parent Loads the lined document in the parent frameset or the window of the frame that contains the link. If the frame containing the link is not nested, then the linked document loads into the full browser window.

   _self Loads the linked document in the same frame or window as the link. This target is implied, so you usually don't need to specify it.

   _top Loads the linked document in the full browser window, thereby removing all frames.

4. Add the alternate text in the Alt box.

   Now your slice is ready to export or to receive a behavior if you'd like to add one.

Text Slices

In Figure 10.4 you can see a field in the Property Inspector called Type. The two Type choices are Image and HTML. So far you have been dealing with image slices only; now let's take a look at what an HTML slice is.

The purpose of having HTML slices (formerly called Text slices) is having a slice area in which you can enter HTML text. You can type in HTML text either from within Fireworks or from your HTML editor. To define a HTML slice, follow these steps:

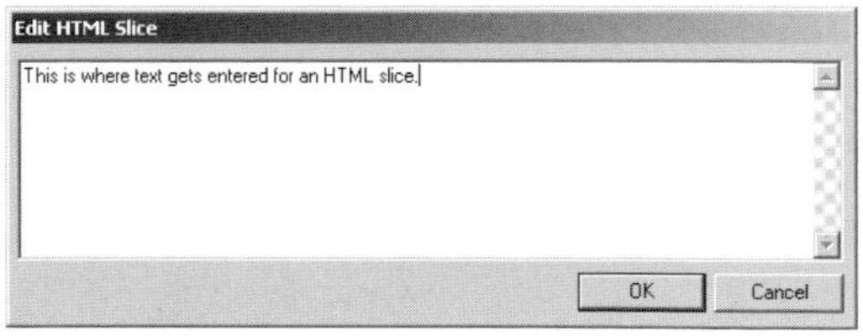

1. Select the slice you want to be reserved for HTML text.

2. In the Property Inspector, choose HTML from the Type field pop-up. If you want to add HTML text from within Fireworks, click the Edit button and the Edit HTML Slice dialog box will open so that you can type it in (Figure 10.6).

Figure 10.6

The Edit HTML Slice dialog box

You can also add the text later in an HTML editor.

That's all there is to it; the slice color will turn a darker green and a label of HTML Slice will replace the Slice label.

Text boxes have no border, cell padding, or cell spacing. As a result, your text will be placed right up against the edge of the area. If there is a bordering image or background, this will most likely be quite unsightly. The problem of no space can be solved by inserting blank text images before and after the text box, or by inserting slices before and after the text box. The extra text boxes or slices can then be filled with the background color or background image of the web page. This can be done in your HTML layout editor (Dreamweaver, for example).

Image File Formats for the Web

The time it takes for your website to load in a browser depends largely on the number of images that need to load and their file size. The two most widely used image formats, and the only two formats that are currently fully supported for the Web, are GIF and JPEG files. It's important that you understand the differences between these two so that you know when to use each.

Web graphics are different from the images that are produced for printing. Fireworks is a web-only environment, so the default resolution of all documents is 72dpi (although you can reset this setting), and the color mode is RGB (which is the color monitors use).

GIF

GIF stands for *Graphics Interchange Format* and is pronounced JIF. GIF, developed for CompuServe in the 1980s, was originally designed specifically for online use. The GIF compression algorithm works better for line art than for photographs. Not only is GIF better for line art, but it is also better for any image that is made up of a lot of flat color. Images such as cartoons, logos, and type are best suited for the GIF format.

GIF and PNG-8 images are indexed to a table of 256 colors. Only 216 of these 256 colors are supported by all browsers. These 216 colors are what are known as *web safe*. You can control the quality of your images and their file sizes by reducing the number of colors. In Fireworks, you can control which colors get eliminated and which ones stay by selecting and locking specific colors.

When you have images with 256 colors or fewer, there is no loss in quality when the image is compressed because of the LZW Lossless compression scheme that the GIF format uses.

As a result of the LZW Lossless compression, the data of the GIF image uses less space on the hard drive because its file size is smaller. The LZW compression algorithm works by determining changes in color within horizontal rows. The fewer color changes in a row of pixels, the more efficient the compression. To see this, look at Figure 10.7, which has horizontal stripes. The file size for this image is 1.17KB.

In Figure 10.8, you will see the same image with the same size except the stripes have been rotated by 90 degrees. Because the vertical stripes add a larger number of changes in a horizontal row, the file size has increased to 4.13KB.

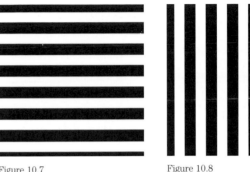

Figure 10.7

A horizontally striped image that compresses to 1.17KB as a GIF file

Figure 10.8

The same striped file rotated vertically increases the GIF file to 4.13KB.

JPEG

Some photographic images contain millions of colors and they would look really bad if they were limited to the 256 colors of the GIF format. That is where the JPEG format comes in. While GIF excels at compressing flat areas of color, JPEG excels at compressing the many colors of a photograph.

JPEG stands for *Joint Photographic Experts Group* and is pronounced Jay-peg. The JPEG compression algorithms work better for photographs than for line art.

The JPEG algorithm compresses the images using *lossy compression*, which means that the lower the quality setting, the fewer pixels are used. You can really compress an image drastically by lowering the quality setting.

The JGEG format has no transparency, however, so if you need a transparent background, you'll have to use a GIF format.

PNG

The World Wide Web Consortium (W3C) has formally endorsed *Portable Network Graphics (PNG)*, pronounced ping. The PNG format was developed for developers who started looking for an alternative to GIF when the patent holders starting charging developers for the use of the GIF export technology (before this point, the GIF technology had been free for many years). PNG has now become an exciting alternative to GIF, but at present, it is only partially supported by Netscape and IE, which makes it not a viable option yet.

Some of the features of a PNG file that are different from the GIF file include support for full alpha channel and graduated transparency, but browsers do not these support yet.

The PNG format uses a lossless compression and decompresses automatically when viewed. PNG uses many different bit depths—8-bit, 24-bit, and 32-bit. In addition, it has Gamma correction capabilities. Once PNG is fully supported by all the browsers, it will be a great alternative to the GIF.

Optimization Methods

Optimization is the most important factor of preparing an image for use on the Web. How you optimize determines how large your file is, which in turn determines how fast your images load on a web page. By slicing an image, you can not only export with GIF, JPEG, or PNG slices in the same document, but you can also apply different settings to specific areas of a JPEG image. This is called *selective JPEG compression*.

In this section, you will see the different tools that are available for setting your optimization choices and the different ways in which you can preview the choices you make.

Optimize Panel

Because most designers we know use the Optimize panel in conjunction with the Property Inspector to set up their optimization choices, we'll discuss this option first. Then, in the following sections, you'll get to see some of the other options. You can then choose which method works best for you.

You can optimize quite a few different formats in the Optimize panel. The ones you will most likely use are GIF, JPEG, and GIF Animation.

The settings in the Optimize panel are used for all slices, defined or undefined, unless you specifically select individual slices and change the settings. These default settings are great if you are exporting all GIF or all JPEG images and the same settings work for everything, but that is rarely the case.

You'll get to look at the specific settings for each format a little later in this chapter, but right now, we're just exploring the different ways to make the optimization choices. Figure 10.9 shows the Optimize panel with a file type of GIF selected.

Figure 10.9

The Optimize panel showing the file format of GIF

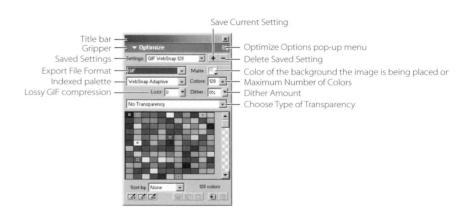

Most of the options seen in Figure 10.9 are available for the majority of the file format choices. You will see the specific options for JPEGs in the "Optimizing Options for JPEG Compression" section. In addition, the color table will be discussed in detail in the "Optimizing for GIF Compression" section.

There are additional optimization choices available in the Optimize Options pop-up menu as seen in Figure 10.10. The grayed-out options on this menu are available for different file formats. For instance, the Progressive JPEG and Sharpen JPEG Edges options become available when the JPEG file format is selected.

In the next section, you will see a couple of different ways to preview how an optimization setting will affect your slice.

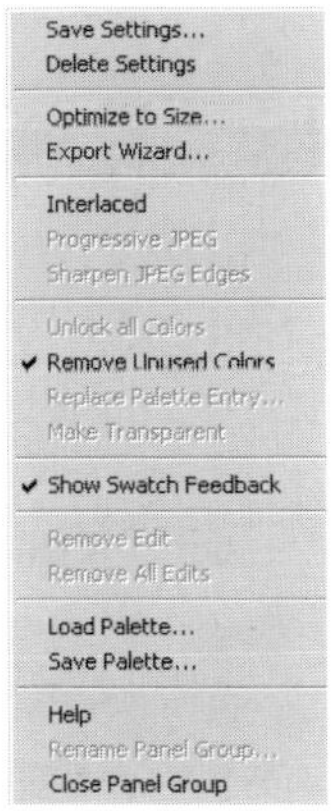

Previewing a Slice

Making optimization choices in Fireworks takes away the guesswork when you use the different preview methods available to you. You can see the changes each setting (such as GIF or JPEG) will make on the file size and the appearance of the image. The preview displays how your image will look in a browser. We will now discuss some of the options you can choose from.

2-Up and 4-Up

In the Document window you will see a 2-Up and 4-Up tab. These options are used for viewing the effects of the optimization you are applying to an image or slice. The 2-Up tab shows you the original image and another one alongside it with optimization settings you have selected.

The tab that is most useful is the 4-Up tab, which allows you to view the original image and three images, each with different optimization settings, at the same time. To change the optimization, select the pane you want to change, and change the setting in the Optimize panel. You can make different choices for each of the three views, and you will be able to see all of the results at the same time. In addition, if you look at the bottom of each view, you can see the file type, the quality (or dither and colors for GIF), the file size, and the approximate time that will be required to load the image in a browser. In addition, you can view GIF and JPEG files at the same time (both in one of the three views) if you desire.

Figure 10.11 shows the 4-Up view. First you will see the original (top left), then a JPEG at 80 percent (top right), a JPEG at 40 percent (bottom left), and a GIF with 128 colors (bottom right). The JPEG at 40 percent is considerably smaller in file size, but you can see some artifacts. Notice that the GIF didn't do well at all and the file size is much larger. You can see this image in the Color section of this book.

Export Preview

You may prefer to use Export Preview (File → Export Preview). In Figure 10.12, we have selected the 4-Up view option and zoomed in a bit. As you can see, the viewing area is much smaller, but you do have the same settings available as in the Optimize panel, as well as a few from the Optimize Options pop-up menu.

Figure 10.10

Additional optimization options available from the Optimize Options pop-up menu

Figure 10.11

The 4-Up view comparing JPEG and GIF optimization settings

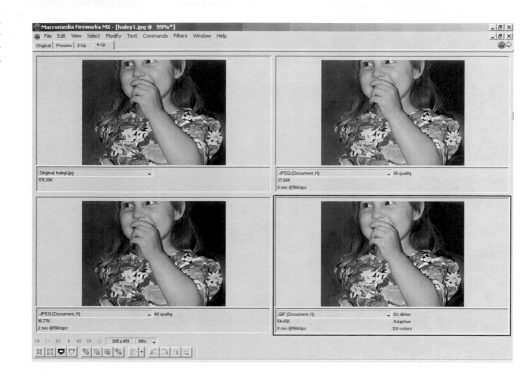

You'll notice that there are a few other options as well, such as the File tab (see Figure 10.13), which allows you to scale your image, and the Animation tab (see Figure 10.14), which allows you to make a few changes to the timing and looping of an animation.

One other option that is available is Optimize to Size. Figure 10.15, which shows the Optimize to Size dialog box, has an arrow pointing to the Optimize to Size icon in the Export Preview dialog box. Here you can type in the maximum file size you want your image to be and it will be optimized accordingly.

Optimizing for GIF Compression

There are quite a few choices you have to make when you are exporting GIF images. Some of the reasons why you might choose GIF over another format are that you want transparency in an image (in which case you have to use GIF compression) or you want to be able to reduce specific colors to lower the file size. This section will detail each of the options you have when you use a GIF compression scheme.

Export File Format

In the Optimization panel, just below Settings, is the Export File Format field. This is simply a menu list (Figure 10.16) of the different formats that Fireworks can export. The three you'll use most often are listed first: GIF, Animated GIF, and JPEG. To see the GIF options that will be discussed in this section, select GIF from this menu.

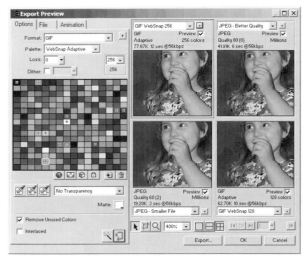

Figure 10.12

The Export Preview dialog box

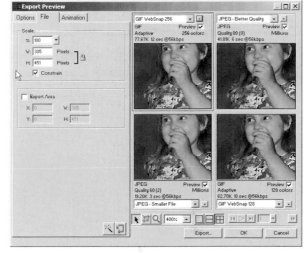

Figure 10.13

The File tab in the Export Preview dialog box

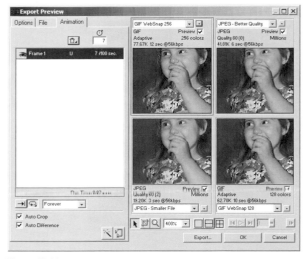

Figure 10.14

The Animation tab in the Export Preview dialog box

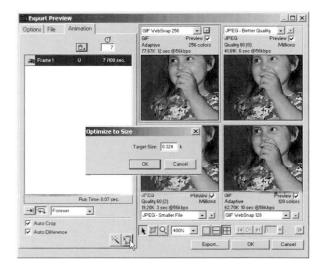

Figure 10.15

The Optimize to Size icon and dialog box

The Indexed Palette

There are nine preset color palettes that can be accessed from the Indexed Palette drop-down menu; each palette makes a different palette of colors available. In addition, you can also customize your own palette and save it with a unique name. Let's look at these palette options.

Figure 10.16

The file formats that can be exported from Fireworks

The WebSnap Adaptive palette This is the default palette for indexed color in Fireworks. Any color that is not web safe will be automatically evaluated and snapped to the closest web safe color, plus or minus seven values. Though this doesn't guarantee that all the colors will be web safe, it does get them close.

If having your images in all web safe colors is important to you, you can use the Find and Replace feature to locate any color that is not web safe and change it.

Adaptive palette This palette allows for a maximum of 256 colors. These 256 colors are not a preset color set, but instead, they are the best 256 colors for your image determined by Fireworks. This palette may contain a mixture of web safe and non–web safe colors.

Web 216 palette This palette converts all colors in the image to their nearest web safe color counterpart.

Exact palette This palette uses the Adaptive palette to automatically find only the exact colors (from the Adaptive Palette) used in the image.

Macintosh palette This palette limits the colors to only those used in the Macintosh operating system.

Windows palette This palette limits the colors to only those used in the Windows operating system.

Grayscale palette This palette uses a range of 256 grayscale values.

Black and White palette This palette uses just those two colors.

Uniform palette This is a mathematical palette based on RGB (red, green, blue) pixel values.

Custom palette This option allows you to use a palette saved from Fireworks or Photoshop.

In the following section, you will begin to look at some of the color and transparency options you have when optimizing a GIF image.

Using the Matte Option

On the right side of the Optimize panel you will see the word Matte. You can probably tell by looking at it that it's a color box; the gray and white checks indicate that it is set to transparent by default. The Matte option allows you to export your image/slice as if it had a background color without changing the canvas background color. This option is particularly important if you want to use the exported image in an environment that is different from the one it was designed in or if the image is going to be used on a variety of different colored backgrounds.

By setting the matte color to that of the destination background, you will eliminate the "halo" effect that is present when you use an image from a different background. You have probably seen countless images with white remnants around the edges that have been placed on a dark background, right? This is what we mean by the halo. You will also get the halo effect when you are using an image that originally had effects such as drop shadows. By setting the matte color to the color of the destination canvas, the "halo" will be the color of the canvas and not so noticeable.

To choose a matte color, simply click the Matte color box and select a color or type in a hexadecimal number and then press Enter (Return for a Mac).

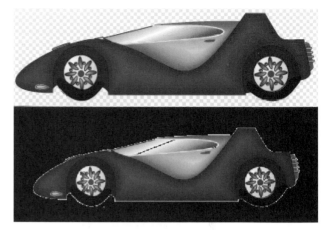

Figure 10.17

The car (top) was exported with the default of a transparent matte resulting in a halo effect around the car (bottom) when placed on a dark background.

> If your image is going to be used on different colored backgrounds, export the image multiple times, changing the matte color for each.

In Figure 10.17 you see a car. On the left it is on a transparent canvas. When it was exported and placed on a black background (on the right) a halo or fringe appeared. Then we exported it without a matte color. Figure 10.18 shows the same image; the only difference is that we exported it using a matte color of black.

> Other settings were used for this export, such as Index Transparency. This option and others are discussed in the following sections.

Colors

You can reduce the size of your image file by reducing the amount of colors used. To do so, choose a number from the Maximum Number of Colors pop-up menu. You can also reduce colors by using the Color table, which is discussed in detail in "The Color Table" section of this chapter.

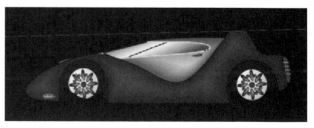

Figure 10.18

The same car exported with the exact same settings except that the matte color was changed to black prior to exporting

> If you choose a color amount from the Maximum Number of Colors pop-up and the number is less than is actually present in your image, Fireworks will delete colors based on the least used colors in the image.

Dithering

Dithering repositions colors to try and simulate colors that don't exist in an image. This gives the illusion of new colors by varying the pattern of dots of color. The best way to demonstrate dithering is to look at a series of images. We will use a sample image of a car that was drawn in FreeHand 10 using gradients and Contour gradients. To maintain image quality, this image would be best exported as a JPEG. But if you needed to have the background transparent, then you would have to export it as a GIF. Let's take a look at how this image will look as a GIF (see Figure 10.19).

The image on the top left is the original copy of the car as a JPEG. (Be sure to check the Color Section of this book to get a better look at these images.) The second image, the one on the top right, is optimized as a GIF with 128 colors; notice the severe banding that results. The image on the bottom left is still using the GIF 128 setting, but the dither has been increased to 100 percent. And finally, the image on the bottom right is just a blown-up version of the one on the bottom left so that you can see the effect better.

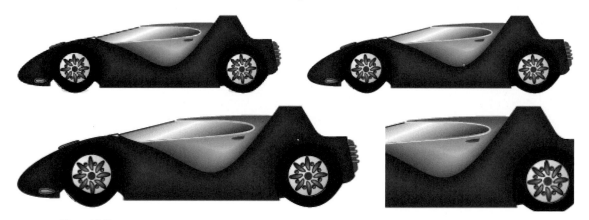

Figure 10.19

The results of dithering

Use the smallest amount of dithering you can. For this image, even 50 percent didn't help it. But for many images you can reduce the dithering.

To compare the differences in file size and quality, take a look at Figure 10.20, which shows the 4-Up view. The first image on the top left is the original; the top right is the GIF and 128 color settings (notice that the file size is 9.57KB). The image below it has the 100 percent dither applied. The file size increased to 10.99KB, which isn't too bad considering the huge difference in appearance.

Please refer to the Color section of this book for a better look at these images.

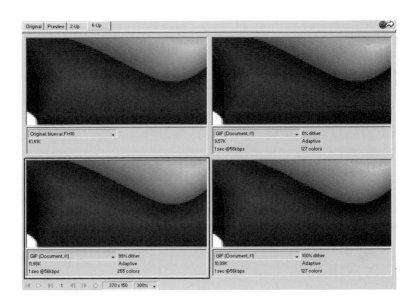

Figure 10.20

The 4-Up view comparing file sizes

Lossy Gif Compression

GIF images normally suffer no degradation of image detail because lossless compression is usually used. But if you'd like to make the file size even smaller, you can choose to use a lossy compression. To do so, choose your compression amount from the field named Loss. But be aware that though your file size may be smaller, it will most likely be distorted—the higher the loss setting the higher the distortion.

Interlacing

Interlacing is an option for GIF files that you are exporting for use on the Web. You can access this option from either the Export Preview or Optimize Options pop-up menu. When a file is interlaced it appears "blockie" or blurry until it loads, so the user sees a blurred copy while the image is loading. If you don't interlace the object, the user won't see anything until the entire image loads.

Transparency

In the Optimize panel, you can see that there are three choices for transparency: No Transparency, Index Transparency, and Alpha Transparency. No Transparency is pretty self-explanatory. When chosen, Index Transparency will make the background color transparent, as well as anything else in your image that is the same color. For instance, if you have a white background and white text, both the background and the text will be transparent. Alpha Transparency will make just the background color transparent.

Test these options for yourself by using these steps:

1. Open a new document that is 200 × 200 pixels and has a white background.

2. Select the Rectangle tool and draw a rectangle.

3. Click the Color box in the Color section of the Tools panel to fill the rectangle with Black.

4. Draw another smaller rectangle in the center of the black rectangle and fill it with White.

5. Click the Preview tab in the Document window.

6. In the Optimize panel, choose Index Transparency. Notice that the white background and the white square are both transparent.

7. Now, while still in the Preview tab, select Alpha Transparency. See how the white square comes back and the background remains transparent?

There is even more control in the Transparency section. For instance, notice the little eyedropper icons below the Transparency options. Figure 10.21 shows the name of the icons. By clicking the Add Color to Transparency icon, you can choose to add colors in addition to the background color that you want to be transparent. By choosing the Remove Color from Transparency icon, you can remove colors you have previously chosen to be transparent. The last choice is the Select Transparent Color; this allows you to choose a color other than the background color to be transparent.

The Color Table

The color table is available for images that are using the Index palette, such as GIF. If you make a change to the optimization settings for your image or you simply don't see a color table, just click the Rebuild button in the lower-right corner. An updated table of colors will be displayed.

Figure 10.21

The Eyedropper tools used to add, delete, and select transparency colors

The Rebuild button is only visible if the colors in the color table don't reflect the most current settings you've chosen.

Select Transparent Color
Remove Color from Transparency
Add Color to Transparency

When you use the color table, you have greater control over which colors get eliminated. You can lock specific colors so that they don't change, you can have colors be shifted automatically to web safe colors, or you can change any color to a different one. With these kinds of options, you can better control which colors are to be included in your color palette for each individual image.

To make any alterations to the colors in your image, just click a color to select it or Shift-click to select multiple colors, and then change the color, delete it, snap it to a web safe color, or lock it. Figure 10.22 shows the labeled icons, which allow you to make these changes. Figure 10.23 shows the swatch feedback of the status of each color.

GIF Animation

GIF files have the added benefit of being able to be used as animations. An animated GIF file contains frames with different images that are all contained in one GIF animation. If you lay out your web pages in an HTML editor such as Dreamweaver, the GIF animation is added just like any other image file, so no special treatment is required.

You optimize a GIF Animation just like any other GIF image—the same options are available.

Be sure that you don't forget to set the optimization of a GIF Animation prior to exporting it. If you forget and leave it as a GIF, the animation will not work.

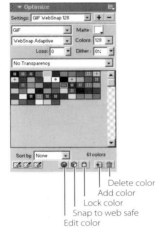

Figure 10.22

Icons in the Optimize panel that allow you to control the colors

Optimizing Options for JPEG Compression

JPEG compression is best used on images such as photographs and gradients. There are a lot fewer options in the Optimize panel for JPEG compression than there were for GIF compression, as you can see in Figure 10.24.

The JPEG format uses *lossy compression*, which means that information is removed from the image. JPEGs are compressed and decompressed when viewed in a browser, which can result in a longer loading time. You have control over quality settings in the Optimize panel; the higher the quality, the less compression.

Here are descriptions of the options that are available.

Matte Here you set the background color of your image. There is no transparency in a JPEG image, so there will always be a background color. The default is white. Click in the color box and use the Eyedropper tool to select another color. You can select a color from the image itself if you'd like.

Smoothing When you lower the quality setting, you may see visible artifacts depending on how low you went. The Smooth option adds a bit of blur to blend the image a bit. You will loose some image sharpness, but it may be a compromise you are willing to make when small file size is a must. The Smooth setting ranges from 0 to 8 with 8 being the highest degree of blur.

Sharpen JPEG Edges The JPEG compression works best on photographs and gradients. But you may have incorporated areas of text or other vector objects with a lot of flat color areas. These areas don't do well with JPEG compression. The Sharpen JPEG command helps alleviate the problem; it is applied only to the flat areas of color, not to the photograph itself. To apply Sharpen JPEG Edges, select it from the Optimize Options pop-up menu.

Figure 10.23

The swatch feedback icons and what they mean

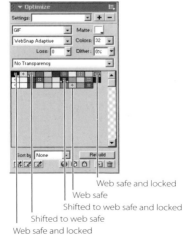

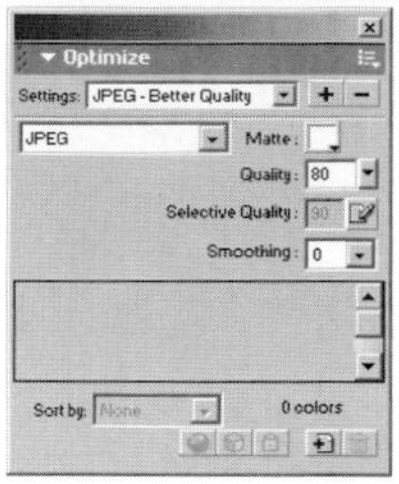

Figure 10.24

The Optimize panel with the JPEG file format selected

Progressive JPEG The Progressive option is similar to GIF interlacing. When the image is loading, it first appears blocky but then it gradually clears as it finishes loading. The drawback is that it is not supported by older browsers (before Netscape 2 and IE 3) and it shows a broken image. If you'd like to use Progressive JPEG, you can access this option from the Optimization Options pop-up menu.

Quality The Quality setting determines how much compression is added to your image. Use the preview options such as the 4-Up tab to view different compression amounts to determine what amount is best for you.

Don't JPEG a JPEG image. It will lose info each time and get considerably worse after the second time. JPEG is good for 24-bit color depth, no less.

Optimizing a JPEG Image

Now that you know what your options are for exporting a JPEG image, you are ready to try them out. For this exercise, we will use a copy of the blue car that you saw earlier in this chapter. It's saved as `car.png` in the Chapter 10 folder on the accompanying CD. This image hasn't been compressed yet, so it's still a PNG file.

1. Open `car.png` from the Chapter 10 folder on the accompanying CD.

2. Select the car, right-click (Ctrl-click on a Mac), and choose Insert Slice.

3. Click the 4-Up tab to view different settings, and click the first image to the right of the original to select it.

4. In the Optimize panel, choose JPEG from the Export File Format area.

5. Click the second image (the one below the original) and apply a quality of 50 percent. You may want to zoom in a bit to see the artifacts that are present.

6. Click the last image and apply a Smoothing of 3. Notice how much better the artifacts look (Figure 10.25). It doesn't look too bad at all. Also note that the file size of this sample is smaller.

To view just the last image with the smoothing to see if it's acceptable in a browser, select it, and then use the arrow in the top-right corner of the Document window and select Preview in Browser.

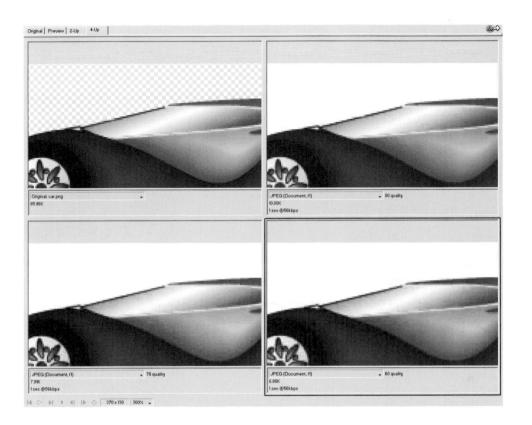

7. Access the Optimize Options pop-up menu and choose Progressive JPEG if you want to see the image gradually load in a browser.

   From the Optimize Options pop-up menu, choose Sharpen JPEG Edges if you have text on an image background or a gradient background.

   Your image is now ready to export. You'll learn how to export later in this chapter.

Selective JPEG Compression

Now that you know how to optimize your images, it's time to look at a feature that was new to Fireworks 4, the Selective JPEG Compression. As you know, you can export images for the Web in GIF and in JPEG format. Well, let's say you have an image with a gradient background. As you know, a gradient is best exported as a JPEG image. Because it's an image background, you will want to keep the file size down, so you decide to export at somewhere

Figure 10.26

This image has a quality of 80, which is fine for the background but results in artifacts around the text and buttons.

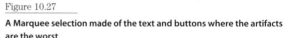

Figure 10.27

A Marquee selection made of the text and buttons where the artifacts are the worst

between 70 and 80 percent; the idea is to use the lowest possible setting while still having an acceptable look. If you have text on this gradient, it may appear blocky or blurred (as shown in Figure 10.26). This occurs when there is too much JPEG compression applied. You can now apply higher quality compression to specific areas, such as the text.

Selective JPEG Compression works in Fireworks by using a mask, but there can only be one mask per document. So if you have a large image that you are slicing up, you can apply Selective JPEG Compression to separate areas of the document, regardless of which slice an area that needs to be better optimized happens to be in. To try it out for yourself, follow these steps:

1. Open the `SelectiveSample.png` file from the Chapter 10 folder on the accompanying CD.

2. In the Optimize panel, choose JPEG and a quality setting of 80 percent. Click the Preview tab. Figure 10.26 shows the result. Click the Original tab before you go to the next step.

3. The artifacts are around the text and buttons only because they are flat areas of color. You can fix these areas by adding a higher Quality setting to them. Do so by clicking the Lasso or Marquee selection tool. Then draw around the area you would like compressed at a higher quality setting. If there is more than one area, then press the Shift key and make your next selection (Figure 10.27).

If you have more than one area to use selective compression on, you must select them all now or you will have to go and begin the edit again. This is because these selections are going to become a JPG mask and there can only be one of those per document.

Figure 10.28

The selection made into a JPEG mask denoted by an overlay of color

Figure 10.29

The quality setting of 90 is added to the selected area, which effectively removed the artifacts.

4. From the menu choose Modify → Selective JPEG → Save Selection as JPEG Mask. You will see an overlay over the selected area (shown in Figure 10.28).

    The Selective Quality option will now be visible in the Optimize panel.

5. Change the view back to Preview.

6. Use the slider to select the quality amount you want. We used a Quality level of 90 for this example. As you can see in Figure 10.29, it takes care of the artifacts around the text and the buttons.

> If you need to try another quality setting, simply change the number in the Selective Quality box in the Optimize panel.

To edit the JPEG mask, you can either delete the mask or start over by choosing Modify → Selective JPEG → Remove JPEG Mask. If you want to simply add to or subtract from the current mask, choose Modify → Selective JPEG → Restore JPEG Mask as Selection. With the Selection active, you can use the Shift key and a selection tool to draw another area or add on or take away from the selection.

Exporting with Fireworks

Before you begin exporting, it's important that you already have your site structure set up. If you set up your folders locally the same way they will be uploaded to a server, it will save you many headaches. If you are using Dreamweaver, and you save in one folder and then move the file, all of your images and links will be broken. For this reason it's better to save in the same folder the file will ultimately be in.

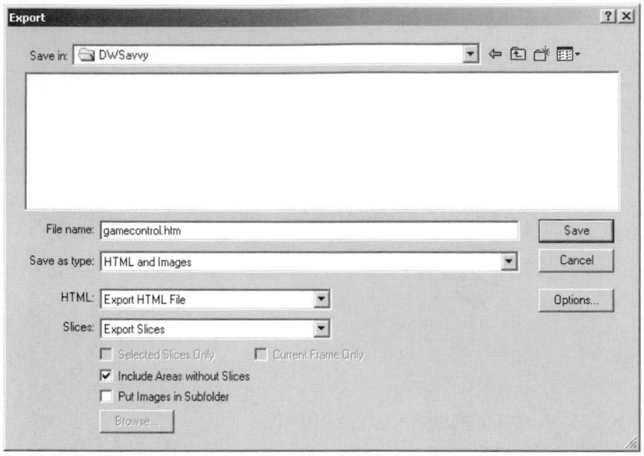

A Fireworks exported document will contain slices and the HTML file that contains the table that will be used to put all the slices back together. If you plan on inserting Fireworks code into a Dreamweaver document, you'll need to save the Fireworks file in the same folder as the Dreamweaver file you will insert the Fireworks code into; if you don't, all the links to your images will be broken.

You can also export Fireworks images that will be compatible with other programs such as Adobe Photoshop and Illustrator as well as Macromedia applications such as Flash and Director and of course, Dreamweaver.

Figure 10.30

The Export dialog box showing the options for the HTML and Images Type

Exporting Fireworks Files

There are many ways to export a Fireworks document. You'll see the basic exporting steps in this section, and then we'll look at the specifics for different types of export in the following sections of this chapter. Figure 10.30 shows the Export dialog box with HTML and Images selected for the Type.

The following steps will walk you through the different settings and options in the Export dialog box.

1. Set the optimization settings you want for your image, slice, and/or document.

2. From the Menu bar, choose File → Export.

3. If your file contains image maps or buttons with rollovers, or you want Fireworks to generate all the code and images, choose HTML and Images from the Save as Type drop-down menu. The HTML and Images option gives you the following Slice choices:

   Export Slices The default. Your slices will be exported as well as any code that is attached to them.

   None Exports as one image (no slices).

   Slice along Guides Doesn't export any JavaScript code used for image maps or rollovers.

   Put Images in Subfolder Gives you the option of separating your images from the HTML file in their own separate folder.

4. If you want to export the images only, then choose Images Only from the Save as Type drop-down menu. The Slices area has the same options available as in step 4.

   For Images Only you can also choose Selected Slices Only and/or the Include Areas without Slices option. There is no option for an Images subfolder because you'd navigate to the proper folder to export into.

5. When you are done choosing your export options, click Save.

> If you select a slice to export or Shift + Select multiple slices to export, the Export Selected
> Slices Only option is not set by default, so be sure to select it.

Using HTML Setup during Export

You may have noticed an Options button when you were checking out the Export dialog box.
If you clicked that button, the HTML Setup dialog box would open. We will now explore the
tabs of this dialog box.

> You can access the same options by choosing File → HTML Setup.

General Tab

Figure 10.31 shows the General tab of the HTML Setup dialog box.

The General tab is where you choose the application you will be using the code in. Your
options are Dreamweaver HTML, FrontPage HTML, Generic HTML, and GoLive HTML.
Choose the file extension name of your choice. The last two options let you choose whether
to include HTML comments and whether or not to use all lowercase letters in the filename.

The Table Tab

You can see the contents of the Table tab in Figure 10.32. In the Space With category, you
can chose between several options, but the most often used option is 1-Pixel Transparent
Spacer. If you choose this option, when you export, you will notice a file called `spacer.gif`.
This is a 1 pixel by 1 pixel transparent file that is used as a spacer to keep a table's integrity.
In some browsers, if there isn't content in every cell, the table will collapse. Fireworks solves
that problem by inserting such a spacer image in all of the empty cells of the table.

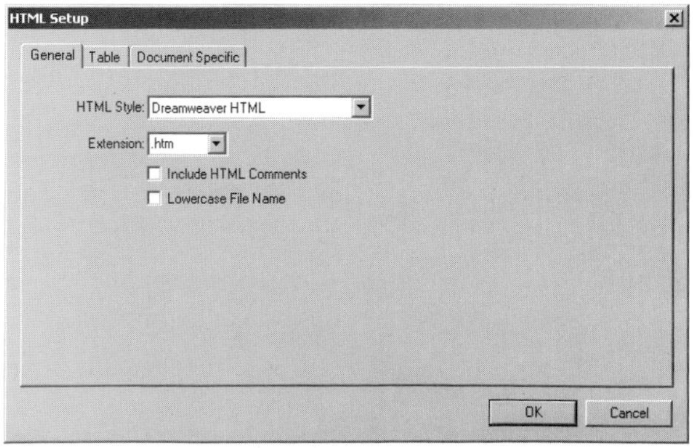

The other options for Space With include Nested
Tables-No Spacers, which places one table into another
table, or Single Table-No Spacers. If your table has an
image in every cell, then Single Table-No Spacers will
work just fine. Be sure to check this method with all the
current browsers to be sure that you get the results you
are expecting.

In the Empty Cells section of this tab is a Contents
field that gives you the option of using a Non-Breaking
Space instead of the Spacer Image; but if you do, be sure
to test your choice in all the current browsers.

Figure 10.31

The General tab

Document Specific Tab

The Document Specific tab (Figure 10.33) is where you go to change the default autonaming of your slices for the current document. You can, of course, override the automatic naming of the slices by naming them individually in the Property Inspector, but you should know how to do it this way too.

The fields you see filled out in the Document Specific tab are the values being used for the autonaming of your slices. Autonaming uses the root name of your document plus the row number and column number. With auto-naming, a file called SelectiveSample would be named `SelectiveSample_r2_c4.gif`, but you can set up a default naming system any way you'd like. For instance, you could use the word "slice" instead of the root name of the file; if you did, your filename would be `slice_r2_c4.gif`.

The down arrows in each category give you some options to choose from. The second row of options is None by default. You can get some pretty long filenames if you really wanted to. The Frames options are for naming exported frames. One of the export options is to export Frames to Files.

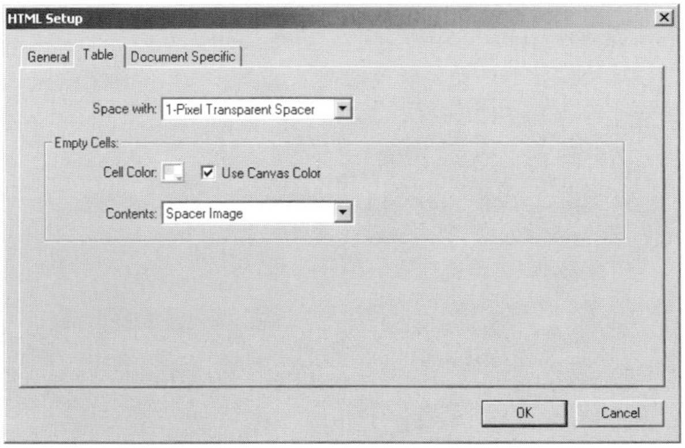

You can also enter an Alternate Image Description in this dialog box. Don't confuse this option with the Alt Tag description found in the Property Inspector. The Alternate Image Description in this tab is used primarily for documents that don't use slices. Alternate tags are what is displayed while an image is downloading all of its various slices or when a mouse cursor passes over the image

If you are exporting a nav bar that you want to generate separate HTML pages, be sure to check the Multiple Nav Bar HTML Pages option. Include Areas without Slices is the default setting. Uncheck it if you'd like it not to be the default. Check UTF-8 Coding if you want it.

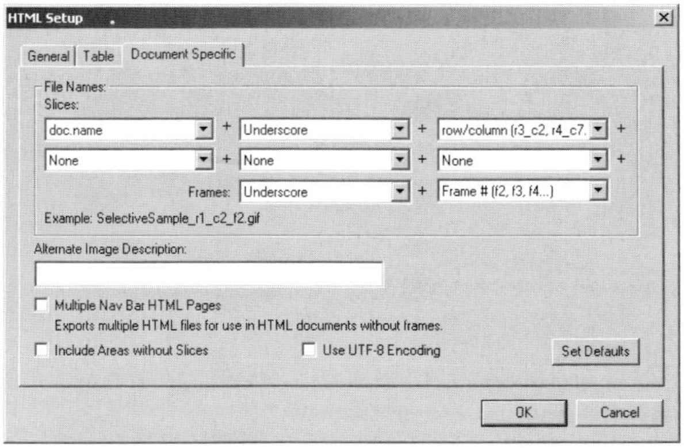

Figure 10.32

The Table tab contents of the HTML Setup dialog box

Figure 10.33

The Document Specific tab with the naming parameters

UTF-8 Coding stands for Universal Character Set Transformation Format. It's an encoding method that allows web browsers to display different character sets on the same HTML page.

When you are done setting up your filename autonaming feature and you have finished entering in an Alternate Image Description, click the Set Defaults button to save.

Exporting Images Only

There are many times when you will design images in Fireworks that you will place in an existing HTML page. Or you may want to place the images into the HTML code yourself. If you use Dreamweaver, it is very easy to do this by simply selecting Insert → Image and browsing to the image you want to place—without ever writing a bit of code. But then there are those of you who wouldn't think of letting a program handle your code; you will want complete control over how your image is coded into the web page. Whatever your reason, Fireworks makes it quite easy to export just one image slice or multiple image slices.

To export images only, follow these steps:

1. Select an image or Shift + Select multiple images you want to export.

2. Choose File → Export and name your file.

3. Click the down arrow in the Save as Type area and choose Images Only.

4. In the Slices area, choose Export Slices.

5. Check the Selected Slices Only option and uncheck the Include Areas without Slices option.

6. Once you've navigated to the folder you want to export into, click Save to complete the export.

Exporting to Macromedia Flash

Exporting to SWF (Flash file format) is becoming more popular with each passing day. It wasn't too long ago that GIF was still the animation option of choice, primarily because the user didn't need to download a separate plugin to see a GIF like they needed to do for a SWF (Flash) file. But based on a recent survey, 96.4 percent of all web users already have the Flash player downloaded, and many more websites are featuring Flash animations instead of GIF. SWF or Flash animation's greatest appeal is not only the tremendous flexibility in design capabilities, but also the small file sizes because Flash is vector based.

You will be amazed at the integration built in between Fireworks and Flash. You can export a Fireworks image or a native Fireworks PNG file as a Flash SWF file. You can also choose to import as either a PNG file or a SWF file, as well as edit bitmaps right from Flash. You can choose to import editable objects—such as text, guides, and images. You can choose to flatten the image; a flattened image is brought into Flash automatically as a bitmap symbol and is then inserted into the Flash Library panel.

To export as Flash SWF, follow these steps:

1. Choose File → Export.

2. In the Save as Type area, select Macromedia Flash SWF.

3. Click the Options button to set your export options. Figure 10.34 shows the Macromedia Flash SWF Export Options dialog box.

4. Choose the options you'd like in the Objects area. Choose Maintain Paths if you want to convert paths into editable Flash paths, or choose Maintain Appearance if you want to convert paths into a bitmapped image.

5. Now choose the Text options. Maintain Editabiltiy will convert Fireworks text into text that is editable in Flash, and Convert to Path will convert the text into a bitmap.

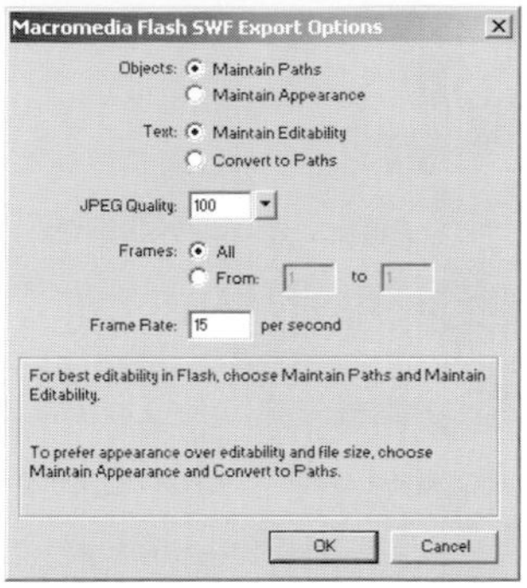

Figure 10.34

The Macromedia Flash SWF Export Options dialog box

6. If you are exporting a JPEG image, select the quality setting you'd like.

7. Then click the All radio button to select all frames or click the From radio button to choose just the frames you want to export.

8. The last option involves setting the Frame Rate per Second. Type a number in the text box.

9. When you are done with your selections, choose OK and then choose Save in the Export dialog box.

SWF exports from Fireworks can be used as they are for web viewing, or they can be inserted into Dreamweaver or another layout editor without even using Flash. But the real purpose of being able to export as a Macromedia Flash SWF file is to be able to reuse the artwork you made in Fireworks in Flash. The term Macromedia uses to describe Fireworks is "a specialized delivery editor."

Vector content will remain vector in Flash, but you should be aware that many actions you can take in Fireworks would be lost when exported for use in Flash. Some of the things lost include Live Effects, Opacity (objects with opacity become symbols with an alpha channel), and blending modes. Masks, slice objects, image maps, and behaviors such as rollovers are lost as well. Other features that are lost include feathering, layers, and some text formatting. Anti-Aliasing will not be maintained on export either, but that won't present you with any problems. The reason Anti-Aliasing it isn't exported is that Flash automatically applies it to documents itself. If you keep in mind that the main reason for using a SWF export from Fireworks is to reuse the art, then you will do fine with few frustrations.

Exporting to Photoshop

If you want to open your Fireworks PNG files in Photoshop, or if someone you send your files to needs or wants to use Photoshop, you can export a Fireworks file as a PSD file. When you export as a PSD, you have the option of exporting with better editability over appearance or better appearance over editability. As you ponder this decision, keep in mind that Fireworks paths will always be converted to bitmap images.

To export for Photoshop, follow these steps:

1. Choose File → Export.

2. From the Save as Type area, select Photoshop PSD.

3. In the Settings area you have four options (see Figure 10.35):

Maintain Editability over Appearance Converts objects to layers, makes deep effects editable, and converts text into editable text. Effects that don't have an equivalent in Photoshop will be discarded.

Maintain Fireworks Appearance Converts object into layers and renders the effects and text into an image.

Smaller Photoshop File Flattens all the objects and layers into one layer, thus producing a smaller file size.

Custom Allows you to select separate setting options for Objects, Effects, and Text. For Objects, you can choose to keep the objects in separate layers or to flatten them into one image. The Effects and Text options give you the choice to maintain Editability or to Render. If you choose Editability, then you or whoever opens the file needs to have the same font or they can choose to change the font. If you choose Render, then the text is converted into a bitmap image.

4. When you are done making your selections, click Save to export.

Exporting or Copying as Vectors (Illustrator AI)

Using Fireworks vector objects in FreeHand, Illustrator, or Flash allows you to use the basic path, fill, and stroke information only. If you want to use the vector shape, this option is viable. If you want to maintain the look of the object (effects added), it is a better idea to produce it in the program you want to use it in.

When you export as a vector object from Fireworks, you will lose all effects, feathering, dither, fills, slices, guides, and most text formatting and blending modes.

If you still want to export a vector shape for FreeHand, Illustrator, or Flash, follow these steps:

1. Choose File → Export.

2. In the Save as Type area, choose Illustrator 7. Once you choose Illustrator 7 the Options button in the Export dialog box appears (shown in Figure 10.36).

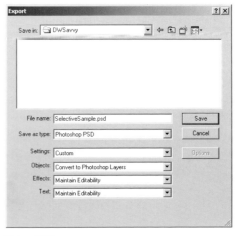

Figure 10.35

The Export dialog box when Photoshop PSD is selected as the export type

3. If you want to keep the elements on individual layers, then select Export Current Frame Only. If you want each frame on a separate layer, then select the Convert Frames to Layers option.

4. To make the export completely for FreeHand, check the FreeHand Compatible check box. Be aware that by checking this box, you will lose bitmap images, but gradients in FreeHand 10 are not lost.

5. When you are finished, click OK.

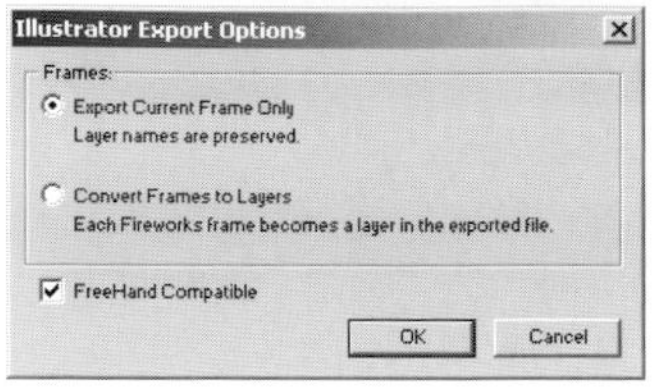

Figure 10.36

The Export dialog box appears after you choose the Illustrator 7 export option and the Options button.

Exporting to Dreamweaver Library

You can export an HTML file with HTML code included as a Dreamweaver Library item (the Pop-Up Menu is an exception). Before you export as a Dreamweaver Library item, you will need to define a local site root folder in Dreamweaver and make a folder called Library (use a capital L). This folder is where you export the Library item. You'll need to do this each time you export a Dreamweaver Library into a new site. This step isn't necessary if you already have a Library folder in the root folder of the target site.

To export as a Dreamweaver Library item, follow these steps:

1. Choose File → Export.

2. In the Save as Type area, click the down arrow and choose Dreamweaver Library.

3. Locate the Library folder to which you want to export.

4. If you want the images put into an image subfolder, check the Put Images in Subfolder option and click Save to export.

Exporting to CSS Layers

By exporting to CSS Layers you can produce style sheets that define how different elements appear on your web page. Cascading style sheets (CSS) is usually used by more experienced users who want to have more control than they get by simply using HTML code. By using CSS layers, they can overlap and stack layers on top of one another, which they can't do with normal Fireworks HTML output.

To export to CSS Layers, follow these steps:

1. When you have your document elements on layers, frames, and/or slices, choose File → Export.

2. In the Save as Type area, choose CSS Layers. Figure 10.37 shows the options that become available once you choose CSS Layers.

3. In the Source area choose how to separate the elements. The choices are Fireworks Slices, Fireworks Layers, or Fireworks Frames.

4. Check the Trim Images check box if you want to discard excess canvas around the images.

5. If you want the exported images in a subfolder, then check the Put Images in Subfolder option.

6. Click Save to export.

Exporting Layers and Frames as Separate Images

You can export all the layers or all the frames of a Fireworks document. Each layer and each frame will export as a separate image. Figure 10.38 shows the Export dialog box when Layers to Files is selected.

To export layers or frames as separate images, follow these steps:

1. Choose File → Export

2. From the Save as Type area, click the down arrow and make your selections—Layers to Files or Frames to Files. You can only export one option at a time, so if you want both layers and frames, you will have to do another export.

3. Check the Trim Images option if you want to automatically trim the images to fit the objects on each layer (or frame). If you want to keep the layer or frame the same size as the document, then uncheck the Trim Images option.

4. When you are finished, navigate to the folder you want to export into and click Save.

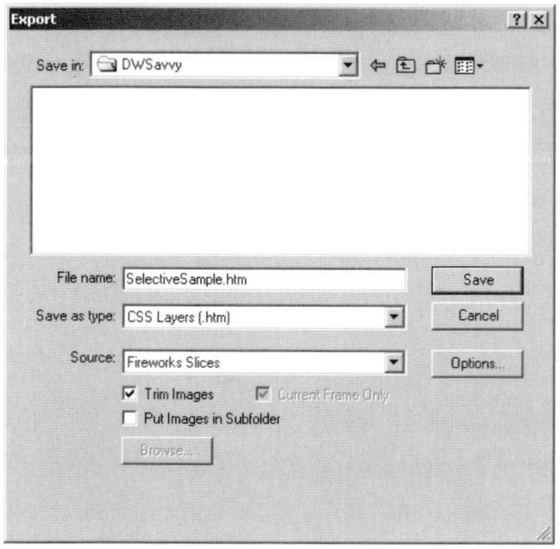

Figure 10.37

The CSS Layer options

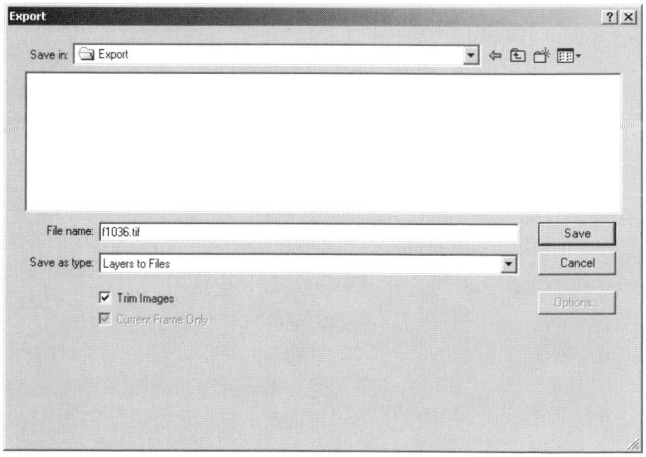

Figure 10.38

The Export dialog box with Layers to Files selected

Exporting an Area or Scaling an Image

In Fireworks, you don't even have to export an entire slice or image. You have the option of exporting just a selected part of an image or document, as well as cropping or scaling an image. When you use the Export Area tool or scale or crop an image, you don't alter the original image—just the exported one.

Using the Export Area Tool

There are times when you may want to export only portions of a document for use in a web page. Or you may want to export part of an image to which you want to assign specialized behaviors in an HTML editor. The Export Area tool is used to define the specific area of a document or image you want to export.

> The Export Area tool is in the pop-up attached to the Crop tool. Click and hold the arrow in the corner of the Pointer tool icon and select the little camera icon to access the Export Area tool.

To export just portions of a document or an image, follow these steps:

1. Select the Export Area tool.
2. Click and drag a Marquee around the portion you want to export.
3. Click and drag the square handles to adjust the selection.
4. Export in one of two ways. You can choose File → Export, name your image, select Images Only in the Save as Type area, and save your image. Or, for more control, you can double-click inside the Export Area Marquee that surrounds the image you want to export. The Export Preview dialog box appears. Here you can control the size of the image area and the optimization settings. When you are finished making your choices, click the Export button. This will bring up the same Save dialog box that you get by using the first option; name your file and click Save.

Using the Export Area Tool with Slices

You can use the Export Area tool in a document that also contains slices. When you select an area to export with the Export Area tool, either option of export (double-clicking inside the image or exporting from the File menu) will give you a warning—when you click the Export or the Save buttons, it will say "Slice objects will be ignored. To get sliced output and behaviors, choose Export Slices." If you want to export the slices, use another export method. The Export Area tool will only export the selected area.

Hands On: Slicing, Optimizing, and Exporting a Web Page

In this tutorial, you will slice a web page, optimize it, and export it. The content of this tutorial is copyrighted, but you can use it to practice on.

Slicing the Web Page

To begin the process, follow these steps.

1. Open the `tutorial.png` file from the Chapter 10 folder on the accompanying CD.

2. Select the Slice tool and make slices as seen in Figure 10.39. The rectangle slice works fine for this whole page.

> The only area you should not slice separately is the list of buttons in the top-right corner and the four image icon labels because they are button symbols with the slices automatically made.

The slices are as follows:

- Contact

- Advertise

- Blank center rectangle—draw a rectangle inside the white lines, and then make a slice of each top line and each side line. Refer to `tutorial2.png` if you need to.

- Four bottom image labels

- Copyright line

- Blank area in the right bottom corner (slice the same way as you did the center blank area)

You can skip the slicing if you want. Just open the `tutorial2.png` file, which has the slices already made.

Figure 10.39

The web page with slices added

Optimizing the Page

Now that the web page is sliced, start the optimizing process by following these steps.

1. Open the Optimize panel, select the Contact slice, and Shift + Select the Advertise slice and the Copyright line. Since this is flat color, choose the following settings:

> Export File Format: **GIF**
>
> Indexed Palette: **WebSnap Adaptive**
>
> Colors: **4**

Dither: 0

Loss: 0

Transparency: **No Transparency**

2. Select the slice over the horse collage and use the following settings in the Optimize panel:

Export File Format: **JPEG**

Smoothing: **0**

Also, uncheck Sharpen JPEG Edges in the Optimize Options pop-up menu.

3. Shift + Select the top and sides of the two blank areas (white lines with yellow stars). Use the following optimization:

Export File Format: **GIF**

Indexed Palette: **WebSnap Adaptive**

Colors: **8**

Dither: 0

Loss: 0

Transparency: **No Transparency**

4. Select the center slice of the blank area and the center slice from the boxed area in the right corner. In the Property Inspector, change the slice Type to HTML. You'll notice a color change of the slices.

5. Shift + Select the four image icons on the bottom and use the following optimization:

Export File Format: **JPEG**

Smoothing: **0**

Also, uncheck Sharpen JPEG Edges in the Optimize Options pop-up menu.

6. Shift + Select the four image icon labels. Use the following optimization settings:

Export File Format: **GIF**

Indexed Palette: **WebSnap Adaptive**

Colors: **16**

Dither: 0

Loss: 0

Transparency: **No Transparency**

When the slices over the labels are exported, there are actually two images in the symbol for a rollover—they will both be exported.

Exporting the Page

You should now be ready to perform the export.

1. Set up the folder you want to export into. Shift + Select all the slices you've optimized so far. That's everything except the links in the top-right corner (white lines with red balls).

2. Choose File → Export using the following settings:

    File Name: Your choice

    Save as Type: **Images Only**

    Slices: **Export Slices**

    Also, check Selected Slices Only, uncheck Include Areas without Slices, and then click Save. That's all there is to exporting all the images except the buttons.

    You could have exported the remaining buttons using the same method as above. The reason they weren't included is because we wanted to demonstrate another technique, which may be useful when you want to export just navigational elements. Here is what you need to do:

1. Marquee-select the remaining buttons (use the Pointer tool to draw a rectangle around all the buttons) and use the following optimization settings:

    Export File Format: **GIF**

    Indexed Palette: **WebSnap Adaptive**

    Colors: **64**

    Dither: **0**

    Loss: **0**

    Transparency: **No Transparency**

    The colors are higher in these buttons because of the gradient in the red ball.

2. Then select the Export Area tool (in the Crop Tool pop-up) and draw a selection around all the buttons.

3. Finally, choose File → Export using the following settings:

    File Name: Your choice

    Save As Type: **Images Only**

    Slices: **Export Slices**

    Then, check Selected Slices Only, uncheck Include Areas without Slices, and click Save.

You are finished exporting an entire web page! Look in the folder you exported to and you'll see all the images, text slices, and rollover images in there.

If you export the page as described in the following sidebar, you can take a look at how it will appear in Dreamweaver in the next chapter.

EXPORTING HTML AND IMAGES

Because you've just finished optimizing all the images for this web page, now would be a good time to try exporting the entire page as a complete web page.

As you prepare to do this, remember that Fireworks doesn't allow you a lot of control over how your tables are formatted. For instance, if you want a fluid design that adjusts your web page to the size of a browser window, you have to code that functionality in Dreamweaver. Fortunately, you can export this entire web page and insert it into a Dreamweaver fluid table.

To export the entire design, follow these steps:

1. Using the same file that you have optimized, choose File → Export and name your file.

2. Choose HTML and Images in the Save as Type field.

3. Choose Export Slices in the Slices field.

4. Click to check Include Areas without Slices.

5. Click to check Put Images in Subfolder.

6. Click Save.

The file is now ready to be placed into a Dreamweaver document.

From Pictures to Pages

In this chapter, you learned the ins and outs of slicing, and you also explored the different file formats that are suitable for the Web. In addition, you learned how to set your optimization settings for the GIF, JPEG, and GIF Animation formats and how to export them all using a variety of export methods.

This chapter concludes the Fireworks section of this book. In Chapter 11, you will begin to lay out a web page in Dreamweaver using tables and layers.

## PART III

Building a Web Page

Finally, we get *to the hands-on, web page design–oriented features of Dreamweaver. With your site set up and your graphical assets gathered, you can start rapidly building the most important pages (such as landing pages for key sections of your site) and then you can really crank on the supporting pages.*

In this part, we show you how to construct web pages out of their component parts. We start with page layout because you have to have some structure in your page design before you can insert text and other elements onto the page. Then we cover the two most common page elements: text and graphics. After a two-chapter digression to cover some more specialized web-page design standards (frames and style sheets), we get to the page element that makes the Web the Web: hyperlinks. This leads neatly into the next part, where we discuss dynamic (interactive) web-page elements.

CHAPTER 11 ■ Page Layout with Tables and Layers

CHAPTER 12 ■ Inserting and Formatting Text Content

CHAPTER 13 ■ Working with Graphics

CHAPTER 14 ■ Interactivity with Framesets and Frames

CHAPTER 15 ■ Cascading Style Sheets

CHAPTER 16 ■ Making and Maintaining Hyperlinks

Page Layout with Tables and Layers

Professionals who design printed material, such as brochures and booklets, expect to be able to position objects anywhere on a page and control spacing precisely. When the Web first appeared without offering that kind of control over the look of a "page," designers couldn't believe it. Then, when popular browsers came out with the ability to render tables exactly, designers regained some degree of precision in placement. With layers, which are still not fully standardized across all popular browsers, designers gain back the lion's share of what they are able to do in print: place images precisely, overlap images, and so on. Still, even today, the rare users who customize their browser's own native style sheet won't see your pages the way you want them to.

This chapter examines the ways you can use tables and layers as page layout tools, including the following:

- **Designing a web page with borderless tables**
- **Using Layout view to draw table cells**
- **Controlling layout by creating layers**
- **Fine-tuning table and layer properties**
- **Creating complex layouts by combining tables and layers**

Selecting a Predesigned Layout

If you're working with tables or layers for the first time, you can save yourself some design time by starting with a template that already contains them. Templates give you the opportunity to build on someone else's experience. If you use a template as a starting point, you can then fine-tune the layout using the techniques described later in this chapter. (See Chapter 4 for an introduction to templates.)

Starting with a Template

In Chapter 4, you learned how to create and apply templates to add consistency to a website. If you create a template that uses tables (as well as layers, which are described later in this chapter), you can carry out that table design throughout your website.

SETTING THE TABLE FOR WEB PAGE LAYOUT

Before you can start using tables as web page layout tools, you need to know the basics about what web page tables are and how they're structured.

Tables were originally included in Hypertext Markup Language (HTML) as a way of arranging data in an orderly way. Tables consist of horizontal divisions called rows and vertical divisions called columns. Each row or column contains one or more subdivisions called cells. Each cell has its own border, as does the table itself. Conventional tables display information in a grid, much like a spreadsheet.

The table below, for instance, has four rows and four columns. The borders around each cell are visible, as is the border around the outer edge of the table itself.

The savvy Web designer can "turn off" the table's border display so that the viewer only sees the contents, not the borders. By filling the table cells with text and images rather than simple figures, the table becomes a tool for designing a whole web page. Dreamweaver gives you plenty of options for creating such tables, as described throughout this chapter.

You can also use a different kind of template—a web page that someone else has designed and that you can use as a starting point for your own site. You just copy the page (or pages; some templates consist of sets of interlinked web pages) to your computer and alter the content to fit your needs.

Where do you find templates? The first and most obvious place to look is Macromedia. Go to `http://www.macromedia.com/software/dreamweaver/download/templates`. You can also purchase some templates that talented web page designers have created and made available. Try Project Seven Development (`http://www.projectseven.com`) or the other sites listed in the Appendix.

It isn't difficult to locate templates that use tables for page layout because they are a very popular starting point for many web page designs. Follow these steps to locate a template and start working with it:

1. Start your browser and go to Macromedia's Dreamweaver templates page (`http://www.macromedia.com/software/dreamweaver/download/templates`).

2. Scroll down and look for a page that's been divided into columns or that has a design similar to one you want to use. Chances are that a columnar layout uses tables.

> You can verify whether or not a web page uses tables by viewing the source code for the page. In Internet Explorer, choose View → Source; in Netscape Navigator, choose View → Page Source. Scan the HTML for tags such as `<table>` `</table>`, which enclose a table; `<tr>` `</tr>`, which define a row within a table; or `<td>` `</td>`, which define a cell.

3. Click Preview to view a close-up of the template in your browser window. The template called Department of History, for instance (see Figure 11.1), uses a common three-column design. The column on the left can be altered to contain a set of links to other parts of your site. The two columns on the right can contain a list of personnel or other facts about your organization.

4. To copy the template, return to the Templates page and click either PC or Mac next to Download. Your system will now begin to download a Zip archive containing the template pages to your computer.

5. Extract the archive to a directory on your computer using WinZip or a similar application.

6. Start Dreamweaver, choose File → Open, and open the `index.htm` file.

Once you have the template open in Dreamweaver, you can begin editing the content. The tables that contain the content appear in the Dreamweaver window (see Figure 11.2).

Figure 11.1

This page uses tables to create the information at the top as well as the main body of information in the center of the page.

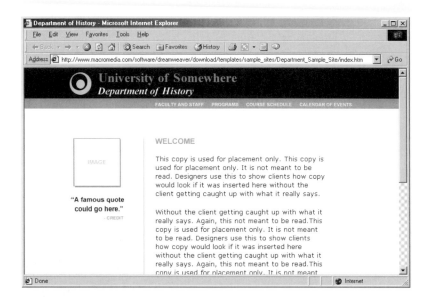

Figure 11.2

Dreamweaver makes it easy to edit tables because borders are always visible in the Document window. You can select images and text within cells and edit them just like regular web page content.

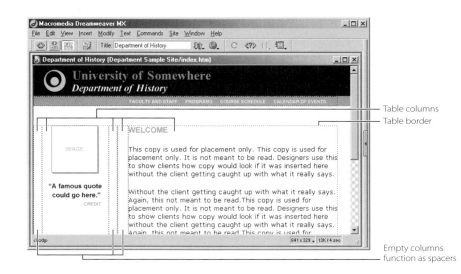

Using a Preset Table Format

Dreamweaver provides you with preformatted tables that give you another sort of design jump-start. They're a great source for innovative ideas of how to present the information within a table—particularly a borderless table. The preset table designs enable you to choose and preview tables that have different background colors assigned to individual rows, and type fonts that are chosen to convey a particular feeling (simple, businesslike, high-tech, and so on).

To view the preset designs, choose Commands → Format Table. The Format Table dialog box opens (see Figure 11.3). Select an option from the list in the upper-left corner of the dialog box to see a preview on the right.

> You can use Dreamweaver's preset table designs at any time, not just when you're first creating a table. To format an existing table, select the table by choosing Modify → Table → Select Table. Then choose Commands → Format Table to open the Format Table dialog box. The design elements you choose are applied to the currently selected table.

Use the controls at the bottom of the dialog box to adjust the attributes of the table. One benefit of doing this is that, when you make a choice, you instantly see the choice reflected in the preview at the top of the dialog box.

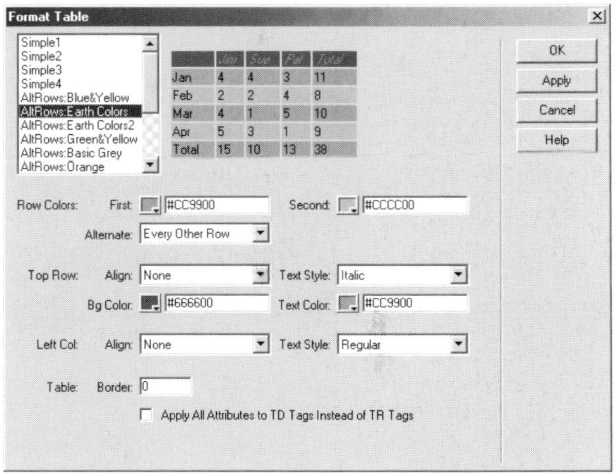

Creating a New Table

If you're coming to Dreamweaver from the traditional design world, it might seem like there aren't a lot of controls over how a web page looks. But using tables as design tools can help designers gain back some of that control.

Web designers have long known that you can divide a page into columns and arrange the contents by using borderless tables—tables with a border width set to zero. The two main options for creating a table from scratch—Standard View and Layout View—are described below.

Figure 11.3

Each row or column within a table can be assigned a color to provide additional graphic interest.

Using Standard View

Standard View gives you a way of creating a table through parts of the Dreamweaver interface that you're already familiar with, such as menus and dialog boxes. Use it if you're not artistically inclined, you don't like to draw, or if you want the control over table attributes that the Insert Table dialog box provides.

> Before you start creating a table from scratch, it's a good idea to sketch out on paper how you want your finished web page to look. That way, you'll know exactly how many rows and columns you'll need before you start filling in the table specifications in the Insert Table dialog box.

It's easy to begin creating tables in Standard View. Just open the page you want to work on in Dreamweaver, and then position the cursor where you want the table to appear. Then, you create the table in one of three ways:

- Click the Table button in the Insert bar, or drag the button right into the Document window.
- Choose Insert → Table.
- Press Ctrl + Alt + T.

No matter which way you chose, the Insert Table dialog box should now appear (see Figure 11.4).

Enter the following specifications for your table:

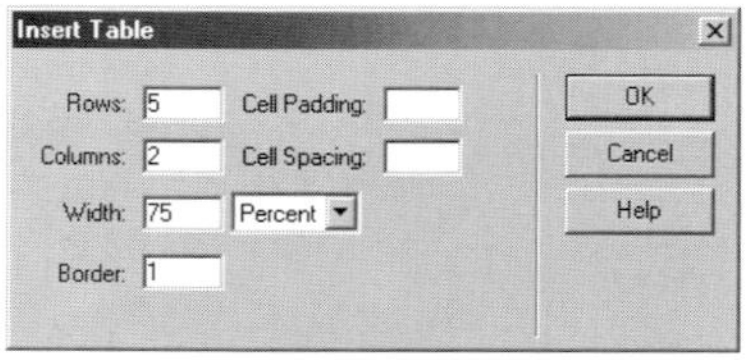

Figure 11.4

The Insert Table dialog box lets you choose the attributes for your table.

Rows Enter the number of rows the table should have.

Columns Enter the number of columns the table should have.

Width The width of a table can be expressed either as a percentage of the width of the page, as displayed in the browser window, or as a fixed number of pixels. Choose Percent or Pixels from the drop-down list to switch between the two types of measurement.

Border Set the border to 0 if you want it to be invisible. (The width shown is in pixels; set the value to 3 if you want a three-pixel-wide border.)

Cell Padding This is optional; it controls the space (in pixels) between the contents of the cell and the cell border.

Cell Spacing This is optional; it refers to the space between cells, in pixels.

You can always make revisions to the table specifications by selecting the Table (choose Modify → Table → Select Table) and then making changes in the Property Inspector.

In order to create a table that is used to design a web page, you should not only set borders to zero, but you may want to create columns or rows that are empty except for a blank space. This creates space between columns that do contain content.

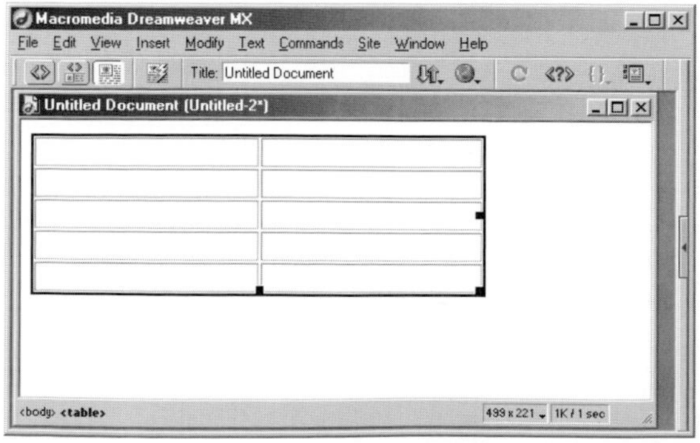

Figure 11.5

This table has two columns and five rows.

Once you're finished entering values in the Insert Table dialog box, click OK. The table appears in your page (see Figure 11.5).

Once the table's outline appears, you need to fill in its cells with content. You do this by clicking within each cell to position the cursor there. You can then begin typing or pasting text or images that you have already copied. You can also choose Insert → Image to insert an image.

Using Layout View

Layout View lets you arrange a page's contents visually. One advantage of using Layout View is that tables and cells drawn in Layout View have a border width set to zero automatically. Another is that you see the table being created as you draw it. To work in Layout View, do one of two things:

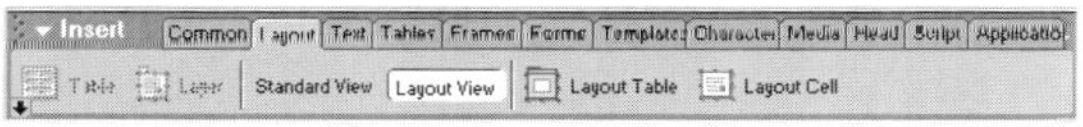

Figure 11.6

The two buttons in the Layout section of the Insert bar let you switch between Standard View and Layout View.

- Choose View → Table View → Layout View.

- Click the Layout tab of the Insert bar and then click the Layout View button (see Figure 11.6).

When you click Layout View and then click either Layout Cell or Layout Table, the cursor turns into a plus (+) sign when you pass it over the Document window.

Layout Cell Click this button, and then drag within the Document window to draw an individual cell within a table.

Layout Table Click here, and then drag within the Document window to create a table.

If this is the first time you've used Layout View, you may want to click Tutorials in the Answers panel. When you do so, the Using Dreamweaver MX window opens and displays the using Tables to Design a Page topic. The instructions will to help you work with the two buttons in the Layout section of the Insert bar.

Let's say you want to draw a table with two columns and only one row—essentially, you can use this table to design the entire web page. Follow these steps:

1. Click Layout View in the Layout section of the Insert bar.

2. Click Layout Table in the Layout section of the Insert bar.

3. Click in the Document window, hold down the mouse button, and drag down and to the right. Release the mouse button, and the table is created (see Figure 11.7).

> The mouse arrow turns into a plus (+) sign when you click Layout Table or Layout Cell. If you click Layout Cell before you create a table, Dreamweaver automatically creates a table to contain the cell that you draw.

4. Resize the table, if needed, by clicking one of the handles around it.

5. Click Layout Cell.

6. Click in the upper-left corner of the table and drag down and to the right to draw a cell.

7. If you need to resize the cell, click it and click and drag one of its handles (see Figure 11.8).

8. Repeat steps 6 and 7 until you have drawn all of the cells you need.

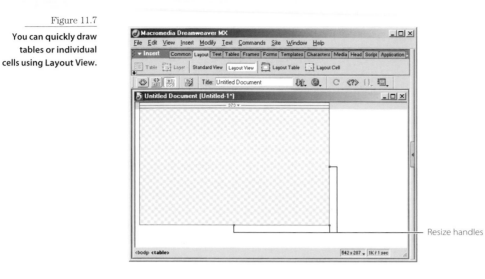

Each time you draw a cell, you need to click Draw Layout Cell first—unless you hold down the Ctrl key as you draw.

You can cut, copy, or paste individual cells within a table just like any other web page contents. If you select a cell within a table, you can view that cell's properties in the Property Inspector so that you can adjust them if you need to. But whether you're working in Layout View or Standard View, Dreamweaver lets you adjust a table or cell by clicking and dragging: in Layout View, you click and drag handles; in Standard View, you click and drag the borders.

Figure 11.8

Click an individual cell to view its properties in the Property Inspector.

Finessing Table Properties

When laying out a page on-the-fly, your initial specifications don't have to be your final ones. As you work with your web page, you'll probably adjust spacing so its contents are readable. When your table covers most of your web page and controls the design for most or all of the page, you'll almost certainly need to adjust the spacing between columns so the columns of your page are far enough apart. (Of course, if you are simply building out a page from a preexisting template, then you probably shouldn't change any of the table settings.)

Maintaining some empty space on a page helps a viewer read the contents more easily and directs the viewer's eye toward the most important contents. This section examines Dreamweaver's tools for fine-tuning the dimensions of a table and its components, including the Property Inspector and the Table submenu of the Modify menu.

Dreamweaver displays tables with dashed lines around the borders. You can view the table without visible borders either by previewing the page in a browser window (choose File → Preview in Browser) or by choosing View → Visual Aids → Table Borders to toggle between turning border display on or off.

Selecting Parts of a Table

Before you can work with a table or individual cells, you should practice selecting them. It's not always easy to select an entire table, row, or column simply by clicking it; you need to know exactly where to click, and what menu options to choose if you don't select exactly what you want the first time.

Selecting in Standard View

The easiest way to select an entire table in Standard View is to choose Modify → Table → Select Table.

You can select a table or rows or columns within it by clicking. Sometimes, clicking parts of a table to select them requires you to place the mouse arrow in exactly the right place. Here are some suggestions:

- Position the arrow just above or below the table to get this four-headed arrow ⊕ . When you click, you select the entire table.

- If you can position the mouse arrow atop a table border, you get this arrow ↧ . When you click, you select the adjacent row or column. (If the arrow points down, you select a column. If the arrow points to the left, you select a row.)

- If you click on a cell border while this double-arrow appears ⇌ , you select the entire table—not the cell. (To select a cell, click and drag across it.)

Selecting in Layout View

It's easier to select individual cells within a table by working in Layout View. You only have to click anywhere within the cell to display the handles around it, which means it's been selected.

However, when it comes to selecting rows that consist of multiple cells, you run into a limitation: you can't select multiple cells by pressing Shift-click (Ctrl-click on the Mac). You can, however, easily select the entire table by clicking the Layout Table label just above its upper-left corner.

Adding a Spacer

One of the advantages of using a table to design an entire web page is that you can easily add space between rows or columns by adding a new row or column that contains only blank space.

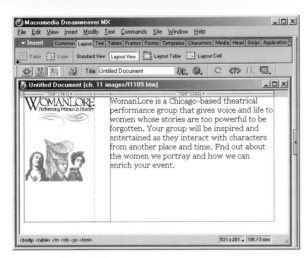

Figure 11.9

You can add table cells to increase space between columns.

In the template table layout shown in Figure 11.9, some "spacer" empty rows and cells have been added to provide extra separation between the column on the left and the large cell on the right, which is intended to hold the main content on the page. If you want to add a few points of space, you can adjust cell spacing or cell padding. But to add large amounts of space, such as a quarter or a half of an inch, consider adding an extra column or row to the table to function as a spacer.

You can easily add a spacer to a table in Layout View. In this case, though, the spacer is a graphic image rather than a row or column. In Layout View, click the down arrow next to the number indicating the size of the column in pixels. Choose Add a Spacer Image from the pop-up menu that appears. If you have not yet used a spacer image in your website, a dialog box appears asking you to choose such an image. Click one of the two options—Create a New Spacer Image, or Choose an Existing Spacer Image File. If you choose to create a new spacer image, Dreamweaver asks you to name the file and choose where you want to save it, and then it creates the image for you.

PERCENTAGES VERSUS ABSOLUTE MEASUREMENTS

The width of a table or of the rows, columns, and cells within it can be expressed in one of two ways:

- As a fixed measurement
- As a percentage of the width of the page or the table itself

Sometimes, tables need to be a constant width. Perhaps one of the cells within a table contains a corporate logo that must be a certain width and must appear on the page; perhaps the cells contain images of objects like autos for sale that need to be a certain width. But there's a big problem with a table that is a fixed width: if the table is 300 pixels wide and the viewer makes their browser window say, 250 pixels, the table won't be completely visible.

In most cases, it's better to make the table a percentage of the browser window width. This enables the table to change in width as the viewer resizes the browser window, so the entire table will always be visible.

Autostretching a Column

When you're working in Standard View, you can adjust the width of an entire table using the Property Inspector. Select the table, display the Property Inspector, and choose Percent from drop-down menus next to the W (width) or H (height) boxes.

If you're working in Layout View, in order to change a table from fixed to variable width, you need to use a Dreamweaver feature called autostretch. *Autostretch* enables you to insert a spacer image in a column of the table. The autostretch column can expand or contract depending on the size of the browser window.

In Layout View, you can make a column a variable width in one of two ways:

- Go to the column you want to make variable and click the down arrow next to the numbers that denote its size. Choose Make Column Autostretch from the pop-up menu.

- In the Property Inspector, select the column you want to make a variable width, and then click the Autostretch button.

When you make a column autostretched, Dreamweaver inserts a spacer image in that column. The image, which is transparent and not visible to a viewer, changes in width along with the browser window. The image changes in width so that the other columns in the column can stay the same width.

> Though it's most common to set the rightmost column in a table to autostretch, you can choose autostretch for any column. But only one column in the table can be set to autostretch.

Adding or Removing Rows and Columns

Use the Modify menu when you need to add or remove rows or columns or make other changes that affect all of the table's rows or columns at the same time. Position the text cursor within the table, then choose Modify → Table. The Table submenu appears.

To add an element, select Insert Row or Insert Column. To add both rows and columns at the same time, choose Insert Rows or Columns, then specify what you want to add in the Insert Rows or Columns dialog box. To delete elements, choose Delete Row or Delete Column.

The options in the bottom section of the Table submenu let you fine-tune cell spacing:

Clear Cell Heights/Widths Sometimes, you add content to a cell that doesn't fill out the cell. To eliminate unnecessary space at the top of the cell, you can either drag the top cell border down or choose this option from the Table submenu.

Convert Widths to Pixels/Percent This option lets you switch the width of the selected cell(s) from a fixed value to a percentage of the table, and vice versa.

The limitation with a nested table is that the width of the table is limited by the width and height of the cell that contains it. However, the nested table can also use small cells of varying size that function as spacers; these spacers enable you to offset cells that do contain contents, as shown in Figure 11.13.

You can import information from a word processing document that has already been formatted in the form of a table. Choose Insert → Table Objects → Tabular Data to display the Insert Tabular Data dialog box. Click Browse to locate the tabular data file you want to add to the current web page.

Designing in Layers

Tables give you a way to design a web page by containing contents within rows, columns, and cells. But the contents of a table's components can't overlap one another, and they can't bleed over the edge of a table border. Designers who want to break through the limitations of the table grid and add sophistication to their web pages can use layers.

A *layer*, like a table, is a container that can hold text, images, colors, and other web page contents. Layers are special because of their dynamic nature: they can be moved around on the page freely, and they can overlap other layers or be nested within larger layers.

For all their flexibility, layers carry one big limitation: they're not supported by older browsers. They require that your visitors use browsers like Microsoft Internet Explorer 4 or Netscape Navigator 4 or later. Other users who try to view a page that contains layers won't see anything at all—unless you create an alternate version of the page using tables instead of layers.

Figure 11.13

Both the nested table and the one that contain it can be "borderless" so that it isn't apparent to the viewer that multiple tables have been used for layout.

Draw a Layer

As usual, Dreamweaver gives you multiple options for creating a layer without having to write JavaScript or other web page code. If you're an artist, you'll probably want to draw a layer. Just follow these steps:

When you are in Layout View you cannot add Layer objects to a page. Make sure you are in Standard View before you start creating layers.

1. Click Draw Layer ▦ in the Insert bar.

2. Position the cursor inside the Document window (the cursor turns into a plus (+) sign), and click and drag down and to the right. Release the mouse button when the layer is the size you want.

Grids make creating layouts or tables a snap—literally. Choose View → Grid → Show Grid to turn on the Grid to draw layers more accurately. If you choose View → Grid → Snap to Grid, the table cells or layers you draw will "snap" (in other words, jump to) the nearest grid line, which can help you achieve precise alignment.

You don't have to worry about drawing the layer perfectly the first time. You can resize it by clicking and dragging one of its resizing handles. These handles only appear when you select the table by clicking the layer's selection handle. You can also move the layer freely around the document window by clicking and dragging its selection handle (see Figure 11.14). Although the border is visible in the Document window, it's invisible when you view the page in a web browser.

If you plan to draw more than one layer at a time, you need to click the Draw Layer button each time—unless you hold down Ctrl (Windows) or Cmd (Macintosh) while you draw each layer in succession.

If you have Invisible Elements turned on, the layer marker appears in the Document window each time you draw a layer on the page. If a layer markers isn't visible and you want to see it, choose View → Visual Aids → Invisible Elements.

Insert a Layer

You can also use Dreamweaver's menus to create a layer. Just position the cursor at the spot on the page where you want the layer to appear. Then choose Insert → Layer while you're in Standard View. A layer instantly appears.

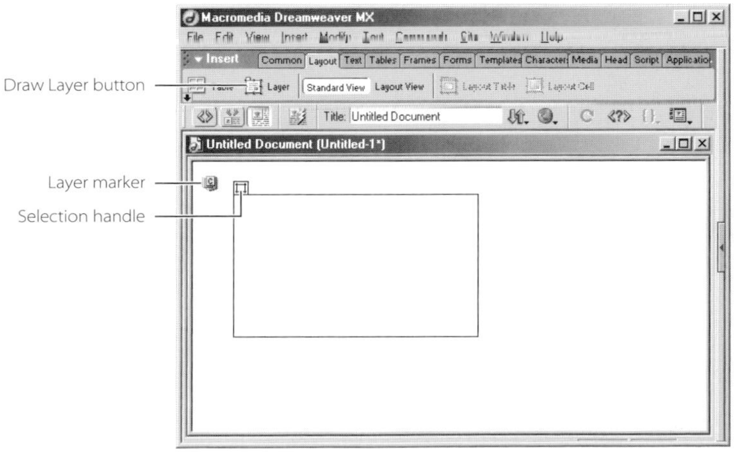

Figure 11.14

You can reposition a layer by clicking and dragging either its selection handle or the handles around its border.

Draw Layer button

Layer marker

Selection handle

The size of a layer when you first insert it is predetermined by Dreamweaver's layer preferences. You can change the preferences if you want: choose Edit → Preferences, click Layers in the Preferences dialog box, and then change the values in the Width and Height boxes.

Use a Tracing Image

Some conventional page layouts are so complex, using overlapping layers of content, that they can only be replicated in Dreamweaver using layers. Dreamweaver lets you use a tracing image as a shortcut that can save you time as well as produce more faithful layouts.

A *tracing image* is a GIF, PNG, or JPEG file that you open in Dreamweaver in the background of the page being displayed in the Document window. The tracing image doesn't show up in the web page, even when it is previewed in a browser. It's only used as a model that you follow when you are assembling the page's contents. You create layers and fill those layers with images and other content that you then drag over the same images and content in the tracing image. When you're done, your web page displays a reasonably close approximation of the original design.

Suppose you scan a printed page that you have saved in GIF, JPEG, or PNG format and that you want to duplicate in a web page layout. Follow these steps to duplicate the image in Dreamweaver:

1. Select View → Tracing Image → Load.

2. In the Select Image Source dialog box, locate the image you want to trace, and then click Open. The Page Properties dialog box appears.

3. Adjust the Image Transparency slider to indicate how transparent you want the tracing image to be, then click OK. The image appears in the background of the web page.

4. Assemble the page, drawing layers over successive parts of the design.

5. Check your design while hiding the tracing image by selecting View → Tracing Image → Hide.

You can follow and try out a more detailed description of this process in the tutorial at the end of this chapter.

> Before you get too far with your tracing, you can align your tracing image with an image or paragraph in the Document window. Choose View → Tracing Image → Align with Selection. The upper-left corner of the element you've selected is aligned with the upper-left corner of the tracing image.

Finessing Layer Variables

You can fine-tune a layer's positioning, size, and properties just as you would with tables. You've got two options: first, if you want to do hands-on adjustment, do it by clicking and dragging the layer. Sometimes, though, you want to really make some precise measurement adjustments, and in that case, you need to use the Layers panel and the Layer Property Inspector.

Using the Layers Panel

When you are working on a web page that contains multiple layers, you can control their visibility and other properties by selecting Window → Layers to display the Layers panel.

The Layers panel displays layers in their stacking order, whether they're actually stacked atop one another or not. The layer at the top of the list is considered to be on top of the stack, and the others follow in order beneath it. You can change the stacking order by doing one of two things:

- Click a layer in the list in the Layers panel and drag it to another position in the list.
- Click the layer's number in the Z column of the Layers panel (see Figure 11.15) and type a higher or lower number to move the layer higher or lower in the stacking order.

You can change the visibility of all layers at once by clicking the eye icon at the top of the panel. You can also click an individual layer's eye icon to toggle between hiding or displaying it. An open eye means the layer is visible; a closed eye means it is invisible.

Using the Layer Property Inspector

Once you've created one or more layers, the Property Inspector gives you a place to manage and adjust them. Some of the items in the Property Inspector are obvious, but others are unique to layers:

Layer ID A default name appears in this box, but you can change it to make it easier to keep track of objects in the Layers panel or if you're writing scripts for the page.

L/T This stands for left and top, and it describes the layer's placement relative to the top-left corner of the page.

Z-Index This refers to the order of the layer in stacking, and it is used in case the currently selected layer is part of a stack of multiple layers.

Vis This describes whether the current layer is initially visible or invisible. Default is usually interpreted by web browsers to mean visible; inherit means the layer uses the same visibility as its parent, if there is one; visible means the layer will be displayed regardless of the parent's visibility; and hidden means the layer will be hidden.

Overflow This tells a browser what to do if the contents of the current layer exceed its borders.

Clip If you need to trim some of the edges of a layer's contents to fit within the layer borders, enter a value here.

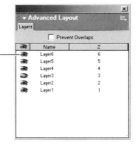

Click the eye icon to toggle between the hiding and displaying layer.

Figure 11.15

The Layers panel lists all the layers in the current web page.

Tag If you know HTML and want to use a tag other than the default DIV to define a layer, enter another tag here (such as SPAN).

You can set properties for more than one layer. To do so, select the layers you want to format, and then enter specifications in the Property Inspector.

The last three items, Tag, Clip, and Overflow, are only visible when you click the expander arrow to display the bottom half of the Property Inspector.

Changing Units of Measurement

By default, layer measurements are expressed in pixels, but you can change this if you're used to working with inches or centimeters. The ability to adjust units of measurement is especially handy if you're using a tracing image that was designed in a common measurement used in printing, such as points or picas. Table 11.1 describes the different layer measurements you can use in the Property Inspector.

Table 11.1

Units of Measurement

UNIT	ABBREVIATION	DESCRIPTION
Pixels	Px	Used in computer graphics; approximately 72 pixels equal one inch.
Points	Pt	Twelve points equal one pica; 72 points equal one inch.
Picas	Pc	Approximately 6 picas equal one inch.
Inches	In	Unit of measurement commonly used in the United States.
Centimeters	Cm	2.54 centimeters equal one inch.
Millimeters	Mm	10 millimeters equal one centimeter.
Percentages	%	Expresses size in relation to the size of the parent layer, if the current layer is nested.

You don't need to capitalize measurements when you enter them, but they do need to follow a numeric value without a space (for instance, 3px or 12pi).

Working with Complex Page Layouts

Tables and layers share a lot of common characteristics: they can contain images and text; they can be assigned background colors; they can be resized; and they can be used to design all or part of a web page.

The differences between tables and layers mean that, for many complex web designs, it's a good idea to combine the two types of objects. Layers, unlike tables, can overlap other objects.

On the other hand, layers don't have visible borders that can be assigned a color and given different widths like tables. Tables give you great control over cell padding and cell spacing, and they're visible to virtually all browsers.

Dreamweaver gives you the best of both worlds by enabling you to use both layers and tables in the same layout, and by letting you convert tables to layers and vice versa as needed.

Combining Tables and Layers

The flexibility with which Dreamweaver lets you use both tables and layers in the same page layout is one of its most powerful features. You can, for instance, draw a layer, position the text cursor within the layer, and then choose Insert → Table to place a table within that layer.

Why would you want to place a table inside a layer? Just click and drag the layer's selection handle to find out: once a table is inside a layer, you can move it freely anywhere on the web page you're designing. You can even overlap tables, if you want, by containing them within layers.

Similarly, if you divide a web page into two or more columns using a table that contains all of the page's content, you can insert two or more overlapping layers into a single column. This not only breaks up a long column of text, but it also adds graphic interest to the page.

Speaking of complex ways to use layers, Dreamweaver MX now gives you the ability to use layers to create a Web page animation. See Chapter 19 for more information.

TABLES VERSUS LAYERS: PROS AND CONS

When is it best to use a table, and when is it best to use a layer? Dreamweaver's flexibility means that this isn't an either/or decision. You can mix tables and layers in the same page. You can also begin working in layers and then convert the layers to tables, and vice versa.

One reason to choose between tables and layers is the browser issue. Use tables when you want your page to be viewed by all browsers or when you have contents that need to be aligned in a grid. As mentioned before, layers aren't supported by version 3.0 and earlier browsers. Use layers when you are sure your viewers are likely to be using browsers that are version 4.0 or later.

Another factor is your own working style. You might be attracted by the flexibility that layers give you in overlapping and stacking content. If so, you can design the page's content using layers. Use them when you need to bleed content over a page or overlap content. You can then convert the layers to tables so that they'll be visible by all browsers. Be aware, though, that you can't convert a single layer or table; you have to convert all the layers or tables on the page.

WHAT HTML CAN AND CANNOT DO

Dreamweaver can enable you to achieve many complex design effects on a web page by combining tables and layers, but it can't do everything. It is limited by the limitations of the HTML. Because HTML isn't a sophisticated layout language like PostScript (which is used by page layout programs like Adobe PageMaker) it can't

- Let you specify exact point sizes or fonts for type.

- Run text around in a circle or abstract design.

- Bleed images off to the edge of a web page.

- Create gradations of color or grayscale.

- Allow you to draw circles, polygons, or other complex shapes.

However, you *can* get some of these effects by creating an image in a graphics program. Just create a file that contains the effects you want in a page layout or graphics program such as Macromedia Fireworks (see Chapter 5), then save the image in GIF, JPEG, or PNG format, and insert it on your web page. (See Chapter 10 for more about understanding web graphics formats and optimizing images for the Web.)

Switching Between Tables and Layers

Another powerful layout feature is Dreamweaver's ability to convert tables to layers and layers to tables. Converting layers to tables has an obvious benefit: your page's contents will be viewable in all browsers. Converting tables to layers has its own benefit: working in layers enables you to position the contents within them in precise, innovative ways.

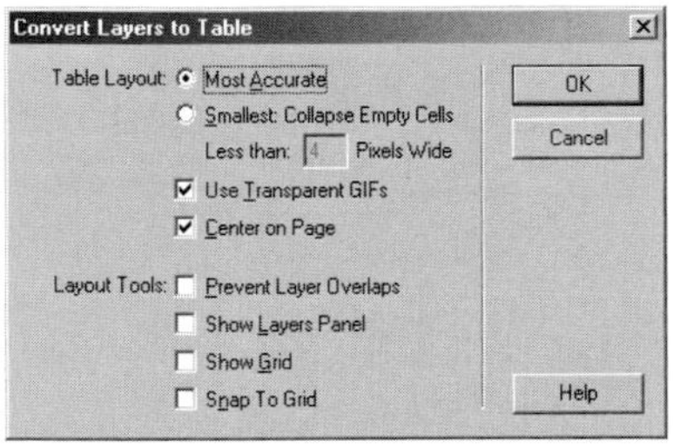

To convert layers to a single table, choose Modify → Convert → Layers to Table. The Convert Layers to Table dialog box appears (see Figure 11.16).

When you're switching from a "layered" layout to one that uses tables, you are likely to end up with lots of tables of all shapes and sizes and a very complex layout. But you can control the conversion with one of the following options.

Figure 11.16

If you convert layers to a table, you can choose options that control how accurately your original layout is duplicated.

Most Accurate Choose this if you don't care about how many table cells will be created—a cell will be created not only for each layer but also for the spaces between layers.

Collapse Empty Cells This means fewer cells will be created, but your original "layered" layout might not be matched exactly.

Use Transparent GIFs If you choose this, a series of transparent GIF images is inserted in the bottom row of the table in order to keep the other rows the same size as in your original layout.

If your layout contains overlapping layers, they won't be converted to a table. You'll have to separate the layers in order to convert them.

Converting a table to layers is similar: choose Modify → Convert → Tables to Layers. The table cells that contain content will be converted to layers, and the Document window will display the grid so that you can reposition the layers if needed. In addition, the Layers panel will open with a list of the layers that have been created.

Hands On: Design a Page with Tables and Layers

Now you can try out some of the ways you can use layers and tables to design a web page. You'll open a tracing image, create a table, add layers, and nest a table inside another table. All of these techniques will help you duplicate an existing printed page design.

In the Chapter 11 folder on the accompanying CD, copy the folder `complex_layout` to your computer. Start Dreamweaver, and open a new blank page. If you want a preview of the completed page, you can open `complex.htm`, which is also in the Chapter 11 folder. The completed page is shown in Figure 11.17.

Open the Tracing Image

Begin by loading a tracing image that you can try to duplicate using layers and tables. Follow these steps:

1. Choose View → Tracing Image → Load.

2. Locate the file `tracing.jpg` in the Chapter 11 folder, and click Open.

Figure 11.17

This web page combines tables and layers for complex layout effects.

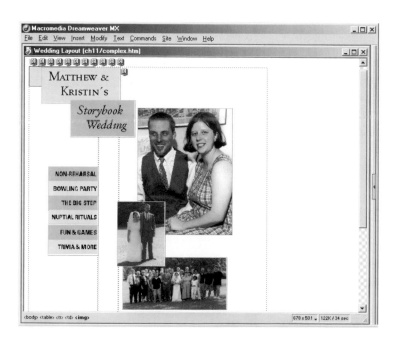

3. In the Page Properties dialog box, adjust the Image Transparency slider to 50%.

4. Click OK.

Add a Table

Next, you'll create a table to contain the page's contents. The primary purpose of the table is to provide a three-column layout. You could trace the layout using only layers, but the table will show up in all browsers and will allow you to create the middle column. The middle column is needed in order to anchor both graphics and photos.

1. Switch to Layout View and click Layout Cell.

2. Draw the first table cell so that it aligns with the right edge of the yellow box. Drag the bottom of the cell all the way to the bottom of the tracer image.

3. Draw the other two table cells as shown in Figure 11.18.

Add Layers

The easiest way to duplicate the graphics and photos in the tracing image is to draw layers over each of them. The layers can overlap, just like the elements in the tracing image.

1. Click Standard View in the Layout tab of the Insert bar.

2. Click Draw Layer, also in the Layout tab of the Insert bar.

3. Draw a layer over the yellow box.

4. Draw a layer over the light red box, overlapping the first and second columns of the table you drew earlier.

Figure 11.18

Drawing a table to enclose the web page contents and establish a three-column layout

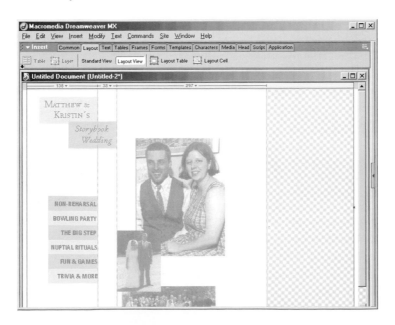

5. Draw layers over each of the photos.

6. Make sure the layers overlap the tracing image graphics and photos as closely as possible. Select each layer's selection handle and move it by adjusting the border if needed.

Insert Graphics

Next, you add graphics to each of the layers you created.

1. Position the cursor in the topmost layer and choose Insert → Image.

2. In the Select Image Source dialog box, choose `Logo1.gif` and click Select.

3. Resize the image to fit in the layer by clicking the handle in the lower-right corner, pressing Shift, and dragging inward.

4. Repeat steps 1 through 3 for each of the following images, from top to bottom: `logo2.gif`, `photo1.jpg`, `photo2.jpg`, and `photo3.jpg`.

> Wherever photos overlap in the tracing image, you should first trace the photos in the back—the photos that are partially hidden. Trace each photo completely, even if part of it is behind another photo. Then trace the photos that are in front. That way, the layers you draw will overlap just like the photos in the tracing image.

Create a Navigation Bar

Next, you create a navigation bar in the left-hand column of the table.

1. Draw a layer over the set of links on the left side of the tracing image.

2. Position the text cursor in the layer.

3. Choose Insert → Image, and insert the file `links1.gif`.

4. Resize the image so that it fits within the table.

5. Repeat steps 3 and 4 for `links2.gif` through `links6.gif`.

6. Associate each of the image files with a link.

7. Save your changes, and check your work by selecting View → Tracing Image Show.

Hopefully this tutorial has acquainted you with some of the ways you can use layers and tables to design a web page. You learned why tables are good for giving structure to a web page, and why layers are good when you need more flexibility and need to overlap objects.

Filling the News Hole

In the magazine business, the space between the ads and design elements on a printed page is sometimes referred to as the "news hole"—the place where you have to fill in some content, er… text, no… what's that w—that's it! words. Next chapter talks about managing the words on web pages.

## CHAPTER 12

Inserting and Formatting Text Content

In the beginning, there was the word, but now we've got pulsating 3-D graphics, animated screechfests, and shiny, beveled, squirmy navigation. But guess what, most—nearly all—of the information on the Web is in the form of plain old text. Yes, it helps if the design of the page is clean and the copy is well groomed. We'll get to that. But in the excitement of interactive networked multimedia, don't overlook the most powerful medium of them all: the written word.

In this chapter, you'll learn about the following topics:

- **Getting words onto pages**
- **Importing copy from Word documents**
- **Editing and proofreading copy**
- **Designing with text (format and style), design, and style**
- **Cleaning up HTML directly**
- **Creating complex layouts by combining tables and layers**

Getting Copy onto the Page

Before you can start inserting text willy-nilly, it helps to gather all your content assets together.

Organizing Your Content

As discussed in Chapter 2, you must try to gather together all of your text content (also known as *copy*) in advance of building your site. At the very least, put together a strict submission, edit, and review schedule with some padding so that you don't end up holding up a launch because the copy isn't ready.

Chances are, you will have to manage copy coming from multiple sources. When this is the case, it can help if you establish what format you'd prefer to receive the copy in (such as Word documents, plain text, HTML files, and so on). Generally, it's preferable to keep the source copy as plain as possible (although fairly standard ways of indicating emphasis, such as italics and boldface, can usually survive the importing process) so you minimize the amount of inappropriate formatting or badly formed HTML tags you have to strip away when you go to clean up the copy.

There are three main ways to get text content onto web pages in Dreamweaver:

- Copy the text from the source document and paste it into the page in Dreamweaver.
- Import the text from Microsoft Word, as HTML.
- Type the text directly.

They're all pretty easy. In fact, if you're at all used to working with word processing programs, then you should find that most of the text-handling you'll have to do feels very familiar.

Inserting Text with Copy and Paste

Copy and paste is not the most powerful method for getting text onto a page, but it's extremely convenient, especially when the source text is not yet formatted (because Dreamweaver will only paste the plain text). The method should be utterly familiar to you already:

1. Select the text you want to copy in the source document.
2. Choose Edit → Copy (or Ctrl + C/Command + C).
3. Switch to Dreamweaver by your preferred method of switching programs.
4. Position the insertion point where you want the pasted text to appear in the web page.
5. Choose Edit → Page (or Ctrl + V/Command + V).
   Figure 12.1 shows some pasted text.

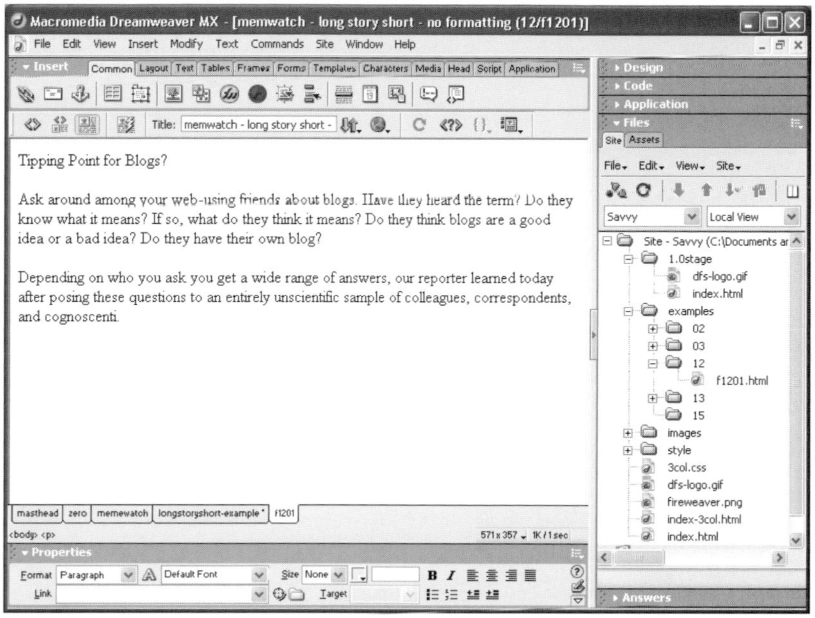

Figure 12.1

Whether the source of the copied text is a Word document, a web page, or an e-mail message, it gets pasted in without any formatting.

Importing Text and Tables (from Word or Excel)

When it comes to importing text created in another program, Dreamweaver has focused on Microsoft Word because, face it, 90 percent of all words are processed in that beloved application. (I made up that statistic and I'm being facetious.) Even the idea of importing implies a greater level of cooperation than is really going on between the two programs. To import a Word document into Dreamweaver (and thus preserve most of its formatting), you must first save it as an HTML file in Word. Then you can import or open it in Dreamweaver.

Dreamweaver can also import tabular data, literally meaning information in tabular form (a table of rows and columns), but that mainly means spreadsheet and database tables, which must be exported from their source applications using a standard text-with-delimiters format. But first, let's talk about Word documents.

Importing a Word Document

Word has a normal Save As command with which you can specify HTML format—the option is listed as Web Page (*.htm, *.html) in the Save As dialog box—and it also has a dedicated Save as Web Page format on the File menu just so no one will miss it. Similarly, you can open a Word HTML file in Dreamweaver the same way you open any web page (use File → Open, or Ctrl + O/Command + O), but if you use the File → Import → Import Word HTML command, then Dreamweaver will automatically bring up the Clean Up Word HTML dialog box to remind you that Word HTML is messy and includes many tags that do not comply with standards (the dialog box will actually cover over another message about corrected HTML, but that is not specific to Word).

> Importing from Word in HTML format and then cleaning up the HTML renders the file illegible to Word, so make sure you have saved a copy of the original document before you clean up the HTML version.

So our advice is to use the Import command, if only because it reminds you to clean up the HTML. Choosing Import Word HTML brings up a variation on the standard Open dialog box (before the cleaning-up step). Browse to, and double-click the file you want to import. Dreamweaver will start to open it and then immediately bring up the Clean Up Word HTML dialog box (see Figure 12.2).

> Would anyone ever need to keep Word's flavor of HTML in a document? Sure! For example, intranet users who have standardized on Microsoft Office and use Internet Explorer, Word, PowerPoint, and so on, seamlessly together might be perfectly comfortable with Word's non-compliant coding.

The options on this dialog box are on two tabs (Basic and Detailed); you might as well look at them all at least once. After the first time you clean up some Word HTML, the dialog box uses your previous selections as the default. Be sure to select the version of Word the imported document was created in with the "Clean Up HTML From" drop-down list.

The basic choices clean up the majority of Word's most egregious HTML output:

Figure 12.2

We generally use all of the available options unless we have a specific reason to want to preserve some Word-style HTML (which is never).

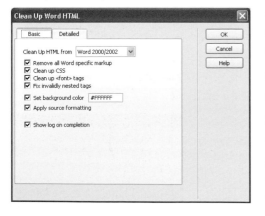

Remove All Word-Specific Markup This option is self-explanatory. If it's only in there to help Word display the document and it's not real HTML, chuck it.

Clean Up CSS Takes out any redundant, unused, or nonstandard style declarations (more about Cascading Style Sheets [CSS] in Chapter 15).

Clean Up <font> Tags Fixes Word's habit of wrapping <font> tags around other tags.

Fix Invalidly Nested Tags Corrects tag entanglements that can render a design incorrectly in a strict browser.

Set Background Color Reminds you that Word HTML documents will get the default gray background unless you set the background to White (#FFFFFF) or some other color.

Apply Source Formatting Permits Dreamweaver to massage the HTML code and make it easier to read.

Show Log On Completion Gives you a detailed "receipt" of all the changes made, which are especially useful in case anything goes wrong with the cleanup.

The choices on the Detailed tab differ depending on the version of Word from which you are importing. If the document was created in Word 97 (for Windows) or Word 98 (for the Mac), then the Detailed tab offers more choices about Word-specific markup and cleaning up `<font>` tags:

- If you checked Remove All Word Specific Markup on the Basic tab, then the Remove Word Specific Markup check box and the Word Meta and Link Tags from `<head>` check box will both be checked on this tab. (If not, not.) The only variation besides having them both checked or both not is having the first checked and the second (relating to the `<head>` portion of the web page) not.

- If you checked Clean Up `<font>` Tags on the Basic tab, then the same option will be checked on the Detailed tab, along with a set of mapping suggestions for Word's use of font sizes 1 through 7. (Dreamweaver suggests turning size 7 into a first-level header, size 6 into a second-level header, and so on, but you can assign any size to any standard HTML formatting tag. (More about HTML tags later in this chapter.)

If the document was created in Word 2000, then the Detailed tab offers different choices for Word-specific markup and some detailed choices about cleaning up CSS:

- If you checked Remove All Word Specific Markup on the Basic tab, then Remove Word Specific Markup will appear checked here with five suboptions—XML within the `<html>` Tags: Word Meta and Link Tags from `<head>`, as with Word 97/98; Word-Specific XML Markup; Word-Style Conditional Tags (of no use outside of Word); and Empty Paragraphs and Margins. Unless you specifically know what you're doing with one of these choices, leave them all checked!

- If you checked Clean Up CSS on the Basic tab, then the same option will be checked here with five suboptions—Remove Redundant Inline Styles, Remove Word-Specific "mso-" Styles, Remove Non-CSS Style Info, Remove CSS from Table Rows and Cells, and Remove Any Unused Styles. Again, unless you're a CSS maven, leave these checked.

When you're ready to cleanup the imported page, click OK. Dreamweaver may take a while to crunch through the file if it's complicated. When finished, Dreamweaver displays the changes.

You can undo or redo a Clean Up Word HTML command, as needed.

Importing Tabular Data

If you need to import a portion of a spreadsheet (such as an Excel document) or a database table, you must first export or save the source data as a tab-delimited text file. *Delimiter* is just a computer science word meaning something that indicates the limit of a field entry—the database equivalent of punctuation. A tab-delimited file separates each field in a record (or cell in a row) from the other fields (cells) using the tab character (or ASCII character 9, for obscurantists). Dreamweaver will actually support any delimiter character you want, but tab is often (as with Excel) the only choice that Dreamweaver supports correctly.

> Excel's Formatted Text (Space Delimited) is not equivalent to Dreamweaver's space-delimited import option. Excel uses a variable number of spaces to suggest formatting (very weak). This just results in a 4-column cell showing up with 23 columns, most of them containing a single space in one row. Stick with tab-delimited text files, trust me!

In most spreadsheet and database programs, you do this by selecting File → Save As, and then choosing an option along the lines of "Text (Tab Delimited File)." Pick a filename, save it, and as always, note where you are saving the file.

Back in Dreamweaver, select File → Import → Import Tabular Data (or click the Insert Tabular Data button on the Insert bar to bring up this dialog box.)

Click the Browse button and find the text document you just saved. Make sure the delimiter shows Tab selected. If you want to control the width of the table in advance, click Set and enter a width in pixels or as a percentage of the browser window. A few more table formatting options are available (but remember, you can format this table all you want once you get the dang thing imported): Cell Padding, Cell Spacing, Border (set to 1 pixel by default), and Format Top Row, which has space options of Bold, Italic, and… wait for it, Bold Italic. (Even more lamely, it sometimes fails to work and only boldfaces the first cell in the top row.) When you become overjoyed with your choices (or before), click OK.

Look, it's a table! (see Figure 12.3).

Entering Text Directly

The third, most humble way of getting text into Dreamweaver is by typing it yourself! Now, for any extended length of copy, this is probably not a good idea. Unless you are also the word-processing expert on the team (even then, I'd expect you'd prefer your own favorite

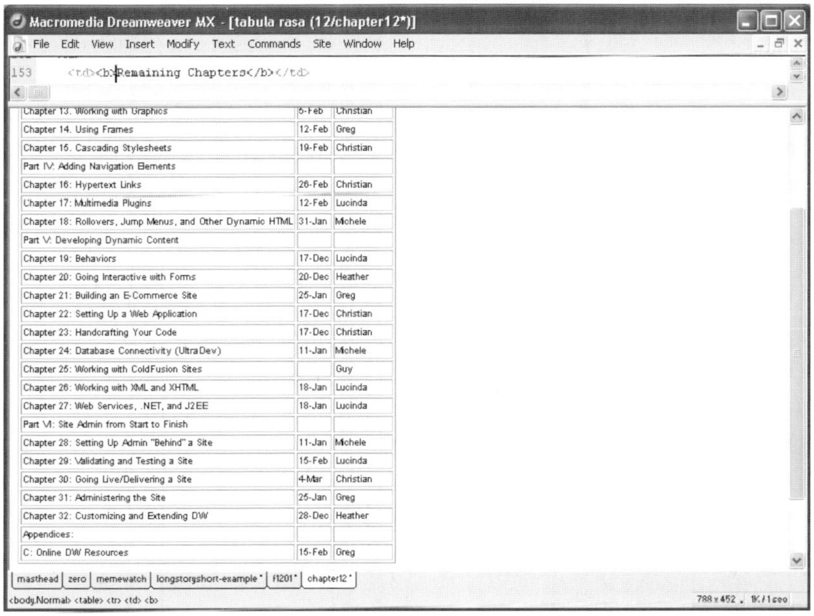

Figure 12.3

Tables, as you saw in Chapter 11, can be used for page layout or to simply place text into rows and columns. Imported data becomes an ordinary table.

word processor for the task), it's probably not the best use of your time. But for small segments of copy, headlines, and minor changes, Dreamweaver is perfectly serviceable. For the purposes of entering text, Dreamweaver more or less functions like a word processor whose output must be compliant HTML.

So just position the insertion point and type. To insert line breaks (single) instead of paragraph breaks (double), use Shift + Enter (or choose the Characters category from the Insert bar and click the Line Break option).

You can also format on the fly if you like (see Figure 12.4). To do so, just boldface a selection or text you're about to type by first pressing Ctrl + B/Command + B or by clicking the Bold button on the Property Inspector, as we'll get to soon.

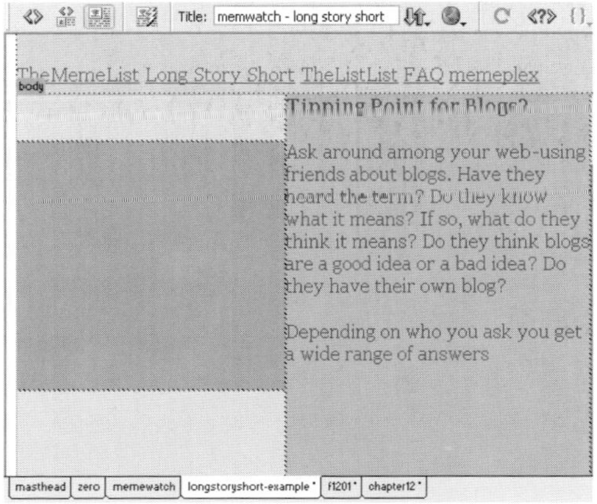

Inserting Special Characters

HTML supports a number of other symbols (mostly commerce and typographical), a few of the most useful of which are on the Characters category of the Insert bar (see Table 12.1).

Figure 12.4

A column of copy partly typed into a layout table—the heading is boldfaced.

Table 12.1

Special Characters

ENTITY	APPEARANCE	USE
Non-breaking space		When multiple spaces are needed or a pair of words needs to be kept together around line breaks
Copyright	©	Used to assert copyright
Registered	®	Used to indicate a registered trademark or service mark
Trademark	™	Used to indicate a trademark
Pound	£	British currency
Yen	¥	Japanese currency
Euro	€	European currency
left quotation mark	"	Curly, smart quote marks look better in print than the old inch mark (")
right quotation mark	"	Same as above. They do, really.
em dash	—	Used for punctuation (not supported by all browsers)

There's also the very useful Other option on the Characters category (the last choice). It brings up a larger selection of special characters in a big dialog box (see Figure 12.5).

Choose the character you want to insert and click OK.

Inserting Dates

Dreamweaver offers a semiautomated date feature that we particularly like (because, really, anyone could have eventually built dialog boxes for character properties and even Cascading Style Sheets, but it takes really smart people to invent or automate new conveniences outside of HTML but managed within Dreamweaver—the Photo Album wizard is another such sign of genius over at Macromedia). Anyway, you can insert the current date into a document at any time by clicking the Date button on the Common category of the Insert bar (or by choosing Insert → Date). Choose a date format in the Insert Date dialog box that appears.

You can leave off the day of the week or the time if you like. The cool part is the Update Automatically on Save check box at the bottom there. If you choose that, then the date always shows the day (or even time) of the last change to the document, which can be useful for your readers in a "This page was last updated…" kind of way when you post your pages live.

The Text in Persistent Page Elements

There are a few other ways that text might appear on one of your pages. Any text in the template used to create your page, for example, will end up on the new page, either editable or not. (See Chapter 4 for the skinny on templates and their editable areas.)

You can also use a server-side include (SSI) to add any content to your pages (Chapter 4 also explains how to work with SSIs). If you do this, then that content won't appear on the page in Dreamweaver or in a preview. To view the complete page, you'll need to view it in a browser directly from the server that is handling the include statements. You can edit the included file, of course, but you have to open it separately to do so.

Editing Text

As with text entry, text editing in Dreamweaver is very similar to text editing in any standard word processing program. You select text by clicking and dragging. You delete a selection by pressing Delete. You can cut (Ctrl + X/Command + X), copy (Ctrl + C/Command + C), or paste (Ctrl + V/Command + V) a selection. And you can drag and drop a selection. As with other word-processing tasks, it doesn't make sense to do too much text editing in Dreamweaver, but for spot corrections here and there it's a breeze.

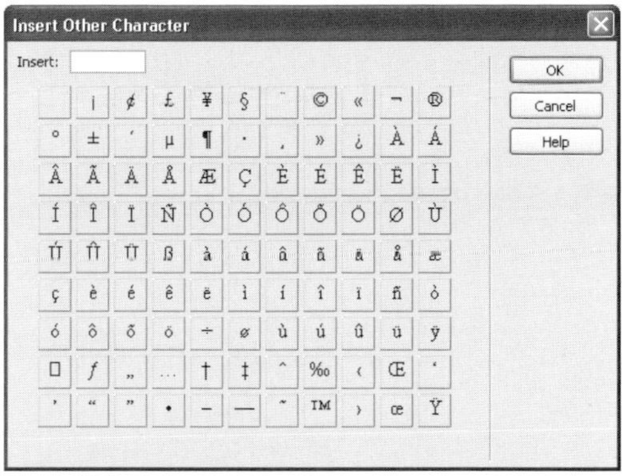

Figure 12.5

For each of these choices, Dreamweaver shows you if it's going to use an entity code (® for ®, for example) or a numerical code (— for —, for example), but this is only useful information if you discover that something is not displaying right.

Doing a Spell Check

To check the spelling of a document (or a selection), select Text → Check Spelling (or press Shift + F7). If Dreamweaver finds any questionable spellings, it will bring up the Check Spelling dialog box (if not, it will pop up a "Spelling check completed" message, and you'll have to click OK to continue).

The dialog box indicates the suspect word (anything not listed in Dreamweaver's dictionary nor added by you in the past). As with spellcheckers in word processors, the dialog box will suggest alternative spellings when possible. Your choices are as follows:

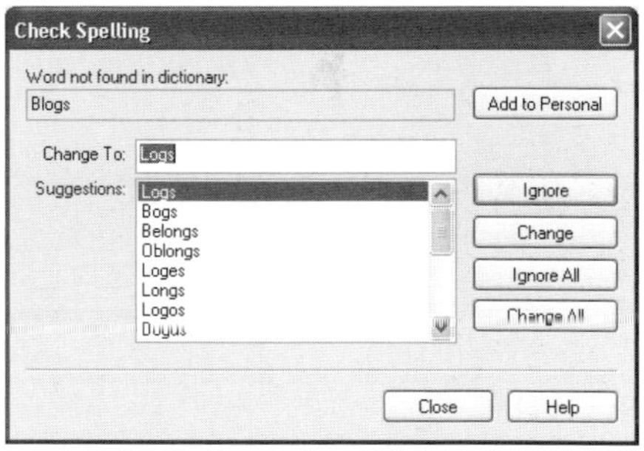

- Accept the top suggestion (listed in the Change To box), select another suggestion, or type your own corrected spelling in the Change To box and then click the Change button, to correct the misspelled word this one time, or the Change All button, to correct it throughout the page.

- Click the Add to Personal button to add the suspect word to your personal dictionary (as when the word is a proper name or other jargon you expect to encounter repeatedly).

- Click the Ignore button to skip the word this one time.

- Click the Ignore All button to skip this word throughout the page.

After you make your decision, Dreamweaver will repeat the process until it reaches the end of the page, at which point it will tell you that is has completed the spelling check and you'll need to click OK to finish.

Editing with Find and Replace

Let's say that you're almost done building a company's site when you learn that the company is changing it's name from, say Dynergix to EnerGlobe, and this means you've got to change any references to the old name throughout the site. Dreamweaver can help.

To find all the instances of a specific word, phrase, or string of characters, use Dreamweaver's find and replace feature, which is—again—analogous to that in word processing programs but is more powerful in one way: you can use it to make changes across multiple files, or even to your entire site.

To start searching, choose Edit ⊕ Find and Replace (Ctrl + F/Command + F).

Find Options

In the dialog box that appears, first decide the scope of your search. In the Find In drop-down list, your choices are Current Document, Entire Local Site, Selected Files in Site, or Folder.

Current Document and Entire Local Site are self-explanatory. If you want to search a specific subset of pages, choose Selected Files in Site (you can switch to the Site panel and choose them now if need be—remember to hold down Ctrl/Command when you are trying to select multiple, discontinuous files). If you want to search all the pages in a folder, select Folder and then choose the folder you want to search with the Browse button.

Figure 12.6

The Find and Replace dialog box.

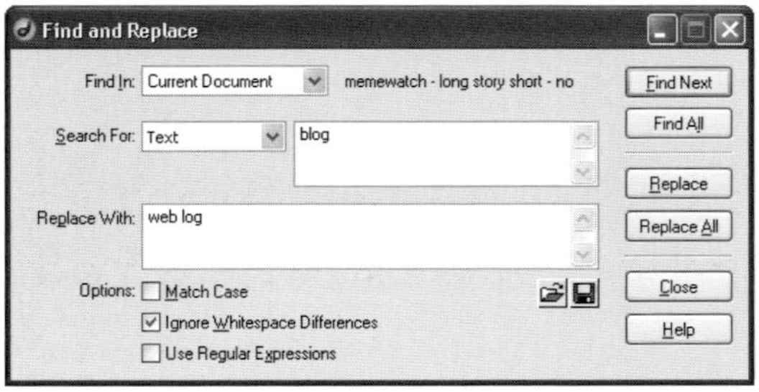

Most of the time, you'll want to leave the Search For drop-down list on Text, although for a company name change, you'd want to make sure that the change is made throughout the HTML code as well, especially in the title section of any page! (See "Working with Raw HTML" later in this chapter, for more on the tag-related choices in this list.) Naturally, you'll need to type or insert the text you're searching for in the box provided (see Figure 12.6).

> Use Ctrl + Enter/Command + Return if you need to insert a line break. (Use copy and paste if you need to insert a new paragraph break.)

Then tab to or click in the Replace With box and type or paste the new text you're replacing the old text with (with which you're replacing the old text?).

- Use the Match Case check box to distinguish proper nouns from common terms.

- Leave Ignore Whitespace Differences checked unless you have a good reason for caring about things like line breaks in the HTML code.

- Only check Use Regular Expressions if you are familiar with Unix-type search syntax. (If you want to learn, the product's manual and help pages—they are the same—include a table of regular expressions with some explanation, though you might be better off with a book like *Perl, CGI, and JavaScript Complete* (Sybex, 2000) or *Mastering PHP 4.1* (Sybex, 2002).

If you expect that you'll need to do this same search again repeatedly, you can save the search by clicking the Save button (the now old-fashioned looking disk icon). Don't change the folder, by the way. Go ahead and save your search to the Queries folder as Dreamweaver suggests.

To reuse a saved search, click the Open icon. Dreamweaver calls this loading a query from a file, and it should open the same Queries folder where the search you're planning to reuse was originally saved.

> If you save or reuse a search, you'll notice that Dreamweaver calls this saving or loading a *query*, not saving a search—it amounts to the same thing. Query is just correct computer science jargon for the request being put to the search function.

Executing the Search

To search for one instances of the text at a time, click the Find Next button. If Dreamweaver finds the text, it will highlight the selection for you, opening the page first if necessary.

To find all the instances of the text at once, click the Find All button. If the Results panel isn't currently open, Dreamweaver will open it to show you its progress:

If you are hunting for your items one at a time, you can decide whether to replace each one individually.

- To make the change, click the Replace button. Dreamweaver will execute the replacement.

- To spare this instance of your item, click the Find Next button.

Either way, Dreamweaver will then automatically look for the next instance of your item. If it doesn't find any more items, it will tell you the search is done.

If you're comfortable making all the changes at once, click the Replace All button (you can do this even if you've already been using the more conservative one-at-a-time Find Next button).

> Be careful not to globally replace something with nothing across your search domain by clicking Replace All when the Replace With box is empty (that is, unless you do want to snip some text out everywhere). Remember you can always Undo an untoward outcome.

When you're done with your replace operation, click the Close button. If you were using the box just to find stuff and not replace it, you can find that same stuff again at any time (until you go and find something else), by pressing Ctrl + G/Command + G or selecting Edit → Find Again.

Formatting Text

There are several ways to format text, each with their own pros and cons:

- Apply standard HTML formatting with the Property Inspector (we'll get to this in the next section).

- Create your own HTML styles using Dreamweaver's feature for naming and saving pre-set HTML formatting choices.

- Use Cascading Style Sheets (CSS) either within a page or linked from a central location.

- For precise control over typeface and appearance, create graphical text.

We'll touch on each of these in this section, but first, it helps to know a little about the basic formatting that is supported by the HTML standard and thus by most or all browsers.

Widely Supported Text Formatting

One of the longstanding ideals of the Web is that form should follow function, and that the formatting, layout, and style (usually called the *design*) of a document are not as important as the information (the content) displayed in it. Of course this is overly simplified—the presentation of information plays a large role in its comprehensibility and usefulness, and in the likelihood that it will get used.

Nonetheless, the goal of keeping the design separate from the information and its structure makes good sense. By structure, we mean information about the purpose of each text element (such as whether it's a heading, a caption, a piece data, and so on), as opposed to the physical design of the copy, meaning its typeface, weight, color, size, and so on. Using style sheets (see Chapter 15) and database-backed sites (see Chapter 24) both offer ways of separating content and structure.

Having said all that, the fact remains that there are certain formatting tags long accepted in the HTML standard, and chances are you'll be using at least some of these in your work:

- Basic typographical enhancements, such as bold and italic, that are interpreted essentially the same way in almost all contexts.

- Standard HTML that communicates structure, such as bulleted and numbered lists.

- Left, center, and right alignment methods that correctly comply with HTML by adding an `align=` attribute to the paragraph or heading tag, or by wrapping a `<DIV>` (divider) tag containing the correct `align=` attribute around the selection.

- Structural tags that have been unofficially associated with certain text effects. For example, there's the way Dreamweaver uses the `<BLOCKQUOTE>` tag to produce indentation effects—this does not comply with the spirit of HTML standards, although it may validate just fine because a validator can't tell semantically whether the text is a quotation or not.

- Tacky `<FONT>` tag-based formatting that, for the time being, works correctly on most browsers. For example, providing a list of preferred typefaces in descending order or specifying a color for the text can be accomplished safely with `<FONT>`, whereas specifying the type *size* consistently across platforms and browsers is not always possible with that same tag.

- Heading tags that may be customized by you, with a style sheet (see Chapter 15), or by the browser.

Formatting Text with the Property Inspector

The Property Inspector makes it really easy to apply most basic formatting options to a selection. To use it, first select the text you want to format.

Then, choose the formatting options you want. (Not all available options are on the Property Inspector. The Text menu contains a few more—which we'll get to in a moment.) Instead of just walking you around the panel, we'll cover the choices in conceptual groups:

- Phrase elements (also called character formatting or text styles)

- Fonts and font lists (typefaces)

- Size

- Color

- Paragraph formats

- Alignment

- Indentation

> **Tipping Point for Blogs?**
>
> Ask around among your web-using friends about blogs. Have they heard the term? Do they know what it means? If so, what do they think it

> If you need to apply the same formatting to a number of different items, do the first one and then, for the rest, just make the selection and then press Ctrl + Y/Command + Y (or choose Edit → Repeat *Last Action*).

Phrase Elements

To boldface or italicize a selection, just click the Bold or Italic button. For other standard HTML character formatting, use the Text → Style submenu. Additional choices include the following:

Strikethrough Not universally supported.

Teletype Traditionally used for monospaced characters.

Emphasis Conceptual, often interpreted as italic and preferred by purists over the italic format because it communicates the purpose of the formatting instead of its appearance, as with Citation.

Strong Conceptual, often interpreted as boldface and preferred by purists over the bold format.

Code Used to display lines of code examples, including scripting languages and markup tags, mainly useful for technical writing, usually interpreted as a monospaced font.

Variable Used to display computer programming-code variables, useful mainly for technical writing, interpreted as italic by most recent browsers.

Sample Used to display sample computer program or script output in technical writing; again, usually monospaced.

Keyboard Used to indicate text the reader should type in technical writing, usually monospaced.

Citation Used for citations, usually interpreted as italic.

Definition Used for the first or defining appearance of a word or phrase in a document.

> You can override a browser's default interpretation of any of these formats using a style sheet (see Chapter 15). You can also apply a longer list of formatting effects, including superscript, subscript, and the now-kitschy Blink effect.

Fonts and Font Lists

Although applying typefaces using the FONT tag is no longer the preferred method, it is widely accepted by most browsers and is still the most common way of controlling typeface. Because you can't be sure what typefaces (fonts) your users have available, it's customary to specify a list of fonts on descending order of preference, such as "Arial, Helvetica, sans-serif." Using this example, if the system has Arial installed, then that font will be used. If not, it will check for Helvetica and use that if possible. Failing that, it will use whatever default sans-serif font is installed. (*Sans serif* is French for "without little thingies on the tips of the letters.")

The Property Inspector offers a few lists of commonly available fonts:

- Arial, Helvetica, sans-serif
- Times New Roman, Times, serif
- Courier New, Courier, mono
- Georgia, Times New Roman, Times, serif

- Verdana, Arial, Helvetica, sans-serif

- Geneva, Arial, Helvetica, sans-serif

To choose one, click the drop-down list button to the right of the Format drop-down list.

If you want to make your own list of preferred fonts, click the list button and choose Edit Font List to bring up this dialog box.

Choose an available font from among those installed on your system (or one of the HTML-defined generic font types, including Cursive, Fantasy, Monospace, Sans-serif, or Serif) from the Available Fonts list box or type the name of a font not present on your system in the text box below and then click the button with the left-pointing guillemets (<<) to add a font to the new sequence in your font list. Repeat to add a second choice (if you wish), a third, and so on. If you change your mind about a font, highlight it and click the right-pointing button (>>) to remove it from the choices.

To add another sequence to the list, click the button with the plus (+) sign. To remove a sequence, highlight it and click the button with the minus (–) sign. To rearrange the order of the list, click the up or down arrow buttons. When you're done editing the font list, click OK.

Size

There are two approaches to setting the size for text in a selection. You can choose a size number ranging from 1 to 7 (with 3 being the default), or you can choose a size *change*, either ranging from –7 to –1 or from +1 to +7. How the exact size or size change is rendered depends on the browser and varies from one platform to the next. The Size drop-down list includes all of these options. Choose one to apply it to the selected text.

Color

As with the other `<font>` tag-based formatting options, setting text color this way is now considered less desirable than using style sheets (Chapter 15), but if you want to add spot color to a selection on the fly, it's awfully convenient. To color a selection, click the color selector on the Property Inspector (hey, that rhymes).

Dreamweaver will only offer web safe colors unless you override the default (by unchecking Snap to Web Safe on the drop-down list you get to by clicking the right-pointing arrow in the upper-right corner of the color picker—do this only when you are sure that the systems that will be used to view the site can handle a wider range of colors).

See Chapter 4 to review how to set up color schemes for pages at your site and Chapter 15 for setting page colors with style sheets.

Paragraph Formats

Most stretches of text in web pages are treated as paragraphs, except for headings, lists, or what's called "preformatted" text, which basically means plain text rendered exactly as is from the HTML source. To change a selection to (or back to) the paragraph type, to a type of heading, or to preformatted text, click the Format drop-down list and choose Paragraph, Heading 1 through Heading 6, or Preformatted. Headings are generally rendered in descending sizes, usually with boldface, although heading formatting can be customized with style sheets, which by now you should know will be discussed in Chapter 15!

There's an old HTML tag called <ADDRESS> that is used to indicate, well, an address, and is usually rendered as italic. Dreamweaver doesn't directly support it, but it knows about it (Dreamweaver also displays it as italic if you insert it). The only way to apply this tag is to enter it directly in Code view. I'll explain about how to do that kind of thing in the last section of this chapter, "Working with Raw HTML."

Various Types of Lists

Similar to paragraph formats are list formats—in that they apply to sections of text and not to specific individual characters. There are several types of lists, each of which have different kinds of items in them, but the first two types of list are by far the most common. The list types are as follows:

- Unordered list (bullets)
- Ordered list (numbers)
- Definition list
- Directory list
- Menu list

To make a selection into an unordered list, click the bulleted list button in the Property Inspector. To make a selection into an ordered list, click the numbered list button.

Definition lists have two types of items, terms and definitions. To make a definition list, select Text → List → Definition List. Dreamweaver automatically treats the first item in the list as a term, the second as a definition, and so on, alternating.

To make a Directory or Menu list, first create an unordered list and then choose Text → List → Properties to bring up this dialog box.

Then choose the type of list you want from the List Type drop-down box.

You can also use this dialog box to customize your bullets or numbering system. To customize the entire list, select a bullet or numbering type in the Style drop-down list. Dreamweaver supports round (Bullet) and square (Square) bullets—although the HTML spec provides for a third kind (Disc—I'm not sure how that differs from round)—and five numbering schemes:

- Number (1, 2, 3…)
- Roman Small (i, ii, iii…)
- Roman Large (I, II, III…)
- Alphabet Small (a, b, c…)
- Alphabet Large (A, B, C…)

You know—the familiar choices from outline numbering—imagine that you're back in some college-level class, copying copious amounts of information from a blackboard that's about to be erased.

You can also start the numbering somewhere besides at 1. Use a numeral even if the list type is Roman or Alphabet.

The List Item part of the dialog box enables you to override the list style for a specific item or restart the numbering of the list with that item.

> HTML and Dreamweaver also support lists within lists. For example, to create a bulleted list within another bulleted list, first apply the bulleted list formatting to the entire list. Then select the items for the sublist and click the text indent button. Dreamweaver will indent the sublist and—for bullets—change the graphical element to indicate another layer down (such as using hollow bullets instead of solid ones for these items).

Alignment

Dreamweaver handles alignment in a way that's smart and compliant with HTML standards. If the selection is a paragraph, Dreamweaver adds the alignment information to the paragraph tag. If the selection is an item that doesn't permit alignment attributes, then Dreamweaver wraps a <DIV> tag around the selection and includes the alignment attribute there.

To align a stretch of text, select it, and then click the Align Left, Align Center, Align Right, or Justify buttons.

Indentation

Dreamweaver offers a serviceable, if not perfectly compliant, approach to indentation using a tag for block quotations. It's preferable to use style sheets (Chapter 15) for indentation, but

if you must, indent a selection by clicking the Text Indent button or outdent it by clicking the Text Outdent button.

> If the selection is already flush left, the Text Outdent button won't do anything.

Formatting Text with HTML Styles

Sometimes you need to apply the same handful of formatting options to a number of different text selections, using them as a kind of consistent style for similar elements in your pages. For example, you might want the first three words of each article to be boldface, one size larger than the rest of the copy, and colored maroon. Dreamweaver offers a pretty cool way of creating and keeping track of these kinds of design choices, which it calls HTML styles.

What Dreamweaver Means by "HTML Style"

All Dreamweaver means by *HTML style* is a saved-and-named collection of formatting choices that you can apply repeatedly. This is not to be confused with the styles in Cascading Style Sheets. Any HTML style you create will exist only in the Dreamweaver software, not in any external reference at the site. Nothing will be maintained or updated automatically. The formatting behaves as ordinary formatting once applied. Really, HTML styles are simply a useful kind of formatting shortcut.

To begin working with HTML styles, first open the HTML Styles panel.

You'll notice that there are two options listed by default: Clear Selection Style and Clear Paragraph Style. These two choices are not styles themselves but commands for removing styles.

Creating an HTML Style

To create a new HTML style, click the New Style button ⊡ in the bottom-right corner of the panel.

This brings up the Define HTML Style dialog box (see Figure 12.7).

Then follow these steps to describe your new HTML style:

1. First give the style a descriptive name that will make sense to you later when you are trying to pick the right style off of the list.

2. Then choose whether this is to be a Selection style (applied only to the characters in a selection) or a Paragraph style (applied to the entire paragraph containing the insertion point).

3. Decide whether this style should accumulate on top of any other styling that was applied to the selection or whether it should replace such styling entirely.

4. Choose a font hierarchy or leave Default Font selected.

5. Choose a size or a size change, or leave None selected

6. Choose a color or leave the color set to Default Color.

7. Choose Bold and or Italic, or click the Other button to add any of the other types of phrase formatting.

8. If you are making a paragraph style, choose paragraph, a heading type, preformatted text, or leave the default None option selected.

   Also for paragraph styles, choose an alignment or leave the alignment buttons uns-elected. (If you choose one by mistake, you'll need to cancel and start over to remove it!)

9. Click OK.

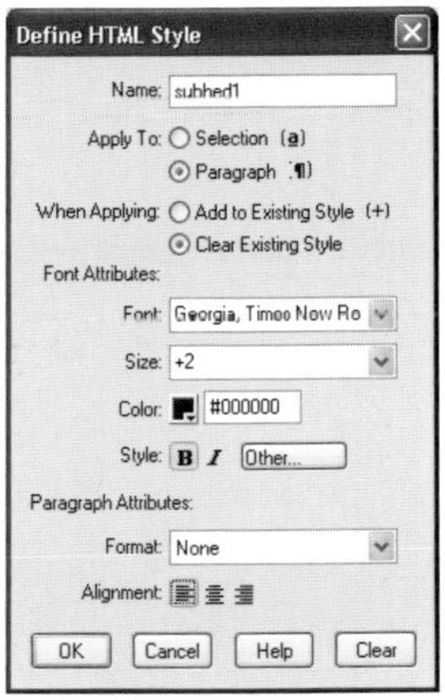

Figure 12.7

Build your HTML style using this handy-dandy set of options.

Applying HTML Styles

To apply an HTML style to a selection or to the current paragraph, click the name of the style in the HTML Styles panel.

Editing HTML Styles

To edit an HTML style, first uncheck Auto Apply so that the style isn't applied willy-nilly when you try to select it for editing. Then click the right-arrow in the upper-right corner and choose Edit from the menu that drops down. Editing a style is just like creating one.

> To create a new style that's similar to an existing one, choose Duplicate from the same drop-down list.

Removing HTML Styles

To eliminate an HTML style, uncheck Auto Apply, choose the style, and then click the Delete Style 🗑 button.

Formatting Text with CSS

Cascading Style Sheets have other applications beyond text formatting (they help with page layout, they can work with scripts, they can be involved with Dynamic HTML, and so on), but they are most stable and effective across platforms as a text-formatting solution. Be sure to check out Chapter 15 to learn how to work with CSS in Dreamweaver. CSS represents one direction of the future in web design.

Graphical Text

If you want total control over the appearance of text (as you sometimes might when you are creating headlines, advertisements, and so on), then you're better off creating graphical or flash text instead of relying on the vagaries of HTML. There are pros and cons to this approach:

It's not really text. One problem with graphical text is that it's actually graphics and not text. It may read just fine to the human eye, but from the computer's point of view, there's no text there. Be sure to include alternative text with any graphical text so that the information will still be available to those who cannot or do not want to view graphics.

But it looks exactly right! The argument for graphical text is that it brings back the level of control over typography that designers have been accustomed to for years in print and other media. Of course, it may only look *exactly* right on your own screen. It's a funny thing about the Web, but you can never be sure exactly how things are going to look for others.

There was an extension for Dreamweaver 4 available at the Macromedia site that enables automatic creation of GIF graphics from HTML text. Most likely this same extension will be updates for MX. (See Chapter 32 for more on using Dreamweaver extensions.)

For more on creating graphical text (in Fireworks), see Part II. Creating Flash Text is covered in Chapter 17.

Working with Raw HTML

Hey, look we're twelve chapters into this book and we've managed to pussyfoot around HTML this whole time! If you're determined to stay away from the code as much as possible, go ahead and skip this last section, but remember that all Dreamweaver really is—for the most part—is an HTML-generating program, a bunch of very clever labor-saving shortcuts for generating clean HTML code. And for that matter, there's no way that Dreamweaver can provide a widget for every conceivable HTML effect. The time may come when you need to edit the code yourself to accomplish the results you seek. When that time comes, this section will help you to have a clue about how HTML works and how Dreamweaver gives you direct access to it.

THERE'S NO ESCAPING HTML

Experienced hand-coders like the authors of this book tend to be somewhat biased. We think it helps to understand the HTML tags, CSS, and other standards used to build the Web. While we're sympathetic to those who'd rather keep things on a visual level, we feel that there are times when there's no substitute from rummaging through the code yourself and rooting out some entangled problem. If you come to agree with us, you may find yourself looking for more detailed sources of HTML information. Of course the best place to start is the World Wide Web Consortium site where the standards are maintained and promulgated (http://www.w3c.org), but you may want to refer to a book, such *Mastering XHTML, Premium Edition,* by Ed Tittel et al. (Sybex, 2002).

Macromedia also thoughtfully provides an HTML reference in a help/reference-style panel (Window → Reference or Ctrl + Shift + F1/Command + Shift + F1). It's a customized interactive version of some other reference books.

Editing HTML in Code View or with the Code Inspector

As you already know if you read Chapter 2 of this book, Dreamweaver can display pages in Design view (what you see is what you get), Code view (just the HTML, ma'am), or in a combined view. You can also switch the placement of Code view portion of the window from above the design portion to below it by selecting View → Design View on Top (see Figure 12.8).

When viewing both the design and code, don't lose track of which panel you're in, or you may end up typing code into the Design view. You can switch between views quickly with Alt + Tab/Option + Tab.

To resize the Code view window, click the divider and drag it up or down.

Using the Quick Tag Editor

If you prefer to work in Design view, you can still edit tags directly using the Quick Tag Editor, which has three modes:

- Insert HTML mode (for inserting new HTML tags into a page)
- Edit Tag mode (for changing an existing tag)
- Wrap Tag mode (for wrapping an opening and closing tag pair around a selection).

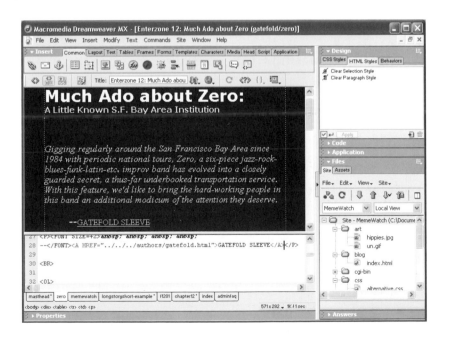

Figure 12.8

You may prefer your code on the bottom, WordPerfect style.

The mode is selected depending on what you do before you invoke the Quick Tag Editor:

- To insert new HTML, just place the insertion point where you want the new code to go.

- To edit an existing tag, first click in Design view or select the object in Design view to which the tag applies and then click the tag you want in the tag selector at the bottom of the page window.

- To wrap a new tag around a selection, first select the text you want to wrap the tag around (it must currently be unformatted).

Then press Ctrl + T/Command + T or click the Quick Tag Editor icon on the right side of the Property Inspector.

The Insert HTML (or Edit Tag or Wrap) dialog pops up showing either the opening and closing angle brackets of an HTML tag (</>) or—for the Edit Tag—the current tag itself.

Now type or edit the HTML code to your liking. Now here's the cool part. If you pause while editing the tag, Dreamweaver will offer you a pop-up list of valid attributes you can apply. If you're editing multiple tags in the Quick Tag Editor, use the Tab key to jump between them.

> The list of attributes offered is stored in a file called `TagAttributeList.txt` in your Dreamweaver installation's Configuration folder. You can edit that file directly in Dreamweaver's Code view if you want to change the list.

When you are done, press Enter and then press Esc to leave the Quick Tag Editor.

Finding and Replacing HTML Tags

Earlier in this chapter, when we discussed editing with Find and Replace, we mentioned that it's possible to use the same tool to make changes in source code. There are three different modes for doing this:

Source Code Works just like regular Find and Replace but sifts through the text in Code view instead of the text shown in Design view.

Specific Tag Works like an ordinary Find and Replace, but looks for a single tag in the code instead of a word in the ordinary text.

Text (Advanced) Enables you to hunt for ordinary text based on the tags that are or are not surrounding it (see Figure 12.9).

> When doing a Find and Replace on source code when both Code and Design views are showing, be careful not to leave the insertion point in the Design view when you next save the page, or the changes made to the source code will be lost.

Layout, Words, ... Pictures!

OK, so far in this part, we've covered laying out web pages with tables and layers, and inserting and massaging text. But as you know, the Web is not a text-only medium. With pictures being worth a thousand words (and who knows how many Euros?), and a whole previous book part on Dreamweaver's sister product Fireworks, it's about time we showed you how to insert graphics into your pages. Well, isn't it?

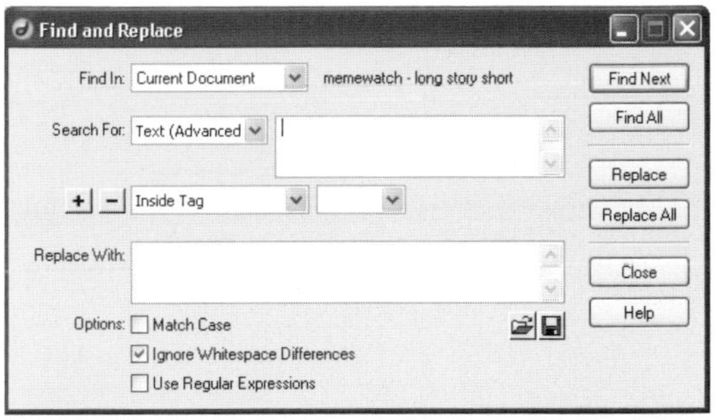

Figure 12.9

Choose Inside Tag or Not Inside Tag, select a tag, and then use the plus (+) button to add further parameters, requiring or excluding attributes of certain values or ranges.

## CHAPTER 13

Working with Graphics

When the Web first became a global reality (around 1994), the supposedly slickest websites were using the <BLINK> tag on their text. If you don't know what that is, be thankful. Very thankful. The first HTML pages I ever wrote had gray backgrounds and all the content was justified left! Try and attract visitors to a site like that nowadays. What few graphics there were, were usually too large and without transparent backgrounds. In other words, all the graphics had visible rectangular edges. Very pocket protector-ish. Now, with the help of applications such as Dreamweaver and Fireworks, you can easily add graphic imagery to your website without having to be a Photoshop guru. Really.

This chapter will cover these basics to get you started:

- **Placing graphics on a page**
- **Fine-tuning the display of images**
- **Designing with placeholders**
- **Modifying a graphic using Fireworks**

Inserting a Graphic

Before we get too far into the mechanics of inserting a graphic into an HTML page for publication on the Web, we'd like to briefly explain the types of graphics that Web browsers can handle and when is a good time to use each of them. Many of these topics were discussed from a Fireworks perspective in Part II of this book, but here we'd like to get into the reasoning behind using—or not using—a particular graphics format in your web page.

GIF Files

GIF files are graphics that have been compressed by indexing the colors in the graphic. This means that if there are shades of different blues or different reds, saving a file to a GIF format will "generalize" the colors so that there aren't so many different shades or variations. This process cuts down on the amount of descriptive information contained in the file, which in turn considerably reduces the file size.

The general rule with GIF files practiced by web designers and graphic designers alike is to only use the GIF format if you do not have gradients (where colors fade into one another or where there are many tones such as skin or grass or sky, and so on.). For the most part, if you stay away from GIF files when you are posting photos, you'll be just fine.

JPEG Files

JPEG files are predominantly used for photographs. Sometimes, if you have a non-photographic image that has many gradients, such as a piece of fine art or a really cool illustration, you may want save your image in the JPEG format. Especially if a GIF version of your image looks horrible. JPEG files have many levels of quality (1 to 100), so you'll want to play with the different levels, making the quality level as low as possible to reduce file size. The best way to do this is to save at a general level, such as 40, drag and drop your image onto a web browser, and see how it looks. If it looks good, leave it. If it looks jagged or pixilated, up the quality level five notches at a time until your image looks presentable.

Placing Your Image

Once you've decided upon a general layout scheme for your web page (as discussed in Part I), you're ready to start placing graphics where you want them.

The process is a fairly simple one:

1. In the Dreamweaver workspace, click the place in your design where you would like to place your graphic. You'll see a blinking cursor that is kind of saying, "I'm waiting for you, pal."

2. Without clicking anywhere else, move your mouse over to the Insert bar (Cmd + F2 on Mac, Ctrl + F2 in Windows), make sure the Common tab is selected, and click the Insert Image button. Figure 13.1 shows you the Insert bar and the location of the button.

When you click the Insert Image button, the Select Image Source dialog box appears (see Figure 13.2). You will now navigate to your computer's hard drive and locate the image you'd like to place into your web page. We'll assume that you've already decided what size your image should be based on your design.

Once you've found and selected your image, you'll notice a small drop-down menu in the Select Image Source dialog box labeled "Relative To:" (just below the URL or path to your image file).

Figure 13.1

Simply place a cursor on your page where you'd like a graphic and press the Insert Image button on the Insert bar to place a graphic in your web page.

If you are publishing HTML that will only appear on your computer (not on the Web) or on a CD or DVD, you should select the Document option because the path (in the code, the page has to refer the browser to the location of the file) will be relative to the HTML document you are working on.

On the other hand, if you are publishing this HTML page to the Web, you may opt to choose Site Root from this drop-down box. Choose this option only if you have already set up a definition for your site by going to Site → Define Sites from the application menu at the top of the screen. (See Chapter 3 for more on setting up your site).

If you work with a site with a "mirror" copy on both your drive and the web server, and you use the Relative To: Site Root, you will have a duplicate of your website/server file and folder hierarchy on your hard drive. This copy will help you keep your file locations organized, thus making it easier to locate files quickly and compare them to the copies on the live web server. The other thing that this process provides—and this is a big benefit—is an exact backup of your site.

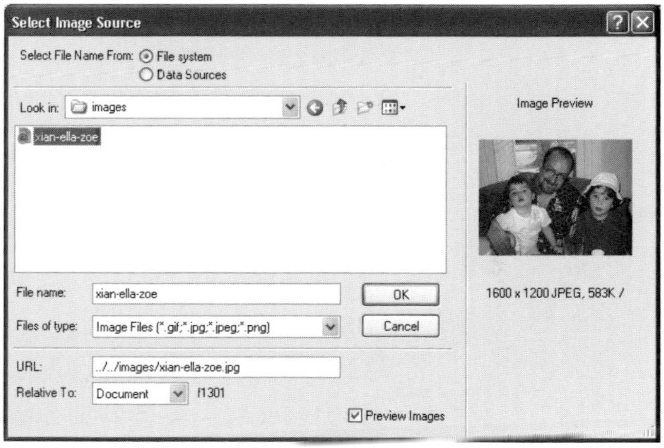

Figure 13.2

Selecting the location of your image relative to a Site Root requires that you set up a site definition for your site as seen here.

Many programmers like to work on their live sites directly on the web server—probably because they know how. That's all fine and good, but if your web server crashes or your service provider goes belly up ("That'll never happen!" Quote circa 1999), you are out of luck. Of course, if you work on your site offline and this happens, you simply upload the latest version of your site files because they live right on your computer.

Because the Select Image Source's Relative To setting is an important one, I'd like to wrap it up with this bit of information—the local root folder in the Site Definition dialog box will act as your `/public_html/` directory, which is the typical directory for web hosting providers. The forward slash ("/") that Dreamweaver will place in front of the path to your image (for example, `"<IMG SRC="/images/file.gif">"`) will be relative to the directory your service provider gave you as your account's public directory.

Make your selection and press Open to insert the image into your page. There it is! Looks good. Now you're done, right? Not quite. You still have to decide on a few image settings so that a web browser knows exactly how you want your image displayed.

CONTROLLING YOUR IMAGE SIZES

One more thing to note when you are creating a layout for your web page is that web pages are viewed on a computer monitor, not on paper. This means that your design and your graphics need to be optimized for this medium. Most novice web designers (I was one of them once) start creating graphics in an application using inches as their unit of measure for determining the size of their graphics. While that isn't technically wrong per se, you'd be wise to start thinking in pixels (the unit of measure for monitor screen resolution).

If you are using a graphics application such as Photoshop, you can change the unit of measure to pixels in Photoshop's preferences. This will get you thinking screen resolution instead of inches and it will help you tremendously when you go to size your images for a particular design. The more control you have over your design and its size, the cleaner your web pages will look to visitors.

Fireworks is specially designed for producing online graphics. It is not geared for print or other media (as contrasted with Photoshop, which has more applications but is not so custom-tailored for web graphics).

Setting Image Options

If your design is simple or you are just placing a graphic onto an empty page just to learn the process, most of the image settings will not apply to you. But if you are trying to make an exact design that needs to have images that fit where they are and work properly in relation to other elements (images, text, and so on) on the page, you will want to work with the Property Inspector (see Figure 13.3). In order to make changes to your image in the Property Inspector, you must select the image (but it will automatically be selected immediately after you place it into your page) by single clicking it.

You'll quickly see that there is a lot of stuff to digest when reviewing the properties of an image. Some properties are more complicated than others, so I'll try and briefly run through each setting so that you can decide which one applies to your particular situation and/or situations to come.

One of the most useful image-related features of Dreamweaver is its automatic placement of the image size in the HTML code. This may seem trivial to some, but it's a huge reason why some sites—even with graphics optimized for the Web—load slowly. If a site has image sizes set properly in the HTML code, the site visitor's browser doesn't have to guess where to place everything. It sees the graphic size and says, "Oh, okay. I know how to lay this page out." It

Figure 13.3

Use the Property Inspector to modify how a browser will display your image.

does this without having loaded the image completely. Without those simple little numbers, the browser has to wait until the images are almost totally loaded in order to "know" where to place everything in order to display the page the way the page designer put it together.

Here are more features to get familiar with when working with images. (You can expand the Property Inspector to show all image-related options by clicking the little arrow in its bottom-right corner.) Naturally, you'll have situations arise when you will need to handle images differently than the norm (for example, large images where you need to have multiple "hotspots," small spacer images where you'll change their size from the original file, and so on)

Image Map Creating an image map allows you to select portions of a single image and make them *hotspots*—clickable areas that send visitors to different URLs using x and y coordinates. This option is typically used with larger images for navigation.

Image Size You'll see the exact pixel size (see, you need to understand pixels!) of your image displayed automatically. You can set this size manually, but be aware of how doing so alters your image when it is displayed in the browser. First, when you make the file size larger, you will probably see the visual quality of your image degrade. Secondly, if you make the size smaller, it may look okay, but the actual file size that a site visitor has to download is larger than it needs to be. Use this feature to visually place a graphic and find the right size, but go back to your graphics editing application and make sure the final image is the exact size you want it.

Image Source (SRC) As you can see, this is the source path to your image.

Image Link This is where you would place a URL (or web address) that you would like to point visitors to if they click your image. You may link to a file in your file structure or to another website altogether. Be aware that if you link to an outside website (off of your domain), you must provide a full path to the URL, such as `http://www.example.com/somewhere/something.html`. (See Chapter 16 for more about hypertext links.)

Image Align This setting can be important depending on how you intend to place your image on your page and how you want it to interact with other elements around it. The default setting is Browser Default. This aligns your image to the left of whatever placeholder it's in, such as a table cell or the entire web browser page. Play with each of these to see what it does for you.

We will explain the Left and Right options here. If you want an image to be displayed within a block or paragraphs of text, you can place the image at the beginning of a line of text and choose the Left or Right Align option. This will align the image and allow the text to "flow" around it on whichever side is away from the alignment setting.

Image Alternate The `ALT` tag is rarely used correctly. `ALT` is an alternate description of your image displayed in text. Originally, it was used for non-graphical browsers (yes, they existed…and still do) so that they could "see" what the image was or what it said. Nowadays, it's used as a descriptor (place your cursor over an image on the Web and see the little text box pop-up) or more importantly for most web designers and/or site owners, it functions as a placeholder for key words used by search engines.

Vertical Space The `VSPACE` attribute is simply a number of pixels (default is "none") that act as a buffer zone above and below your image. This option and the Horizontal Space option are typically used if you are placing an image that is surrounded by text or other images and you do not want the other content right up against your image.

Horizontal Space `HSPACE` is the same as `VSPACE`, but it's for the left and right side of your image rather than the top and bottom.

Link Target If you are using frames or if you want to control how the browser handles a link, this is the place to choose your options. Most of these pertain to frames. If you'd like to have a new browser window pop up over the window with your site displayed, choose "_blank".

Low Source This is another old-school style of placing images on a web page. You have the option of creating a very low quality version of your image and having it load first while the original, more detailed image is still loading. This was designed for the overwhelming number of site visitors who were using 28.8K modems—way before DSL, cable modems, and so on. We recommend that you use this feature only when you have a very large graphic—which you should avoid using anyway.

Border If you add a link to an image, Dreamweaver automatically places a "0" value in the Border setting. If you have a link associated with an image, the browser will automatically place a colored border (usually blue) around the entire image to indicate that it is a hotspot.

You don't want that, trust us. If you have an image that does not have a link, you can add a border (in pixels again) to give it some structure. Use a one- or two-pixel border around a photo for a nice touch.

Image Align Part II You'll notice three buttons on the far right of the box for aligning your image. These are for quickly centering your image (click the center one—duh!) or aligning left and right without having to go to the drop-down list.

Edit In Dreamweaver's preferences, you can associate the Edit button with an image editor. By default, clicking it will open Fireworks, but you can set it to open whatever application you use.

Designing with Image Placeholders (When the Art Isn't Ready Yet)

Sometimes you need to lay out your pages without having the final versions of the artwork ready. This is no problem. Use Dreamweaver's Insert Image Placeholder button (right next to the Insert Image button on the Common tab of the Insert Bar) to insert a dummy image tag. This brings up a dialog box where you can specify the height and width of the placeholder.

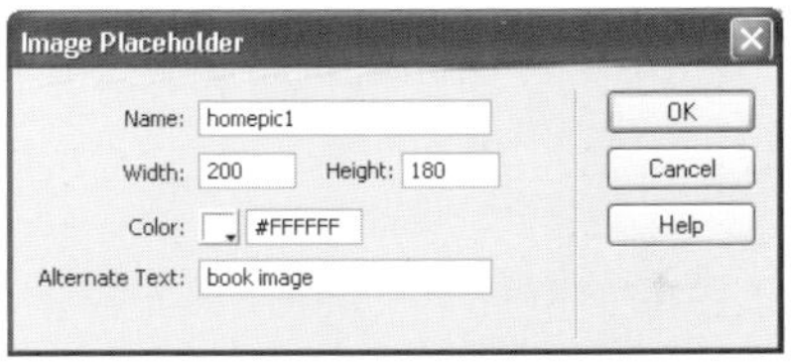

Choosing a color for the placeholder is optional, but it's a good idea to give it a name, just to remind you what's supposed to go there eventually. Dreamweaver will show a box to represent the image for now (see Figure 13.4).

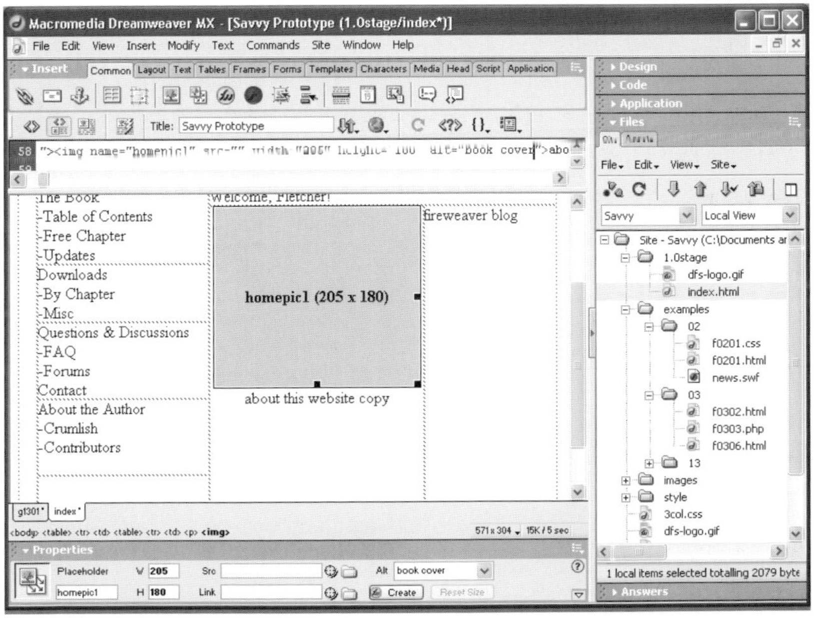

Figure 13.4

A placeholder has properties just like those of a real image.

When you have the art ready, click the placeholder to choose the image to insert, or create the image directly in Fireworks by clicking the Create button in the Property Inspector.

Modifying a Graphic Using Fireworks

Often, you'll find that the image you created or were given to place in your web page won't look right. It might be a bit too large or you may need to crop it down to focus in on an object or a person. The problem is so common that Macromedia developed Fireworks specifically to provide that sort of functionality in the Dreamweaver context.

Opening Fireworks

Fireworks is a completely separate application from Dreamweaver, even though it seems like there is a seamless transition between the two applications, which is of course exactly what Macromedia was shooting for. While you can always launch Fireworks directly, if you are already in Dreamweaver and the image you want to edit is visible in your web page, you can double-click the image to open it in Fireworks. You can also click the Edit button in the Property Inspector, or right-click (Ctrl-click on the Mac) the image and choose either Edit in Fireworks or Optimize in Fireworks. (Optimizing images in Fireworks is discussed at length in Chapter 10.)

> If you have already modified the graphics application selected in Dreamweaver's preferences, you will have to launch Fireworks directly from your computer's hard drive.

Once you've opened your image in Fireworks, you'll need to familiarize yourself with the tools that are available. For this chapter, we're going to discuss basic graphic editing features in Fireworks as they pertain to placing images into a web page. (See Part II for more in-depth discussion of Fireworks' capabilities.)

Notice that Fireworks is aware that you've launched the program from Dreamweaver to work on a specific image. The Done button gives you the ability to finish your changes and then switch right back to Dreamweaver and update the image (see Figure 13.5).

Resizing Your Image

Have you ever taken an image directly from your web page and resized it only to have it go all jagged or just look plain ugly? Oh yeah, I know you have. I can tell by your reaction. The reason why is because you either A) tried to resize a GIF image or B) tried to enlarge a JPEG image.

GIF files are smaller to download because their colors have been indexed—remember what we talked about with gradients earlier in this chapter? This means that if you try to enlarge this image, you're really only "stretching" it without actually reindexing the colors from the original RGB or CMYK image (the high-res version you or someone else originally started with). Sometimes you can get away with a small enlargement or reduction without

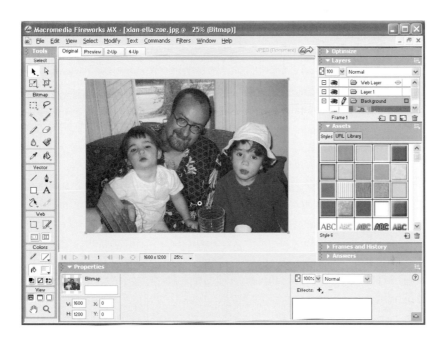

Figure 13.5

Fireworks knows when you're "editing from Dreamweaver" and offers you the Done button for one-click roundtrips.

much loss of quality, but you'll have to eyeball that yourself. As a rule, you should load your original high-resolution file and resize the image from there. If you don't have another image, you'll need to change the image to an RGB-based format in Fireworks in order to convert the image to a format that will allow itself to be re-sized. Granted, this isn't the best way to do this—you may still have image degradation.

Converting an Object to an Image

Once you've opened your image in Fireworks, you can convert it to a format that will allow you to resize your image slightly, while trying to keep it looking all right. If you are only changing the size one way or the other a tiny bit (I highly recommend that you not try to enlarge or reduce too much with a GIF image—get the original file so that you can retain the clarity of the image), you can probably get away with converting the image to JPEG, resizing it, and then converting it back to a GIF file (using the Optimize panel) before importing it back into Dreamweaver.

You can choose JPEG from the drop-down list in the Optimize panel. Now, choose Modify → Image Size to bring up the Image Size dialog box. Because we've got you thinking in pixels now (right?), modify one area of the pixel settings to the size you want. As we mentioned before, shrinking the image will work more than enlarging it because when you shrink an image, you have more pixels to work with and when you enlarge it, you are actually forcing the image to add more pixels—sometimes it's ugly. By default, Fireworks will preserve the width/height ratio. This means that if you change only the width value, the height value will proportionately go right along with it. If you deselect this feature, you'll end up with a stretched look to your image (you've done that before too, huh?).

Once you've made your size change, click OK. If that size doesn't work, press Ctrl + Z (or Cmd + Z on the Mac) to undo the size change. You'll notice that after you make a size change in Bitmap mode, your image returns to being an object as far as Fireworks is concerned. You'll have to double-click it again to return to Bitmap mode if you want to make more changes to it.

Figure 13.6

The Export wizard can help you determine the best format in which to export your image for use outside of Fireworks.

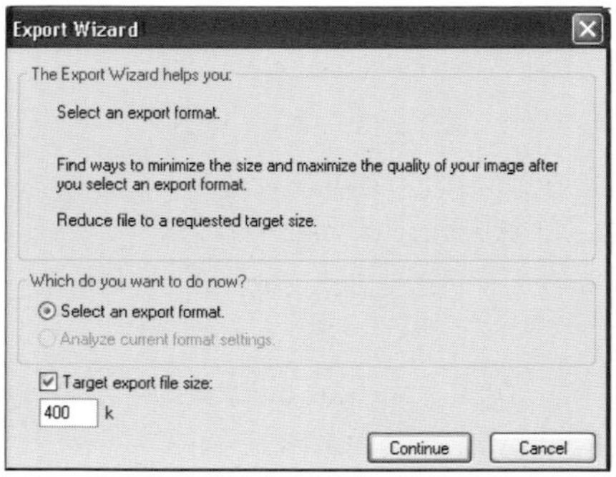

With your image still in JPEG mode, choose File → Export Wizard. When this dialog box comes up (see Figure 13.6), it will ask you questions about how you will use your image so that Fireworks can determine for you the best format in which to export your image (pretty cool, huh?). As you see in Figure 13.6, the Export wizard provides all kinds of options for exporting the image outside of Fireworks. You can change to different formats and actually preview what the file will look like with that particular setting. You can also choose transparency options, and much more. Because the image in this example was already a GIF file, that same format (GIF) is the best one to choose for optimal file size and clarity in this case.

I recommend that you save any changes to an existing image to a new filename (unless of course you have the highest quality source image stored elsewhere). Call it image2.gif or something. This is especially important if you don't have the original high-res file to go back to. There's nothing worse than shrinking an image size, changing your mind, and finding out that you overwrote the larger image size. Ouch.

When you are finished in Fireworks, click the Done button. Fireworks keeps running but gets out of the way and returns you to Dreamweaver, where your image has been updated. Like what you see?

Can You Imagine?

What you've learned in this chapter should help you tremendously with putting together a clean, quickly loading site—a goal that many, many web designers miss completely. In the next chapter, you'll learn how to work with frames (and when not to work with frames at all).

## CHAPTER 14

Interactivity with Framesets and Frames

The first few chapters in this part showed you how to design and add text and graphics to web pages. Before we proceed to the more exotic kinds of objects you can put on a web page, we'd first like to show you some further layout options in this chapter— frames and framesets. A *frame* is a subdivision of a web page that appears in a browser window. A web page can be divided into two or more frames; each contains an individual web page with its own URL, content, and hyperlinks.

At one time, frames were overused, wasting screen real estate. Worse yet, they interfered with ordinary bookmarking of websites, usually hiding the content away from the base URL of a page's master frameset. But they do have their place, especially when a complex web design is required. Luckily, Dreamweaver makes it a matter of point and click.

This chapter examines the ways you can use frames to your benefit and add interactivity to your site; the following topics highlight these uses:

- **Creating an interactive frameset**
- **Using Dreamweaver's predefined frames objects**
- **Adding navigation bars, targeted frames, and other linking options**
- **Fine-tuning borders, scrollbars, and other frame properties**
- **Creating NoFrames content to reach the widest possible audience**

Creating a New Frameset

As usual, Dreamweaver gives you a variety of options for performing the task at hand—in this case, creating frames. But before you can begin to create a frames-based web page, you need to know something about such a page's component parts.

When you divide a web page into frames, you create a set of frames called a *frameset*. The term comes from the HTML command used to contain the frames instructions, <FRAMESET> </FRAMESET>. Figure 14.1 shows the HTML for a simple frames page displayed in Code view.

Figure 14.1

Frames commands are contained within the body of a web page and are enclosed by <FRAMESET> </FRAMESET>.

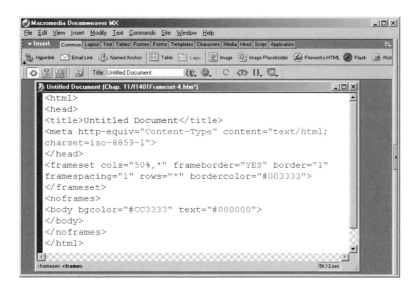

The HTML shown in Figure 14.1 describes a web page that has been divided into two frames, as shown in Figure 14.2.

In a web page that consists of two frames, those two frames each contain their own web page. But there's also a third page—the frameset page—that contains the instructions that describe the number of frames as well as their sizes and attributes.

Designers considering whether or not to create frames on a page should keep in mind that Dreamweaver's options for creating frames aren't as visually oriented as with tables or layers. You can't draw frames, as you can with layers. You can't use Layout View to create or edit frames, as you can with tables. You can create a frameset instantly with the Insert bar or use the Frames submenu of the Insert menu, however, as described later in the sections "Using a Predefined Frameset" and "Creating Frames from Scratch."

Figure 14.2

A web page with two frames that actually contains three separate documents—one for each frame and one for the frameset page.

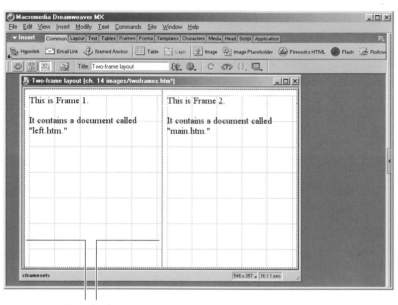

Frame border

USING FRAMES APPROPRIATELY

When you're planning your page layout, take a moment to consider whether frames are appropriate for the purpose you want to achieve. Many designers and web surfers alike are opposed to frames because they are so frequently misused. (In fact, there's a whole web site devoted to banning the use of frames—see http://www.noframes.org).

Look around the Web and see what kinds of frames layouts work and which ones don't. You'll probably encounter no-nos like these:

Too many frames Viewers are intimidated by the large number of frames and easily get confused.

Confusing links You make find links to other websites that have themselves been divided into frames. An entire frames page appears within a frame in your frameset.

Recursive frames A web page is divided into frames. One of the frames contains a set of nested frames. One of those nested frames contains nested frames, and so on. Too many layers of such recursive frames can cause your visitor's browser to crash.

Frames can cause other problems for your visitors. Some have older versions of web browsers or handheld devices with browsers that don't support frames display. You will have to create alternate NoFrames content so they'll see something on your site (see "Creating

continued on next page

USING FRAMES APPROPRIATELY (CONTINUED)

NoFrames Content" later in this chapter). In addition, frames layouts can look awful in a small browser window, and pages contained within frames can't be bookmarked.

Most websites that use frames effectively use just three or four frames per page. The site shown here is a good example of what *not* to do because the layout is far too complicated for most users.

You don't always have to use frames. You can divide web page content into multiple sections using tables or layers, as described in Chapter 11. You can also add a navigation bar without placing it in a frame (see Chapter 9). And the most common reason to use frames is to keep one sort of content static and always on screen while the content of other frames changes. The static content is usually a logo, or an ad, or a navigation bar.

As a savvy web designer, you will use frames only when it's necessary to display multiple web pages at the same time, and when you know the viewer will benefit from being able to have separate pages on your site interact with one another using frames.

Framing Your Layout

Now that you have a realistic idea of the limitations of frames layouts, it's about time you tried to create your own frames so that you can learn about their many benefits.

For many designers, the first step is to draw your frameset on paper before you start to use Dreamweaver. That way, you'll decide to use one of the Insert bar's predefined frame layouts or to create one from scratch. In order to make such a sketch, you need to know about the various components that make up a frameset as well as the tools for adjusting frames—the Frame Property Inspector and the Frames panel.

Individual Frames

A frame in a frameset has to be saved separately with a filename that's separate from the frameset page's filename and the filenames of other frames in the set. To save a frame, click to position the text cursor within it. Then choose File → Save Frame As. Be sure to save every individual frame you create with a separate filename.

> Instead of clicking in each frame separately and choosing File → Save Frame As, choose File → Save All. Dreamweaver prompts you to save each frame successively as well as the frameset page. Be sure to give the frameset web page a name that clearly describes the frameset as a whole so that you don't confuse it with an individual frame's web page.

Each frame, as a separate web page, has its own properties. You have to set them separately using the Property Inspector (see "Modifying Frames and Framesets" later in this chapter).

Each frame also has a name that's separate from the filename of the web page it contains. For instance, a frame on the left side of a frames-based page might contain a web page named `links.htm`. But the frame itself might be named `left` or `links`. You can name a frame using the Property Inspector.

Frame names are important when you want to target links—you create a hyperlink in one frame and target a frame named Main so that the linked content appears there. (See "Targeting Linked Content" later in this chapter for more on this.)

When you design a web page with a set of frames, which page within those frames contains the title that the viewer sees in the browser's Title bar? The frameset itself has its own title, and that's what the user sees. When you want to edit the title, open the frameset page in Dreamweaver and enter a title that describes the whole frameset in the title box.

Frame Borders

Each frame within a frameset is enclosed by a border on all four sides, much like that of a table. You can click and drag the border that's within the Document window (as opposed to a frame border that's around one of the edges of the web page) to quickly resize a frame.

By default, the borders you see around the frames in Dreamweaver are only guides to help you design the page. When you preview the page in a browser window, the borders aren't actually visible because, by default, their width is set to zero.

You can change the border width—and even assign a color to borders—by following these steps:

1. Click any frame border. A dashed line appears around all borders in the frameset to show that the entire frameset has been selected. The tag `<frameset>` also appears in the status bar to indicate that the frameset has been selected.

2. Choose Window → Properties (or press Ctrl + F3) to display the Frames Property Inspector if it's not already displayed (see Figure 14.3).

3. Enter a value other than 0 in the Border Width box to assign a width to the frameset's borders.

4. Choose Yes from the Borders drop-down list to display borders in the browser window.

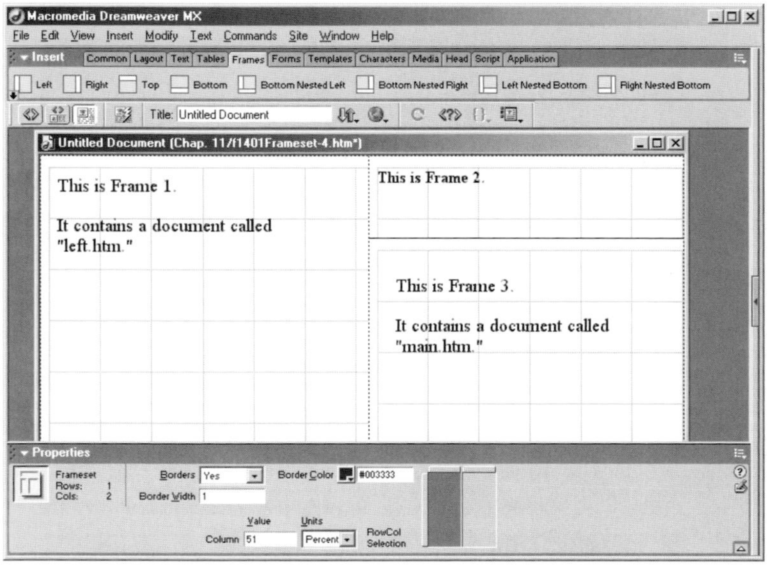

Figure 14.3

Click a border to select the frameset and adjust borders and other properties in the Frames Property Inspector.

If you select the entire frameset, you can only change the borders for all of the frames at once. But you can assign different colors to the borders of an individual frame. Begin by either Alt-clicking within the frame or by clicking that frame in the Frames panel. Then display the Property Inspector for that frame and click the Border Color box to select a color.

The Border drop-down list contains two other options. Choose No if you don't want borders to appear in the frameset. Choose Default if you want to leave it up to the user's browser settings to determine whether or not frame borders are displayed.

The Frames Panel

The Frames panel, which appears when you choose Window → Others → Frames or press Shift + F2, provides a miniature representation of the frames within a frameset. The Frames panel also gives you a clear, visual way to select either an individual frame or an entire frameset.

When you click a frame in the Frames panel, the borders of that frame are highlighted to indicate that it's currently selected (see Figure 14.4). Once an individual frame is selected, you can adjust its properties in the Frame Property Inspector.

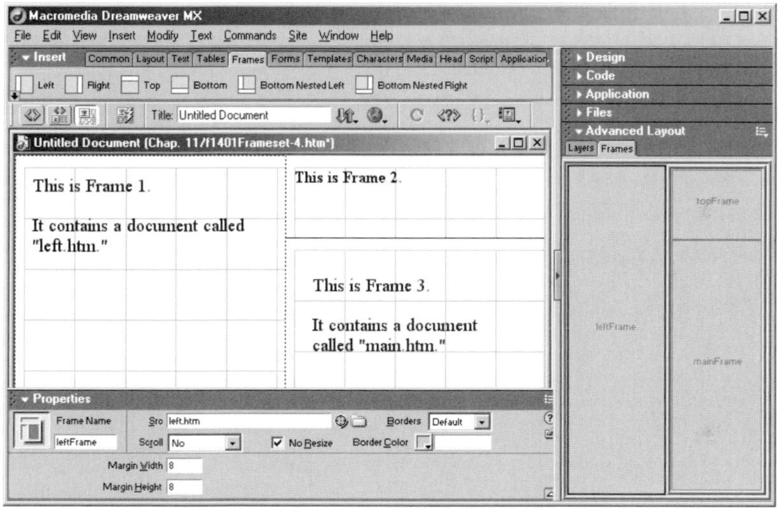

Figure 14.4

The Property Inspector displays attributes for a single frame when you select that frame in the Frames panel.

To select a single frame, Alt-click (Option + Shift + Click for the Macintosh) anywhere within it.

Rows and Columns

Like tables, framesets are divided into rows and columns; when you divide a page into two vertical frames—one on the left and one on the right (as shown in Figure 14.2)—you create a frameset with two columns. If you split one of those frames into two horizontal frames, you create two rows within that column of the frameset.

When you select a frameset and view the Property Inspector, you see a RowCol Selection box (see Figure 14.5) that you can use to adjust width and height. (See "Specifying Row Height and Column Width" later in this chapter.)

Figure 14.5

The frames in a frameset are arranged in rows and columns just as in tables.

Using a Predefined Frameset

Now that you know how frames are organized, you can start creating your own framesets. Dreamweaver provides you with preformatted frames layouts that give you another sort of design jump-start. If you haven't worked with frames before, or if you just want to save some time, look at the predefined frames layouts first.

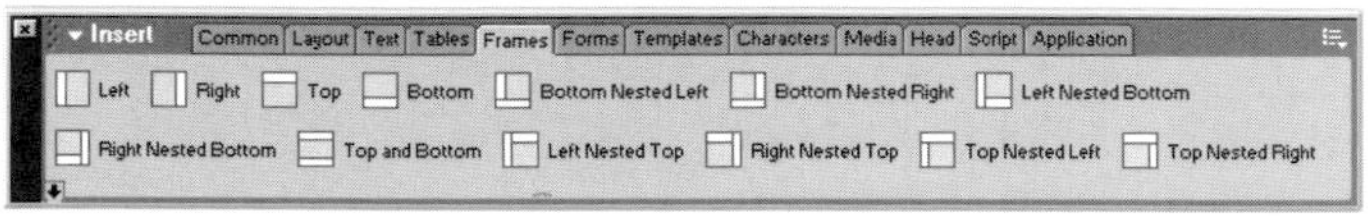

To view the preset designs, choose Window → Insert to display the Insert bar. Then click Frames in the set of tabs at the top of the Insert bar. A set of common frames designs appears (see Figure 14.6). Click an option to instantly create the frameset in the Document window.

Figure 14.6

The Insert bar presents you with a set of common frameset arrangements that you can quickly add to a web page.

You can use Dreamweaver's preset frame designs at any time, not just when you're first creating a frameset. To format an existing frameset, select it by clicking directly on a frame border. Then click the design you want in the Insert bar. The design is applied to the currently selected table.

You can also use the Insert menu to create one of the predefined frame designs. Choose Insert → Frames and then select an option from the Frames submenu: Left, Right, Top, Bottom, Bottom Nested Left, Bottom Nested Right, Left Nested Bottom, Right Nested Bottom, Top and Bottom, Left Nested Top, Right Nested Top, Top Nested Left, or Top Nested Right. The problem with using the Insert menu is that you can't preview the arrangement before you insert it. However, if you don't like the layout you've chosen, just choose Edit → Undo and choose another one.

Creating Frames from Scratch

You don't have to use the predefined frame layouts, of course. You can insert your own frames one at a time. Or you can start with one of the predefined arrangements and then modify it to suit your needs.

You can use the Modify menu to create a frameset or modify one you've already created. You can also split a web page or a frame within a page into two frames.

> Make sure you've configured Dreamweaver to display frame borders to make it easier to work on framesets. Choose View → Visual Aids → Frame Borders to see the borders displayed in the Document window while you are assembling your pages. When you want to preview your pages, you can turn the borders off by choosing View → Visual Aids → Frame Borders once again. That way, you'll be able to see the page as your viewers will see them. (You can, of course, choose File → Preview in Browser to preview the page, too.)

Inserting Frames

A single web page can be considered a frameset that only consists of a single frame. Thinking of a page this way comes in handy when you want to create a new frame. You do it by splitting the current single frame. Follow these steps:

1. Display the web page you want to divide into frames, or position the text cursor within a frame you want to divide.

2. Choose Modify → Frameset.

3. Choose one of the following options from the Frameset submenu:

    Split Frame Left Creates a frame to the left of the current one.

    Split Frame Right Creates a frame to the right of the current one.

    Split Frame Up Creates a frame above the current one.

    Split Frame Down Creates a frame beneath the current one.

The Frames submenu comes in handy when you want to create an unusual frames layout, such as three or four horizontal frames in succession, or when you want to adjust an existing frameset.

Dragging Frames

If you're a fan of clicking and dragging, Dreamweaver gives you the option of creating frames with your mouse. Remember that every web page, whether or not it has already been divided into frames, has a border around it. You can use this border to split the page into two frames by following these steps (make sure frame borders are visible by choosing View → Visual Aids → Frame Borders if necessary):

1. Click the left or top border of the currently displayed web page.

2. Drag the border into the Document window in one of the following ways:

    - Drag the top border (the mouse arrow becomes a two-headed arrow when it is positioned over the border) down to split the page into two horizontal frames.

    - Drag the left border to split the page into two vertical frames.

    - Drag the corner (the mouse arrow becomes a four-headed arrow) to split the page into four frames (see Figure 14.7).

You can also drag an inner frame border—one that's already a frame border and within the Document window rather than around the edge of the Document window. For an inner border, Alt-drag (Option-drag for the Macintosh) to split the frame into two frames.

Saving Framesets

Once you've created a frameset, you need to save it. This isn't as straightforward as choosing File → Save to save a stand-alone web page. You need to save both the frameset page and its component frames before you can preview the frames page in a browser.

When you use Dreamweaver to create a frame, a blank document is created within that frame and given a temporary filename. The first frame you create is given the temporary name Untitled-1, the second becomes Untitled-2, and so forth. The frameset page is called UntitledFrameset-1.

To save a frameset, you first need to select it by clicking any frame border. Then you can choose from the following options:

- Choose File → Save Frameset Page to save only the frameset page and not the individual frames.

- Choose File → Save Frameset As to save the current frameset with a different name.

When you click anywhere in an individual frame, a different set of frame-related File menu options appears:

- Choose File → Save Frame to save the currently selected frame.

- Choose File → Save Frame As to save the current frame with a different name.

- Choose File → Save Frame as Template to save the current frame as a template that you can use to create similar pages (see Chapter 4).

Whether you select a frameset or an individual frame, choose File → Save All Frames to save all frames in succession. Dreamweaver displays the Save As box and highlights the frame you're being prompted to save (though you might need to move the Save As box slightly to see which frame is being highlighted so that you can give it the name you want).

Modifying Frames and Framesets

Simply creating frames with a few mouse clicks and menu choices is only part of the way Dreamweaver helps you "frame" web pages. Once your frames layout is in place, you add content to the frames as you would any other series of web pages. Then you can modify the attributes of each frame using the Frame Property Inspector or the Frames panel.

The following sections describe how to turn scrollbar display on or off, keep a user from changing a frame's size, or make other adjustments.

Changing a Frame's Appearance

Frames pages, like conventional web pages, need to complement rather than clash with their contents. But there's no reason why you need to limit yourself to a default white background for every frame. By giving your frames some visual interest, you can dramatically improve the overall appearance of your website.

At the same time, you can make the content being presented within the frames more readable by controlling alignment and other visual attributes. The ultimate goal is to get your message across in a compelling way so that the viewer will explore your site.

Adding Colors

Each individual frame in a frameset can have its own background color. By changing the background color of a single frame, you can call attention to a logo or section. On the other hand, for a simpler look, you can assign the same background color to the frames-based page by first assigning that color to all of the frames within it.

To add color to a frame's background, follow these steps:

1. Click anywhere in the frame you want to adjust.

2. Choose Modify → Page Properties to display the Page Properties dialog box.

3. Click the color box next to Background and select a color from the color picker that appears (see Figure 14.8).

4. Click OK to close Page Properties and return to the Dreamweaver window, where the frame displays a page with the new background.

Figure 14.8

Dreamweaver's color picker helps you assign a background color to an individual frame page.

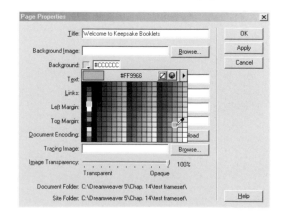

Alt-clicking within a frame displays the Frame Property Inspector, which enables you to assign a color to that frame's border but not to the background of the web page within the frame. Simply click within the frame to adjust the current page's background. But remember that you're only adjusting the *currently* displayed page. If the contents of the frame change due to clicks on hyperlinks in other frames, you'll need to adjust the backgrounds of all the pages that might appear in that frame.

Adjusting Frame Margins

Another way to make a frame's contents more readable is to adjust the margins. The margin of a frame is the space between any one of the four borders and the text or images within them. By default, the margin space is about 8 pixels. By making the margin bigger, you can call attention to contents within the frame.

To adjust margins, follow these steps:

1. Alt-click to select the frame you want to adjust.

2. Choose Window → Properties to display the Property Inspector if it isn't already displayed.

3. Enter values in the Margin Width and/or Margin Height boxes.

4. To see the changes on screen (see Figure 14.9), press Enter or click the miniature frames layout on the left-hand side of the Property Inspector.

By setting margins to 0, you can make the frame's contents "bleed" to the border. This enables you to align the images in one frame with images in another frame.

Figure 14.9

Increasing frame margins can direct more attention to a frame's contents.

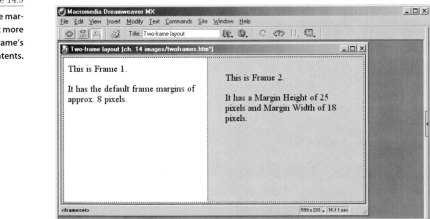

Specifying Row Height and Column Width

Dreamweaver makes it easy to change the size of frames: simply drag borders until each frame is the size you want. An alternative is to select one or more rows or columns and enter a value in the Property Inspector. However, you need to begin not by selecting a specific frame but by selecting the entire frameset. To do so, follow these steps:

1. Click directly on a frame border to select the frameset.

2. Click the expander arrow in the bottom-right corner of the Property Inspector to display the expanded version if you need to.

3. Click a row or column in the RolCol Selection Box on the far right side of the Property Inspector (see Figure 14.10). When you click a row, all the frames in that row are selected. When you click a column, all the frames in that column are selected.

Figure 14.10

Select a row or column in your frameset so that you can specify a different height or width, respectively.

You can express the size of a row or column within a frameset as a fixed number or pixels or as a relative value. Select the frameset, view the Property Inspector, and select the row or column you want to adjust by clicking the RowCol Selection box on the right side of the Property Inspector. Then choose one of three measurements from the Units drop-down list:

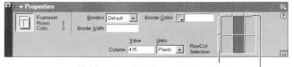

Click here to select the row to the right.

Click here to select the column below.

Pixels Assigns a specific pixel size to the frame. The frame size will remain constant no matter what the size of the browser window.

Percent Expresses the row or column size as a percentage of the frameset height (for a row) or width (for a column).

Relative Describes the size of the selected row or column in relation to other frames that have been given pixel or percentage measurements.

If you choose Pixels, enter a number of pixels in the Value box. If you choose Percent or Relative, enter a percentage in the Value box.

If you have trouble selecting a row or column in the RowCol Selection box, click one of the rectangles either above the top row or to the left of the first column.

If you are used to working with HTML, an alternative to dragging frame borders or using the RowCol Selection box is to edit the HTML code:

1. Alt-click to select the frame you want to edit.

2. Choose View → Code to open the frameset in Code view. The frameset code is highlighted.

3. Specify a precise width for columns or height for rows by changing the values that follow the FRAMESET tag. For instance, the two-column layout shown in Figure 14.9 is described by the following HTML:

```
<frameset cols="241,*" frameborder="NO" border="0" framespacing="0"
rows="*">
```

The `"241,*"` value after the COLS attribute means that the frameset contains two columns. The first column is 241 pixels wide. The width of the second one is not a fixed value; rather the width as symbolized by the asterisk (*) varies depending on the width of the browser window. You can change 241 to a different value or give a fixed value to the second column. You can also use percentages rather than fixed values or asterisks—the first column can be 40 percent of the browser window width and the second 60 percent, for instance.

A special case arises when the web designer specifies a fixed value for a frame and the viewer's web browser is too small to display the frame in its entirety. For example, if a web page has been divided into two columnar frames, one 241 pixels and the other of varying width, and if the viewer reduces the browser size to, say, 200 pixels, the frame will appear to be cut off. Any text in the frame will rewrap to fit the browser window. But any images wider than 200 pixels won't appear at all.

Putting the Viewer in Control

Some frame attributes are ones that give the viewer the ability to use frames or view their contents. Remember that frames can be difficult to view for those whose web browsers are older or who have only a limited amount of screen real estate to allocate to the web browser window. You can provide some enhancements to help visitors use your frames layout.

As stated earlier in this chapter, when you first create a frameset, border widths are set to 0. Although frames without visible borders can be useful in some circumstances, one of your first adjustments should be to change border width to 1 or some other value to help viewers understand that frames are being used and to keep them from being disoriented.

Controlling Scrollbar Display

By default, Dreamweaver displays scrollbars when a frame's contents can't be displayed in their entirety. For instance, when the text in a frame extends beyond the length of the Document window, a scrollbar appears on the right side of the frame so that you can scroll down and edit all of the frame's text. If images extend beyond the width of the frame, scrollbars appear at the bottom of the frame so that you can view them.

But you don't always need scrollbars. For instance, if a frame only contains a single logo or banner ad, it doesn't make sense to include scrollbars that interfere with the image (see Figure 14.11).

By selecting the frame and changing the Scroll drop-down list in the Property Inspector, you can specify one of four settings:

Yes Means that the frame will always display scrollbars, even if they are not needed.

No Means that the frame will never display scrollbars.

Figure 14.11

Some contents, like images, don't need scrollbars and you should turn them off.

Auto Means that the frame will display scrollbars only when needed.

Default Means that the viewer's browser can determine whether scrollbars should be shown. Most browsers use Auto as the default—they show scrollbars if the frame's contents aren't fully shown.

By choosing Auto or Default, you enable your visitors to control how the frames appear. Because you can't control the size of the browser window, it makes sense to give visitors control over scrollbars unless you're absolutely sure that the Yes or No options should be used. The four scrollbar options apply to both horizontal and vertical scrollbars.

Allowing Frame Resizing

By default, when a frame is created, the viewer can resize that frame by dragging its borders. If you want to let visitors to your website resize a frame, Alt-click the frame, then make sure the No Resize box is unchecked in the Property Inspector.

You might not always want to give viewers the ability to resize a frame, however. If one of your frames displays an ad that a customer has paid to display on your pages, you don't want to give visitors the chance to obscure part of it. To prevent resizing, select the frame and make sure the No Resize box is checked.

> To delete a frame, Alt-click to select it, then press Delete. Or, if you're a fan of clicking and dragging, click the frame, hold down the mouse button, and drag the frame off of the page. Release the mouse button, and the frame is gone.

Adding Navigation Elements to Frames

When you divide a page into frames, links get more complicated. A link in one frame should cause the viewer's browser to display some new content. The question is: where should that content appear? Should it appear in another frame in the frameset, the current frame, or a new web page?

By *targeting* a link in a frame, you make sure that link produces the effect you want. Targeting a link means that you select a destination page—the target page—that displays the file that you have associated with the link.

This section describes one of the most useful features of frames: their ability to interact with one another through hyperlinks. By the way, Part IV of this book discussed navigation elements and linking in greater detail.

Targeting Linked Content

It's important to select a target for the content that is associated with a link when the link occurs in a frames-based web page. Unless you identify a target where the linked content will appear, the content will appear in the same frame in which the link appeared before you clicked it.

For example, if one of your frames contains a set of links leading to the various important pages on a website, chances are you want those links to remain on screen while someone explores your site. If someone clicks one of the links and it is replaced by a new page, that person might have a hard time navigating your site.

To target a link in a frame, follow these steps:

1. Create the text, image, or other object you want to turn into a link.

2. Identify the file to link to in the Property Inspector's Link field by doing one of the following:

   • Enter the URL for the file in the Link box. This should be a relative URL—a URL that describes the location of the file in relation to the file that contains the link.

   • Click the folder icon and select the file in the Select File dialog box.

   • Click the Point to File icon and drag it to a file, such as a web page that's displayed in another frame in the Document window.

3. Select the location where the linked content should appear by choosing an option from the Target drop-down list in the Property Inspector. This list includes all the frames in the currently displayed frameset as well as four other options:

Figure 14.12

A link in one frame is often targeted to an adjacent frame.

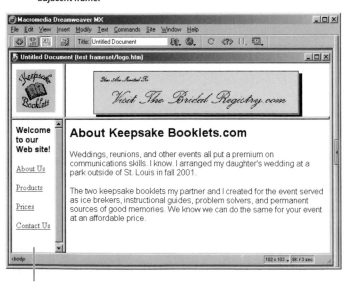

Links in this frame are targeted to an adjacent frame.

_blank Causes the linked file to open in a new, blank browser window.

_parent Opens the linked file in the parent frameset. This applies when you have nested one frameset inside another.

_self Causes the linked file to open in the same frame that contained the link.

_top Opens the linked content in the top level of all frames, replacing all other frames.

Most designers who use frames target linked content to open in an adjacent frame. In one common arrangement, a row of links in a frame on the left side of the page causes content to appear in a larger frame to the right, as shown in Figure 14.12.

ASSIGNING BEHAVIORS TO FRAMES

You can also control how frames interact with one another and display linked content by assigning behaviors to them. To do so, you create the frameset and add content. Select an object in one of the frames, and then display the Behaviors panel. Click the plus (+) sign, then choose one of the following frames-related behaviors from the Actions pop-up menu:

Set Text of Frame Replaces the content and formatting of a frame with the content you specify. The content can include any valid HTML. Use this action to dynamically display information.

Go to URL Lets you specify one or more documents to open in targeted frames. You create a link, then identify multiple documents to open in different frames. Go to URL, in other words, lets you change the contents of multiple frames in response to a single mouse click.

Insert Jump Menu Lets you create a pop-up menu with a series of clickable list items. Each item can be targeted to a frame in your frameset.

Insert Navigation Bar Lets you create a row of clickable buttons that can be linked to individual frames.

Creating NoFrames Content

Frames aren't going to be viewable by the growing number of wireless users who access the Web with handhelds, phones, pocket PCs, or other small devices. The handful of web surfers who still use old versions of web browsers won't be able to see frames, either. For such users, you need to set up NoFrames content.

> *NoFrames* pages are alternate versions of frames-based pages that use other design elements, such as tables, to present the same content. Browsers that can't view frames will instead see the NoFrames content, so they can still get an idea of what's on the frames page.

In addition, most of the programs used by Internet search services (commonly called *spiders*) don't index frames pages. A commercial site that wants to get listed on search services so that customers can find it needs to provide the spiders with keywords, site descriptions, and basic information about the site in a NoFrames page, not in one of the frames pages.

The Edit NoFrames Content command lets you see what viewers who can't see frames see. After you create a frameset, edit the NoFrames content as follows:

1. Save your frameset. You may want to copy some content from one of your frames for use in the NoFrames page.

2. Choose Modify → Frameset → Edit NoFrames Content. A new blank page appears in the Document window, replacing your frames pages.

3. Enter the NoFrames text in the Document window or paste any text you have copied.

4. To return to your frames layout, choose Modify → Frameset → Edit NoFrames Content again.

For some designers, NoFrames content is as simple as a sentence saying, "This page is designed with frames, and your browser does not support them." Others attempt to duplicate the frames layout with tables. The important thing is to provide alternate content so that some viewers won't see a blank browser window when they come to your frames-based page.

Prevent Others from Framing Your Pages

Some websites that contain links to other websites (for example, the Internet index site About.com) choose to "frame" the remote site's pages. When a visitor to About.com clicks a link to another website, the new site's content opens as a frame in a frameset. The originating site's content frames the new site. The purpose of such "framing" is so that the visitor always has a link to the original site that contained the link. However, many web designers are offended by the thought that their web pages would appear beneath another site's name, logo, and advertisements for other websites.

If your site already contains frames, it can be confusing for your frames-based pages to appear as a frame in someone else's frameset. You can, however, prevent other sites from framing your own pages. Add the following JavaScript code to the HEAD section of any pages you want to block from being framed:

```
<Script Language=JAVASCRIPT TYPE="TEXT/JAVASCRIPT">
  <--! Hide script from old browsers
  if(top.location != self.location)
  { top.location =self.location }
  // end hide from older browsers -->
```

You can use the preceding script to prevent framing of conventional web pages as well as frames-based pages. The HTML Goodies website has an alternative script for preventing framing—check it out at `http://www.htmlgoodies.com/tutors/yesnoframes.html`.

Hands On: Design a Frames-Based Page

Now you can try out frames yourself by designing a web page. You'll divide a page into frames, add a navigation bar to a frame, target links to open in another frame, add layers, and create an alternate NoFrames page.

In the Chapter 14 folder on the accompanying CD, copy the folder `frames_layout` to your computer. Start Dreamweaver, and open a new blank page. If you want a preview of the completed page, you can open `KeepsakeFrames.htm`, which is also in the Chapter 14 folder on the CD. The completed page is shown in Figure 14.13.

Create the Frameset

To begin, create a frameset that you can work with. Follow these steps:

1. Start Dreamweaver.

2. In a new blank Document window, choose View → Visual Aids → Frame Borders.

3. Click and drag the upper-left corner of the frame border into the center of the Document window, then release the mouse button.

   The web page is split into four frames.

4. Click and drag the part of the frame border where the four frames intersect so that the frames resemble those in Figure 14.14.

Add Images

Next, you'll add content to your frameset. The two frames in the first row of the frameset are intended to hold images, and the frame on the left will preset a set of links. These three frames are static: their contents don't change. The fourth, largest frame in the frameset is mobile— its contents change in response to links.

1. Choose Site → New Site and define a site where you can locate this frameset unless you have a site already open in Dreamweaver.

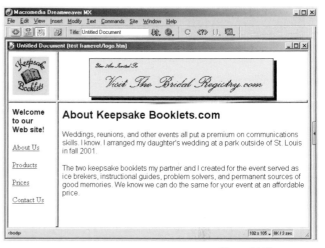

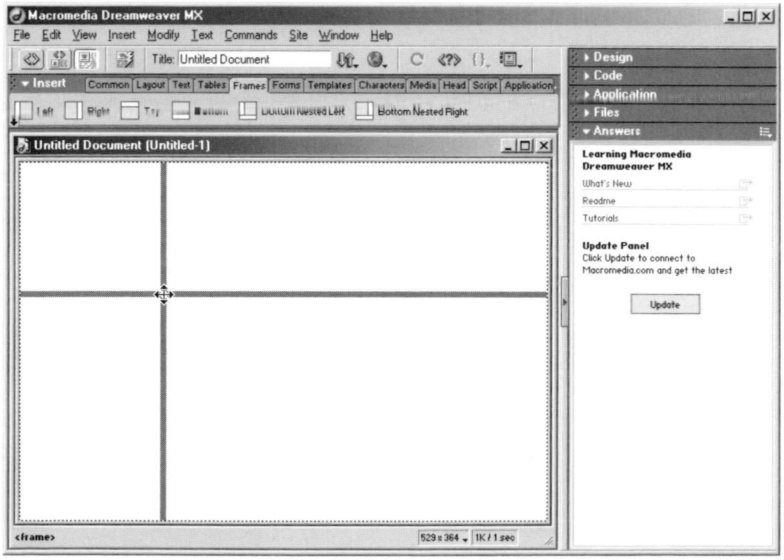

Figure 14.13

This web page uses frames to add interactivity and to present multiple pages simultaneously.

Figure 14.14

Divide a web page into four frames.

2. Position the text cursor in the small frame in the upper-left corner and choose Insert ➔ Image.

3. In the Select Image Source dialog box, locate the file `logo.png` in the `frames_layout` folder and select it.

4. Resize the image by Shift-clicking and dragging the handle in the lower-right corner if you need to.

5. In the Property Inspector, select No from the Scroll drop-down list to turn off scrollbars.

6. Position the text cursor in the other frame in the top row and insert the file `ad.gif`, following steps 3 and 4.

7. Drag the frame border just beneath the first row of the frameset to fit more closely around the two images if you need to.

8. In the Property Inspector, select No from the Scroll drop-down list to turn off scrollbars.

Insert Web Pages into the Frames

You've got a number of options for adding content to your frame. In this case, you don't have to type content from scratch. You'll add a complete web page that's provided in the `frames_layout` folder to each of the remaining two frames.

1. Position the cursor in the lower-left frame and choose File ➔ Open in Frame.

2. Choose the file `links.htm` in the `frames_layout` folder and click Select to insert it in the frame.

3. Position the cursor in the lower-right frame and choose File ➔ Open in Frame.

4. Choose the file `index.html` in the `frames_layout` folder and click Select to insert it in the frame.

5. Click any frame border to select the frameset and enter a title in the Title box. This is the frameset title that the viewer will first see upon visiting your frames-based page.

Save the Frames

Now that you've created the frameset and added content to all frames, you'll save your frames and the frameset page itself.

1. Choose File ➔ Save All Frames.

2. In the File Name box of the Save As dialog box, enter a name for your frameset, such as **KeepsakeFrames.htm**, then click Save.

3. The Save As dialog box reappears so that you can save one of the individual frames. You may have to move the Save As dialog box to the side slightly so that you can see which frame is highlighted. Assign a filename to the frame and click Save.

4. Repeat step 3 for the other top row frame in the frameset. (If you inserted web pages into the bottom two frames, you don't have to save them.) Your page should look like the one shown in Figure 14.15.

Figure 14.15

Save the frameset page and each of the four frames and you have a basic frameset.

Target Links

Next, you need to target each of the links in the links.htm page you inserted into the lower-left frame.

1. Click the About Us link.

2. In the Property Inspector, choose mainFrame from the Target drop-down list.

3. Click the Products link and repeat step 2.

4. Repeat this process for other two links.

5. Choose Save All Frames to save your changes. You can now preview your page in a browser window and test out your links.

> If you want frame borders to appear in the browser window, click a frame border and enter a value other than 0 in the Border Width box in the Property Inspector.

One Holy Grail

One of the dreams of the designers of the Web is to be able to separate content from presentation (also called formatting or style). The CSS (Cascading Style Sheets) standard offers a forward-thinking approach to this goal. The use of frames to divide pages or handle persistent navigation is, frankly, a little out-of-date. CSS, the topic of the next chapter, is—at least according to some—the future of web design.

## CHAPTER 15

Cascading Style Sheets

In the eternal battle to separate content from presentation on the Web, CSS (Cascading Style Sheets) is a powerful weapon. It's also, in some ways, a well-kept secret. For the most part, this is because the popular browsers of the last few years (Internet Explorer and Netscape) implemented the CSS standard only partially, and inconsistently to boot. With the advent of CSS 2.0 and the appearance of better-behaved browsers, it has become more practical to use style sheets in recent years, although if your audience largely uses Netscape 4.7, then they're not ready for it yet.

After explaining a little bit about how style sheets work and what they can do, we'll show you how Dreamweaver MX makes working with CSS easier than ever. Here are the topics we'll discuss:

- **The pros and cons of CSS**

- **Internal and external style sheets**

- **Understanding the box model**

- **Applying CSS styles with the Property Inspector**

- **Working with the CSS Styles panel**

- **Making, attaching, editing, and viewing a style sheet**

Why Use Style Sheets?

Because style sheets abstract (separate) out the style rules for anything from a single document to an entire site, using them makes it easier to update, correct, or otherwise change the look-and-feel of a page or site without individually recoding all the formatting tags. There are other ways to separate content from presentation:

- Use a database to assemble documents on-the-fly using a single web boilerplate file that can be changed once to affect an entire dynamic site. (we'd call that file a template but that might be confusing.) See Chapter 24 for more on developing database-driven sites.

- Use Dreamweaver templates to establish the look-and-feel for a site (as discussed in Chapter 3).

- Use server side includes (SSIs) to reuse single instances of page elements.

> If your approach includes trying to be as forward-looking as possible, use CSS with XHTML and XML (which are discussed in Chapter 26).

Drawbacks to the use of CSS relate mainly to poor backward-compatibility:

- There is a lack of support for style sheets in 3.0 version browsers (as well as flawed support in Netscape 4.7).

- There are projects where the site has already been built using HTML-based text formatting (as discussed in Chapter 12).

Nonetheless, within the next year or so, we believe the use of CSS will take hold as a well-adopted standard, and it will behoove you to become familiar with it now. Support for CSS in Dreamweaver MX is leaps and bounds beyond that in previous versions. Now all we could ask for is a more visual interface or the ability to preview styles as you're defining them.

What to Use Style Sheets For

OK, so it's obvious that style sheets control "style," but what does that mean? For many people, previous experience with Microsoft Word provides one of example of how styles can be defined and then applied to the contents of a document, but Word's styles are primarily focused on text formatting, which is only one of the applications of CSS. Style sheets can also define how links will appear in different circumstances and how your pages will be laid out (without using any tables or layers!).

With CSS, you can apply style definitions to existing tags or create new subclasses of existing tags, each with their own style. You can also define freestanding styles that can be applied to any number of different tags.

Formatting with Styles

Text formatting options include font (typeface, size, color, weight, and so on), alignment, indentation, and paragraph spacing.

Link formatting options allow you to specify how links will look when unclicked, when hovered over, when being clicked, and after having been clicked.

Layout with Styles (The CSS Box Model)

Page layout options are governed by something called the CSS *box model*. In CSS layout, a box is defined as a series of nested rectangular frames around a content rectangle. The outermost frame is the margin and is always transparent, next comes the border, then the padding (which gets the same background as the content area), and finally the content box. These areas can be defined as the same on all four sides or with different specifications for top, bottom, left, and right.

For a diagram of the CSS box model, visit `http://dreamweaversavvy.com/examples/15/boxmodel/`.

How Styles Are Applied

CSS styles are applied to content using tag selectors. If you've redefined a tag entirely, then the ordinary HTML tag functions as the CSS style selector. When you need to apply multiple styles to variants of the same tag (for example, when you are defining different types of paragraph tags for different design elements), and when you want to be able to apply a style to many different tags, then you define the style as a class or id. (Classes and id's can be specified for one specific tag or defined individually and applied to any tag or selection of text.)

CSS also provides for *pseudo-classes*, which are distinctions applied to text and links that the browser, what the CSS definition calls the user agent (UA), determines when displaying the document. The most common application of pseudo-classes is for link formatting. They are called pseudo-classes because you don't actually apply the classes manually: you can't! There's no way to know when building a page whether the link will ultimately have been clicked or not. It doesn't make any sense to apply that determination in advance. This is something only the browser can do.

Similarly, the other common use of a pseudo-class is paragraph formatting applied to the first line of a paragraph. Until the page is rendered in a browser window, there's no way to know which words will end up on the first line, but the UA can make this determination on-the-fly and apply small caps (for example) to the first line when displaying the page.

Types of Style Sheets

There are essentially two different types of style sheets: external and internal. You apply external style sheets to documents by either *linking* to them or *importing* them. Dreamweaver supports both approaches. Internal style sheets are defined directly within the document (in its `<head>` area), and Dreamweaver can export an internal style sheet to an external document so that it can be used by multiple web pages. But frankly, style sheets only make sense to us if you make them external and share them with multiple documents!

CSS also permits styles to be defined and applied *inline*—directly within the body of the HTML document—but again we don't really see the benefit of doing this most of the time.

For Further Reading on CSS

There is much more to say about CSS and its capabilities—at least an entire book's worth—so we'll have to leave the background explanation where it stands for now so that you can start working with Dreamweaver's CSS tools. If you want to learn more about CSS, start by visiting some of these sites:

- Access the original CSS specifications at `http://www.w3.org/TR/REC-CSS1`.
- Read the inimitable Jeffrey Zeldman's "CSS in the Real World" lecture at `http://www.zeldman.com/lectures/css/`.
- Browse the New York Public Library's Online Style Guide (CSS: Steal These Style Sheets) at `http://www.nypl.org/styleguide/css/opensource.html`.
- Visit Eric Costello's site, which contains many examples including `http://glish.com/`, `http://glish.com/css/`, and `http://glish.com/css/7.asp`.
- Look at Eric Meyer's site, which also has many CSS examples: `http://www.meyerweb.com/eric/css/`.
- View WebMonkey's guide to style sheets at `http://hotwired.lycos.com/webmonkey/reference/stylesheet_guide/`.
- Absorb BrainJar.com's overview, which offers some help understanding the box model, and also contains links to other CSS resources: `http://www.brainjar.com/css/using/`, `http://www.brainjar.com/css/positioning/`, and `http://www.brainjar.com/css/resources.asp`.
- Try the Web Design Group's guide to style sheets at `http://www.htmlhelp.com/reference/css/`.
- Take in the Web Standards Project's website, which promotes the use of CSS, among other standards: `http://archive.webstandards.org/`.

- Stop by a site for testing CSS2 at `http://www.xs4all.nl/~ppk/css2tests/`.

- Get assistance by visiting Box Lessons at `http://www.thenoodleincident.com/tutorials/box_lesson/`.

- Take a look at the Box Model Hack at `http://www.tantek.com/CSS/Examples/boxmodelhack.html`.

- Learn about some more stealable CSS designs at `http://www.bluerobot.com/web/layouts/`.

CSS Tools in Dreamweaver

There are two main ways to create and apply CSS styles in Dreamweaver:

- Using the CSS mode of the Property Inspector (see Figure 15.1)
- Using the CSS Styles panel (the CSS Style tab of the Design panel [see Figure 15.2])

The Toggle CSS/HTML Mode button

Figure 15.1

Click the Toggle CSS/HTML Mode button (it initially looks like a capital A) to switch the Property Inspector to CSS mode.

Both of these offer the same range of options in two different ways, but you'll probably use whichever you're more comfortable with. We prefer to use the Property Inspector most of the time, especially for applying styles, but the CSS Styles panel can be more convenient, ergonomically speaking, when creating or editing a long list of styles.

In fact, no matter which tool you use to access these features, whenever you create or edit a style, you're going to end up at the CSS Style Definition dialog box (see Figure 15.3).

Figure 15.2

The CSS Styles panel has one mode for applying styles and another for editing them.

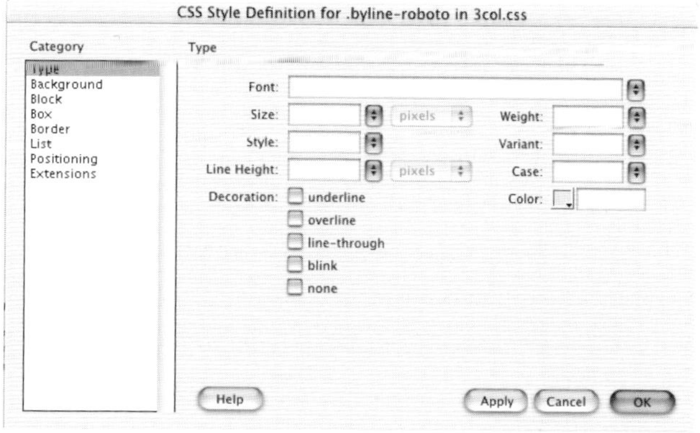

Figure 15.3

The CSS Style Definition dialog box compactly offers a wealth of CSS definition options organized into eight categories.

Working with Styles

Working with styles boils down to three things:

- Making new styles
- Applying existing styles
- Editing existing styles

The hard part of all of this is not Dreamweaver. The program's interface enables you to develop CSS styles relatively quickly, but you still have to have some idea of how CSS works, because there's little visual feedback as you're working your way through multiple categories in dialog boxes.

Making a Style

To make a new style, follow these steps:

1. Choose New CSS Style in the Property Inspector or click the New CSS Style button ⊞ in the CSS Styles panel.

> If the new style you're making is largely similar to an existing style, then skip ahead to "Editing a Style" so that you can base the new style on a duplicate of the existing one and save some effort.

2. After you have done this, the New CSS Style dialog box will appear (see Figure 15.4).

3. Now, select the type of style you want to make:

   - Choose Make Custom Style (Class) for styles that might be applied to multiple tags.
   - Choose Redefine HTML Tag to establish a style for a specific tag.
   - Choose Use CSS Selector to create pseudo-class styles (such as link formatting).

4. Now type or choose the selector for the new style, using the pop-up menu next to the name box.

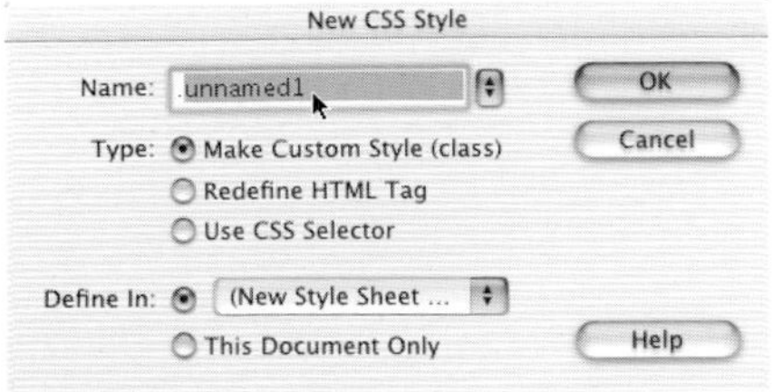

   - If you are making a custom style, Dreamweaver will suggest a name such as `.unnamed1` to remind you to start your class name with a dot. Give the selector any name that makes sense to you.
   - If you are redefining an HTML tag, the pop-up menu will show all the available tags. Choose one.
   - If you are defining a pseudo-class style, the pop-up menu will offer the four link style choices: `a:link`, `a:visited`, `a:hover`, and `a:active`. Choose one.

Figure 15.4

The New CSS Style dialog box

5. Then indicate if this style is internal to the current document only or part of a style sheet. You can choose to create a new style sheet at this point (as discussed later in this chapter), but you won't be prompted to name and save the new style sheet until you click OK.

6. Click OK. Name and save the style sheet if you're making an external one. The CSS Style Definition dialog box will appear (refer back to Figure 15.2).

Now you're ready to define your style. The settings you wish to apply may well be scattered over five or six of the categories, so we recommend checking each categories to determine whether its options are applicable. For each of the categories, we'll give you some context to understand the purpose of the options.

Type Options

When styling type, you can select a font or font list, Choose Edit Font List in the pop-up menu to create your own font lists, size (use pixels since most of the other measurements are interpreted differently on different platforms, thus defeating the purpose of CSS), weight, style, variant (small caps or not), line height, case (capitalization), decoration (underline and its variations), and, perhaps most importantly, color.

Background Options

Choose the Background category to define the background color or pattern for this style element (see Figure 15.5).

If you use an image, you can have it repeat across (repeat-x) or down (repeat-y) or both (repeat). In the Attachment choice, you also can determine if the background will scroll with the page or stay fixed. Finally, you can position the image horizontally and vertically.

Block Options

Options in the Block category control spacing and alignment (see Figure 15.6).

The spacing and alignment choices are fairly self-explanatory (remember to use pixels as the measurement when possible). The Display option permits you to define whether the style is applied to inline text (without starting a new box or paragraph) or as a block. There are a number of other choices for specific layout situations, such as table headers and the like.

Figure 15.5

Choose a background color or image here.

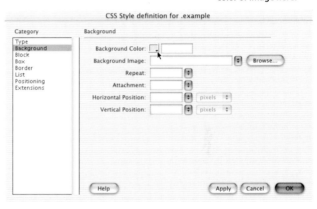

Figure 15.6

Choose text alignment, indentation, and display options here.

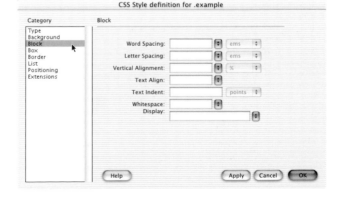

Box Options

The Box category controls most of the features of the box model we described earlier (see Figure 15.7).

First define the box's height and width. (The most important thing to remember here is that padding is added to the size of the box and not subtracted from it!) Then decide if you want the box to float left or right.

Then define the padding and margins. If you want margins or padding that differ on each side, uncheck the Same for All check box.

Figure 15.7

Define the box dimensions, padding, and margin here.

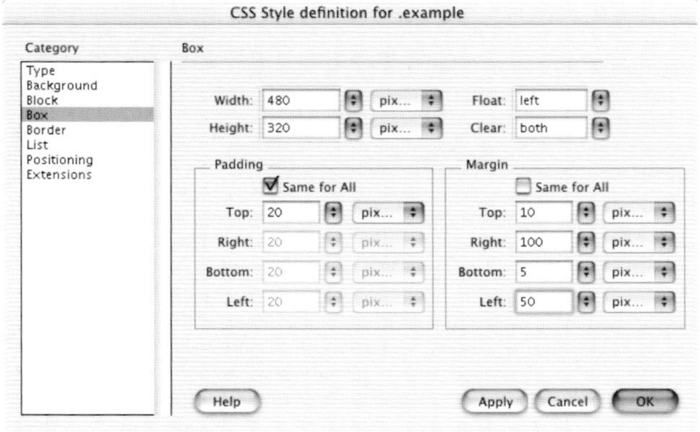

Border Options

The Border category controls the other element of the box model—the optional border inside the margins and outside the padding (see Figure 15.8).

Here you should choose a style for the border (solid, dashed, groove, ridge, and so on), then define a width (use pixels if you need precise control), and then choose a color for the border. Remember that the background color for the style will fill the box and padding out to the border, and that the margins will be transparent (meaning they will pick up an underlying background, if there is one).

List Options

List options are useful only for list elements (obviously), such as ordered (numbered) and unordered (bulleted) lists. You can use them to define the bullet symbol or image and to control positioning of list elements.

Positioning Options

Positioning options are useful for sophisticated page layout where you need to place boxes precisely on the page relative to other elements or relative to the page itself.

Extensions Options

Extensions options include the relatively mundane choice of calling for a page break before or after the styled element (useful when pages are printed), to

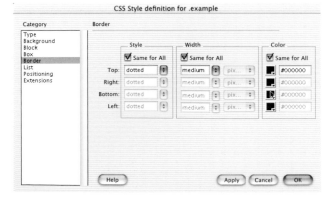

Figure 15.8

Get that wavy-edged chartreuse border you always wanted.

funky cursor substitutes (such as a crosshairs symbol), to a number of filter effects that may or may not be supported by your target browsers.

Finishing

When you are done defining your style, click OK. The new style will now appear in the pop-up menu on the Property Inspector and the style list on the CSS Styles panel.

Applying a Style

To apply a style, first select the text or other objects you want to apply it to and then select it with the Property Inspector (or make sure the CSS Styles panel is in Apply mode and then click the name of the style you want to apply).

Editing a Style

To edit a style using the Property Inspector, choose Edit CSS Style in the pop-up menu. If no style is currently selected, this brings up the Edit Style Sheet dialog box (see Figure 15.9).

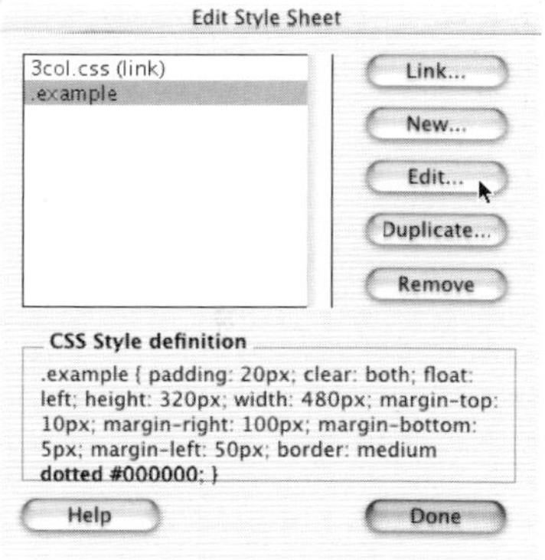

From here, you can choose one of two options:

- To edit an existing style, choose it and click the Edit button.

- To duplicate an existing style, click the Duplicate button, edit the name in the Duplicate CSS Style dialog box, and click OK. Then click the Edit button.

To skip the Edit Style Sheet dialog box, select the style in your document (either select text formatted with the style, or select a tag with a style, such as p.example, in the status bar, or with the CSS Styles panel to Edit mode, select the style you want to edit, and then click the Edit Style Sheet button ▣.

Either way, you arrive at the Style Definition dialog box. See "Making a Style" above for an explanation of the various categories and options there.

Figure 15.9

Edit or duplicate an existing style here.

Working with Style Sheets

Just as with individual styles, there are three main things you do with style sheets:

- Make them

- Attach them

- Edit them

We'll take them one at a time.

Making a Style Sheet

So far, you've seen how to create, apply, and edit a single style. A style sheet is a collection of styles. If you've been making your styles within the current document, you can export them to an external style sheet so that they'll be available to any document. You can also just choose to create a new style sheet when you first make a style and then add all subsequent styles to that sheet (as described in "Making a Style" above).

To export a set of styles as a style sheet, follow these steps:

1. Select File → Export → CSS Styles. This brings up the Export Styles as CSS File dialog box (see Figure 15.10).

2. Choose a folder for the style. It often makes sense to put all your style sheet files in the same folder at a site.

3. Give the style sheet a name. Dreamweaver will take care of adding the .css extension.

4. Click Save.

Attaching a Style Sheet

To make the styles in a style sheet available to a new document, all you need to do is attach the style sheet to the document (using either the link or the import method. In most cases,

either method works fine. If you attach multiple style sheets to a single document (and there's no stopping you from doing this), then linked style sheets will be read first with imported style sheets read afterward, superseding any styles with the same names).

To attach a style sheet, choose the Attach Style Sheet option in the Property Inspector or click the Attach Style Sheet button in the CSS Styles panel.

Either way, the Link External Style Sheet dialog box appears. Once it does, follow these steps to complete the process of attaching a style sheet:

Figure 15.10

Export your styles to an external style sheet all at once.

1. Browse to the CSS file you want to attach (or type a URL if you want to use a style sheet located elsewhere on the Web).

2. Then choose the method for attaching the file, Link or Import.

3. Then click OK. The styles in the style sheet are now available to the current document.

Generally, it won't matter what method you use for attaching the style sheet, but some designers use the import syntax to hide style sheets from older, noncompliant browsers.

One easy way to make a style sheet available automatically to a given class of pages at your site is to link the style sheet to a template file and then attach the template to the documents in question (or build new documents based on the template). See Chapter 4 for more about working with templates.

Editing a Style Sheet

Editing a style sheet is merely a matter of editing the styles in the style sheet, as described above in the section "Editing a Style." However, if you are a hand-coder, you can edit your style sheets directly just by opening them in Dreamweaver. Use File → Open or double-click the style sheet file in the Site panel (or the Site window in the floating layout). Dreamweaver will open the CSS file as code only (see Figure 15.11). You can now hand-edit the code.

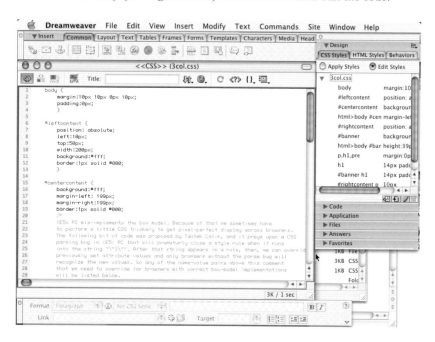

Figure 15.11

A style sheet file in Code view

You can edit a style sheet with an external editor by right-clicking (or Ctrl-clicking) on the style sheet's icon or the open file and choosing Edit With → Browse, or Edit → Edit with External Editor. Use the latter if you've set up an external editor or if you use Windows, in which case Dreamweaver will set up the evaluation copy of TopStyle that comes with it as an external editor for style sheets.

Previewing Styled Pages

Dreamweaver does its darnedest to render CSS-styled pages accurately, following the CSS 2.0 specification, but it doesn't always get everything right (for instance, it doesn't always render borders). The fact is, your pages may very well look different in different browsers, so you will probably want to preview them.

Viewing a Style Sheet Layout

To preview a page in a browser, select File→ Preview in Browser → *browser name*. You can add browsers with File → Preview in Browser → Edit Browser List. Any good web designer, developer, or information architect should have older versions of Internet Explorer and Netscape available as well as Opera and Mozilla (two relatively CSS-savvy browsers). So make sure you have these too, unless you know for sure that your user is standardized on a specific browser, of course.

Design-Time Style Sheets

One approach that some developers use to get around inconsistent style sheet interpretation by different browsers is to use scripting to serve up different style sheets depending on the user agent (browser) at any given time. If you need to do this, you will find that it becomes increasingly difficult to design pages without being able to see how the pages will render depending on which style sheets are being attached. Fortunately, Dreamweaver includes a feature called Design Time Style Sheets that allows you to select which style sheet(s) you want to use for displaying on-the-fly while you are designing.

To choose or hide style sheets, select Text → CSS Styles → Design Time Style Sheets, or right-click (or Ctrl-click) on the CSS Styles panel and choose Design Time Style Sheets. Either move brings up the (can you guess?) Design Time Style Sheets dialog box.

Use the top portion of this dialog box to choose one or more style sheets to control display of the pages. Use the bottom portion to choose style sheets to hide (prevent from controlling the display of pages).

Get Hip to Hyper

So far in this part, you've learned how to lay out pages and populate them with text and graphics. You've seen how to work with framesets (if you must), and now you've been initiated into the mysteries of CSS 2.0. But there are also page elements that connect your web page to other pages or objects, or that make things happen. In Chapter 16 you'll learn how to weave together pages with hypertext links.

## CHAPTER 16

Making and Maintaining Hyperlinks

In some sense, hyperlinks (also known as *hypertext links* or just *links*) are the essence of the Web. Linking together individual web pages, using navigational links that follow a strict order, and using ad hoc links from anywhere to anywhere, is what weaves the fabric of the any given site. To work with links, you need to understand a little about the folder (directory) structure of your site and how references are made from one page to another. Dreamweaver makes this as easy as possible for you, but we'll still start you off with some fundamentals (skippable if you're already an old hand) so that you know what you're doing.

Here are the topics with which you will become familiar:

- **Understanding links, anchors, and paths**

- **Making a link with the Property Inspector**

- **Inserting a link**

- **Creating links from the site map**

- **Making an image map**

- **Managing Links with the cache**

- **Checking and fixing links**

Some Fundamental Concepts About Links

One of the unique aspects of the Web as a medium is that the "page-turning" mechanisms are built into the content of the pages. Hidden in the HTML of your web pages, tags indicate *anchors* that are either the source or destination of a link, or the location (in the form of a URL or a *relative path*) of a destination. When these tags surround text or images, they can trigger behaviors (scripts).

> The work *link* is also used to refer to files associated with an HTML document, such as a style sheet that can be referred to with a Link tag in the Head of a document. This should not be confused with the kind of hyperlinks that we're discussing in this chapter.

Anchors Aweigh

Links on the Web connect two anchors—one in the source document (that is, a link *from* a web document, usually activated by clicking), and one in the target document. Most of the time, only the source anchor requires a specific tag.

Where From?

To create a link, you insert an anchor tag (the HTML syntax is `<a href="`*`address`*`">` *`linktext`*`</a>`) that specifies an href (a hyper-reference) in the form of a URL or path and filename. With Dreamweaver, you can avoid the hand-coding, of course.

Where To?

Most of the time, the specification of the address or path in the link's href attribute sufficiently defines the target anchor. When it's necessary to reach a specific section of a document (as in a page with a dynamic table of contents), you can insert *named anchors*. This is the same HTML anchor tag `<a>` with a different attribute (`name="`*`anything`*`"`), by the way. Dreamweaver provides a shortcut for this as well.

What Will Happen?

Links from one HTML document to another tell the browser to load the target page and possibly go to the named anchor somewhere in that page (or, alternatively, go to some named anchor elsewhere on the current page), but a link can refer to any kind of file. If the user's browser knows what plugin or helper application to invoke in order to display or play back the target file, then the user will experience the link as if they were directly opening the file. If not, the user will be given the opportunity to save the file.

Similarly, links can be made to run scripts. See Chapter 19 for more on scripts and how to trigger them.

> If you want a link to open a new mail message from the user to an address (such as a webmaster@ or info@ address), the HTML syntax is `<a href="mailto:`*youraddress*`">`*linktextor-image*`</a>`, but of course you don't really have to know this because Dreamweaver provides a specific shortcut for inserting a mailto link (on the Common tab of the Insert bar).

Paths Lead to Destinations

When specifying an href, you can use either an absolute form (a complete URL, such as `http://groups.yahoo.com/group/dreamweaversavvy/messages`) or a relative form. A relative path can be relative to the current document or to the root of the current site. To specify a path relative to the current document, do not precede the path with a forward slash. To specify a path relative to the root of the site, start the path with a forward slash. To indicate "up one level" in a path, you use the Unix format (../).

Understanding the Different Kinds of Links

Hyperlinks are often called hypertext and the medium of the Web is often referred to as hypertext. More properly, the Web features hypermedia—the nonlinear ("hyper") linking process that connects more than just text. The most common types of links, then, are the following:

Text links The basic link—highlighted text. You select, hit, or click it and something happens.

Image links Just like text links, but the thing you indicate, press, or click is a picture instead of text (pictures can, of course, still include text).

Image maps These are complicated image links with variously shaped regions called hotspots, each of which links to an individual destination.

Navigation menus These are a specific flavor of text or image (but usually image) links that are dedicated to holding down a consistent set of navigation links throughout a site or section of a site. These often include multiple behaviors, appearing as you roll or hover over them, when you select them, or after you have selected them and are hovering over them, and so on. See Chapter 18 for the straight skinny on these so-called jump menus.

How to Deal with the Design Issues Posed by Links

One last conceptual topic deserves mention before we get into the nitty-gritty of inserting links into pages: link color schemes. When designing your pages, if you don't specify a color scheme for links (before, during, and after they're clicked) versus regular text, then your viewers will see whatever their browser shows by default (links are usually blue and underlined before they're clicked and purple afterward in comparison to the rest of the text, which is black).

There are several approaches to standardizing your use of colors at a site, including basing pages on templates, using the Page Properties dialog box to set the colors for a specific page (or template), or through the use of CSS styles and style sheets. To use one of these approaches, do one of the following.

- Use Modify → Page Properties (Ctrl/Cmd + J) to select colors for the text, background, link, visited link, and active link portions of a specific page or template.

- See Chapter 4 for a discussion of using templates to maintain consistency among such page elements as link coloring.

- Use Cascading Style Sheets (CSS) (as discussed in Chapter 15) to control color *and appearance* of links as compared to regular text, including how the link should look when the mouse pointer hovers over it.

Inserting Links

Naturally, there are about 17 different ways to insert links into a web document with Dreamweaver. Well, maybe not quite that many, but it seems that way. We'll run through the most useful techniques and you'll probably end up using just one method most of the time, but, as you'll see, some of the methods are more convenient in particular situations.

> Save your document before you insert links or you'll have to wade through various reminder dialog boxes and Dreamweaver will use absolute references to your local files until it knows how they relate to the current document (Dreamweaver can't know this until you've saved your document at least once).

Entering a Link with the Property Inspector

As is often the case with Dreamweaver, most of the time we find it easiest to make a link by just selecting the source and entering the target information into the Property Inspector. If you don't have the Property Inspector visible, make it so with Window → Properties or Ctrl/Cmd + F3. Then follow these steps:

1. Select the text (or image) that will trigger the link.

2. Indicate the href target using any of these four techniques:

    - Type a URL or relative pathname and filename in the Link box on the Property Inspector (see Figure 16.1).

Figure 16.1

**Typing a link directly
into the Property
Inspector**

- Click the pop-up menu next to the Link box to get a list of recently linked-to addresses (Figure 16.2).
- Click the Point-to-File icon (shown in Figure 16.3) and then point to a file in the Site panel (or Site window in the floating layout). You may have to do some window rearranging to get a clean sightline).

Figure 16.2

**Choosing a recent link in
the Property Inspector**

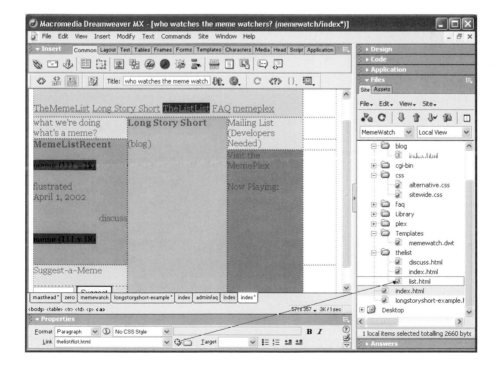

Figure 16.3

**Using the Property
Inspector's Point to File
icon to select a link
from the Site panel**

- Click the browse icon and choose a file from the Select File dialog box that results (see Figure 16.4). If it's not already within your site, Dreamweaver will offer to copy it there for you.

> You can use Point-to-File even without going through the Property Inspector—just select the source text for the link, hold down the Shift key, and then point to the target document in your Site panel.

Using the Insert Hyperlink or Insert Email Link Commands

To insert a link entirely (as opposed to turning existing text into a link), click the Hyperlink button on the Common tab of the Insert bar for links to documents, or click the Email Link button on the same panel for mailto links. (You can also choose Insert → Hyperlink or Insert → Email Link to get the same effects.)

Creating an Ordinary Hyperlink

When you insert a hyperlink, Dreamweaver brings up the Hyperlink dialog box (see Figure 16.5).

Figure 16.4

Browsing to your link anchor through the Select File dialog box

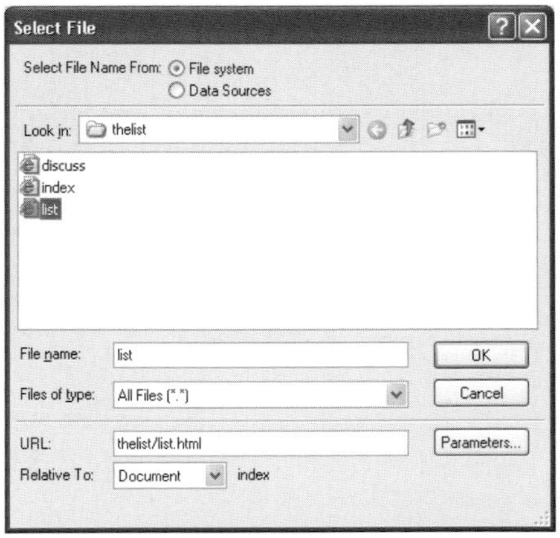

Figure 16.5

The Hyperlink dialog box enables the rapid assembly of a hypertext link.

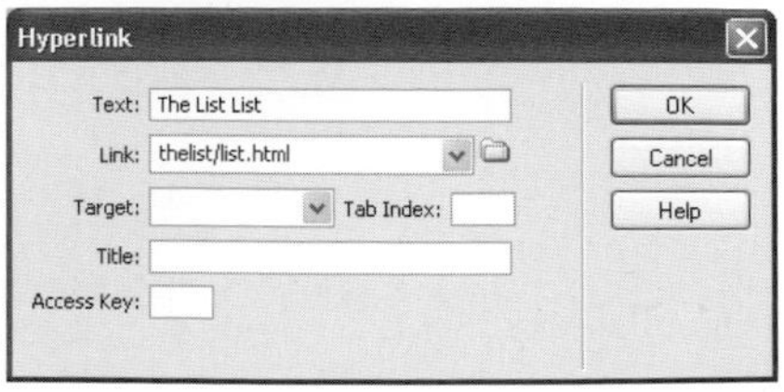

To insert a link, follow these steps:

1. Type the link text in the Text box.

2. Press the Tab key and then enter the link target address, or choose it from the pop-up menu or by browsing (there's no Point-to-File option on this dialog box).

3. Optionally, most often if you are using frames, you can direct the link toward a target window or frame, using the Target pop-up menu. The Target menu will include frames defined in the frameset of your current page, if any, as well as these standard target names:

    _blank The linked page comes up in a new browser window.

    _parent The linked page comes up in its parent window (if any) or the full window (removing all frames, if any).

    _self The linked page comes up in the same frame (if any) as the source.

    _top The linked page comes up in the full window (removing all frames, if any).

4. Optionally, enter an ordinal number in the Tab Index box.

5. Optionally, type a label for the link in the Title box. This will create a tool tip that appears if the user hovers the mouse over the link.

6. Optionally, type a single keystroke in the Access Key box. If the user clicks Ctrl/Cmd + *AccessKey* while viewing this page, this will activate the link.

7. Click OK.

Creating an E-Mail Link

When you insert an e-mail link, Dreamweaver brings up the (much simpler) Email Link dialog box (shown in Figure 16.6). When this figure appears, follow these steps:

1. Type the link text in the Text box.

2. Type the e-mail address in the E-Mail box.

3. Click OK.

Figure 16.6

The Email Link dialog box

Creating a Named Anchor

When you need to designate a target area in a document, you must first name it with an anchor tag. To do so, first select the target area and then click the Named Anchor button (or select Insert → Named Anchor). This brings up the Named Anchor dialog box shown here.

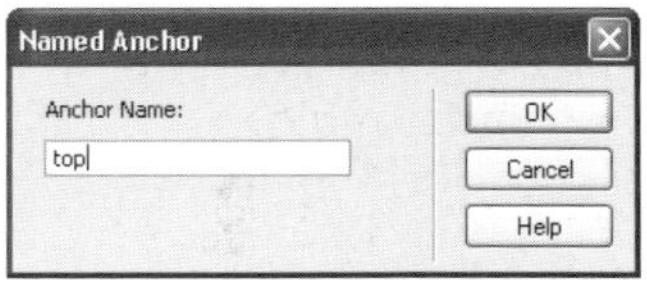

All you need to do to create a named anchor is type a name in the Anchor Name text box and click OK.

Then, any time you are making a link targeted at this anchor, you will either use "*#thatname*" as the href or append *#thatname* to the end of the path- and filename or URL.

Making a Link with the Make Link Command

For some reason, this only works in Design view, but if you select your source text, you can also create a link by selecting Modify → Make Link (Ctrl/Cmd + L). This brings up the Select File dialog box (refer back to Figure 16.4). Use it to browse to a destination file or to enter a URL.

Making Links from the Site Map

The same Point-to-File icon available on the Property Inspector can also be used with the Site Map view in the Site panel. Click the Expand/Collapse button first to maximize the Site panel if you're working in the integrated MX workspace. (If you are using the floating layout, just choose the Site Map view in the Site panel.) Figure 16.7 shows a set of links created directly from the site map.

To create a link in this view, follow these steps:

1. Select the document *from* which you want to link.

2. Click the Point-to-File icon and hold down the mouse button.

3. Drag to the file you want to link *to* in your Local Files view (see Figure 16.8).

4. Repeat as necessary.

Figure 16.7

When starting a project, you can insert the basic navigation links into the key pages for a site from the Site Map view.

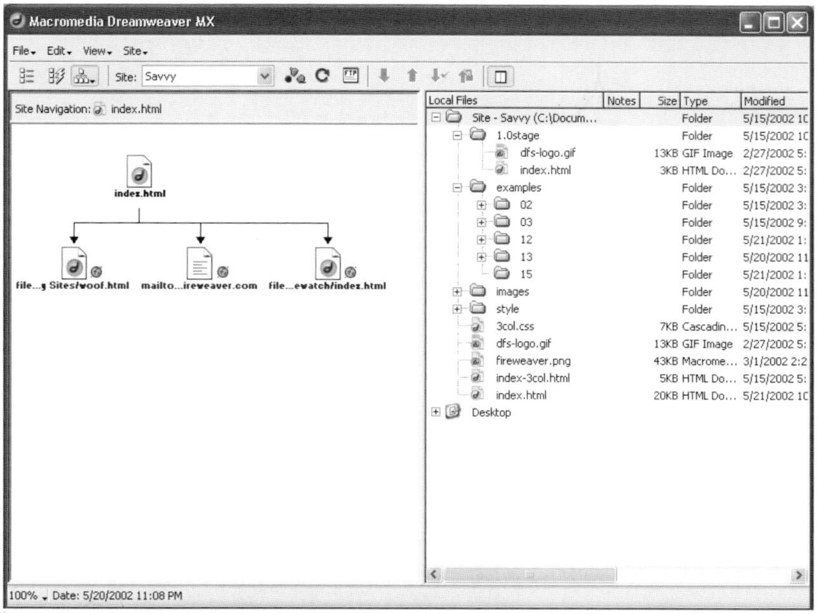

Figure 16.8

Use the Point to File to link up files quickly through the Site Map view

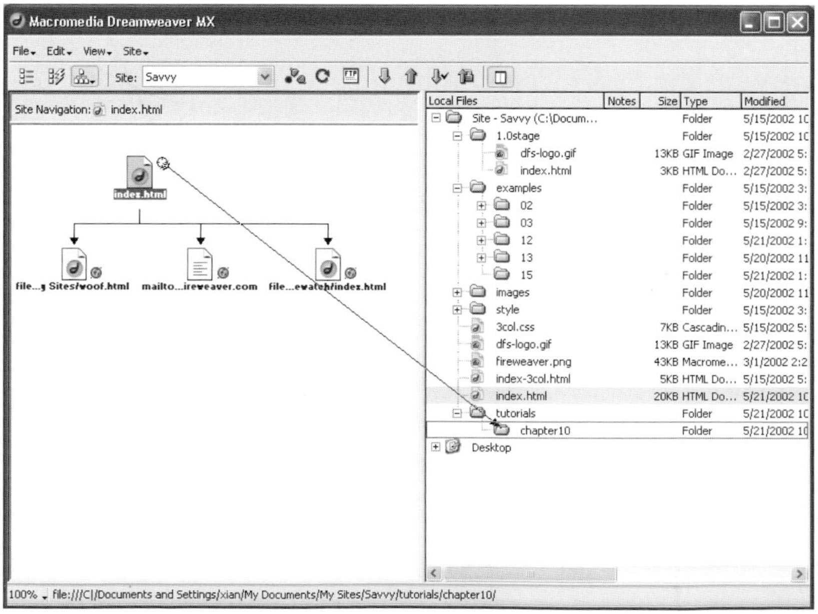

Because some links can trigger scripts or behaviors, you may need to insert a placeholder for the destination of the link until you can add the relevant behavior, such as "`javascript:;`" (the word "javascript" followed by a colon and then a semicolon). See Chapter 19 for more on behaviors.

Building Image Maps

An image map is a graphic with one or more designated hotspots that function as links. The first types of image maps to be supported on the Web were processed by web servers and hence called *server-side* image maps. These simply sent x and y coordinates from the selected point in the image, and the server would determine what link that particular (x,y) pair corresponded to.

These have now been largely supplanted by *client-side* image maps that are interpreted by the user's web browser. This means that all the shape and link information is stored in the page—in fact, the information is stored in the tag for the image. When the user hovers over a hotspot on a client-side image map, they can actually see the target of the link in the status bar (unless you've overridden this info, as discussed in Chapter 19) instead of a series of x and y coordinates. Dreamweaver only makes client-side image maps, but this should not be a problem!

If you prefer, you can make your image maps in Fireworks and then import them into Dreamweaver, as discussed in Chapter 9.

The process for creating an image map is straightforward:

1. Insert an image or placeholder onto a page.
2. Select the image or make sure it's selected.
3. Expand the Property Inspector to show all available options (see Figure 16.9).
4. Draw circles, rectangles, and/or irregular shapes on the image to indicate the hotspot areas (see Figure 16.10).

Rectangles and circles are drawn from upper left to lower right. For rectangles, this means that you should drag from the top-left corner to the bottom-right corner of the rectangle. For circles, this means that you should drag from an imaginary top-left corner of an invisible square containing the circle.

Figure 16.9

An image has been inserted and highlighted and the Property Inspector has been expanded to show the image-map creation features.

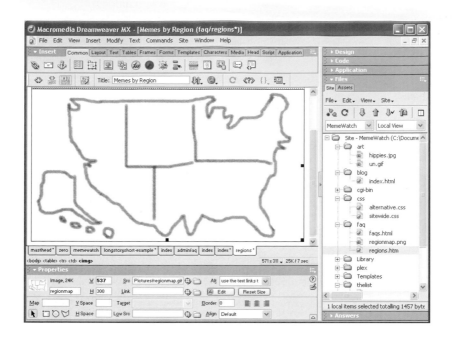

Figure 16.10

After indicating a rectangular hotspot and a round one, we're now specifying an irregular shape by clicking from corner to corner.

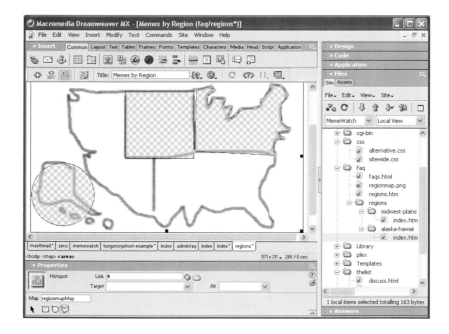

5. Select each hotspot with the Property Inspector (see Figure 16.11) and supply a desti-
    nation address in the Link box that appears in the top half of the Property Inspector
    (much as you would to select an ordinary link in the Property Inspector, as discussed in
    the previous section).

6. Indicate a default link (for the rest of the image), if so desired, by clicking outside of all
    the hotspots and specifying a link destination for the image as a whole.

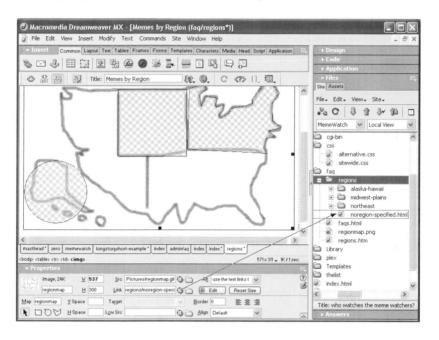

Figure 16.11

**Expand the Property
Inspector to see the
hotspot options
needed to build an
image map.**

Avoiding or Fixing Broken Links

Though it's definitely a time-saver to be able to create links automatically using Dreamweaver's
various shortcut features, and it minimizes the risk of typos in pathnames when you can select
a link by browsing, perhaps the most valuable advantage to be gained from links by using
Dreamweaver is the ability to track, manage, and correct links across your entire site. Without
a site-management tool, one of the banes of web publishing is the fact that hand-coded pages
may contain broken links, especially after a site revision that involves renaming or moving
pages. Without Dreamweaver (or a similar tool), hunting for all the broken links and fixing
them by hand can be prohibitive.

Managing Links as You Go

Figure 16.12

The General category of the Preferences dialog box

To enable Dreamweaver so that it can help you maintain working links, you have to first turn on Link Management (if it's not already turned on) and create a cache for the site (if the site does not already have a cache created).

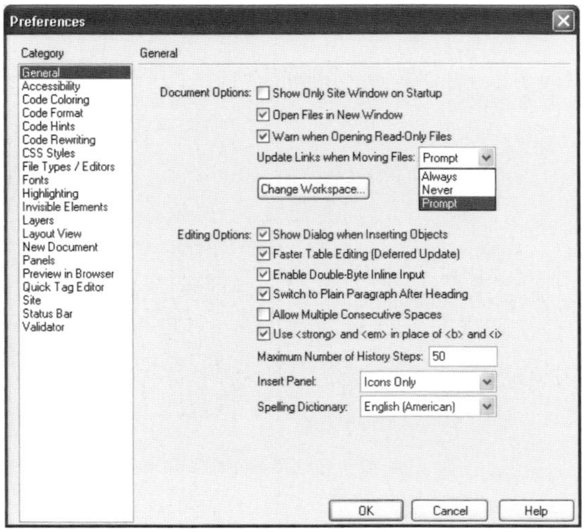

Turn On Link Management

To turn on Link Management, follow these steps:

1. Open the Preferences dialog box (Edit → Preferences/Dreamweaver → Preferences).

2. Select the General category (see Figure 16.12).

3. In the Document Options area, next to Update Links When Moving Files, select Always or Prompt. (If you select Always, Dreamweaver will automatically correct links to or from documents whenever you move them. If you select Prompt, Dreamweaver will always check with you first before correcting such links.)

4. Click OK.

Figure 16.12

The General category of the Preferences dialog box

If you did not create a cache when you first defined your site (see Chapter 3), you should do so now. To do this, select Site → Edit Sites, select the current site, and in the Local Info category, click the Enable Cache check box, and then click OK.

Allowing Dreamweaver to Update Links for You

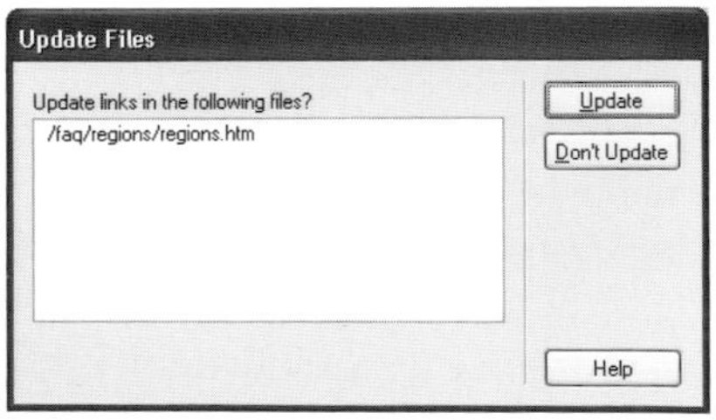

Figure 16.13

The Update Files dialog box lists the files identified as needing some links corrected.

Once Link Management is turned on, you can freely move documents around your site without worrying about tracking down all the affected links (including those links from other documents to the moving file and the links from that file to other documents) and correcting them by hand.

When you move a document, Dreamweaver will either fix affected links automatically without checking with you first for confirmation (if you selected Always in the previous section), or it will double-check with you first by listing all the links it intends to correct (see Figure 16.13).

Click the Update button to allow Dreamweaver to proceed. Dreamweaver will track its progress until the changes are completed.

Manually Changing a Link throughout Your Site

In addition to this passive approach to changing links, you can also redirect all links to any specific destination with a single change (much like the Find/Replace feature). This is most useful when the link points outside your current site and can't be simply redirected by moving the destination file, or when you want to redirect all links to a file before deleting it. To do this, follow these steps:

1. Choose Site → Change Link Sitewide. This brings up the—wait for it…—Change Link Sitewide dialog box (see Figure 16.14).

2. Enter the old link address in the Change All Links To box (the top one).

3. Press the Tab key and enter the new link address in the Into Links To box below.

4. Click OK.

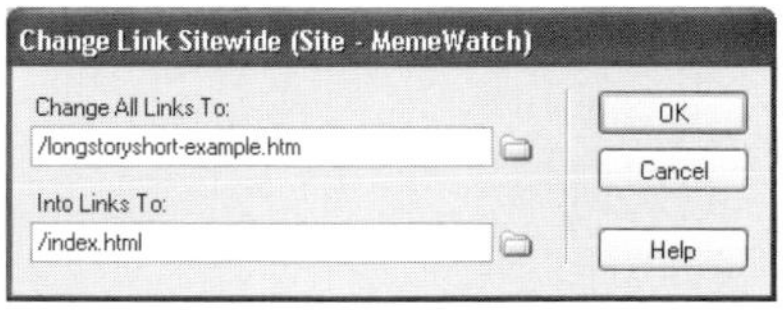

Figure 16.14

Make global link-changes here in the Change Link Sitewide dialog box

If you select a document before doing these steps, Dreamweaver will suggest the address of the selected document as the link to change.

Editing Links from the Site Map

If you're rearranging some of the basic navigational or structural links in your site, you might want to consider doing this from the Site Map view of the Site panel. To change a link from the Site Map view, right-click/Ctrl-click the file representing the destination link and choose Change Link from the context menu that pops up.

Then browse to a new destination file or type a URL directly to indicate a destination outside the current site. Then click OK. Dreamweaver will update the link for you.

Testing and Checking Links

In large, complicated sites, links can still end up broken—either from being typed incorrectly or from being changed without Link Management updating all affected files. In an ideal world, you wouldn't have to worry about this, but fortunately you can check individual links to make sure they go where they're supposed to, you can check all links throughout your site, and you can have Dreamweaver fix any broken links it finds.

Testing a Single Link

You've probably noticed by now that hyperlinks shown in Dreamweaver are not "active" as they would be in a web browser; that is, you can't click a link and automatically browse to or open the destination of the link. However, for documents in your local site, you actually can

browse through the links—just hold down Ctrl/Cmd and then double-click the link in Design view. If the destination is a local file, Dreamweaver will open it. If the destination is a web address, Dreamweaver will explain that it can't open "http, mailto, or other remote addresses".

Checking All the Links in a Site

You can actually check links for a single document, any sub portion of a site, or across an entire site.

For more on testing a site before it goes live, see Chapter 29.

To check links for one document or a subset of a site, the steps are as follows:

1. Open a document or select any number of files and folders in the Site panel.

2. Select File → Check Links in the Site panel in Windows, or File → Check Page → Check Links on the Mac (Shift + F8).

3. Dreamweaver creates a report on broken and external links displayed in the Results panel group (see Figure 6.15).

4. To see broken links, choose Broken Links in the drop-down list. To see links to external sites (which Dreamweaver can't check), choose External Sites.

To check links for the entire site, follow these steps:

1. Select Site → Check Links Sitewide.

2. In the Link Checker tab of the Results panel, you can view broken and external links across the site as well as orphaned files (files in the local folders that are not linked from anywhere within the site).

Figure 16.15

View a report of broken links in the Link Checker tab in the Results panel

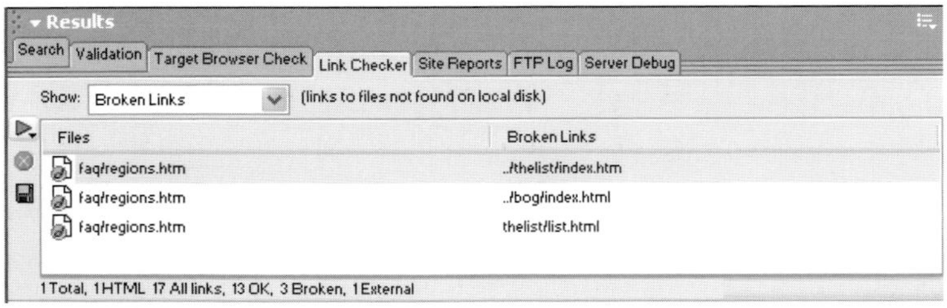

Files	Broken Links
faq/regions.htm	../thelist/index.htm
faq/regions.htm	../bog/index.html
faq/regions.htm	thelist/list.html

Show: Broken Links   (links to files not found on local disk)

1 Total, 1 HTML 17 All links, 13 OK, 3 Broken, 1 External

Search | Validation | Target Browser Check | Link Checker | Site Reports | FTP Log | Server Debug

Fixing Broken Links

Naturally, you can fix any broken links you find manually by using the techniques discussed earlier in this chapter, or you can do it directly from within the Results panel. To do so, follow these steps:

1. Select a broken link in the Broken Links column of the Broken Links report.

2. Click the Folder icon that appears.

3. Browse to the correct destination file.

4. Press the Tab or Enter key.

5. Dreamweaver will prompt you if there are any other broken links to the same file you just selected. If there are, click Yes to correct them all at once.

Dreamweaver automatically uses the Check Out feature to hold any files that have changed so that they can be updated on the remote site if you have File Check In/Check Out turned on, as discussed in Chapter 3.

Updating Links—Publishing the Changes

Once you've corrected links in the local version of a site, if the site is already live on a remote server, you'll need to update the remote site with all the changes. The easiest way to do this is with the Synchronize command:

1. Select Site → Synchronize. This brings up the Synchronize Files dialog box, shown in Figure 16.16.

2. Select Entire *site name* Site and then select Put Newer Files to Remote.

3. Click the Preview button.

4. When Dreamweaver has compared the local and remote files and indicated the documents that need updating, uncheck any files you don't want updated and then click OK (Figure 16.17).

5. When the synchronization is complete, click the Save Log button if you wish to keep a record of the update.

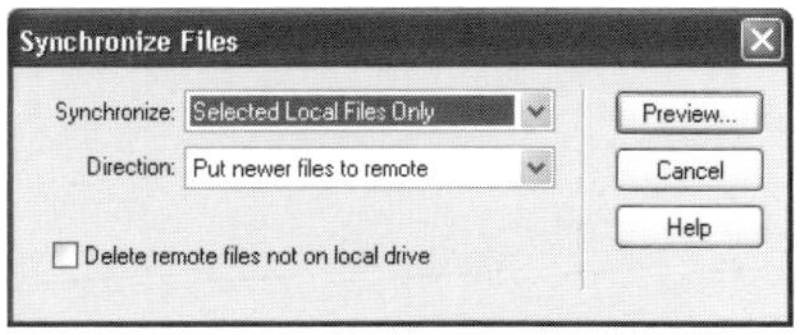

Figure 16.16

Update corrected links to your remote site with the Synchronize Files dialog box

Figure 16.17

The Synchronize command makes you preview the intended changes so you have a chance to verify the files to upload before proceeding.

Put the Multi in Multimedia

Now you know how to create and manage the links that make your website an interconnected part of the Web and not a series of disconnected web pages. In the next chapter, we'll look at the various types of multimedia plugins you can exploit in your pages to go beyond the basic text-and-pictures version of the Web. Or, if you want to continue with links and navigation, skip ahead to Chapter 18, where we discuss jump menus and other forms of dynamic HTML.

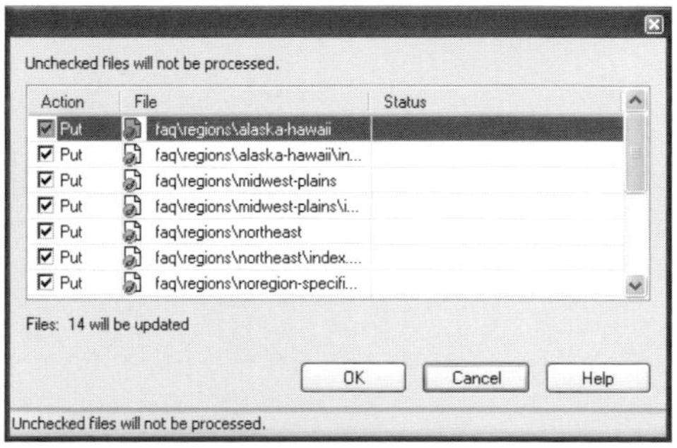

## PART IV

Inserting Dynamic Content

The previous *part discussed the most common types of page elements (text, graphic, layout and design tags, and hyperlinks), all of which contribute to a static (nonmoving) web page. But the Web is a dynamic medium: it moves, and it interacts with the user. It doesn't just sit there.*

In this part, we show you how to add multimedia objects to your pages, how to insert dynamic navigation elements, how to use Dreamweaver's catalog of behaviors to add interactivity to your site without having to master programming languages, how to build interactive forms, and how to set up a site for e-commerce.

CHAPTER 17 ■ Adding Multimedia

CHAPTER 18 ■ Rollovers, Navigation Bars, and Jump Menus

CHAPTER 19 ■ Behavioral Science

CHAPTER 20 ■ Going Interactive with Forms

CHAPTER 21 ■ Building an E-Commerce Site

Adding Multimedia

Multimedia elements can add exciting visual and auditory content to attract visitors and to keep them returning to your site. In the early days of the World Wide Web, web pages contained only text and still images. Today, web pages can include these and interactive images, animated GIFs, Flash movies, Shockwave movies, Java applets, and sound and video files.

You must learn how to use multimedia elements wisely so they don't become a liability and deter visitors from your site. You should also be aware that many multimedia files are extremely large and may require a long download time for visitors using dial-up modems. In addition, other multimedia files may require the user to have a plugin installed in order to view the file.

This chapter reviews factors you should consider when you are making decisions about using multimedia content, and details information about using Dreamweaver to insert this content in your pages. Topics include the following:

- **Deciding to include multimedia**

- **Understanding web audio and video formats**

- **Using multimedia players**

- **Adding sound and movies**

- **Adding media elements**

- **Controlling media elements**

- **Launching and editing Flash MX files from Dreamweaver MX**

Deciding to Include Multimedia

When you make a decision about including multimedia elements, you are performing an important part of the site design process. But first be sure that the multimedia element is necessary. Start with these questions:

- What is the overall purpose of the site? Is multimedia content necessary to meet these goals?
- Does the multimedia element add content that can't be provided in any other way?
- Does the multimedia element enhance the rest of the page content?

Second, take a look at your audience definition, and pay particular attention to the following issues:

- Which browsers and browser versions is your audience most likely to be using to access your site?
- What kind of Internet connections is your audience likely to use?
- What percentage of your audience is likely to have broadband access?

Bandwidth is a very important issue to consider when you are using multimedia on the Web. Your site visitors will likely include users with both *broadband* connections and *narrowband* connections. Broadband connections are high-speed—200Kbps (kilobits per second) or higher—and include most Digital Subscriber Lines (DSL), cable modems, T1, and T3 connections. Narrowband connections are less than 200Kbps, and include dial-up modems.

Third, be sure to consider how you're going to obtain multimedia files for the pages. Are you planning to create the multimedia files yourself or do you plan to contract with someone else to do this? If you're going to create them yourself, evaluate these issues:

- Do you have the necessary software and other materials (video camera, sound files, and so on) to do this?
- Do you already know how to use the software and materials, or do you need to plan on additional site development time to learn these skills?

If you've reviewed these issues for your website and have decided to go ahead with including multimedia elements on the pages, you're ready for the next steps: choosing multimedia file types, choosing a server, and deciding whether to use a multimedia player.

Understanding Web Audio and Video Formats

Many different types of files can be used for audio and video on the Web. The following two sections of this chapter review the features of the most popular audio and video files.

Web Audio

There are six file types commonly used for web audio. Each type has advantages and disadvantages for use on the Web.

MIDI (Musical Instrument Digital Interface) MIDI files (with the `.midi` or `.mid` extensions) contain synthesized music. MIDI files are supported by most browsers, and don't require a *plugin* (a program that is used to view effects that the browser doesn't support by itself). The sound quality is very good, and the files are relatively small, making MIDI a very good choice for web audio. Special hardware and software are required to synthesize MIDI files.

WAV (Waveform Extension) WAV files (with the `.wav` extension) contain high quality sampled sound. WAV files are supported by most browsers and don't require a plugin. You can record your own WAV files, but the large file size limits their use on the Web.

AIFF (Audio Interchange File Format) AIFF files (with the `.aif` or `.aiff` extensions) contain good quality sampled sound. AIFF files are supported by most browsers and don't require a plugin. You can record your own AIFF files, but, like WAV files, large file size limits their use on the Web.

AU (basic Audio) AU files (with the `.au` extension) contain acceptable quality sampled sound. AU files are supported by the widest range of browsers and don't require a plugin.

MP3 (MPEG Audio Layer 3) MP3 files (with the `.mp3` extension) contain outstanding quality sound. The MP3 format is a compressed format that greatly reduces the size of the files. MP3 files can still be very large, however. MP3 files can be *streamed*—the file plays as it downloads, rather than having to wait for the whole file to download before it starts to play. The disadvantage of the MP3 format is that it requires a browser plugin or helper application.

RA, RAM (RealAudio) RealAudio files (with the `.ra`, `.ram`, or `.rpm` extensions) contain high quality streaming sound in a compressed format. Real Audio files have a smaller file size than MP3 files. RealAudio files require the use of RealPlayer software, either a browser plugin or a helper application.

Which audio format you choose will depend on what sound files you have available for your site. You can record your own sounds if you have a sound card and a microphone. You can also find thousands of sound samples on the Web—just be sure a sound file is in the public domain before you publish it on the Web.

FindSounds.com is a search engine for finding sound effects and sample sounds on the Web. Visit their site at `http://www.findsounds.com`.

Web Video

There are five file types commonly used for web video. Video files tend to be extremely large, however, so you must be sure a large video file is essential before you add it your site.

AVI (Audio Video Interleave) The AVI file format (with the `.avi` extension) was originally only supported on Windows platforms but is now also supported on the Mac platform. AVI files are often used for short video clips that aren't streamed. You can embed the AVI file in your page or create a link to it. In either case, the file must download entirely before playback can begin, so don't forget to keep it short!

MPEG (Moving Picture Experts Group) MPEG files (with the `.mpg` extension) are the most widely supported video file format on the Web. The MPEG file format is highly compressed so that the video file size can be made as small as possible. MPEG files, like AVI files, are often used for short video clips that aren't streamed.

QuickTime, RealMedia, Windows Media QuickTime, RealMedia, and Windows Media files are the most common web video file formats for streaming video. Each of these file formats requires a helper application unless the specific multimedia player is already installed on the user's computer.

Using Multimedia Players

Multimedia players are integrated packages of software that support almost all multimedia file types available on the Web. There are both free and commercial versions of all of the following multimedia players.

Real Player RealPlayer supports streaming audio and video including RealAudio and RealVideo as well as several other media types available as plugins. The RealOnePlayer is currently the newest version of the RealPlayer software. RealOnePlayer combines features of RealPlayer and RealJukebox so that you can organize your media files or burn CDs. It also includes a built-in web browser for downloading media files. Although the preset defaults in the RealOnePlayer allow you to use it for every media file type, you can uncheck those selections during the installation process.

You can download the RealOnePlayer from `http://www.realone.com`.

QuickTime QuickTime supports over 200 types of digital media types, including MP3, MIDI, AVI, AVR (*Avid Video Resolution*), streaming media, and digital video. The newest version of QuickTime is QuickTime 5. QuickTime 5 creates streaming media in HTTP, RTP (Real-Time Transport Protocol), and RTSP (Real Time Streaming Protocol) formats, and it also works with Cakewalk, After Effects, Cubic VR, and Premiere files. Flash 4 files are now supported, and QuickTime 5 also includes increased support for SMIL (Synchronized Multimedia Integration Language) and for XML import.

You can download the QuickTime player from `http://www.apple.com/quicktime`.

Windows Media Player The Windows Media Player includes seven features: a CD player, an audio and video player, an audio CD burner, portable device file transfer, a media guide, a media library, and Internet radio. The Windows Media Player supports streaming media files. The newest version is the Windows Media Player for Windows XP. Windows Media Player 7.1 is the newest version for Windows 98, Windows Me, and Windows 2000, and versions are also available for several other platforms including the Mac OS X platform.

You can download Windows Media Player from `http://www.microsoft.com/windows/windowsmedia/EN/default.asp`.

> For more information on the features of the newest multimedia players, check out "Media Player Update" by Adam Powell at `http://hotwired.lycos.com/webmonkey/99/24/index4a.html`. For more details on embedding a multimedia player in a web page, see his article "Embedding a Windows Media Player" at `http://hotwired.lycos.com/webmonkey/01/49/index2a.html?tw=eg20020111`.

Adding Sound and Movies

Both sound and movie files are often very large files, so be sure to consider whether audio or video enhancement of your pages is worth the download time.

Adding Audio Files

Sounds that can be a part of pages include background sounds that play as soon as the page loads, sounds that play when the user clicks a link, or sounds that are part of other multimedia files such as Flash animations or video files.

CHOOSING A SERVER FOR MULTIMEDIA CONTENT

Another important issue to consider when you are adding streaming multimedia content to your website is the choice of a server for streaming multimedia files. Most web servers use HTTP, but streaming web servers that use RTSP and other protocols are becoming increasingly available. Streaming media files can be served from an HTTP server, but the media file download is not synchronized, so playback might not be synchronous either! Pauses in playback are also more likely to happen when you are using HTTP for downloading streaming media files.

For more information on streaming media, visit `http://www.streamingmedia.com`.

Additional Flash movie properties can be included by clicking the Parameters button in the Property Inspector. To pass additional parameters to the Flash movie, it must be designed to accept these additional parameters.

Editing Links in Flash Movie Files

You can also edit links in a Flash movie file in Dreamweaver Site Map view.

1. Set a home page for the site. If you have already designated a home page for the site, skip to step 6.

2. Open the Site menu and select Edit Sites (Site → Edit Sites).

3. Select the site in the Edit Sites window and click the Edit button.

4. Choose the Advanced tab in the Site Definition window.

5. Select Site Map Layout and enter a URL in the Home Page text box or browse to a file from the folders icon to the right of the text box.

6. Open the Site window and click the Site Map icon under the menu bar.

7. Open the View menu and select Show Dependent Files (View → Show Dependent Files). The link appears below the Flash movie file.

8. Right click the link and select Change Link from the pop-up menu.

9. Type the new URL in the URL text box or click the folder to the right of the text box to browse to the new file.

10. To change the link in the entire site, open the Site menu and choose Change Link Sitewide.

11. Type the new URL in the Change All Links To text box, or click the folder to the right of the text box to browse to the new file.

Launch and Edit Features for Flash

Dreamweaver MX includes launch and edit features for Flash. If you have both Flash MX and Dreamweaver MX installed on your computer, you can update Flash movies that have been added to your Dreamweaver pages. To launch and edit Flash files from Dreamweaver, select the Flash file icon in Design view, and then open the Property Inspector (Window → Properties) and click the Edit button.

When the Edit button is clicked, Dreamweaver launches the Flash program and attempts to find the Flash source file for the selected Flash movie file . You can then work in Flash to make changes to the source file and re-export it as a movie file. The Flash document window shows that you are editing from Dreamweaver. Flash closes after exporting the new movie file, and the focus returns to Dreamweaver. You can preview the new movie in Dreamweaver itself, as detailed in the preceding tip.

The Flash source file is a different file type (.fla) than the Flash movie file (.mov). When you edit Flash files from Dreamweaver, you are editing the Flash source file and re-exporting it as a Flash movie file.

Cloaking Flash Files

When you create Flash movies, save the Flash source files and the Flash movie files in a Dreamweaver defined site. This makes the source files easy to locate for you, as well as anyone else working on the site files.

If you want to protect the source files (this applies to any source files, not just Flash source files) from being updated, you can cloak the folder that contains the source files. You can also cloak specific file types. Cloaking enables you to exclude folders from certain Dreamweaver operations, including the following:

- GET
- PUT
- Asset panel contents
- Check In
- Check Out
- Undo Check Out
- Check links sitewide
- Change links sitewide
- Library updating
- Reports
- Search/replace sitewide
- Select newer local
- Select newer remote
- Synchronize
- Template updating

To cloak a folder, follow these steps.

1. Open the Site menu in the Site panel and select Edit Sites (Site → Edit Sites…).
2. Choose the site you wish to edit from the Edit Sites dialog box and click the Edit button.
3. Click the Advanced tab of the Site Definition Wizard.
4. Select Cloaking. This enables cloaking for this site if you have previously disabled it. (Cloaking is enabled by default.)

5. Select the folder you want to cloak.

6. Open the Site menu in the Site panel, select Cloaking, and then Cloak/Uncloak (Site → Cloaking → Cloak/Uncloak). You can also do this by right-clicking (Ctrl-clicking in Macs) on the folder in the Site panel and then choosing Cloak/Uncloak from the pop-up menu that displays. You can also enable cloaking for the site from this pop-up menu.

A red line is displayed through the Folder icon, indicating that the folder is cloaked.

Adding Media Elements

Many other media elements can be added to your pages in Dreamweaver. These files can include Netscape plugins, ActiveX controls, Java applets, PDFs, and animated GIFs.

Adding Netscape Plugins

Most multimedia files require plugins in order to be viewed in Netscape Navigator. Plugins act as though they are part of the browser and extend the capabilities of the browser. The most popular plugins are the Java plugin (for viewing Java applets) and plugins for Adobe Acrobat Reader, Apple QuickTime player, Macromedia Flash player, and RealNetwork's RealPlayer.

> For more information on Netscape plugins, see "About Plug-ins" at `http://home.netscape` `.com/plugins/manager.html`.

Developers can create new plugins for Netscape Navigator by using the Plugin API. For more details, see "Plug-in Basics" at `http://developer.netscape.com/docs/manuals/` `communicator/plugin/basic.htm#1009627`.

> Internet Explorer for Windows beginning with versions 5.5 SP2 and 6.0 no longer supports Netscape-style plugins. This does not affect Mac users or Netscape users. Windows users can restore support for Netscape-style plugins by downloading an ActiveX control from Apple at `http://www.apple.com/quicktime/download/qtcheck/`.

To add a Netscape plugin, use the Insert bar and click the Media tab, and then click the Plugin icon (Figure 17.1). Browse to the media file from the Select File display box, or enter the URL of the media file.

Netscape supports the `embed` element for inserting multimedia files. When you add a plugin to your Dreamweaver page, an `embed` element with an `src` attribute (the location and filename of the multimedia file) and `width` and `height` attributes is automatically created.

To specify additional attributes for the embed element, follow these steps.

1. Select the Plugin icon in Design view.

2. Open the Property Inspector (Window → Properties). The top part of the window displays the most commonly used properties for the Plugin object. To see all the properties, click the down arrow in the lower-right corner of the Property Inspector (Figure 17.4).

3. Insert values for any attribute you want to include in the embed element.

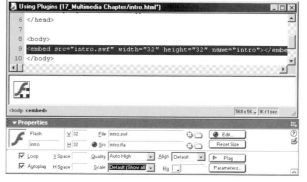

Figure 17.4

Plugin Property Inspector—full view

Table 17.2 lists the most common properties of the Plugin object.

The Property Inspector also includes a Parameters button. Click this button, or right-click the Plugin icon on the Dreamweaver page to open the Parameters dialog box. The Parameters dialog box can be used to add attributes specific to the type of object being inserted and can be used with embed, object, and applet elements.

Click the plus (+) button and enter a name and a value to add a parameter. To remove a parameter, select it in the Parameters dialog box and click the minus (-) button. You can also change the order of parameters by selecting a parameter in the Parameter dialog box and then using the up and down arrow buttons.

To preview plugin content in the Document window, select a media element you have inserted and choose View → Plugins → Play. To play all the media elements on the page, choose View → Plugins → Play All. You can also play a media element by selecting it, and then opening the Property Inspector (Window → Properties) and clicking the Play button. Only media objects that use the embed element can be played in the Document window in this way. The appropriate plugin to play the file must be installed on your computer.

PROPERTY	DESCRIPTION
name	Identifies the plugin, used in scripting
width	Identifies the width of the plugin
height	Denotes the height of the plugin
src	Describes the path (location and filename) to the plugin file
Plg Url	Contains the URL of the pluginspace attribute[1]
align	Shows the alignment of the plugin
vspace	Specifies the vertical space above and below the plugin
hspace	Denotes the horizontal space to the left and right of the plugin
border	Specifies the width of the border around the plugin

Table 17.2

Common Plugin Properties

[1] The browser uses this URL to download the plugin if the viewer does not already have it installed.

Adding ActiveX Controls

ActiveX controls are small programs that add functionality to a web page. ActiveX controls use the ActiveX technologies developed by Microsoft.

> For further information on ActiveX, see "Introduction to ActiveX Controls" at `http://msdn`
> `.microsoft.com/library/default.asp?url=/workshop/components/activex/intro.asp`.

To add an ActiveX control, use the Insert bar and click the Media tab, then click the ActiveX icon. Browse to the media file from the Select File display box, or enter the URL of the media file.

Internet Explorer supports the `object` element for inserting ActiveX controls. When you add an ActiveX control to your Dreamweaver page, an `object` element with an `src` attribute (the location and filename of the multimedia file) and `width` and `height` attributes is automatically created.

To specify additional attributes for the `object` element, follow these steps.

1. Select the ActiveX icon in Design view.

2. Open the Property Inspector (Window → Properties). The top part of the window displays the most commonly used properties for ActiveX objects. To see all the properties, click the down arrow in the lower-right corner of the Property Inspector.

3. Insert values for any attribute you want to include in the `object` element.

Table 17.3 lists the most common properties of the ActiveX object.

	PROPERTY	DESCRIPTION
Table 17.3	name	Identifies the ActiveX object, used in scripting
Common ActiveX	width	Denotes the width of the ActiveX object
Properties	height	Declares the height of the ActiveX object
	classid	Identifies the ActiveX control to the browser[1]
	embed	Adds an embed element within the object element[2]
	align	Shows the alignment of the ActiveX object
	src	Denotes the source of the data file to be used for a Netscape plugin[3]
	vspace	Specifies the vertical space above and below the ActiveX object
	hspace	Specifies the horizontal space to the left and right of the ActiveX object
	base	Denotes the URL of the ActiveX control
	Alt img	Identifies the image file to be displayed if the browser doesn't support the `object` element
	id	Denotes an optional ActiveX id parameter
	data	Identifies the data file for the ActiveX control to load

[1] The browser uses the class id to find the ActiveX control associated with the ActiveX object on the page. If the browser doesn't find the ActiveX control, it will download it from the URL value given for `base`.

[2] If the ActiveX control has a Netscape plugin equivalent, the `embed` element activates the plugin.

[3] This option only works if the `embed` element is included.

Additional ActiveX properties can be included by clicking the Parameters button in the Property Inspector (as described in the preceding section on Netscape plugins), which results in the Parameters dialog box being displayed (Figure 17.5). To choose which additional parameters to include, check the documentation for the ActiveX control you're using.

Figure 17.5

Parameters dialog box

Adding Java Applets

Applets are small programs written in the Java programming language. You can use Java applets to add interactivity and animation to your pages. These applets can be embedded directly in your pages. Though applets are usually quite large, they don't require the additional download of a plugin or helper application. Applets can be viewed in most browsers, including both Netscape and Internet Explorer.

To add a Java applet, use the Insert bar and click the Media tab and then click the Applet icon. Browse to the applet file from the Select File dialog box, or enter the URL of the applet file.

Java applets use the `class` file extension. For simple applets, you only need to know the name of the applet to use it on your page. For more complex applets, you need to specify additional attributes, as follows:

1. Select the applet icon in Design view.

2. Open the Property Inspector (Window → Properties). The top part of the window displays the most commonly used properties for applets. To see all the properties, click the arrow in the lower-right corner of the Property Inspector (Figure 17.6).

3. Insert values for any attribute you want to include in the `applet` element.

GETTING TECHNICAL—*OBJECT* AND *EMBED* ELEMENTS

The object element is used by Internet Explorer (which is the browser included with Windows 9x/NT/2000/XP) and also by other browsers that support ActiveX controls. The embed element is used by Internet Explorer for the Mac, Netscape, and also by other browsers that support Netscape-style plugins.

The object and embed elements can both be used separately or together for inserting multimedia content on a page. If they are used together, the embed element is nested within the object element. Browsers that support the object element ignore the nested embed element, and those that don't support the object element ignore it, and use the embed element instead.

The embed element is deprecated as of XHTML 1.0, but an equivalent element is not available in HTML or XHTML. (In other words, there is currently no option that uses the embed element and includes both cross-browser compatibility and web standards compliance.)

Table 17.4 lists the most common applet properties.

Table 17.4

**Common Applet
Properties**

PROPERTY	DESCRIPTION
name	Identifies the applet, used in scripting
width	Denotes the width of the applet object
height	Denotes the height of the applet object
code	Specifies the location (URL) of the Java file on the server
base	Specifies the folder containing the applet[1]
align	Specifies the alignment of the applet object
alt	Denotes the alternative content that should be displayed if the browser doesn't support Java or if Java is disabled[2]
vspace	Denotes the vertical space above and below the applet object
hspace	Denotes the horizontal space to the left and right of the applet object

[1] *This attribute field is filled in automatically when you select an applet.*

[2] *To make alternative content accessible in both Netscape and Internet Explorer with Java disabled (as well as text browsers), use both an image and an* alt *attribute to specify alternative content.*

For complex applets, you may need to specify additional attributes. Additional applet properties can be included by clicking the Parameters button in the Property Inspector to open the Parameters dialog box (Figure 17.5). To decide which additional parameters to include, check the documentation for the applet you're using.

Adding PDFs

Portable Document Format (PDF) is a file format that saves formatting information from desktop publishing programs. PDF files can be viewed in a browser, and you can insert links to PDF files on your web pages. PDF files preserve the fonts, colors, graphics, and original formatting of any document. The Adobe Acrobat Reader, which is needed to view a PDF file, can be downloaded for free from http://www.adobe.com/products/acrobat/readstep2.html.

To insert a link to a PDF file, use the Insert bar and click the Hyperlink icon; then enter a URL in the Link text box or click the folder to the right of the text box to navigate to the PDF file location.

> When you are uploading your site files to a web server, be sure to upload PDF files in the same mode you use to upload graphic files. For example, if you use WS-FTP for file transfer, choose binary mode for uploading a PDF file.

Adding Animated GIFs

Animated GIFs were one of the first multimedia elements to be added to web pages. They continue to be popular because their file sizes are usually small and because they are easy to create. You can create animated GIFs in graphics programs such as Fireworks, Photoshop,

ImageReady, or Animation Shop. You can also use software specifically developed to create animated GIFs, such as Gif Construction Kit (Windows) or GifBuilder (Mac). All of these programs include tools to combine individual GIF images into an animated GIF.

> Gif Construction Kit is available as shareware. It can be downloaded at http://www
> .sharewarejunkies.com/8gh3/gifcon.htm. GifBuilder is available for free download at
> http://homepage.mac.com/piguet/gif.html.

You can add an animated GIF to a page in the same way you add any image. Use the Insert bar and click the Image icon. Select the animated GIF file in the Select Image Source dialog box.

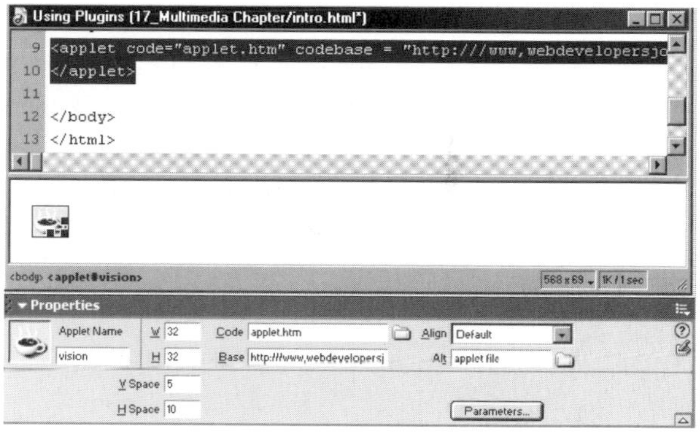

Using Dreamweaver Behaviors to Control Media Elements

The following three Dreamweaver behaviors can be used with media elements:

Control Shockwave or Flash Stops, starts, rewinds, or goes to a specific frame in a Shockwave or Flash movie.

Play Sound Plays a sound when a specified event occurs.

Check Plugin Checks to see if site users have a specific Netscape-style plugin installed, and sends them to different URLs based on whether or not the plugin is installed.

Figure 17.6

Applet Property Inspector

> For more information on using Dreamweaver behaviors, including details on the preceding three behaviors, see Chapter 19.

GENERATOR OBJECTS

Macromedia Generator files can be used to serve dynamic web content. Generator files can be created with Flash 4 or 5 using the Generator authoring templates included with the Flash software. These Generator files can then be served on a web server running Generator server software.

With the recent release of Flash MX, Macromedia has announced that it plans to stop further development of Generator and focus on dynamic content and client application development using Flash. But Generator can still be used, and Generator objects can be added to Dreamweaver pages. Previous versions of Dreamweaver have included a selection for Generator objects in the Media tab of the Insert bar. This feature is not available in Dreamweaver MX.

For more information on Flash MX, visit http://www.macromedia.com/software/flash/.

Hands On: Launching and Editing Flash MX Files from Dreamweaver MX

If you have both Dreamweaver MX and Flash MX, you can launch and edit Flash MX from within Dreamweaver MX. You can edit your Flash source file, re-export it into Dreamweaver as a Flash movie, and then preview it in Dreamweaver.

1. Open `multimedia.html` from the Flash Tutorial folder within the Chapter 17 folder on the accompanying CD.

2. To preview the Flash file inserted in this page, click the Flash icon in Design view. Open the Property Inspector (Window ➤ Properties) and click the Play button in the bottom half of the Property Inspector. (If you don't see the Play button, click the down arrow in the bottom-right corner of the window to display the full Property Inspector.)

3. After you've previewed the Flash movie, click the Stop button in the Property Inspector.

4. Then click the Edit button. This launches the Flash MX application from Dreamweaver.

5. The Flash source file (`tutorial.fla`) for the Flash movie file (`tutorial.swf`) opens in a Flash window labeled "Editing From Dreamweaver"(Figure 17.7).

6. In Flash, open the Library panel (Window ➤ Library) to access the library items for the Flash source file.

7. Double-click the icon labeled "Opening Text" to edit the Opening Text graphic. Make sure you choose the graphic and not the movie clip. Any changes you make to the graphic symbol will also be changed in the movie clip.

8. Using the arrow tool from the Flash Tools panel, select the graphic symbol in the symbol editing window (see Figure 17.8).

9. Choose the text tool from the Flash Tools panel, and highlight the 4 in the text box. Type **MX** in place of the 4.

10. Open the Property Inspector (Window ➤ Properties) in Flash. Select the graphic symbol in the symbol editing window.

11. From the Font window, change the font from Impact to your choice of another font in the drop-down menu.

12. Change the font size in the Font Size drop-down menu to the right of the Font window.

13. Change the font color in the Text Fill Color box to the right of the Font Size menu (see Figure 17.9). Click the B (Bold) button to the right.

Figure 17.7

"Editing From Dreamweaver" window in Flash MX

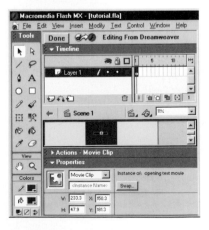

14. Once you have completed editing the Flash file, click the Done button in the upper-left
    corner of the Flash file window. This exports the new movie file to Dreamweaver. It will
    have the same filenamc as the original Flash movie file (`tutorial.swf`).

To view our version of the new HTML page with the edited Flash file, open `multimedia_`
`complete.html` from the Chapter 17 folder of the accompanying CD.

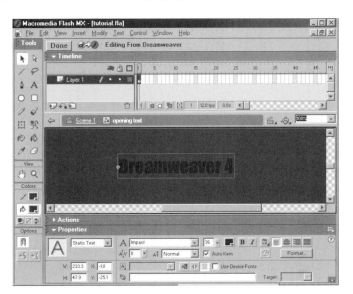

Figure 17.8

Editing a graphic symbol in Flash

Figure 17.9

Changing properties of a graphic symbol in Flash MX

To Add Multimedia or Not to Add Multimedia...

The decision to add multimedia elements to your pages is the essential question to answer during the site planning process. Once you've made the decision, it is easy to use Dreamweaver to add multimedia files.

There are many additional ways to add dynamic content to your Dreamweaver pages. See the next chapter for details on adding jump menus and DHTML features.

## CHAPTER 18

Rollovers, Navigation Bars, and Jump Menus

What is it about fancy drop-down menus or rollovers that make us say to ourselves, "Ooh, that's cool!" Even old pros who've been designing sites since 1994 say the same thing when they see a clean rollover effect on a web site—even a simple one. Maybe it's that we like movement on the Web. Not too much movement, of course. No, it's just a subtle color change or a new icon that pops up. Just enough of a change to show us that we are involved, individually, in the navigation of this particular site. Maybe it makes us feel special.

Well, with Dreamweaver, the mystery of the rollover and the pop-up (or drop-down) menu will all but disappear for you. You no longer have to learn everything about JavaScript or go hunting on the Web for some hacked script that you spend all night debugging, eventually waking up with half a keyboard imprinted on your face. That's just not pretty. Besides, do you have any idea how hard it is to get drool out from between the keys?

Here are some topics covered in this chapter that will help you out:

- **Making rollovers**

- **Making a navigation bar**

- **Using Dreamweaver's Flash buttons**

- **Making a jump menu**

- **Digging into the JavaScript code**

Gathering Your Graphic Assets

Remember that Dreamweaver is not a graphics program and that you'll need to prepare your images first, most likely in Fireworks (see Part II for more on working with Fireworks). In fact, you may choose to create your navigation elements entirely in Fireworks (as discussed in Chapter 9), but with Dreamweaver MX, you no longer need to do so. As long as you have the images prepared (including whatever variations you want to display when a graphic link is hovered over, active, or current), you can assemble your jump menus and navigation bars directly in Dreamweaver.

If you have already created your entire interactive image in Fireworks (whether it be a simple rollover, a jump menu, a navigation bar, or something more complex), you can insert it into your document in Dreamweaver with Insert → Interactive Images → Fireworks HTML. Then you just browse to the Fireworks file and click OK. See Chapter 9 for more information on this approach.

Making a Rollover

A *rollover* is a graphic that changes appearance when hovered over. It's really just two different graphics with a little bit of scripting that tells the browser to swap one image in for the other.

To make a rollover, follow these steps:

1. Position the insertion point where you want the image to appear.

2. On the Common tab of the Insert bar, click the Rollover Image icon 🖼 (or select Insert → Interactive Images → Rollover Image).

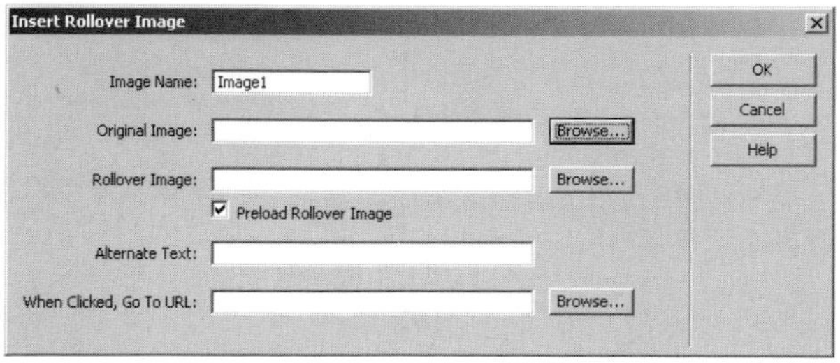

Figure 18.1

The Insert Rollover Image dialog box makes it simple to drop a rollover onto your page.

3. On the Insert Rollover Image dialog box that appears, type a name for the image (see Figure 18.1).

4. Browse to the original image (the one that should be displayed by default).

5. Then browse to the rollover image (the one that should be displayed when the action takes place—hovering, clicking, and so on.).

6. Type alternate text for nongraphical browsers.

7. Browse to the destination for the rollover, assuming that you're using the interactive image as a link.

8. Click OK. Dreamweaver inserts the rollover.

> Dreamweaver won't display the rolling-over action for you. You'll need to preview your page in a browser (by pressing F12) to see the image in action.

By default, Dreamweaver makes rollovers that respond to the mouse when it is hovering over the image. If you want to make a rollover that responds to another action, such as clicking, use the Behaviors feature to add an Action called Swap Image (see Chapter 19 for more on working with behaviors).

Making a Navigation Bar

As with rollovers, before you can insert a navigation bar into the pages of your site, you first have to prepare the images that will appear as the links, menu choices, or buttons.

For each button, you'll need up to four images: one for the initial state of the button, one for when the mouse is hovering over the button, one for when the button has been clicked, and one for when the button has been clicked and the mouse is hovering over the button.

Once you have the graphic images ready, Dreamweaver makes the assembly of even complicated nav bars rather easy.

To make a single navigation bar available to numerous pages in your site, insert the bar into a template and then attach the template to your pages (or build your pages based on the template). See Chapter 4 for more on templates.

To make a rollover, follow these steps:

1. Position the insertion point where you want the navigation bar to appear.

2. On the Common tab of the Insert bar, click the Navigation Bar icon ![icon] (or select Insert → Interactive Images → Navigation Bar).

3. On the Insert Navigation Bar dialog box that appears, type a name for the first button (see Figure 18.2).

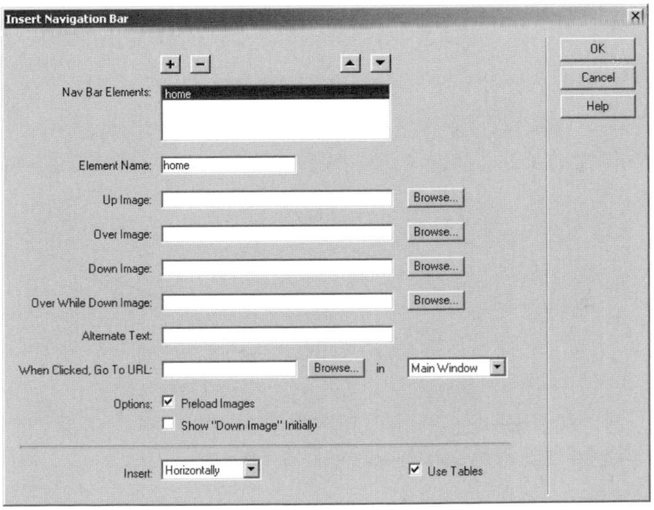

Figure 18.2

The Insert Navigation Bar dialog box streamlines the process of assembling a nav bar.

4. Browse to the original image (the one that should be displayed by default, when the button hasn't been clicked and nothing's hovering over it), called the Up Image.

5. Then (optionally), browse to the Over Image, (displayed when the mouse is hovering and the button is still unclicked).

6. Then (optionally), browse to the Down Image (displayed when the button is clicked and the mouse is not hovering).

7. Then (optionally), browse to the Over While Down Image (displayed when the button is clicked and the mouse is hovering).

8. Type alternate text for nongraphical browsers.

9. Browse to the destination for the rollover, assuming that you're using the interactive image as a link.

10. If the current button represents the current page (as, for example, a Home button would do on the home page of a site), click the Show Down Image Initially option.

11. To add the next button, click the Add Item button (the plus (+) sign at the top of the dialog box) and then repeat steps 3 through 10. Do this as many times as needed.

12. Indicate if the nav bar is to be inserted vertically or horizontally.

13. Click OK. Dreamweaver inserts the navigation bar.

Using Dreamweaver's Flash Buttons (and When Not To)

In the past, if you wanted to add some Flash animated buttons to your site, you had to purchase ($$) the Flash application and then (yikes!) actually learn it. A very cool feature introduced in Dreamweaver 4 was the ability to create Flash rollover buttons right within Dreamweaver. Now, with zero knowledge of Flash and without even having the program installed on your computer, you can quickly add simple Flash buttons to your site.

Should You Even Use Flash Buttons?

One of the decisions you have to make is whether or not you should use Flash elements in a Dreamweaver document. Macromedia (and many other web experts) believe that 70–90 percent of web visitors have the Flash plugin installed in their browsers. The problem—in our estimation—is that not all of these web visitors are 1) using high-speed Internet connections, and 2) have high-speed computers.

Certainly one can argue that Flash files are vector art and are, in some cases, smaller files than most JPEG photos, but that's not necessarily the case. Flash files are sometimes bothersome to slower computers because they still have to redraw on the screen in a timely manner. There are cases when a user on a 486 or Pentium I machine who is connecting to the Internet via a 56K modem (meaning, at best, 48K) finds that Flash buttons don't load right away or don't load at all.

Remember, just because a web visitor has the Flash plugin installed in their browser doesn't mean that they have the most current version. We certainly don't want to scare you from using Flash elements in your site—for the most part, they are pretty harmless at this point—rather we'd like to simply make you aware of all sides of the issue of whether or not to use Flash.

The point is, you have to know your audience. Read log files (or get a report from a client) to see what versions of web browsers the visitors are using (the newer the better for Flash elements). Recognize the make up of the site audience. For instance, if your site caters to schoolteachers, be aware that they may or may not have the latest software. On the other hand, if you are catering to a younger audience, say teenagers, they are more apt to make sure that they have the latest and greatest software and plugins and you are probably just fine.

As long as you know your target audience, you'll be able to make decisions about Flash and other non-standard elements on your pages. This knowledge will make for better sites (more visitors able to see them!) and for better business for you and/or your client since sites that work tend to bring visitors and keep them coming back for more.

Flash Rollover Buttons

Rollover buttons will make your site more interactive. To add a rollover button, follow these steps:

1. Open an HTML document in Dreamweaver and place your cursor where you'd like to add a Flash button.

2. In the Media tab of the Insert bar (usually located along the left side or top of your screen), choose the Insert Flash Button icon 🔵 to open the Insert Flash Button window (see Figure 18.3).

3. From the list of button styles, single click a style name to view the sample in the Sample window above the style name selection. You can scroll down the list to see more styles.

4. Next, type the text into the Button Text field as you want it to appear on the Flash button.

5. Next, choose the font and font size for your text.

6. Place the URL that you'd like your Flash button to link to in the Link field.

7. You can then choose a Target if you are using frames, or if you want a separate browser window to pop up and display the URL content, enter it in the Target field.

8. Click OK to save you changes.

Now that you've learned how to add a Flash button, let's discuss getting more button styles.

Figure 18.3

It's a virtual breeze to incorporate a Flash button rollover into Dreamweaver.

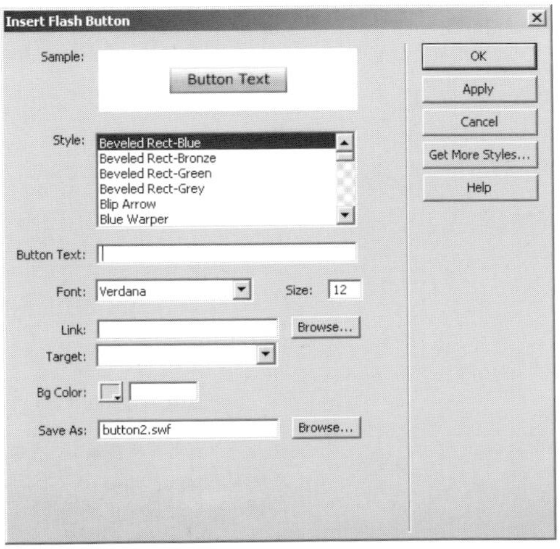

GETTING MORE BUTTON STYLES

If you don't find the button style you like, you can click the Get More Styles button at your right. This will launch your browser and take you to Macromedia's website where you can import more styles.

You should realize, however, that the Flash buttons are a fixed size. For instance, your text may not fit the button style you chose in the Style list. In order to make it work with a particular style, you may have to change font size and/or fonts.

Matching Your Background

A really cool feature of Flash buttons is Bg Color. If you want to place your Flash button over a background color or graphic, you want any background on the button (some buttons aren't perfectly square and will show white squared corners by default) to blend with it. To make sure this happens, click on the Bg Color square of the Insert Flash Button window, and with the eyedropper tool that appears as your cursor, "reach" over and click your web page's background color; you have just selected it as the background color of your Flash button. Another way to accomplish this is by typing the HTML equivalent of your background color into the Bg Color field (such as, #FFFFFF for white).

Saving and Previewing

Now that you have finished creating your Flash button, just click the Browse button to the right of Save As to locate the directory where you'd like to save your Flash button. Make sure to name it so that it's easy to find and identify.

To preview your new button before you save it, click Apply. This will show you your button on your page and you won't even have to leaving the Insert Flash Button window. This way, if your font isn't what you were expecting or the font size isn't right, you can quickly make a change and click Apply again to view it. When you are satisfied with its appearance, click OK and you are finished. The window will close, taking you back to your web page.

On-the-Fly Resizing

Unlike GIF and JPEG files, Flash buttons are vector graphics. This means that you can resize them on-the-fly while still retaining their clarity and even proportions.

To do so, just follow these steps:

1. Click your new Flash button. Notice that you now see several little black handles (see Figure 18.4).

2. Click and hold the handle on the lower right of your button.

3. Next, hold down the Shift key and drag your mouse either inward to make the button smaller or outward to make the button larger. By holding down the Shift key, you can retain the button's proportions rather than having them get stretched out one way or another.

When you let go of the mouse button, the Flash button will redraw to its new size and shape. Cool, huh?

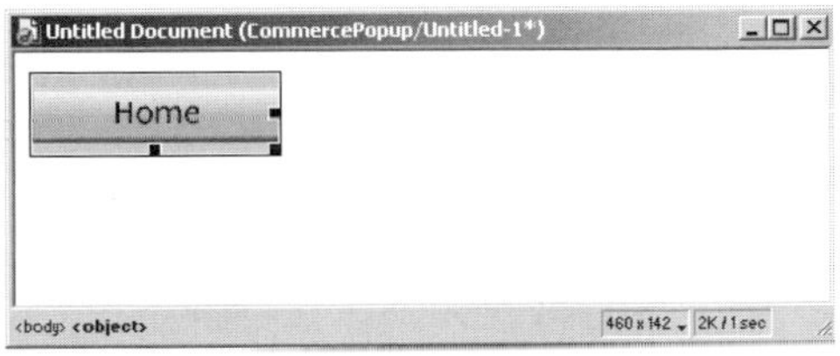

Figure 18.4

Because Flash buttons are vector graphics, resizing them doesn't cause "jaggedness" or blur the image the way it would for a bitmap image.

Testing and Editing Your Flash Button

When you single click the new Flash button you created earlier, you will notice something new in the Property Inspector, which is usually at the bottom of your screen. (If you don't see the Property Inspector, you can get to it by choosing Window → Properties.) There's now a green play button in the Property Inspector whenever you have a Flash element selected. This gives you the opportunity to see your Flash button in action right within Dreamweaver. You may need to double-click in the Property Inspector to expand it (if you don't see the play button initially).

Click the Play button in the Property Inspector (circled in Figure 18.18) and then move your cursor over the Flash button to see how the rollover effect works. You can also click it to see how the other states will look in a browser. Notice that when you click Play, the button now says Stop. Once you are done playing with, er, testing your Flash button, click Stop to go back to editing your web page.

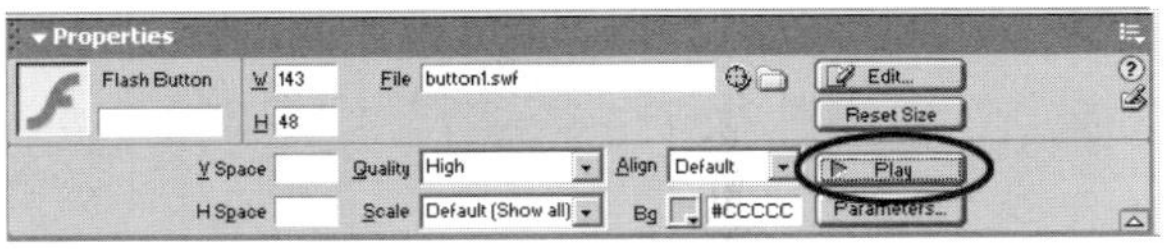

Figure 18.5

Click the Play button in the Property Inspector to test your new Flash button.

To make changes to your Flash button, simply double-click it to open the Flash Button dialog box. Make your changes as you did when you first created it, click Apply to see them, and click OK to save them and go back to working on your web page.

Figure 18.6

The Flash text feature is very similar to the Flash buttons.

Creating Flash Text

Almost identical to Dreamweaver's Flash button feature is Flash text. Basically, this feature is exactly like the Flash button feature—the only difference is that there isn't a graphical button involved. All aspects described previously (with the exception of the button styles) apply to Flash text.

To insert Flash text, follow these steps:

1. Choose the Insert Flash Text button in the Tools panel. The Insert Flash Text dialog box opens (see Figure 18.6).

2. Choose the font, font size, and alignment.

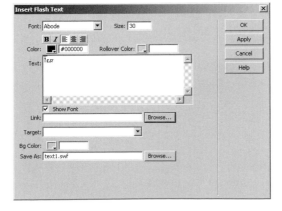

3. Next, choose the color of your text and then choose the color of the rollover text (when a mouse cursor is placed over the text).

4. As you did in the Flash button window, choose your link, target, and background color (to match your web page background), and then save the Flash text file to your computer.

5. Click Apply to preview your Flash text just as you did for the Flash button.

6. Once you've finished with the settings, click OK.

Want to edit the Flash text later? Double-click the Flash text item to open the Flash text settings box. Simple!

Making a Jump Menu

A jump menu is a pop-up menu in a document that is visible to your site visitors; it contains links that allow them to go to other documents or files. You can create links to documents in your website, documents on other websites, e-mail links, links to graphics, or links to any file type that can be opened in a browser.

Jump menus allow for more link options in a smaller amount of space on a page.

There are three basic components of a jump menu:

- A menu selection prompt, such as a category description for the menu items, or instructions, such as "Choose one." This is an optional element.

- A list of linked menu items from which a user chooses an option, which causes a linked document or file to open. This is a required element.

- A Go button. This is an optional element.

Figure 18.7

Search Category jump menu

Figure 18.7 displays a jump menu that shows your search categories. This jump menu also uses the optional Go button, so this is a combination of two elements, although Dreamweaver let's you create them together.

Inserting a Jump Menu

Because the jump menu must be part of a form object, Dreamweaver automatically creates one if you don't already have one defined. Therefore, to insert a jump menu into your document, you use the Jump Menu form object.

1. Select Insert → Form Objects → Jump Menu. This opens the Insert Jump Menu dialog box shown in Figure 18.8.

2. To create a selection prompt, type the prompt text in the Text field of the dialog box.

3. Under Options, select the "Select first item after URL change" check box, then click the plus (+) button to add a menu item.

4. In the Text field of the Insert Jump Menu dialog box, type the text you want to appear in the menu list.

5. In the When Selected, Go to URL field, select the file to open by browsing for the file, or entering the file's path.

6. In the Open URLs In pop-up menu, select a location in which the file will open, either the main window, or a frame.

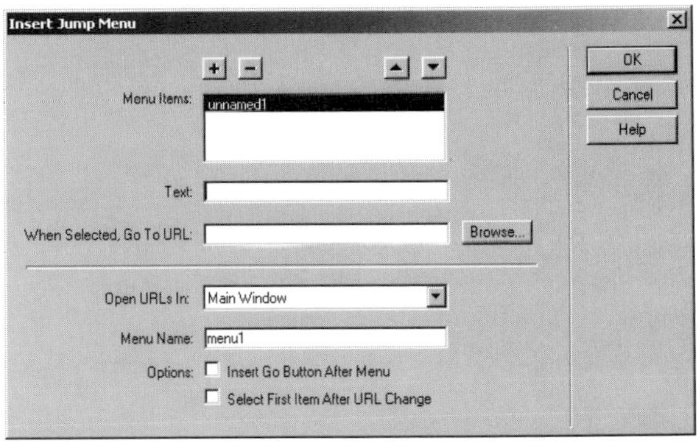

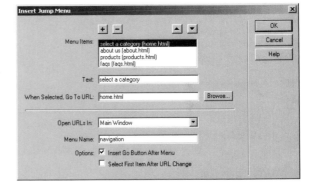

Figure 18.8

Insert Jump Menu dialog box

> If your target frame doesn't appear on the Open URLs In pop-up menu, close the Insert Jump Menu dialog box and name the frame.

7. If you want to add a Go button instead of a menu selection prompt, under Options, select the Insert Go Button after Menu option.

8. To add additional menu items, click the plus (+) button and repeat steps 3 through 6 of this procedure (see Figure 18.9).

9. Click OK.

Figure 18.10 shows both the jump menu and the Go button the user sees from the information entered for Figure 18.9.

You can also write your own DHTML code to create jump menus for your website, as we'll discuss shortly. But first we'll look at how to make changes to your jump menus.

Figure 18.9

Completed Insert Jump Menu dialog box

Editing Jump Menus

In order to make jump menu changes, use the Property Inspector or the Behaviors panel. You can change the list order or the file an item links to, or you can add, delete, or rename an item. However, if you are changing the location in which a linked file opens, or even adding or changing a menu selection prompt, you must use the Behaviors panel.

Figure 18.10

Jump Menu and Go Button

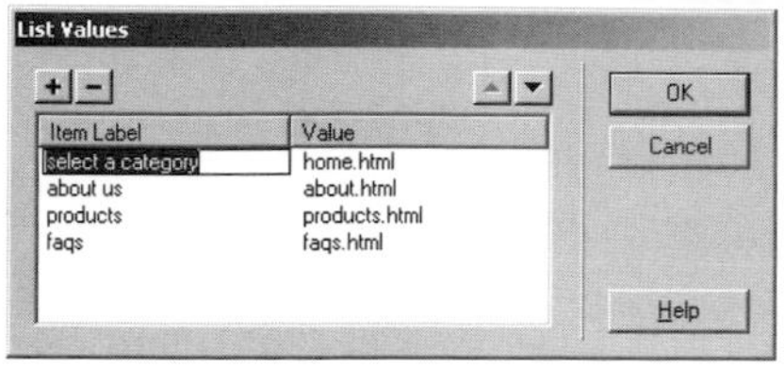

Figure 18.11

List Values dialog box

In order to edit a jump menu item using the Property Inspector, follow these steps:

1. In the Property Inspector, choose Window → Properties.

2. In the Document window's Design view, select the jump menu object.

3. The List/Menu icon should appear in the Property Inspector.

4. In the Property Inspector, click the List Values button. Figure 18.11 shows the List Values dialog box that displays as a result.

5. Make changes to the menu items, then click OK.

As with any software application, there are always different ways of doing something. If you're using frames as a destination for your jump to take the user to a new page then the user can't navigate backwards. Though being able to navigate back to where they user started from is handy, it can be worked around.

Troubleshooting Jump Menus

As just mentioned, once users choose a jump menu item, they will not be able to reselect that menu item if they navigate back to that page, or if the Open URL In field specifies a frame. You have to work around this problem, and there are two ways to do it.

First, you can use a menu selection prompt, such as a category, or a user instruction, such as "Choose one." This menu selection prompt is reselected automatically after each menu selection.

Second, you can use a Go button, which allows a user to revisit the currently chosen link.

Select only one of these options per jump menu because they cannot be used at the same time on the same jump menu.

Now we're going to discuss how to insert jump menus using DHTML (dynamic HTML), which is just an old-fashioned name for combining Cascading Style Sheets (CSS) and JavaScript. (See Chapter 15 for more on CSS.)

Using JavaScript to Direct Your Jump

When you enter JavaScript, you always begin your code with the following in the head of your document, otherwise the browser doesn't know it needs to run the script.

```
<script language="JavaScript"><!-

//-></script>
```

Then you should make a list of all the drop-down layers in the JavaScript so that most of the functions can be automated:

```
ftest_droplayer=new Array()
ftest_droplayer[0]="drop1"
ftest_droplayer[1]="drop2"
ftest_droplayer[2]="drop3"
ftest_droplayer[3]="drop4"
ftest_droplayer[4]="drop5"
ftest_droplayer[5]="drop6"
```

After you have done this, you should build two functions: one that shows any particular layer, and another that makes sure all the layers are hidden. Creating a function to hide all the layers is easier than trying to hide one specific layer. This doesn't seem too bad, right? We haven't had any complications yet—well, now here comes a complication. Remember that we mentioned that all browsers view code differently?

Well, Netscape and IE need different code, which means that a browser checker is needed. You add your browser check information at the top of the script. A browser checker determines if the user is running Netscape or IE.

```
//simple browser check
ftest_v4=(parseInt(navigator.appVersion)>=4 &&
parseInt(navigator.appVersion)<=5)?1:0
ftest_ns=(document.layers && ftest_v4)?1:0
ftest_ie=(document.all && ftest_v4)?1:0
```

Because you've created the browser checker, you now use the commands `if(ie)` and `if(ns)` to apply bits of code only to the appropriate browser. For example, `if(ie)` means that if the user has IE as their browser, this happens. JavaScript functionality can now be written.

Adding JavaScript Functions

As mentioned earlier, the JavaScript is entered after the browser check in the script. The following functions check the state of the browser.

```
//code for drop layers

function ftest_showdrop(thelayer){
  ftest_keep=thelayer; ftest_hideall(); ftest_showitnow=1
  ftest_showit(thelayer)
  }

function ftest_showit(thelayer){
  if(ftest_ie){ eval(ftest_droplayer[thelayer]+
'.style.visibility="visible"') }
```

```
     if(ftest_ns){ eval('document.'+ftest_droplayer[thelayer]+
'.visibility="show"');}
       }

function ftest_hidedrop(){
   ftest_keep=-1; setTimeout('ftest_hideall()',500)
       }

ftest_keep=-1

function ftest_hideall(){
    for(i=0;i<ftest_droplayer.length;i++){
      ftest_hideit=0; ftest_checkmousepos(i)
      if(ftest_ie && ftest_keep!=i){
        if(ftest_hideit){
eval(ftest_droplayer[i]+'.style.visibility="hidden"') }
          }
      if(ftest_ns && ftest_keep!=i){
        if(ftest_hideit){
eval('document.'+ftest_droplayer[i]+'.visibility="hide"') }
          }
        }
      }
```

This script monitors the conditions, and if they are right, it either shows a particular drop from an onmouseover command when you ask it to, or it hides all the layers, following a 500 millisecond delay after the onmouseout command. Note that neither the onmouseover nor onmouseout command appears in this code; they have yet to be added.

Before we can add these, we have to deal with another little problem. Netscape doesn't support onmouseover for layers. This means that when you roll off the buttons in Netscape, the menu disappears even if your mouse is still over the menu. To get around this, we need to add a checker that looks at the position of the mouse and the position of the visible layer and checks to see if the cursor is over the layer. This is the function called by ftest_checkmousepos in the previous code sample.

Now we're going to compare the mouse position to the layer position. Once again we're using the if(ftest_ns) and if(ftest_ie) commands to check each browser. This browser check code is placed at the end of the code.

```
//deal with cursor over layer

document.onmousemove = ftest_getmousepos
if (ftest_ns) document.captureEvents(Event.MOUSEMOVE)
```

```
function ftest_getmousepos(e){
  if(ftest_ns){ftest_mousex=e.pageX; ftest_mousey=e.pageY}
  if(ftest_ie){ftest_mousex=event.clientX; ftest_mousey=event.clientY;}
  }

function ftest_checkmousepos(i){
  if(ftest_ie){
    ftest_x_min=eval(ftest_droplayer[i]+'.style.pixelLeft')
    ftest_x_max=ftest_x_min+eval(ftest_droplayer[i]+ '.style.pixelWidth')
    ftest_y_min=eval(ftest_droplayer[i]+'.style.pixelTop')
    ftest_y_max=ftest_y_min+eval(ftest_droplayer[i]+ '.style.pixelHeight')
    }
  if(ftest_ns){

    ftest_x_min=eval('document.'+ftest_droplayer[i]+'.left')
    ftest_x_max=ftest_x_min+eval('document.'+
ftest_droplayer[i]+ '.clip.width')
    ftest_y_min=eval('document.'+ftest_droplayer[i]+'.top')
    ftest_y_max=ftest_y_min+eval('document.'+
ftest_droplayer[i]+ '.clip.height')
    }
  if (ftest_mousex>=ftest_x_min &&
ftest_mousex<=ftest_x_max && ftest_mousey>=ftest_y_min
&& ftest_mousey<=ftest_y_max){
  ftest_hideit=0; setTimeout('ftest_hideall()',500)
    }
  else { ftest_hideit=1 }

  return ftest_hideit
  }
```

This code just decided whether the mouse was over the menu item, since Netscape has this extra sensitivity. Now we're going to use the onmouseover and onmouseout commands to call the functions at the relevant times. First you'll need an onmouseover command for the drop-down headers, which looks like this:

```
<a href="#" onmouseover="ftest_showdrop(1)"><b>Menu
2</b></a>
```

Make sure you change the 2 in Menu2 in this code to the number of your layer according to the array you set up to define your layers. The last piece of code you need to write is an onmouseout command, ftest_hidedrop(), so your link looks like the following:

```
<a href="#" onmouseover="ftest_showdrop(2)"
onmouseout="ftest_hidedrop()" ><b>Menu 2</b></a>
```

Whew! That was a lot of code to get your jump menu items up and running!

SOME MORE WEB SITES TO CHECK

Here are some sites that you may find useful.

    http://www.anybrowser.com/

As its name implies, AnyBrowser increases your visibility and makes your site viewable
by any browser. This site include tutorials and other valuable information for your
website.

    http://www.geocities.com/bgx_2000/ultradev/listsubm.htm

This site gives you code to create three types of jump menus: those with appending
parameters, those that use a list to submit a form, and those that use a jump menu to
submit a form.

    http://tom.me.uk/scripting/dropdowns.asp

This site shows code for drop-down jump menus and talks about problems and
workarounds.

Keeping It Simple

So now you know how to create rollovers, jump menus, and navigation bars in Fireworks and
Dreamweaver. Treat your newfound knowledge like a loaded pistol—don't abuse the power
it wields. Remember that rollovers—from a design point of view—should be used to enhance
an already clean website design. Your site should already have great—not just good—navigation
that is easy to use and even easier to understand, and colors and graphics should not detract
from the content and purpose of the site.

Keep it simple and clean—subtly integrate your rollovers into your existing design and
you'll be just fine. In other words, make sure that you don't make your fancy-schmancy
rollovers the focus of the site. Unless, of course, your site is about rollovers, in which case
you could have written this chapter yourself and saved us the trouble!

In Chapter 19, we'll take a look at other dynamic behaviors Dreamweaver automatically
helps you put into your pages.

Dreamweaver MX and Fireworks MX Color Tutorials

The Web is a color medium—like television and magazines and the front page of the New York Times. In this section, we'll demonstrate some of the more colorful features of Dreamweaver MX and Fireworks MX.

First we'll show you one basic application of the cool new nested template feature in Dreamweaver MX. Then we'll explore some Fireworks MX techniques, including adding strokes to images, working with text effects, using the Dodge tool, and optimizing an image. Next we'll show you the different ways to choose colors in Dreamweaver. Lastly, we'll showcase a colorful page design with CSS.

Working with Nested Templates

One of the new features in Dreamweaver MX is nested templates—templates that are based on existing templates. (For more information on using Dreamweaver templates, refer to Chapter 4.) When would you want to use this feature? Well, let's say that every page at your site is going to have the same banner across the top of the page, but some of the pages will also have a navigation bar down the left side of the page, some will have several columns of copy, and others will have a single text area below the banner.

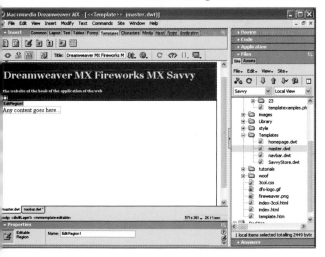

In order to efficiently maintain consistency, you can create a base template that designates the banner at the top of the page. Then you could create three or more nested templates from the base template. Here's how you would do it.

To create a new template from scratch, click the Make Template button on the Templates tab of the Insert bar. Give your base template a filename and save it. Now create the content that you will want to appear on every page, and designate the rest of the template as an editable region (bordered in aquamarine).

Be sure to save your changes.

To base a nested template on the template you've already created, first make an ordinary page from the existing template (also called an "instance" of the template), by choosing File →

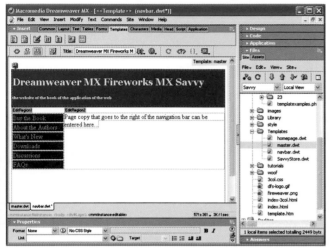

New, selecting the Templates tab and your current site, and then double-clicking the name of the template you just created.

Then click the Make Nested Template button on the Templates tab of the Insert bar. Save the new nested template. Now you can define further editable areas in addition to the content that will pass through (regions bordered in orange are passed through from the parent template).

Develop pages for this section of the site using the nested template you just designed. For sections of the site that require other variants of the master design, create new nested templates from the base template.

Adding Strokes to Images

One easy way to put a border around an image in Fireworks MX is to make a rectangular path around the object and then either expand the path and add a fill color, or use the Property Inspector to customize the path—on the Property Inspector, click the Stroke Category pop-up menu and choose Stroke Options. (See Chapter 6 for more on adding strokes to images.) Here's a border made with a solid color and a stroke of a slightly different color (in the Air-brushed category with an 8-pixel tip and the Oilslick texture centered over the stroke).

Here's a clear view of the resulting image with border (the Oilslick texture is very subtle as it blends one color into the main fill color for the border).

Working with Text Effects

You can add a text effect easily by clicking the Add Effect button on the Property Inspector. (Refer to Chapter 7 for more on working with text effects in Fireworks.) To add additional effects, click Edit Effect and then click the plus (+) button to select each effect.

This text has an inner glow and a motion trail.

This text has the inner glow and a drop shadow, with the motion trail turned off (but not deleted—so you can turn it back on again later if you want; this is useful for making comparisons).

This text has a marble effect added, the inner glow turned off, and the drop-shadow retained. (When the text is selected, as in this illustration, the Property Inspector shows the text properties.)

Using the Dodge Tool to Lighten an Image

This image looks too dark.

If you use the Dodge tool carefully, you can gently lighten an area. (Refer to Chapter 8 for more on using the Dodge tool.) In a traditional darkroom, "dodging" decreases the amount of light hitting the photo-sensitive paper, thus making the resulting image brighter. The Dodge tool in Fireworks "desaturates" (lightens) an area based on the values you enter in the Property Inspector.

Use the Range pop-up menu to adjust Shadows (dark areas), Midtones, and Highlights (light areas), individually. Experiment with each to see their effects.

To lighten the entire image, select the Dodge tool (you may have to click and hold on the Blur tool to change it into the Dodge tool), and, in the Property Inspector, set Size to 100, Edge to 100, and Exposure to 50. Then drag the tool over the entire image. Notice how much brighter and more detailed the image appears.

To treat different areas of the image differently, try applying the above midtone settings to just the top two-thirds of the image, then select Highlights in the Property Inspector, decrease the size to 25, and click the Dodge tool over the white portion of the umbrella, the lights, and white flowers. This gives a more subtle clarity to the image.

Optimizing an Image

Before exporting a Fireworks MX image for use in Dreamweaver MX, take the time to optimize it by finding the ideal balance between quality and file size. (See Chapter 10 for more discussion of optimization.) High quality is important, but so is making sure that your pages will download rapidly for all users. The Preview feature in Fireworks enables you to compare up to four different versions of your image side-by-side.

To rapidly compare optimization choices, click the 4-Up Preview and select Window → Optimize (F6). Then, for each of the preview areas, you can choose different optimization options.

- The original image (upper-left) is a TIF and is very large (nearly 1500K).

- Turning the image into a GIF (lower-left) with a 30% dither loses a lot of quality and only gets the thing down to a little over 420K.

- Choosing the JPEG option that tries to maintain maximum quality (upper-right) manages to get the file down to about 112K.

- The JPEG option that trades off more quality gets it down to under 35K with adequate image quality!

Speaking of dithering, this 4-Up Preview shows how three different dither settings affect a GIF image (all four view are zoomed in 300%).

- The original image has a nearly continuous tone.

- The GIF in the upper-right has 0% dither and the continuous tone is clearly rendered in a series of discrete color areas.

- The GIF in the lower-left has 99% dither, which roughens the edges of the color areas but still leaves them looking blocky.

- The GIF in the lower-right has 100% dither, which manages to blur the jumps in color tone more effectively.

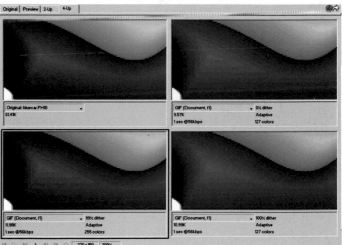

IMAGE BY DAVID D. BUSCH

Setting Page, Text, and Link Colors

One of the ways that you maintain a consistent look-and-feel across an entire website is by standardizing the use of color on each page. Page elements that can be given default colors include the page's background, ordinary text, and link text. (See Chapter 12 for further discussion of text formatting.) Link text can have a different color depending on whether it's never been clicked, is currently being clicked, or has already been clicked. Any of these colors can be added to the Asset Manager or hardwired into a template (as discussed in Chapter 4).

To indicate your color preferences for a page, select Modify → Page Properties (Ctrl + J/ Cmd + J). On the Page Properties dialog box that appears, choose the related pop-up menu to select colors for page background, text, links, visited links, and active links.

Each time you open the color menu, you can choose a color from the palette shown, choose one from elsewhere on your screen, or use your system's built in color picker. Dreamweaver's color palette can display colors using a number of different formats, which are shown here.

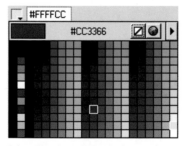

Color cubes (showing related colors together)

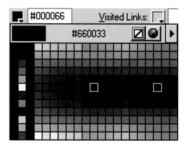

Continuous tone (showing colors in a spectrum)

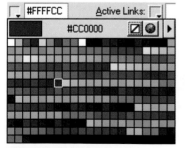

Windows OS (showing the colors of the Windows palette)

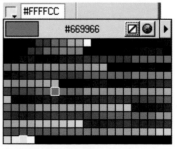

Mac OS (showing the colors of the Mac palette)

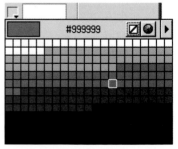

Grayscale (showing shades of gray)

For all these cases, you have the choice of having the color palette snap to the web safe colors or to display a wider range of colors (some of which will not be rendered accurately on all browsers).

If you prefer to choose colors using the color chooser built into your operating system, then choose the System Color Picker option on any color palette.

This first image what you get in Windows XP and the second is what Mac OS X users see.

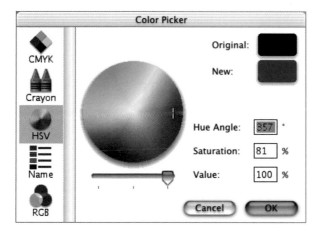

When you're done, click OK.

Using CSS for Text Formatting and Layout

With Cascading Style Sheets (CSS), you can define a look-and-feel for any design element at your site and then invoke it just by attaching the style sheet to a page and using CSS commands to format your elements. (Refer to Chapter 15 for an introduction to CSS.) You can use CSS to control both text formatting and page layout (through the CSS box model). Together these two screenshots show the code that will produce a web page that has a two-column page layout with a header area on top, a menu box in the left column, and a content area in the right column.

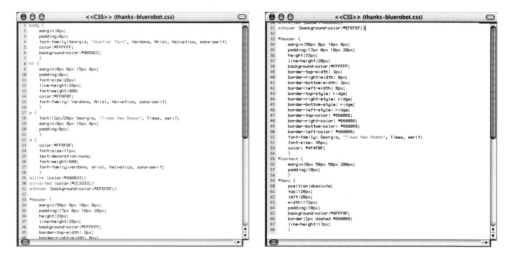

And here's what a web document designed using this CSS file would look like.

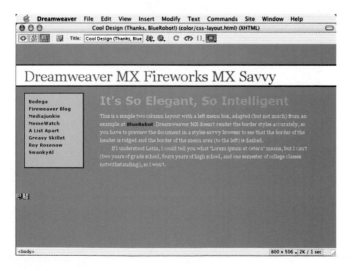

## CHAPTER 19

Behavioral Science

Behaviors provide an easy way to create interactive pages. Dreamweaver includes 25 built-in behaviors that are simple to use and do not require prior knowledge of JavaScript. Additional behaviors are available from Macromedia and third-party vendors. Experienced JavaScript users can also customize the built-in behaviors or create new ones.

This chapter covers the following topics related to Dreamweaver's behaviors:

- **Introducing Dreamweaver's built-in behaviors**

- **Using behaviors with layers and timelines**

- **Generating Flash objects**

- **Creating animation using layers and timelines with behaviors**

Introducing Dreamweaver's Built-in Behaviors

Behaviors are a combination of *events*—a browser's response to changes on a page, such as the page being loaded, or a user moving the cursor over an image—and *actions*—event handlers that use scripts to respond to an event. Events are generated by browsers in response to a change in a page. For example, a browser generates an `onClick` event when a user clicks on an object, such as an image. The browser then checks to see if any action (event handler) is associated with an `onClick` event for that object (the image) and if there is one, it calls the action (in the form of a JavaScript statement or function) attached to the `onClick` event for that object.

Dreamweaver behaviors are designed to be cross-browser compatible, but the availability of specific actions and events depends on the browser and the browser version.

For more information on browser compatibility issues, see Chapter 29.

Using Behaviors and Events

To use a behavior in Dreamweaver, you must follow these steps:

1. Select an object (a page element, such as `body` or `img`).

2. Open the Behaviors panel (Window → Behaviors, or Shift + F3).

3. Choose an action to attach to the object.

4. Use the default event associated with the chosen action, or click the down arrow in the Events column of the Behaviors panel to open the Events menu, and choose a different event.

In the upper-left corner of the Behaviors panel (see Figure 19.1), there is a plus (+) button, which is used to add an action and an event, and a minus (–) button, which is used to delete a selected action and event. When you click on the plus (+) button, the Action menu shows the actions that can be associated with the selected object. Unavailable choices for that object are grayed out.

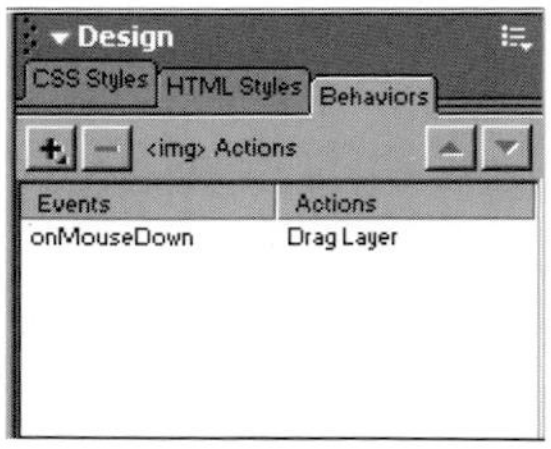

A default event is shown in the Behaviors panel once an action is selected. The menu of events that is available for a particular action is determined by the choice of target browser. Newer browsers include more events. The target browser(s) is specified by choosing the Show Events For option in the Action or Events menu. The target browser

Figure 19.1

The Behaviors panel

determines which events are shown in the Events menu for the chosen action. The Show Events For submenu includes the following target browser choices:

- 3.0 and Later Browsers
- 4.0 and Later Browsers
- IE 3.0
- IE 4.0
- IE 5.0
- IE 5.5
- IE 6.0
- Netscape 3.0
- Netscape 4.0
- Netscape 6.0

Dreamweaver MX includes IE 5.5, IE 6.0, and Netscape 6.0 in the Show Events For submenu. If you are using Dreamweaver 4, you can add Netscape 6.0 to the menu of browser choices in the Show Events For submenu by downloading the free Netscape 6 Pack from Macromedia at `http://www.macromedia.com/support/dreamweaver/downloads.html`. An Internet Explorer 6 Pack is not yet available, but all actions supported in Internet Explorer 5.0 are also supported in Internet Explorer 6.0.

Table 19.1 shows all the events available in the Events menu. The actual choices displayed in the Events menu vary, depending on the selected action and the target browser.

> If an event name is displayed in parentheses in the Events menu, that event can only be used with a link. If the selected object is not a link, Dreamweaver automatically adds a null link. The format for a null link is `<a href="javascript:;">link object</a>`. The behavior is attached to the link object, which can be text, an image, or another object on the page.

> In addition to the events shown in Table 19.1, many additional events are available for use in scripts. As with the events listed above, the choice of target browser determines which events can be used. Internet Explorer 6 supports more events than any other browser at the present time. A list of events that can be used with Internet Explorer 6 can be viewed at `http://msdn.microsoft.com/library/default.asp?url=/workshop/author/dhtml/reference/events.asp#om40_event`.

Detailing the Built-in Behaviors

Behaviors are named for the 25 actions that are included in Dreamweaver. These built-in behaviors are detailed in the following pages.

Table 21.1

Events and Browser Support

EVENT	BROWSERS SUPPORTED	DESCRIPTION
onAbort	IE4+, NS4+	The user stops the browser from completely loading an image.
onAfterUpdate	IE4+	A bound data element finishes updating the data source.
onBeforeUpdate	IE4+	A bound data element has been changed and the element has lost focus.
onBlur	IE4+, NS3+	A specified element loses focus.[1]
onBounce	IE4+	The contents of a marquee element reach the boundary of the marquee.
onChange	IE3+, NS3+	The user changes a value on the page.
onClick	IE3+, NS3+	The user clicks a page element.
onDblClick	IE4+, NS4+	The user double-clicks a page element.
onError	IE4+, NS3+	A browser error occurs when a page or page element is loading.
onFinish	IE4+	The contents of a marquee element complete a loop.
onFocus	IE3+, NS3+	A specified element gains focus.[2]
onHelp	IE4+	The user clicks the browser's Help button or Help menu.
onKeyDown	IE4+, NS4+	The user presses any key.
onKeyPress	IE4+, NS4+	The user presses and releases any key.[3]
onKeyUp	IE4+, NS4+	The user releases any key.
onLoad	IE3+, NS3+	A page or an image completes loading.
onMouseDown	IE4+, NS4+	The user presses the mouse button.
onMouseMove	IE3+, NS6	The user moves the mouse while over a specific element.
onMouseOut	IE4+, NS3+	The user moves the mouse pointer off of a specific element.
onMouseOver	IE3+, NS3+	The user moves the mouse pointer onto a specific element.
onMouseUp	IE4+, NS4+	The user releases a pressed mouse button.
onMove	NS4+	A window or frame is moved.
onReadyStateChange	IE4+	The state of the specified element changes.[4]
onReset	IE3+, NS3+	A form is reset to default values.
onResize	IE4+, NS4+	The user resizes a window or frame.
onRowEnter	IE4+	The data source changes the current row.
onRowExit	IE4+	The data source is about to change the current row.
onScroll	IE4+	The user scrolls up or down.
onSelect	IE3+, NS3+	The user selects text in a text field.
onStart	IE4+	The contents of a marquee element begin a loop.
onSubmit	IE3+, NS3+	The user clicks the Submit button in a form.
onUnload	IE3+, NS3+	The user leaves the page.

[1] *For example, a user clicks in a text field in a form, and then clicks outside the text field.*

[2] *For example, a user clicks in a text field in a form.*

[3] *This event combines* onKeyDown *and* onKeyUp.

[4] *This event is for objects that can have states, such as Loading, Initializing, or Complete.*

Call JavaScript

The Call JavaScript behavior lets you attach custom JavaScript code to an event. This JavaScript can be original code or from a JavaScript library.

In the Call JavaScript dialog box, enter the name of a JavaScript method or function, as shown in Figure 19.2, or enter one line of JavaScript code.

Figure 19.2

Calling a JavaScript function using the Call JavaScript dialog box

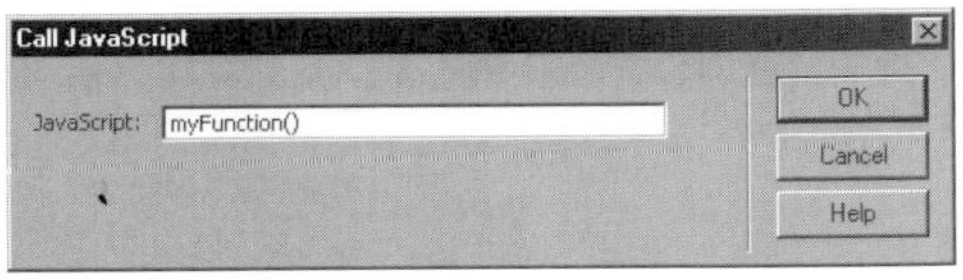

Change Property

The Change Property behavior dynamically changes the value of a property of 11 HTML elements including `div`, `form`, `img`, `layer`, `span`, `select`, `textarea`, and additional form elements such as check boxes, password fields, radio buttons, or text fields. Only certain properties of these 11 elements can be changed, depending on the specific element and the target browser.

Once you have selected a page element and added a Change Property action, the Change Property dialog box appears. From this dialog box, follow these steps to add a dynamic change to the value of a property.

1. Choose an object from the Type of Object menu.

2. Choose the name of the object from the Named Object menu.

3. Choose the property you want to change from Property → Select, or click the Enter radio button and type the property's name. If you choose Select, you also need to choose a target browser and browser version. If you want to target more than one browser, you need to apply more than one Change Property action. The choice of target browser is important. Different browsers support different properties for some HTML elements.

Figure 19.3

Change Property dialog box

A Change Property action is used in the animation tutorial at the end of this chapter to change the border color of the image dynamically. The border changes from lavender to red as the animation plays.

Figure 19.3 shows the Change Property action for a `div` object. The `backgroundImage` style property is selected, and IE 4 is chosen as the target browser. The New Value for this property is `cat.gif`.

Knowledge of HTML and JavaScript is required to use the Call JavaScript and Change Property behaviors. You can obtain more information about HTML, JavaScript, and Cascading Style Sheets (CSS) through Dreamweaver's Reference panel (Window → Reference, or Shift + F1).

Check Browser

The Check Browser behavior directs the user to a specific page depending on the user's browser and version. This behavior can be attached to a body element or can be used with a null link.

When the Check Browser action is added to an object, the Check Browser dialog box is displayed. In this dialog box, follow these steps.

1. Enter the version number of Netscape Navigator to check for. The default is 4.0.

2. Choose an action from the menu. This action tells the browser what to do if it is Netscape Navigator version 4.0 or later. The choices in this menu are

   - Go to URL

   - Go to Alt URL

   - Stay on This Page

3. Choose an action from the second menu (otherwise). This tells the browser what to do if it is not Netscape Navigator 4.0 or later.

4. Repeat steps two and three for Internet Explorer.

5. Choose an action from the menu labeled Other Browsers.

6. Enter values for URL and Alt URL, or click the Browse button to navigate to a file. For a URL on a different site, you must enter an absolute path, such as `http://www.macromedia` `.com/support/dreamweaver/`.

Figure 19.4 shows the Check Browser dialog box.

Check Plugin

The Check Plugin behavior directs the user to a specific page depending on whether they have a specific plugin installed.

When the Check Plugin action is added to an object, the Check Plugin dialog box is displayed. In this dialog box, follow these steps.

Figure 19.4

Check Browser dialog box

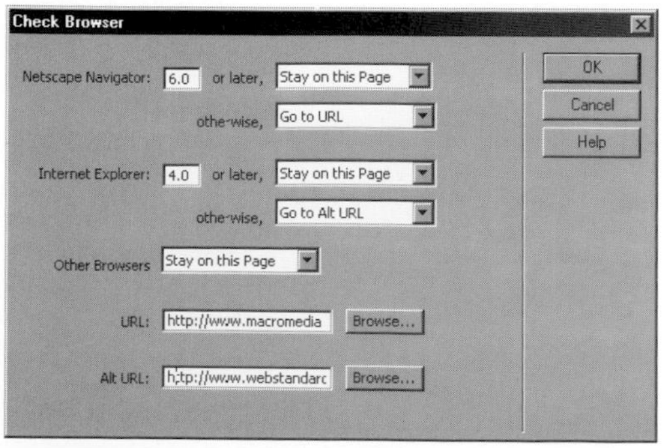

1. Choose a plugin from Plugin → Select. The five choices are

   - Flash

   - Shockwave

   - Live Audio

   - Quick Time

   - Windows Media Player

Plugins can't be detected by using JavaScript in Internet Explorer. If you select a Flash or Shockwave plugin in the Check Plugin dialog box, VBScript code will be added to your page in order to detect those plugins in Internet Explorer in Windows. No plugins can be detected in Internet Explorer on a Mac.

2. Alternatively, enter the exact name of a plugin in Plugin → Enter. On a PC, the exact plugin names can be found in Netscape Navigator in the Help menu (Help → About Plugins). On a Mac, choose About Plugins from the Apple menu.

3. Enter a URL in the If Found, Go to URL text box. If you want users to stay on the page if they have the plugin, leave this text box blank.

4. Enter a URL in the Otherwise, Go to URL text box.

If detection is not possible, the user is sent to the URL specified in Otherwise, Go to URL. Because the user may have the plugin even though it is not detected, you may want the user to be directed to the address specified in If Found, Go to URL. In this case, check the box labeled "Always go to first URL if detection is not possible."

Figure 19.5 shows the Check Plugin dialog box.

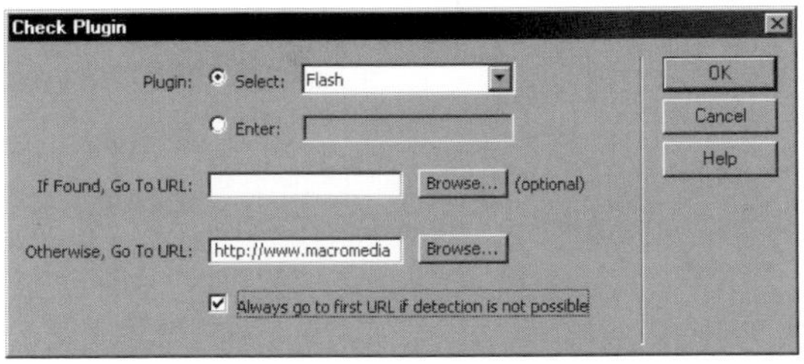

Figure 19.5

Check Plugin dialog box

Control Shockwave or Flash

The Control Shockwave or Flash behavior directs a Shockwave or Flash animation to play, stop, rewind, or go to a specific frame in the animation. More information on using behaviors with Flash is presented in the section "Using Flash Objects," later in this chapter.

To attach an action to a Shockwave or Flash movie, follow these steps.

1. Insert a Shockwave or Flash movie on the page (Insert → Media → Shockwave, or Insert → Media → Flash).

To use this behavior, the media file extension must be .dcr, .dir, .swf, or .spl.

2. Open the Property Inspector (Window → Properties).

3. Enter a name for the movie in the blank text field in the upper-left corner of the Property Inspector. The movie must have a name in order to use the Control Shockwave or Flash action.

4. Open the Behaviors panel, and add Control Shockwave or Flash. The Control Shockwave or Flash dialog box is displayed.

Figure 19.6

**Control Shockwave or
Flash dialog box**

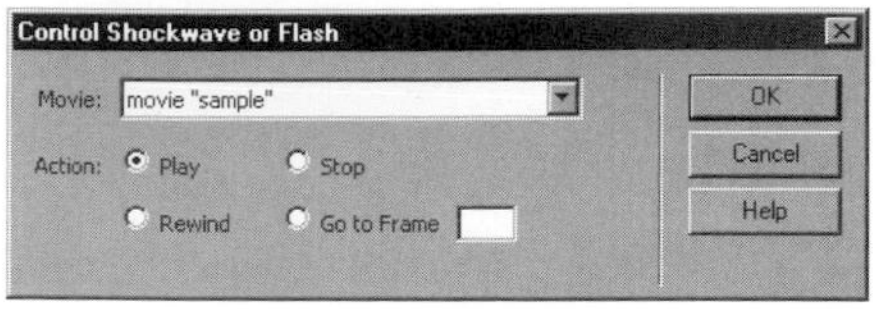

5. Choose a movie from the Movie menu.

6. Choose one of the four available actions:

- Play   • Rewind

- Stop   • Go to Frame

Figure 19.6 shows the Control Shockwave or Flash dialog box.

If you choose the Go to Frame action, you must enter a frame number in the box next to that choice.

Drag Layer

The Drag Layer behavior allows the user to drag a layer. This behavior can be used to create movable elements on a page. More information on using behaviors with layers and timelines is presented later in this chapter in the section "Using Behaviors with Layers and Timelines."

To attach a Drag Layer action to a layer, follow these steps.

1. Insert a layer (Insert → Layer).

2. Open the Property Inspector (Window → Properties) and note the name for the layer in the text field in the upper-left corner. A default name is assigned by Dreamweaver, such as Layer 1, but this name can be changed in the Property Inspector.

3. Select the body element.

The event that triggers the Drag Layer action must occur before the user can drag a layer, so it's generally easiest to attach this action to the body element (using an onLoad event).

4. Open the Behaviors panel and choose Drag Layer. This choice will not be available if a layer is selected. The Drag Layer dialog box is displayed. By default, the Basic tab is shown in front.

5. Choose a layer from the Layer menu.

6. Choose Constrained or Unconstrained from the Movement menu.

7. For constrained movement, enter pixel values in the Up, Down, Left, and Right fields. The pixel values are relative to the starting position of the layer.

For vertical movement only, enter 0 in the Left and Right fields. For horizontal movement only, enter 0 in the Up and Down fields.

8. Enter pixel values in the Drop Target Left and Top fields to specify the exact spot where the layer should be dragged. These values are relative to the top-left corner of the browser window. Specifying a drop target is optional.

9. Click Get Current Position to enter the layer's current Left and Top values. Use this option only if the current position is the target position for the layer.

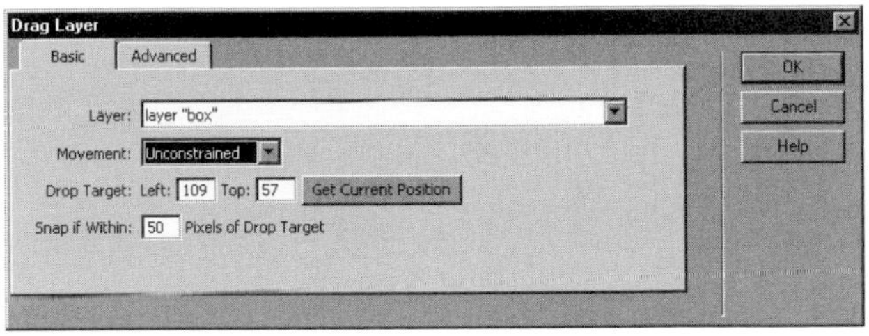

Figure 19.7

Drag Layer dialog box, Basic tab

10. Enter a pixel value in the Snap if Within field to specify how close the user must get to the target before the object snaps to the target.

Figure 19.7 shows the Basic tab in the Drag Layer dialog box.

Take a look at the Advanced tab of the Drag Layer dialog box. Use the options on this tab to create a drag handle or specify the layer's position relative to other layers.

You can also use the Advanced tab to specify code that should be executed under different conditions. Enter JavaScript code in the Call JavaScript field to repeatedly execute the code while the layer is being dragged, or add JavaScript code in the When Dropped: Call JavaScript field to execute the code when the layer is dropped. You can also check the Only if Snapped box to specify that the code should be executed only if the layer has been dragged to the drop target.

> Knowledge of JavaScript is required to use the advanced features of the Drag Layer behavior.

Figure 19.8 shows the Advanced tab in the Drag Layer dialog box.

Go to URL

The Go to URL behavior opens a new page in the current window or in a specified frame.

When a Go to URL action is added, the Go to URL dialog box is displayed. In this dialog box, choose a frame or window from the Open In list, and then enter a URL in the URL field. Figure 19.9 shows the Go to URL dialog box.

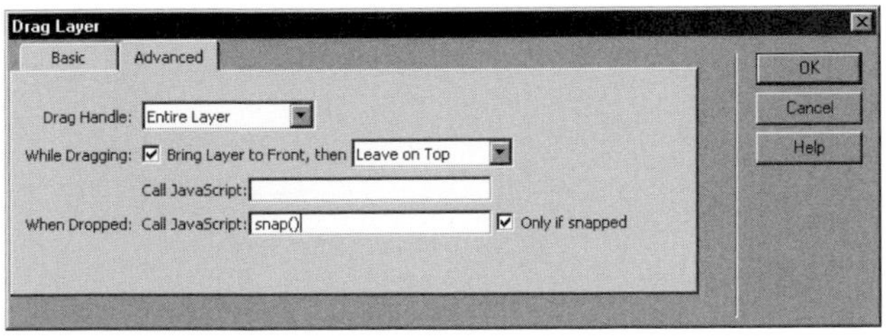

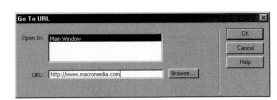

Figure 19.8

Drag Layer dialog box, Advanced tab

Figure 19.9

Go to URL dialog box

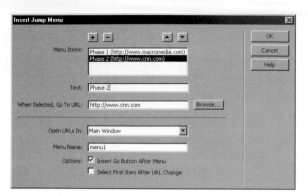

Figure 19.10

**Insert Jump Menu
dialog box**

Jump Menu

Jump menus are created from the Insert menu (Insert →
Form Objects → Jump Menu). It is not necessary to use the
Behaviors panel to attach the Jump Menu behavior to an
object. However, the Behaviors panel can be used to edit
an existing Jump menu.

Select the Jump menu, open the Behaviors panel, and
double-click Jump Menu in the Actions column. The Insert
Jump Menu dialog box is displayed with the current settings for the menu (Figure 19.10) Edit these settings as
desired, and click OK.

For further information on jump menus, see Chapter 18.

Jump Menu Go

The Jump Menu Go behavior associates a Go button with an already existing Jump menu. A
Go button is not always necessary but is useful when Jump menus are used in frames.

When a Jump menu is inserted (Insert → Form Objects → Jump Menu), an Insert Jump Menu
dialog box is displayed (see Figure 19.10). At the bottom of the dialog box, check the option
Insert Go Button after Menu to insert a Go button next to the Jump menu.

Figure 19.11

**The Jump Menu Go
dialog box**

You can use a different image for the Go button instead of the
default image. Select the object that you want to be the Go button.
Open the Behaviors panel, and add Jump Menu Go. The Jump Menu
Go dialog box displays (Figure 19.11). Choose a menu for the Go
button to activate from the Choose Jump Menu drop-down list.

Open Browser Window

The Open Browser Window behavior opens a pop-up browser window. You can choose
the properties of this window, including its size, toolbars, and name. If you don't specify any
properties, the pop-up window will have the size and properties of the window it was
launched from.

When an Open Browser Window action is added, the Open Browser Window dialog box is
displayed. In this dialog box, follow these steps to add a pop-up window:

1. Enter a URL in the URL to Display text box, or click the Browse button to navigate to a
   file to display—for example, a new window that displays a larger graphic.

2. Enter pixel values for Window Width and Window Height. If you leave these fields blank,
   the new window will have the same size as the window it was launched from.

3. Specify the attributes of the new window. These include

- Navigation Toolbar (includes Back, Forward, Home, and Reload buttons)

- Location Toolbar (shows the URL of the page being displayed)

- Status Bar

- Menu Bar (includes File, Edit, View, Go, and Help menus)

- Scrollbars as Needed

- Resize Handles (allow the user to resize the window)

4. Enter a name for the new window in the Window Name text field. This enables you to specify this window in JavaScript code, and allows you to use this window as a target in a link.

Figure 19.12 shows the Open Browser Window dialog box.

Figure 19.12

Open Browser Window dialog box

Play Sound

The Play Sound behavior plays a sound when a specified event occurs—for example, an audio clip that plays when the page is loaded.

> Audio files may require audio plugins or specific types of media players. For more information on web audio and other multimedia files, see Chapter 17.

Figure 19.13

The Play Sound dialog box

When a Play Sound action is added, the Play Sound dialog box is displayed. In this dialog box, enter a path and filename or click the Browse button to navigate to a sound file.

Figure 19.13 shows the Play Sound dialog box.

Popup Message

The Popup Message behavior creates a JavaScript alert box that displays the message you specify. Pop-up messages are used to present information to the user. You can display a text message, or you can display other information by including JavaScript functions, variables, or expressions in the text. To use JavaScript code in the text, enclose it in curly braces { }. For example:

```
The current time is {getTime()}
```

When a Popup Message action is added, the Popup Message dialog box is displayed (see Figure 19.14). In the Message text area, enter a text message (and/or JavaScript code if you are experienced with JavaScript).

Figure 19.14

Popup Message dialog box

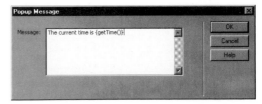

Preload Images

The Preload Images behavior is used to load images that may not appear when the page is first loaded; for example, when the user is using a Rollover link, a second image appears when they move the mouse over the first image. If the image is preloaded, it is displayed immediately because there is no delay waiting for the image file to download.

> If you are using the Swap Image behavior, there is no need to add the Preload Images behavior—just check the Preload Images option in the Swap Image dialog box.

When a Preload Images action is added, the Preload Images dialog box is displayed. In this dialog box, follow these steps to preload images into the browser cache so there's no delay to download them after an action is triggered:

1. Enter the path and filename of the image you want to preload in the Image Source File text box at the bottom of the dialog box, or click the Browse button to navigate to an image file.

2. Click the plus (+) button at the top of the dialog box to add this image to the Preload Images list.

3. Repeat steps 1 and 2 to add additional image files.

4. Select an image from the Preload Images list and click the minus (–) button at the top of the dialog box to remove an image from the list.

> For more information on creating rollovers and preloading images, see Chapters 9 and 18.

Figure 19.15 shows the Preload Images dialog box.

Set Nav Bar Image

The Set Nav Bar Image behavior is used to edit the properties of a navigation bar image; for example, it can be used to change the display and/or actions associated with the images in a navigation bar. You can specify different images for each state of the navigation button (Up, Over, Down, Over While Down) as well as adding more complex actions to this behavior, such as changing the state of more than one image at a time when a user moves the mouse over an image.

A navigation bar can be created by using the Insert menu (Insert → Interactive Images → Navigation Bar).

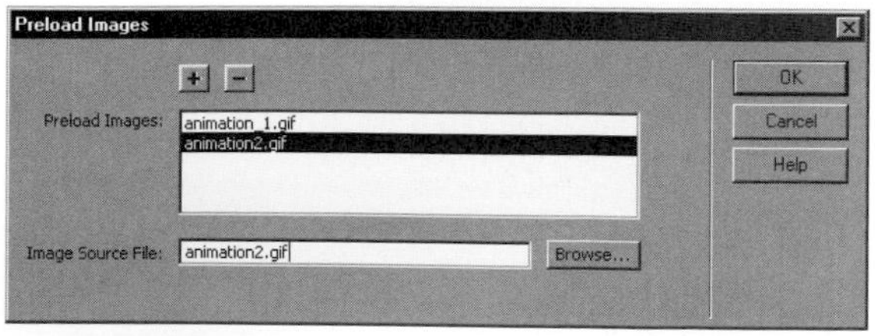

Figure 19.15

Preload Images dialog box

> For more details on creating a navigation bar, see Chapter 9.

To edit an existing navigation bar image, follow these steps.

1. Select an image in the navigation bar.

2. Open the Behaviors panel, and double-click the Set Nav Bar Image action in the Actions column. By default, the Basic tab of the Set Nav Bar Image dialog box displays.

3. In the Set Nav Bar Image dialog box, the Element Name text field displays the name of the selected image. This name is the same one that is displayed in the Property Inspector under Image, (size of file), or it can also be specified by using a `name` attribute in the `img` element.

4. Edit the options in this dialog box. These include the following:

   • Up Image (path and filename)

   • Over Image (path and filename)

   • Down Image (path and filename)

   • Over While Down Image (path and filename)

   • When Clicked Go to URL (URL in window or frame name)

5. Choose additional options by clicking the check boxes listed under Options:

   • Preload Images

   • Show "Down Image" Initially (can be used to let the user know their location in the site)

Figure 19.16 shows the Basic tab in the Set Nav Bar Image dialog box.

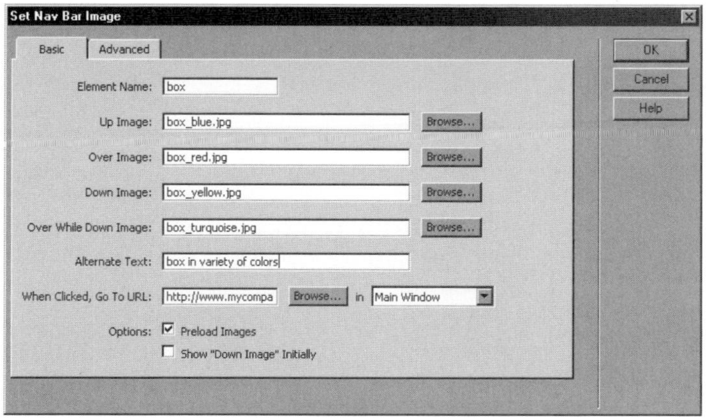

Figure 19.16

Set Nav Bar Image dialog box, Basic tab

Clicking a navigation bar image causes all other images in the navigation bar to automatically be restored to their Up state. To change the state of other images in the navigation bar to something other than their Up state, use the Advanced tab of the dialog box. This creates multiple rollovers—when the state of more than one image is changed by a single event.

1. In the "When element (element name) is displaying" menu, choose an image state:

   - Over Image or Over While Down Image (to change the display of another image when the selected image is clicked)

   - Down Image (to change the display of another image when the user moves the mouse over the selected image)

2. Select another image on the page from the Also Set Image list.

3. Enter the path and filename of the image to be displayed in response to the image state of the selected image, as specified in step 1, or click the Browse button to navigate to an image file.

   Figure 19.17 shows the Advanced tab in the Set Nav Bar dialog box.

Figure 19.17

Set Nav Bar Image dialog box, Advanced tab

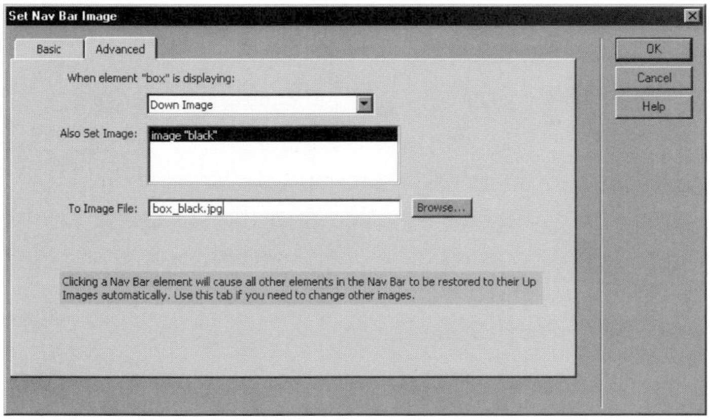

Set Text of Frame

The Set Text of Frame behavior replaces the content and formatting of a specified frame with the content and formatting that you specify. The content can include HTML code as well as JavaScript functions, properties, variables, or expressions. To include JavaScript, enclose it in curly braces {}; for example, here is how you would display the current date:

```
Today's date is {getDate()}.
```

To add a Set Text of Frame action, follow these steps:

1. Create a frameset (Insert → Frames) and choose the appropriate option for the type of frameset you want to create (Left and Top, Split Right, and so on).

For more information about framesets and frames, see Chapter 14.

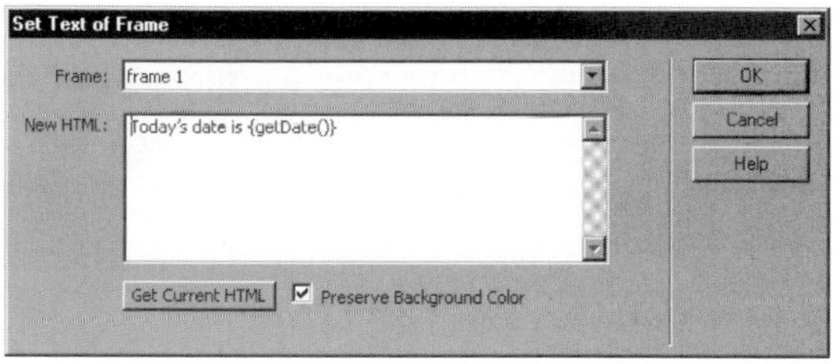

2. Select an object.

3. Open the Behaviors panel and click the plus (+) button to open the Actions menu.

4. Choose Set Text → Set Text of Frame. The Set Text of Frame dialog box appears.

5. Choose the target frame from the Frame menu.

6. Enter text, HTML source code, and/or JavaScript code in the New HTML text area field. You can also click the Get Current HTML button, which will copy the HTML content of the body element in the current target frame into the New HTML field where it can be changed. However, this only works when you are updating the source code in the body element. Any other code in the targeted frame will be lost—for example, the code in the head element.

7. Check the Preserve Background Color box to maintain the background color of the frame when the new frame contents appear.

Figure 19.18 shows the Set Text of Frame dialog box.

Figure 19.18

Set Text of Frame dialog box

Set Text of Layer

The Set Text of Layer behavior replaces the content and formatting of an existing layer with the content and formatting that you specify. The current layer attributes are preserved. The new content can include text, HTML source code, and JavaScript functions, properties, variables, and expressions. To include JavaScript code in the new content, enclose it in curly braces { }; for example, here is how you would display the current time:

```
The current time is {getTime()}.
```

To add a Set Text of Layer action, follow these steps.

1. Create a layer (Insert → Layer).

2. Select an object in the layer and open the Behaviors panel.

3. Click the plus (+) button and select Set Text → Set Text of Layer from the Actions menu. The Set Text of Layer dialog box displays.

4. Choose the target layer from the Layer menu.

5. Enter a text message, HTML source, and/or JavaScript code in the New HTML text area field.

Figure 19.19 shows the Set Text of Layer dialog box.

Figure 19.19

Set Text of Layer dialog box

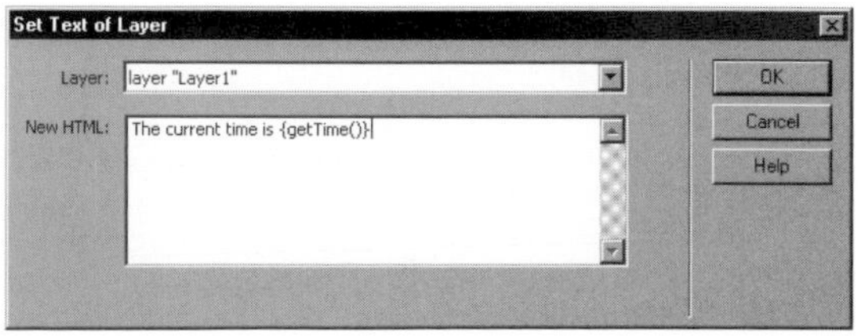

Set Text of Status Bar

The Set Text of Status Bar behavior displays a message in the status bar at the bottom of the browser window. With the Set Text of Status Bar behavior, you can associate this message

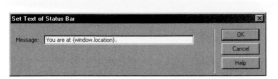

Figure 19.20

Set Text of Status Bar dialog box

with an event, such as displaying a status bar message when the user moves the mouse over a specified image. The status bar message can be text, or you can include JavaScript functions, properties, variables, or expressions. To include JavaScript code, enclose it in curly braces { }; for example, here is how you would display the URL of the current page:

```
You are at {window.location}.
```

When a Set Text of Status Bar action is added, the Set Text of Status Bar dialog box displays. In this dialog box, you can enter a text message and/or JavaScript code.

Figure 19.20 shows the Set Text of Status Bar dialog box.

Set Text of Text Field

The Set Text of Text Field behavior replaces the content of a selected text field in a form with the content you specify. The new content can be text, or you can include JavaScript functions, properties, variables, or expressions. To include JavaScript code, enclose it in curly braces { }; for example, here is how you would display the current day of the week:

```
Today is {getDay()}.
```

To add a Set Text of Text Field action, follow these steps.

1. Create a text field (Insert ➔ Form Objects ➔ Text Field).

2. Select the text field, and open the Property Inspector.

3. Type a name for the text field in the blank text field in the upper-left corner of the Property Inspector.

4. Open the Behaviors panel and click the plus (+) button to add an action.

5. Choose Set Text ➔ Set Text of Text Field from the Actions menu. The Set Text of Text Field dialog box displays.

6. Select the target field from the Text Field menu.

7. Enter text and/or JavaScript code in the New Text text area.

   Figure 19.21 shows the Set Text of Text Field dialog box.

Show-Hide Layers

The Show-Hide Layers behavior shows or hides one or more layers on a page. This behavior can be used to change the layer display as a user interacts with a page. For example, when a user moves the mouse over an image, another layer becomes visible, and this layer presents information about the image.

To add a Show-Hide Layers action, follow these steps.

1. Insert a layer (Insert ➔ Layer).

2. Open the Property Inspector (Window → Properties) and note the name for the layer in the text field in the upper-left corner. A default name is assigned by Dreamweaver, such as Layer 1, but this name can be changed in the Property Inspector if you choose.

3. Deselect the layer by clicking the Document window, and open the Behaviors panel.

4. Click the plus (+) button and select Show-Hide Layers from the Actions menu. The Show-Hide Layers dialog box displays. If this choice is unavailable in the Actions menu, make sure you don't have a layer selected.

5. Select the target layer from the Named Layers list.

6. Click Show to make the layer visible, Hide to make the layer hidden, or Default to restore the default visibility of the layer.

7. Repeat steps 4 and 5 for any other layers to change the layer visibility.

Figure 19.22 shows the Show-Hide Layers dialog box.

Swap Image and Swap Image Restore

The Swap Image behavior replaces one image with another. This behavior is used to create rollovers. The replacement image must have the same height and width as the original image, or the display of the replacement image may appear distorted.

For more information on creating rollovers, see Chapter 9 and Chapter 18.

To add a Swap Image action, follow these steps.

1. Insert an image (Insert → Image).

2. Open the Property Inspector (Window → Properties) and enter a name for the image in the text field in the upper-left corner of the window. The Swap Image behavior can be used without naming the images; however, Dreamweaver automatically assigns default names to images (for example, Image 1, Image 2, and so on) if no image names have been assigned before the Swap Image action is added. It is much easier to identify an image if it has a name that means something to you.

3. Repeat steps 1 and 2 to add additional images.

Figure 19.21

Set Text of Text Field dialog box

Figure 19.22

Show-Hide Layers dialog box

4. Select the image (or one of the images) and open the Behaviors panel.

5. Click the plus (+) button and select Swap Image from the Actions menu. The Swap Image dialog box displays.

6. Select the image you want to swap from the Images list.

7. Enter the path and filename of the new image in the Set Source To field, or click the Browse button to navigate to an image file.

8. Repeat steps 6 and 7 to change additional images. Use the same Swap Image action to change additional images if you want the Swap Image Restore action to restore all of them.

9. Click in the Preload Images box to preload the additional images when the page is loaded.

Figure 19.23 shows the Swap Image dialog box.

To add the Swap Image Restore behavior, click the Restore Images onMouseOut check box in the Swap Image dialog box. This behavior restores the original image when the user moves the mouse off of the image.

Go to Timeline Frame

The Go to Timeline Frame behavior goes to a specific frame in a timeline. A timeline can be used to create animation by changing the position, size, visibility, and stacking order (*z-index*) of layers.

> For more information on using timelines with layers and behaviors to create animation, see "Using Behaviors with Layers and Timelines," later in this chapter, and also see the tutorial entitled "Creating an Animation Using Layers, Timelines, and Behaviors" at the end of this chapter.

To add a Go to Timeline Frame action, follow these steps.

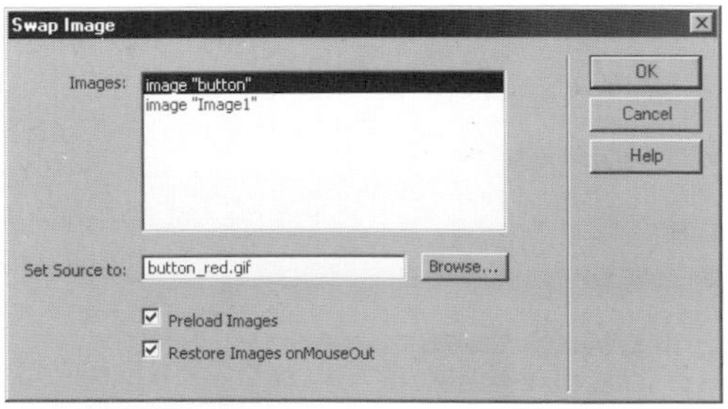

1. Open the Timelines panel (Window → Timeline).

2. The Timelines panel should contain horizontal purple animation bars if the document contains a timeline. If the Timelines panel is blank, the document does not contain a timeline. For more information on creating a timeline, refer to "Using Behaviors with Layers and Timelines" later in this chapter.

3. If the document contains a timeline, select an object on the page to which to attach the Go to Timeline Frame action. This object can be the body element or any other element on the page.

Figure 19.23

Swap Image dialog box

4. Open the Behaviors panel, click the plus (+) button, and select Timeline → Go to Timeline Frame from the Actions menu. The Go to Timeline Frame dialog box should display.

5. Select a timeline from the Timeline menu.

6. Enter a frame number in the Go to Frame field.

7. If you want a portion of the timeline to loop, enter a number in the Loop field to specify the number of times you want it to loop.

> Setting a loop is only valid if the Go to Timeline Frame action is attached to a frame in the timeline using the Behavior channel in the Timeline window.

The Go to Timeline Frame behavior stops the animation at a specified frame. If you want to play the animation starting at this frame, you need to add a Play Timeline behavior in addition to the Go to Timeline Frame behavior. Just add it to the same object as the Go to Timeline Frame behavior, and make sure that it is listed below the Go to Timeline Frame action in the Behaviors panel.

> The Go to Timeline Frame behavior is not used to control a Shockwave or Flash movie. Use the Control Shockwave or Flash behavior instead.

Figure 19.24 shows the Go to Timeline Frame dialog box.

Play Timeline

The Play Timeline behavior starts a timeline at the first frame. The user can click a button or a link to start the timeline manually, or you can make the timeline play automatically when the user moves the mouse over a link, image, or other object on the page.

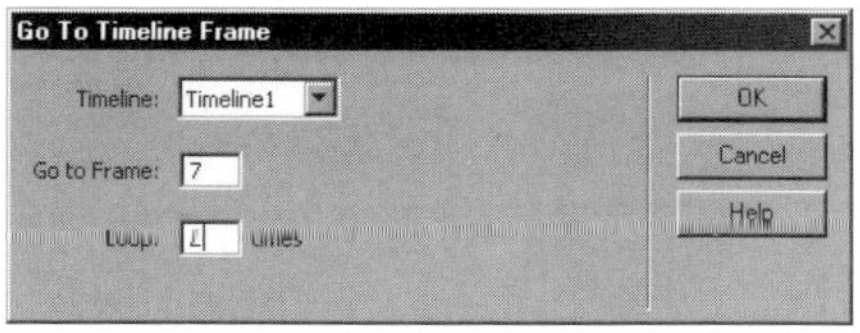

Figure 19.24

Go to Timeline Frame dialog box

To add a Play Timeline action, follow these steps.

1. Open the Timelines panel (Window → Timeline).

2. The Timelines panel should contain horizontal purple animation bars if the document contains a timeline. If the Timelines panel is blank, the document does not contain a timeline.

3. Select an object and open the Behaviors panel.

4. Click the plus (+) button, and select Timeline → Play Timeline from the Actions menu. The Play Timeline dialog box displays.

5. Select a timeline from the Play Timeline dialog box.

A Play Timeline action is automatically attached to the body element and the onLoad event when you select Autoplay in the Timelines panel.

Figure 19.25 shows the Play Timeline dialog box.

Figure 19.25

**Play Timeline
dialog box**

Stop Timeline

The Stop Timeline behavior stops a timeline. You can allow the user to click a button or a link to stop the timeline manually, or you can make the timeline stop automatically when the user moves the mouse over a link, image, or other object on the page.

To add a Stop Timeline action, follow these steps.

1. Open the Timelines panel (Window → Timeline).

2. The Timelines panel should contain horizontal purple animation bars if the document contains a timeline. If the Timelines panel is blank, the document does not contain a timeline.

3. Select an object and open the Behaviors panel.

4. Click the plus (+) button, and select Timeline → Stop Timeline from the Actions menu. The Stop Timeline dialog box displays.

5. Select a timeline from the Stop Timeline dialog box. You can select one timeline to stop, or you can choose the **ALL TIMELINES** option to stop the playback of all timelines on the page.

Figure 19.26 shows the Stop Timeline dialog box.

Figure 19.26

**Stop Timeline
dialog box**

Validate Form

The Validate Form behavior checks the content of specified text fields in a form to make sure that the user has entered a value in required fields and that the user has entered the correct type of information for the field. The Validate Form action can be used with an onSubmit event to check for entries in all required text fields when the user clicks the Submit button. It can also be used with an onBlur or onChange event to validate individual fields as the user fills out the form.

To add a Validate Form action, follow these steps.

1. Insert a form (Insert → Form).

2. Insert a text field (Insert → Form Objects → Text Field). Repeat this step to add additional text fields to the form.

3. To validate individual fields, select a text field and open the Behaviors panel. To validate multiple fields, when the user clicks the Submit button, select the form element and open the Behaviors panel.

4. Click the plus (+) button and choose Validate Form from the Actions menu.

5. If you are validating an individual field, select that field in the Named Fields list. If you are validating multiple fields, select a field in the Named Fields list.

6. Check the Value Required check box if the field must contain an entry.

7. Choose one of the following Accept options:

Figure 19.27

Validate Form dialog box

Anything This option checks to make sure that a field contains an entry, but no particular type of entry is necessary.

Email Address This option checks to see whether a field contains @.

Number This option checks to see whether a field contains only numerals.

Number From This option checks to see whether a field contains a number within a specified range.

8. If you are validating multiple fields at once, repeat steps 5, 6, and 7 for each field you wish to validate.

If you select the form element before adding a Validate Form action, the onSubmit event is automatically selected. If you select an individual text field before adding a Validate Form action, check that the event is onBlur or onChange. The onBlur event occurs whether or not a user has changed anything in the text field, but the onChange event occurs only if the user changes the contents of the text field.

Figure 19.27 shows the Validate Form dialog box.

Show Pop-Up Menu

The Show Pop-Up Menu behavior is a new behavior in Dreamweaver MX. The Show Pop-Up Menu behavior allows you to add or edit a Dreamweaver MX pop-up menu or edit a Fireworks MX pop-up menu inserted in a Dreamweaver MX document.

You can use the Show Pop-Up Menu dialog box to add a horizontal or vertical pop-up menu, and to edit the color, text, or position of the menu.

To add or edit a pop-up menu, follow these steps:

1. Select an object to attach the Show Pop-Up Menu behavior to, and open the Behaviors panel (Window → Behaviors, or Shift + F3).

2. Click the plus (+) button in the Behaviors panel and select Show Pop-Up Menu from the Actions pop-up menu. The Show Pop-Up Menu dialog box (Figure 19.28) displays.

3. From the Show Pop-Up Menu dialog box, set any of the following options. Each option is on a separate tab in the dialog box.

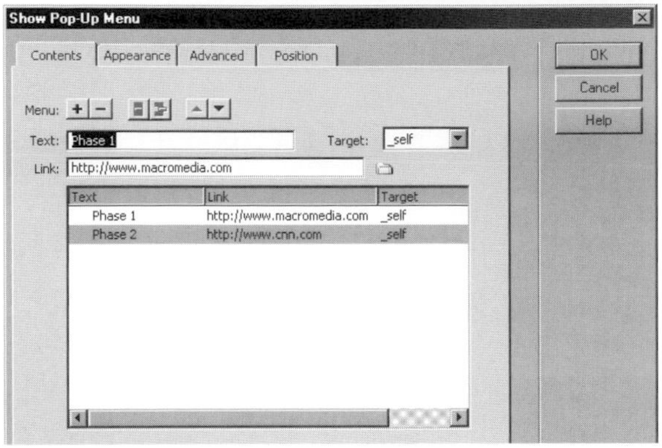

Figure 19.28

**Show Pop-Up Menu
dialog box**

Contents This option is used to specify the name, structure (outdent or indent), URL, and target for any individual menu item.

Appearance This option is used to specify the appearance of the up and over states and to choose a font for the menu item text.

Advanced This option is used to specify the properties of the menu cells, including cell width, cell height, cell padding, cell spacing, text indent, menu delay, and border properties.

Position This option is used to specify the position of the pop-up menu relative to the triggering image or link.

Figure 19.28 shows the Show Pop-Up Menu dialog box.

Using Behaviors with Layers and Timelines

Dreamweaver behaviors can be combined with layers and timelines to create interactivity and animation on web pages.

A *layer* is a rectangular box that can contain any number of page elements. Layers can be stacked on top of each other to create dynamic effects when associated with behaviors; for example, a layer's visibility can be associated with an `onMouseover` event so that the layer is visible only when the mouse moves over another object on the page. Layers can also be combined with both behaviors and timelines to create animated effects, such as an image that moves across the page in response to the page being loaded (`onLoad` event).

Layer Properties

A layer has the following properties:

- Dimensions (height [H] and width [W] in pixels)
- Position on the page (relative to the top-left corner of the window or the parent layer, specified with pixel values for Left [L] and Top [T])
- Formatting (background image and color)
- Visibility (visible or hidden)
- Stacking order (z-index)
- Overflow (handling contents with larger dimensions than the layer)
- Clipping (displaying a rectangular piece of a layer)
- Layer ID (name)
- Tag (associated HTML element—`div`, `span`, `layer`, or `ilayer`)

Additional properties can be used when a layer is associated with a layer or ilayer element. However, layer and ilayer are supported only in Netscape Navigator 4 and above. For more information on layers, see Chapter 10.

To view all the properties of a selected layer, open the Property Inspector (Window → Properties).

Using Behaviors with Layers

Three built-in Dreamweaver behaviors can be used with layers:

Drag Layer Allows the user to move a layer by dragging it.

Show-Hide Layers Changes the visibility of a layer when a specified event occurs.

Set Text of Layer Replaces the content of a layer with the new content you specify.

For more information on these behaviors, refer to the previous discussion.

Dreamweaver also includes an optional command that automatically includes JavaScript code in the head section of your document so that it can fix a bug in Netscape 4.*x*. Netscape 4.*x* causes layers to lose their positioning coordinates if the browser window is resized. To prevent this from happening, this JavaScript code instructs the page to reload whenever it is resized, which restores the layer positioning coordinates. To insert this command, open the Commands menu and select Add/Remove Netscape Resize Fix.

A simple animation can be created by dragging a layer. The previous section of this chapter includes detailed information on the Drag Layer behavior.

Using Timelines

Timelines provide a mechanism for animating layers by allowing you to change layer properties (position, size, visibility, and stacking order) in a timed sequence. You can also change image source files or call other Dreamweaver behaviors at specified points (*frames*) in the timeline.

To open a timeline, press Alt + F9 (Option + F9 for the Mac) or select Window → Others → Timelines, which displays the Timelines panel, as shown in Figure 19.29.

Figure 19.29

Timelines panel

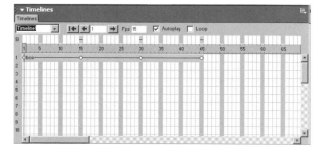

The top row of the Timelines panel includes the following (from left to right):

- Timeline Selector menu

- Rewind button

- Previous Frame button

- Current frame number

- Next frame (right arrow)

- Fps (frames-per-second)—playback speed

- Autoplay—playback begins when the page is loaded

- Loop—playback repeats specified number of times or infinitely

The bottom half of the Timeline panel shows numbered rows of frames called *channels*. Each channel represents an individual layer of animation.

Layers can be added to a timeline by selecting a layer and choosing Modify → Timeline → Add Object to Timeline. A new purple animation bar then appears in one of the channels of the timeline. By default, the animation bar consists of 15 frames, but this can be extended by dragging the white dot in the last frame.

The white dots in the animation bar represent keyframes. A Dreamweaver animation automatically has a keyframe at its beginning and end. A *keyframe* is a point in an animation where the position of a layer changes (or any layer properties are modified). To add a keyframe, click in a frame in the Timelines panel, and press Shift + F6 (or Modify → Timeline → Add Keyframe). When you add keyframes to a timeline, you specify the position of the layer at certain points in the timeline. Dreamweaver calculates the intermediate positions of the layer in the frames in between specified keyframes.

You can modify any layer properties (visibility, size, z-index, size, and so on) at keyframes—not just layer position. To do so, select a keyframe in a channel, and then open the Property Inspector (Window → Properties). You can then edit any properties of the layer. Enter the Layer ID value to access the properties of another layer.

You can control the rate of movement in an animation by adding or deleting the number of frames between keyframes. Add frames by dragging a keyframe to the right. Delete frames by selecting them and then choosing Modify → Timeline → Remove Frame.

Directly above the frame numbers in the Timeline panel is the Behaviors channel, labeled B. To add a behavior to a timeline, click the desired frame in the Behaviors channel and then open the Behaviors panel to add a behavior. You can't select an event to go with this action—the action is triggered when the playback reaches the specified frame.

Three built-in Dreamweaver behaviors can be used to control the playback of an animation:

Play Timeline Starts a timeline when a specified event occurs.

Stop Timeline Stops a timeline when a specified event occurs.

Go to Timeline Frame Jumps a timeline to a specified frame when a specified event occurs.

For more information on these behaviors, see the previous sections.

> A tutorial using layers and a timeline to create an animation is available at the end of this chapter.

Using Flash Objects

Dynamic Flash objects, including Flash buttons and Flash text, can be created in Dreamweaver. These objects, best used in moderation, can be simple additions to the interactive visual elements of your page.

> Flash objects can be effective interactive visual objects on a page. The Control Shockwave or Flash behavior can be attached to Flash animations to control the playback, but these playback features do not apply to other interactive Flash objects.

Flash objects include Flash buttons and Flash text. These Flash objects are small Flash files that can be created in Dreamweaver.

Inserting a Flash Object

To insert a Flash object, follow these steps.

1. Place the insertion point where you want to insert the Flash object.

2. Click the appropriate button in the Insert bar (or select Insert → Interactive Images → select Flash Button, Flash Text, or Flash HTML).

3. A dialog box appears. You can specify a Flash source file and other parameters for the object.

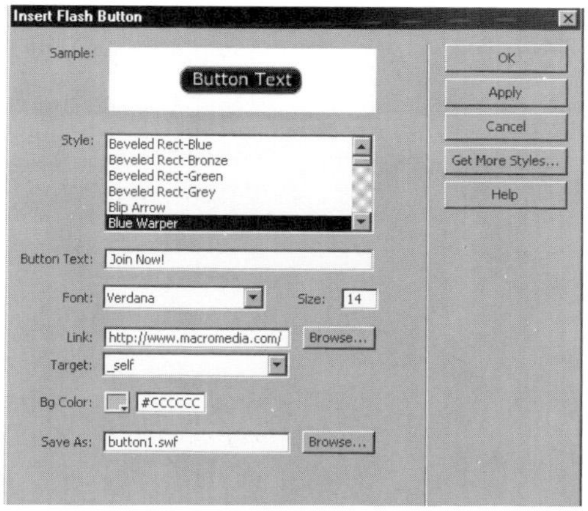

Figure 19.30

Insert Flash Button dialog box

Making a Flash Button

To create a Flash button, follow these steps:

1. Place the insertion point where you want the Flash button to appear.

2. Click the Insert Flash Button icon in the Insert bar (or select Insert → Interactive Images → Flash Button).

3. The Insert Flash Button dialog box (see Figure 19.30) displays.

4. Select a button style from the Style menu. The button image is then displayed in the Sample field.

5. Enter text in the Button Text field.

6. Choose a font from the Font menu, and enter a font size in the Size window.

7. Enter a URL in the Link field, or click the Browse button to navigate to a file.

8. If you want the link to open in a specific frame or window, choose a target from the Target menu.

9. Click the Background Color field to choose a color from the color palette, or enter a color name or hexadecimal color value in the blank text field.

10. Enter a filename in the Save As field to name the Flash file. Dreamweaver supplies a default name, such as `button1.swf`, if no other name is entered. You can also click the Browse button to navigate to a file.

Creating Flash Text and Specifying Text Properties

To create Flash text, follow these steps.

1. Place the insertion point where you want the Flash text to be inserted.

2. Click the Insert Flash Text icon in the Insert bar (or Insert → Interactive Images → Flash Text).

3. The Insert Flash Text dialog box (see Figure 19.31) displays.

In the Insert Flash Text dialog box, choose the features you wish to specify, as shown in the following steps:

1. Select a font from the Font menu of True Type fonts on your system.

2. Enter a font point size in the Size field.

3. Click the **B** for bold and/or the *I* for italic to change the font style.

4. Click the alignment icons to change the font alignment.

5. To choose the color of the text, click the Color field and choose a color from the color palette, or enter a color name or hexadecimal color value in the blank text field. To choose the color that the text will appear during a rollover, click the Rollover Color field and choose a color from the color palette, or enter a color name or hexadecimal color value in the blank text field.

6. Enter the text in the Text field.

7. Select Show Font to see the font displayed in the Text field.

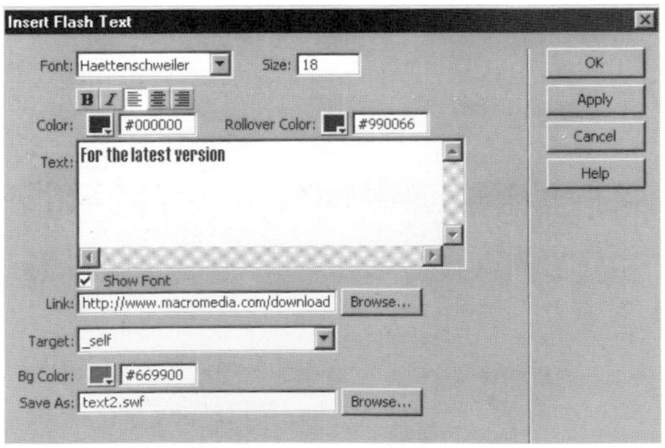

Figure 19.31

**Insert Flash Text
dialog box**

8. Enter an absolute URL or a document-relative URL in the Link field or click the Browse button to navigate to a file. Site-relative URLs can't be used for links because browsers don't recognize them in Flash movies.

9. Use the Target menu to select a target window or frame for the link.

10. Click the Bg Color field to choose a color from the color palette, or enter a color name or hexadecimal color value in the blank text field.

11. Enter a filename in the Save As field to name the Flash file. Dreamweaver supplies a default name, such as `text1.swf`, if no other name is entered. You can also click the Browse button to navigate to an SWF file on your computer if you wish to overwrite a previously saved SWF file.

Setting Additional Properties of Flash Objects

To set additional properties of Flash objects, follow these steps.

1. Select a Flash object and open the Property Inspector (Window → Properties), as shown below in Figure 19.32. Here are some of the properties you can choose from:

   - Name
   - Dimensions (width and height in pixels)
   - File (path to the Flash object file)
   - Align
   - Bg (background color)
   - ID (Optional Active X ID parameter)
   - V Space (vertical white space around button)
   - H Space (horizontal white space around button)
   - Quality (quality parameter for the `object` and `embed` element)
   - Scale (scale parameter for the `object` and `embed` elements)

Other features that can be accessed from the Property Inspector include the following:

Figure 19.32

Property Inspector, Flash object

Edit Opens the Flash object dialog box.

Reset Size Resets the button to the original movie size.

Play/Stop Preview the Flash object in the document window.

Parameters Opens a dialog box for adding additional parameters.

For more information on the Control Shockwave or Flash behavior, see the previous section of this chapter, "Introducing Dreamweaver's Built-in Behaviors."

Behaviors in Fireworks are similar to Behaviors in Dreamweaver. They are used to attach behaviors to interactive image elements, such as rollovers and image maps. Fireworks also has a Behaviors panel that can be used to attach a behavior to a slice or hotspot in a Fireworks file. If a Fireworks rollover file is exported to Dreamweaver, the file can be edited in Dreamweaver's Behaviors panel.

Hands On: Creating an Animation Using Layers, Timelines, and Behaviors

You can create animations on your web pages using layers, timelines, and behaviors. In this tutorial, you will create a simple Dreamweaver animation that moves an image across a page and attaches behaviors to the image to create animated effects.

Inserting a Layer and Setting Layer Properties

Begin creating your animation by inserting a layer and setting layer properties:

1. Open the file named `animation_begin.html` from the Chapter 19 folder of the accompanying CD.

2. Insert a layer on this page (Insert → Layer).

3. Select the layer and open the Property Inspector (Window → Properties).

4. Set the layer properties as shown in Figure 19.33.

Inserting an Image in a Layer and Inserting the Layer in a Timeline

Insert an image into your new layer and then insert this layer in a timeline:

1. Insert the image file named `box.jpg` into the new layer by placing the insertion point within the layer and inserting the image using Insert → Image.

2. Select the image and open the Property Inspector. Set V Space 7, and H Space 10.

3. Insert the layer in a timeline. First select the layer, then choose Modify → Timeline → Add Object to Timeline (see Figure 19.34).

Figure 19.33

Setting layer properties

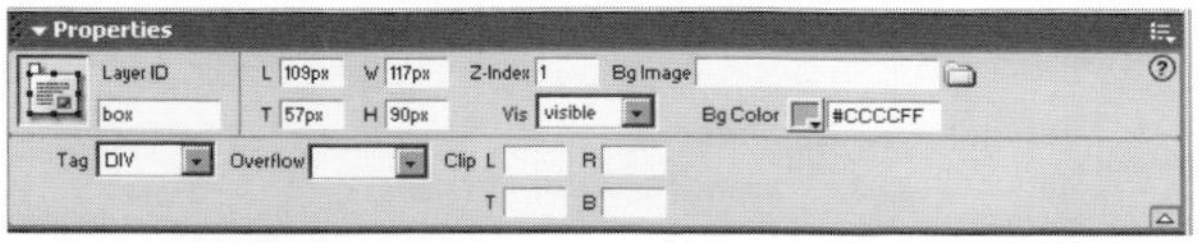

Adding Frames to the Timeline

Add additional frames and keyframes to your timeline:

1. Create additional frames in the timeline. Click and drag the keyframe in Frame 15 of the Timeline to Frame 45 of the timeline.

2. Insert additional keyframes in Frame 15 and Frame 30. Select Frame 15 in the Timelines panel, then choose Modify → Timeline → Add Keyframe (Figure 19.35). Repeat for Frame 30 in the timeline.

3. Select Frame 15 in the Timelines panel. Open the Property Inspector and change the values for the layer's position. Change L to 200px and T to 100px.

4. Repeat steps 2 and 3 for Frame 30. Change L to 300px and T to 200px.

5. Repeat steps 2 and 3 once more for Frame 45. Change L to 400px and T to 300px.

Figure 19.34

Adding an object to the Timeline

Adding Behaviors to a Timeline

Add behaviors to frames in your timeline:

1. Add behaviors to Frames 15, 30, and 45. Click Frame 15 in the Behaviors channel (above the frame numbers in the Timelines panel). Open the Behaviors panel. Click the plus (+) button and select Popup Message from the Actions menu.

2. Enter **Hello world!** (or your own message) in the Popup Message dialog box.

3. Note that there is now a horizontal dash across Frame 15 in the Behaviors channel of the Timelines panel. This indicates that a behavior has been attached to this frame (see Figure 19.36).

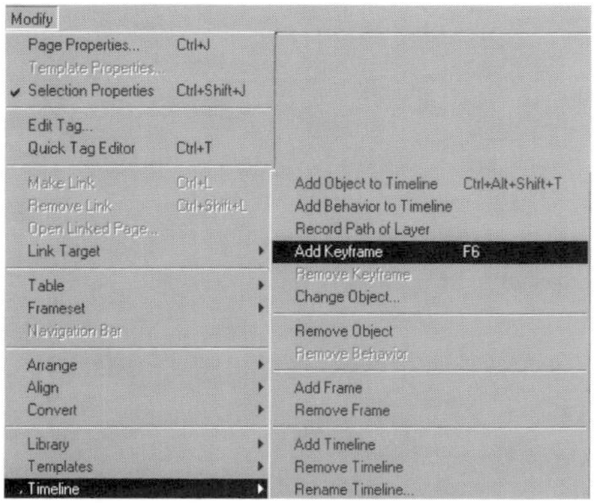

Figure 19.35

Adding keyframes

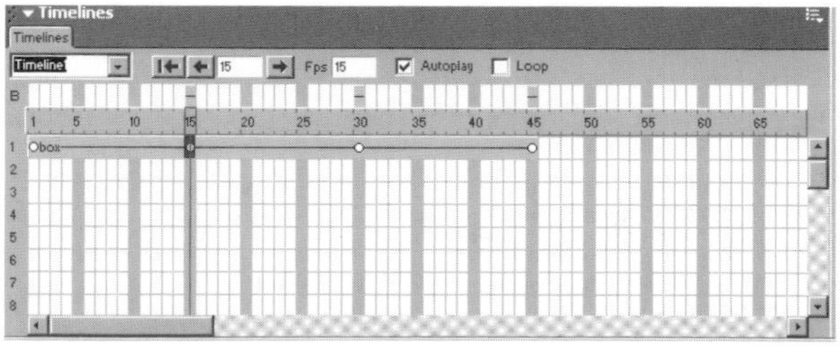

Figure 19.36

Adding a behavior to a timeline

4. Repeat step 1 for Frame 30, but this time, select Change Property from the Actions menu.

5. Make the following selections in the Change Property dialog box:

   - Type of Object: DIV

   - Named Object: div "box"

   - Property: choose Select Radio Button, then choose `style:backgroundcolor` from the Select menu.

   - New Value: red

6. Repeat step 1 for Frame 45, but this time select Set Text → Set Text of Status Bar from the Actions menu.

7. Enter **That's All, Folks!** in the Message field in the Set Text of Status Bar dialog box.

Adding a Behavior to the Body Element

Add a behavior to the body element so that the animation begins to play when the page loads:

1. Close the Timelines panel and then select the `body` element in the `animation_begin .html` file.

2. Open the Behaviors panel, click the plus (+) button, and select Timeline → Play Timeline from the Actions menu.

3. Choose the appropriate timeline from the Play Timeline menu in the Play Timeline dialog box.

Previewing the Animation

Save your file and preview the file in a browser:

1. Save the HTML file as `animation_end.html`. Preview the file in a browser to see if your animation works properly. The Change Property behavior will not work properly if viewed in Netscape Navigator 4.x, but all four behaviors will work in Internet Explorer 4.0 or higher and in Netscape Navigator 6.0 or higher.

2. If your `animation_end.html` file is not working properly, or if you would like to view the completed file, open the `animation_complete.html` file from the Chapter 19 folder of the accompanying CD.

That's All, Folks!

There, now we've covered the essentials of behaviors, but as you have seen, behaviors work closely with many other Dreamweaver features. To further advance your skills and knowledge in creating interactive and dynamic web pages using Dreamweaver, Fireworks, HTML, and JavaScript, see the next chapter, Chapter 20, where you'll learn how to use forms to create interactivity on your pages.

Going Interactive with Forms

Any time you submit information online, you fill out a form. Forms can range from complex collections of fields such as a survey, to a single field that allows you to select a file to download. The front-end experience of filling out a form is easy to grasp and familiar to most software users. The back-end automation of a form, which controls how the information is processed, is a black box to most users. But if you want your forms to *do* anything, then you or your team will have to be comfortable "under the hood," to mix metaphors shamelessly.

Forms are used in a variety of situations. No matter how you use your form, it remains a tool for collecting information or enabling interaction with your site, and it operates through a collection of CGI scripts (or Java applets, or other coded routines), and HTML form elements.

This chapter explains how to create forms using the tools provided within Dreamweaver with the following topics:

- **Using the various elements of HTML forms**

- **Using CGI-based form-processing scripts with forms created in Dreamweaver**

- **Editing CGI scripts from within a text editor**

- **Creating target pages for form responses**

- **Accentuating information processed using hidden form data**

- **Using a form to process a search request**

Exploring Form Elements

HTML forms, as created by Dreamweaver or any other HTML editor, use a combination of HTML elements and attributes to define, collect, and process the information requested by the website owner or administrator.

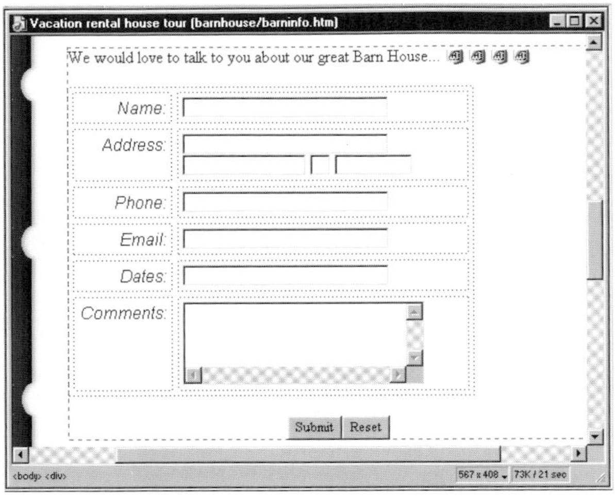

Figure 20.1

Form collecting lodging reservations

Dreamweaver allows you to create HTML-based forms using its built-in form field controls located on the Insert bar. These elements are used to create the form structure, text fields, buttons, radio buttons, check boxes, images, file fields, list/menu selections, hidden tags, labels, fieldsets, and legends that are discussed in the following sections. Once all of these form objects are combined, you will find that your form can be an efficient collection of fields that can collect the information you require, as shown in Figure 20.1.

The formatting of this form is controlled by using a series of table cells that allow you to align each label, as well as each text field, into separate columns, while still keeping the information easy to read and readily accessible to the individual filling out the form. If you don't have a form that fits on a single screen, as shown here, break the form into sections so that the form doesn't become an overwhelming, monotonous task for your site visitors.

Specifying Your Form Structure

Dreamweaver uses the HTML `<form>` tag to create the foundation box of any form on your web page. The form itself has only three attributes—`name`, `method`, and `action`—all of which are accessible through the Property Inspector, which is shown in Figure 20.2.

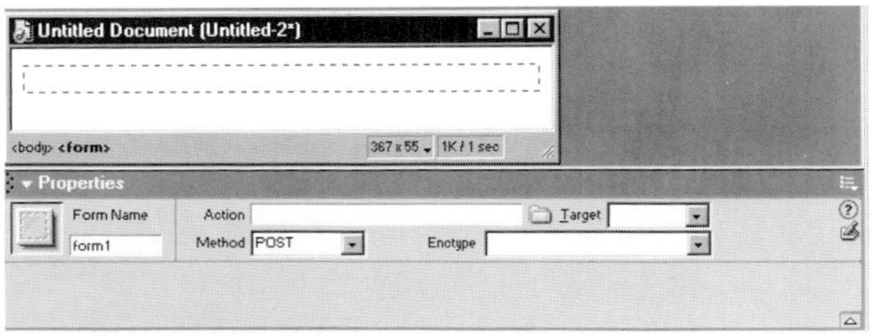

Figure 20.2

Form properties

To insert a form into your Dreamweaver document, select Insert → Form, or use the tools shown on Forms tab on the Insert bar. This inserts the `<form name="form1" method="post" action=""> </form>` tags into your document. The form itself, when seen through the Design view (View → Design view) as shown in Figure 20.2, appears as a red dashed outline on your screen. To add your form objects, text, and formatting, you must place your cursor in this red box prior to the addition of your information.

Although Internet Explorer doesn't require the `<form>` tag to be present in order to display form objects, Netscape Navigator does.

The Property Inspector for each form in your document contains these three fields which correspond to the `<form>` tag's attributes of the same name:

The Name Field This stores the name used to reference the form in scripts. You can place any unique alphanumeric string, such as `form1` or `contact_form`, in this field. This field corresponds to the `name` attribute of the `<form>` tag.

The Method Field This drop-down list has two options: GET or POST. The GET HTTP method will append the contents of the form fields to the URL specified in the `action` attribute. If you wish to use the GET method to submit your form data, you must limit your form content to ASCII character strings under 8KB. The POST HTTP method sends the form data directly to the CGI script or Java applet specified by the `action` attribute. There are no restrictions on the amount of information that can be submitted using the POST method. POST can also be used to send binary information, such as files and images. This field corresponds to the `method` attribute of the `<form>` tag.

The Action Field The Action field on the Property Inspector specifies the file/script name and location that will receive the contents of the form when the Submit button on the form is pressed. This field corresponds to the `action` attribute of the `<form>` tag.

Most of the time, the contents of the action field will specify the name of the CGI script (`.cgi`), a Perl program (`.pl`), a Java applet or Java Server Page (`.jsp`), a ColdFusion document (`.cfm`), an Active Server Page (`.asp`), a Hypertext Preprocessor file (`.php`), or one of any number of other formats for coding HTTP behaviors. Some examples of strings that can be used to specify an action are

```
http://www.myserver.com/cgi-bin/formmail.pl
http://www.myserver.com/mydocument.cfm
/cgi-bin/links.pl
/myprocessingdocument.asp
scripts/login.php
```

Once you have set each form attribute, your `<form>` tag will look something like the following in your Code view (View → Code View):

```
<form name="form1" method="post"
    action="/cgi-bin/formmail.pl">
</form>
```

Using Form Text Fields

There are three types of text fields used in HTML forms: single-line text fields, multiline text fields, and password text fields. Although the function of these three fields is much the same, their appearance and abilities widely differ. *Single-line text fields* contain, understandably, a single line of text and are typically used to collect information such as names and addresses or other short-phrase answers. *Multiline text fields* can contain and display multiple lines of text including comments, full paragraph queries, and in-depth descriptions of problems and solutions that you wish to share with, say, an online discussion board. *Password text fields* substitute asterisks for the entered text to keep sensitive information private.

To insert a text box into your Dreamweaver document, select Insert → Form Objects → Text Field. As you can see from the TextField Property Inspector (shown in Figure 20.3), the difference between these three types of text fields is controlled by setting the values in the PI's property fields. Each of these properties corresponds to an attribute of the same name, or a similar name, for the `<input type="text">` tag.

The Name property The TextField Name field on the Property Inspector stores the name used by scripts to reference the text field. You can place any unique alphanumeric string in this field, such as `text1` or `contact_name`. This property corresponds to the `name` attribute of the `<input type="text">` tag.

The Char Width property The Character Width attribute sets the total number of characters that are visible in the field. This property corresponds to the `size` attribute of the `<input type="text">` tag.

The Max Chars property The Maximum Characters attribute sets the total number of characters that can be stored in the field. This property corresponds to the `maxwidth` attribute of the `<input type="text">` tag.

The Wrap property The Wrap attribute allows the contents of a multiline text field to wrap to a second line in the text box, rather than run continuously on a single line. This property corresponds to the `wrap` attribute of the `<input type="text">` tag.

The Type property The Type property specifies that the box should be drawn as a single line, a multiline, or a password field. This property corresponds to the `type` attribute of the `<input>` tag.

The Init Val property The Initial Value attribute sets up the value that will originally be displayed in the field when the HTML document is displayed. This property corresponds to the `value` attribute of the `<input type="text">` tag.

The following sections show each of the three types of text fields in action.

Figure 20.3

Text Field properties

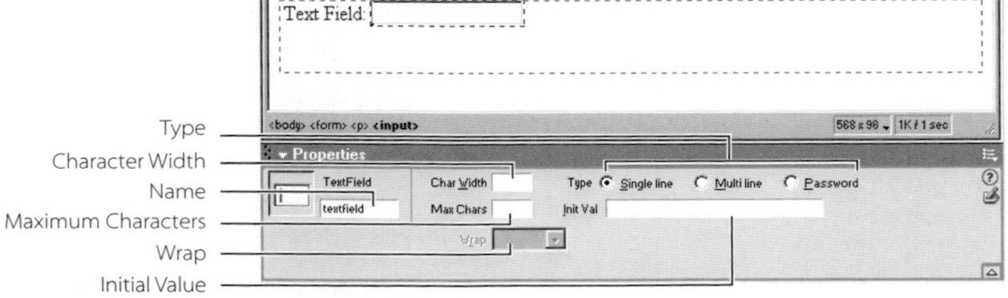

Type
Character Width
Name
Maximum Characters
Wrap
Initial Value

Single-Line Text Fields

Single-line text fields are best used to collect answers to single phrase requests (such as "What is your name?" or "What is your Address?" or even "What Product do you wish to order?"). Anything that requires a more complex answer (such as "How do you feel about widgets?") should be answered in a multiline text field, as shown in the next section.

When you select Insert → Form Objects → Text Field, a single-line text field is created automatically, as seen in Figure 20.3. You can ensure that you are creating a single-line text field, and not a password field, by selecting Single Line from the Type property in the Property Inspector.

Multiline Text Fields

Multiline text fields are best used to collect answers to complex questions, such as "How do you use widgets at home compared with how you use them at work?" or "What is your favorite vacation?" If you have a request that will require more than a single line of text to answer, you should give the visitor the space to answer it fully.

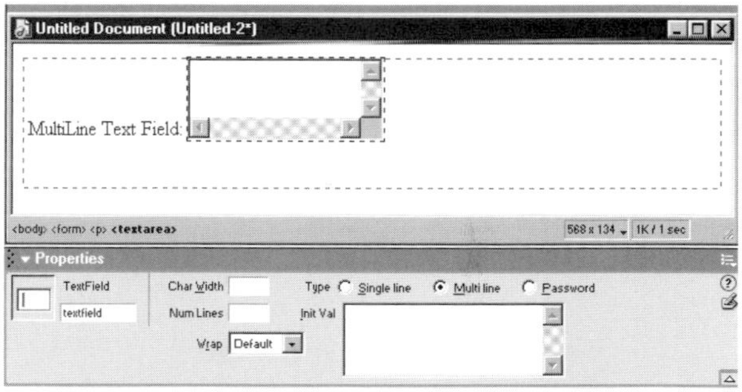

As we saw, when you selected Insert → Form Objects → Text Field, a single-line text field was created automatically. To change this into a multiline text field, select Multi Line from the Type property in the Property Inspector. Notice how the `max chars` property is replaced by a `num lines` property. Dreamweaver allows you to specify the character width and number of lines for a multiline text field, but not a maximum number of characters. As odd as this restriction may sound, it exists because a multiline text field isn't created using an `<input type="text">` tag, but is created using a `<textarea>` tag, which doesn't support an attribute specifying a maximum number of characters.

In Figure 20.4, you can see a sample of a two-line text box. You can make your boxes display as many lines as you wish, but keep in mind that it is more comfortable to fill out a form in which the space allotted is neither too small, nor so large that it seems as if you are requesting a small novel.

Figure 20.5

A password text field displayed through Internet Explorer

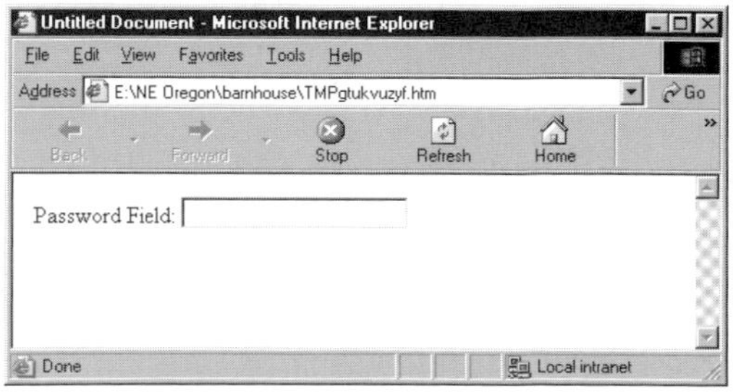

Password Text Fields

Password text fields look just like single-line text fields in Dreamweaver, but users' entered text displays as asterisks (see Figure 20.5). If you are asking the visitor for a password or wish to hide a credit card number you are collecting, the use of a password text field is handy and makes visitors feel that your site is more secure.

> Password text fields hide the information displayed on screen, but they do not encrypt the data as it is sent through your server. Do not use password text fields to collect private data unless you are also encrypting the form contents before you deliver it through e-mail or store it in a database.

To change a single-line text field into a password text field, select Password from the Type field in the Property Inspector.

Inserting Check Boxes and Radio Buttons

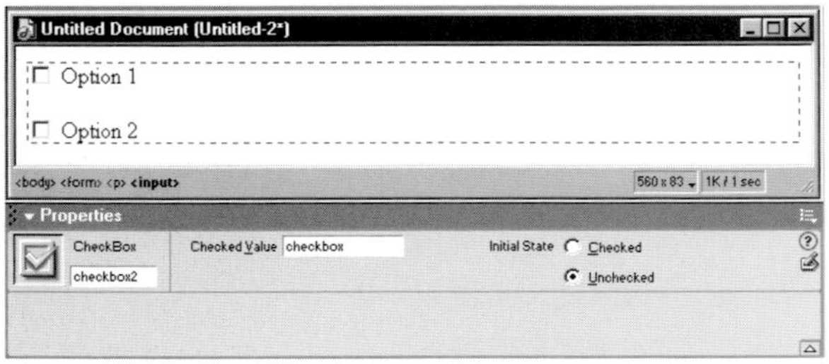

Figure 20.6

Check boxes and the Check Box Property Inspector

Check boxes and radio buttons serve a similar purpose in forms. They both allow you to select from a list of options, or objects, and make one or multiple selections. Radio buttons force a single selection, while check boxes allow you to make multiple selections.

To insert a check box into your form, select Insert → Form Objects → Check Box. In Figure 20.6, you can see two check boxes with their Property Inspector.

The properties for check boxes include these:

The Name Property The Check Box Name property on the Property Inspector stores the name used to reference the check box in scripts. You can place any unique alphanumeric string in this field such as `box1` or `career_farmer`. This property corresponds to the `name` attribute of the `<input type="checkbox>` or the `<input type="radio">` tag.

The Checked Value Property This property stores the value that will be sent to the form's processing application when the form is submitted. This property corresponds to the `value` attribute of the `<input type="checkbox>` or the `<input type="radio">` tag.

The Initial State Property This property can be set to either Checked or Unchecked to control how the check box first appears. This property corresponds to the `checked` attribute of the `<input type="checkbox>` or the `<input type="radio">` tag.

Both check boxes and radio buttons have the same available properties on the Property Inspector, but radio buttons must be grouped in order to force a single selection to be made. To group radio buttons together, you must give all of the radio buttons in that group the same name (shown as "RadioGroup2" in Figure 20.7). This will force the form to allow only one of the buttons to be checked at a time, and send only one value to the form's processing script when the form is submitted. Because radio buttons work as part of a group, you can only set the Initial Value of one radio button to be checked. All others will automatically be reset to Unchecked. (You can also leave them all unchecked.) Check boxes allow you to set multiple boxes to be checked.

You can also create a series of radio buttons using the new Radio Group option in Dreamweaver MX. To create a series of radio buttons, which are automatically part of the same group, follow these steps:

1. Select Insert → Form Options → Radio Group.

2. Type a name for the group in the Name field. This will be the name applied to all the radio buttons used in this group.

3. Click the plus (+) button to add additional radio buttons, or use the minus (−) button to remove buttons that have already been added.

4. Use the up and down arrow buttons to control the order in which the radio buttons are displayed on your page.

5. Select either Line Breaks (
 tags) or Table in the Lay Out Using option to control the layout of your radio buttons.

Once you have completed your selections, the Radio button group will be created as shown in Figure 20.7.

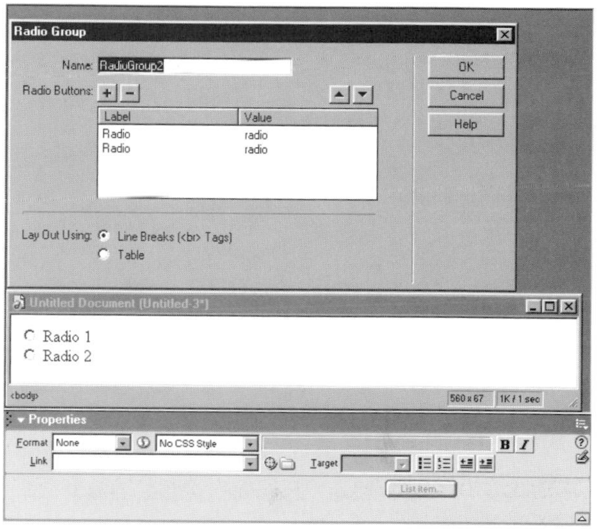

Figure 20.7

A selection of radio buttons, the Radio Button Property Inspector, and the new Radio Group dialog box, which automatically groups radio buttons for you

Using Form File Fields

One of the great things about the Internet is its ability to share files and other documents. For instance, you can add a File field to your HTML forms and allow people to send you files from their own computers.

To add a File Selection field to your form select Insert → Form Objects → File Field. File fields, as shown in Figure 20.8, allow users to use the Browse button to search their own hard drives. Once a file is selected, the filename and location appear in the text field next to the button. A Submit button then uses this information to send the file to your server.

CONCERNS WITH UPLOADED FILES

Don't have files that have been uploaded to your site automatically sent to your e-mail or some other system that may automatically try to execute the file. This is a great way to get and spread viruses. Keep in mind that many mail clients now have a preview pane that automatically shows and activates the contents of the message as soon as it is selected in your mailbox. Instead, you should have all files sent to a secure location where they can be inspected for viruses and other bugs well in advance of them interacting with your personal computer.

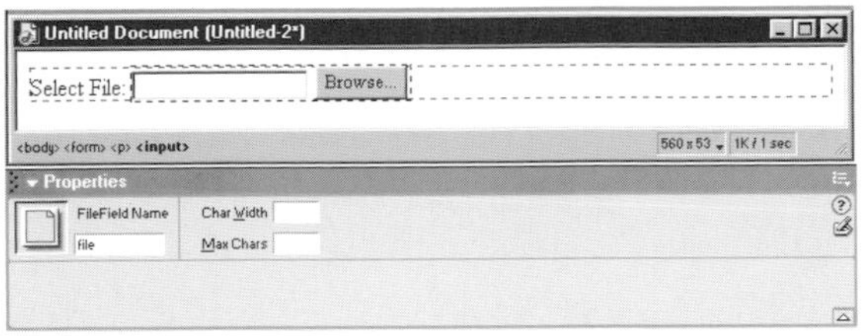

Figure 20.8

Selecting a File field allows you to share files using web forms.

As you can see from the File Field Property Inspector, file fields have the following properties that need setting:

The Name property The File Field Name field on the Property Inspector stores the name used to reference the File field in scripts. You can place any unique alphanumeric string in this field, such as `file1` or `upload_file`. This property corresponds to the `name` attribute of the `<input type="file">` tag.

The Char Width property This property sets the total number of characters that can be visible in the text portion of the File field. This property corresponds to the `type` attribute of the `<input type="file">` tag.

The Max Chars property This property sets the total number of characters that can be stored in the text portion of the file field. This property corresponds to the `type` attribute of the `<input type="file">` tag.

Creating List/Menu Form Selections

List/Menu fields, as shown in Figure 20.9, allow you to create a list of options that can be selected either from a list of constantly visible items, or from a drop-down menu system. Lists are great for providing immediate access to just a few settings from which multiple selections can be made, while menus work better when you are trying to force the selection of a single option from a long list of options.

To add a List/Menu selection to your form, select Insert → Form Objects → List/Menu.

As you can see from the List/Menu Property Inspector, these fields have the following properties:

The Name property The List/Menu property on the Property Inspector stores the name used to reference the field in scripts. You can place any unique alphanumeric string in this field such as `list1`, `menu1`, or `site_urls`. This property corresponds to the `name` attribute of the `<select>` tag.

Figure 20.9

Form showing the same options in both a list and menu format

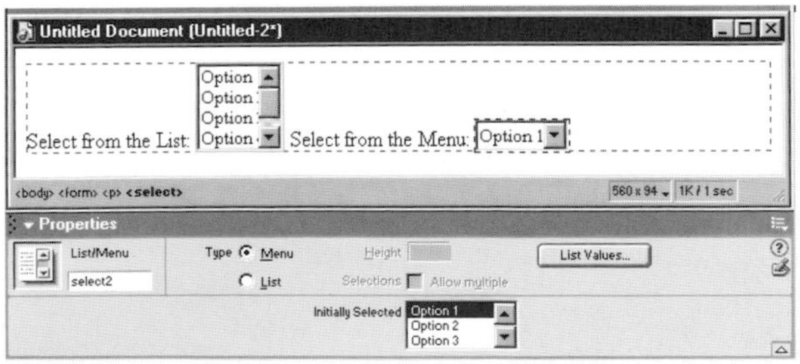

The Type property This property specifies that the field should be drawn as a list or drop-down menu. This property corresponds to the `type` attribute of the `<select>` tag.

The Height property This property sets the total number of lines that can be visible simultaneously in a List field. This option isn't available when the Type property is set to Menu. This property corresponds to the `size` attribute of the `<select>` tag.

The Selections: Allow Multiple property This property allows you to select a series of options from a list. This option isn't available when the Type property is set to Menu. This property corresponds to the `multiple` attribute of the `<select>` tag.

Figure 20.10

List Values dialog box

The List Values property This button opens the List Values dialog box, shown in Figure 20.10, which allows you to add (+), remove (–), and move the options on your list or menu. Each option you add is stored within a series of `<option></option>` tags in your HTML document.

The Initially Selected property This property selects the item in your list or menu that will be highlighted by default when the form first loads. This property corresponds to the `selected` attribute of the `<option>` tag.

Using Form Images

Figure 20.11

Form images

Admittedly, forms can be somewhat boring to view at times. By using images in place of Submit buttons or even Reset buttons, you can spruce up the appearance of your pages. Image fields on forms look much like any other image on your web pages (see Figure 20.11), but they have the added function of working like buttons when you wish them to.

To insert an Image field into your form, select Insert → Form Objects → Image Field. As you can see from the Image Property Inspector, these fields have the following attributes:

The Name property The Image field Name property on the Property Inspector stores the name used to reference the field in scripts. You can place any unique alphanumeric string in this field, such as `image1` or `image_option`. If you set the name of the image to "Submit" and then click it, the image will function the same as if you clicked a Submit button. This property corresponds to the `name` attribute of the `<input type="image">` tag.

The W property The Width property sets the width, in pixels, of the image being displayed. This property corresponds to the `width` attribute of the `<input type="image">` tag.

The H property The Height property sets the height, in pixels, of the image being displayed. This property corresponds to the `height` attribute of the `<input type="image">` tag.

The Alt property The Alternate Text property specifies the text that will appear if the image can't be loaded for any reason. This property corresponds to the `alt` attribute of the `<input type="image">` tag.

The Src property   The Src property identifies the location of the image file on the server. This property corresponds to the `src` attribute of the `<input type="image">` tag.

The Align property   The Align property controls the alignment of the image on your document. This property corresponds to the `align` attribute of the `<input type="image">` tag.

Inserting Form Buttons

Buttons are used to submit form information to the processing application. Now, they don't all have to be labeled Submit, or Reset. When you are working with a search form, the button is often labeled Go or Search. At other times, you will have a button labeled Browse to help you find a file, or even Open to load a new website off of a menu list. The sample buttons, shown in Figure 20.12, give you just a few examples of the types of labels that can be sported on your Form buttons.

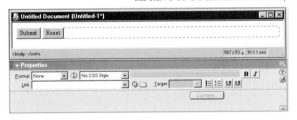

Figure 20.12

Form buttons

To insert a button into your form, select Insert → Form Objects → Button. As you can see from the Button Property Inspector, these fields have the following attributes that need setting:

The Name property   The Button Name field on the Property Inspector stores the name used to reference the field in scripts. You can place any unique alphanumeric string in this field. This property corresponds to the `name` attribute of the `<input type="submit">`, the `<input type="reset">`, or the `<input type="button">` tag.

The Label property   The Label property sets the text that appears on the face of the button, such as Submit, Reset, or Go. This property corresponds to the `value` attribute of the `<input type="submit">`, the `<input type="reset">`, or the `<input type="button">` tag.

The Action property   The Action property controls the function of the button. The actions that you can choose from are Submit Form, Reset Form, and None. When set to Submit Form, the button's action will send the form data to the processing application, and the `type` attribute of the `<input>` element will be set equal to "submit." When set to Reset Form, the buttons action will reset all of the values in the form to either a blank state, or to the value specified in the form object's Initial Value field and the `type` attribute of the `<input>` element will be set equal to "reset." When set to None, the button will require a script to manipulate the processing of the information from the form and the `type` attribute of the `<input>` element will be set equal to "button."

Using Hidden Fields

Hidden fields are invisible to visitors and are used to provide specific information to the form's processing application. For instance, in the `formmail.pl` script, a hidden field is used to identify the recipient of the form content, while another hidden tag is used to specify the target page that will be loaded when the script is done processing the form information.

To add a hidden field to your HTML form, select Insert → Form Objects → Hidden Field. As you can see from the HiddenField Property Inspector, these fields have the following attributes that need to be set:

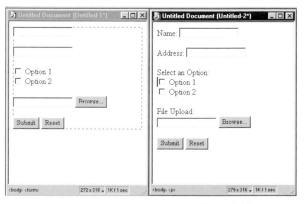

The Name property The HiddenField Name field on the Property Inspector stores the name used to reference the field in your processing script. You can place any unique alphanumeric string in this field such as `Target` or `Recipient`. This property corresponds to the `name` attribute of the `<input type="hidden">` tag.

Figure 20.13

Unlabeled forms make no sense to your site visitors.

The Value property The Value property sets up the value that will be sent to the processing application when the script is submitted. Values can be anything from e-mail addresses to JavaScript code. This property corresponds to the `value` attribute of the `<input type="hidden">` tag.

Adding Form Labels

Forms don't do you a lot of good without labels for each of the form's fields. For instance, which form in Figure 20.13 is easiest to read and understand? Obviously it's the one on the right with the labels that let you know exactly what information is expected in each field.

For those of you who have actually read the HTML 4.01 or the XHTML specification, you may remember that there is actually a `<label>` element that provides labels for your form elements. Although this feature has been missing in previous versions of Dreamweaver, it is now available in Dreamweaver MX.

To add a label using Dreamweaver, select Insert → Form Objects → Label. This opens the Code view, in addition to your Design view, allowing you to directly modify the name of your label, as shown in Figure 20.14. Type in the text you wish to appear as a label between the `<label></label>` tags.

Once you have typed in the appropriate label text, press F5, or click the Refresh button in the Property Inspector. This will update all of the information you have updated in Design view as well as in Code view.

Using Fieldsets and Legends for Form Organization

Dreamweaver MX has incorporated support for the `<fieldset>` and `<legend>` tags. The sole purpose of the `<fieldset>` tag is to group sets of form elements, while the `<legend>` tag provides a label for those groups. By dividing your form fields into groups, you can make their relationships easier to comprehend (for your site visitors) and still improve the function of

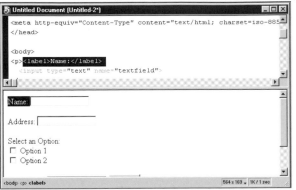

tab-based navigation methods. When you use the `<legend>` tag with your `<fieldset>` tag, you can provide a description for the group of controls.

For instance, assume you are taking a survey and wish to know an individual's age range. By creating a `<fieldset>` tag that holds all of the radio buttons representing the age range values, and by adding a legend to that `<fieldset>` tag, you end up with a meaningful combination of elements that can then be interpreted by your processing application in a more succinct manner.

If you wish to add your own `<fieldset>` and `<legend>` elements, you can add them manually in Code view (View → Code View) or use the Insert → Form Objects → Fieldset element. Either way, you will need to modify the code in Code view to show the legend for your fieldset. Your code, once complete, would look something like this:

Figure 20.14

You must edit the HTML code to add a label using Dreamweaver's installed feature.

```
<form action="..." method="post">
 <p>
 <fieldset>
  <legend>Contact Information</legend>
  Last Name:
  <input name=" lastname" type="text" tabindex="1">
  <br>
  First Name:
  <input name=" firstname" type="text" tabindex="2">
  <br>
  Address:
  <input name=" address" type="text" tabindex="3">
  <br>
  ...more contact information...
 </fieldset>
<fieldset>
   ...more form controls...
</fieldset>
</p>
</form>
```

Enhancing Forms with Hidden Tags

Hidden tags are commonly used to collect information on forms and pass it to the forms' processing applications without the site visitors' knowledge. Although some people don't like not knowing what information their computer is sending out, this isn't necessarily a bad use of form controls. Sometimes hidden tags are used to provide detailed instructions as to which target page to load after the processing application is complete. At other times, they can be used to specify which e-mail address should receive the content of the form.

Hidden tags can also be used to collect such information as what browser a visitor is using or what their IP address is. You can accomplish this by adding JavaScript code to the values of your hidden form field.

The following sample statements send the last modified date of the document that they are submitting their information through to the form processor as part of the hidden information in the file.

```
<input type="hidden" name="hiddenField"
        value="{document.lastmodified}">
```

To learn more about JavaScript, check out *Mastering JavaScript Premium Edition* by James Jaworski (Sybex, 2001).

Implementing Jump Menus

Dreamweaver includes the ability to automatically create a series of menus that will jump you between documents in your site, or between sites on the Web. These *Jump menus* function by associating a series of URLs with items shown in a Menu field. When a site visitor selects one of the menu options, a JavaScript program loads the associated page in the specified target window.

To insert a Jump menu in your document, follow these steps:

1. Select Insert → Form Objects → Jump Menu. This opens the Insert Jump Menu dialog box shown in Figure 20.15.

2. Fill in the Text and the When Selected, Go to URL field with the name and the URL of the site, or document, you wish to load when that menu option is selected.

3. Click the plus (+) button to add a new entry.

4. Repeat steps 2 and 3 until you have added all of the possible websites you wish to mention to your list of menu items.

5. In the Open URLs In field, select the frame or Main window that will be used to display the documents when the menu selection is made.

6. Type the name of the menu in the Menu Name field.

7. Check the Insert Go Button after Menu check box if you wish to allow your visitors to make a selection, and then press Go to load the new page, rather than have their selection initiate the loading procedure.

Figure 20.15

Insert Jump Menu dialog box

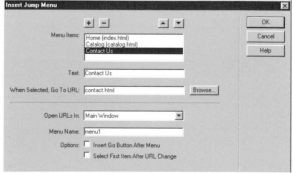

Figure 20.16

8. Check the Select First Item after URL Change check box if you wish the menu to be reset after every document load. This option only has meaning if you are loading your pages into a frame within the current window. When this check box isn't checked, your check box always displays the last selected option.

Jump menus can have multiple options and configurations, as shown in Figure 20.16.

Working with CGI Scripts

All forms must be processed or they just sit there and don't do anything. You have a lot of options for processing those forms, but Common Gateway Interface (CGI) scripts are probably the most common. CGI scripts can be used to e-mail the contents of your form to you or to another designated individual, to write the information collected in the form to a database, or to post the information to another web page. They can also be used as the input to search a database. No matter what your goal is, you need to become a bit more familiar with CGI scripts in general before you start using them.

CGI Script Requirements

Depending on the type of web server you are using, most CGI scripts will be created in either Perl or C. Perl is typically the language used to develop CGI scripts for use on a Unix/Linux platform; C is most commonly used on Windows platforms.

If you are using Perl-based CGI scripts, your server must have

- A compatible version of Perl installed

- A properly configured `cgi` directory

- The proper CHMOD settings for each directory and file in your `cgi-bin` directory

Compatible Version of Perl

Although most Unix/Linux-based servers do have Perl installed, they may have an older version than the one for which your script is designed. You can find out the requirements for your script by reading its documentation; then you can find out what version of Perl you are running on your server by checking with your server administrator.

Properly Configured *cgi* Directory

There are typically two options for using CGI scripts on your Unix/Linux-based web server. The first, and most common, is to run all of your programs out of a `cgi-bin` directory, which has been configured in your server files to store and run Perl and CGI files. The second commonly used option is to use a CGI-wrapper that will allow scripts to run on a server but also allows the server administrator more security over the types of scripts that can be run, who can run them, and how they are run.

Proper CHMOD Settings

CHMOD is a Unix command, an abbreviation of "change mode"—it is used, among other things, to assign read/write privileges for directories.

You must have proper file access settings for each file used by your CGI script in order for this script to work properly. There are varieties of permission settings that can be used for these files, but you should always set those permissions to be just what you need to run the script without giving away any extra access.

CHMOD permissions on Unix and Linux machines are broken down into Users, Groups, and Others identification classifications. Each of these groups is allotted permissions individually. These permissions are controlled by the assignment of a numerical value to that specific set of users. Permission values are Read = 4, Write = 2, and Execute = 1. In order to apply a Read and Execute permission to an owner, you would add the assigned numerical values and come up with a 5 for your user group. For instance

User= Read + Write + Execute = 7

Group= Read + Execute = 5

Other = Read + Execute = 5

If you were to type in the command CHMOD myfile 755 you would be stating that it is OK for anyone to read or execute the file, but only you can modify it.

Once all of your file permissions are correct, your cgi directory is properly set up and installed, and you have a valid version of Perl running on your computer, you are ready to start writing and testing the CGI scripts you wish to use.

Understanding Different Perl Versions

There are many versions of Perl that are available for use on Unix/Linux computers, as well as Windows and Macintosh servers. Perl first became available to the world in 1987, and it has been growing ever since. The majority of the scripts you find on the Internet were designed for one of the versions of Perl 5, which has been available since 1994. The most recent version of Perl is Perl 5.006, released in January 2000.

When you are deciding on a version of Perl to run on your system, it would be best to use Perl 5.004 or newer because all previous versions of Perl were subject to buffer overrun security errors. This security flaw would allow nefarious individuals to flood your CGI scripts and their associated memory buffers with too much information too fast, causing your scripts to break down, run erratically, or in some cases, even provide access to otherwise secure memory on your web server. Overall though, Perl 5 is extremely stable and easy to program.

If you are interested in keeping up with the times, you may want to look into the "Topaz Project," also called Perl 6. This project is a from-the-ground-up rewrite of the Perl core. As of this writing, Perl 6 isn't available for general use, but if you want to learn more about it, visit `http://www.perl.org`. There is a mailing list there for people that are interested in working on the project or in keeping abreast of the changes.

Using the Perl Declaration

One of the primary pieces of any Perl script is the Perl declaration that identifies the location of the Perl interpreter on your machine. This statement is typically located at the top of every PL or CGI file running on a Unix or Linux box. If this statement doesn't properly identify the location of Perl, then none of your scripts will work, even if everything else on the server is properly configured. Common Perl declaration statements include these:

```
#!/usr/bin/perl
#!/usr/local/bin/perl -wT
```

One of these statements typically occurs in the first line of your Perl script and identifies the location of the Perl module and what options must be used when you run it. Specifically, these statements tell the Unix/Linux shell where to find Perl, and then they pass the rest of the script to that program where it can be executed.

Of course, the path specified in this statement will change, depending upon where your copy of Perl is installed. For instance, if you have multiple versions of Perl on your system, you may have a `perl5` directory, rather than just a `perl` directory.

```
#!/usr/bin/perl5
#!/usr/local/bin/perl5 -w
```

The -w switch shown in the second statement produces warning messages when the Perl program is run. Without this switch, you won't receive any error messages, other than those generated by the software that you are using to view the results of your Perl program. Whenever you are testing out a script, be sure to turn warnings on. This will help you keep a log of errors and find hundreds of erroneous code lines deep in your program.

Using Languages Other Than Perl

CGI scripts can be developed in many languages. Perl has been known to use the best constructs of C, awk, and sed, so using a strict version of C isn't much different from using Perl. It just depends on what you know best, and which language your server supports. A CGI program can be written in any language that allows it to be executed on the system; some possibilities include the following:

- Any Unix shell script
- AppleScript
- C/C++
- Fortran
- Perl
- TCL
- Visual Basic

The configuration of your server may force you to use a language other than Perl, or C, with which you may be comfortable. Most Unix/Linux servers come with a Perl interpreter. Most Windows servers come with either a Visual Basic or C/C++ compiler. And most Apple servers come with a version of the AppleScript compiler. These four languages are easily used by most people, and therefore, it is rare to see a TCL or Fortran CGI script nowadays.

Outside of the consideration of the server's current software installation, you also need to take into account how the script will run. For instance, Perl, Unix shell scripts, and TCL are interpreted languages. C, C++, and Fortran are compiled languages, so you must compile them before placing them in the `cgi-bin` directory of your web server.

An additional consideration for choosing a language for writing CGI scripts is your task. For instance, C++ is a full-fledged programming language that allows you to create just about anything that you can think of. Perl doesn't have the full features of C++, and therefore it may limit you in the tasks that you can accomplish with it. C code is faster than Perl, and Perl is generally faster than TCL. So speed also might play a factor in your decision.

Editing a CGI Script

CGI scripts written in Perl are simple text files, nothing more complicated than that. When you need to edit a Perl CGI script, you will often need to modify variable values, define new variables, add fields to databases, or even modify the HTML created by your script.

Because Perl-based CGI scripts are simple text programs, you can easily view and modify their source code in a program such as Windows Notepad (shown in Figure 20.17) or in PICO on your Linux box.

Figure 20.17

Windows Notepad shown with the easily modifiable formmail.pl **script**

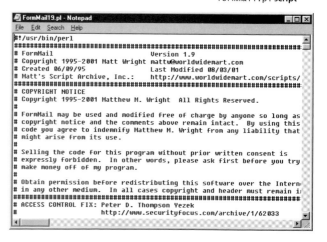

When you go to modify your documents, simply open them in your text editor and scroll down through the mix of comments and code to find the section you wish to modify. Read the comments carefully as you go. They will tell you what portion of the script you are in, what it does, and what the variables are referring to, as seen in the following code snippet

```
# Variable Definitions
#
# $sitetitle
#     Identifies the title to use for all instances
#     of the <title> elements in the resulting HTML
#     documents.
$sitetitle = 'Happy's Wholesale Haven'

# $siteadmin
#     Identifies the login name of the individual
#     that has administrative control over pages.
$siteadmin = 'beaudiddley'
```

In order to modify this code, you simply need to follow the existing format and add or update the information it contains. For instance, in the `$sitetitle` variable, if your site's name isn't `'Happy's Wholesale Haven'`, then you need to modify this path to represent the actual title of your site. It could be something like `'WebGuru's Script Haven'`.

After you are done making changes to your CGI scripts, you will need to re-upload them to your web server. When you do, make sure that you set the script back to its original CHMOD settings, discussed previously.

Creating Target Pages

After the user completes a form and submits the data (usually by clicking a Submit button), the script runs, and the user has to be given a new page to land on. This resulting page is called a *target page*. Target pages are used by form processing applications as a destination for the script after the information in the form has been processed. In the case of a simple form e-mail processing script, the page might just be something as simple as a "Thank You" with links to the primary areas of your website.

If you are processing your form information with ColdFusion, JavaServer Pages, or Active Server Pages, then your target page might be a lot more complicated. For instance, assume that you have a survey that runs off of a ColdFusion server. The target page might be the compiled answers for your survey and a list of suggested reading based upon the answers that you made.

In general, when you are creating a target page for your form processing script, you need to ensure that it has the following features:

- Links to every primary page on your website
- Contact information (phone, e-mail, and so on) for your company
- Verification that their information was properly received

- Assurance that they will be getting a response in an appropriate time frame

- A description of how they should expect to receive a response to any questions they may have posed

Target pages, with all of this information, may look like the simple page shown in Figure 20.18.

Creating your target page is no different than creating any other page in your website. Simply use the tools you learned of in Part II of this book to create a page, preferably one with a format similar to what is found in the remainder of your website, that can be used to reassure your visitors that they have submitted information to your company and your company only.

Figure 20.18

A simple target page for an e-mail processing application

Hands On: Build a Search Form

The process of building a search form on your web page can be either very simple, or very difficult, depending upon the software that you are using for completing the search. To install a search form in your document, complete the following steps:

1. Download and install your chosen search script into your `cgi-bin` directory on your web server. Be sure to read all of its documentation so that you don't have to repeat steps multiple times. CGI scripts, especially on Unix/Linux machines, require that file permissions are set correctly for every file on the machine. So be especially careful when setting these permissions.

SCRIPT ARCHIVES ON THE WEB

You can find free CGI scripts online that will do everything from create a search engine, to a guest book, to a shopping cart, to a calendar. Visit any of these sites to get 'em:

- eXtropia (http://www.extropia.com)

- Matt's Script Archive (http://www.worldwidemart.com/scripts)

- BigNosedBird.com (http://bignosebird.com)

- Perl Archive (http://www.perlarchive.com)

- CGI Resource Index (http://www.cgi-resources.com)

- MegaCGI cgi scripts (http://www.megacgi.com)

As you might have guessed, there are many other script archives available on the Internet. If you wish to find them, simply type "cgi scripts" into your favorite online search engine and wait for the thousands of links to come back to you.

Search County
Businesses and Events:

- select a category - ▼

Business Name Search

Return to Home

Figure 20.19

Search form using a category drop-down list.

2. Open your HTML document in Dreamweaver and select Insert → Form.

3. Give the form a meaningful name such as SearchForm.

4. Set the method to either GET or PUT depending upon the instructions provided with your search script. Most searches tend to use GET.

5. Set the Action field to point to the CGI script that will process the information contained in the search field.

6. You are now ready to add the search field to the form. Type a label for the field (see Figure 20.19).

7. Add a Text field, or in this case, a Menu List field, that can be used to type in the search term by selecting Insert → Form Objects → List/Menu.

8. Provide a name for your field. The search script may designate this name, but, in most cases, it can be any name you want.

9. Add the Submit button by selecting Insert → Form Objects → Button.

10. In the Submit Property Inspector select Type: Submit and label the button either Submit or Search so that its function is obvious to all of your site visitors.

You are now done creating the search form. The HTML code created by theses steps is shown in the following code:

```
<form name="SearchForm" method="get"
action="http://www.wallowacountychamber.com/cgi-bin/links/search.cgi">
 <p align="center">Search County Businesses and Events:</p>
    <p align="center">
      <select name="menu1"
          onChange="MM_jumpMenu('parent',this,0)">
        <option value="/pages/">
          - select a category -</option>
        <option value="/pages/Agriculture/">
          Agriculture</option>
        <option value="/pages/Arts/">Arts</option>
        <option value="/pages/Boosters/">
          Boosters</option>
        <option value="/pages/Business/">
          Businesses</option>
        <option value="/pages/Camping/">
          Camping</option>
        <option value="/pages/Churches">
          Churches</option>
        <option value="/pages/Communications/">
          Communications</option>
        <option value="/pages/Education/">
```

```
                    Education</option>
            <option value="/pages/Events">Events</option>
            <option value="/pages/Gift_Shops/">
                Gift Shops</option>
            <option value="/pages/Government/">
                Government</option>
            <option value="/pages/Insurance/">
                Insurance Agencys</option>
            <option value="/pages/Kids_Activities/">
                Kids Activities</option>
            <option value="/pages/Lodging/">
                Lodging</option>
            <option value="/pages/Medical/">
                Medical Services</option>
            <option value="/pages/Non_Profit_Orgs">
                Non Profit Groups</option>
            <option value="/pages/Outfitters_Tours/">
                Outfitters and Tours</option>
            <option value="/pages/Real_Estate/">
                Real Estate Agencys</option>
            <option value="/pages/Recreation/">
                Recreation</option>
            <option value="/pages/Restaurants/">
                Restaurants</option>
            <option value="/pages/Retail/">
                Retail Stores</option>
            <option value="/pages/Service_Orgs/">
                Service Groups</option>
            <option value="/pages/Timber/">
                Timber Companies</option>
            <option value="/pages/Transportation">
                Transportation</option>
        </select>
        <br>
    </p>
</form>
```

From Forms to Transactions

Forms are the fundamental means of interactivity on the Web, the primary way that a website's user may respond or give information. When interactions are tied to transactions, you have e-commerce—online behavior that generates payments. Chapter 21 takes you through the process of developing an e-commerce site.

## CHAPTER 21

Building an E-Commerce Site

Dreamweaver makes starting up an e-commerce website practically as easy as swiping a credit card, whether you're a business tycoon or a web design expert.

Because e-commerce websites have different goals, they require different strategies than informational or community-building websites. To reach your ultimate goal—getting potential customers to purchase your goods or services—you need to make products easy to find and select, provide good customer service, and process transactions.

In addition to setting up your site in the most appealing way, you will need to perform other strategies that fall into the category of traditional business activities; it's up to you to accomplish many basic tasks the old-fashioned way. Dreamweaver can't do much to help you write a good sales pitch, solve a shipping problem, or satisfy a customer who calls you with a question about your products. But the software *can* help you design your store's look-and-feel. Dreamweaver can also provide a starting point for important back-end activities like shopping carts.

This chapter explores the following topics:

- **Establishing a graphic identity**

- **Marketing your website**

- **Setting up a sales catalog**

- **Creating a shopping cart**

- **Processing online transactions**

Creating an Identity for an Online Store

All of the activities that go into creating a website—creating a look-and-feel, gathering compelling content, organizing the pages, going live, and performing ongoing maintenance—become more critical when your website represents some or all of your income. This section presents a quick rundown of what creating a graphic identity means when your goal is e-commerce.

E-commerce refers to the process of generating revenue through transactions that take place on the Internet. Business-to-consumer (B2C) e-commerce occurs between a website that has something to sell and an individual who wants to buy it. Business-to-business (B2B) e-commerce involves the exchange of supplies between companies.

Why care about developing a look and feel for your site? Here are a few reasons:

Trust and confidence A consistent graphic identity builds trust and confidence in customers who might be reluctant to shop and make purchases online due to security concerns.

Communication Your visual image strikes a chord with customers you have already identified as the people you want to reach, the people who are likely to need and buy what you have to offer.

Like any website, an e-commerce site conveys its look-and-feel through color, type, and graphics. Your company's name—not just your "brick and mortar" name, but your domain name—makes your store easy to find and revisit. Be sure to pick a short, understandable domain name that reflects what you do and is easy for your customers to remember and type into their browsers' Address box.

Creating a Logo

A *logo*—a small graphic image that includes the name of your company and, often, a drawing that visually represents the product or service that you provide—plays one of the most important roles in creating an online store's identity. (The logo, together with the site's look-and-feel, contribute to the online aspect of what's called the *branding* of your store.) A good logo gets your company's name across in a single glance while also establishing color and type choices that will be used consistently throughout the site.

If you create your own logo with, you can easily add it to your Dreamweaver website (for more on Fireworks, please refer to Part II). But suppose your organization already has a logo for its printed material that you or your designer have created using a popular program like Adobe Photoshop. Such an image can't be put online as a Photoshop file because it's too complex; it needs to be compressed using one of the standard image formats used on the Web—GIF, or JPEG, or PNG (see Chapter 10 for more information about these graphics formats).

With Fireworks, you can open images that are currently in non-web-friendly formats and that have multiple layers, such as the logo shown in Figure 21.1. Fireworks lets you optimize the image for the Web so that you can import it into Dreamweaver.

Using Color and Type

Every website needs good color and type selections. Other chapters have covered the basics of using color and type to get your message across. But you may be wondering what issues are specific to choosing color and type for an e-commerce site. It's all a matter of matching what your customers want to what you or your company has to offer.

Matching Customer Tastes

The best colors for an online store are ones to which your customers will respond positively, and ones that will not interfere with the presentation of your sales items. If you're looking to reach customers with conservative tastes, or if your products reflect traditional values, use simple color schemes. The Fairytale Brownies site (`http://www.brownies.com`) shown in Figure 21.2 doesn't do anything fancy. It uses a simple white background with American-as-apple-pie red and blue as accents. Other sites use vivid colors and garish backgrounds to reach a youthful audience looking for excitement—check out the Aggressive Skate and Snowboard site (`http://shop.store.yahoo.com/buyskates/index.html`) for an example of eye-catching type and color.

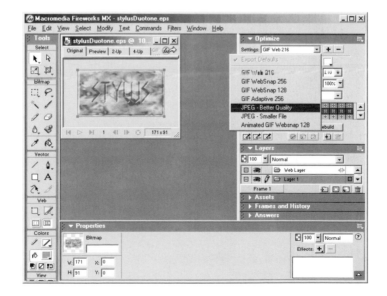

Figure 21.1

To prepare a logo for an e-commerce site, use Fireworks to import images in other file formats, such as this Encapsulated PostScript (EPS) image. Then use the Settings or file format drop-down lists to specify a format such as GIF or JPEG for the Web.

Figure 21.2

Successful e-commerce
sites match color and
type selections to the
tastes of their target
audience. The color and
type choices should
also match the product
being sold and the
emotion it produces in
the customer.

Matching Corporate Colors

The shipping company FedEx's website (`http://www.fedex.com`) has been around almost as long as the web itself and has won awards for e-business. Yet, the colors on the site aren't ones that naturally go together: orange and dark blue. However, the colors are those seen on the company trucks, uniforms, and envelopes.

If you are creating an e-commerce site that functions as an outgrowth of an existing brick-and-mortar business, your website can be a great place to build your brand recognition. To match colors your organization uses on its existing printed material, use the eyedropper. The Dreamweaver eyedropper lets you choose a color that you have scanned from one of your corporate publications. Click anywhere on your screen—even outside your Dreamweaver windows—to select the color with the eyedropper.

> A *pure play* is a company that operates only online. A *brick-and-mortar* business has a physical location where customers can shop. Many brick-and-mortar businesses are developing websites so that they can do *cross-channel e-commerce*—selling both online and through their physical store (for example, Barnes & Noble, Booksellers).

Let's say you've scanned a piece of stationery and the colors you see on screen are the ones you want to duplicate on your website. Start up Dreamweaver and follow these steps to do the copying.

1. Open the file that has the color you want to duplicate. This file can be in a program other than Dreamweaver, such as the web browser window shown in Figure 21.3.

2. Click the color box in Dreamweaver's Property Inspector. The color picker appears, and the mouse arrow turns into the eyedropper.

3. Hold down the mouse button when you move from the Dreamweaver window to the window that contains the color you want. (You need to have the browser window and Dreamweaver window both visible on your screen to do this.) This keeps the eyedropper on screen even when you move outside of Dreamweaver. When you pass the eyedropper over the desired color, that color appears in the color sample box in the upper-left corner of the color picker.

4. Release the mouse button. The selected color appears in the color box in the Property Inspector. You can now assign the color to text or images on your web page.

Style sheets give you another way to develop an online identity for your store by applying colors consistently from page to page. Cascading Style Sheets (CSS) also let you specify type size and leading (the space between lines) precisely, if you want to emulate the look of printed publications. (See Chapter 15 for more about style sheets.)

The key word is *emulate*. You won't be able to exactly duplicate printed type specs on your Dreamweaver web page. Nor should you; most of the typefaces used in print won't display on the Web unless viewers have those same fonts installed on their own computer systems, and there's no way you can guarantee that. Stick to common type fonts that your user is likely to have installed on their system, such as Arial, Verdana, or Times Roman.

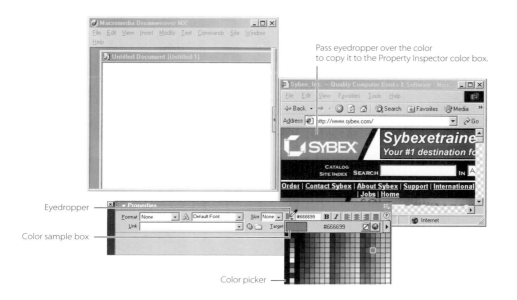

Figure 21.3

Dreamweaver helps you promote your brand through your e-commerce site. Use the eyedropper to copy your corporate colors, even if they appear in another application.

Marketing Your Site

An e-commerce site owner needs to do targeted, smart marketing to build traffic. Traffic can make or break an e-commerce site. Attract enough visitors, and you can earn revenue by charging other businesses to place advertisements on your site. Attract shoppers who are already looking for what you have to offer, and you make sales. This section runs through the basics of marketing your online store.

Listing with Search Services

How do potential customers find their way through the scores of web stores to the one you've just set up with Dreamweaver? Chances are they search for you or your products by entering a word or phrase in a search engine's search box, for example: `http://www.google.com`. When they submit the information, a search program scours a database of web pages and their contents and returns pages that contains the desired word or phrase.

BE A PROFILER: IDENTIFY YOUR IDEAL CUSTOMERS

One of the most important aspects of online marketing is something you need do on your own before you even start up Dreamweaver. Know exactly whom you want to reach. Only when you identify those people can you market your goods and services to them.

How do you get to know them? Here are some suggestions:

- Find them online. Single out websites where your likely customers hang out. Lurk in newsgroups to get a feel for their concerns; ask them questions in chat rooms.

- Create customer profiles. Try to describe three of your customers in as much detail as possible. Tell yourself where they live, how they dress, what they do for a living. Print out the profiles, paste them on your bulletin board near your computer, and keep them in mind when you create content for your site.

- Talk to people who already buy what you have to offer at your competitors' stores.

- Talk to experts in your field.

Most people who shop online are looking to save time and money. They are too busy to drive, park, and trudge through shopping malls. They want efficiency and good service as well as good value. Check out the demographics information at CyberAtlas (`http://www.cyberatlas.com`). You'll find some useful information there about online shoppers and their characteristics. Once you know who these people are, you can then market to them.

Search services use special programs that scour the Web's contents and build a database that anyone can search. If you tap your toes long enough, your site will probably be added to the search service's database automatically. To enhance the effectiveness of this type of search, add as many descriptive words about your site into the keywords on your site. This way, you'll get pulled up more often by web searches (more about this can be found in the "Adding Keywords" section that follows).

But instead of just waiting for a search engine to list you, you can register your site and add yourself to the database. To register, you fill out a form that provides the service with your store's name and URL, as well as a description of what you do. As you may have guessed, filling out each service's form can be time consuming. You can streamline the process by using a service that submits your site's information to multiple search sites at once. Some will submit your information to a handful of sites for free and to a larger number of sites for a fee. Check out SiteOwner.com's Submit It! Free service (`http://www.siteowner.com/sifree.cfm`).

If you can get your site listed on Yahoo! (`http://www.yahoo.com/`), you'll get visitors because this indispensable index to the Internet is so popular. It's worth taking the time to register there, though it can take weeks to get your site registered with them, and the staff people who review applicants' sites might even reject you. Ouch!

Adding Keywords

The way you present your online store is an essential component of your marketing success. For that reason, be sure you go behind the scenes to add keywords to the home page of your site.

Keywords are a series of terms you create that describe your business or the goods or services you sell. For a site that sells hardware, you might add keywords like `hardware`, `tools`, `repair`, `building`, `electrical`, `paint`, and so on. Adding keywords increases the frequency with which you site appears in a search service's list of results. If the user's search term matches one of your keywords, your site is presented in the list.

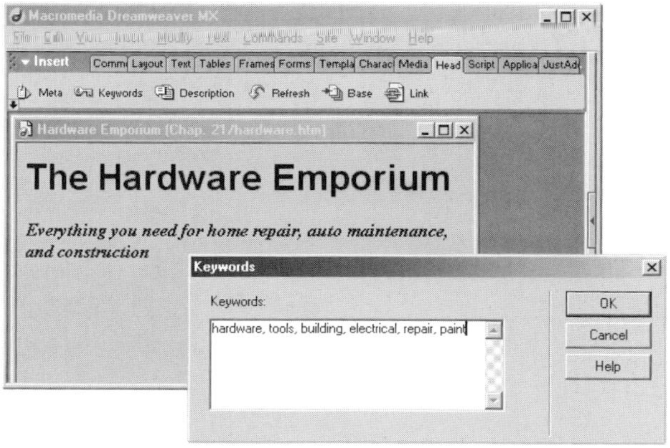

You add keywords by clicking the Keywords button in the Head section of the Insert bar (see Figure 21.4). Type the keywords in the Keywords box of the Insert Keywords dialog box, and then click OK.

Advertising with Banners

Advertising on the web is becoming a big business. The most common online ads take the form of rectangular graphics (usually one inch by four or five inches in size)

Figure 21.4

Adding keywords to your site's home page increases your chances of being found by a potential customer using a search service.

called *banners*. They appear on a web page and publicize someone else's website. When viewers click the graphics, their browsers go to the sites being advertised. The site that displays the ad usually charges a fee for displaying these banners. The fee is either based on the popularity of the site doing the displaying, the number of times the page bearing the ad is viewed, or the number of times visitors click through to the advertiser's site (these are called *clickthroughs*). Banners can be expensive to place on sites that receive a lot of traffic—for instance, Yahoo! charges thousands of dollars for the privilege of placing ads on some of its more popular index pages.

You can save money and still market your business by exchanging banners with other websites. First, you need to create a banner for your own site, either in Fireworks or by using an online service such as the Banner Generator (`http://engine.coder.com/creations/banner`). Once you have your banner, you can trade it with other websites using a service such as Microsoft bCentral's free Banner Network (`http://www.bcentral.com/products/bn/default.asp`).

A Dreamweaver extension called Add To Favorites lets you take a proactive approach to making your website easier to find. Once you install the extension, you identify a link or image on one of your web pages and then add the behavior to it. The behavior causes a dialog box to appear when the visitor clicks the link or image on one of your web pages. The dialog box gives the user who uses Microsoft Internet Explorer the option of instantly adding your site to the Favorites menu. If the user clicks OK, your site is automatically added to the list of favorites. Go to the Macromedia Exchange for Dreamweaver page (`http://www.macromedia.com/exchange/dreamweaver`) and search for the Add To Favorites extension.

Processing Transactions

Many activities go into making an e-commerce operation successful. But there's only one that really counts as far as your bottom line is concerned: getting your customers to close the deal. Online shoppers like to be able to complete purchases within a few mouse clicks. The closer you can get to making the transaction process a no-brainer, the more likely you are to generate sales.

This section discusses how to use Dreamweaver as a starting point to create the essentials of completing purchases online—a sales catalog, a shopping cart, and a credit card processing system.

Creating an Online Catalog

Many e-commerce websites force shoppers to do an excessive amount of searching just to figure out how to purchase something. The first thing you can do to avoid such confusion is to create a well-organized sales catalog. An effective online catalog

- Consists of a set of web pages that presents sales items with clear descriptions and (usually) photos.

- Contains buttons or links that enable the shopper to store the items in a shopping cart for later purchase.

- Includes links to other parts of the company's catalog, as well as to all other parts of the website, so that the shopper can jump from one sales category within the catalog (such as men's formalwear) to another (such as children's outerwear).

Dreamweaver's predesigned web page components include several catalog layouts. They contain the features that are essential to virtually all online catalogs, and you should browse through them before you start to create catalog pages on your own. Open the site you want to contain the catalog, and then follow these steps:

1. Choose File → New to open the New Document dialog box.

2. Click Page Designs in the Category column.

3. Click one of the Catalog options at the top of the Page Designs column to view a preview and description on the right side of the dialog box.

4. Click the catalog layout you want, and click Create. The catalog page is created.

For example, if you click Commerce: Product Catalog A, the layout shown in Figure 21.5 appears. You can add your images and type your descriptions, replacing the placeholder text.

When you think about catalogs, you probably think about selling discrete consumer goods. However, you can describe your services if you are in a service field and don't sell individual commodities. The most important thing is to anticipate what customers want from your catalog. Ideally, your website should provide customers with the look-and-feel of walking into a store and approaching a sales clerk who will handle the entire transaction in real time—with no delays in processing, with strong customer service, and with complete answers to questions.

Some web hosting services that specialize in e-commerce, like Microsoft bCentral (http://www.bcentral.com) for small business solutions, include utilities that streamline the process of creating a catalog. If you don't want to create your catalog from scratch, consider signing up with such a service.

Figure 21.5

Dreamweaver MX provides predesigned layouts you can use to create a sales catalog.

Keep It Fresh

If you update your catalog on a regular basis, you give your customers an incentive to return to your site. Be sure to include links to new items, seasonal sales, and inventory clearances in a prominent place on your home page.

Don't be reluctant to sprinkle words like New! or Sale! liberally around your home page or other parts of your site. Also consider compiling a mailing list of your customers' e-mail addresses

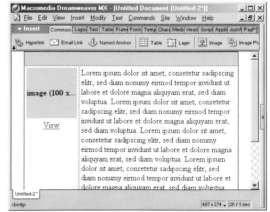

so that you can send them announcements of upcoming promotions to remind them of your site and to encourage them to revisit it—Amazon.com does this on a weekly basis, sending out ideas about what you might like that is new, and what items in their warehouse of inventory are on sale.

Keep It Organized

Divide your sales items into categories and subcategories, if that's possible. This not only makes your total selection seem less intimidating, but it makes it easier for the shopper to immediately hone in on the specific item that they want. You can set up jump menus (see Chapter 18) to lead people from one category to another instantly.

Make It Complete

Shoppers on the Web have an insatiable desire for information. Don't hold back when it comes to images and descriptions of your products. At the same time, you don't have to present everything all at once. In the catalog page shown in Figure 21.6, you see a thumbnail of the product, a brief description, and the price. Shoppers can click the small image to view a larger version, and they can click the links in the right-hand column for further product details. Related products are presented at the bottom of the page.

It doesn't matter whether each catalog page contains a single item or a group of items—only that it's easy to navigate the site and do the shopping. It's generally better to present only the bare essentials about an item on a catalog page, while giving shoppers the option of clicking elsewhere to find out more. Inviting prospective customers to explore your site further keeps them involved; the longer they stay on your e-commerce site, the more likely they'll make a purchase.

Figure 21.6

The page from the Sybex online book catalog contains all the essentials.

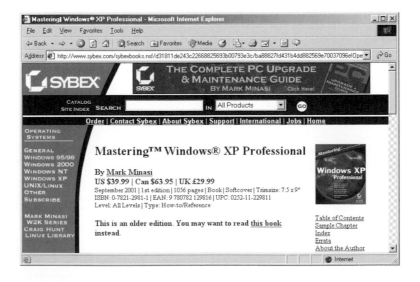

Creating a Shopping Cart

A *shopping cart* is software that performs the same function as the metal device you push around a brick-and-mortar store. Dreamweaver doesn't come with a built-in shopping cart. You have several options for adding one to your e-commerce website. You can write your own shopping cart program and install it on the server that hosts your site; you can add an extension to Dreamweaver that adds a cart to your site (see the tutorial at the end of this chapter); or you can choose to host your site with a company that provides you with a cart as part of its services.

When combined with an online catalog, the shopping cart performs another set of essential e-commerce functions. First, it enables shoppers to make selections. By clicking Add to Cart, or a similarly named button, items are stored in the cart (see Figure 21.7). Once shoppers have added an item to the cart, they have the option of either continuing to shop for more selections or proceeding to the checkout area.

The cart stores the catalog items that customers select in a safe location—a secure server that uses encryption to protect customer information. When the customer decides to check out, the cart totals up the selected items and gives the shopper the option of rejecting items that they don't want. Finally, the cart contains a button labeled Proceed to Checkout that sends the shopper's browser to an area where payment and shipping information is requested so that the transaction can be completed. Figure 21.8 shows Rich Media Technologies, Inc.'s JustAddCommerce shopping cart, which can be installed as a Dreamweaver extension. It's used as the shopping cart for The Silver Connection (`http://www.silverconnection.com`), an online jewelry store.

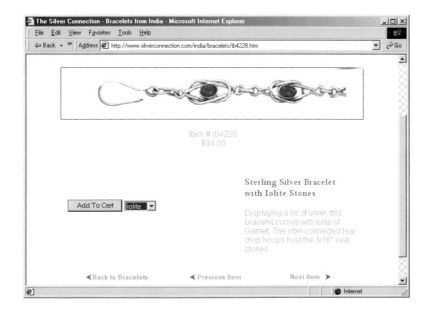

Figure 21.7

A shopping cart gives e-commerce website owners an Add To Cart button that they can add to each page of their sales catalog. Shoppers click the button to store the selected item in the cart until checkout.

The version of JustAddCommerce that you download from Macromedia Exchange doesn't include any credit card processing. However, another version of JustAddCommerce does enable you to apply for a merchant account so that you can do real-time processing online if you don't already have this ability. This is called the JustAddCommerce Real Time Processing, and it costs $399. Find out more at `http://www.richmediatech.com/justaddcommerce/index.asp`.

The New Document dialog box includes a shopping cart layout you can add in a flash. Just open the web page that you want to contain the shopping cart, position the cursor where you want the cart to appear, and follow these steps:

1. Choose File → New to open the New Document dialog box.

2. Click Page Designs in the Category column.

3. Click Commerce: Shopping Cart in the Page Designs column.

4. Click Create.

A shopping cart layout appears in the current page (see Figure 21.9).

Processing Credit Card Payments

Some shoppers, squeamish about online security, prefer to pay for their web-based purchases by phoning or faxing their credit card billing information and shipping address. For that reason, you should include your phone and fax numbers on your web pages. But you should also make it possible for shoppers to follow their impulses and complete transactions in just a minute or two by submitting their credit card data to you online. There are two options for obtaining what you need: you can do it yourself, or you can sign up with other online businesses that will do some or all of the work for you.

Doing It Yourself

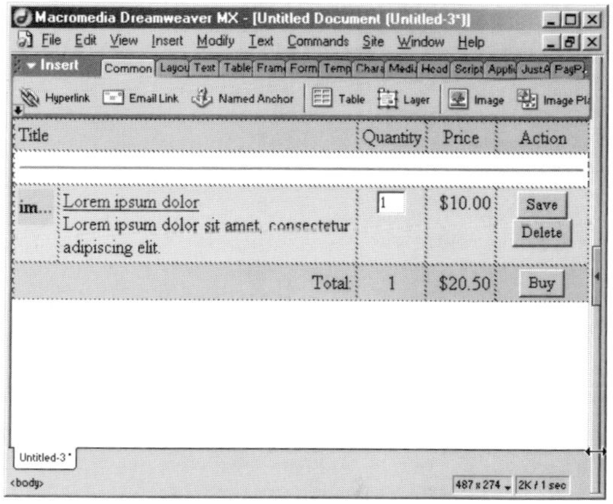

If you're the do-it-yourself type and you want to process your customers' sensitive financial information, you need to set yourself up with the following:

- A merchant account with a financial institution that can charge the customer's credit card and credit your account. Expect to wait anywhere from several days to several weeks for your application to be approved; you'll also have to pay application fees of $300 to $800 as well as "discount fees" of 1 to 4 percent per transaction.

- A secure server that protects your customers' credit card numbers and other personal information with Secure Sockets Layer (SSL) encryption.

Figure 21.9

Dreamweaver MX includes a predesigned shopping cart you can add with a single mouse click, and then customize to suit your needs.

- Point-of-sale (POS) hardware or software that transmits your customers' credit card numbers to your bank. The hardware device is a terminal of the sort that most retail stores use. The software is a program like Authorizer (`http://www.atomic-software.com/othersite/windows.html`). Both communicate with the bank through your modem.

It's not difficult to find online businesses that are eager to set you up with merchant accounts. (Perhaps you've received unsolicited e-mail messages from some of these organizations already.) You can check out a well-established online financial institution like Wells Fargo Bank (`http://www.wellsfargo.com`) or scan the lengthy list of merchant account providers on Yahoo!'s site (at `http://dir.yahoo.com/Business_and_Economy/Business_to_Business/Financial_Services/Transaction_Clearing/Credit_Card_Merchant_Services/`).

If you have an existing store and already process credit cards, you should probably stick with that bank for your online transactions. The advantage of using your current financial institution is that it saves you the trouble of having to shop around for a credit card vendor, and as an existing customer, you're more likely to have your merchant account application approved.

But if you're starting up a new web-based business, consider the many shortcuts to the merchant account application process that are provided by e-commerce hosting companies. You don't have to shop around for a financial institution; you don't have to convince them that your online business is a "real" one; and since the merchant already has an affiliation with your hosting service, you're likely to be approved. But be sure to read the fine print— credit card merchants affiliated with e-commerce hosts are likely to carry the same "hidden" charges such as application fees and "discount fees" as traditional banks. (The term "discount fee" is commonly used to describe the charges the financial institution makes you pay it for each transaction it processes.)

Letting Your Host Do the Processing

You can save yourself some time and trouble by renting web space on the system of another company that already has credit card processing systems in place. In this situation, you pay a fee to a website that sets you up with a merchant account, provides you with the forms you need, gives you space on a secure server, verifies the customer information, and processes the data.

At Yahoo! Store, for instance, you pay a $49.95 per month for a hosting fee, plus 10 cents per item per month, plus a 0.5 percent fee for each transaction, and a 3.5 percent revenue share on transactions that originate on the Yahoo! Network. Despite all these charges, being a Yahoo! merchant has its advantages. For instance, as a Yahoo! Store merchant, you can use an affiliated credit card payment service called Paymentech, and the process of applying for a merchant account will be streamlined. Paymentech processes applications in three days or less, so you will be up and running in no time. However, there are charges here too. Paymentech charges a monthly service fee of $22.95 for processing credit card purchases. In addition, it offers you a "discount fee" of 2.32 percent plus a 20-cent transaction fee to MasterCard International Inc. or Visa International as well.

Similarly, if you pay $24.95 per month to become a Microsoft bCentral merchant, you can apply to Cardservice International to become a credit card merchant. If you are a bCentral customer and have 10 sales or less per month, Cardservice will process credit card transactions for 3.5 percent of each transaction plus a fee of 50 cents per transaction, but it won't charge you a monthly fee. If you have more than 10 sales per month, Cardservice charges $19.95 per month, offers you a 2.35 percent transaction fee, and charges you 20 cents per transaction.

Obtaining a merchant account through your web host doesn't mean you're not involved with completing transactions. On the contrary, you need to answer questions, handle returns, make sure items are shipped, and be able to track shipments if they're lost or delayed.

Having read about all the fees you have to pay to be a credit card merchant, you might wonder why you should go through all the trouble in the first place. The main reason is that online shoppers love to purchase with credit cards. Filling out forms and clicking a few buttons is what they're used to. If you force shoppers to send in checks or phone in credit card information, you won't get as many sales.

Some online merchants prefer to process credit card payments themselves rather than leaving the work to a processing service. When they do this, they assume responsibility for making sure that the credit card number is valid, that the customer's name is correct, and that the credit card limit has not been reached. That way, they can be on the watch for obvious signs of fraud, such as a billing address in one country and a shipping address in another country.

Some credit cards, like American Express and Discover, may not be covered by the merchant account you obtain through your web host. If you want to accept these cards, you need to apply to the credit card companies separately.

Hands On: Create a Shopping Cart

As stated in the section "Creating a Shopping Cart," the New Document dialog box includes a predesigned shopping cart design that you can add to a web page in a flash. But that's only the front end of the cart, the part that the user sees. To get the cart to actually function, you need to manually capture session variables yourself using ColdFusion, ASP, or ASP.NET (see Chapters 25 and 27).

Alternatively, you can add full shopping cart functionality to your e-commerce website using WebAssist.com's easy-to-use WA PayPal eCommerce Toolkit extension to Dreamweaver. The extension creates Add to Cart and other buttons to your site. The buttons are linked to the website of PayPal (`http://www.paypal.com`), a popular online payment service. PayPal acts as a payment broker, accepting credit card payments on your behalf without your having to apply for a merchant account. You do have to sign up for an account with PayPal, and you have to pay a transaction fee on any sales you make.

Before you download and install the software, be sure to you've obtained the Extension Manager as described in Chapter 32. Then go to the WebAssist.com home page (`http://www.webassist.com/home/home.asp`) and click the WA PayPal eCommerce Toolkit link. Your browser displays the WA PayPal eCommerce Toolkit extension page. Click the Get Now! button to begin the download process. Once you download the extension, double-click the file to install it. The Extension Manager window opens with information about how to access the extension within Dreamweaver.

The WA PayPal eCommerce Toolkit is free, and it comes in a file that is only 123K in size. At this writing, the product's home page indicated that it supported Dreamweaver 4, but it works with MX as well.

After you read this information, follow these steps to add a shopping cart extension to Dreamweaver.

1. After you have installed the WA PayPal eCommerce Toolkit, in order to use it within Dreamweaver, you need to first quit Dreamweaver, if it is already running, and then restart it.

2. Open the catalog page on your website on which you want to include the shopping cart functionality.

3. Choose Window → Insert to display the Insert bar, if necessary, and then click the PayPal tab, which is added to the Insert bar when you install the extension.

4. The PayPal tab contains three buttons. They enable you to add an Add to Cart button, a Single-Item Purchase button, and a View Cart button. To begin, click the PayPal AC Button.

These steps assume that you've already set up a business account with PayPal. In order for the system to work, however, your customers need to be PayPal customers, too. PayPal is a popular system used frequently on auction sites like eBay, and it doesn't take long to sign up to be a registered PayPal user. But customers who aren't already familiar with PayPal might be scared off by the extra step involved, and you should provide an alternate means of purchase for them.

5. When the Insert PayPal Add to Cart Button dialog box appears, enter the e-mail address you used to obtain a PayPal account in the PayPal Account box, then click Next.

6. In the next dialog box, click the button next to the type of Add to Cart button you want, then click Next.

7. In the next dialog box, enter the information about the product that the shopper will select by clicking this button, such as its name, product number, the price, and so on. When the shopper clicks the button, this information will be stored in PayPal's shopping cart.

8. Click Next to go the next dialog box, where you have the chance to enter the URL of the your company logo so that your customers will see it on your PayPal payment pages.

9. Click Next to move to the next dialog box, where you can enter the URL of the pages you want your customers to see after they have completed a payment (such as your home page).

10. Click Next. The next dialog box lets you review the information you've entered. When you've done so, click OK to close the Insert PayPal Add to Cart Button dialog box. An Add to Cart button should now appear in the Dreamweaver window. You can cut and paste it as needed on your catalog web page.

11. Repeat steps 3 through 9 to add a Single-Item Purchase button and a View Cart button to your pages. When you're done, return to Dreamweaver. The checkout form with the options you just specified appears in the Dreamweaver window. You can then customize the form using Dreamweaver's form tools.

12. When you're done customizing the form and the Add To Cart buttons you may want to use, you've created the basic "front end" for your shopping cart.

Now you can upload your catalog pages to your web server as described in Chapter 30.

The preceding steps have led you through the process of using Dreamweaver to create the front end of a fully functional e-commerce shopping cart. You made your cart fully functional by uploading your checkout form to the PayPal network (that's the back end). Now all you have to do is administer your website and make those sales!

Putting the e- In Everything

Sure, a basic e-commerce storefront is just the tip of the iceberg when it comes to e-business, but that's what some of your customers will be looking for. For more sophisticated business-to-business, business-to-employee, or business-to-supplier sites (often called corporate or enterprise portals) you'll want to pull together most of what there is to learn in this book, from designing pages, to working with forms, databases, and XML, and finally to administration, which is coming up.

## PART V

Developing Web Applications

With this MX version, *Dreamweaver has become more than a designer's tool for constructing file-based websites: it is now a full-featured development environment for database-backed web applications. In this part, we show you how to set up web applications in Dreamweaver; how to customize, streamline, and automate your coding workspace; how to tie your pages to database tables; how to work with ColdFusion sites; how to incorporate the XML and XHTML standards into your site; and how to work with cutting-edge technologies such as .NET and other web services standards.*

CHAPTER 22 ■ Building Web Applications

CHAPTER 23 ■ Handcrafting Your Code

CHAPTER 24 ■ Database Connectivity

CHAPTER 25 ■ Working with ColdFusion

CHAPTER 26 ■ Working with XML and XHTML

CHAPTER 27 ■ Working with Emerging Technologies—Web Services and .NET

Building Web Applications

In Part I, before you got started making pages, you learned how to set up a website in Dreamweaver. If you're building a dynamic, database-backed site (also known as a web application), there are a few more steps you will need to take to set up a testing server. Dreamweaver handles a number of different popular server models (ASP, JSP, and PHP with MySQL), and the process for each is analogous, though the specific steps vary somewhat. This chapter will show you how to get set up so that you can start coding your site.

- Building and testing web applications

- Choosing between JSP, ASP, ASP.NET, ColdFusion, and PHP

- Working with a local or remote web server

- Working with an application server

- Setting up the site in Dreamweaver

Designing and Testing Web Applications

The difference between developing web applications and developing static sites in Dreamweaver starts with the setup. You set up the local site the same way for web apps as you do for non-database websites (as discussed in Chapter 3). The remote site can be the same if you plan to test your applications on a remote server, or it can be set up to point to a web server running on your local computer or network. Finally, you set up your application server as the test server so that you can see your dynamic processes in action as you build them.

Choosing a Supported Server Model

To build a web application, you have to decide what type of server technology it will run on. The biggest factor in this decision may be your client's, your own, or an existing infrastructure. If you have to build or install the application yourself, then consider issues such as budget, compatibility, and future scalability. Dreamweaver supports a pretty broad range of server models, from Microsoft's latest web services gambit (.NET), through Macromedia's own ColdFusion server, to open source frameworks based on Java or Apache/PHP/MySQL:

The JSP Model JSP stands for Java Server Pages. JSP is popular with Unix users and non-Microsoft shops.

The ASP and ASP.NET models ASP stands for Active Server Pages and is a Microsoft standard. The .NET framework is another MS standard (for web services). See Chapter 27 for a further discussion of .NET site development.

The ColdFusion model ColdFusion sites run on the ColdFusion MX application server using the ColdFusion scripting language. Dreamweaver is now closely integrated with ColdFusion because ColdFusion MX is another Macromedia application in the same suite of products.

The PHP model PHP is an open source scripting language and application server most often used with MySQL databases. The term PHP, by the way, is the just another "recursive acronym" (good examples include GNU, which stands for Gnu's Not Unix, and PINE, which stands for Pine is not Elm). Officially it stands for "PHP: Hypertext Preprocessor." More cleverly it's also said to stand for "Pre- Hypertext Processor."

Setting Up Your Web Server

In order to run an application server for the purposes of testing your site in production, you first need a web server. If you use Windows, you may have a web server (PWS or IIS) already installed or even running on your machine. If you use Mac OS X (10.1 or later), then you already have the Apache server installed. You may also prefer to work with a web server installed at a remote location.

Though ASP sites can be developed on PWS or any version of IIS, ASP.NET sites require IIS 5 running on Windows 2000 or XP Pro systems. You can still develop ASP.NET sites anywhere, but you need the aforementioned setup to test them as you go.

Setting Up Your Application Server

You'll use the application server to test your site while it's in development. Most application servers can be downloaded and installed on a local or network machine. You may also be working with a host or client who has the app server you need installed on a remote site.

Table 22.1 shows some web locations where popular application servers can be obtained. If any of the URLs listed in the table are no longer active, check the website for this book, `http://dreamweaversavvy.com/` for updated links.

When setting up an application server, be sure to define a root folder for the application you're building.

APPLICATION SERVER	DOWNLOAD SITES
JRun	`http://www.macromedia.com/software/jrun`
IBM WebSphere	`http://www-4.ibm.com/software/webservers/appserv/download.html`
Tomcat	`http://jakarta.apache.org/tomcat/`
Sun Chili!Soft ASP	`http://www.chilisoft.com/chiliasp/default.asp`
Microsoft .NET Framework	`http://msdn.microsoft.com/netframework/downloads/`
ColdFusion MX	`http://www.macromedia.com/software/coldfusion/`
PHP	`http://www.php.net/downloads.php` (and, for Mac OS X users who want to run PHP on their built-in Apache server) `http://www.entropy.ch/software/macosx/php/`

Table 22.1

App Servers and Download Sites

Setting Up Your Web Application as a Dreamweaver Site

Once you've got the infrastructure in place, setting up your dynamic site or web application in Dreamweaver is no more complicated than it is for setting up an ordinary static site full of HTML pages.

Defining the Local Folder

Defining the site starts with setting up your local folder for staging copies of your files, which is really not any different from how you would do it for a static site (see Chapter 3 for more discussion on this).

Select Site → New Site. This brings up the Site Definition dialog box. If the wizard is showing, click Advanced. You should automatically start in the Local Info category, but if you don't, click Local Info (see Figure 22.1).

Give your site a memorable name, browse to the local root folder, and indicate the eventual URL of the site for link-checking purposes.

Defining the Remote (Root) Folder

Next, set up access to your web server. Choose the Remote Info category, and start by choosing an Access type (see Figure 22.2).

Here's how to choose the right Access type:

FTP Choose FTP if the web server is at a remote host without any special source-code security database running.

Local/Network Choose this if the web server is on your local computer or network.

RDS Choose this option if the web server is a ColdFusion MX server.

SourceSafe Database Choose this if you are collaborating on a project where the code is stored in a SourceSafe database.

WebDAV Choose WebDAV if your code is secured using the WebDAV extensions to HTTP.

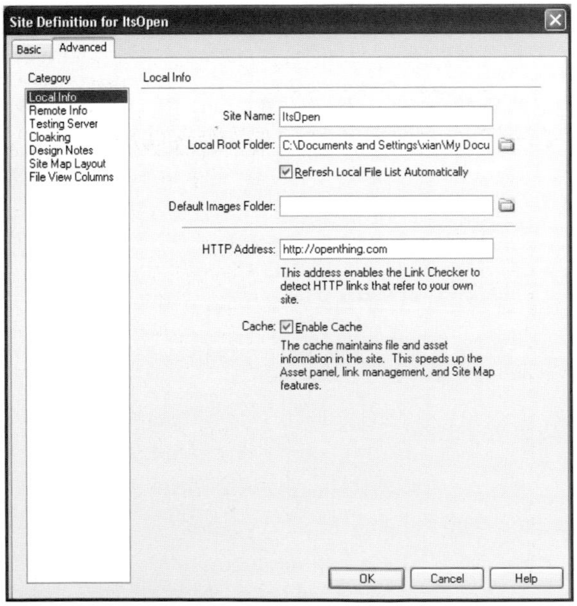

Figure 22.1

Always start with the Local Info category in the Advanced tab of the Site Definition dialog box.

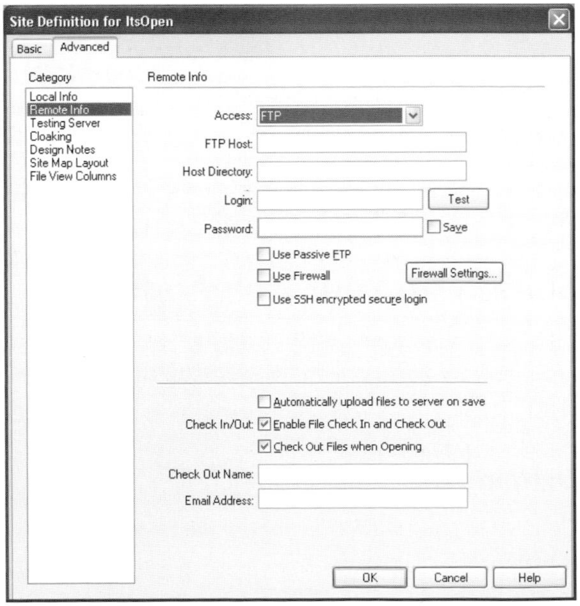

Figure 22.2

Set up your web server as the remote site.

Depending on your choice, indicate the path to the local/network server, the FTP login information, or the RDS, SourceSafe, or WebDAV settings (path, username, and password).

If you're collaborating on this site, click the Check In/Check Out option. (RDS, Source-Safe, and WebDAV will all require Check In/Out automatically.) See Chapter 3 for more discussion of these remote setup options.

Defining the Testing Server

Finally, set up your applications server as the testing server for your site so that Dreamweaver will know how (where) to process your dynamic components. To do so, choose the Testing Server category in the Edit Sites dialog box (see Figure 22.3).

For your server model, choose one of the following options:

ASP JavaScript For ASP sites using JavaScript as the scripting language.

ASP VBScript For ASP sites using VBScript as the scripting language.

ASP.NET C# For ASP.NET sites using C# ("C-sharp") as the scripting language.

ASP.NET VB For ASP.NET sites using Visual Basic as the scripting language.

ColdFusion For ColdFusion sites. (If you choose ColdFusion, you must tell Dreamweaver whether the site contains Dreamweaver MX pages, Dreamweaver UltraDev pages, or both.)

JSP For JSP sites.

PHP MySQL For PHP sites (MySQL is the only database type supported for PHP sites).

After choosing a server model, you need tell Dreamweaver how to get access to the testing server and where to find the site's root folder on the testing server:

Access Choose FTP if the application server is remote or Local/Network if the application server is on your local computer or network.

- If you choose FTP, Dreamweaver will suggest the FTP server and path to your remote server. Use that if the test server is the same server as the remote server. Otherwise, replace it with the correct FTP server and path information for your testing server.

- If you choose Local/Network, Dreamweaver will suggest the local site's root folder for the Testing Server Folder. Use that or browse to the correct local folder.

Figure 22.3

Tell Dreamweaver the server model you're working with and the location of your application server here.

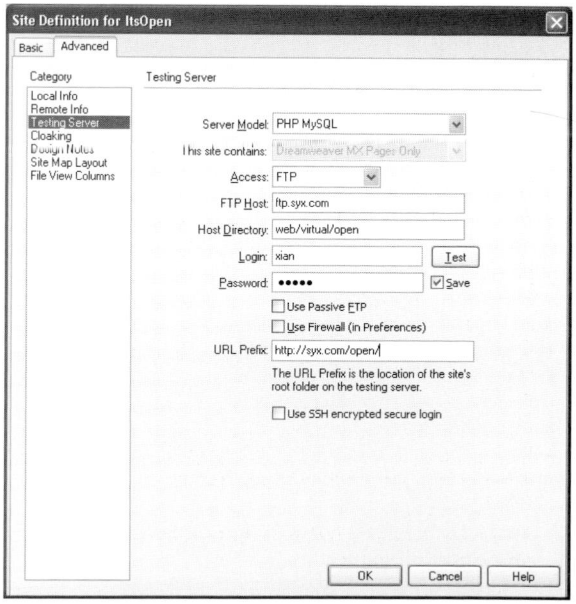

URL Prefix For URL Prefix, indicate the site's root folder. This is the web address of the application server, including the root folder specified when you (or someone else) set up the app server. If the app server is on your own computer, the URL will start with `http://localhost/`.

> If the root folder of the application server is not within your site hierarchy, you will need to create a symbolic link (also called a *shortcut* in Windows or an *alias* on the Mac) to the directory, and then indicate the symbolic link here.

Then click OK. You're now ready to start building a dynamic site.

Connecting to the Database

The final ingredient in your web application is your database. After the testing server is up and running and the application server is working, you'll need to connect to a database to actually get anything dynamic happening on your pages. With an active database connection, you can build pages that take input from forms and return results that are reported out directly from the data tables. Refer to Chapter 24 to see how to work with databases in detail.

Delving into the Code

If you're building a web application, then you'll probably be writing some scripts for accessing the data in your database and displaying it dynamically at the site. The more you get into working with the code, as opposed to page layout and other design issues, the more you may want to work in Code view. Chapter 23 shows you how to set up a coding environment to your liking in Dreamweaver. If you'd rather plow ahead and start hooking up to databases, skip to Chapter 24.

Handcrafting Your Code

Dreamweaver gives you the option of seeing how the sausage is made, or not. It's up to you. But if you're going to be coding applications, you have no choice: you have to see, touch, and smell your code. OK, there's no way to literally smell it, but trust me, I've seen some mighty stinky code.

So, though Dreamweaver was clearly created to automate and insulate you from the raw code of any website you're designing, the fact is that it has evolved into a powerful, timesaving coding environment as well.

Here are some of the issues we'll be discussing in this chapter:

- **Setting up your coding environment**

- **Writing code longhand or with a plethora of shortcuts**

- **Printing your code (finally!)**

- **Working with an external or integrated editor**

- **Working with tag libraries and custom tags**

- **Debugging your code**

The Ergonomics of Coding

Working with code involves an entirely different approach to the project. You see it as lines of code, whether script files, HTML pages, or database queries. The minute-to-minute habits that define the actual real-world user experience for humans using a piece of software will be different when you are working with code than they are when you work from a design-centered perspective. So, if you prefer to work directly with code and want to use Dreamweaver as your *coding environment*, set aside a little time (less than half an hour) to decide how you'll view, enter, and edit code.

Viewing the Code

If you plan to do most of your work directly at the code level, then you'll probably work in Code view (or possibly Code and Design view but with the design portion kept pretty short) using Design view only for previewing a page, if that. To choose a view, do one of the following:

- To view just code, select View → Code.
- To view both code and design, select View → Code and Design. (To reverse the positions of the code and design panes, select View → Design View on Top.)

If you're more comfortable viewing design in one window and code in another, choose Windows → Others → Code Inspector.

Figure 23.1

Designating code-only file formats

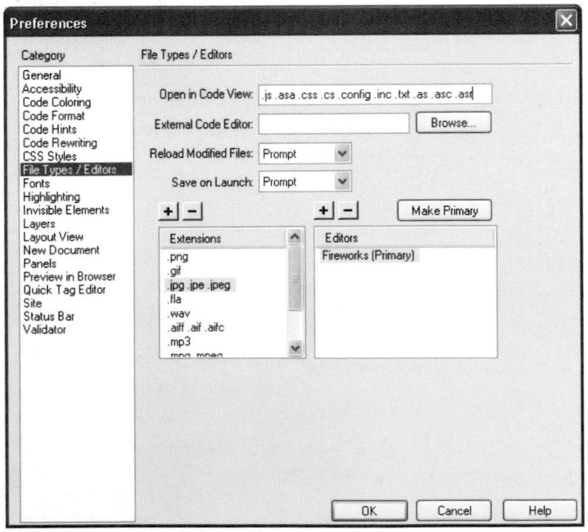

Some documents, such as script files, only make sense in Code view. They don't present visual information and therefore don't have a Design view. You can tell Dreamweaver that files with specific extensions should always be opened in a code-only view (the Code and Design and Design options are disabled). To do so, go to your Preferences dialog box (Ctrl + U/Cmd + U), and in the File Types / Editors category, add the file extension (preceded by a dot, as in `.txt`) to the list in the Open in Code View box, and then click OK (see Figure 23.1).

Windows-using code jockeys may want to choose the HomeSite/Coders variation of the integrated MX workspace (as discussed in Chapter 3).

Code Display Options

If you are new to coding, you can probably skim or skip this section because Dreamweaver's default settings for code display are as good as any to start with. If you have some longstanding preferences for the look and structure of your code, possibly developed while you were working in some other coding environment or application, then this section will tell you how to overrule the default preferences for such options. First, though, there are a few simple Code view options you can toggle easily from the View → Code View Options submenu shown here.

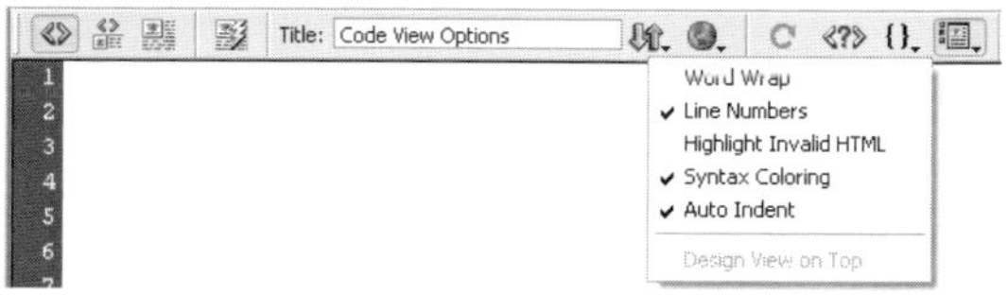

> In Code and Design view, additional options will appear on this pop-up menu (Hide All Visual Aids, Visual Aids, Head Content, Rulers, Grid, even Tracing Image and Design View on Top), but none of these deal with how the code is displayed, so we will ignore those options here.

Word Wrap This option makes sure that lines are visible even if the code window is narrow (see the next section for setting limits for hard word-wrapping when entering code).

Line Numbers This option shows or hides the numbers (We like to see them—it makes it easier to discuss the code).

Highlight Invalid HTML This is what it sounds like. The only reason you might want to turn this off is if you are deliberately inserting fragmented HTML, as you would do when you are expecting embedded scripts to complete the pages dynamically when they are loading.

Syntax Coloring This turns the colors on and off. We like syntax coloring. For us, it makes the code easier to read.

Auto Indent It is a good idea to use this option to automatically structure your code. It keeps things nice and tidy.

For advanced code-format, structure, and display options, start by going to the Preferences dialog box (Ctrl + U/Cmd + U). The four categories related to Code preferences are clustered together (see Figure 23.2).

The Code Format Category

The Code Format options are generally straightforward, but the context of each may not be clear. Remember, features accumulate in mature software to meet recognized needs for both large and small numbers of users. You may

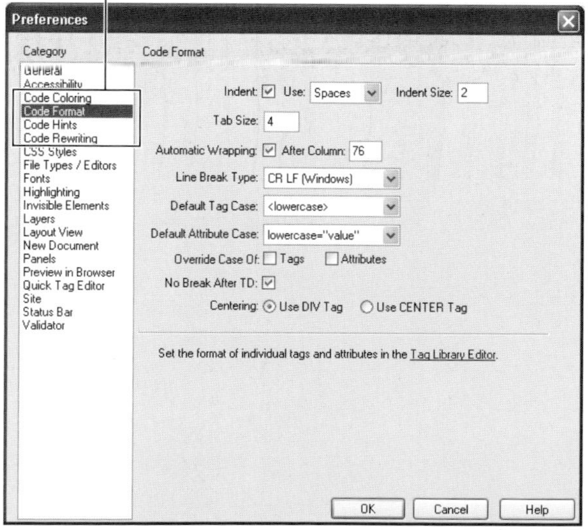

Figure 23.2

Code Format is the primary code-related category in the Preferences dialog box, but there are three others.

not care about some of the options, which is fine. Most of them are very easy to understand, but here are a few tips you may find helpful:

Automatic Wrapping After Column In this context, a column means the width of a single character. The default column number (line length in characters) before word-wrapping is set to 76, which is considered a number safely shy of the old 80-character maximum for certain terminals. Pick a lower number if you like, but we don't recommend going up to or over 80.

Line Break Type This determines which ASCII character is used to indicate a new line in your code's text files. Don't necessarily choose the option that corresponds to your own platform! Choose the one that corresponds to the platform of the eventual production (live) server. If you are developing on a PC but going live on a Unix (or Linux) box, for example, choose LF (Unix), not CR LF (Windows).

Default Tag Case and Default Attribute Case The default tag and attribute case (that is, lower- or uppercase) used to be an aesthetic choice or a matter of legibility, but if you are concerned with forward-compatibility, you should bear in mind that XML and XHTML require lowercase for tags and attributes.

Centering Centering with the `center` tag is a backward-compatible approach that should be avoided if possible (this will depend on what browsers your audience is known to use), but some—those who prefer CSS and standards-compliant design, would consider the `div` tag not that much more forward-looking, although it is supported by XHTML as of this writing. (CSS mavens would recommend creating a `.center` style that could be attached to any tag.)

The Code Coloring Category

The next most useful code-related category is Code Coloring. It stores all the color-syntax choices for an incredible number of file types (see Figure 23.3).

To change any one scheme to your own preferences, select it in the Document Type box and click the Edit Coloring Scheme button. In the resulting dialog box, choose any element, change its color (or background color, or make it bold and/or italic), and repeat as often as you like before clicking the OK button to seal the changes.

The Code Rewriting Category

Use the Code Rewriting category to control whether and how Dreamweaver will change the code for imported documents (see Chapter 11 for a discussion of this in the context of importing Word or FrontPage files). By default, Dreamweaver now maintains a "hand's off" posture, but you can check Rewrite Code and then specify any of several specific situations in which Dreamweaver is authorized to make changes.

For instance, if you were using an earlier version of Dreamweaver (2.0 or 3.0) to try to help the team speed up some `.asp` development, you could offer to enter your copy changes directly into the files, using Dreamweaver for the editing and the FTP. At the time when these versions of Dreamweaver were current, the software would clean up imported files by default, and consequently strip all the scripts from your first attempt. We have since learned how to overrule that option, but it is no longer really a concern because now Dreamweaver protects you from yourself unless you explicitly enable rewriting, and even then, it defaults to excluding a long list of known scripting formats that should not be exposed to this kind of scrutiny (see Figure 23.4).

The Code Hints Category

The Code Hints category mainly enables you to turn off hints (Why? Probably if you find them annoying.), or change the speed with which they pop up as you are entering code (more on this later).

Advanced Setup

If you are going to be working with additional custom tags or libraries of tags that Dreamweaver doesn't inherently recognize, you can extend Dreamweaver by importing tag libraries and custom tags, and you can create and edit custom tags with the tag editors. But, first, a few definitions are in order:

Tag library A collection of tags associated with a programming language or some other custom set of tags, defined with XML or through some other convention. The tag library defines how each tag is to be displayed.

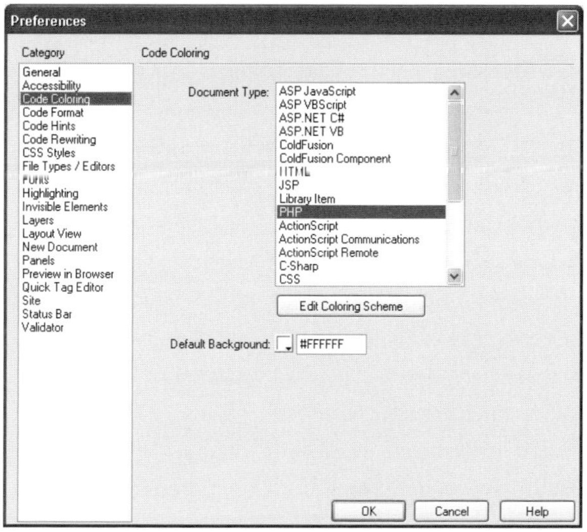

Figure 23.3

The scrolling Document Type box shows only a partial list of the types of files that Dreamweaver can parse for syntax coloring.

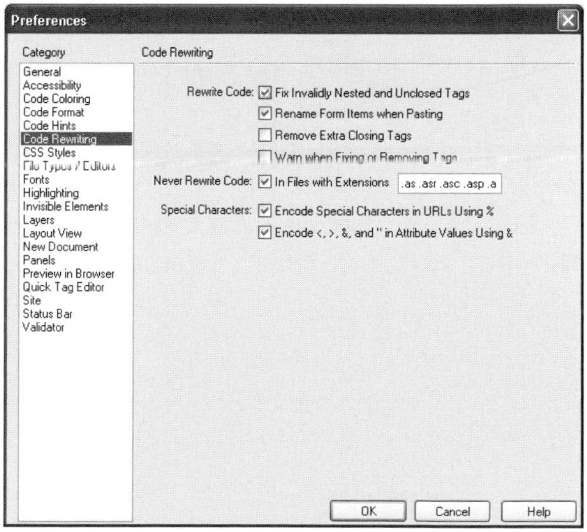

Figure 23.4

You won't accidentally overwrite ASP, JSP, or PHP files (among others) if you leave the Never Rewrite Code option checked.

Custom tag A tag that is defined by an XML Document Type Definition (DTD) file or by an external tag library (Dreamweaver supports ASP.NET, JSP, and JRun).

Tag Library Editor An editor that enables you to make, change, and delete tag libraries and to import custom tags.

> A *tag editor* is something else entirely—it is one of Dreamweaver's many helpful shortcuts for inserting tags, which will be discussed in the next major section of this chapter. The *Quick Tag Editor* is a tool for inserting tags, primarily from Design view.

To work with libraries and custom tags, choose Edit → Tag Libraries. The Tag Library Editor dialog box comes up with the HTML tag library expanded, but you can collapse it to see the base set of libraries with which Dreamweaver ships (see Chapter 23.5).

Making, Editing, and Deleting Tag Libraries

You can make a new library easily. Just click the plus (+) sign at the top of the Tags list box in the Tag Library Editor dialog box and select New Tag Library on the pop-up menu (see Figure 23.6). Then type the library name and click OK. It's immediately added to the list of libraries and made available to HTML files. You can then check off any other file formats that might need access to your new library.

Adding tags to a library is a two-step process—first you add the tags and then you specify the attributes for the tags you've added.

To add tags to your empty new library, click the plus (+) sign and choose New Tags, and then (making sure that the correct library is selected), type a list of tags separated by commas and no spaces, and click OK. Dreamweaver will specify the end tags unless you don't want it to.

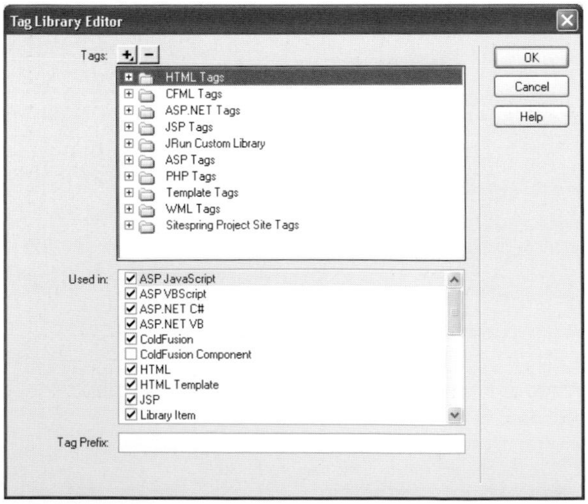

Figure 23.5

The Tag Library Editor dialog box represents Dreamweaver's collected wisdom about how to display many sets of tags with legibility-enhancing structured formatting.

To customize the display of a new tag, decide whether and where line breaks should appear within the tag, and whether the tag should get formatting and indentation, or just one or the other, or neither. You can also choose a case for the tag, bearing in mind that XML and XHTML will expect lowercase. If you choose mixed case, you'll have to show Dreamweaver exactly which characters are uppercase and which are lowercase (see Figure 23.7).

To add attributes to a tag, click the plus (+) sign and choose New Attributes, and then (making sure that the correct library and tag are selected), type a list of attributes separated by commas and no spaces, and click OK.

To customize the display and allowable values for an attribute, choose a case (same comments as for tags) and an attribute type. If you choose Enumerated, list the allowable choices in the Values box (see Figure 23.8), and you know the drill (comma, no space between entries).

To delete an attribute, tag, or library, click the minus (–) sign.

> Be careful with that minus (–) sign! Dreamweaver gives you a chance to think twice before deleting an entire library, but it deletes tags and attributes without quarreling, and those deletions are irreversible.

Figure 23.6

Making a new tag library

Importing Custom Tags

To import a library of custom tags from an external source, click the plus (+) sign and choose one of the ASPNet, DTDSchema, or JSP submenus. Each represents a different custom tag source that Dreamweaver can understand. Choosing Import XML DTD or Schema, for example, brings up a dialog box where you can browse to a source file or enter a URL for an external source. Several modes for importing JSP tag libraries are supported (file, folder, and server), and the ASP.NET option includes the choice of importing only selected tags.

When you're finished destroying your tag libraries (no, I mean, *enhancing* them, yeah) click OK.

Figure 23.7

Describing the tag format for a new tag.

Figure 23.8

Select the case and type of the attribute, and sometimes the allowable values.

Writing Code

Despite the color and indentation, code is basically meant to be typed and read as raw, unformatted text. There's a reason that coders have often preferred to do all their word-processing in bare bones text-editing environments. On that level, it's silly for us to be telling you how to write code. You type it in the window. End of story, right? Well, not really. It's true that you will type in code, either most of the time or just some of the time, but you may also cut it from another source and paste it in place, and that's really just the beginning.

> Changes made in Design view always update Code view automatically, but changes made in Code view do not reciprocate. To see code changes reflected in Design view, you must either save the file (generally a good idea anyway—use Ctrl + S/Cmd + S) or refresh the view without saving by clicking the Refresh button in the Property Inspector, pressing F5, or selecting View → Refresh Design View. Whatever's easiest for you to remember.

Structuring Your Code

If you aren't using Auto Indent (see the previous major section) or if you want to override the automatic indenting while you're entering code, use Edit → Indent Code to indent the selection or Edit → Outdent Code to push it back.

> In addition to syntax coloring and structured code, be sure to use comments in anything complicated so that others can tell what your intentions are even if you're not around to narrate the code personally.

Using Code Shortcuts

Dreamweaver offers a plethora of shortcut tools to help you insert code. At times the number of these seems almost ridiculous, and to some extent, this wealth of tools represent the software's legacy as products like HomeSite and ColdFusion Studio have been brought into the Macromedia fold and features have been duplicated for compatibility's sake. But there's no harm in it. Chances are you will use three of these approaches from time to time and mostly ignore the rest.

Code Hints While-U-Type

As soon as you type the < symbol, the Code Hints menu pops up.

You can press the Esc key to make this pop-up go away, or you can just start typing and the pop-up Code Hints menu will jump to the tag you appear to be typing. Hit Enter to accept the suggestion at any time. A matching closing tag appears immediately after your insertion point as soon as you close the tag so that you can start typing anything that you need to put between the opening and closing tag. Or, instead of closing the tag, you can type a space and then the Code Hints pop-up menu will show you available attributes. (Code Hints can also show available functions and methods.)

Inserting Tags with the Tag Chooser

To choose and insert a tag directly from a library, press Ctrl + E/ Cmd + E or choose Insert → Tag to bring up the Tag Chooser (see Figure 23.9).

Choose a library and then a tag, and click the Insert button. The flexible Tag Editor dialog box will appear and prompt you for attributes if any are required. If there are only a few settable attributes for a tag, the Tag Editor dialog box may be compact, as shown here for the base tag:

For other tags, multiple categories of options can be applied, including tag-specific options, style sheets, language, events (`onHover`, `onJohnson`, `onDonner`, `onBlitzen`) categories, "browser version" categories, and so on, based on the features of each tag.

Click the Close button when you are done inserting tags.

Inserting and Storing Snippets

Just because you want to work with raw code and not in Design view, that's no reason to turn your nose up at useful shortcuts (such as keyboard shortcuts, as discussed in Chapter 32). Hardcore coders find it useful to maintain a library of boilerplate code samples that can be pasted in place with very little tweaking. The tool for managing such useful pieces of code (or *snippets*, as Dreamweaver calls them) is the Snippets panel (the Snippets tab of the Code panel), which you can bring up with Window → Snippets if you don't already have it showing. Here is what it looks like.

The panel is seeded with some existing snippets—mostly drawn from the design templates that ship with Dreamweaver.

To insert a snippet, follow these steps:

1. Position the insertion point or select the code you want to surround with the snippet.

2. Then browse to, preview, and double-click the snippet you want to insert.

Figure 23.9

The Tag Chooser is overkill for run-of-the-mill tags, but for scripts and complicated attributes you may find it helpful.

To store a new snippet, follow these steps.

1. If you have an example (even if it's just close but not exact) of the entire snippet (including any surrounded material, if necessary to get the opening and closing part of the snippet, where applicable), select it.

2. Then click the New Snippet button 🔁 .

3. In the Snippet dialog box that appears (see Figure 23.10), type a name for the new snippet (it has to work as a legitimate filename, so avoid funky characters).

4. Press Tab and type a (optional) description.

5. Click Wrap Selection if this snippet is supposed to surround the selection or Insert Block if not.

6. Depending on your choice in step 5,
   - Type or edit the opening code in the Insert Before box, and type or paste the closing code in the Insert After box, for wrapping snippets.
   - Type or edit the code in the Insert Code box for block snippets.

7. Decide if the snippet should be previewed in the panel as code or design.

8. Click OK.

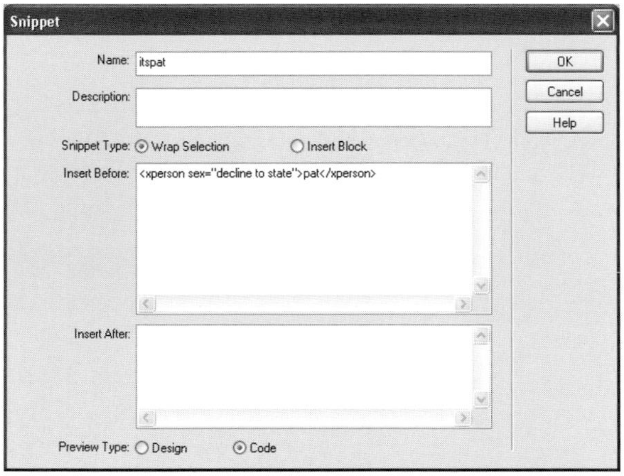

Figure 23.10

If you made a selection first, it will appear in the Insert After or Insert Before box.

Use short bits of dummy copy to indicate replaceable text in snippets. Snippets are not interactive dialog boxes like tag editors. They just insert or surround the selection with whatever you tell 'em to.

DESIGN-ORIENTED SHORTCUTS

Note that you can also insert tags using several shortcuts that are more suited to Design view editing, all of which are discussed in Chapter 11. These shortcuts include the following:

- The Quick tag editor, for inserting individual tags quickly. This is accessed through a pop-up menu that appears when you point to the actual tag or the tag selector.

- The Text tab of the Insert bar, including the Font tag editor.

- The Property Inspector, which shows status but also enables you to apply formatting and some other attributes quickly.

Editing Code

Unless you always type (or insert) your code flawlessly and never need to make any changes, you'll want to know how to edit your code as well. As with code entry, you can edit code by hand, of course deleting and inserting characters at will, but to avoid further typos and mistakes, consider using these shortcuts.

> When making sure you have the right tags selected before editing them, you can use Edit → Select Parent Tag and Edit → Select Child.

Using a Tag Editor

To edit an existing tag, right-click or Ctrl-click it to access the pop-up menu; select Edit Tag. This brings up the tag editor for the selected tag. (As discussed in Chapter 11, access the pop-up menu from a tag in the Tag Selector at the bottom of a document window to gain access to the Quick tag editor for that tag.)

Using the Tag Inspector

To view and edit code in Tag Inspector, first choose the Tag Inspector tab in the Code panel (or select Window → Tag Inspector). The Tag Inspector shows all the tags in your document. Highlight a specific tag to see its attributes displayed (see Figure 23.11).

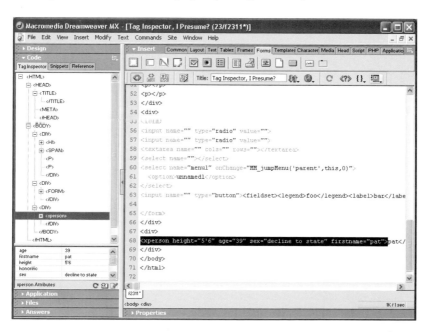

Figure 23.11

If you like to see your tags abstracted from the document, use the Tag Inspector to edit them.

To edit the attributes, click in the second column and type a new value, or use the available shortcuts, such as the color picker, as shown here.

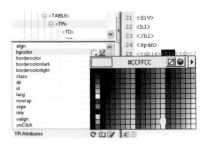

Cut, Copy, Paste

While in Code view, you can use the ordinary Cut (Ctrl + X/Cmd + X), Copy (Ctrl + C/Cmd + C), and Paste (Ctrl + V/Cmd + V) shortcuts available in most applications on the planet.

Search and Replace

When you need to make global changes to your code, you can use Edit → Find and Replace, as discussed in Chapter 11. Use any of these Search For options:

Source Code Source Code is the simplest choice, meaning that you just want to work with raw code for your replacing fun.

Text (Advanced) Text (Advanced) offers a number of choices for complicated searches within or between tags. (The first choice is to search for text either inside tags or not inside them, but if you click the plus (+) sign, you'll see that you can start adding extra conditions about tag attributes and contents.)

Specific Tag Specific Tag is straightforward but also enables you to closely specify the exact tag-and-attribute combination you are searching for and to perform a wide range of actions (shown here) on any matches.

Code Navigation

If you are working on a script file with functions, you can instantly jump to any function with the Code Navigation button **{}.** in the Document toolbar.

Hold down Ctrl (Windows) or Option (Mac) to see all functions in alphabetical order.

REGULAR EXPRESSION SUPPORTED

Regular expressions are a Unix standard for specifying searches with remarkable precision. Like all Unix-type syntax, regular expressions involve a list of teeny (single-character mostly) commands and switches. The Find and Replace box supports regular expression-based searches. Just check the Use Regular Expressions option. For a good online resource about regular expressions beyond the brief introduction in the Dreamweaver documentation, see the website http://sitescooper.org/tao_regexps.html (A Tao of Regular Expressions).

Printing Your Code

With previous versions of Dreamweaver, one had to use all kinds of workarounds to print out source code. Dreamweaver MX, though, now features a Print Code command on the File Menu (Ctrl + P/Cmd + P).

Using an External or Integrated Editor

If you have an HTML or plain text editor that you prefer for your coding, Dreamweaver isn't jealous. It will "play nicely" with that external editor. In fact, the Windows version of Dreamweaver comes bundled with HomeSite, a popular HTML editor now part of the Macromedia family. On the Mac side, Dreamweaver has always closely integrated with BBEdit and at times has shipped with trial or demo versions of that program. Beyond that, you can choose any external editor you want.

Figure 23.12

Browse to your preferred external editor.

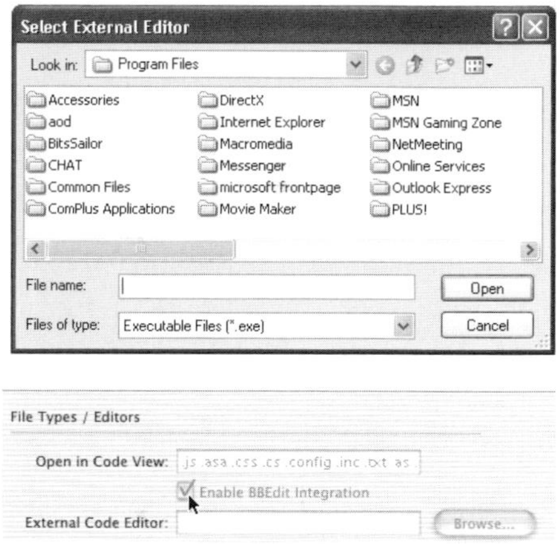

Setting Up an Editor

To set up an external editor, go to the Preferences dialog box and choose the File Types/Editors category (see Figure 23.12).

Mac users only must uncheck the Enable BBEdit Integration option to integrate with a different editor.

After you have made the appropriate choice depending on your operating system, browse to the application you want to use.

For the Reload Modified Files option, choose Always, Never, or Prompt to determine whether Dreamweaver will automatically reload file changes in the external editor, not do so, or ask you each time.

Similarly, the Save on Launch option determines whether Dreamweaver automatically saves the current file before opening it in an external editor, or never does so, or asks you each time.

Launching an External Editor

To open a file in an external editor (whether "integrated" or not), select Edit → Edit with *external editor name*. When you are finished editing, save the document in the external editor and switch back to Dreamweaver. To change the settings that govern whether Dreamweaver saves the document before you go to the external editor or reloads it when you come back, see the previous section.

Roundtrip HTML

Dreamweaver calls its approach to HTML and code from other sources "Roundtrip HTML." Because it's too easy for software applications to break code inserted externally, in the interests of cleaning it up, Dreamweaver is completely configurable, enabling you to disable code rewriting entirely or for certain file types (as discussed in Chapter 11 and earlier in this chapter).

Debugging Your Code

If you've got Dreamweaver highlighting any invalid HTML (as discussed at the beginning of this chapter), and cleaning up any imported code, and if you're using tag libraries and choosers and editors and an inspector to insert everything, then your code should all be valid and functional, right? Well, no. You can always insert stuff where it doesn't belong or delete something that breaks a working set of nested tags. For that matter, if you're writing script for applications, there are all kinds of errors you can include in your code undetected.

There are a few things you can do, though, to comb through your code and keep it as clean and bug-free as possible. For example, you can

- Make sure that opening and closing tags are balanced
- Clean up your HTML or XHTML code
- Validate your HTML or XHTML code
- Debug your JavaScript code
- Debug your ColdFusion code

If you're unfamiliar with debugging concepts, such as setting break points, or stepping through code, then this section of this chapter will not be enough to get you completely up to speed, but if you are familiar with such basic debugging concepts, you can learn how to apply them in Dreamweaver.

Balancing Your Tags and Braces

One quick way to check for egregious errors is to make sure that all of your opening and closing tags are balance or, in the case of script code, that all of your braces are balanced.

- To balance your tags in an HTML document, select a tag and choose Edit → Select Parent Tag (Ctrl + [/Cmd + [). Repeat this until you arrive at the <HTML> and </HTML> tags.
- To balance your braces in a script file, put the insertion point inside a function and select Edit → Balance Braces. The entire expression between the braces will be selected. Repeat this to work your way through surrounding braces.

Cleaning Up HTML (or XHTML)

You can have Dreamweaver review and clean up all of the HTML in your document at once by selecting Commands → Clean Up HTML. This brings up the Clean Up HTML/XHTML dialog box, as shown here. Dreamweaver can also clean up XHTML, as discussed in Chapter 26.

These options are fairly self-evident but here are a few comments:

- Don't use the (Remove) Non-Dreamweaver HTML Comments option if you tend to insert comments manually, because Dreamweaver will only recognize the types of comments the software itself inserts, such as to mark off areas in templates.

- For the (Remove) Specific Tag(s) option, you can list multiple tags, separated by commas. You only need to list the opening tag of any pair.

- We recommend that you use the Show Log On Completion option so that you can see what Dreamweaver did!

Click OK when you're ready.

Validating Your HTML Code

Another way to check your code for errors is to validate it ().

Validating your code is easy, but it's a crucial step to take before handing anything over. You can also use it as a quick-and-dirty debugging tool to detect errors quickly. To validate your HTML code select File → Check Page → Validate Markup. Dreamweaver will display any errors it finds on the Validation tab of the Results panel (see Figure 23.13).

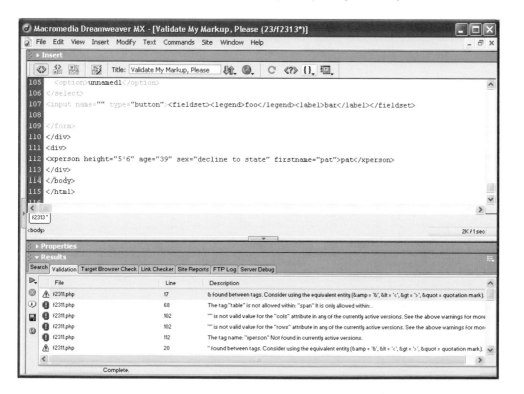

Figure 23.13

Validate your code before you're through.

Debugging JavaScript Code

To debug a JavaScript file, select File → Debug in Browser and choose a browser. In Windows, you can choose Internet Explorer or Netscape. On a Mac, you must choose Netscape. Only Netscape 4.0 is supported for debugging purposes (not Netscape 6.0 or later).

Dreamweaver launches the browser along with the Debugger dialog box. While debugging, you have several things you can do:

- To start the debugger, click the Run button.
- To stop it at any time, click the Stop Debugging button. The debugger displays any syntax errors it finds (see Figure 23.14).
- Click an error once to select it and see its description.
- Double-click an error to go directly to it in the code.

When the debugger finds errors, a JavaScript Syntax Errors window displays them. You'll need to reassure your browser that the script is safe by clicking OK and Grant, or Yes and OK, depending on the platform.

To see where the script goes off-track (that is, to find errors of logic in the code), set breakpoints to stop the code from executing at a specific line to allow you to see variable values and states at that moment in the code, or step through the code one statement at a time. Here's how you work with breakpoints:

- To set a breakpoint, position the insertion point where you want the breakpoint to occur in the code, and then click the Set/Remove Breakpoint button. A red dot appears in the code to mark the breakpoint.

Figure 23.14

The Debugger dialog box catches syntax errors and enables you to find logical errors.

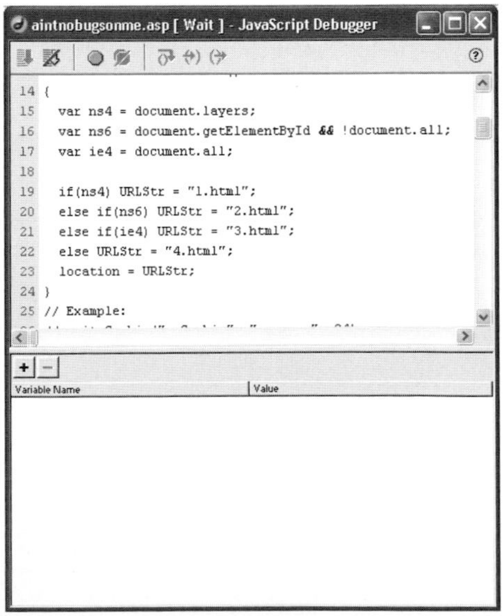

- To remove a single breakpoint, position the insertion point at the breakpoint and click Set/Remove Breakpoint.
- To remove all the breakpoints at once, click Remove All Breakpoints.

In addition to stopping the code at breakpoints, you can also step through or over statements one at a time. When the debugger stops at a statement, you have two choices: You can step over it and proceed to the next one, or you can step into a function to see how it executes. After stepping into a function, you can naturally step out of it as well. The commands for stepping into and out of functions are simple:

- To skip a statement, click the Step Over button.
- To step into a function, click the Step In button.
- Once you're in a function, you can skip the rest of the statements by clicking the Step Out button.

| If the statement you step into is nonstandard, the debugger will step over it instead. |

Watch the variable list pane, shown here, at the bottom of the debugger window to see the values of variables as the statements execute.

To diagnose problems, you can plug in new values for variables. Just select an item in the variable column and click the value in the value column. You can then enter any value you like.

Debugging ColdFusion Code

If you are a ColdFusion developer running Dreamweaver on a PC, then you can use Cold-Fusion MX as your Dreamweaver testing server (see Chapter 25 for more on working with ColdFusion applications).

To start debugging, click the Server Debug icon in the Document toolbar. Dreamweaver opens an internal Internet Explorer window (using the famous integration with the Windows operation system) and a Server Debug panel.

In addition to showing you all the pages, queries, variables, and values involved in executing this ColdFusion code, the Server Debug panel will also trap errors by listing Exception categories when the server runs into problems.

Expand an Exception category to find out more about the error. Then click the page's URL in the Debug panel to edit and correct the error.

To stop debugging, just switch back to Code view (View → Code).

Coding an Application

So you've set up Dreamweaver to build a web application and you've got your coding environment working the way you want it to. Now the time has come to plunge into the heart of any application: the data tables. In Chapter 24, you'll learn how to work with databases, add logic with scripting languages, and insert dynamic content into your web pages.

Database Connectivity

It has been great learning to create static pages, but now we're going to tackle a whole new beast—working with live databases. And yes, it really is a beast. The amazing thing about Dreamweaver MX is that this version allows you to do back-end management of your web pages, thereby creating dynamic content powered by a database. No other application integrates databases so well.

This chapter will help you determine whether a dynamic page is right for you, and then it will help you with the nuts and bolts of creating that dynamic page to impress your relatives, friends, and your business partners. Topics addressed in this chapter include the following:

- **Learning the basics of Dreamweaver MX**

- **Working with databases**

- **Mastering web database concepts**

- **Conquering server-side includes**

- **Troubleshooting database problems**

The Basics of Dreamweaver MX

You're probably asking yourself, how can Dreamweaver MX help me build dynamic, database-driven web pages?

Well, we'll tell you. Dreamweaver MX now incorporates features that used to be sold separately as Dreamweaver UltraDev. This version allows you to pick a development model, make a database connection, and create pages with dynamic content tags in them. Essentially, Dreamweaver MX creates a framework for building database-driven pages. Database-driven pages allow you to create websites like `http://www.amazon.com` where information is remembered about you and your purchase history, as well as your billing and shipping information. There are two major components of creating an interactive web page: the web server and the database. Both of these will be discussed fully throughout the course of this chapter.

The Birthing of a Dynamic Page

The birth of dynamic pages is simple. All dynamic pages begin as blank or static pages. First you build a static page, and then you transform it into a dynamic one. Your page might start out simply with some logos, text, and links to the rest of your site, and a table. In order to make this information dynamic, you could modify the table to display information gathered from a database. In order to create dynamic pages, you would follow a four-step process:

1. Lay out the page.
2. Define a Dreamweaver MX data source.
3. Add dynamic content.
4. Add server behaviors.

Three of these four steps seem self-explanatory, but the server behaviors may be perplexing. *Server behaviors* are functions that you can assign to a web page after you establish a database connection and a query. These could be actions like moving to the next record, deleting a record, or inserting a record.

To build Web applications in Dreamweaver MX, you need the following:

- A web server
- An application server that runs on your web server, or a web server that doubles as an application server, such as Microsoft's Personal Web Server (PWS) or Internet Information Server (IIS)
- A development model
- A database
- A database driver that supports your database

Implementing a Web Server

A web server allows anyone to look at your web pages from a browser. The web server is even more important when you have dynamic content because it performs the process of dynamically building your pages. If we weren't creating dynamic pages, then we could simply access the files locally without using a web server. Technically, this process is conducted through an application server, which dynamically generates web pages from code on the server.

The easiest way to go is to use the Microsoft web server that is available with your operating system. Depending on what version of Windows you're running, this web server will either be Internet Information Server (IIS) or Personal Web Server (PWS). We'll talk about IIS first because it is available with the most advanced versions of Windows, such as XP and 2000. Macromedia recommends using Windows 2000 Professional for optimal development results.

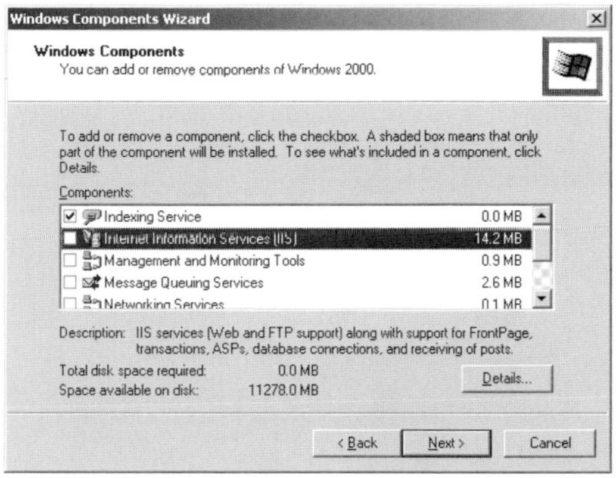

Figure 24.1

The Windows Components wizard for IIS installation

Installing Internet Information Server (IIS)

IIS is Microsoft's enterprise-class web server. It has a built-in application server for processing Active Server Pages (ASP). It will create a directory structure including inetpub and wwwroot as follows: C:\Inetpub\wwwroot. This directory is the default location from which IIS will publish documents.

In order to install IIS, go to the windows Control Panel → Add/Remove Programs → Windows Components, which is shown in Figure 24.1.

> If your computer is connected to the Internet, be sure you have the latest patches for IIS, otherwise your computer may become infected with various lethal and unpleasant viruses Information regarding IIS security can be found at http://www.microsoft.com/windows2000/ technologies/web/default.asp.

Using Personal Web Server (PWS)

PWS is similar to IIS except that it is older. It is supported by Windows 98 instead of current versions of Windows. Like IIS, it also has a built-in application server for ASP pages, and it also serves pages out of the C:\Inetput\wwwroot directory.

To install PWS, use your Windows 98 CD; browse to Add-Ons → PWS, and select setup.exe. The Microsoft Personal Web Server Setup dialog box displays, as shown in Figure 24.2.

Using a Macintosh

If you're using a Macintosh, you will use a Java Database Connectivity (JDBC) driver to connect to an Access database, or any Open Database Connectivity (ODBC) data source, located

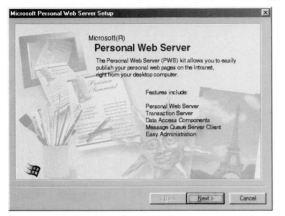

on a Windows server. If you don't have access to a database with a JDBC driver, you can install the client and server components of the RmiJdbc driver that is available on the Dreamweaver MX CD and at the Dreamweaver MX Support Center. The RmiJdbc driver allows you to connect to the Access database at runtime and "view" the database at design time. This means that you can view the database in development mode using the JDBC-to-ODBC driver.

Moving right along, we will now discuss development models, the differences between them, and what might be the best environment for you to use.

Figure 24.2

Microsoft's Personal Web Server Setup dialog box

Selecting a Developmental Model

Dreamweaver MX produces your dynamic content web pages by placing snippets of code where you tell it to perform data related functions. Dreamweaver MX does its best to hide the details of the code from you so that you don't have to be a programmer to use it. It does however support several types of code, so you must pick which type you will use. Your choice of development model will also affect how you connect to the database, which we'll talk more about later. ASP, JSP, and ColdFusion are development models. Each uses a different programming language and application server. ASP pages typically are written with Visual Basic code, while JSP typically uses Java code, and ColdFusion uses the ColdFusion programming language.

Active Server Pages (ASP) Active Server Pages (ASP) was developed by Microsoft. ASP functions can be called from either JavaScript or VBScript, which are two languages used to call code. ASP code is actually executed by the application server, which in the case of ASP is usually IIS or PWS.

Active Server Pages.NET (ASP.NET) ASP.NET is a new development model from Microsoft. It works much the same as the ASP model but it supports the Microsoft .NET framework. In order to use ASP.NET you must download and install the ASP.NET framework, which is available from the Microsoft website (`http://www.asp.net/download.aspx`). ASP.NET includes support for Visual Basic and C#. C# is a new, full featured object-oriented programming language from Microsoft.

Java Server Pages (JSP) Java Server Pages (JSP) are generated by running Java scriplets (which are written in Java which was developed by Sun). If you choose to have Dreamweaver MX insert JSP snippets of code, you'll need to have an application server that is able to execute this code. You may still use IIS, but you'll also need a separate application server. Two popular choices are WebSphere (by IBM) and Jserv, an Apache add-on. In addition, you'll need the Java Development Kit (JDK) from Sun. It is a free download, available from `http://java.sun.com/products/`.

PHP Dreamweaver MX supports the PHP dynamic page development model. You must have a PHP application server installed before you can process PHP pages. The PHP application server can be downloaded from the PHP site (`http://www.php.net/`). There is a separate file to download depending on if you use IIS or Apache.

ColdFusion ColdFusion is a development system by Macromedia. The language used by ColdFusion is called ColdFusion Markup Language (CFML). Like ASP, for ColdFusion, you'll need a web server—either IIS or PWS, for example. You'll also need Macromedia's ColdFusion Application Server.

Once you've selected the development model you'd like to use you should specify it. You need to specify the type of developmental model because once Dreamweaver knows what you're using it inserts code based on the development model type. If you're using JSP, Dreamweaver inserts Java code. The development model is defined as part of the site definition. To select a model, select Define Sites from the Site menu and then click the New button. You can modify the name and location that Dreamweaver MX uses to store your site. On the Application Server tab the Server Model drop-down list has the three development model choices that were listed above: JSP, ASP, and ColdFusion.

Once you've picked a development model, you can also specify the remote folder where Dreamweaver MX uploads your code. Your code has to reside in the same directory that the web server/application server publishes from in order for it to be viewed. This is generally not the same directory that your project resides in. For example, if you are using IIS, the remote folder could be `c:\Inetpub\wwwroot\test`.

Databases

Databases provide a way to store information that remains constant between your visits to a web page. There are several major vendors of databases, including Microsoft and Oracle.

Microsoft offers two database choices: Access and SQL Server 7 or 2000. Access is good for setting up a small, simple database when you're first learning about how a database works and are not concerned with performance. SQL Server 7 and 2000 are more complicated to setup and run, but they offer more database procedures than Access and they have the power to handle many simultaneous web users.

In addition, Oracle offers their $9i$ database, which supports many users as well as complex logic that can be built in to the database. SQL Server and Oracle$9i$ fight for major website dominance, but currently, Oracle is the industry leader for busy websites.

MySQL is another database option that you should consider. MySQL is available for free from `http://www.mysql.com/downloads/index.html`. It's available for free because it's open source, and it is supported on the Mac OS X, as well as Windows, and Linux. MySQL supports ODBC connectivity. ODBC is useful because Dreamweaver also supports ODBC.

Oracle is a more robust system, but also more complicated and pricey compared to free MySQL. In addition Oracle requires more resources, including CPU memory and if you're just starting out, you probably want to use MySQL.

Drivers

Dreamweaver MX builds pages that access the database through one of the three standard protocols described here. The drivers tell Dreamweaver MX how to "talk" to each type of database. You can think of them as translators.

ODBC The most common and flexible way to build pages is by using Open Database Connectivity (ODBC). ODBC connections are managed under the Windows ODBC Connection Administration screen. Database vendors provide ODBC drivers with their database to allow easy access by applications. Dreamweaver MX supports any database that provides an ODBC driver.

OLE DB Native ASP applications talk to databases through a standard called OLE DB. Because database vendor support for OLE DB is still very sparse, the usual method for ASP applications is to use an OLD DB driver that translates OLE DB into ODBC. Even though ODBC is less efficient than talking to the database through OLE DB directly, it is better supported.

PICKING THE RIGHT DATABASE

If you are going to create a large site, don't bother even booting up Microsoft Access; go full-steam ahead to a database like SQL Server, or Oracle. If these choices seem too enterprise-wide and too big for your needs, you could use Access with a SQL database engine. The Access SQL database engine processes SQL commands.

However, enterprise databases like SQL Server give you programming and business logic within the database (often referred to as stored procedures). Picking the right database is important because you don't want a lot of rework if you make significant changes to your pages.

JDBC JSP applications talk to databases natively through Java Database Connectivity (JDBC). If your database supports JDBC directly, this is the fastest way to go. Oracle and IBM's DB2 provide JDBC drivers. For compatibility, Sun also provides a bridge driver that translates JDBC into ODBC, thereby allowing you to use any ODBC supported database. See `http://industry.java.sun.com/products/jdbc/drivers` for more information on JDBC drivers available from Sun.

> ColdFusion accesses the database using the same methods as ASP.

Defining a Data Source

When you begin building a dynamic page, you need to define at least one data source. The *data source* is the description of the database that you will use to query and store information. The data source definition includes all of the information that Dreamweaver needs to access the database and a name for the connection. Required information includes the type of connection, such as ODBC, OLE DB, or JDBC; the database name; and the login.

Any data source that you define is added to your list of data sources in the Data Bindings panel, which you use to add dynamic content to your page. To define a data source, follow these steps:

1. Open the Databases window; if it isn't already open on your screen, select Databases from the Window menu.

2. From the plus (+) sign menu, select Data Source Name. This opens a window in which you can select a DSN.

3. Click the radio button to use a local DSN, which is defined on your local computer instead of on the server.

4. Select a DSN to use from the DSN drop down list. Dreamweaver uses a naming convention where connection names start with "conn." For example, connCompass could be a name of a DSN.

5. DSN points to ODBC database connections. If you want to create your own DSN, click the Define button on the Data Source Name window. This button is a shortcut to the Windows Control Panel's ODBC Data Sources applet, which defines DSNs. However, you don't need to define one since Macromedia provides a sample Microsoft Access database called Compass, as designated in the Data Source Name field of the ODBC Microsoft Access Setup window (see Figure 24.3).

6. After you define your data source, it is a good idea to test your database connection definition by pressing the Test button.

Figure 24.3

ODBC Microsoft Access Setup window

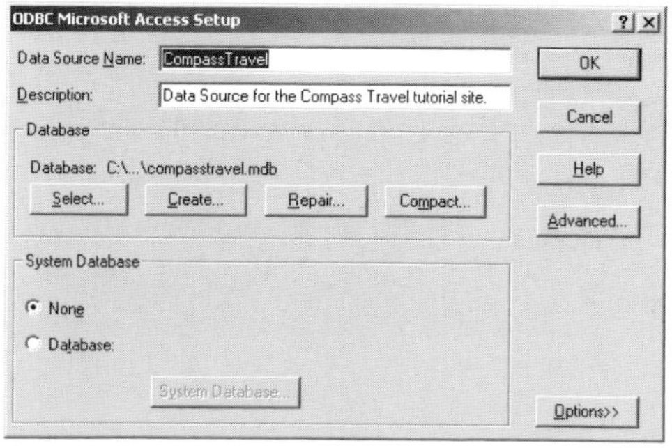

If you've chosen to develop in JSP, you'll have more choices when you create a new database. These choices will include Oracle, MySQL, IBM DB2, and Sun's JDBC-to-ODBC driver. Each of these drivers requires you to enter some information in the URL field. The required information needs to be enclosed in brackets. For example, the Sun ODBC driver requires that the ODBC DSN be entered in the URL field where it says "odbc dsn"—for the Compass DSN, you would type `jdbc:odbc:[Compass]` for the actual entry.

Now that you've defined your connection, we'll further develop how results from the database are processed. A recordset is a subset of the data source, so a data source allows you to define one or more recordsets. Database filters allow you to specify which records of a recordset you are interested in. Both recordset and database filters are discussed below.

Defining a Recordset

Before you can work with the data from a table that is made available through a Data Source, you must define a recordset. The recordset specifies which table and columns will be selected when you retrieve data.

To define a recordset, select RecordSet from the plus (+) sign menu on the Data Bindings window. Your choices for columns include All or selecting which ones you want to include.

The final parameter on the RecordSet definition screen is the sort parameter. This parameter allows you to select the order in which records are returned. The result columns and ascending or descending can be selected.

Defining a Database Filter

Once you have selected the table, you can further limit the records that are returned by defining a database filter, otherwise you'd get everything in the table, which is useless for your purposes. The filter is the same as the WHERE clause used in the Structured Query Language (SQL). By using this filter/clause, you limit the rows returned from a database query. Dreamweaver MX gives you the choice of using their GUI to select the WHERE clause or specifying the SQL WHERE clause yourself. We'll talk more about using SQL to do an advanced query in "Exploring SQL," later on in this chapter.

The GUI allows you to select not only which column to filter by, but also the type of comparison, and where the comparison value comes from. Possible sources include a URL parameter, a form variable, or an entered variable.

In order for you to manage the dynamic objects on your web pages, you'll need to use the Dynamic Bindings and Server Behaviors windows. We'll now talk about where these new windows are located, and introduce you to setting up your page with Dreamweaver MX.

Dreamweaver MX Window Components

Just like the main page in Photoshop, you get a blank window with smaller windows surrounding it when you load Dreamweaver MX, as shown in Figure 24.4. Use the Window menu to display or hide various windows or to customize your main window.

Main Window

In the main window, you can view pages in either Code or Design view. Design view provides a representation of what the page will appear like in a web browser, and Code view displays the actual HTML and development model–specific code of the page.

The main window also has a special mode called Live Data mode. This mode allows you to preview the data that appears in your page from the database without having to view the pages using the web server and the application server. Be aware though, that the functionality of the Live Data mode is limited; in other words, you cannot preview advanced functions. For example, you wouldn't be able to preview the function that causes you to move to the next record in a record set.

Should you encounter problems using the Live Data feature, a good site to check for troubleshooting information is `http://www.macromedia.com/support/ultradev/ts/documents/common_server_errors.htm`. This site has solutions to common application server problems. These tips also apply to problems that you might encounter while you are viewing the pages directly off of your web server.

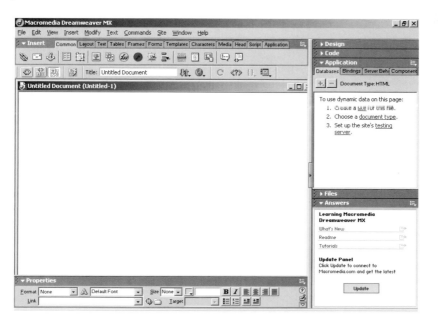

Figure 24.4

Dreamweaver MX's main window

Figure 24.5

The Data Bindings panel

Data Bindings/Server Behaviors Window

The Data Bindings/Server Behaviors window, which is accessed through the Window menu or through the Application Building pop-up menu, is used to define data driven objects for your web page. The current server model is displayed in this window. For example, "ASP-VBScript" represents an ASP server model using VBScript to call the ASP functions. The plus (+) and minus (–) buttons of each tab are used to add and remove data objects and bindings.

Data binding allows you to define the sources of data for you dynamic content; server behaviors allow you to move through and manipulate that data. The Data Binding/Server Behavior window is a one-stop reference for the dynamic data that is being used on the current page. You'll need to set up a query on the Data Binding tab before you can add server behaviors to your page. Figure 24.5 displays menu items that are available from the Data Bindings/Server Behaviors window.

The Server Behaviors tab lists existing server behaviors that are present on the current page that you are editing. To remove an existing server behavior from a page, select the server behavior and press the minus (–) button.

Properties Window

The Properties window allows you to set the properties for objects on your page. Properties are contingent on the type of object. For example, text objects have parameters like font size and family, and form objects have parameters like target page and invocation type (GET or POST methods).

Site Files Window

The Site Files window displays the files that are part of the current active project. Both the local files (the ones that you are currently working on) and the remote or application server files are displayed. After you've made changes to the local files, you can retransmit your changes to the remote directory by using the blue up arrow in the window's toolbar, as evidenced in Figure 24.6.

The main reason you're using Dreamweaver MX is to include dynamic content on your web pages. Next, we'll introduce you to the concept of adding any dynamic content to your page, including radio buttons, images, lists, and text.

Figure 24.6

The Site panel

Adding Dynamic Content to Your Page

Once you've defined a database connection or another source of dynamic data such as a session variable, you may want to include some dynamic content on your page. If you are in Live Data view, you will see the dynamic text as soon as you enter it. Otherwise, you'll see a placeholder that describes the data source of the text.

In this section we discuss the various types of dynamic content that are added to your page. These include dynamic text, lists or menus, radio buttons, and images. All of these items are customized by database information.

Figure 24.7

Select a recordset from the drop-down list.

Inserting Dynamic Text

The simplest dynamic object to work with is dynamic text. To insert dynamic text into a page, do the following:

1. Select the Data Bindings tab from the Data Bindings/Server Behaviors window. You can also get to this window by selecting Data Bindings from the Window menu.

2. Select the data source from the list of available sources. In the case of a recordset, select the column of the recordset to include.

3. Select the text to replace or the point to insert your dynamic text from the Design view of your page.

4. Click the Insert button or simply drag the data source from the Data Bindings window to the insertion point.

Inserting Dynamic List/Menus

What if you want to dynamically change the contents of a list or menu in your page? No problem; just follow these steps.

1. Insert a list/menu item into your page.

2. From the Server Behaviors window, click the plus (+) sign.

3. Select Dynamic Element → Dynamic List/Menu.

4. A dialog appears in which you must select the recordset as well as the fields that will populate both labels and values (see Figure 24.7).

5. Make your selections and click OK.

Inserting Dynamic Radio Buttons

What if you want to dynamically set whether a check box is checked based on a data source? To do so, you'll need to specify the data source and the value you want to see in it for the check box to be checked. Do the following to set the initial value:

1. Insert a radio button item into your page.

2. From the Server Behaviors window, click the plus (+) sign.

3. Select Dynamic Element → Dynamic Radio Buttons. A dialog box appears from which you can select the recordset as well as the fields that will populate both labels and values (as shown in Figure 24.8).

4. Make your selections and click OK.

Figure 24.8

Dynamic Radio Buttons dialog box

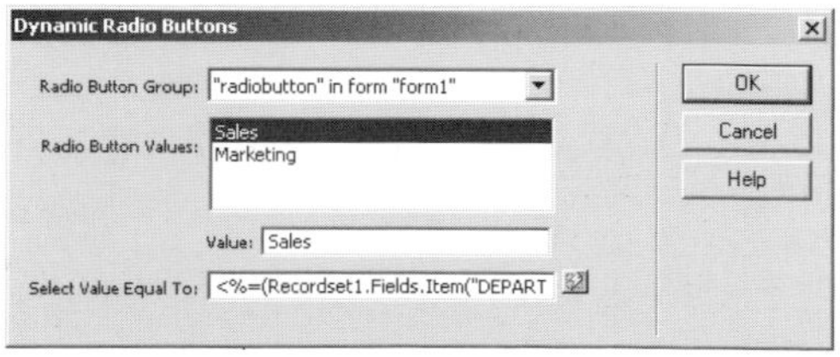

An example of when this might be a good idea is if you need to have a radio button on your page that indicates which department an employee is part of. The radio button's value defaults to the value that matches in the database column. By using the default database value the user won't have to change the selection.

Inserting Dynamic Images

Oracle allows you to store binary images to display on your web page, however Dreamweaver doesn't allow for this functionality, which means that you must keep the images on the web server and use your database to figure out which image to use. Once you have your images on the web server, you can set up Dreamweaver to dynamically generate the image source path for the image you want. First you'll need to store the filenames of the images in a table before they are viewable by the end user. You can then add the image tag to your site by doing the following:

1. Add the image by selecting Image from the Insert menu.
2. Click the Data Source check box.
3. Select the column that contains the image location information (as shown in Figure 24.9).

An example of what might be in your Image Source database column is `Sales.jpg` if the department is Sales and `Marketing.jpg` if the department is currently Marketing. Both `Sales.jpg` and `Marketing.jpg` must be in the same directory, and that directory must be specified in the static part of the image path.

Now that we've added dynamic content, you're probably wondering how to get rid of it if you decide to revamp your site. You can either delete content, or change it.

Changing or Deleting Dynamic Content on Your Page

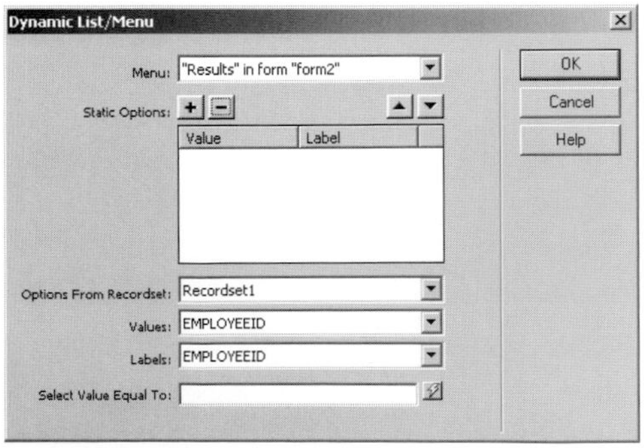

Figure 24.9

Dynamic List/Menu dialog box

Often, we'll insert content on our web page that needs to change, or be deleted completely. The easiest way to change the dynamic content on your page is to select it from the Server Behaviors window (as seen in Figure 24.10). When you double-click an entry, you are allowed to edit its properties. And by selecting an entry and clicking the minus (–) sign, you can delete a Server Behavior.

Defining a Search and Result Page Set

After you've added your dynamic content, you need to consider how your users will be accessing your website data. The user may want to specify parameters for their search, and then they'll want to see a page with results. For example, say you're searching through the employee records and you want to see all the records that match a last name. You would create this type of interaction for the user by defining a search and result page set.

A typical web page interaction for retrieving database records is to have your user specify search parameters on a search page using a form. This page, which we'll call the search page (it's actually just taking the search parameters), then calls the results page with the user's search criteria sent as URL parameters. The results page does the actual database query.

The results page takes the parameters from the search page and plugs them into the filter section (WHERE clause) of a recordset. Depending on how you set up your results page, you can display one record or a whole set of records at one time. The results page can also be a stepping-stone to viewing details of a record or record deletion page.

Figure 24.10

Server Behaviors panel

Setting Up the Search Page

To set up your search page, start with a new page, preferable with "search" in its name. This page will need a form object to contain one or more parameters with which the user will search. You should change the names of the variables for each form object to reflect what the fields will hold. This makes it easier to match up the parameters when you define you recordset filter.

If you have only one search parameter, you can use Dreamweaver MX's simple Recordset query on the results page. Otherwise, you'll need to use the advanced SQL WHERE clause.

You'll also need to include a search button on your form for the user to press when they have finished entering their parameters. The form needs to have the destination page set in its parameters and a submission type of GET.

Setting Up the Results Page

To set up your results page, start with a new page. It helps if you include "results" somewhere in its name. Add the recordset to the results page by selecting recordset from the Add menu of the Data Bindings/Server Behaviors window. Select all of the columns that you want to be part of your recordset. If you have only one search parameter, you can specify it using the simple version of the recordset definition window. If you have multiple search parameters, you'll need to use the advanced WHERE clause to add all of them. Be sure to specify URL parameter as the source of your filter parameters.

You may now add the Recordset field to a table row as described earlier in the "Inserting Dynamic Text" section. If you'd like to use a repeating range, you may also set that up to display more than one record. A Live Preview, accessed by the Live Data command in the View menu of the result page, displays the first record or records of a recordset. Up until this point, you may have been using a sample database, such as the Compass database that comes bundled with Dreamweaver MX. You will now learn how to set up your own database.

Designing Your Database Schema

A *database schema* is a set of user-defined tables and columns that holds all the dynamic information that your website uses. Because this is referred to so often, it is vital that you lay out the database tables correctly. In the section, you will see how to lay out your database tables. If you don't design your database properly, you will experience problems not only while you are developing your site, but also with the end user performance.

Grouping Data Together into Tables

You should group the data that you are collecting logically. For example, if you are collecting human resources information, you will want to group data like the following:

EMPLOYEE	DEPENDENTS	DEPARTMENT
Employee ID	Employee ID (links to the Employee table)	Employee ID (links to the Employee table)
First Name	First Name	Department Name
Last Name	Last Name	Head of Department
Gender	Gender	Location
Start Date	Relationship to Employee	
Department Name (links to Department table)	Birth Date	
Extension		
Birth Date		
Home Phone		
Supervisor ID (links to another entry into Employee table)		

In our example, we broke up the information to allow employees to have any number of dependents without duplicating all of the employee information for each dependent entry. Likewise, department-specific information is stored only once for each department, and only the name of the department needs to be stored with the employee record. In your database, try and find redundant data and put it in a separate table, as we did in this example. Setting up your database in this way eliminates performance problems, as well as page errors.

However, there's more to defining tables than just the column names, we also need to define how the tables are accessed and the type of data they store.

Primary Keys

Each table should have a field that is used by default to look up the rest of the entries in the table. This field is called the Primary Key field and it usually has a unique value for each record in the table. For the employee table, the primary key is the Employee ID because each employee has a unique employee ID. This unique ID streamlines the lookup process. For example, the employee ID can also be used to lookup an employee's information in another table such as the Dependents table.

Data Types

Each column in a database table has a data type associated with it. The most common types are character strings, numbers, dates, and Booleans. When you create a table, either through a GUI interface or using SQL, you will need to specify the types for tables.

> Boolean logic is a form of algebra in which all values are reduced to either TRUE or FALSE. For example, the expression 3 < 7 (3 is less than 7) is considered Boolean because the result is TRUE. Any expressions which contain relational operators, which the less than sign (<) is, are Boolean. The following operators are Boolean operators: AND, OR, XOR, NOR, and NOT.

Let's use an employee table as an example. You can see below, that the Employee ID has a data type of Number.

COLUMN	TYPE OF DATA	SQL TYPE
Employee ID	Number	NUMBER
First Name	Character String	VARCHAR(30)
Last Name	Character String	VARCHAR(30)
Gender	Character ('M' or 'F')	CHAR
Start Date	Date	DATE
Department Name	Character String	VARCHAR(30)
Extension	Number	NUMBER
Birth Date	Date	DATE
Home Phone	Number	NUMBER
Supervisor ID	Character String	VARCHAR(30)

Table 24.1

Employee Table

> The number specified after VARCHAR is the maximum length of the string that the database will store.

Dreamweaver MX attempts to isolate you from the language used to query the database, which is fine, but you should have some basis in understanding the language used, so we will now briefly discuss SQL.

Exploring SQL

SQL describes both Database Manipulation Language (DML) and Database Definition Language (DDL) operations in a standard way. DML operations are instructions to add, update, or delete data rows. DDL operations instruct the database to create or delete database objects, such as the tables and indexes that are used to speed up access to rows in a table.

In this section you'll learn how to create and drop database objects such as tables and indexes. You'll also learn how to add and remove data from the database tables.

Creating and Dropping Tables with SQL

Dreamweaver considers SQL to be an advanced option, but don't worry, with a little practice, it's really quite simple. Let's start with an example of a DDL statement that is being used to create the employee table in SQL.

```
CREATE TABLE employees
(employee_id      NUMBER,
 first_name       VARCHAR(30),
 last_name        VARCHAR(30),
 gender           CHAR,
 start_date       DATE,
 department_name  VARCHAR(30),
 extension        NUMBER,
 birth_date       DATE,
 home_phone       NUMBER,
 supervisor_id    VARCHAR(30)
)
```

The column names have their spaces replaced by underscores because spaces are not allowed in user defined database names. The case of the text in the statement is driven more by convention. Commands and keywords are typed in caps while user defined names, such as the table name and column names, are typed in lowercase. Typically, databases consider table and column names to always be uppercase unless they are enclosed in double quotes when defined, but it's best not to use the mixed-case names.

Dreamweaver MX user groups advise users to learn how to write Visual Basic Script or JavaScript. However, if you learn SQL, your website can have more elaborate interactions. Learning how to write SQL or Stored Procedures may be difficult at first, but in the long run it will pay off because you will have snazzy, complicated web pages!

To remove the Employees table with a SQL command, execute the following:

```
DROP TABLE employees;
```

Remember to use this command with caution because once you drop a table it is permanently removed. You might need to remove a table if you've decided to split up the information in one table into two tables. You may find that as you add information to a table that it becomes clear that several tables should represent that information.

Creating and Dropping Indexes with SQL

A *database index* is a special database object that speeds up access to rows in database tables if it is given queries on the indexed field. The nuts and bolts of an index are built using a b-tree (binary tree index). We will not go into too much detail here about how this works because you are not required to know how to use it. What is important about indexes is that they speed up access to rows. The downside of using indexes is that they use more database space and take up additional processing time when you are adding records. To create an index that makes querying up rows from the employee table based on first name and last name faster, you would use the following query:

```
CREATE INDEX employee_name
                ON employees (first_name,
                                        last_name);
```

If you've created an index that you aren't really using, you should delete it in order to release its resources and to speed up inserts into the database. To delete the employee_name index we just created, execute the following command:

```
DROP INDEX employee_name;
```

In general the syntax to drop an index is

```
DROP INDEX [index name];
```

If you drop a table, all indexes associated with it are automatically dropped.

Selecting Rows from a Table

Now that we've gone over the basics of how to create database objects with SQL, we'll move on to selecting data from an existing table. The command that is used to select data is naturally called SELECT. The following is the basic syntax for the SELECT command:

```
SELECT [COLUMNS]/[*]
FROM table
[WHERE] column=value;
```

To select the employee name and phone extension from the Employees table use the following:

```
SELECT first_name,
               last_name,
               extension
   FROM employees;
```

To select an employee name and phone extension from employees in the Sales department, use the following:

```
SELECT first_name,
               last_name,
               extension
   WHERE department = 'Sales'
      FROM employees;
```

Dreamweaver allows you to build SELECT queries by using the filter portion of the Recordset definition screen, an example of which is shown in Figure 24.11. You can use the more advanced and flexible WHERE clause of the SELECT statement by clicking the Advanced button of this screen.

Figure 24.11

Recordset dialog box

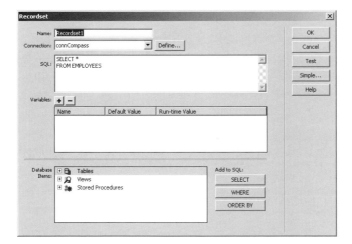

The SQL portion of this window shows the actual SQL query that Dreamweaver is using for the current filter. You can modify the text in the SQL window directly, or you can use the Database Items tree view to select items to be included (the Select button), limited by (the Where button), or the order in which records are returned (the Order By button). The Database Items tree and these action buttons are present to help you write the SQL query.

In order to streamline your process, you should write your database code in your database. Ask any Oracle or SQL Server guru and they will tell you that it's handier to write the code in the database instead of in Dreamweaver MX because by doing so, you keep your code in the application instead of on a web page. If you end up making a platform change down the road, all of your code won't have to be rewritten.

Inserting Rows into a Table

To insert rows into a database table, use the SQL command `INSERT`. `INSERT` uses the following syntax:

```
INSERT INTO table_name (column1, column2,...)
                VALUES (value1, value2,....)
```

For example, to add an employee to our Employees table you could use the following statement:

```
INSERT INTO employees (employee_id,
                                 first_name, last_name, gender,
                                 start_date, department_name,
            extension,
                                 birth_date, home_phone,
            supervisor_id)
                VALUES (1,
                              'Bob','Smith','M',
                              '13-NOV-2001','Engineering',3923,
                              '11-JAN-1950','(612)823-2312',2);
```

This statement creates an employee whose name is Bob Smith and who works in the Engineering department. The list of columns can be omitted if you specify the values in the same order as they are listed in the table definition and you provide all of the values.

Deleting Rows from a Table

Now that you have added rows to your database table, you may wish to delete some. This can be done with the SQL DML command `DELETE`. `DELETE` uses the following syntax:

```
DELETE FROM table_name WHERE column_name = value;
```

The `DELETE` command syntax is very similar to the syntax of the `SELECT` command except matched rows are deleted instead of displayed. To delete the row we just added/execute the following:

```
DELETE FROM employees WHERE employee_id = 1;
```

Though we could have also specified the WHERE clause as `first_name = 'Bob'`, it is safer to use the primary key, which we know is unique. Otherwise, we could end up unintentionally deleting all employees with the first name of Bob.

Now that you've worked with database objects, which make up a database schema, we'll talk about how to manipulate data from the web page.

Manipulating Database Records

Records are generally displayed as collections of dynamic database text on your web page. By default, only the first record of a recordset displays on your page. Server behaviors are used to display and manipulate database records. As you add server behaviors to your page, they appear in the list of in-use server behaviors in the Server Behaviors window.

We will now discuss inserting and removing database records; the database would be useless if you didn't have the ability to add and remove data from it. You might as well be using a book for your database.

Inserting Database Records

You may want to give your users the ability to add records to the database. For example, in the employee database scenario that we were discussing earlier, a manager may want to add a new employee.

To insert database records, you would need to perform the following steps:

1. Set up a page with a form that has fields for all of the columns you want entered.

2. Add the Insert Records Server Behavior from the Server Behaviors tab. In the Insert Records window, you will be able to define which table you will be adding to, the page you want to go to after you perform the insertion (which should inform the user that the insert was successful), and the appropriate HTML form's field to database table column that is mapped during insertion. This mapping defines which field in the form contains the data for each database column when inserting the data.

3. For each field in the form, select the data type from the Dreamweaver MX drop-down list.

4. Click OK to add the Server Behavior to your page.

Dreamweaver MX also provides a live object called Record Insertion Form that further automates the process of building pages to insert records. The Record Insertion Form window asks for the same information as the Insert Records server behavior, but it also creates the form for you.

Removing Database Records

You may also want to give your users the ability to delete a record. Using our employee database example, this scenario might arise—an employee leaves the company and you want to delete that record from the Employees table. Typically, such a deletion is done in a multistep process:

1. Create a new page by selecting File → New. This will be your Search page. The simplest search page simply displays all records from a recordset as deletion candidates.

2. From the Server Behaviors plus (+) sign pop-up menu, select Go to Detail Page. The page must have a Go to Detail Page Set server behavior to launch the delete page.

3. In the Go To Detail Page window, leave Link: as Create New Link. This tells Dreamweaver MX to create the link for you that indicates the deletion.

4. Set Detail Page to `delete.asp` by entering **`delete.asp`**.

5. Select Recordset1 from the Recordset drop-down list. Then select Code from the Column drop-down list. This tells Dreamweaver where to get all of the details for the record you are about to delete.

6. From the Site window, double-click `delete.asp` to open the delete page. Dreamweaver will have already added the code to display the record.

7. To add a Delete button, you must add a form to hold it and choose a location for it. To do so, click to the right of the table of information for the displayed record and select Insert → Form. A new form appears below the record.

8. To Add the Delete button, select Button from the Form Objects submenu of the Insert menu.

9. In the Properties window for the button, change Label from Submit to Delete.

10. You'll now add the Delete Record server behavior by selecting Delete Record from the Server Behaviors plus (+) sign menu. The Delete Record server behavior window is shown in Figure 24.12.

Figure 24.12

Delete Record dialog box

11. In the Delete Record server behavior window, select your database connection from the Connection drop-down list.

12. Then select which table to delete from by selecting it from the Delete From Table drop-down list.

13. Select the recordset from the Select Record From drop-down list that you used in the search page.

14. Select the unique key column from the Unique Key Column drop-down list. This corresponds to the key value that your delete page used to display the record. The Delete By Submitting drop-down list should specify the form name to which you added your delete button.

15. Specify the page to which you want to go to in the After Deleting, Go To field. If the deletion was accomplished successfully (without a database error), you will be sent to the page you specify here. The detection of database problems is handled for you by the server behavior.

16. Click OK to add the server behavior. Your delete page is now complete.

Dreamweaver also provides you with the ability to change database records through stored procedures.

Stored Procedures

Dreamweaver MX includes support for database stored procedures. *Stored procedures* are pieces of code that reside within the database. A stored procedure can take parameters, and when executed, it modifies data in the database. Stored procedures also have the advantage of being able to execute programming logic, such as conditional statements, whereas plain SQL cannot. Not all databases support stored procedures, however. Specifically, Oracle and SQL Server do; Access and MySQL do not.

> How you create stored procedures varies by database and is beyond the scope of this chapter. To learn how, consult a database administrator or your databases documentation.

Dreamweaver MX displays available stored procedures in the database on the Database tab of the Application window. The stored procedures appear under the tree branch called Stored Procedures.

The way that you add a stored procedure to your page varies slightly depending on the development model you are using. In general, you should follow these steps:

1. Go to the page that you want to add the stored procedure call to and select Command (Stored Procedure) from the pop-up menu that appears when you click the plus (+) sign of the Bindings panel.

2. From the Command dialog box's Connection drop-down list, select the database where the stored procedure you want to add resides.

3. Choose Stored Procedure from the Type drop-down list. This tells the Command dialog box that you want to execute a stored procedure.

4. Select the stored procedure to call from the Stored Procedures tree branch in the Database Items box. This tells Dreamweaver MX which procedure to call.

5. If your procedure requires parameters, associate them in the Variables table to variables from your page. For each variable, click the plus (+) sign and enter the name and Run-Time Value (which variable your form puts the value into). You may want to create a page that collects the information to send to the procedure before it is called.

6. Click OK on the Command dialog box to accept your stored procedure execution options. Dreamweaver will now add the code to your page.

Dreamweaver MX also provides server behaviors that allow you to move through record-sets; this is discussed in the next section. It's important to be able to view more results from a recordset.

Navigating Recordsets

Naturally, the web page user wants to be able to step through records when there is more than a single record. One of the ways to make this happen is to assign images or text to the server behaviors that are responsible for moving to the next or previous record in a recordset. To assign the server behaviors for navigation, follow these steps:

1. First add images or text to your page that indicate the action.

2. Then select the image or text that indicates you are interested in moving to the next or previous records.

3. From the Server Behaviors panel, select Move to Record from the plus (+) sign's pop-up menu.

4. The Move to Record dialog box has options for moving to the next, previous, first, or last record. Select one of these options and then select OK.

5. Repeat steps 2–4 for each direction you want on your page.

6. Then upload your pages to a server because Live Data does not support these server behaviors.

7. After your page is uploaded, view it using your web browser. You will be able to use the icons you created to move through a recordset.

If all the records displayed do not fit on the page, you'll use a Repeated Region to specify how many are displayed at a time.

Repeated Region

A repeated region is a server behavior that allows you to display dynamic content, for example, database records. This means that the formatting assigned to the first record is assigned to all subsequent records. When you define a repeated region you select the recordset and how many records to display at a given time. Use the Repeated Region dialog box to define the recordset and the number or records to display. If a repeated region is used and all of the records cannot be displayed at once, the server behavior displays the next set of records.

To apply a repeated region, follow these steps:

1. Select the table row of one of the fields of the recordset that you are already displaying on your page.

2. Click the `<tr>` tag in the footer of the window to select the entire row.

3. Next, select Repeated Region from the Add Server Behaviors menu.

4. The Repeated Region is automatically added to the page.

Sometimes you'll want to add a group of server behaviors all at once to accomplish a goal. Adding a group of server behaviors simultaneously is similar to running a macro. For example, in Word you can create a macro using VBScript that will install an entire set of styles for the user to access while creating a document. In the database world, this is called using Live Objects.

Live Objects

Dreamweaver MX provides the ability to add Live Objects to your site. Live Objects are really just collections of server behaviors that are packaged together to do a task. An example of a Live Object is a Navigation bar. You can build this yourself as we discussed in "Navigating Recordsets" or you can use the Live Object to do it all at once. The following Live Object allows you to get more detail about a record.

Master/Detail Pages

A master/detail page is a Live Object that Dreamweaver MX allows you to zoom in on. On the master page, generally, fewer columns are displayed about each record. When a user clicks the master record, a detail page displays with all of the recordset information. You create only one detail page that is used no matter which master record the user selects to zoom on.

The master/detail pages can be created using a Live Object (Insert → Live Objects → Master Detail Page Set) to do everything at once or piecemeal by using server behaviors (Plus Menu → Go to Detail Page). To apply a detail page, insert text or an image indicating details into the row of the resultset and apply the detail record to it. Figure 24.13 shows an example of the Go to Detail Page parameters window

Figure 24.13

Go to Detail Page dialog box

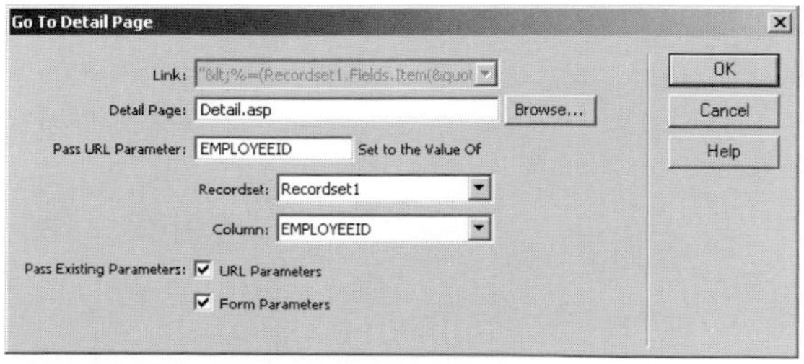

The detail page options specify which page to jump to for details as well as the URL parameter to send to the detail page. This parameter is generally going to be the primary key of the resultset.

Troubleshooting

Dreamweaver MX is certainly very powerful and flexible when it comes to building the code to make your dynamic web pages run. Unfortunately, you may still encounter problems when you try to execute the pages that Dreamweaver MX has built. We'll discuss some of the strategies for minimizing the pain this may cause you and also how to avoid some of these problems.

The first time that you'll notice problems is when you attempt to use the Live Preview feature. The Live Preview feature displays the Live View of your page by actually running the code on the page though the application server. You will likely see the same type of errors here as you would when you execute the code by using your browser to access it though the web server as the code is executed through the application server regardless.

You may want to display the Code view of the page that is giving an error and check the code that Dreamweaver MX has built for you. Because you may need to do this, you should understand the code that your development model uses.

Application Server Problems

Macromedia recommends running the latest version of Windows 2000 Professional if you're on a PC. This should minimize errors with IIS, especially the processing of the ASP code on your pages. Make sure that you have installed the latest Microsoft Service Pack. You should be running at least Service Pack 2. The service packs are available from the following address: `http://www.microsoft.com/windows2000/downloads/servicepacks/default.asp`.

Most of the errors you will encounter happen during the application server's processing of the page. Both Macromedia and the vendor who makes your application server should have pages with problem FAQs and/or searchable databases of problems.

The error type appears in the page that your application server returns. Here is an example of such an error:

```
Error Type·
        Provider (0x80004005)
        Unspecified error
        /MyTutorialSite/Results.asp, line 10
```

Macromedia's help page for Application Server errors is `http://www.macromedia.com/support/ultradev/ts/documents/common_server_errors.htm`. This web page also provides links to the help sections of all of the major application server vendors.

Database Problems

If you are experiencing a database access problem, it will appear when you try to process your page. ODBC/Access database errors can be permission related. For instance, you may see this error:

    80004005 - Couldn't use '(unknown)'; file already in use.

This indicates that you probably have a Windows 2000 file permissions error. The files in question are either the project files in IIS's wwwroot directory or the file and directory that hold the MDB file. This location can be found by checking the ODBC data sources applet definition for the database. Assign these files to access groups that the IIS server belongs to.

Under Windows 2000, the application servers access files as the user IUSR_[*machine name*]. You can go to Control Panel → Administrative Tools and select the Computer Management applet to give more permission to that user or to change each of the files that may need access to be updateable by that user or "Everyone."

If you are having a problem getting the results you expect from a database query, try executing the query outside of Dreamweaver MX. Each database provides its own interface for executing SQL queries. For example, Oracle's tool is called SQL*Plus. The SQL query executed on its own with the parameters that you wish Dreamweaver MX to search by will tell you if your query is correct.

Backups

It's a good strategy to periodically back up your project files (specified in the local directory section of your site definition). This way, should you encounter a problem with your site after adding functions, you can go back to the last working version without having to start all over. At the very least, you should backup the file that you're currently working on.

In conclusion, keep an eye out for problems and always remember to backup your website so that you don't have to start all over.

Hands On: Rapid Development of a Master Detail Page Set

In this tutorial, we will take you through the steps of defining a Master Detail page set that zooms in on Location records from the Global.mbd database that Macromedia provides with Dreamweaver MX. We will use the ASP JavaScript development model, but the steps in the tutorial are the same for any development model.

To Develop a Master Detail Page Set, perform the following steps:

1. Set up your site to use your locally defined application server to process the ASP pages (or another application server if you have chosen to use a different development model).

2. Define a database connection named connGlobal, and point it to the `Global.mdb` file by selecting Data Source Name from the plus (+) sign drop-down list of the Database tab of the Application window.

3. Type **connGlobal1** in the Data Source Name dialog window's Connection Name text box.

4. Select GlobalCar from the Data Source Name drop-down list of the Data Source Name dialog box and click OK.

5. Now create two new pages for your site by selecting File → New. Call them `testMaster.asp` and `testDetail.asp`. Use File → New File from the Site tab to add these files.

6. On the testMaster page created in the last step type **Master Page Test** (this is cosmetic only, but it will help you identify the Master page).

7. Create a recordset to retrieve locations from the Global database by selecting Recordset (Query) from the plus (+) sign's drop-down menu on the Bindings tab.

8. In the resulting Recordset window, type **Recordset1** in the Name field.

9. Set the connection to connGlobal1 from the Connection drop-down list. Then select Locations from the Table drop-down list. Leave Columns set to All.

10. Click OK to add the Master Detail Page Set.

11. Click after the Master Page Test text. Press the Enter key to add a new line on the Master Page.

12. Insert the Master/Detail object at the line you just added. From the main document window, choose Insert → Application Object →Master Detail Page Set.

13. From the Insert Master-Detail Page Set window that appears (see Figure 24.14), select Recordset1 from the Recordset drop-down list.

14. Then use the minus (–) sign to remove all but LOCATION_NAME, CITY, and STATE_COUNTRY from the Master Page Fields list. This defines which fields to include on the master page.

15. Then select LOCATION_NAME from the Link to Detail From drop-down list, and select CODE from the Leave Pass Unique Key drop-down list.

16. Next, use the Browse button to select `testDetail.asp` using the file selection dialog that appears.

17. Use the minus (–) button to remove CODE and REGION_ID from Detail Page Fields list. This list defines which fields to include on the detail page, so by removing these items, you have eliminated them from the detail page.

Figure 24.14

Insert Master-Detail Page Set

18. Click OK to save your changes and close the Insert Master-Detail Page Set window.

19. Save the `testMaster` and `testDetail` files, and then upload the files to the application server (by highlighting each file and pressing the up arrow icon on the Site tab).

20. Finally, test the testMaster page by entering a URL (`http://127.0.0.1/mytutorial-site/testMaster.asp`, for example) into your web browser for the project directory appended with the file name, which is `testMaster.asp`. Figure 24.15 shows how the Master Detail Page Set window will appear through your web browser.

You can now zoom in on a database record using pages that were created by the Master Detail Page Set Live Object.

Figure 24.15

Testing Master-Detail page set

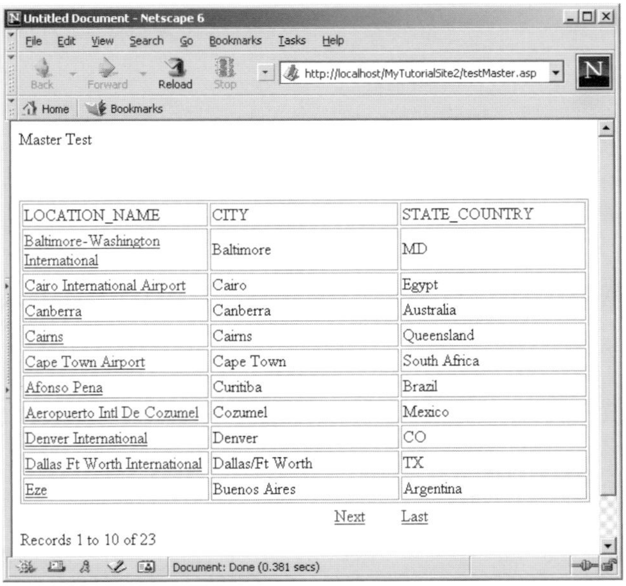

Dynamic Sites with ColdFusion

Dreamweaver MX makes creating database-driven dynamic pages easy. All different kinds of objects can be dynamically generated. Dreamweaver MX allows you to go back and change your dynamically linked object options. A variety of databases and development models are supported for ease of use and personal preference. Now that Macromedia also owns the ColdFusion MX server product, Dreamweaver includes support specifically designed for that server model. The next chapter helps you work with ColdFusion-based sites. As your expertise with the development model and database grows, Dreamweaver MX allows you to manipulate the code directly, if you so desire. You can also use Dreamweaver MX to customize your own live objects and extensions. Good luck creating your web interactions with a database that you are comfortable with, and may your dynamic content rock!

## CHAPTER 25

Working with ColdFusion

Macromedia's server product, ColdFusion, is a popular application server whose core rests in the execution of template files. These template files have `.cfm` extensions and use ColdFusion Markup Language (CFML), a tag-based language, to direct logic and invoke functionality through the server. More than any other web scripting language, CFML has the benefit (with a few exceptions) of working in a fashion that Dreamweaver understands—using tags.

When Macromedia acquired Allaire, they got more than just ColdFusion and JRun; they also got the HomeSite product line, which included the two HomeSite derivative tools—ColdFusion Studio and JRun Studio. Both were essentially HomeSite on steroids, and it was ColdFusion Studio that garnered most of the attention. When it came time to update Dreamweaver, the decision to grab some of the ColdFusion Studio market placed many requirements on the development team. This chapter will highlight some of the features meant to entice ColdFusion developers into using Dreamweaver.

The following topics will be discussed in this chapter:

- **Exploring the features of ColdFusion**
- **Setting up a Dreamweaver site for ColdFusion**
- **Connecting to ColdFusion data sources**
- **Setting up bindings**
- **Using server behaviors**

Important Features for ColdFusion Developers

Because working with ColdFusion templates is not unlike working with other tag-based files, Dreamweaver excels in its tool applicability. The sheer number of built-in parsing tools, commands, and behaviors makes working with ColdFusion templates incredibly easy. Here are some of the best examples.

Code Editor

The core of the Dreamweaver tool, for a ColdFusion developer, is the editor, or Code view, as it is called in Dreamweaver. The Code view portion of the UI is extremely flexible about its presentation of files. Dreamweaver allows you to have multiple files open at once, and they can be stacked in workbook fashion (like Excel and ColdFusion Studio) or in a more traditional Multi-Document Interface (MDI) style. The MDI style allows you to see two or more files simultaneously which can be very useful when migrating code.

Beginning with Dreamweaver MX, some of the more powerful features found in ColdFusion Studio, Tag editors, and Code Hints, have been incorporated into the editing environment for the developer.

Tag Editors One of the truly powerful features of ColdFusion Studio is the Tag editor. Merely by right clicking a tag the user can launch a dialog box that will assist with the completion of the tag's attributes. This is not unlike the Property Inspector in Dreamweaver.

Code Hints Another feature that ColdFusion Studio users will find familiar in Dreamweaver is Code Hints. This mechanism provides typing assistance for the developer by displaying a pop-up menu of tags and attributes. The developer can select a desired tag or attribute from the display and it will be inserted. This display automatically updates as the developer continues to type—trying to match names to the letters being typed. How quickly the pop-up menu is display is a configurable setting that can be adjusted in the Preferences dialog box.

Property Inspector

A tried and true staple of the Dreamweaver interface, the Property Inspector is the forerunner to the Tag editors. While the distinction between the Property Inspector and the Tag editors is a bit hazy, it turns out that toggling between the two is not a dramatic change for the developer.

Application Panel Group

Nothing will really prepare the ColdFusion Studio user for the power that Dreamweaver UltraDev users have known for some time through the Application panel group. This panel group includes four panels that contain tools for creating application logic with the click of a few buttons. Though there will be some familiar points of functionality, the overall toolset is a major leap ahead for ColdFusion developers in all strata.

Databases Panel

This panel is analogous to the Database tab in ColdFusion Studio. It provides a view of the data sources configured with the ColdFusion Administrator on the targeted server. The ability to drill down via a tree view into each data source, each table or view or stored procedure within that data source, and the fields within each aforementioned constituent of that data source is a powerful UI metaphor. This metaphor has been reused by other database applications and should, hopefully, be familiar to you already.

The pop-up menu associated with each table or view or stored procedure will allow you to view the data resulting from a selected item or refresh the entire list.

What appears to be missing from this panel, from a ColdFusion Studio user's perspective, is the Visual Query Builder. Not to fear though, Dreamweaver MX has a powerful solution on the Data Bindings panel.

Data Bindings Panel

This panel allows the developer to manage all the queries and variables for a template from a single GUI interface. What's more, as with UltraDev, Dreamweaver MX allows the cacheing of queries for testing during development time.

Though features of this panel aren't much different from ColdFusion Studio's Visual Query Builder tool, and the Recordset tool isn't nearly as nice from a drag-and-drop perspective, the panel is considerably more powerful. What this panel can do that Studio's Visual Query Builder cannot do is look at data sources that have been abstracted with variable names. The common practice of defining a variable in the `Application.cfm` for use as the `CFQUERY` tag's `DATASOURCE` attribute can be handled from this interface and will remain persistent not only while working in a template but for the whole configured site.

Server Behaviors Panel

The closest things that ColdFusion Studio has to compare to server behaviors offered by Dreamweaver are snippets and wizards. However, these do not compare to the scriptable versatility in even the basic kit that comes with Dreamweaver MX.

There are some similarities between the Server Behaviors panel and the Data Bindings panel when it comes to managing recordsets, but that is where the similarities end. A server behavior (SB) not only provides tools for creating recordsets but also for manipulating them by inserting, updating, and deleting records within them. There are SBs for conditional logic that will insert CFIF statements, authentication tools, and HTML Form tools for creating elements bound to CFML variables.

The single most powerful feature of this panel, though, is its ability to be extended. Custom behaviors can be added, and in fact, they can be created using existing behaviors as templates. For more details on server behaviors see Chapter 22.

Components Panel

One of the new features of the yet-to-be-released ColdFusion MX are ColdFusion Components or CFCs. CFCs are a powerful new language extension for building reusable components in CFML. The Components panel is Dreamweaver's tool for creating and manipulating CFCs. Unfortunately, because ColdFusion MX is still in beta status, real discussions about this feature cannot be had. However, using it to create CFCs does yield some information about the way that CFCs will be written and how they might function.

This feature will undoubtedly be a major draw for advanced ColdFusion developers once ColdFusion MX is released.

Setting Up a Dreamweaver Site for ColdFusion

Configuring a site specific for handling ColdFusion is not that much different than configuring one for other application servers, see Chapter 22 for more on setting up web applications in general.

The Site editor can be launched by selecting "Edit Sites…" from the drop-down list on the Site panel. Clicking the New button will launch the Site Definition wizard, which operates in two modes: basic and advanced. The Site Definition's basic mode, accessed by clicking the Basic tab, is a wizard mode that will walk you through setting all the site configurations.

A ColdFusion configured site is required before any of Dreamweaver MX's ColdFusion features can really be explored. The following process will help you set up the site needed for the other exercises in this chapter.

1. Launch the Site panel (Window → Site).

2. Select Edit Sites from the drop-down list.

3. Click the New button on the Site editor.

4. Select the Advanced tab on the Site Definition wizard.

5. Select Local Info in the Category list on the left and set the values as they are shown in Figure 25.1.

6. Select Remote Info in the Category list on the left and set the values as they are shown in Figure 25.2.

7. Select Testing Server in the Category list on the left and set the values as they are shown in Figure 25.3.

Connecting to ColdFusion Data Sources

Opening your ColdFusion site allows the various ColdFusion-specific features of the Application panel group to be enabled. The Databases panel will display a four or five step prompter if there is no prior information available for connecting to your ColdFusion site.

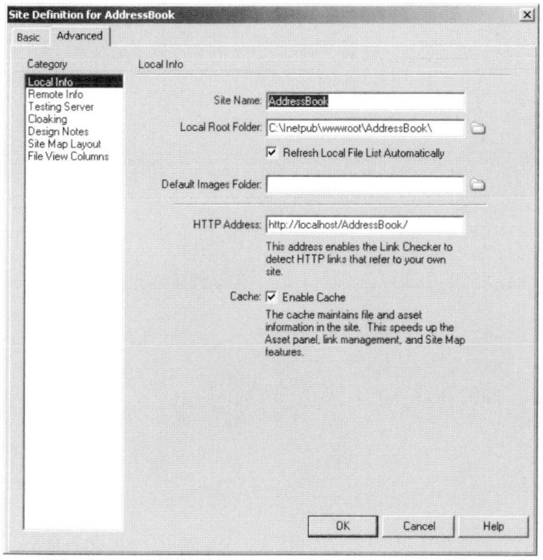

Figure 25.1

AddressBook Site's Local Info settings

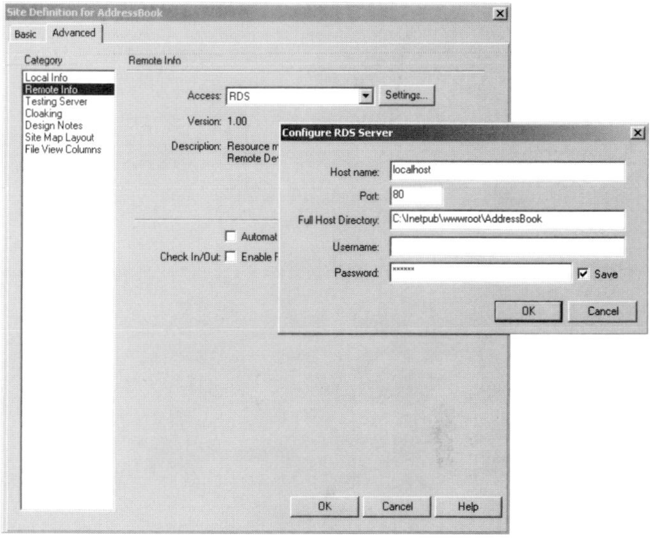

Figure 25.2

AddressBook Site's Remote Info settings

The prompter steps are as follows:

1. Create a site for this file.

2. Choose a document type.

3. Set up the site's testing server.

4. Specify the RDS login information.

5. Create a ColdFusion data source.

If everything in your site configuration is set up, you have only to click the login link for step 4. This will display the RDS Login dialog box and allow you to get authenticated, provided that a ColdFusion Studio/RDS client password has been configured in the ColdFusion Administrator. Once this is done, all of the data sources configured with that ColdFusion Server will be displayed.

Follow these steps to connect to the AddressBook database:

1. Select the AddressBook site on the Site panel.

2. Open a new ColdFusion template. Select File → New, and from the resulting dialog box, click the General tab. From the General tab, click the Dynamic Page

Figure 25.3

AddressBook Site's Test Server settings

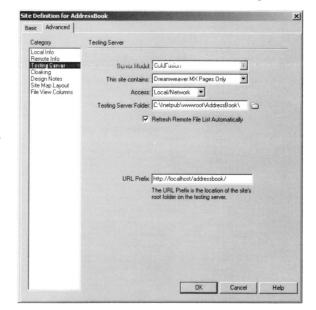

entry in the Category list. Then from the Dynamic Page list select ColdFusion. It is necessary to have a dynamic page open (specifically a ColdFusion page in this case) otherwise the panels in the Application panel group will be grayed out and inaccessible.

3. Click the RDS login information prompter and log in if a list of databases is not displayed in the Databases panel of the Application panel group.

4. Inspect the AddressBook database.

Setting Up Bindings

There are many powerful capabilities on the Data Bindings panel—each individually worthy of discussion. If you have not read about the Data Binding panel in Chapter 24, you should pause and do so now.

A common practice in developing database-backed applications is to abstract the data source name to a variable. This makes pointing the application at different test and production databases a little easier. Typically, third-party development environments don't handle this abstraction very well; but this is not the case with Dreamweaver. Using the Data Source Name Variable binding tool, a developer can identify to Dreamweaver, within the context of a ColdFusion site, the variable used to abstract the name of the data source. Once this is done, the variable is available to server behaviors and recordsets. Using this variable, the results of the query used in the recordset can even be viewed during development by Dreamweaver.

The following steps will walk you through setting up this binding.

1. Remove all of the HTML and save the blank ColdFusion template created in step 2 of the process described in the previous section as `Application.cfm`.

2. Insert a variable into this template from the Bindings panel (by clicking the Add button and selecting the CFParam menu item from the resulting pop-up menu), and set the following values in the resulting dialog box:

   Name: **Datasource**

   Default: **AddressBook**

   Type: leave empty

3. Bind the variable created in step 2 as the Data Source Name Variable (by clicking the Add button and selecting the Data Source Name Variable menu item from the resulting pop-up menu), and set the following values in the dialog box:

   Variable Name: **Datasource**

   Data Source: **AddressBook**

4. Save the template.

Using Server Behaviors

The basic toolkit of server behaviors that comes with Dreamweaver seems paltry when contrasted with the nearly 100 tags (and roughly double that in functions) of CFML. While this is
true on the surface, most of the Dreamweaver SBs center on the two most common operations facing a developer when building a ColdFusion application: gathering data in forms and
manipulating database content.

Using the exercises in the following two sections as examples, you will explore the point-
and-click power that Dreamweaver SBs provide you as a ColdFusion developer. While the
exercises seem rather involved, with 14 steps and 5 steps respectively, they really aren't at
all difficult.

Creating the Main Page

Here you will walk through the steps to create the main page of the AddressBook application
that we worked with earlier in the chapter. What will be produced is a simple page that displays
groups of records from the database and allows the user to scroll through them using back
and next image buttons on the page (not to be confused with the Back and Next buttons of the
browser). There is a hyperlink for creating new records that we will tend to in the next section.

1. Create a new ColdFusion template. Select File → New, and from the resulting dialog box,
   click the General tab. From the General tab, click the Dynamic Page entry in the Category list. Then from the Dynamic Page list select ColdFusion. Once this is done, immediately save it as `index.cfm`.

2. From the Server Behaviors panel, add a Recordset object to the template by clicking the
   Add button and selecting the Recordset menu item from the pop-up menu. Click the
   Advanced button on the Recordset dialog box and set the values as shown in Figure 25.4.

3. Insert a `<table>` tag into the `<body>` tag using the Insert bar, (from the Insert bar select
   the Common category and click the Insert Table button) and set the following values
   in the Tag editor:

   Rows: 2

   Cell Padding: 2

   Columns: 3

   Cell Spacing: 0

   Width: 75%

   Border: 0

Figure 25.4

Recordset dialog box

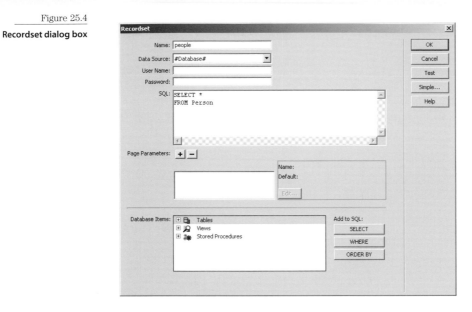

4. Using the Property Inspector (Window → Properties), select each of the table cells in the first table row and make the following changes:

   Horz: **Left**

   Header: Make sure this is clicked.

5. Replace the non-breaking spaces in the first table row's three table cells with the following values: Name, E-mail, and Tools.

6. Replace the non-breaking space in the second table row's first table cell with two SBs. Click the Add button and select the Dynamic Text menu item from the pop-up menu. From the resulting Dynamic Text dialog box, expand the people Recordset, select the Firstname field and click the OK button. Repeat this to select the Lastname field as well. This will insert two CFOUTPUT blocks displaying two variables from the CFQUERY:

   ```
   <td><cfoutput>#people.firstname#</cfoutput> <cfoutput>#people.last
   name#</cfoutput></td>
   ```

7. Replace the non-breaking space in the second table row's second table cell with a Dynamic Text SB. Click the Add button and select the Dynamic Text menu item from the pop-up menu. From the resulting Dynamic Text dialog box expand the people Recordset, select the email field and click the OK button.

8. Replace the non-breaking space in the second table row's third table cell with two empty `<img>` tags. Using the pop-up menu, launch the Tag editor and set the following general values for each:

> Source: `edit.gif`
>
> Alternate Text: **Edit a Person**
>
> Border: 0

and

> Source: `delete.gif`
>
> Alternate Text: **Delete a Person**
>
> Border: 0

9. Select the entire `<tr>` block that is the second row of the table, insert a Repeat Region SB (click the Add button and select the Repeat Region menu item from the pop-up menu), and set the following values in the resulting dialog box:

> Recordset: **people**
>
> Show: **10 Records at a Time**

10. Replace the non-breaking space in the third table row's first table cell with two empty `<img>` tags. Using the pop-up menu, launch the Tag editor and set the following general values for each:

> Source: `back.gif`
>
> Alternate Text: **Back**
>
> Border: 0

and

> Source: `next.gif`
>
> Alternate Text: **Next**
>
> Border: 0

11. Wrap each of the two `<img>` tags created in Step 10 in empty hyperlinks from the Insert bar (from the Insert bar select the Common category and click the Hyperlink button).

12. While the cursor is in the first empty hyperlink (wrapping the `<img>` tag and loading `back.gif`), add the Move to Previous Page SB (click the Add button and select the Move to Previous Page menu item from the pop-up menu) and set the following values:

> Link: Select the empty hyperlink around `back.gif`
>
> Recordset: **people**
>
> Pass Existing URL Parameters: Make sure this is checked.

13. While the cursor is in the second empty hyperlink (wrapping the `<img>` tag and loading `next.gif`), add the Move to Next Page SB (click the Add button and select the Move to Next Page menu item from the pop-up menu) and set the following values:

    Link: Select the empty hyperlink around `next.gif`

    Recordset: **people**

    Pass Existing URL Parameters: Make sure this is checked.

14. Replace the non-breaking space in the third table row's third table cell with a hyperlink from the Insert bar (from the Insert bar select the Common category and click the Hyperlink button) and set the following values in the tag editor:

    Text: **New Person**

    Link: **AddPerson.cfm**

    Target: leave empty

    Tab Index: leave empty

    Title: **Add a New Person**

    Access Key: leave empty

The resulting ColdFusion template (see Listing 25.1, which can also be found in the Chapter 25 folder on the accompanying CD), while not truly complex, does contain a considerable amount of code. The beauty of this is that nearly all of it was produced via point and click.

Listing 25.1

Main page (index.cfm)

```
<cfset CurrentPage=GetFileFromPath(GetTemplatePath())>
<cfparam name="PageNum_people" default="1">

<cfquery name="people" datasource="#Datasource#">
select * from Person
</cfquery>
<cfset MaxRows_people=10>
<cfset StartRow_people=Min((PageNum_people-
1)*MaxRows_people+1,Max(people.RecordCount,1))>
<cfset EndRow_people=Min(StartRow_people+MaxRows_people-1,people
    ↪.RecordCount)>
<cfset TotalPages_people=Ceiling(people.RecordCount/MaxRows_people)>
<cfset QueryString_people=Iif(CGI.QUERY_STRING NEQ
    ↪"",DE("&"&CGI.QUERY_STRING),DE(""))>
<cfset tempPos=ListContainsNoCase(QueryString_people,
    ↪"PageNum_people=","&")>
```

```
<cfif tempPos NEQ 0>
<cfset QueryString_people=ListDeleteAt(QueryString_people,tempPos,"&")>
</cfif>

<html>
<head>
<title>AddressBook</title>
<meta http-equiv="Content-Type" content="text/html; charset=iso-8859-1">
</head>

<body>

<table width="100%" border="0" cellpadding="2">
  <tr>
    <th align="left">Name</th>
    <th align="left">Email</th>
    <th align="left">Tools</th>
  </tr>
  <cfoutput query="people" startRow="#StartRow_people#" maxRows="
   →#MaxRows_people#">
    <tr>
      <td>#people.firstname# #people.lastname#</td>
      <td>#people.email#</td>
      <td><img src="edit.gif" alt="Edit a Person" border="0"> 
   →<img src="delete.gif" alt="Delete a Person" border="0"></td>
    </tr>
  </cfoutput>
  <tr>
    <td><a
href="<cfoutput>#CurrentPage#?PageNum_people=#Max(DecrementValue(PageNum
   →people),1)##QueryString_people#</cfoutput>"><img src="back.gif"
   →alt="Back" border="0"></a> <a href="<cfoutput>#CurrentPage#?
   →PageNum_people=#Min(IncrementValue(PageNum_people),TotalPages_people)
   →##QueryString_people#</cfoutput>"><img src="next.gif" alt="Next"
   →border="0"></a></td>
    <td> </td>
    <td><a href="AddPerson.cfm" title="Add a New Person">New Person
   →</a></td>
  </tr>
</table>

</body>
</html>
```

New Records

The following steps will walk you through creating a form for adding new records to the database's Person table.

1. Create a new ColdFusion template. Select File → New, and from the resulting dialog box, click the General tab. From the General tab, click the Dynamic Page entry in the Category list. Then from the Dynamic Page list select ColdFusion. Save it as `AddPerson.cfm` (the link that you created in step 14 of the previous exercise).

2. Create a `<form>` tag within the `<body>` tag of this document and from the Property Inspector, make the following changes:

   Form Name: **NewPerson**

   Action: leave empty

   Method: **POST**

3. Add eight `<input>` tags within the `<form>` tag for each of the eight fields in the Person table. Set `name` attributes to correlate to field names in the table and the `type` attributes for each of them should be "text."

4. Add a Submit button to the `<form>` tag.

5. Add an Insert Record SB (click the Add button and select the Insert Record menu item from the pop up menu) and set the values in the resulting dialog box as they appear in Figure 25.5:

   The resulting ColdFusion template (see Listing 25.2, which can also be found in the Chapter 25 folder on the accompanying CD) contains a considerable amount of ColdFusion code inserted by the Insert Record SB.

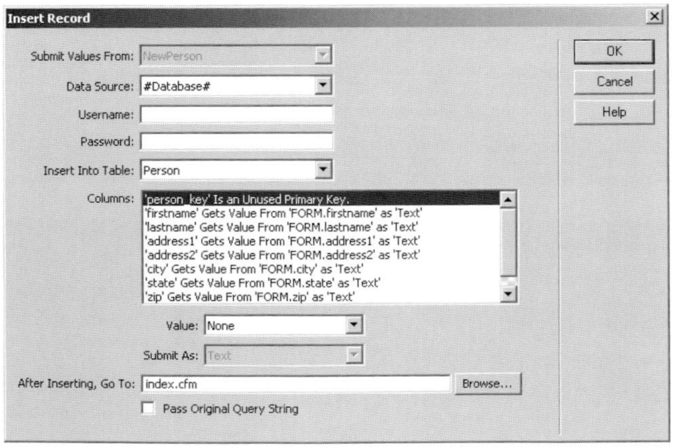

Figure 25.5

The Insert Record dialog box

Listing 25.2

New Person Page (*NewPerson.cfm*)

```coldfusion
<cfset CurrentPage=GetFileFromPath(GetTemplatePath())>
<cfif IsDefined("FORM.MM_InsertRecord") AND FORM.MM_InsertRecord EQ
    ➝"NewPerson">
<cfquery datasource="#Datasource#">
INSERT INTO Person (firstname, lastname, address1, address2, city,
    ➝"state", zip,
email) VALUES (
<cfif IsDefined("FORM.firstname") AND #FORM.firstname# NEQ "">
'#FORM.firstname#'
<cfelse>
NULL
</cfif>
,
<cfif IsDefined("FORM.lastname") AND #FORM.lastname# NEQ "">
'#FORM.lastname#'
<cfelse>
NULL
</cfif>
,
<cfif IsDefined("FORM.address1") AND #FORM.address1# NEQ "">
'#FORM.address1#'
<cfelse>
NULL
</cfif>
,
<cfif IsDefined("FORM.address2") AND #FORM.address2# NEQ "">
'#FORM.address2#'
<cfelse>
NULL
</cfif>
,
<cfif IsDefined("FORM.city") AND #FORM.city# NEQ "">
'#FORM.city#'
<cfelse>
NULL
</cfif>
,
<cfif IsDefined("FORM.state") AND #FORM.state# NEQ "">
'#FORM.state#'
<cfelse>
NULL
```

continued

continues

```
</cfif>
,
<cfif IsDefined("FORM.zip") AND #FORM.zip# NEQ "">
'#FORM.zip#'
<cfelse>
NULL
</cfif>
,
<cfif IsDefined("FORM.email") AND #FORM.email# NEQ "">
'#FORM.email#'
<cfelse>
NULL
</cfif>
)
</cfquery>
<cflocation url="index.cfm">
</cfif>
<html>
<head>
<title>New Person</title>
<meta http-equiv="Content-Type" content="text/html; charset=iso-8859-1">
</head>

<body>

<form action="<cfoutput>#CurrentPage#</cfoutput>" method="POST"
    →name="NewPerson">
  <table>
    <tr>
      <td>First Name:</td>
      <td><input name="firstname" type="text"></td>
    </tr>
    <tr>
      <td>Last Name:</td>
      <td><input name="lastname" type="text"></td>
    </tr>
    <tr>
      <td>Address:</td>
      <td><input name="address1" type="text"></td>
    </tr>
    <tr>
      <td>Address (Line 2):</td>
      <td><input name="address2" type="text"></td>
```

```
      </tr>
      <tr>
        <td>City:</td>
        <td><input name="city" type="text"></td>
      </tr>
      <tr>
        <td>State:</td>
        <td><input name="state" type="text"></td>
      </tr>
      <tr>
        <td>Zip:</td>
        <td><input name="zip" type="text"></td>
      </tr>
      <tr>
        <td>Email:</td>
        <td><input name="email" type="text"></td>
      </tr>
      <tr>
        <td colspan="2"><input type="submit" name="submit" value=
     →"Submit"></td>
      </tr>
    </table>
    <input type="hidden" name="MM_InsertRecord" value="NewPerson">
  </form>
  </body>
  </html>
```

Continuing Work

The AddressBook application is intensely simple. It could easily be expanded in a number of different directions. The main page (`index.cfm`) alone has numerous opportunities for continuing exercises and exploration. Here are some exploration options:

Delete Form You can use the Delete Record SB to create a form to delete existing Person records from the database. Link it to the obvious image on the main page's Delete icons displayed for each record in the Tools column of the table.

Edit Form You can use the Update Record SB to create form to edit existing Person records in the database. Link it to the obvious image on main page's Edit icon that is displayed for each record in the Tools column of the table.

State Dropdown You can update the edit form using the Dynamic List SB (Add → Dynamic Form Elements → Dynamic List) to display content from the State table in the database. This will replace the previous edit field for state codes.

To the Bleeding Edge

The sheer power of the features in Dreamweaver MX truly makes rapid application development in ColdFusion possible. Just leveraging the server behaviors could improve a developer's productivity massively. Further still, the extensibility of Dreamweaver means that as new features come available in the future versions of ColdFusion, Dreamweaver will be able to adapt without a serious need for upgrade. The last two chapters in this part cover some of the most relevant technologies in database-backed business-to-business applications: XML (and XHTML), and web services (including both .NET and J2EE approaches).

## CHAPTER 26

Working with XML and XHTML

HTML is fine for most person-to-machine interactions, but machines have a hard time reading HTML. This is because HTML is mostly formatting information (which machines don't care about) and links (which they do), and machines don't read the content the way humans do. Basically, machines read data and need metadata or some sort of context to help them understand the meaning or applicability of that data. For day-to-day websites, this may not be very important. But for B2B (business-to-business) websites, it can make or break the project.

One way that both humans and machines can understand is to encode the meaning or metadata surrounding data at a website with XML (Extensible Markup Language), which is used to create custom markup languages (XML applications). You can design your own language by creating a set of tags that describe the content they contain. You can use this set of custom tags to specify a structure for the content of your XML document.

This chapter covers the following topics:

- The basics of XML

- Importing and exporting XML using XML templates

- Creating custom third-party tags using XML

- XHTML in Dreamweaver

- Validating XML and XHTML documents

- Using and modifying Dreamweaver menus

XML Concepts

One of the most important and basic features of XML is extensibility. *Extensibility* means that, in contrast to HTML, there is no core set of tags that make up the language. You can create whatever tags you need to structure your XML document so that the content is in a form that meets your needs. If you give your tags meaningful names that describe the content, it is easy for you and others to understand what information is contained in the document.

> Dreamweaver itself is partly written in XML as well as HTML and JavaScript. For example, the configuration of your menus is stored in an XML file. Dreamweaver also supports the use of XML, through the use of Dreamweaver templates to import and export XML.

Creating XML documents requires planning. If you are sharing XML documents with a larger group or industry, it's very important to make sure that the XML documents are structured in a consistent way so that the information can be accessed and exchanged easily and efficiently.

For example, to create an XML document (`inventory.xml`) that can be used for parts inventory information, follow these steps:

1. Start the XML document with an XML declaration like this one:

   ```
   <?xml version="1.0"?>
   ```

   This XML declaration tells the processor that this is an XML file, and it also specifies which version of XML is used in the document. Version 1.0 is currently the only version of XML available, so it's the only one we can specify in our XML declaration!

2. Add a root element to the document. In this case, the root element is `inventory`. Everything that follows the XML declaration is contained within this root element.

   ```
   <inventory>
   ```

3. Add a `part` element. This element is the first child of the `inventory` element.

   ```
   <part>
   ```

4. Add the child elements of the `part` element. These child elements contain information about a specific part in our inventory.

   ```
   <name>Maxwell Silver Hammer</name>
   <description>12" hammer with silver coating on head</description>
   <warranty>lifetime</warranty>
   <weight>5 lbs</weight>
   <cost_retail>25.00</cost_retail>
   <cost_wholesale>12.50</cost_wholesale>
   <discount>yes</discount>
   <shipping>7.95</shipping>
   <stock>5</stock>
   ```

5. Add a `supplier` element. This element is the second child of the `inventory` element.

```
<supplier>
```

6. Add the child elements of the `supplier` element. These child elements contain information about the supplier of this specific part.

```
<name>Ralph's Hammer Company</name>
<address1>1445 E. Lake Avc</address1>
<city>Santa Fe</city>
<state>NM</state>
<zip>87501</zip>
<phone>505-982-9886</phone>
<fax>505-983-5572</fax>
```

7. Close the `supplier` tag, the `part` tag, and the `inventory` tag to complete the document.

```
    </supplier>
  </part>
</inventory>
```

The complete markup for `inventory.xml` is shown in Listing 26.1 and is also included on the accompanying CD.

Listing 26.1

XML File for Inventory Data (*inventory.xml*)

```
<?xml version="1.0"?>
<inventory>
  <part number="1971">
    <name>Maxwell Silver Hammer</name>
    <description>12" hammer with silver coating on head</description>
    <warranty>lifetime</warranty>
    <weight>5 lbs</weight>
    <cost_retail>25.00</cost_retail>
    <cost_wholesale>12.50</cost_wholesale>
    <discount>yes</discount>
    <shipping>7.95</shipping>
    <stock>5</stock>
    <supplier>
      <name>Ralph's Hammer Company</name>
      <address1>1445 E. Lake Ave</address1>
      <city>Santa Fe</city>
      <state>NM</state>
      <zip>87501</zip>
      <phone>505-555-9886</phone>
      <fax>505-555-5572</fax>
    </supplier>
  </part>
</inventory>
```

The markup in XML documents is often indented, as shown in Listing 26.1, to highlight the underlying structure of the document.

This XML document (`inventory.xml`) illustrates the following basic rules of XML syntax:

An XML document must contain a root element that contains all the other elements in the document. The XML declaration, links to other documents, and comments are the only components that can be outside of the root element container. The root element in this example is `inventory`.

Every element must have a closing tag. Most commonly, XML elements contain content, either text or data, and need both an opening and a closing tag. However, XML can also include empty elements (elements that contain no content). Empty elements can use a combined opening and closing tag

```
<warehouse/>
```

or can use separate opening and closing tags

```
<warehouse></warehouse>
```

Empty elements often include attributes, but the attributes are contained within the tag itself: `<warehouse branch="east"/>`.

Elements must be properly nested. If you open one element and then open a second element before you close the first one, you must close the second element before you close the first one. For example, this is correct XML syntax:

```
<apples>
<oranges>
</oranges>
</apples>
```

This is incorrect:

```
<apples>
<oranges>
</apples>
</oranges>
```

Unlike HTML, XML syntax has strict rules that must be followed. XML documents will not function correctly if the syntax is not correct.

XML is case sensitive. Case matters in XML. The elements `APPLES`, `Apples`, and `apples` are three different elements in XML. It doesn't make a difference which case you use, but you must be consistent.

All attribute values must be quoted. An attribute's value must be enclosed in either single or double quotation marks, for example:

```
<part number="1971">
```

An XML document that follows the rules of XML syntax is a *well-formed* XML document. An XML document that is well formed will display in a browser; however, the display itself varies with the browser. Internet Explorer 6 displays the source code of the XML document. Figure 26.1 shows `inventory.xml` as displayed in Internet Explorer 6.

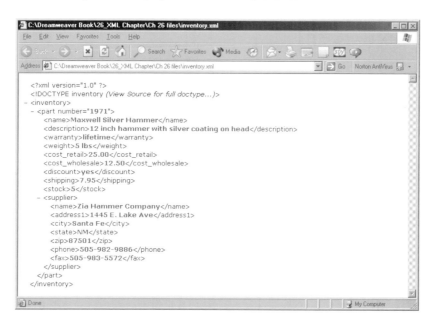

Figure 26.1

`inventory.xml` in **Internet Explorer 6**

Unlike Internet Explorer 6, Netscape 6 displays the content of all the tags. Because XML does not include any information about the presentation of the content, the content is displayed in a straight line without any formatting. Figure 26.2 shows `inventory.xml` as displayed in Netscape 6.

Style information can be added to an XML document by using a Cascading Style Sheet (CSS) or Extensible Style Language Transformations (XSLT) style sheet. Since the content is separated from the style, XML information exchange is not limited to the Web, but it can also be used on other devices such as wireless appliances.

In addition to being well formed, XML documents should be valid. To determine if an XML document is valid, test it against another document that specifies the rules for the structure of the XML document. Either a *document type definition (DTD)* or a

Figure 26.2

`inventory.xml` in **Netscape 6**

schema can be used for validating XML documents. A DTD is a set of rules for the elements and attributes in a document. The syntax of a DTD is based on *Standardized General Markup Language (SGML)*, the parent language of many other markup languages, including XML and HTML. A schema is also a set of rules for a document's structure. Schemas are written in XML itself.

For additional information about XML, check out the following online resources:

- The W3C XML 1.0 specification at `http://www.w3.org/TR/2000/REC-xml-20001006`

- XML tutorial at `http://www.w3schools.com/xml/default.asp`

- IBM Developer Works at `http://www-106.ibm.com/developerworks/xml/?nx-1021`, which offers several XML tutorials including "Intro to XML" and "Validating XML"

- "What the Hell Is XML?" an article by Troy Janisch at `http://www.alistapart.com/stories/hellxml/`

- "How Should My XML Look? Using Style Sheets with XML", an article by Jennifer Kyrnin at `http://html.about.com/library/weekly/aa110600a.htm`

- "Validating XML: A Pretty Complete Primer" by J. Eisenberg at `http://www.alistapart.com/stories/validate/`

Importing and Exporting XML with XML Templates

XML can be imported and exported from Dreamweaver by using templates. The templates can be used to import XML content into the editable regions of a template and then display that information as part of an HTML page. Content can also be exported from the editable regions of a template to create an XML file.

For more information on using templates, see Chapter 4.

XML must be formatted in a very specific way in order to be imported into a Dreamweaver template, and any XML exported from Dreamweaver will also be formatted in this way. Dreamweaver uses CDATA (character data) sections to enclose any content contained in your XML tags, as shown in the following example:

```
<name><![CDATA[Maxwell Silver Hammer ]]></name>
```

This example shows the fourth line of markup from the `inventory.xml` file after it has been converted to Dreamweaver XML format.

CDATA sections are used in XML documents to enclose any content that you would like to display, but not parse. Because these sections are not available to the XML parser, your content will not be available for validation. The structure of your document can still be validated, just not the content that is enclosed in CDATA sections. If your content is mainly text, validating the content may not be a big issue. If your content is mainly data, however, validating the content is a major advantage of using XML.

XML Schema, the newest XML validation tool, offers sophisticated datatyping that allows you to create very specific rules for the format of valid content.

The easiest way to get your XML document into a format that's compatible with Dreamweaver is to create a Dreamweaver template, use the template to create an HTML page, and then export the editable regions from this HTML page to create an XML file. This XML file can then be used to create other XML files in a format that can be imported into Dreamweaver. To do this, follow these steps:

1. Open the `inventory.dwt` file from the Chapter 26 folder of this book's accompanying CD. This is a template file created in Dreamweaver in order to display XML inventory information. Figure 26.3 shows `inventory.dwt` in Dreamweaver's Design view (View → Design).

   As you look at this view, you will see that the names of the XML elements are the same as the names of the editable regions in the Dreamweaver template. This is so that Dreamweaver knows where to insert the XML content.

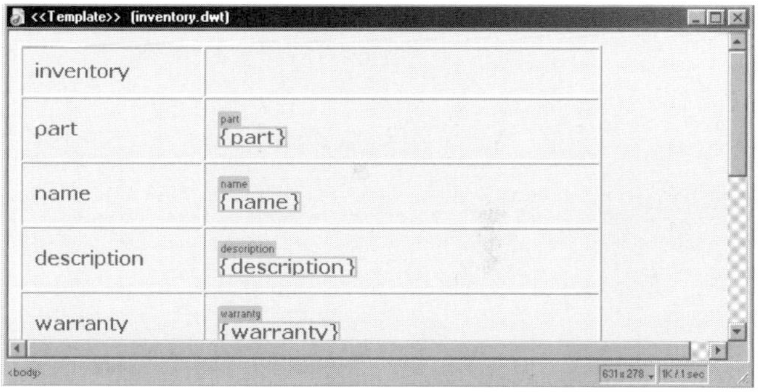

2. From the `inventory.dwt` file, choose File → Import → Import XML into Template. An Import XML dialog box displays, as shown in Figure 26.4. Choose the XML file you wish to import.

Figure 26.3

inventory.dwt in
Design view

3. If your XML document is not in Dreamweaver XML format (it does not have all the content enclosed in CDATA sections), the new HTML page that is created by Dreamweaver may show no XML content, or may display content incorrectly. Generally, in this case, the HTML file looks the same as the template file; in other words, no content has been inserted.

   If the XML file you choose to import is already in Dreamweaver XML format, the HTML file that's created will display the data correctly. In this case, you don't need to go through the rest of the steps that follow—you're done!

Figure 26.4

Import XML dialog box

4. If the XML file is not in Dreamweaver format, you will need to add XML content to the appropriate areas in this HTML file, as shown in Figure 26.5. Save this file as `inventory.html`.

5. From the `inventory.html` file, choose File → Export → Template Data as XML. The Export Template Data as XML dialog box displays, as shown in Figure 26.6.

6. Click a radio button to choose the type of notation for the XML file. You can choose either Use Standard Dreamweaver XML Tags or Use Editable Region Names as XML Tags. The standard Dreamweaver XML tags use an `item` element. The name of the item element is the same as the name of the editable region. Listing 26.2 shows markup for `inventory2.xml` (also included on the accompanying CD). This file uses Dreamweaver XML tags. The content is exactly the same as our original file, `inventory.xml`, but the tag structure is different. This file has a root element named `templateItems` that includes a `template` attribute that specifies the path and filename of the template file (`inventory.dwt`).

7. If you choose to use editable region names as XML tags, your XML file will use the names themselves as tags, and no Dreamweaver `item` elements will be included. The markup in that case will be similar to `inventory3.xml`, shown in Listing 26.3. The root element is still `inventory`, but it now includes a `template` attribute to specify the path and filename of the template file.

Figure 26.5

An HTML file
(`inventory.html`)
created by importing
an XML file

Listing 26.2

Using Standard Dreamweaver XML Tags (*inventory2.xml*)

```
<?xml version="1.0"?>
<templateItems template="/Templates/inventory.dwt">
    <item name="doctitle"><![CDATA[    <title>Inventory</title>
]]></item>
    <item name="part"><![CDATA[1971]]></item>
    <item name="name"><![CDATA[Maxwell Silver
      Hammer ]]></item>
    <item name="description"><![CDATA[12
      inch hammer with silver coating on head]]></item>
    <item name="warranty"><![CDATA[lifetime]]></item>
    <item name="cost_retail"><![CDATA[25.00]]></item>
    <item name="cost_wholesale"><![CDATA[12.50]]></item>
    <item name="discount"><![CDATA[yes]]></item>
    <item name="shipping"><![CDATA[7.95]]></item>
    <item name="stock"><![CDATA[5]]></item>
</templateItems>
```

Listing 26.3

Using Editable Region Names as Tag Names (*inventory3.xml*)

```
<?xml version="1.0"?>
<inventory template="/Templates/inventory.dwt">
    <doctitle><![CDATA[
<title>Inventory</title>
]]></doctitle>
    <part><![CDATA[1971]]></part>
    <name><![CDATA[Maxwell Silver
      Hammer ]]></name>
    <description><![CDATA[12
      inch hammer with silver coating on head]]></description>
    <warranty><![CDATA[lifetime]]></warranty>
    <cost_retail><![CDATA[25.00]]></cost_retail>
    <cost_wholesale><![CDATA[12.50]]></cost_wholesale>
    <discount><![CDATA[yes]]></discount>
    <shipping><![CDATA[7.95]]></shipping>
    <stock><![CDATA[5]]></stock>
</inventory>
```

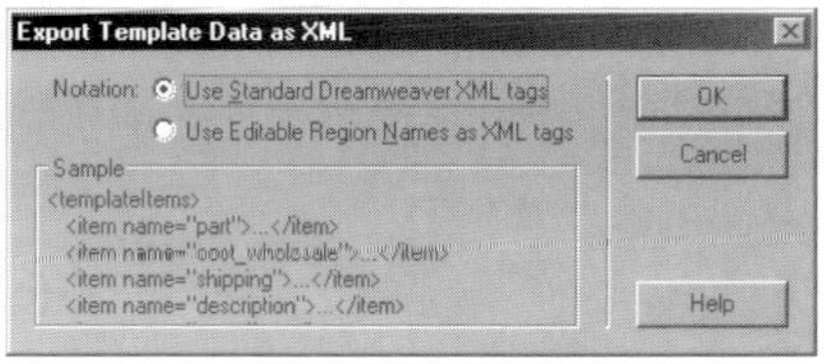

Figure 26.6

Export Template Data as XML dialog box

The exported XML file can be used to create other XML files with the same structure but different content. Because these XML files are in Dreamweaver XML format (either using item elements or using editable region names as tag names), they can be directly imported into Dreamweaver templates to create HTML files.

Third-Party Tags: Creating Custom Tags Using XML

Dreamweaver can be extended to support the use of custom tags through its third-party tag feature. This feature is not limited to custom tags to be used in XML documents, but it can include custom tags for other applications such as ColdFusion, PHP, ASP, or JSP. In Dreamweaver MX, custom tags are a very useful feature that are used to incorporate server-side processing information in an HTML page.

When you define a custom tag in Dreamweaver, a tag database file is created that defines how Dreamweaver reads and interprets the tag. The tag database file is saved as an XML file in the ThirdParty Tags subfolder of the Configuration folder.

You can create two kinds of custom tags: HTML-style tags that include an opening and a closing tag, or string-delimited tags that are empty tags without a separate opening and closing tag. The <br> tag in HTML is an empty tag because it contains no content and has no opening and closing tag. ASP tags are string-delimited tags that start with <% and end with %>, as shown in the following example that specifies that the scripting language used in this ASP file is VBScript:

```
<%@ Language = VBScript %>
```

An empty tag in XML and XHTML includes a forward slash before the closing angle bracket to close the tag. For example, an HTML <br> tag would be formatted in XML and XHTML as <br/> or <br />. The extra space before the closing angle bracket allows empty tags to display properly in browsers.

A custom tag consists of one XML element, `tagspec`, with up to seven attributes:

tag_name The `tag_name` attribute specifies the name of the custom tag.

tag_type The `tag_type` attribute specifies whether a tag is empty or nonempty. This attribute is ignored for string-delimited tags because they are always empty.

render_contents The `render_contents` attribute specifies whether the contents of the tag rather than an icon should appear in the Design view of a document. It is a required attribute for nonempty tags but is ignored for empty tags. Values are Boolean (`true` or `false`).

content_model The `content_model` attribute specifies what kind of content is allowed in the tag and where the tag can appear in the document. There are four choices for the value of this attribute:

> **block_model** Block-level elements that can appear only in the body of the document or within other block-level elements such as `div`.
>
> **head_model** Elements that contain text content and that can only appear in the head section of the document.
>
> **marker_model** Elements that can contain any valid HTML code and that can appear anywhere in the document, usually used for inline tags.
>
> **script_model** Elements that can appear anywhere in the document, usually used for markup that Dreamweaver should not parse, such as ASP markup.

start_string The `start_string` attribute is used to mark the beginning of a string-delimited tag. A string-delimited tag can appear anywhere in the document where a comment can appear. If this attribute is used, an `end_string` attribute is also required.

end_string The `end_string` attribute is used to mark the end of a string-delimited tag. If this attribute is used, a `start_string` attribute is also required.

detect_in_attribute The `detect_in_attribute` attribute specifies whether to ignore everything between a `start_string` value and an `end_string` value even if this information appears within an attribute. This attribute is usually set to `false` for string-delimited tags. The default value is `true`.

parse_attribute The `parse_attribute` attribute specifies whether to parse the attributes of the tag.

icon The icon attribute specifies the path and filename of the icon associated with the tag. It is required for empty tags and for nonempty tags whose contents are not displayed in Design view.

icon_width The icon_width attribute specifies the width of the icon image in pixels.

icon_height The icon_height attribute specifies the height of the icon image in pixels.

To create a custom tag for the description element in inventory.xml, the following markup could be used:

```
<tagspec tag_name="description" tag_type="nonempty"
         render_contents="true" content-model="marker-model">
```

The markup is then saved in an XML file and placed in the ThirdParty Tags subfolder in the Dreamweaver Configuration folder. You can save more than one custom tag in the same XML file.

You can now access this tag for any Dreamweaver document. Figure 26.7 shows the Code and Design view for the description.html file. The content of the description tag is displayed in the Design view window.

Figure 26.7

description.html—
Code and Design view

Importing Tags from XML Files

Dreamweaver MX allows you to import tags from an XML DTD (Document Type Definition) or XML Schema document. These imported tags are added to the Tag Library and then are available for use in Dreamweaver MX.

To add XML tags from an XML document, follow these steps:

1. Open the Tag Library editor (Edit → Tag Libraries).

2. Click the plus (+) sign and choose DTDSchema from the drop-down menu, and then select Import XML DTD or Schema File.

3. Enter the filename or URL of the DTD or schema document in the File or remote URL box, or click the Browse button to the right of the box to navigate to the DTD or schema file.

4. If you want to identify a tag as a part of a specific tag library, enter a prefix for the tags in the Tag Prefix box.

5. Click the OK button.

These tags are now available for you to use when you are creating Dreamweaver MX documents.

Supporting XHTML in Dreamweaver

XHTML (Extensible Hypertext Markup Language) is HTML written in XML syntax. XHTML is a transition between HTML and XML, and it provides an easy and useful way to write code that is compliant with W3C standards.

Dreamweaver MX includes support for XHTML documents in its basic configuration, and it allows you to create XHTML documents as well as convert HTML documents to XHTML documents.

XHTML is a reformulation of HTML using XML syntax. It is very similar to HTML but uses the stricter XML syntax rules. The basic rules of XHTML syntax are the same as the rules for XML syntax in the "XML Concepts" section earlier in this chapter. Dreamweaver MX automatically applies the following rules of XHTML syntax to the XHTML files it creates:

- The root element of the document must be the `html` element. XHTML files are saved with an `.html` file extension.

- If the character encoding of an XHTML document is anything other than UTF-8, an XML declaration that includes the character encoding is included in the document, as shown in the following:

  ```
  <xml version="1.0" encoding="iso-8859-1"?>
  ```

- A `DOCTYPE` declaration must precede the root element, such as the transitional XHTML 1.0 doctype shown in the following example:

  ```
  <!DOCTYPE html PUBLIC ""-//W3C/DTD XHTML 1.0 Transitional//EN""
      "http://www.w3.org/TR/xhtml1/DTD/xhtml1-transitional.dtd">
  ```

There are three types of XHTML doctypes: strict, transitional, and frameset. A doctype is required for a valid XHTML document. Dreamweaver MX automatically uses the transitional XHTML doctype for any XHTML document that is not in frames, in which case it uses the frameset XHTML doctype. The strict XHTML doctype is not available in Dreamweaver MX, although you can always manually change the doctype to XHTML strict.

Other rules for valid XHTML include the following:

- The XHTML namespace must be associated with `html` root element, as in the following example:

  ```
  <html xmlns="http://www.w3.org/1999/xhtml">
  ```

- Use an `id` attribute in addition to a `name` attribute (with the same value) to identify elements.

- Attributes that do not include a value, such as `checked` in a check box form element, must include a value in XHTML. This is specified by using the attribute name for the value—for example `checked="checked"`.

- All `script` and `style` elements must include a `type` attribute. Any `script` elements must also include a `language` attribute.

- All `img` and `area` elements must include an `alt` attribute.

The complete markup for a simple XHTML file named `xhtml_example.html` is shown in Listing 26.4 and is also accessible on the accompanying CD. Note that all attribute values are quoted, even color name attributes such as `white`.

Listing 26.4

An XHTML Document Created in Dreamweaver MX (*xhtml_example.html*)

```
<!DOCTYPE html PUBLIC ".//W3C/DTD XHTML 1.0 Transitional//EN"
    "http://www.w3.org/TR/xhtml1/DTD/xhtml1-transitional.dtd">
<html xmlns="http://www.w3.org/1999/xhtml">
<head>
<title>XHTML sample</title>
</head>
<body bgcolor="#ffcccc" text="white">
<hr />
<p>This is an XHTML file. It is saved as an HTML file so that browsers can
display it.</p>
<br />
</body>
</html>
```

XHTML is easy to learn, and helps ensure that the documents you create are W3C standards compliant.

> The W3C provides a free online validator for XHTML documents at `http://validator`
> `.w3.org/file-upload.html`. For information about validating XHTML documents in
> Dreamweaver MX, see the next section, "Validating XML and XHTML Documents."

It's easy to create XHTML documents in Dreamweaver MX. There are three options for creating XHTML documents.

To create a new XHTML document, follow these steps:

1. Open a new file (File → New).

2. In the Category column, select Basic Page.

3. In the Basic Page column, select HTML.

4. Check the box labeled Make Document XHTML Compliant.

5. Click the Create button.

To convert an HTML document to an XHTML document, follow these steps:

1. Open an existing HTML file (File → New).

2. Convert it to XHTML (File → Convert → XHTML).

> If the HTML document is part of a frameset, each frame and the frameset document must be selected and converted separately. See Chapter 14 for more information on saving documents in frames and framesets.

And follow these steps to create XHTML documents by default:

1. Open the Preferences dialog box (Edit → Preferences).

2. Select the New Document category.

3. Select a document type and check the Make Document XHTML Compliant box.

For more information on XHTML, check out the following:

*   "XHTML: The Clean Code Solution," an article by Peter Wiggin at `http://www.oreillynet.com/pub/a/network/2000/04/28/feature/xhtml_rev.html`

*   "What is XHTML?" an article by Jennifer Kyrnin at `http://html.about.com/library/weekly/aa013100a.htm?once=true&`

*   The XHTML Resource page at `http://xhtml.startkabel.nl/`, which includes links to XHTML articles and tutorials

*   XHTML tutorial at `http://www.w3schools.com/xhtml/`

*   The XHTML section of the W3C HTML home page at `http://www.w3.org/MarkUp/`, which includes links to all of the W3C XHTML specifications

Validating XML and XHTML Documents

Dreamweaver MX supports validation of XML and XHTML documents (as well as several other types of documents) through the built-in Validator. Using the Validator helps you find tag and syntax errors in your code and helps ensure that your XML and XHTML documents work properly.

You can set preferences for the Validator, including the tag-based languages it should check against, the problems it should check for, and the types of errors it should report. To set these preferences, follow the following steps:

1. Open the Validator Preferences dialog box (Edit Preferences → Validator).

2. Check the boxes for the tag libraries you want to validate against.

3. Click the Options button. The Validator Options dialog box displays.

4. Check the boxes in the Display option list for the types of errors you want to be included in the Validator report.

5. Check the boxes in the Check For option list for the problems the Validator should check for.

6. Click OK to close the Validator Options dialog box, and then click OK again to close the Validator Preferences dialog box.

Once you have set the Validator preferences, you can run the Validator for a document by following these steps.

1. Open an XML or XHTML file.

2. Select Check Page from the File menu, and then select Validate as XML from the drop-down menu (File → Check Page → Validate as XML).

3. If there are no errors in your document, the message No Errors or Warnings is displayed in the Results panel below the document.

4. If the Validator found errors, the error messages are displayed in the Results panel. Double-click an error message to highlight the relevant code in the document.

5. Right-click (Ctrl-click on a Mac) in the Results panel to save the report as an XML file or to open the report in a browser.

XML Behind the Scenes: Dreamweaver Menus

Dreamweaver offers several ways to customize and extend the basic Dreamweaver program. Dreamweaver is unusual in that it allows you access to the program files themselves so that you can customize the program to meet your needs.

> For more information on extending and customizing Dreamweaver, see Chapter 32.

An XML file, `menus.xml`, found in the Configuration/Menus folder contains configuration information for the menus and keyboard shortcuts in Dreamweaver. To change Dreamweaver menus, you need to edit the `menus.xml` file. (Remember to save a copy of the original `menus.xml` file before you make any changes to it!)

The `menus.xml` file is written to be parsed by Dreamweaver itself, so it may not work properly if you edit it in an XML editor. For the best results, edit it in a standard text editor like Notepad, Simple Text, or EditPad (available at `http://www.editpadpro.com/`).

The `menus.xml` file is a collection of XML elements that specify the menu bars, menus, and keyboard shortcuts. There are four XML elements for menu bars and menus included in this file:

menubar The `menubar` element specifies a Dreamweaver menu bar. It contains one or more `menu` elements, and must include an `id` attribute, which specifies a unique identifier for the menu bar. Each menu bar, menu, and menu item should have a unique `id` value. The following example shows the `menubar` element for the Dreamweaver styles menu bar:

```
<menubar id="DWStyleContext">
```

menu The `menu` element specifies a menu in a menu bar. It can contain one or more `menuitem` and `separator` elements, and it must include `id` and `name` attributes. The name attribute specifies the name of the menu. The following example shows the menu element for the Dreamweaver styles menu:

```
<menu name="CSS Style Popup" id="DWContext_CSSStyle">
```

menuitem The `menuitem` element specifies a menu item in a Dreamweaver menu. It must include `id` and `name` attributes, and it may also include any of the following optional attributes:

key This attribute specifies the command that this menu item performs.

enabled This attribute specifies JavaScript code to determine if the menu item is currently enabled.

command This attribute specifies a JavaScript expression that is executed when you select this item from the menu.

file This attribute specifies the name and path of an HTML file that contains JavaScript that controls the menu item.

arguments This attribute specifies the arguments to be passed to the JavaScript file used in the file attribute.

The following example shows the first `menuitem` element in the Dreamweaver styles menu:

```
<menuitem name="_Edit..."
enabled="dw.cssStylePalette.getSelectedStyle().length > 0"
command="dw.cssStylePalette.editSelectedStyle()"
id="DWContext_CSSStyle_Edit" />
```

You must specify either a command attribute or a `file` attribute for each `menuitem` element.

separator A `separator` element is used to create a dividing line between menu items. There are no required attributes for a `separator` element. Because the `separator` element is an empty element (has no content), the markup is as follows:

```
<separator />
```

Dreamweaver allows you to modify any part of the menu bar. An individual menu, for example, the File menu, can be changed by adding, deleting, or modifying the `menuitem` and `separator` elements contained in the `menu` element for the File menu.

The following example shows the New File menu item in the File menu of the Dreamweaver Main window menu bar:

```
<menubar name="Site Window" id="DWMainSite" platform="win">
  <menu name="_File" id="DWMenu_MainSite_File">
    <menuitem name="_New File"   key="Cmd+Shift+N"
```

```
enabled="dw.getFocus(true) == 'site'
&site.canMakeNewFileOrFolder()"
command="site.makeNewDreamweaverFile()"
id="DWMenu_MainSite_File_NewFile" />
```

The `menubar` element includes an optional `platform` attribute that specifies that this menu bar is only valid for the Windows platform.

The tutorial in the following section shows how to modify a Dreamweaver menu and how to create submenus.

Hands On: Modifying Your Dreamweaver Menus

In this tutorial, you will learn to modify the Style submenu in the Text menu of the main Dreamweaver window. Because the actual `menus.xml` file in the Dreamweaver program is the configuration file for all the Dreamweaver menus, you are not going to actually modify your copy of that file. Instead, you will modify the `text_menu.xml` file that is included on the accompanying CD for this book. You will learn how to modify the Dreamweaver menu configuration file without taking any risk of overwriting your original file by mistake!

1. Open the `text_menu.xml` file on the CD. This file includes the XML markup for the style submenu of the text menu in the main Dreamweaver window. The complete markup is also shown later in Listing 26.5.

2. Refer to Listing 26.5. The first line of this listing shows that this is the Main menu bar, the second line specifies the Text menu, and the third line specifies the Style submenu of the Text menu. Only the Style submenu is included here. The actual Text menu includes many additional submenus.

```
<menubar name="Main Window" id="DWMainWindow">
    <menu name="_Text" id="DWMenu_Text">
        <menu name="_Style" id="DWMenu_Text_Style">
```

3. Review the contents of the Style submenu, which consists of a group of `menuitem` and `separator` elements. For each `separator` element, a horizontal rule is displayed in the menu or submenu.

4. Note that each `menuitem` element contains these attributes: `name`, `key`, `file`, `arguments`, and `id`. The following markup is the first `menuitem` element in the Style submenu:

```
<menuitem name="_Bold" key="Cmd+B" file="Menus/MM/Text_Style.htm"
 arguments="'B'" id="DWMenu_Text_Style_B" />
```

Here, the `name` attribute identifies this as the Bold style. Because the name is preceded by an underline, the letter B will be underlined to indicate a shortcut for the Windows platform. The `key` attribute shows the keyboard shortcut to apply this style to a selection. The `file` attribute shows the path to the file named `Text_Style.htm`. This file contains the JavaScript that controls the Bold text style. The `arguments` attribute specifies that B is the argument to be passed to the JavaScript in Text_Style.htm. The id attribute shows the unique id for this menuitem element in the menus.xml file.

> Do not change the value of the id attribute or you may make the menu item inaccessible to JavaScript commands and functions.

5. Change the order of the menuitem elements following the first separator element by cutting and pasting the individual lines of markup. Move the _Emphasis and St_rong menu items to the top of this group, as shown in the following:

```
<menuitem name="_Emphasis" file="Menus/MM/Text_Style.htm"
    arguments="'EM'" id="DWMenu_Text_Style_EM" />
<menuitem name="St_rong" file="Menus/MM/Text_Style.htm"
    ="'strong'" id="DWMenu_Text_Style_STRONG" />
<menuitem name="_Strikethrough" file="Menus/MM/Text_Style.htm"
    arguments="'S'" id="DWMenu_Text_Style_S" />
<menuitem name="_Teletype" file="Menus/MM/Text_Style.htm"
    arguments="'TT'" id="DWMenu_Text_Style_TT" />
<separator />
```

6. Delete the _Teletype menuitem element.

7. Add a separator element between the _Italic and _Underline menuitem elements.

8. Save this file as text_menu_revised.xml.

 The complete markup for text_menu_revised.xml is shown in Listing 26.2 and is also included on the accompanying CD.

Listing 26.5

XML Code for Text Menu (text_menu.xml)

```
<menubar name="Main Window" id="DWMainWindow">
  <menu name="_Text" id="DWMenu_Text">
   <menu name="_Style" id="DWMenu_Text_Style">
      <menuitem name="_Bold" key="Cmd+B" file="Menus/MM/Text_Style.htm"
arguments="'B'" id="DWMenu_Text_Style_B" />
      <menuitem name="_Italic" key="Cmd+I"
file="Menus/MM/Text_Style.htm" arguments="'I'"
id="DWMenu_Text_Style_I" />
      <menuitem name="_Underline" file="Menus/MM/Text_Style.htm"
arguments="'U'" id="DWMenu_Text_Style_U" />
     <separator />
      <menuitem name="_Strikethrough" file="Menus/MM/Text_Style.htm"
arguments="'S'" id="DWMenu_Text_Style_S" />
      <menuitem name="_Teletype" file="Menus/MM/Text_Style.htm"
arguments="'TT'" id="DWMenu_Text_Style_TT" />
```

```
        <menuitem name="_Emphasis" file="Menus/MM/Text_Style.htm"
arguments="'EM'" id="DWMenu_Text_Style_EM" />
        <menuitem name="St_rong" file="Menus/MM/Text_Style.htm"
arguments="'strong'" id="DWMenu_Text_Style_STRONG" />
        <separator />
        <menuitem name="_Code"
file="Menus/MM/Text_Style.htm" arguments="'code'"
id="DWMenu_Text_Style_CODE" />
        <menuitem name="_Variable" file="Menus/MM/Text_Style.htm"
arguments="'var'" id="DWMenu_Text_Style_VAR" />
        <menuitem name="S_ample" file="Menus/MM/Text_Style.htm"
arguments="'samp'" id="DWMenu_Text_Style_SAMP" />
        <menuitem name="_Keyboard" file="Menus/MM/Text_Style.htm"
arguments="'kbd'" id="DWMenu_Text_Style_KBD" />
        <separator />
        <menuitem name="Citati_on" file="Menus/MM/Text_Style.htm"
arguments="'cite'" id="DWMenu_Text_Style_CITE" />
        <menuitem name="_Definition" file="Menus/MM/Text_Style.htm"
arguments="'dfn'" id="DWMenu_Text_Style_DFN" />
    </menu>
    </menu>
</menubar>
```

Listing 26.6

Revised XML Code for Text Menu (*text_menu_revised.xml*)

```
        <menubar name="Main Window" id="DWMainWindow">
    <menu name="_Text" id="DWMenu_Text">
    <menu name="_Style" id="DWMenu_Text_Style">
        <menuitem name="_Bold" key="Cmd+B" file="Menus/MM/Text_Style.htm"
arguments="'B'" id="DWMenu_Text_Style_B" />
        <menuitem name="_Italic" key="Cmd+I"
file="Menus/MM/Text_Style.htm" arguments="'I'"
id="DWMenu_Text_Style_I" />
        <separator />
        <menuitem name="_Underline" file="Menus/MM/Text_Style.htm"
arguments="'U'" id="DWMenu_Text_Style_U" />
        <separator />
        <menuitem name="_Emphasis" file="Menus/MM/Text_Style.htm"
arguments="'EM'" id="DWMenu_Text_Style_EM" />
        <menuitem name="St_rong" file="Menus/MM/Text_Style.htm"
arguments="'strong'" id="DWMenu_Text_Style_STRONG" />
        <menuitem name="_Strikethrough" file="Menus/MM/Text_Style.htm"
arguments="'S'" id="DWMenu_Text_Style_S" />
```

continued

continues

```
            <menuitem name="_Teletype" file="Menus/MM/Text_Style.htm"
    arguments="'TT'" id="DWMenu_Text_Style_TT" />
            <separator />
            <menuitem name="_Code" file="Menus/MM/Text_Style.htm"
    arguments="'code'" id="DWMenu_Text_Style_CODE" />
            <menuitem name="_Variable" file="Menus/MM/Text_Style.htm"
    arguments="'var'" id="DWMenu_Text_Style_VAR" />
            <menuitem name="S_ample" file="Menus/MM/Text_Style.htm"
    arguments="'samp'" id="DWMenu_Text_Style_SAMP" />
            <menuitem name="_Keyboard" file="Menus/MM/Text_Style.htm"
    arguments="'kbd'" id="DWMenu_Text_Style_KBD" />
            <separator />
            <menuitem name="Citati_on" file="Menus/MM/Text_Style.htm"
    arguments="'cite'" id="DWMenu_Text_Style_CITE" />
            <menuitem name="_Definition" file="Menus/MM/Text_Style.htm"
    arguments="'dfn'" id="DWMenu_Text_Style_DFN" />
        </menu>
      </menu>
    </menubar>
```

This file could be copied and pasted into the appropriate section of the markup in
`menus.xml` to actually change the display of the Style submenu in the Text menu, as shown in
Figure 26.8.

> Listing 26.5 and 26.6 do not include an XML declaration at the beginning because they are
> not actually a separate XML file but are part of `menus.xml`.

The steps in this section describe very simple modifications to a Dreamweaver menu. Although some modifications are indeed this easy, other changes can be quite
complex. Many menu items include JavaScript or
Dreamweaver commands that may be difficult to modify
correctly without a good background in using and writing
JavaScript.

Figure 26.8

**Modified Style sub-
menu in the Text menu**

VIEWING JAVASCRIPT SPECIFICATIONS FOR STYLES IN DREAMWEAVER

Step 4 in the tutorial above specifies that the Text_Style.htm file is the source file for the Bold style information. The Text_Style.htm file contains the JavaScript that controls the Bold style for text. If you would like to view the JavaScript, open Text_Style.htm in a browser (Configuration → Menus → MM → Text_Style.htm). View the page source to see the JavaScript code. Here's the JavaScript code for the Bold text style:

```
function receiveArguments()
{
  var what = arguments[0];
  if (dw.getFocus(true) == 'html' || dw.getFocus() == 'textView') {
    if (what == "B") {
      dw.getDocumentDOM().source.wrapSelection("<b>", "</b>");
    }
```

This code inserts <b> and </b> tags around the selected text in the HTML file.

Why Should You Care About XML?

XML and its associated technologies are one of the most rapidly growing areas in web development today. Even if you never deal with "data" on the websites you design, XML can also be used to efficiently update and maintain the text content of web pages. Check out the resources listed at the end of the "XML Concepts" section earlier in this chapter to continue your introduction to XML. Future versions of Dreamweaver are very likely to include much more support for XML and XHTML.

In the next chapter, you'll learn about using emerging web technologies with Dreamweaver MX, including how to use special types of XML files (WSDL and SOAP files) to add web services to your pages, and you will also find out how to use the .NET framework with Dreamweaver MX.

## CHAPTER 27

Working with Emerging Technologies—Web Services and .NET

Dreamweaver MX features extensive support for web development, including support for many server-side languages (ASP, ASP.NET, ColdFusion, JSP, and PHP) and emerging web technologies.

While the preceding chapters in this section offered more information on web application development, connecting to databases, using ColdFusion, and using XML and XHTML, this chapter focuses on using Dreamweaver to access web services and .NET.

Both web services and the .NET framework can be used with Dreamweaver MX to create dynamic web applications. *Web services* are remote applications (accessed via a web page) that carry out specific tasks or functions. Through the use of web services technology, the Web can be accessed not only to share information but also to share services. Microsoft *.NET* is the Microsoft platform for XML web services, and it can be used in Dreamweaver with ASP.NET to create web applications.

This chapter includes the following topics:

- **Understanding web services**

- **Accessing web services**

- **Adding a web service to a page**

- **Understanding .NET**

- **Using ASP.NET**

Understanding Web Services

Web services allow digital services, such as currency conversion, language translation, and user authentication, to be shared. The web services platform includes WSDL (Web Services Description Language), SOAP (Simple Object Access Protocol), and UDDI (Universal Description, Discovery, and Integration Service). Any language can be used to develop a web service application and web service applications can be run on any platform.

Web services allow application developers to combine software components from different web service providers to create distributed applications. Web service applications are made available by web service providers that can be located through online registries. The registries use UDDI to describe the services available from various web service providers.

Many registries are available, including the following.

XMethods (`http://www.xmethods.com`) Lists publicly available web service applications.

SalCentral (`http://www.salcentral.com/salnet/webserviceswsdl.asp`) Provides a search engine that looks for commercial web service applications that meet your criteria.

Microsoft UDDI Registry (`http://uddi.microsoft.com/default.aspx`) Offers free copy of the UDDI registry, but you must register to use it.

Dreamweaver MX allows you to create web pages (using JSP or ASP.NET) that can interact with web service applications. A web client can connect to a web service application via this page, and can use the application as needed. Dreamweaver, however, is not a tool for creating the web service applications themselves.

In order to create a web page that accesses a web service application, you need to know the server implementation and the protocol used. This information is available as part of the online registry listing, or directly from the service provider.

> For information on using JSP for web services, see "Getting Started on Developing Web Services" at `http://dcb.sun.com/practices/howtos/developing_webserv.jsp`. For details on using JSP in Dreamweaver, see Chapters 22 and Chapter 24.

Accessing Web Services

A web service is accessed from a web page. A typical scenario involves a web browser that sends a request to a web server for a particular page. The page is a portal to dynamic content—news stories, for example. The page on the web server makes a call to other servers that supply updated news content. After the latest news information is obtained from the web service providers, the information is inserted into the web page and returned to the web browser.

The three major components of the web services platform (WSDL, SOAP, and UDDI) provide the technology that supports this dynamic information transfer.

WSDL

To access a web service application, your web page needs a way to communicate with the application to determine the programmatic interface (available methods and parameters). WSDL is the proposed standard for this communication. WSDL is an XML format that describes the basic form of web service requests with different network protocols. It can be extended to any network protocol or message format.

Each web service includes a WSDL file that describes the bindings, methods, and data inputs and outputs. WSDL defines a *service* as a collection of ports. A *port* is specified by associating a network address with a binding. A *binding* is a protocol and data format specification for a specific port type.

> For more information on WSDL, see "Web Services Description Language (WSDL) Explained" at `http://msdn.microsoft.com/library/default.asp?url=/library/en-us/dnwebsrv/html/wsdlexplained.asp`.

WSDL 1.1 is a W3C Note as of March 2001 (`http://www.w3.org/TR/2001/NOTE-wsdl-20010315`). The W3C Note describes bindings with SOAP 1.1, HTTP GET/POST, and MIME (*Multipurpose Internet Mail Extensions*), but it is not limited to these bindings. More information about current W3C work in the web services area is available on the W3C Web Services Activity page at `http://www.w3.org/2002/ws/`.

SOAP

The web page requesting the service and the web service application usually communicate using SOAP, although other bindings can also be used. SOAP is a protocol that is independent of platform and language. A SOAP message is an XML document that is sent via a transport protocol—usually HTTP, but SOAP can also work with other transport protocols.

SOAP 1.2 is currently a W3C Working Draft and consists of four basic parts:

- An envelope that describes what's in a message and how to process it
- A set of encoding rules for application-defined data types
- A convention for remote procedure calls (RPCs) and responses
- A binding convention for exchanging messages using an underlying protocol

The latest version of the working draft was released in December 2001 and includes three parts:

- Part 0: Primer (`http://www.w3.org/TR/2001/WD-soap12-part0-20011217/`)
- Part 1: Messaging Framework (`http://www.w3.org/TR/2001/WD-soap12-part1-20011217/`)
- Part 2: Adjuncts (`http://www.w3.org/TR/2001/WD-soap12-part2-20011217/`)

3. In the Components panel (see Figure 27.1), choose Web Services from the drop-down menu in the upper left. Click the plus (+) button to the right of the pop-up menu and choose Add Using WDSL. The Add Using WSDL panel (also called the Web Service Chooser dialog box) is displayed.

4. In the Add Using WDSL display box, specify the URL of the web service you want to use.

5. If you don't know the URL, click the globe to the right of the URL text box and select one of the web service registries. The four selections are IBM Public UDDI, IBM Test UDDI, Microsoft UDDI, and XMethods UDDI. Dreamweaver will launch your specified primary browser and open the selected registry. You can also select Edit UDDI Site List to add additional registries or web service providers to the list, or you can select Edit Browser List to change the primary and secondary browsers. Select a web service from this registry, and enter the URL in the URL of the WSDL File text box.

6. Select a proxy generator that supports your chosen web service server model from the Proxy Generator drop-down menu at the bottom of the Add Using WSDL display box. (Implementation information is provided as part of the registry listing so that you can determine if the web service is available for your chosen web service server model.) Be sure that the selected proxy generator is installed and configured on your system.

Figure 27.5

Web service listing in the Components panel

7. Enter a username and password if requested by the proxy generator, and then click OK.

8. The web service now appears in the Components panel (Window → Components) and can be inserted in a web page (Figure 27.5).

The proxy generator then creates a proxy for the web service and *introspects* it. Through introspection, the proxy generator queries the internal structure of a web service proxy and makes its methods, properties, and interface available through Dreamweaver. An introspector can be chosen in the Default Proxy Generator dialog box (Figure 27.4) from the drop-down menu labeled Introspect Compiled Proxy.

> For more details on using the Web Services Chooser dialog box to generate a proxy, see "Completing the Web Services Chooser dialog box" in Dreamweaver Help (Help → Using Dreamweaver).

Once you have selected a web service and generated a proxy, you can insert the web service on your web page.

1. Switch to Code view (View → Code).

2. Open the Components panel (Window → Components), select the web service name, and drag it into the Code view window.

3. In the Components panel, click a method of the web service and drag it into the Code view window. Dreamweaver then adds the method and dummy parameters to the page.

4. Edit the inserted code with the data types, parameter values, and service instance names as required by the web service application.

When you use Dreamweaver to upload your site files to a web server, Dreamweaver automatically copies the pages, the proxy, and any necessary library files to the web server. These items must be available to the web server or your pages will not be able to communicate with the web service application. If you do not use Dreamweaver to upload your site files, make sure you include the proxy and any necessary library files.

Understanding .NET

Microsoft .NET is the Microsoft XML Web Services platform. The .NET platform includes four main areas

Smart clients and devices "Smart" client software that allows PCs and smart devices to access XML Web Services.

XML Web Services A core set of web services.

.NET servers Servers that integrate XML and XML Web Services in a distributed computing model. These include .NET Enterprise servers and Windows 2000 servers—other .NET servers are in development.

Developer tools Visual Studio .NET and the .NET Framework.

The .NET Framework

The .NET Framework is Microsoft's programming model for developing and using XML Web Services. It consists of three major components:

Common language runtime Takes responsibility for executing the application and making sure that all application dependencies are met.

Unified core classes Ensure that any type of application uses the same core classes; these classes also support code reuse.

Presentation classes Include ASP.NET, ADO.NET (for loosely coupled data access), XML Web Services, and Windows forms (for smart client applications).

The .NET Framework supports the integration of applications using different programming languages and allows application developers to use any programming language to develop applications.

The .NET Framework SDK is a free download (`http://msdn.microsoft.com/downloads/`). For more information on .NET and the .NET Framework, check out the following articles:

- "What is .NET?" at `http://www.microsoft.com/net/defined/default.asp`

- ".NET Framework Features Overview" at `http://msdn.microsoft.com/netframework/prodinfo/features.asp`

- ".NET Framework Developer's Guide: Getting Started" at `http://msdn.microsoft.com/library/default.asp?url=/library/en-us/cpguide/html/cpcongettingstartedwithnet-framework.asp`.

Using ASP.NET

If you are developing and testing dynamic web pages, you need both a web server and an application server. (The application server is also called a testing server in Dreamweaver MX.) The application server is software that assists the web server to process web pages that include server-side scripts. When a client browser requests a dynamic page from a web server, the web server sends the page to the application server for processing, and then returns the page to the browser.

Dreamweaver supports five server technologies: ASP, ASP.NET, ColdFusion, JSP, and PHP. The application server you choose depends on the server technology. The application server for ASP.NET is the .NET Framework.

To use ASP.NET in Dreamweaver MX, you need the following:

- Windows 2000 or Windows XP Professional

- Web server software—IIS 5 or higher on your computer or a networked Windows computer

IIS may already be installed on your computer. You can check by searching for a folder named `Inetpub` that IIS creates during installation.

- Application server software—.NET Framework (`http://msdn.microsoft.com/downloads/`)

- A root folder for the web application

To create a root folder, follow these steps.

1. Open `C:\Inetpub\wwwroot\` on the system running IIS.

2. Create a new folder for your web applications within the `wwwroot` folder.

3. Open the IIS Administrative Tool (select IIS from Administrative Tools in the Control Panel), and choose Web Sites → Default Web Site. Right-click the new folder you created in step 2, and select Properties.

4. Select the Scripts option in the Execute Permissions text box.

Your web server is now ready to serve pages from the root folder in response to HTTP requests from browsers.

> You must define a Dreamweaver site (Site → New Site) in order to create dynamic web pages.

After receiving an HTTP request from a browser, the web server will serve any page that is contained in the wwwroot folder or subfolders. Once you have a web server, an application server, a defined Dreamweaver site, and a root folder (whew!) you are almost ready to create and test dynamic pages. The next step is to specify a folder for processing your pages:

1. Open the Site Definition window (Site → Edit Sites). The Edit Sites dialog box displays.

2. In the Edit Sites dialog box, select the site from the list. Click the Edit button, which causes the Site Definition dialog box to display.

3. Click the Advanced tab.

4. From the Category list, select Remote Info. The Remote Info screen displays (Figure 27.6).

5. Choose Local/Network from the Access drop-down menu.

6. Click the folder icon to the right of the Remote Folder box. Browse to the root folder you created.

7. From the Category list, select Testing Server. The Testing Server screen displays (Figure 27.7).

8. Choose Local/Network from the Access drop-down menu.

9. Make sure the Remote folder you specified in the Remote Info category is the same as the one shown in the Testing Server Folder box. If not, click the folder icon and browser to the correct folder.

10. In the URL prefix box, enter the root URL. The root URL is the URL you enter in a browser to serve the dynamic page you're testing. For example, if the path specified in the Remote Folder box is C:\Inetpub\wwwroot\ MyApplications, you would enter http://localhost/MyApplications. Dreamweaver suggests a URL prefix, but you must check to make sure it's correct.

11. Click OK, then click Done.

Okay, you're almost ready to test your dynamic pages (at last!). The last step is to upload your files to the web server.

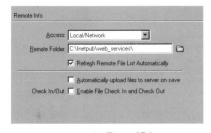

Figure 27.6

Remote Info screen

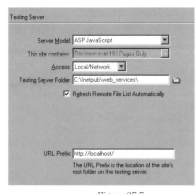

Figure 27.7

Testing Server screen

You need to upload the files to the web server even if the web server resides on your computer. Otherwise, certain features in Dreamweaver MX, such as Live Data view, may not function correctly.

Figure 27.8

Site folder in the Files tab

To upload your files, follow these steps.

1. Open the Site panel (Window → Site).

2. Select the Site folder from the list in the Files tab (Figure 27.8).

3. Click the blue up arrow icon on the toolbar.

4. A warning dialog box displays "Are you sure you wish to put the entire site?" Click OK.

Dreamweaver copies all of the site files into the folder you specified to process your dynamic pages.

Okay, are you ready to test your dynamic pages? All right, if you're sure… You can preview and edit your dynamic pages by using the Live Data window. To access the Live Data window, open the Live Data window (View → Live Data). Dreamweaver automatically sends a temporary copy of the dynamic page to the application server for processing. The resulting page is displayed in the Live Data window and the temporary copy on the server is deleted. That's it! If the application server has any problems returning a page, a warning box will display with suggested sources of errors and possible solutions.

Figure 27.9

Live Data Settings dialog box

If the page expects URL parameters from an HTML form using the GET method, you can enter that data in the text box on the toolbar of the Live Data window. Click the refresh icon (circle-arrow) after entering the data.

You can also enter the data in the Live Data Settings dialog box (see Figure 27.9). To do so, open the Live Data Settings dialog box (View → Live Data Settings), and enter data in the Name and Value columns. For example, if the parameter name is city and the value is Chicago, you would enter `city=` in the Name column, and `Chicago;` in the Value column.

You can also test your dynamic pages by previewing them in a browser (F12). Complete the Testing Server category in the Site Definition dialog box before you preview the page. For more details, see "Previewing dynamic pages in a browser" in Dreamweaver Help (Help → Using Dreamweaver).

Emerging Technologies

Both web services applications and the .NET platform are currently emerging technologies that are still in development and rapidly evolving. With public web service applications such as those listed in the XMethods registry (`http://www.xmethods.com`) and the free download of the .NET Framework, you can test out these new technologies in Dreamweaver MX.

Dreamweaver MX provides an extensive development environment with a GUI interface, and it is a great milieu for using these emerging web technologies to create dynamic web pages.

In the final part of this book, you'll learn how to prepare a site (or web application) for turnover to a client, how to test the site and then go live with it, and how to maintain it throughout the rest of its lifecycle.

## PART VI

Site Administration from Start to Finish

Too many designers, architects, and consultants build websites that look great when they launch and then slowly begin to gather dust when it becomes apparent that nobody put any thought into how to maintain them. To build websites that last, remember that the administrator of the site is a user too. There should be a convenient and well-designed interface for administering the site if you expect anyone to bother to do it.

In this part, we'll show you how to set up the administration features needed on the backend of a web site, how to make sure your site is compatible with the browsers your audience will be using, how to handling the turnover of a site ("going live"), and how to administer a website after the launch. As a bonus, the last chapter deals with customizing and extending Dreamweaver to get the most possible out of the application.

CHAPTER 28 ■ Setting Up Administration Behind a Site

CHAPTER 29 ■ Checking Browser Compatibility

CHAPTER 30 ■ Going Live or Delivering the Site

CHAPTER 31 ■ Administering the Site

CHAPTER 32 ■ Customizing and Extending Dreamweaver

Setting Up Administration Behind a Site

In order to get your site up and running, you need to have your back-end administration set up as well. This means that you must establish levels of security, administration, and different access levels for your website. Security is an important issue in this time of Internet hackers and destructive e-mail worms and viruses; so it's in your best interest to designate some sort of access control for your website.

Your site's security is also a reflection on your level of professionalism. Users trust you to keep their data confidential. In order to do this, you will need to establish roles for various users and follow a protocol of user and content administration.

This chapter addresses all of these security related features and topics including the following:

- **Developing user administration**

- **Administering content**

- **Personalizing your website**

- **Establishing groups and roles**

- **Using passwords and security**

Developing User Administration

Dreamweaver MX gives you the tools that will help you restrict user access to your website. Here are examples of what could result from the several levels of security you choose to provide:

- Users could register when they arrive at the site for the first time.
- Users could log in every time they visit the site.
- Only certain authorized users could view specific pages.

Before we get into the specifics of how to set up such levels of security, we'll first discuss the components you need to begin creating a secure site. Here are some specifics.

You need to have a database table that stores your users' pertinent information, and you need a form that allows entry of personal data, including a user ID and a password. The database table you create holds this form's information so that it can be recalled every time the user logs in to your system.

In addition, you will also need two server behaviors: Insert Record, which updates the database user information; and Check New Username, which ensures that the username each user enters is unique. Refer to Chapter 24 for more information about these and other server behaviors.

Creating Your Database Table and Assigning Privileges

When you create your database table to store the user information, think about what type of data you want to collect from the user—their username, password, name, address, and phone number, for instance—and set up the table columns accordingly. Remember to create as many columns as you need to store each type of data that you want to collect in its own column. For example, if you only want to collect a username and password, then your database table would just have two columns.

The following steps will show you how to create a user's table using Oracle; however, each database works differently, so the process for Oracle may not be identical for Access, SQL Server, or MySQL.

1. Log in to the database. Remember, to do so, you must have "create table access."

2. Execute the following SQL command:
   ```
   CREATE TABLE users {
   username varchar(20),
   password varchar(10)}
   ```

3. Log out of the database.

If you want to assign different privileges to different users, make sure you create a privileges column in your database table. To do this, you would first create a database column that specifies each user's access privileges, and then you would assign each user one of the following privilege types: Administrator, User, or Guest.

A programmer will tell you that they don't like the extra work of having to assign individual privilege types when they are having a database store security information, so instead, they will assign a default level of security to this Security column so that each user has a standard level of security—let's say User. Then they would go back and give higher or lower security to individual users based on what permissions they want to give those specific users.

When you are assigning levels of security, remember that a single user cannot have multiple levels of security. Because of this rule, if you want to set up multiple privileges for a certain page of content, you will need to set those privileges at the page level instead of at the user level. Here's how you do it:

1. From the page you want to restrict, click the Server Behaviors panel.

2. Click the plus (+) button, and from the resulting pop-up menu, select User Authentication → Restrict Access to Page. The Restrict Access to Page dialog box displays.

3. Click the Username, Password, and Access Level radio button to assign individual access levels to different users.

4. A list displays in the Select Levels box. Click the access levels you want that are valid.

5. Click OK.

> If you want to prevent unauthorized users from accessing a particular page, you can use Dreamweaver MX's server behavior, Restrict Access to Page. This redirects the user to another page if the user attempts to access the protected page. (This page will typically say something to the effect of "You are not permitted to access this page, with a way to return to the accessible areas of the site.) Restrict Access to Page only protects HTML pages, however. There is no security available in Dreamweaver MX for other types of files, such as images, audio, and Word documents.

After you add security to your page, you need a way to allow users to set up accounts. This can be done with a registration page, which will be the first page your users access.

Creating a Registration Form

A registration page is a form that your front end uses to collect information from the user. It is in this form that you specify that the user should create a username, a password, and any other additional information you want to collect.

To create such a form in Dreamweaver MX, follow these steps:

1. Select Insert → Form. This creates an empty form on your Dreamweaver page where you can add in username and password text fields.

2. To establish text fields on this form, for example User and Password fields, select Insert → Form Object → Text Field. This creates a text field in which the user can add their information.

3. Add text labels to your fields by choosing Insert → Form Objects → Label.

4. After your fields are designated, add a form Submit button by using Insert → Form Objects → Button.

You now have everything you need on your form to capture login information.

In order for your form to store the information it collects in the database, you'll need to add an Insert Record server behavior. In the next section, you'll learn how to add the Insert Record server behavior to save the user's registration information.

Adding Server Behaviors

Figure 28.1

The Server Behaviors panel

Whenever you need to add a server behavior, you use the Server Behaviors panel to do so (see Figure 28.1). This window lists the active server behaviors on your page; in addition, it lists the new behaviors that can be added. During the process of making a registration page for you users, you will use this window to add two server behaviors: Insert Record and Check New Username server, which will be discussed in more detail in the following sections.

Whenever you add, change, or delete information, your database needs to reflect these changes. Let's go over how to save these registration changes to the database.

Updating the Database with the Insert Record Server Behavior

In order to update the database table of users, follow these steps to use the Insert Record server behavior (see Figure 28.2).

1. In the Server Behaviors panel, click the plus (+) button and select Insert Record. The Insert Record server behavior window displays.

2. To specify the table of users in the database, select the database to use from the Connection drop-down list. Also select the table to insert into from the Insert Into Table pop-up menu.

3. In the After Inserting, Go To box, enter the page that should be opened after the log in information is inserted into the table.

4. In the Get Values From pop-up menu, select the form that was used to obtain the user's username and password.

5. Map each value in the login form to the database column it will be stored in. For each field in the form, first highlight the field from the Form Elements list and then select the database column it uses from the Column drop-down list as well as the data type from

the Submit As menu. For example, the Username form field should map to the Username database column as a text data type.

6. Click OK.

This figure shows the Insert Record dialog box after these steps have been used to fill in its values with sample data.

> The *data type* is the kind of data the column in your database table is expecting (text, or numerals). Password or username columns usually expect text, but sometimes numbers might be used.

Speaking of login forms, while we are talking about users sending their password to your site, let's consider the security of their password. When the web user enters their login information on the web page, the data will not be secure if it is being sent over the Internet in an unencrypted form, in fact, it could be intercepted. To put your user at ease, you might be better off using the more secure Secure Socket Layer (SSL) encryption, or by checking your web server software for additional security measures that you can add to your site.

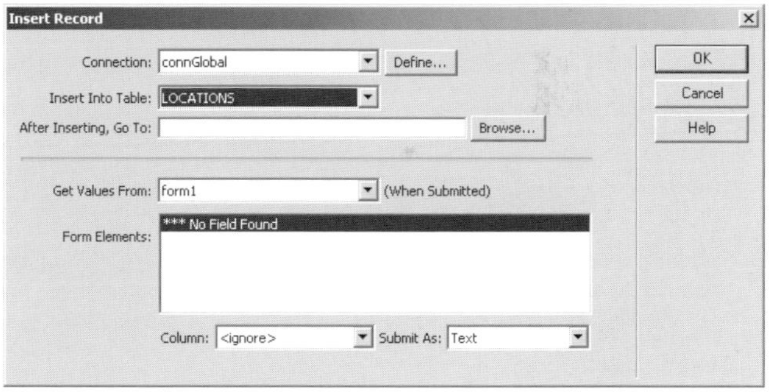

Figure 28.2

Insert Record dialog box

In addition to providing such security features, when you are managing your site, you could also use a unique username to dynamically change the look of a web page based on the user's role or group. This information for their personalized page would be stored with their username and password. When the user requests a personalized page, content is dynamically shown or hidden based on the users role. We'll discuss personalization in greater detail later on in this chapter.

Making Sure Usernames Are Unique

No matter what the size of your site, you will find that getting users to use unique information is a challenge. It seems like everyone likes to use their initials, or their dog's name as a username, and when this happens, you end up seeing a lot of identical usernames. To avoid this problem, you need to set up your database to check its tables to see if a specific username is unique.

To have your database check for existing usernames, use the Check New Username server behavior (see Figure 28.3).

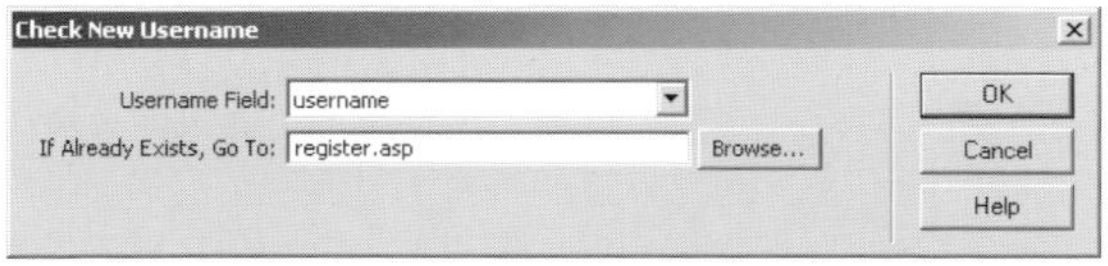

This dialog box specifies the field to check and the page to go to if the username already exists. By using this behavior,

Figure 28.3

Check New Username dialog box

when a new user clicks Submit, or Enter (whatever button name you've selected to indicate that the user has completed filling out the data), this server behavior compares the username they just entered with all the registered usernames stored in the database.

When the Check New Username performs its search, one of two things can happen. One would be that no matching username is found, and the other would be that a matching username is found. If there isn't a match, Insert Record creates a new record for that user and lists the username that they chose.

But if there is an existing record, Check New Username cancels the Insert Record function and delivers an error to the user. This is the process that you should follow to find out if the username is unique.

1. Click the plus (+) button from the Server Behaviors panel and choose the Check New Username from the User Authentication sub-menu.

2. From the Username Field drop-down list of the Check New Username window, specify the form field name that contains the user's username.

3. Use the Browse button to select a page to go to if the username already exists. This page should tell the user to pick a different username.

4. Click OK to save your changes.

The registration process is now complete. Once they are registered, your user will have a login name and a password that they will use every time they enter your site, or the portions of it that they visit if they are restricted to specific groups.

Login Pages and Processes

Now that you can register users, you'll need a login page to authenticate them each time they visit your site. When a user completes a successful login, Dreamweaver MX places their login information in a session variable. After logging in, the user will be able to access the pages that match their access level as long as their current session is open.

To add a login page, follow these steps.

1. Start with a new page by Selecting New from the File menu of the main screen.

2. Add a form object, by selecting Insert → Form, that creates an empty form in which you can add username and password fields.

3. Use Insert Form → Objects → Text Field to add field definitions so that your users understand what data to enter in each separate field.

4. After your fields are designated, add a form Submit button by using Insert → Form Objects → Button.

5. You may now add the Log In User server behavior (see Figure 28.4 for an example of how the Log In User dialog box can be filled out) to your page. Click the plus (+) button

from the Server Behaviors panel and choose the Log In User from the User Authentication sub-menu.

6. The Log In User dialog box prompts you for the name of the form you just created. In this case, the form name was fmLogin.

7. Then use the Browse button to select the pages that the user will be sent to after successful and failed logins.

8. You can then select the database table that holds the access information from the Validate Using Connection drop-down list.

9. Select the table that is used for validation from the Table drop-down list.

10. Select the username column from the Username Column drop-down list.

11. Select the password column from the Password Column drop-down list.

12. Click OK to save your changes.

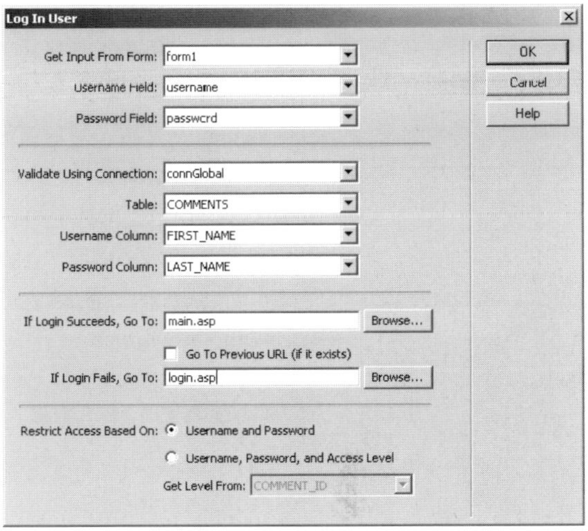

Figure 28.4

Log In User dialog box

This produces a functional login page. You'll still need to develop the static content, attach a template or style sheet, and otherwise finish the design of the page (as discussed in Parts III and IV of this book.)

If you want to make your login process Amazon-slick, you can use a cookie to identify your users, as we will discuss next, and no, we're not talking about the kind you eat! *Cookies* store information on the browsing user's computer for later reference by your site.

Using Cookies to Store Persistent User Data

Cookies are data structures used by a website to deliver data to a user, store user information, and sometimes return that stored information to a website. This means that websites can "remember" user information in order to deliver their custom preferences, and allow the use of passwords. For example, a cookie could be used to automatically default to the user's username on the login page (or even skip the login page altogether and automatically log in the user). Automatically logging in a user is obviously less secure than requiring them to enter their password every time.

To gather cookies from a user, you need a request object that allows your login page to either default to the username or even completely log in the user. All you need is a place in your database to store the cookies, and the `Request.Cookies` ASP routine to check for the cookie and loop up, or associate, the user ID.

The `Request.Cookies` routine allows you to retrieve the values from a user's cookie file when it is sent to you in an HTTP request. Currently HTTP is stateless, which means that the web server doesn't store any information about a particular HTTP transaction, so each subsequent transaction is like the first one.

For security's sake, users should be able to log out of your site. If you don't make your users login every single time they access your site, or if the information is incredibly sensitive, you can provide a logout button for your users to end their session. For example, a bank site, usbank.com, requests usernames and passwords when users log in order for the database to show the user their customized information. Because this is a banking site, the information is secure, so they also have a logout button in order to closeout the display of sensitive information.

Logging Users Out

Security conscious users will want the ability to log out of a website (so that someone else using the same computer cannot access their information). Dreamweaver MX provides the Log Out User server behavior to accomplish this (see Figure 28.5).

This server behavior offers two ways to tie the login behavior to the site. You can create a logout link (you may want to include it in your navigation bar or template header) that invokes the behavior or you can choose to have the logout server behavior launch automatically when the page that contains it loads. The login page should usually be the page that you specify to go to after logout.

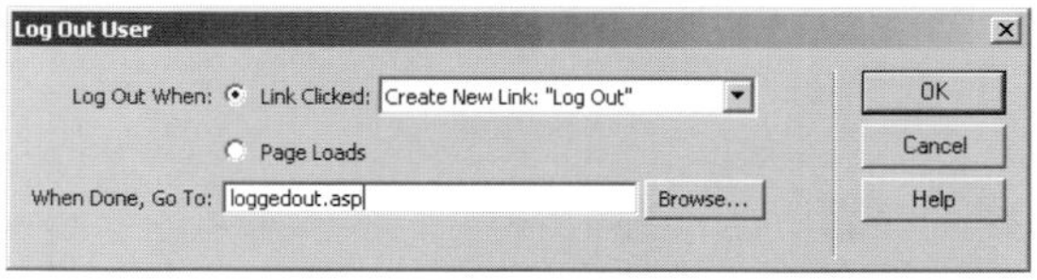

Figure 28.5

**Log Out User
dialog box**

Now that we've talked about registering and logging in and logging out users, let's discuss security restrictions to your pages.

Page Access Restriction

As we mentioned in the beginning of this chapter, you can secure your web pages individually so that a user doesn't have access, or you can give users a privilege value that restricts them to using only the portions of your website that you allow them to view. In either case, when the user attempts to access a restricted page, the user is redirected to another page that alerts them of their access faux pas. When you want to restrict access to a page, you use the Restrict Access server behavior (see Figure 28.6).

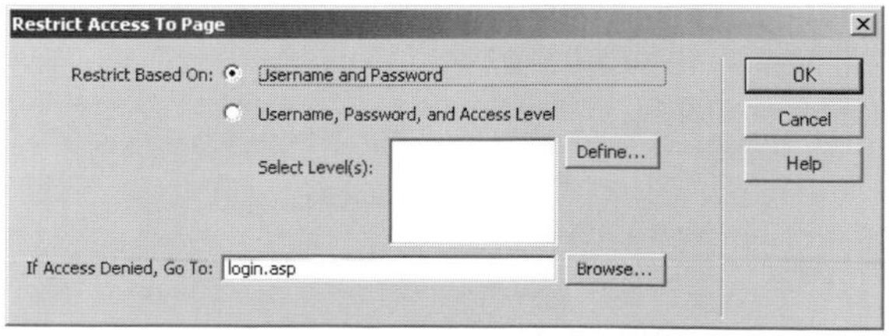

Figure 28.6

**Restrict Access to
Page dialog box**

The options that you can control from this dialog box include restricting access to include which access levels are valid for the page and which page to go to if the user isn't logged in. Usually, the login page is specified as the Access Denied Go To page.

Restricted pages should always contain a link to logout.

Now that who is logged in has been established, we can customize the content to a specific user based on their role or group; this is also called *personalization*.

Developing a Portal

A web portal provides several informative tools that are dynamically created for the user. With a portal, you can structure your information in categories and subcategories; in addition, you can manage and change the hierarchy of the categories. When portalization is being used, your user's searches will include searches within categories, titles, summaries, texts, and authors of information.

In addition, portals let you do many cool things:

- Manage files available for download.

- Manage ad banners.

- Manage target links.

- Rate content based on user feedback.

- Allow users to register and manage their own profile and password.

- Make sure that user logins are secure.

The following website discusses the potential benefits of using a portal: `http://www .4eit.com/portals.htm`

Adding Personalization Features

Once you know who is logged in to your site, you may want to do more than just whimsically restrict or grant access to pages and sections of your site. Groups of users who perform the same functions (roles) can all be assigned the same access privilege. Whether you've grouped your users by role or you simply want to exploit an attribute of their database profile, you've got plenty of choices of ways that you can personalize their web experience. Generally, users are happiest when they are presented with a higher ratio of information that is relevant to them.

Let's use an e-commerce site that sells clothing as an example. A user with a registration profile that specifies that their home state is Minnesota could be offered an initial page with heavy winter coats featured, whereas a user from Arizona might be offered windbreakers.

As this example illustrates, by using the demographic and personal information you have about a user, you can customize every small detail of the web page that they will see. This unique treatment enhances the user's experience and also increases the probability that they will continue using your site. For example, if you are a frequent purchaser on Amazon.com, your cookies alert the site that it is you who is viewing, and then Amazon.com offers suggestions for new purchases in music, books, and toys (wherever your interest was in prior purchases). This customization of their site probably makes you feel special—almost as if you had a personal sales associate to guide you to purchases based on your likes and dislikes.

THE 'PORTAL' BUZZWORD DURING THE DOTCOM DAYS

The term *portal* has come and gone several times in successive waves of the Internet tulip-bulb type craze of the late '90s and early '00s. It first appeared as jargon for directory sites, such as the early Yahoo! Site, meaning a categorized site of links to other resources. The "portal" was supposed to be the doorway to those other sites. Competing terms that didn't catch on included things like launchpad, jumping-off point (or jumpzone, or something "kewl" like that).

As Yahoo! developed into more than just a directory of web pages and started offering multiple services (free e-mail, stock listings, news headlines, maps, greeting cards, auctions, etc.), the term portal came back, or it never went away but its meaning mutated to mean a full-service site or a site that offered a range of services. What stayed the same was the underlying goal that you will make our portal your browser's home page, you will start at our portal every time you go online, and you will view plenty and plenty more of our ads.

The third-wave meaning for portal is still all around us, in the form of the *enterprise portal*, *corporate portal*, *vertical portal* (also *vortal*), *federated portal*, and so on. Most of the time this refers to a sort of uber-site for an organization (or enterprise), combining three types of web sites or applications:

- An enterprise's **website**, public-facing and high-profile site

- An enterprise's **intranet**, private, secure, employee-facing site

- An enterprise's **extranet**(s), access-restricted, secure, partner/supplier/vendor-facing site

In the grand unified portal theory, an enterprise portal should use one common architecture, and combine security, profiling, personalization, customizing, and—most importantly—the web-enabling of traditional business processes (with self-service as the ultimate goal), meaning everything from sales, through HR interactions, to supply-chain management and beyond. Of course, one problem with any such big-picture scheme is that it tends to ignore an enterprise's existing fragmented and differently implemented "facts on the ground."

Incrementalism seems to be the real way of the Internet, so whether you or your client is building the ultimate portal from the ground up or simply remodeling one corner of your enterprise's web sprawl, there's plenty of work to be done. Roll up your sleeves.

Here are some other things to consider.

Changing the presentation of a page   Though you may just send different groups of users to different pages, you can also make more subtle changes such as including a different CSS definition for different roles. Either the path of the CSS definition or the name of the definition can be generated dynamically. This changes the way the page appears and feels but not the content. For example, users in the USA might see a page with red, white, and blue, while users from Germany would see yellow, red, and black (the colors of the German flag).

Modifying the content of a page   You can also change the content of your pages by using the Show Region server behaviors as well as all of the other dynamic objects, such as dynamically changing images.

Your end users aren't the only ones who benefit from dynamically building pages based on their login. You can create profiles and groups for administrators to help you or them get the job done faster.

Another feature common to portals and other intentional web communities is a posting board, which is similar to a bulletin board, where people can share information on any given topic.

Incorporating Discussion Boards

A portal is built by combining several tools to inform and empower users. One of the most important tools of a website that uses portals is that it lets users on the site share information. The most basic way for users to share information is though lists that can be expanded upon or added to through the web interface. This posting board framework (the framework allows the users to add topics and reply to messages) can be used to implement many useful sections of a portal. For example, a company intranet site may have an announcement listing that displays on the main portal page. Each announcement was submitted by a portal user and appears in brief. If the portal user clicks the announcement, they get the full announcement.

These lists use a mix of Dreamweaver MX features to display. For instance, in the example of the company's intranet announcement, the announcement list was dynamically generated from a database table that holds announcements. The newest announcements appear first on the page (this is accomplished by selecting Using and Order By in the filter). Also, in this example, users can click the announcement's subject to view more information (which is held in a master/detail page set). Users also have the ability to add their own announcement via an Insert page that uses a form and an Insert Row server behavior. The web user sees only the page on which to add their announcement—the database and structure of the form are hidden from them. Other portal features can be built using the same idea as this announcement example.

Reducing Site Maintenance

A big advantage of dynamically altering pages based on roles is that doing so reduces the total number of pages that must be maintained. If users in different roles are simply given a different set of pages to access, the number of supported roles multiplies by the number of pages that must be maintained. By using dynamically generated pages, you can reuse much of the content, and thus keep the overall number of pages that you have to maintain to a minimum.

Because the customized information that appears on a dynamically modified site may be sensitive, you may consider using authorization levels to view the new registrants before you allow them to access your site.

For example, an online drugstore (say, Walgreens.com) might have unique features that require this kind of site—such as those that let you view your prescription history and request refills online. In order to use these features, you must first provide information to the site that includes a username, password, real name, address, and telephone number. Also, even though you just entered all your data, Walgreens.com still has to verify that you are who you say you are, and in order to do this they send you a PIN (Personal Identification Number) through the mail. After you receive the PIN, you go back to Walgreens.com, and enter your PIN. Your pre-existing information is then activated in the database, and you can now log in with your previously established username and password.

On the website's end of things, here is what just happened. After receiving the PIN, Walgreens.com upgraded your privilege level so that you would have access to your own records. In order to mirror this scenario on the site that you are building, you would add an extra column to your database table that will store the user's access privileges, and you would also have to use the Restrict Access to Page server behavior to redirect unauthorized users to another page.

Subscription-based access like the type just described and portalization aren't always the same things. Using portals can also help you organize your data.

Testing, 1, 2 …

As you can see, setting up the crucial back end aspects of a website can be an exciting adventure for a person with a little thought, creativity, and knowledge. You can enhance your website in a myriad of ways, and all of these can help ensure that your users (or community members) come back again, and again, and again. You can use what you've learned here to create a customized and secure site. Next, you will learn about how to test your site for usability before going live.

## CHAPTER 29

Checking Browser Compatibility

Browser compatibility continues to be a major issue for web designers. Unless you are designing pages for a very specific audience—an office intranet where everyone is using computers with the same operating system and the same browser, for example—it is necessary to design pages with browser compatibility in mind. You should also test your pages in multiple browsers before uploading them to a web server.

This chapter covers the following topics:

- **Defining the target audience**

- **Evaluating browsers for JavaScript, CSS, and XML support**

- **Testing browser compatibility in Dreamweaver**

- **Avoiding common problems**

Defining the Target Audience

The vast majority of web surfers are using computers with the Windows operating system. As of October 2000, according to statistics from Statmarket (`http://www.statmarket.com`), Windows users make up 93 percent of the web audience, Mac users make up 3 percent, and the remaining 4 percent includes users of all other platforms combined.

Internet Explorer 5 is currently the most popular browser for web surfers, but IE 6 is gaining in popularity. Overall, as of April 2002, global statistics at `http://www.thecounter.com` showed that 90 percent of the web audience used Internet Explorer, 5 percent used Netscape Navigator, and the remaining 5 percent used other browsers, such as Opera and Mozilla.

Keeping these statistics in mind, look at your target audience again. Which browsers are they likely to use? Do your pages include JavaScript or CSS? Do your pages include special features that require the latest browsers, such as XML or CSS absolute positioning support? Are your pages viewable by users with disabilities? You should review all of these important issues at the beginning of the site design process, and again during the testing phase.

> See Chapter 1 for more information on audience definition and site planning.

Evaluating Browsers

All browsers support basic HTML, but browser support varies widely for JavaScript, CSS, and XML. If you are using these additional features in your pages, it is very important to evaluate and test the browser support for the specific features you want to include.

Table 29.1 provides general information about browser support for JavaScript, CSS, and XML. In addition to the most popular browsers, Internet Explorer and Netscape Navigator, Opera has been included. Although Opera does not have a large number of users in the United States, it is much more popular in Europe. If your site targets an international audience, it may be important to include Opera in your browser evaluation and testing.

Table 29.1

Browser Support for JavaScript, CSS, and XML

BROWSER	JAVASCRIPT VERSION	CSS VERSION	XML
Explorer 6	1.5 ECMA[1]	CSS1, partial CSS2	Yes
Explorer 5.5	1.5 ECMA	CSS1, partial CSS2	Partial
Explorer 5.0	1.3 ECMA	CSS1, partial CSS2	Partial
Explorer 4.0	1.2 ECMA	CSS1	No
Netscape 6	1.5 ECMA	CSS1, partial CSS2	Partial
Netscape 4.7	1.3 ECMA	CSS1	No
Opera 6	1.4 ECMA	CSS1, CSS2	Yes
Opera 5	1.3 ECMA	CSS1, CSS2	Yes

[1]ECMA is an open standard for JavaScript.

Table 29.1 provides general guidelines for browser support, but for information about support of specific features, check out the following sources:

- WebReview's Browser Compatibility Chart at `http://www.webreview.com/browsers/browsers.shtml`

- WebReview's CSS master grid at `http://webreview.com/style/css1/charts/mastergrid.shtml`

Information regarding browser support of specific CSS, HTML, and JavaScript features is also available in Dreamweaver itself. Choose the Window menu, and select Reference. A Reference window displays. From this window, choose O'REILLY CSS Reference, O'REILLY HTML Reference, or O'REILLY JavaScript Reference, and then choose the specific feature you are interested in from the drop-down list. Browser information is shown to the far right of the feature name.

Dreamweaver includes built-in JavaScript in Dreamweaver behaviors. (For more information on Dreamweaver behaviors, see Chapter 19.) A target browser(s) is specified by choosing the Show Events For item in the Action or Events menu of the Behaviors panel. The target browser determines which events are shown in the Events menu for the chosen action. The Show Events For submenu includes the following target browser choices:

- 3.0 and Later Browsers
- 4.0 and Later Browsers
- IE 3.0
- IE 4.0
- IE 5.0
- IE 5.5
- IE 6.0
- Netscape 3.0
- Netscape 4.0
- Netscape 6.0

Testing Browser Compatibility in Dreamweaver

Dreamweaver includes two features for testing pages in browsers and determining browser compatibility: Preview in Browser and Check Target Browsers. You can also modify browser profiles or create new ones to customize your testing.

Preview in Browser

The Preview in Browser feature allows you to view your pages in the browser(s) of your choice.

Pages don't have to be saved in order to use this feature, so you can test them at any time. All browser-related functions work in Preview mode, so you can test JavaScript and CSS functions as well as links, plugins, and ActiveX controls. Although absolute and relative URLs function in preview mode, root-relative links can only be viewed if the file is on a server.

To use the Preview in Browser feature, select Preview in Browser from the File menu in the page you want to preview, and then choose one of the browsers from the list. You can also add or remove browsers from the list by choosing File → Preview in Browser → Edit Browser List and then clicking the plus (+) button to add a browser to the list, or the minus (–) button to delete a selected browser from the list.

You can also specify a primary browser and secondary browser. This enables you to use function keys to activate Preview in Browser. F12 opens the current page in the primary browser, and Control + F12 (Cmd + F12 for the Mac) opens the current page in the secondary browser.

> You can include up to 20 browsers in the Browser List. You must, however, have all these browsers installed on your computer.

Dreamweaver MX also includes a Debug in Browser selection in the File menu. The Debug in Browser feature allows you to check for syntax errors in any JavaScript included in the page you are testing. The debugger checks for syntax errors in the JavaScript for that page and lists any errors in the Results panel. In this window, select an error, then click the Go to Line button in the lower-right corner to go to the line of code where the error is located. To view line numbers in your code, choose View → Code View Options → Line Numbers. You can check for logical errors in your JavaScript code by using Preview in Browser.

Check Target Browsers

The Check Target Browsers feature allows you to check for any elements or attributes that are not supported by the target browser. Dreamweaver uses preset browser profiles for Netscape Navigator versions 2.0, 3.0, 4.0, and 6.0, for Internet Explorer versions 2.0, 3.0, 4.0, 5.0, 5.5, and 6.0, and for Opera versions 2.1, 3.0, 3.5, 4.0, 5.0, and 6.0. These profiles can be modified, and new browser profiles can be created.

Check Target Browsers can be used to check a document, a directory, or an entire site. Dreamweaver generates a Check Target Browsers report that opens in your Target Browser Check panel in the Results panel group. This report includes the following:

- The name and location of the files with errors
- The specific line where the error occurs

- A description of the error

Here are some ways to use the Check Target Browsers feature.

- To check a file, save the file first. The check is done on the last saved version of the file. With the file open in Dreamweaver, choose File → Check Page → Check Target Browsers. When the Check Target Browsers window displays, select a browser from the list, and then click the Check button.

- To check a folder or a site, select Window → Site to open the Site panel. Choose the correct site from the drop-down menu on the left, and then select a folder from the site files. Open the Results panel (Window → Results). Click the Target Browser Check tab, and then click the green arrow at the top left and choose "Check target browsers for entire site" or "Check target browsers for selected files/folders in site." When the Check Target Browsers window displays, select a browser from the list, and then click the Check button.

> Check Target Browsers checks only HTML files, not scripts. To check the JavaScript in your pages, use Dreamweaver's JavaScript Debugger. To use the debugger, go to the File menu and select Debug in Browser; then choose a browser from the list. This list is the same as the Preview in Browser list.

Using Browser Profiles

Browser profiles are text files that include detailed information about the elements and attributes supported by specific browser versions. The browser profile files are contained in the `Configurations/BrowserProfiles` folder in the Dreamweaver application folder.

The following code shows an excerpt from the browser profile for Internet Explorer 5.0.

```
<!ELEMENT BaseFont >
<!ATTLIST BaseFont
     Class
     Color
     Face
     ID
     Lang
     Size
     Style
     Title
>
```

The browser profiles are very similar to Document Type Definitions (DTDs) and are mainly written using DTD syntax. These files specify exactly which elements and attributes a particular browser supports. HTML pages can be tested, or validated, against the browser profiles. In the preceding code example, the `BaseFont` element is specified as a valid element in this browser. The additional lines of code specify that the `BaseFont` element can contain any of the listed attributes.

> Browser profiles can also include warnings, error messages, and suggested substitutions for the unsupported element or attribute.

Browser profiles must have a very specific structure to function correctly. The rules for this structure include the following:

- You must use a unique profile name. This name appears in the Check Target Browsers list, and it must appear as the first line of the document, as shown in the first line of code in the Internet Explorer 5 profile:

  ```
  Microsoft Internet Explorer 5.0
  ```

- You must use the following form for the second line, which identifies this document to Dreamweaver as a browser profile:

  ```
  PROFILE_TYPE=BROWSER_PROFILE
  ```

- You may use only the following elements in a browser profile:

  - `!ELEMENT`, which are HTML elements

  - `!ATTLIST`, which is made up of HTML attributes for a specified element

  - `!Error`, which adds an error notice in the Check Target Browsers report

  - `!msg`, which are messages in plain text that are added to error notices

  - `!htmlmsg`, which are messages in HTML that are added to error notices

- You may not use HTML comments `<!-- -->` in a browser profile. You can include comments by using `--` at the beginning of a line.

- You can include `!Error` within `!ELEMENT` or `!ATTLIST`.

- You must include a space in the following locations: before the closing angle bracket (>) in an `!ELEMENT` declaration, after the opening parenthesis in a list of attribute values, before the closing parenthesis in a list of attribute values, and before and after each pipe (|) in a list of attribute values.

For example, the format for the `BR` element is shown in the following excerpt from the Internet Explorer 5 profile:

```
<!ELEMENT BR Name="Line break" >
<!ATTLIST BR
    Class
    Clear ( left | right | all )
    ID
    Language
    Style
>
```

The first line is an element declaration for the HTML element `BR`. A `Name` attribute is optional, but if it is included, this name (`Line break`) can be used in error messages. Otherwise, `BR` will be used in error messages.

The second line is an attribute list declaration. The `BR` following `!ATTLIST` specifies that this is a list of valid attributes for the `BR` element. These attributes include `Class`, `Clear`, `ID`, `Language`, and `Style`. In addition, the valid values for the `Clear` attribute are `left`, `right`, or `all`. The pipe symbol (`|`) stands for "or."

To edit a browser profile, open an existing profile in a text editor (Notepad, SimpleText, or another text editor of your choice).

If you don't want to see an error message for a particular unsupported element or attribute, change its format. For example, to stop seeing error messages for the `style` element in Netscape 3, change its format from this:

```
<!ELEMENT Style !Error >
```

to this:

```
<!ELEMENT Style >
```

If you edit a browser profile, save the profile with a new file name. This preserves the original profile in case you want to use it again.

To add a custom error message, add either `!msg` or `!htmlmsg` after `!Error`. For example, you can modify the error messages for the attributes of any element that includes attributes. Take a look at this code from the Netscape Navigator 3 browser profile for the `UL` element and its attributes:

```
<!ELEMENT UL name="Unordered List" >
<!ATTLIST UL
      Type ( disc | circle | square )
      Class !Error
      ID    !Error
      Style !Error
>
```

This can be modified to include messages regarding errors, as shown in the following:

```
<!ELEMENT UL name="Unordered List" >
<!ATTLIST UL
      Type ( disc | circle | square )
      Class !Error !msg "Netscape Navigator 3 does not support the Class
attribute."
      ID    !Error !htmlmsg "<b>Netscape Navigator 3 does not support the
ID attribute.</b>"
      Style !Error
>
```

To create a new browser profile, follow these steps:

1. Open an existing profile in a text editor (Notepad, SimpleText, or other text editor of your choice).

2. Replace the profile name in the first line of the browser profile file.

3. Add any new elements or attributes using the format shown above for the BR element and its attributes.

4. Delete any elements or attributes not supported by the browser. If you are creating a profile for a new browser, it is unlikely you will need to delete any elements or attributes.

Avoiding Common Problems

Browser compatibility issues are best addressed by preventing them from taking place. Take a close look at your target audience, including which browsers and platforms they are most likely to be using to view your pages. The more features you add to your pages—including complex layouts, JavaScript, CSS, animation, interactivity, and multimedia content—the more likely you will have problems with browser compatibility.

Browser Detection and Version Control

Sometimes it is easiest to include different versions of pages for different browsers rather than trying to design one page that will display the way you want in several browsers. JavaScript can be used to include browser detection and direct users to different pages depending on the browser version they're using to view your page.

> For an excellent free browser detection script, see "The Ultimate JavaScript Client Sniffer, Version 3.03" at `http://www.mozilla.org/docs/web-developer/sniffer/browser_type.html`.

Designing for Browser Compatibility

To design the most browser-compatible page, consider the following when you design the pages for your site:

- Don't save browser-compatibility testing until the last moment. It's much easier to make changes early in the design process. Test your pages in multiple browsers (and on both the PC and the Mac platform, if possible). Web designers tend to use the latest, greatest browsers, but that is often not the case with your audience.

- Allow some flexibility in your design layout. Don't expect your pages to look the same in all browsers and all platforms—they won't! A pixel-precise design may work well in some browsers, but it is unlikely to work the way you had in mind in all browsers.

- Use multimedia elements wisely and offer viewers the choice of listening to audio files and viewing long segments of animation.

- Specify margin width, margin height, and left margin and top margin attributes in the body element to ensure that browsers display your page margins in a similar way.

- Use layers wisely. If possible, use tables instead of layers to lay out your pages.

- Be especially careful when you are using CSS. Use the Reference panel and the Check Target Browser feature to check if a particular CSS feature is supported.

- Think twice about including several complex features in a single page. Be sure these features are really necessary to convey the intent of your page.

Web Standards

As you can see, browser compatibility is very complex, and a major headache for most web designers and web developers. Newer browsers—including Netscape 6.*x*, Internet Explorer 6.0, and Opera 6.0—are designed to be much more compliant with the web standards developed by the Worldwide Web Consortium (W3C) and make it much easier to design a single version of a page that will display approximately the same in each of these browsers. Although browsers are certainly nowhere near being totally compliant with web standards, these newer browsers are a huge step in the right direction.

> For more information on web standards, visit the Web Standards Project site at http://www .webstandards.org (this site is currently being retooled as Web Standards Phase II—the old site is still available at http:// archive.webstandards.org) and A List Apart at http://www.alistapart.com.

Your audience, however, is likely to include viewers using older browsers. In particular, as long as your audience includes viewers using 4.*x* browsers or earlier, you will have to carefully consider browser compatibility issues.

Resources for Exploring Browser Compatibility Issues

A good start to exploring browser compatibility issues is to learn the features of the browsers well. For more information about specific browsers, see the following:

- "IE 6 Overview" at http://hotwired.lycos.com/webmonkey/01/30/ index3a.html?tw=eg20010824

- "Why Netscape 6 Woes Are Your Best Friends" at http://www.webreview.com/2001/ 01_19/webauthors/index03.shtml

- "Why Don't You Code for Netscape?" at http://www.alistapart.com/stories/netscape/

For more complex browser compatibility issues, particularly if you are using DHTML (JavaScript and CSS) in your pages, see the following:

- "Common Browser Implementation Issues" at `http://www.webreview.com/browsers/browser_implementation.shtml`

- "Browsers! Browsers! Browsers! A Strategic Guide to Browser Interoperability" at `http://www.webreview.com/2000/12_29/strategists/index01.shtml`

- "Scripting for the 6.0 Browsers" at `http://www.scottandrew.com/weblog/articles/dom_1`

Getting Ready to Launch

Before you go live with a new site or project, it's natural to want to get everything "just exactly perfect." Of course, this is an ideal result that is statistically almost possible to achieve (particularly if perfection is defined subjectively, usually by the person paying the bills). However, you now know how to plan around the likely browsers your audience will be using, and you can validate your site code one last time using the methods described in Chapter 23. In the next chapter you'll finally get to that most important milestone, the site launch, also known as "going live."

## CHAPTER 30

Going Live or Delivering the Site

Some people say that web projects never end, and they're not just talking about how a website requires round-the-clock babysitting for its entire life. No, what they mean is that it's sometimes hard to hand the code over to your client (or boss, or whomever) and say, "I'm done." The best way to deal with this is to plan it in advance. Put a milestone at the end of the project plan called "Turnover," and list all the things you'll need to do to wash your hands of a finished project with a clean conscience—things like I'll discuss in this chapter:

- **Final testing and QA**

- **Section 508 accessibility standards**

- **Finding or preparing a host server**

- **Going live (from staging to production)**

- **Exporting a site as a single XML file**

- **Transferring just the right files**

- **Documenting your work**

Quality Assurance and Final Testing

I know we just got done with a lot of testing in Chapter 29, but that was validation—making sure that your code won't break in any of your user's browsers. When a project is concluding, on the other hand, there may be subphases for a few other types of testing:

Usability testing The final stage. Though usability testing can start during storyboard/thumbnails, it can continue when HTML templates have been made, and it can be done even here at the end of a project to avoid costly post launch retro-fixes.

QA Quality assurance testing. This must be completed before turnover.

User-acceptance testing This may be carried out on the production server like a beta test before the site or application officially goes live. Though it's a bit late in the game to make changes, if users aren't going to adopt your new application or site, then it is worth making changes so that they will.

Usability Testing

Though you can test a site's interface reasonably well from mockups and prototypes, there's no real substitute for watching first-time users attempt to navigate and use your final site code. To facilitate this process, design a series of procedures you want to see tested, and then ask your subjects to attempt to accomplish them. Don't give them any help or feedback; just observe what the users do when presented with the interface. Some large-scale projects can benefit from highly quantitative testing done in lab conditions, but even on a shoestring budget you can find some way to bring people into your office (or home) and watch them interact with your site.

QA Testing

Like usability testing, QA testing could warrant an entire book to itself, but I will address it here briefly. The classic way to do quality assurance testing is to design a "coverage matrix" of features and functionality based on the user requirements you gathered at the beginning of the project. The same people who did the analysis and requirements gathering can also design the QA tests, or you can bring in a specialist for the end game. In addition to testing the features and functionality, the QA expert will identify what platforms and web browsers the intended audience will be using and then they will test each procedure in every possible environment.

Often, you grab every warm body you can, and set them up in front of Internet Explorer for Windows NT, Opera for OS X, Mozilla for Windows XP, and so on. In each environment, each tester needs to work their way through the coverage matrix and log any bugs they find. Bugs are prioritized in a three- or five-point scale (examples of priority types might include "serious," "minor," and "suggested enhancements"), and then the top-priority bugs are fixed in the time permitted—ideally you would get to everything except for perhaps some nice-to-have enhancements that don't break the site for anybody if they don't get added.

> Dreamweaver's Sitespring product is designed to integrate with Dreamweaver and enable collaborative project management and client-relations tracking.

User-Acceptance Testing

User-acceptance testing is often confused with usability testing, but it is different. It is less scientific and usually involves bringing some of the intended end users in to test the site after it has been handed over (as discussed in the next few sections) but before it has officially gone live. Similar to what you would do for usability testing, you can develop a set of tasks for the user-testers to perform, but it's not as important to avoid helping them or commenting on the interface. If problems arise that aren't egregious, they can possibly be addressed through the help material, documentation, and training. The primary goal of user-acceptance testing is to verify that the site operates as intended and can be comprehended and used effectively by those who are going to be stuck with it once you're on to your next project.

Meeting Section 508 Accessibility Standards

The U.S. Federal Government has mandated a set of accessibility standards (in the 1998 Rehabilitation Act), usually referred to as "Section 508" standards collectively, for sites developed for the government or using government funding. These have become de facto standards for other organizations and it is becoming more common for Section 508 compliance to show up as a requirement in RFPs (requests for proposals).

> See Chapter 3 for a discussion of how to turn on prompting for accessibility attributes when you are designing your sites.

As a result, it is important that your site meets these standards. To run an accessibility report to make sure your site complies, follow these steps.

1. Select your site from the Site pop-up menu in the Site panel.
2. Choose Site → Reports. This bring up the Reports dialog box.
3. Select Entire Current Local Site in the Report On pop-up menu.
4. Click the Accessibility check box (see Figure 30.1).
5. Click the Run button. Dreamweaver analyses your site and produces a report, keyed to the Section 508 regulations (see Figure 30.2).
6. Double-click any line in the report to jump to the problem code and fix it, if need be.

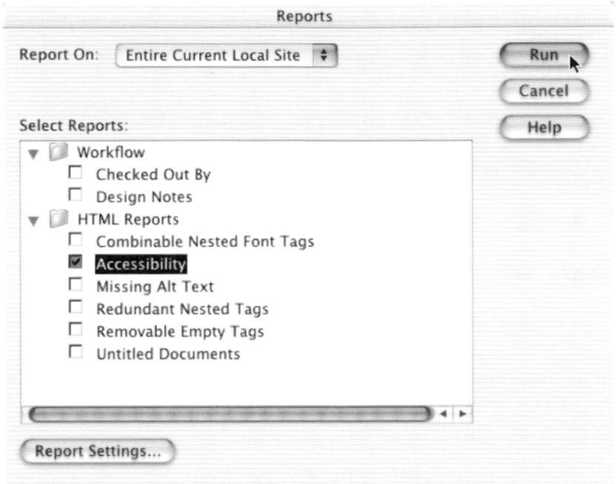

Figure 30.1

Getting ready to check the accessibility of an entire site

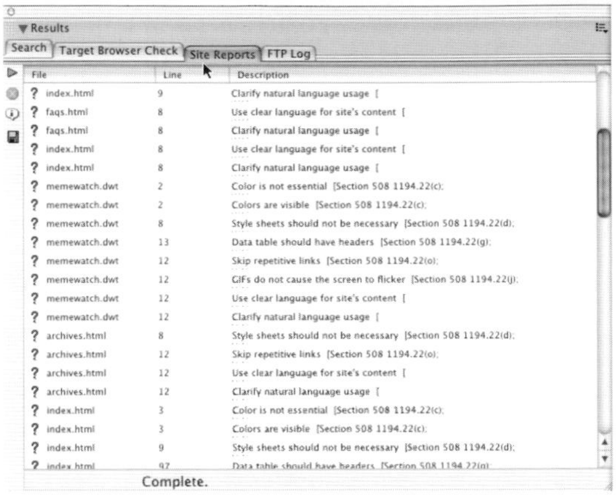

Figure 30.2

It looks like we've got a lot of code to clean up to make sure our site is as compliant as possible.

Even if your client or employer does not require total compliance with Section 508 standards, you may still benefit from reviewing the accessibility of your site from this perspective. For more information about the guidelines, see the government's site at `http://www.section508.gov/`, which describes, among other things, the Buy Accessible program. Note that this site is itself compliant with the standards (of course).

From Staging to Production

The big step you take at turnover or when your site goes live is moving the site from the staging environment (whether that's a testing server, a local version of the site, or what have you) to a production environment, meaning a live environment that makes the site or application available to the public (or to its intended audience—this may be on a secure intranet, after all).

If you are building your own site and do not have access to an Internet host, then you'll need to contract with a hosting service and set up an FTP account for publishing the site live. You should be able to do this inexpensively, assuming your site is not too large and the expected traffic not high enough to require premium pricing. (If you are developing a high-traffic site, then you need to factor the costs of hosting the site into your business model!) There are many sources of opinion available online about hosting providers. The market changes rapidly and we wouldn't feel comfortable recommending anyone specific in this context.

In any case, the staging server and the production server should be set up exactly the same way. If there are services enabled, they should be configured the same way and the directory structure of one should mirror the other.

Turnover (At Last!)

There are two different ways to upload a finished site to a production server from your test-ing/stating environment:

- Export the entire site as a single XML file.

- Synchronize the local site with a remote site.

The first approach makes sense when you won't have regular access to the production server but need to deliver or send the site to the new server for installation.

The second approach works best when you can set up the production server as your remote site (as opposed to using the staging server as a remote site and keeping a local site in addition).

Exporting a Site as XML

It's easier than it sounds to export a site as XML. Just follow these steps.

1. Choose Site → Edit Sites.

2. Click the Export button. A dialog box appears asking if you are exporting the site merely for a backup or to "share with others" (see Figure 30.3).

3. Choose the latter choice because your passwords and local paths are not relevant.

Export Site

Are you exporting this site to back up your settings or to share your settings with other users?

○ Back up my settings (includes login, password, and local paths).

○ Share settings with other users (does not include login, password, or local paths).

OK

Cancel

Help

Figure 30.3

The Export Site dialog box

4. Another "Export Site" dialog box appears (this one is like a Save As dialog box). Choose a folder and a filename for the site export.

5. Click Save.

6. Click Done.

To import the XML version of an entire site, the process is similar.

1. Choose Site → Edit Sites.

2. Click the Import button.

3. Browse to and select the STE file.

4. Click the Open button. Dreamweaver unpacks the site and adds it your list of sites.

5. Click Done.

So, one way to make a clean handoff of site code is to simply deliver the XML (STE) file exported from the completed site.

Synchronicity

Another, more common way of delivering the final site is to put it all from your local server to a remote server. If you've been using a staging or testing environment as your remote server, you should first synchronize that entire version of the site with your local copy, and then set up the production ("live") server as your remote server and synchronize again.

Cloaking Folders and Files

If there are any folders or files on the local server that don't belong in the official release of the site, you can "cloak" them before synchronizing so that they will be ignored during the mass put of folder and files to the remote server.

> Besides hiding files and folders from the synchronize command, cloaking also hides them from the PUT and GET methods, Check In and Check Out, reports, "select newer," all sitewide operations, Asset panel content, and template and Library updating.

To cloak a folder or file, first make sure that cloaking has been enabled. To enable cloaking, select Site → Cloaking → Enable Cloaking. (Similarly, to turn off cloaking, select Site → Cloaking → Disable Cloaking.)

To have all files of a specific type cloaked automatically, select Site → Cloaking → Settings, and then on the Advanced tab of the site Definition dialog box, click the Cloak Files Ending With check box and enter the file extensions of any file types you want to cloak (see Figure 30.4).

Figure 30.4

Dreamweaver can automatically cloak all the files of a specific type for you.

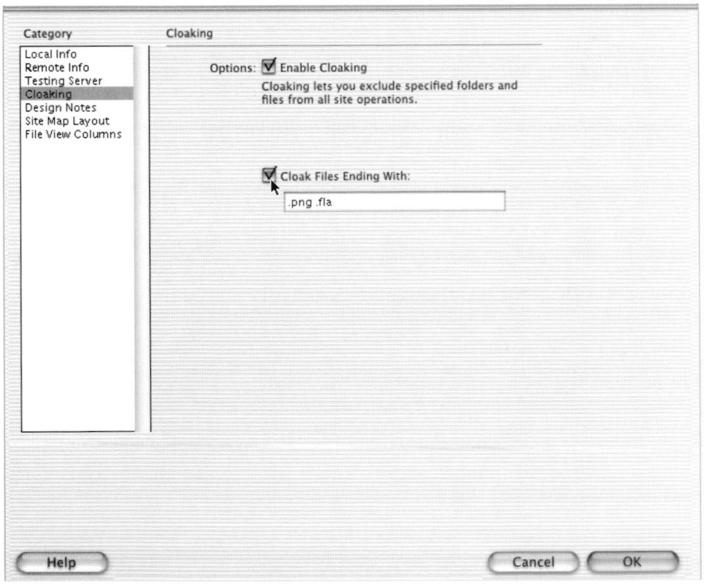

To cloak a specific folder or file, select it in the Site panel and then choose Site → Cloaking → Cloak. Cloaked files appear struck through with a red line, as shown here. (Naturally, to "decloak" a specific folder of file, use Site → Cloaking → Uncloak.)

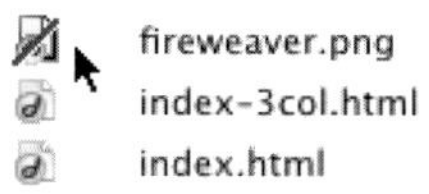

fireweaver.png

index-3col.html

index.html

You can also uncloak all cloaked files at your site in one fell swoop by choosing Site → Cloaking → Uncloak All.

> Be aware that the step of uncloaking all files at the site is irreversible. Dreamweaver will "forget" which files and folders were cloaked and if you change your mind, you will have to recloak each file or folder individually.

Synchronizing to the Remote Server

When the time comes to duplicate the site on the production server, the easiest way to do this is with the site Synchronization feature. This is simply an automatic way of handling the PUT operation for the entire site.

> See Chapter 3 for an explanation of getting, putting, Check In, and Check Out.

To upload your site this way, follow these steps:

1. Choose Site → Synchronize. The Synchronize Files dialog box will appear (Figure 30.5).

2. Select the Select Entire Site option in the first pop-up menu.

3. Select Put Newer Files to Remote in the second pop-up menu.

4. Click the "Delete remote files not on local drive" check box if you're sure there's nothing at the remote site aside from the files you're uploading that should be preserved.

5. Click the Preview button. Dreamweaver will list the files to be put to the remote server. Uncheck any files you don't want put there (see Figure 30.6).

6. Click OK. Dreamweaver will report "synchronization complete" when done.

7. To save a record of the upload, click the Save Log button.

8. Click Close.

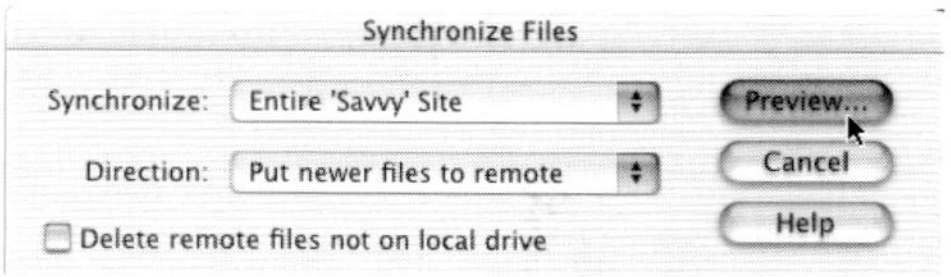

Figure 30.5

The Synchronize Files dialog box

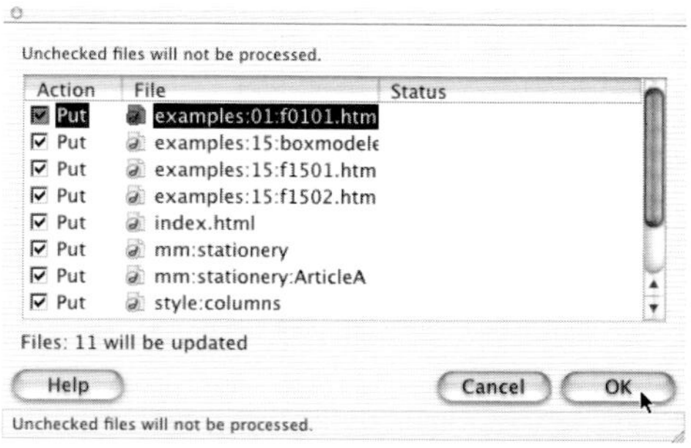

Figure 30.6

Files to be updated

Teach Them to Fish: Knowledge Transfer

Once you've handed over the code for a site, your project may still involve supporting whoever will have to work with and maintain the site (if this is not you). Dreamweaver can help with some aspects of what's called *knowledge transfer* (which is just consultant jargon for training your client to help them understand how their new system works). Here's a list of some of the key aspects of knowledge transfer, with notes on whether Dreamweaver can be of any help in executing each process:

- By supplying the client with the site templates, you will make it easier for them to maintain and update the site in the future. If you did not use templates in the building of the site, you still may want to create templates from the key pages for this purpose. See Chapter 4 for an explanation of templates.

- You must use clean, readable code if you may have to maintain a site or application developed by someone else. Dreamweaver can structure and highlight your code (as discussed in Chapter 23). You can also insert comments into your code to help explain it using the Comment button 🗩 on the Common tab of the Insert bar, as shown here (it brings up a dialog box; type your comment and click OK).

- You can add design notes to any file that might benefit from explanation, by choosing File → Design Notes. (Enter your notes in the primary text box and then click OK.)

- You should provide the client with documentation (a manual for maintaining the site) or—at minimum—a clean copy of the requirements used to develop the site. Dreamweaver can't help with this!

- You should also provide the client with training. Again, Dreamweaver won't help you with this.

- And then there's always good old-fashioned hand holding.

The Long Haul

So, now you know what to do at the end of a web development project. You go live with your new site, or you deliver a working site or application to your client, and that's the end of the story, right? Well, no. The Web is not a printing press and a website is not a book. Most websites and some web application require constant maintenance and oversight, which brings us to Chapter 31.

Administering the Site

In Chapter 3, you learned how to use some of the Dreamweaver tools that enable you to set up and organize a website. Once you have published your site, the same tools allow you to perform the ongoing maintenance that keeps your content fresh and your pages usable. Ongoing website administration may not be glamorous, but it's essential—it's what keeps visitors coming back consistently.

Luckily for anyone tasked with having to keep a website running smoothly, Dreamweaver offers an unmatched range of tools for keeping track of files, cleaning up HTML, and collaborating with members of a team. This chapter examines the typical website administration functions you'll need to perform once your site is online. They include the following:

- **Managing content with the Site Map and Files List views**
- **Synchronizing your local site with online files**
- **Collaborating with your team using Check In/Check Out and Design Notes**
- **Making your workflow run smoothly**
- **Keeping records of changes and backups**

Managing Content

Your website might start out at a manageable size—say, three to six pages—but it can soon begin to grow exponentially and at a rapid rate. If your site presents an online catalog of goods for sale, for example, you will need to delete items as they go out of stock and change descriptions as prices change. On the other hand, if you are managing a corporation's informational website, you will also need to perform regular updates of personnel, financial information, press releases, and more.

When your website contains hundreds or even thousands of files, even a single change, such as renaming a file or repairing a broken link, can have big consequences. Happily for both experienced and expert webmasters, Dreamweaver presents you with a toolbox full of utilities for keeping track of your site's content.

Using the Site Map and File List Views

The first challenge faced by many website administrators is simply being able to get an overview of all of the files the website contains. Some like to get a visual picture of how their site is organized. Others prefer to view the folders, subfolders, and files in the form of a hierarchical list. Dreamweaver gives you access to both ways of viewing your site's content through the Site panel. In Figure 31.1, the left half of the Site panel, which shows the remote site, displays the site's contents in Site Map view. The right half shows the local version of the site in File List view.

If you want to view only the visual map of your website, click the Site Map button in the Site panel toolbar and hold down your mouse button until a pop-up menu appears. Choose Map Only from the pop-up menu to make the Site panel display only the Site Map view. Choose Map and Files so that the Site panel displays both the Site Map and the File List as shown in Figure 31.1.

Figure 31.1

Site Map view (left) gives you a picture of how your files and folders are linked. File List view (right) shows folders and files in a hierarchical list.

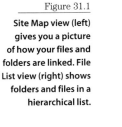

The Site panel, which contains the Site Map and Files List views, lets you do much more than just see your site; it gives you a way to perform routine administrative functions. Not only that, but when you use the Site panel to create or rename files or move documents from one location to another, you can instantly see the result and how the change fits into the overall structure of your site.

If you have a server set up on your computer, such as Apache or Internet Information Server, you can test your site locally before publishing your files. Clicking the Testing Server button in the Site panel toolbar lets you view the files you have on your local testing server.

In order to work both on the local version of your site and on the one you've already published, you need to define your site as described in Chapter 3, and connect to it with FTP or another protocol (see Chapter 30). Then continue by opening the Site panel, and choosing the site's name from the Site drop-down list to open your local Files List view. Then choose Site → Connect to connect to your remote site. When you have both the remote and local sites open in the two panes of the Site panel, you can start moving files between the two.

> FTP isn't the only option you have for gaining access to your website and transferring files. If the server that hosts your website supports it, you can also connect to your remote website using the WebDAV (Web-based Distributed Authoring and Versioning) and Visual SourceSafe protocols. These let you do source-control and version-control integration.

Moving Files

Dreamweaver, like some FTP programs, uses the terms Get and Put to move the files between your website and your filesystem. Choose Site → Get to move a selected file from the remote server to your computer; choose Site → Put to move a file from your local site to the remote server.

Selecting a single file in either the remote or local pane of the Site panel moves that file when you select Get or Put. But you can also select multiple files and then move them all at once. Shift-click to select contiguous folders or files; Ctrl-click (Cmd-click on a Macintosh) to select discontiguous folders or files.

You can configure Dreamweaver to automatically save files before you put them on the remote site. Choose Edit → Preferences to open the Preferences window. Click Site in the Category List in the Preferences window, check the box next to Save Files before Putting, and then click OK.

Creating and Deleting Files

The Site panel makes it easy for you to revise the content of both your remote and local websites. You can remove or create both individual files and folders. To create a new folder, either in the remote site or on your local directory, follow these steps:

1. Select the folder that you want to contain the new folder.

2. Do one of the following:

    - Choose File → New Folder (Site → Site Files → View → New File on a Mac).
    - Press Ctrl + Alt + Shift + N (Cmd + Shift + Option on a Mac).

The new folder is created. The default name New Folder is highlighted so that you can type a new name and then press Enter to rename it.

To add a new file to the site, the steps are similar:

1. Select either the folder that you want to contain the new file or an existing file in the folder that you want to contain the file.

2. Do one of the following:

    - Choose File → New File (Site → Site Files → View → New File on a Mac).
    - Press Ctrl + Shift + N (Cmd + Shift + N on a Mac).

The new file is created. The file's name is highlighted so that you can type a new name and then press Enter to rename it.

Double-click the file's icon in the Site panel to open the file in a new Dreamweaver window so that you can edit it.

If you connect to your site with FTP, Dreamweaver will disconnect you if you're inactive for more than 30 minutes. You can change this limit: choose Edit → Preferences, click Site, and replace the number 30 in the Disconnect after 30 Minutes Idle box.

Renaming Files and Folders

You can rename an existing file or folder on either the remote or local site by following these steps:

1. Highlight the file's name in one of two ways:

    - Right-click the file or folder (Windows) or click and hold down on the file (Mac) and choose Rename from the pop-up menu.
    - Click the file and choose File → Rename (Windows) or Site → Rename (Mac).

2. Type the new name and press Enter.

If your site presents content generated by a small- to medium-sized company, you might suddenly find yourself awash in content. Consider adding on a program designed to automate content creation.

Synchronizing Local and Remote Sites

After you've created, deleted, or renamed files in one pane of the Site panel, you need to make sure your changes are carried over to the other pane of the window. Rather than making you search and replace files and folders one by one, Dreamweaver saves you time and effort by enabling you to automatically synchronize both sites.

Before you synchronize, you need to identify which version of the site is the newest. With both the remote and local versions of the site open in the Site panel, choose either Edit → Select Newer Local or Edit → Select Newer Remote. Dreamweaver compares the file creation dates of the files with their counterparts in the opposite pane of the Site panel. The newer files are highlighted. Then follow these steps:

1. If you only want to synchronize specific files or folders, select them in either the Local or Remote pane of the Site panel. If you want to synchronize the entire site, select the top-level folder in either the Local or Remote pane.

2. Choose Site → Synchronize. The Synchronize Files dialog box (see Figure 31.2) appears.

3. Choose one of the following options from the Synchronize drop-down list:

   Entire Site Synchronizes all files in the remote and local versions of the site.

   Selected Local Files Only or Selected Remote Files Only Selected Local Files Only appears if an item in the Local pane was most recently selected, and Selected Remote Files Only appears if an item in the Remote pane was most recently selected. These options only synchronize selected files.

4. Choose an option from the Direction drop-down list:

   Put Newer Files to Remote Moves the local files that were more recently modified to the Remote pane and replaces the earlier versions of those files.

   Get Newer Files from Remote Moves the remote files that were more recently modified to the Local pane and replaces the earlier versions of those files.

   Get and Put Newer Files Moves the most recently modified versions of the files in both the Local and Remote panes to the opposite panes.

5. Check the box at the bottom of the Synchronize Files dialog box if you want to delete files on the destination pane that don't have corresponding files in the origin pane. (This option doesn't appear if you choose Get and Put Newer Files.)

6. Click Preview. Dreamweaver compares the files in the local and destination panes but it doesn't actually replace any files. If no selected files in the originating pane are newer than those in the destination pane, a dialog box appears telling you that no synchronization is necessary. If

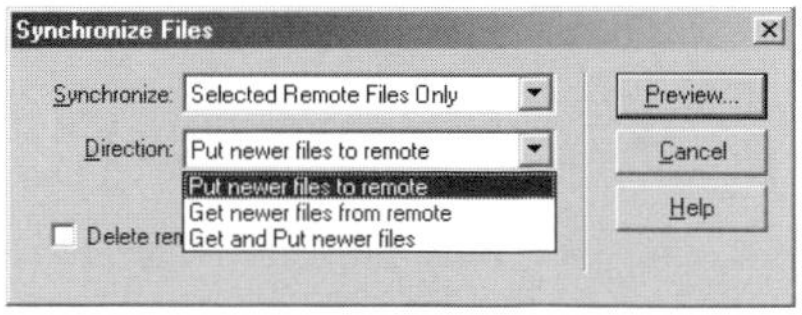

Figure 31.2

You can make the local and remote versions of your website match, thus updating your remote site with a single command, using the Synchronize Files dialog box.

synchronization is necessary, a new dialog box, simply called Synchronize, opens with a list of any files that need to be synchronized (see Figure 31.3).

7. Deselect any items in the Synchronize dialog box that you don't want to replace. When you are ready, click OK to transfer files and replace older versions if necessary.

If you want to verify whether an individual file or folder in one location exists in the other location, Dreamweaver can save you some time looking. Right-click the folder you want to locate and choose either Locate in Remote Site or Locate in Local Site from the pop-up menu. When Dreamweaver finds the file, it is highlighted in the opposite pane of Site panel. The Locate in Remote/Local Site command is especially helpful if the file you're looking for is buried within folders and subfolders and would take some searching to find otherwise.

Cleaning Up Your HTML

It's up to the editors and writers who create content for your site to make sure the words that make up your web pages are free of grammatical errors and typos. (Of course, if you're doing everything yourself, you need to proofread the content as well as design the web pages.) But no matter what, it's up to you to make sure your site's behind-the-scenes content—its HTML code—has the correct syntax.

If you create all of your content from scratch using Dreamweaver, you can be certain that your HTML is correct. But few webmasters type all the text themselves in the Dreamweaver window. More often, they import text from word processing programs such as Microsoft Word, which adds unnecessary HTML commands to your web page code. You can tell Dreamweaver to clean up the code, whether it comes from Word or from another source. Dreamweaver gives you the option of automatically cleaning up the HTML when it opens a file, or when you manually tell it to perform a cleanup.

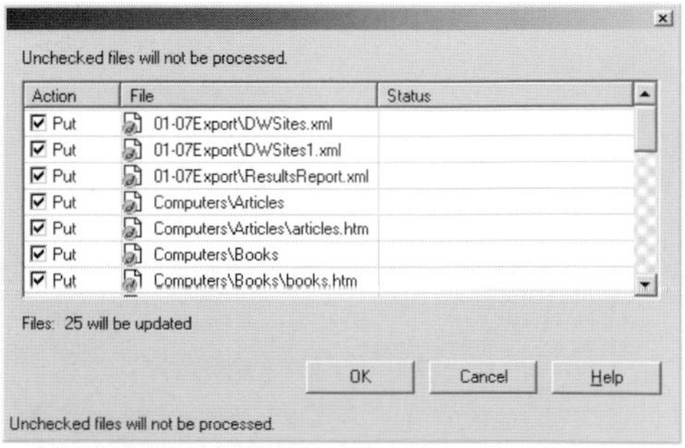

Automatic Cleanup

Dreamweaver, by default, is set to automatically cleanup files when it opens them. When you open a Word file in Dreamweaver, for instance, Dreamweaver opens the file as well as the Clean Up Word HTML dialog box. Clicking OK in this dialog box tells Dreamweaver to start cleaning up the file's HTML. You can either disable automatic cleanup or adjust the cleanup preference by adjusting the Code Rewriting preferences. Follow these steps:

1. Choose Edit → Preferences to open the Preferences dialog box.

2. Select HTML Rewriting from the Category list. The HTML Rewriting preferences appear.

Figure 31.3

The Synchronize dialog box gives you additional control over the synchronization process. You can deselect any files that you don't want to change before any are actually replaced.

3. If you want Dreamweaver to display a list of the tags it has repaired after opening a file, check the box next to Warn When Fixing or Removing Tags.

4. If you want to exempt a particular type of file from the cleanup process, delete it from the list in the box next to In Files with Extensions.

5. Deselect one of the following code rewriting options if you want to leave a particular code feature as is:

   - Fix Invalidly Nested and Unclosed Tags

   - Remove Extra Closing Tags

   - Encode Special Characters in URLs Using %

   - Encode <, >, &, and " in Attribute Values Using &.

6. Click OK.

   If you aren't fluent in writing or editing HTML, it's a good idea to leave the default code rewriting settings alone. You can always examine a file's HTML manually by choosing Code or Code and Design from the View menu of an open document.

Manually Cleaning Code

You can instruct Dreamweaver to clean up an HTML file at any time, whether it's origin is a word processing document or an HTML coder who did a messy markup job. Open the file, and follow these steps:

1. Choose Commands → Clean Up HTML. (Choose Commands → Clean Up Word HTML if you're working with a Word document.) The Clean Up HTML/XHTML dialog box appears (see Figure 31.4).

2. Select the options you want to enable:

   Remove Empty Container Tags Deletes tags that have no content, such as <p></p>.

   Remove Redundant Nested Tags Removes any tags that are enclosed by other tags and that aren't necessary, such as the tags around the word really in <i>This jalapeno cheese is <i>really</i> spicy!</i>.

   Remove Non-Dreamweaver HTML Comments Removes any comments that programs other than Dreamweaver added to your file.

   Remove Dreamweaver Special Markup Removes any Dreamweaver-generated comments in the file.

   Remove Specific Tag(s) Lets you identify one or more tags you want to delete.

Figure 31.4

Part of website administration involves cleaning up your web pages' HTML so files appear the same in all browsers, and no "extra" commands appear online by mistake.

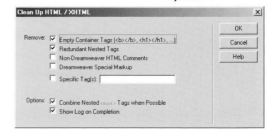

Combine Nested `<font>` tags   Combines two or more font tags (such as the commands that control font color and size) when they control the same text.

Show Log on Completion   Tells Dreamweaver to present a log of the changes it made after cleanup is complete.

3. Click OK to start the cleanup.

Cleaning up your HTML isn't just a matter of good housekeeping. It ensures that your website content will appear the way you want, with no "extra" tags showing in your pages, and no extra spaces due to unnecessary commands.

> Don't forget to take advantage of the Assets panel when you are called upon to perform ongoing website maintenance. The Assets panel enables you to select groups of items quickly, or move individual assets to or from a website. See Chapter 4 for more about the Assets panel.

Workflow

Workflow is all about getting the tasks associated with creating a website done efficiently and on deadline, and getting everyone on your production team to work in a cooperative way. It means collaborating efficiently with the members of your production team and communicating effectively with your clients.

Part of maintaining smooth workflow is up to you: you need to set a schedule and make sure everyone in your workgroup knows what they're supposed to do. But you can take advantage of some special Dreamweaver utilities to improve your communication and make sure your website progresses smoothly—Design Notes and Check In/Check Out.

Communicating with Design Notes

Sticky notes are great, but you can't attach them to a web page that exists not on paper but on a computer screen. With that limitation in mind, Dreamweaver provides a counterpart called Design Notes—computer files that can contain messages and that can be electronically attached to web pages.

Design Notes enable you to attach important information to your files. When coworkers open the files, they can view the information. The notes stay with their files when the files are copied, moved, or renamed. You might record the file's author or the program in which the file's contents were originally created. You can also communicate less technical information, such as the individuals who need to approve the document, or policy decisions that went into its creation.

Enabling Design Notes

Before you can begin using Design Notes, you have to set up this feature for the website on which you're working. Follow these steps:

1. Choose Site → Edit Sites… to open the Edit Sites dialog box.

2. Select a site and click Edit to open the Site Definition dialog box.

3. In the Category list, click Design Notes.

4. Check the box next to Maintain Design Notes, if it's not already checked, to enable Design Notes for this site.

5. If you need to share your Design Notes with your coworkers, make sure Upload Design Notes for Sharing is selected.

6. Click OK to close the Site Definition dialog box and Done to close the Edit Sites dialog box.

If you are working alone on your site, deselecting the Upload Design Notes for Sharing option can save some time when you transfer files from one location to another. However, when this option is deselected, your Design Notes won't be transferred when you upload your files to your remote server.

Creating Design Notes

Once you have enabled Design Notes, you can start attaching them to files within your site. Open the file to which you want to attach a note, and choose File → Design Notes to display the Design Notes dialog box (see Figure 31.5).

> You can also right-click a file's name in the Site panel and choose Design Notes from the pop-up menu to open the Design Notes dialog box.

In the Basic Info tab, you can choose a status to assign to the file to remind you or your coworkers exactly where the file stands in the production process. You enter notes about the file in the Notes text box. Check the Show When File Is Opened box if you want the Design Notes file to appear whenever the file is opened.

In the All Info tab, you can add information about the file in the form of name-value pairs. You might enter type of information (such as **Author** or **Date**) in the Name field and then the specific data (such as **Becky** or **1/7/02**) in the Value field. If you need to enter another name-value pair, click the plus (+) sign; to remove a name-value pair click the minus (−) sign.

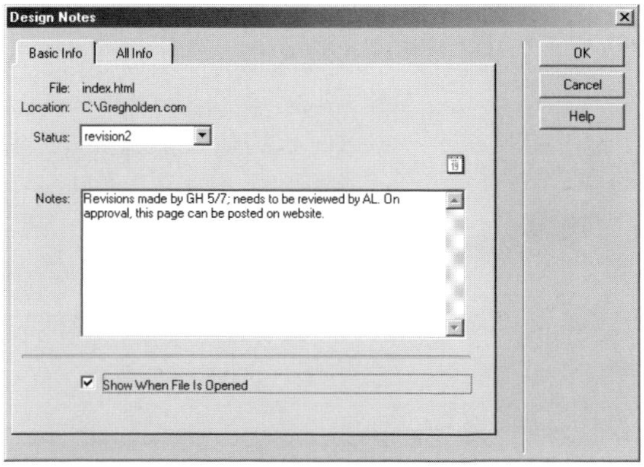

Figure 31.5

Use this dialog box to designate a status for a file such as Draft, Beta, or Needs Attention, and to type Design Notes that you can share with your coworkers.

When you're done, click OK. The notes are saved in a subfolder of your website named _notes. Each Design Notes file is assigned the filename extension .mno. A file that has Design Notes attached to it is given a special icon in the Notes column of the Site panel (see Figure 31.6).

You can run a report that generates a list of all the files in a site that have Design Notes attached to them. To do so, open the site, choose Site → Reports, check Design Notes in the Workflow section of the Reports dialog box, and click Run.

In order to view notes for an individual file, you or your coworkers can do one of two things:

- Right-click the file's icon in the Site panel and choose Design Notes from the pop-up menu.

- Select the file in the Site panel and choose File → Design Notes from the Site panel menu bar.

If the author of the notes checked Show When File Is Opened, the Design Notes will appear when the file is opened.

Web pages are only the most obvious kinds of files that can have Design Notes attached to them. You can also attach Design Notes to images, Flash animations, Java applets, and other website contents. You can attach Design Notes to web page templates, but be aware that any documents created with the template don't inherit its Design Notes.

Using Check In/Check Out

After a website has been created and is online, you might be called upon to perform regular updates. You might receive new files from writers, and editors and designers might need to work on pages to change colors or images. When you're part of a larger workgroup of individuals with different responsibilities, you need to keep track of who has worked on a file, and when the work was completed, so as not to duplicate effort or miss important stages. The need to track workflow becomes more important if more than one team member needs to work on a web page, and if workers are scattered in different locations.

The Check In/Check Out system of file management that you learned about in Chapter 4 can be just as useful for ongoing website administration as it is for site creation. You can use Check In/Check Out even if you're the only one doing the work on the site. For instance, you can enter different check-out names depending on which computer you're working on (such as **GregH-Production Mac**, **GregH-Home PC**, and so on) so that you know where the most recent changes are located should you forget to check a file back in.

Figure 31.6

You or your team members can identify a file that has Design Notes by the icon in the Notes column of the Site panel.

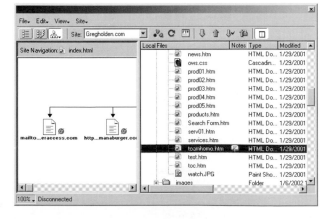

MANAGING CONTENT WITH DREAMWEAVER TEMPLATES

All the Design Notes in the world won't prevent coworkers from changing parts of your site that they aren't supposed to tamper with. Even a Design Note that says "Don't Change This!" doesn't guarantee that they won't click a heading and delete it accidentally, or change the look of boilerplate text that isn't supposed to be altered.

Unless, that is, you mark such content as non-editable through the use of Dreamweaver's Templates. You can use templates to create your own content management system, by only allowing certain contents to be changed. As you learned in Chapter 4, templates can contain regions that you specify as either editable or non-editable. By using templates to design your site, you can restrict what others can change. This enables contributors to input content without compromising site design.

Dreamweaver MX also gives you the ability to designate regions of a template as "optional." You can set parameters that let either the template author (that's you) control which regions show and hide without letting a user edit the content, or, alternately, you can let your colleagues edit content and specify whether the region shows or hides. See Chapter 4 for more information about creating editable regions in templates.

In terms of ongoing maintenance, it's particularly useful to keep in mind that you can activate Check In/Check Out on some sites and make it inactive on others. Use Check In/Check Out when you're revising files on your local site. When the revisions are done and you want to move new files to the remote server and/or delete outdated files, you can disable Check In/Check Out to save time. This also makes sense if you're the only one authorized to publish files on the remote server and there's no chance of confusing your work with anyone else's.

Journaling and Rollback

Guarding against lost data is an essential part of ongoing website administration. Once your site is online, you need to protect yourself and your clients or employers against viruses, security breaches, or disasters that can not only take a site offline but can force you to spend considerable time rebuilding a site.

Dreamweaver can help you guard against such disasters by enabling you to perform such functions as journaling and rollback. By using reports to keep track of the most recent versions of your files, you gain the ability to return to the last correct version of your website when something goes wrong.

A journal is a record of transactions you've conducted or events you've encountered over a period of time. In the world of computer software, *journaling* is the process of keeping a record of system writes so that you can know what files have been copied to a filesystem recently. *Rollback* is a term usually used in connection with databases. If data is lost or the current database becomes corrupted in some way, a system administrator needs to roll back to the most recent correct version.

Generating Reports

Most web hosting services provide you with log file reports that analyze how your site has been used. You can also generate reports that tell you when files were created or modified or when they were moved to the server.

Dreamweaver has a built-in reports utility of its own, but it's primarily used to track Design Notes and Check In/Check Out records as well as specific HTML problems such as bad external links or unnecessary tags.

You can, however, create your own website journal of recent changes, and thus have a higher degree of control over the information you need, by installing some Dreamweaver extensions.

The Site Import Export Extension

The Site Import Export Extension, provided by Macromedia, enables you to save configuration information for a website. You can export the data to a file that you can either share with your coworkers or open up in case your files are damaged. The extension produces an electronic "snapshot" of a site that can help others work on it or even recreate it if necessary.

To use the extension, go to the Macromedia Exchange for Dreamweaver site (`http://www.macromedia.com/exchange/dreamweaver`) and search for Import Export Extension. Download and install the file as described in Chapter 32. Quit Dreamweaver if it is already running, then restart the program to start using the extension. Once you've got the extension up and running, the following steps show you how to start using it.

1. From the Document window's File menu, choose File → Export → Site. The Export Site dialog box opens.

   The Import Export Extension adds the Site option to the Export submenu of the File menu— but only in the Document window. The Site panel's File menu does not contain Import or Export options.

2. If you want to export all of your websites, select All. If you want to export fewer sites, select Selected. Shift-click to select adjacent websites; Ctrl-click to select non-adjacent site names.

3. Click Export. The Select Destination for Exported Site dialog box appears.

4. Navigate to the folder in your filesystem that you want to contain the exported site data, or click the New Folder button to create a new folder.

5. Click Select to export the website data.

6. When a dialog box appears telling you that the data has been exported, click OK.

The exported website information appears with the generic name `DWSites.xml` in your selected location. To view the file, you can either open it in the Dreamweaver window or import the file by choosing File → Import, locating the site file, and clicking OK. You have to restart Dreamweaver in order to view the site, which is added to the list of sites in the Edit Sites dialog box.

The Site Summary Reports Extension

Another extension provided by Macromedia, Site Summary Reports, is intended for users who are migrating to Dreamweaver from another popular website design tool—Microsoft FrontPage. But the extension works just as well with Dreamweaver-created sites. It enables you to create reports listing different types of information about the files in your site. You can use the extension to report on all files created or modified after a certain date, which can prove helpful if you need to roll back to a previous version. After you download and install the extension, quit and restart Dreamweaver if necessary. Then follow these steps:

1. Open the site that you want to report on.

2. Choose Site → Reports.

3. The Site Summary Reports Extension adds a new category to the Reports dialog box: FrontPage Migration Kit (see Figure 31.7). Check one or more of the options in this category. If you want a list of files created in a certain period of time, click either File Creation Date Range or File Modification Date Range.

4. Choose an option from the Report On drop-down list, such as Entire Site.

5. Click Report Settings.

6. In the File Creation Date Range dialog box (which appears if you have selected File Creation Date Range or File Modification Date Range), specify the start and end dates you want to report on.

7. Click OK to return to the Reports dialog box.

8. Click Run.

Report results appear in the Results panel (see Figure 31.8). To save your results, click Save Results. Choose the location on your computer or network where you want to save the file, and click Save. You can then open the file either with Dreamweaver or with a text editor.

Figure 31.7

Clicking one of the new report options under the FrontPage Migration Kit category can help you take a snapshot of your site so that you can restore it if need be.

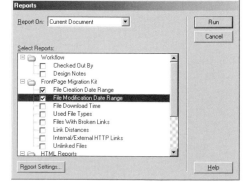

Another extension, Web Kitchen, lets you sort only files modified after a certain date. It also includes utilities for such website maintenance functions as finding and replacing text, repairing instances of "smart" quotes, going word counts, and converting accent marks. You can download a 30-day trial version from the Macromedia Exchange for Dreamweaver website and then purchase the product for $99 from Matterform Media. Find out more at `http://matterform.com/webkitchen/help/frames.php?page=general/list.htm`.

Figure 31.8

The Site Summary Reports Extension provides you with lists of files created or modified after a certain date.

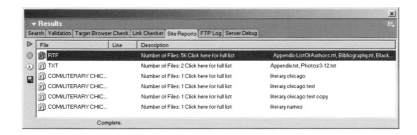

Rolling Back Your Site

Of course, it's important to save information about your site and compile a list of recently created or modified files. But in order to move back to a previous version of the site, you've got to *save* a backup version in a place where you can retrieve it easily.

It's up to you to come up with a schedule for making regular backups and then observe that schedule. If you use a backup program, such as one of the popular Retrospect packages by Dantz Development Corporation (`http://www.retrospect.com`) you can schedule your backups to take place automatically. Here are some other ideas:

- Take a snapshot of your site map and save it as a bitmap image so that you can retrieve it in case you need to re-create links. Open the site, choose File → Save Site Map from the Site panel menu bar, assign a name to the site map image, and click Save.

- Duplicate your site by choosing Site → Edit Sites…, and then clicking Duplicate in the Edit Sites dialog box. A copy of the site is created and stored in `C:\Program Files\ Macromedia\Dreamweaver 5\Configuration`. Move the duplicate to a safe location so that you can retrieve it if your server or your local computer is damaged.

- Like many webmasters, you may want to mirror your site on a completely different server so that people can get access to it if the original server goes down.

In late 2001, the online news service CNET reviewed several backup software packages. You can read the review at `http://www.cnet.com/software/0-806180-7-2376963 .html?tag=st.sw.806180-7-2376964-rost.back2.806180-7-2376963`.

Hands On: Updating an Existing Website

Now try out some of the common website administration tasks in a project. You'll update a website template, change some basic content, adjust the site navigation, and use Dreamweaver's link checking feature.

From the Chapter 31 folder on the accompanying CD, copy the folder `sample_website` to your computer. Start Dreamweaver, and define the site by choosing Site → New Site…, then locating and naming the site in the Site Definition dialog box. Then open the site by displaying the Site panel, then choosing the site from the Site drop-down list. If you want a preview of the completed site, you can open `corrected_website`, which is also in the Chapter 31 folder on the accompanying CD. The site maps of both versions are shown in Figure 31.9.

Correcting the Website Template

The Stylus Media website contains seven separate web page files, each created from a template called `StylusTemplate.dwt`. Your first administrative task is to change the template, something that frequently occurs as organizations change their products or services.

1. Open the `StylusTemplate.dwt` template file, which is located in the Templates folder in `sample_website`.

2. At the bottom of the template page, change 2001 to 2002.

3. Add a new editable region after the editable region labeled Heading. Position the cursor just after the word Heading.

4. Press Shift + Return to move to a new blank line.

5. Choose Modify → Templates → New Editable Region.

6. In the New Editable Region dialog box, enter **Subhead**.

7. Click OK.

Figure 31.9.

Before (left) and after (right) routine maintenance of sample website

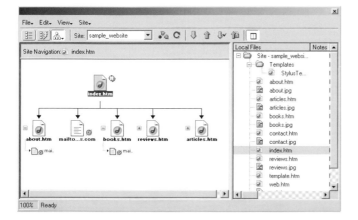

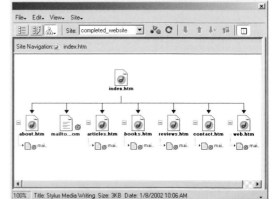

8. Replace the placeholder word *Subhead* with **Stylus Media**.

9. Select the words Stylus Media. In the Property Inspector, choose the Arial typeface group, font size 1, and press Return. The new subheading is shown in Figure 31.10.

Figure 31.10

Edited website template

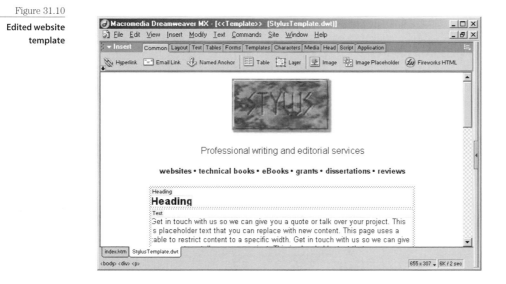

Change Website Content

Next, you'll fulfill one of the most common website administrative tasks—changing the basic content on your web pages. Suppose your client has directed you to change the words "editorial services" at the top of every web page to "content management." The quickest way to make the change across the entire site is to use Find and Replace.

1. From the Document window menu bar, choose Edit → Find and Replace.

Figure 31.11

Making textual changes across an entire website

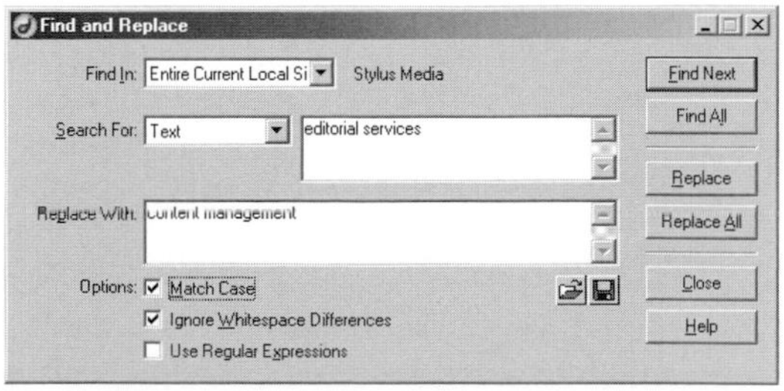

2. In the Find and Replace dialog box (see Figure 31.11), choose Entire Current Local Site from the Find In drop-down list.

3. Enter **editorial services** in the box next to the Search For drop-down list.

4. Enter **content management** in the Replace With box.

5. Check the Match Case box.

6. Click Find All.

7. When a dialog box appears telling you the changes have been made, click OK.

Adjusting Website Navigation

Next, you'll perform another common administrative task—you'll change the navigation for your site. Go to the Site panel, and view the site map for the sample website. You'll notice that although there are seven files in the site, only five are included in the map. You need to make sure the home page index.htm links to all of the six second-level pages.

1. In the Site Navigation pane of the Site panel, click the file index.htm to select it.

2. Drag the Point-to-File icon  to one of the pages not included in the site map, contact.htm, in the Local Files panel (see Figure 31.12). Release the mouse button when contact.htm is selected. The file is added to the map.

3. Repeat step 2 for the file web.htm to add it to the site map.

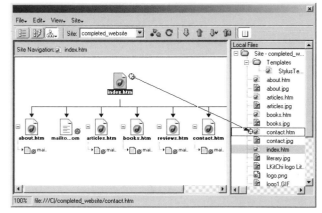

Figure 31.12

Changing the navigational structure of a website

Checking Links

Checking the links in a website and repairing those that are broken is another common administrative task that you'll perform. Here's how.

1. Choose Site → Check Links Sitewide from the Site panel's menu bar.

2. Click Close to close the Link Checker window after it reviews the links in your site.

Changing a Link

Next, you'll change an e-mail link that occurs on each of your site's web pages.

1. Select the file index.htm in the Local Folder pane of the Site panel.

2. Choose Site → Change Link Sitewide.

3. In the Change Link Sitewide box (see Figure 31.13), enter **mailto:jdoe@mywebsite.com** in the Change All Links To box, and enter **mailto:webmaster@stylusmedia.com** in the Into Links To box.

4. Click OK.

5. In the Update Files dialog box, click Update.

6. Double-click any one of the files in the website to view it and check the link.

Figure 31.13

Changing a link sitewide

Extend Your Reach

Granted, website administration isn't the most thrilling part of going online. But like seeing your doctor for checkups or getting your oil changed, it's a necessary part of keeping a site healthy as it grows. After all, sites that undergo regular tune-ups maintain regular visitors and stay useful for their owners—and that's the ultimate goal of using Dreamweaver.

Next, you'll learn how to do some *really* exciting things with Dreamweaver. First, you'll discover how to extend your reach and make the program work just the way you want by customizing it. Then, you'll learn how to extend Dreamweaver's own reach by installing extensions that enable Dreamweaver to do even more amazing things.

## CHAPTER 32

Customizing and Extending Dreamweaver

You might not find all of the features you want straight out of the box with Dreamweaver, but its extensibility allows you to create or download extensions for the features you need. You can add, or download, any of the premade third-party extensions available from the Macromedia Exchange for Dreamweaver website. You can also modify your menus and shortcut keys, record macros to create shortcuts for multiple steps that you repeat often, add objects to your Insert bar, and even change the way that Dreamweaver's dialog boxes and default document template appear.

In the following sections of this chapter, you will find descriptions of how to completely customize and modify your Dreamweaver interface and functionality:

- ■ **Using the Extension Manager**

- ■ **Setting up custom shortcut keys**

- ■ **Changing the default template**

- ■ **Making custom commands (macros)**

- ■ **Making custom menus**

- ■ **Adding objects to the Insert bar**

- ■ **Changing dialog boxes**

Using the Extension Manager

Though Dreamweaver is incredibly malleable (in how many other programs you know can you edit the menus and dialog boxes yourself?)—you might quite naturally find it a little intimidating to start mucking around in the software's innards without some practice or a few examples to follow. Fortunately, the community of Dreamweaver users has already collectively developed and tested quite a few extensions that you might find handy. You can download these examples from the Macromedia Exchange for Dreamweaver site at http://www.macromedia.com/exchange/dreamweaver/.

These extensions have been provided by Dreamweaver end users or the Macromedia developers. Other software companies that work closely with Macromedia also create some of the extensions. To learn how to create your own extensions and share them with others, refer to the "Creating Extensions" section later in this chapter.

Not all of the extensions are available for both Windows and Macintosh operating systems. The pages that describe each extension will list the operating systems for which the selected extension is available.

Using the Macromedia Exchange for Dreamweaver Site

The purpose of the Macromedia Exchange for Dreamweaver website is to provide a forum where developed additions for Dreamweaver and Fireworks can be shared. The extensions provided on this website come with no warranty of functionality, so you should be careful when you add any extension into your installation of Dreamweaver or Fireworks.

You can open the Macromedia Exchange for Dreamweaver site, using any of the following options:

- Visit the website directly at http://www.macromedia.com/exchange/dreamweaver/.
- Select Help → Dreamweaver Exchange.
- Select Commands → Get More Commands.
- Select File → Go to Macromedia Exchange from the Extension Manager menu bar, or click the Go to Macromedia Exchange tool on the toolbar.
- Select Get More Styles inside the Insert Flash Buttons (Insert → Interactive Images → Flash Buttons) dialog box.
- Select Get More Behaviors from the plus (+) menu in the Behaviors dialog box.

The Macromedia Exchange for Dreamweaver website also has sections for the previous versions of Dreamweaver Ultradev (http://www.macromedia.com/exchange/ultradev) and Flash (http://www.macromedia.com/exchange/flash).

Extension Categories

As you browse the Macromedia Exchange for Dreamweaver website, you will see that the many different extensions for Dreamweaver and Fireworks are divided into different categories. Each category provides a collection of extensions that should assist you when you go to develop your own websites. The categories available within Exchange are listed here:

Accessibility Provides features that make using your website easier for people using portable devices, MSN TV (formerly known as WebTV), speech synthesizers, and other related hardware. The extensions here also include controls for creating and setting cookies, adjusting image attributes, validating your HTML code, and for assessing the accessibility of your pages.

App Servers Provides extensions for querying, viewing, and formatting data that is fed to your web page dynamically using server-side languages such as Active Server Pages (ASP), ColdFusion, Java Server Pages (JSP), and Apache's PHP. This category even includes the addition of search functions and a Java-based web mail system.

Browsers Provides controls for checking on browser versions, redirecting pages, adding pages to your Favorites/Bookmark lists, controlling the appearance of your document titles, and controlling the toolbars on your browser window.

DHTML/Layers Provides extensions and updates that support the dynamic web components on your pages. The extensions in this category provide capabilities such as aligning your layers, creating scrollable and draggable layers, and adjusting the stacking order of your layers dynamically.

eCommerce Provides links to shopping carts, counters, banner advertising systems, and site searches that can be easily installed on your pages without the problems associated with trying to run customizable Common Gateway Interface (CGI) scripts, or other more complex systems.

Extension Development Provides links to a variety of extensions, which assist you in developing your own extensions.

Fireworks Provides all of the extensions that can be used to help Dreamweaver use Fireworks functions to complete tasks faster than would be possible without an automatic system.

Flash Media Provides sets of new Flash button images, text, and other Flash objects.

Learning Provide sets of extensions that allow you to easily create learning/testing-oriented web pages. The ever-popular CourseBuilder extension is included in this category.

Navigation Provides commands that allow you to create more dynamic effects, such as button rollovers, in your navigation bars. Some of these extensions provide lists of site structure, while others create collapsible menus, format Cascading Style Sheet (CSS) styles on your menu text, and check all of the links on your pages.

Productivity Provides additional features that will help you get more done faster on your existing sites. You can use one of these extensions to add additional Meta tags to your document templates, while others create calendar pages, automatically title documents, and update document dates and times.

Rich Media Provides extensions that add multimedia to your web page. Some of these extensions work with audio files, while others allow you to insert movies, CAD drawings, and news services.

Scripting Provides sets of commands that can be used to rotate banner images, test colors, adjust CSS code, and create dynamic form fields. All of the extensions in this category work with extensive JavaScript that will be added to your document.

Security Provides extensions that keep your pages from being set up inside of a frame on another site; they also help restrict the language used in form submittals.

Style/Format Provides a list of customized CSS effects that can be added to your documents.

Tables Provides access to extensions that work directly with Open Database Connectivity (ODBC) databases to populate your tables, as well as controls that change the formatting axis of the table, and its appearance.

Text Provides advanced text formatting options, such as changing character case, inserting math symbols, and displaying your text in graduations of color.

Downloading Extensions

When you find an extension, either using the category listing or the Search function, you are taken to a page devoted to the extension you selected. On this page, you can read about the extension, discuss the extension in a chat group, or rate the extension, and you will find a link from which you can download the extension.

To download an extension, you will need to be a member of the Macromedia site. This registration is free, and once you complete the registration information, a cookie is placed on your computer so that you will be recognized whenever you visit the Macromedia website. Keep in mind that all of the extensions you see on the Macromedia Exchange for Dreamweaver website are not free. Some of them are for sale, with or without a free 30-day trial. Read the extension explanation page carefully for information about the extension with which you are working.

Once you have found the extension you want, you'll want to download it. Notice that on the right-hand side of the extension's page there are links to both Windows and Macintosh versions of the extension, if both are available. Extensions are written in combinations of HTML documents and JavaScript files which are just standard text files. This makes it is relatively easy for a developer to provide the same functionality for both operating systems.

Extensions are stored in MXP files that are used to install the appropriate files for the extension by the Extension Manager. MXP files are specific to the Macromedia Extension Manager. You most likely won't see these types of files anywhere else on your computer. The Extension Manager reads them in a fashion similar to WinZip and a ZIP file, collecting the information it needs out of the MXP file and placing that information where it needs to be stored.

To start the download process, all you have to do is click the link for your operating system, which will automatically trigger the download to start, and then wait for the download to complete. After the download is finished, you can start the Extension Manager and install the extension.

> If you don't have a copy of the Extension Manager, or you wish to download the latest copy, go to the main Macromedia Exchange for Dreamweaver page at http://www.macromedia.com/exchange/dreamweaver.

Installing Extensions

Once you have downloaded your extensions, you need to start the Extension Manager to install them. The Extension Manager, shown in Figure 32.1, can be opened in a variety of ways:

- Select Commands → Manage Extensions from within Dreamweaver.
- Select Help → Manage Extensions from within Dreamweaver.
- Select Start → Programs → Macromedia Extension Manager → Macromedia Extension Manager from your Windows desktop.
- Double-click the Extension Manger application in your Finder window on your Macintosh.

The Extension Manager is installed automatically with Dreamweaver 4 and MX, but not all of the extensions available for Dreamweaver 4 will work in Dreamweaver MX. You will need to check the extensions documentation to find out for which versions compatibility exists.

To complete the installation of your extension, follow these steps:

1. Select either the Install New Extension button on the Extension Manager toolbar, or select File → Install Extension (Ctrl + I in Windows or Cmd + O on a Macintosh).

2. When the Select Extension to Install dialog box opens, select the MXP file you wish to add to your installation.

3. Answer any questions, including the licensing statement, that are required during the installation of the extension.

4. Restart Dreamweaver if prompted.

5. Ensure that the new extension is checked in the Extension Manager.

Figure 32.1

Dreamweaver Extension Manager

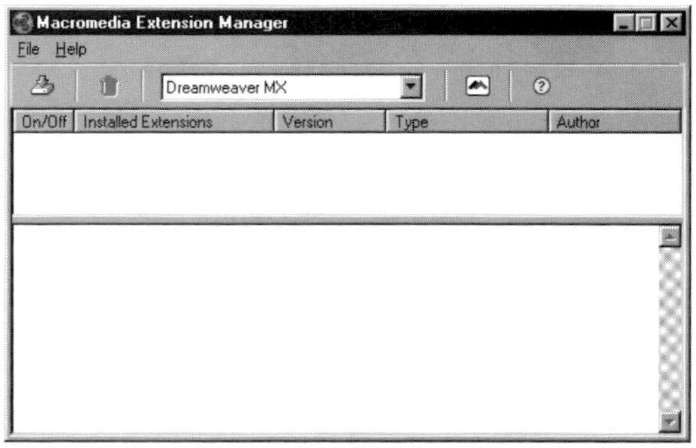

To find out how to run the extension, select the extension in the list of installed extensions, and read the information about the extension in the lower window of the Extension Manager. In this location, you will find the instructions for starting, using, and configuring the options in this extension.

Using Extensions

Once you have downloaded and installed your extensions, you will be able to use them as you would any other feature of Dreamweaver. In Figure 32.2 you can see a copy of Dreamweaver's Insert bar showing a variety of additional objects, which you can use to add functionality to your web pages.

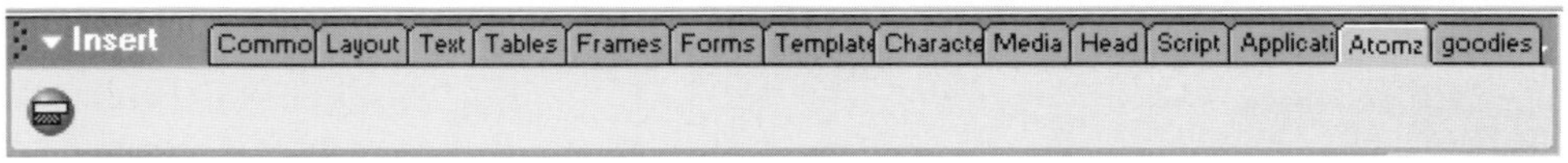

Figure 32.2

Additions to the Insert bar made by Dreamweaver extensions

Other extensions will be found on your Commands menu, as shown in Figure 32.3.

To use the new extension(s), simply select it from your objects or commands, and answer any of the prompts that control the configuration of the extension. For assistance with any of the extensions you download off of the site, you will need to return to the extension's page and ask your questions in the chat group, if it is available.

Creating Extensions

You can create your own Dreamweaver extensions if you know HTML and some JavaScript, but the detailed description that would be required to teach you how to create a fully functional extension is outside of the scope of this book. Hopefully the information and resources provided here will point you in the right direction.

Figure 32.3

Additional options on the Commands menu

Resources for Creating Extensions

There are many books and websites devoted to the development of Macromedia Dreamweaver and Fireworks extensions. If you have questions about developing your own extensions, check out these Macromedia resources first.

- Select Help → Extending Dreamweaver in the Dreamweaver window. This takes you to the Extending Dreamweaver web-based manual. This manual takes you through the nitty-gritty details of how Dreamweaver works, and how the files used in the creation of an extension must be formatted. If you look on your Dreamweaver installation CD, you will find both the `Extending Dreamweaver.pdf` and the `Extending Fireworks.pdf` files that document how to extend both of these programs.

- Select Help → Creating and Submitting Extensions in the Extension Manager. This option takes you to a document that provides an overview of the process used to create and submit extensions to the Macromedia Exchange for Dreamweaver website. Before you submit an extension to Macromedia to be added to the Exchange, be sure to read this file thoroughly.

- Open the `http://www.macromedia.com/support/dreamweaver/extend.html` document to read more about extensions themselves and how to customize Dreamweaver in general.

- View the files that were installed by other extensions, and see how they accomplished their appointed task.

Extension Creation Overview

In general, extensions are no more difficult to create than your own customizations to Dreamweaver. The following steps should help outline the extension creation process for you.

1. Create the primary HTML file that serves as the base file for the extension. This file references the JavaScript program that is created in step 2.

2. Create the JavaScript files that will actually provide the functionality for the extension. In some cases, the JavaScript will be a part of the HTML file; other times it will be an external JavaScript (`.js`) file that must be called and loaded when the extension is used.

3. Create the icons, or menu items, that will be used to start the extension once it is installed within Dreamweaver.

4. Ensure that your dialog boxes, and other effects comply with the Macromedia UI Guidelines available from `http://dynamic.macromedia.com/MM/exchange/ui_guidelines.jsp`. This document tells you how things must function and appear in order for them to be accepted into the Exchange program.

5. Complete a thorough testing procedure of your extension on multiple operating systems, multiple system configurations, and with multiple browsers. Macromedia also provides some instructions for testing extensions at `http://dynamic.macromedia.com/MM/exchange/about_testing.jsp`.

6. Create a staging area on your computer, and move the relevant extension files to that location. This must be done before the files can be packaged.

7. Create a MXI file (Macromedia Extension Installation) that specifies the locations and controls used when installing the extension. You can view the `blank.mxi` file located in the `Extension Manager/Samples/Dreamweaver` folder in your Extension Manager installation. Within this MXI file, you will need to define shortcut keys, menu options, object buttons, and so on. You can find additional information on formatting this file and other extensions related customizations at the Macromedia Exchange for Dreamweaver website `http://www.macromedia.com/exchange`.

8. Open the Extension Manager, and select File → Package Extension. This will start the packager that creates an MXP file out of the individual pieces of your extension. This file contains compressed versions of all of the pieces you created in the previous steps. Because of the nature of the files, you can typically use the same MXP file on both a Windows or Macintosh platform.

9. Test out the MXP file you just created on your own machine, preferably with a fresh install of Dreamweaver so that none of your old pieces and parts from previous tests or the creation of the extension are still hanging about. At this point, you need to retest all of the features of the extension so that you can be sure they all work as expected.

10. You can now submit the extension to the Macromedia Exchange for Dreamweaver site using the File → Submit Extension option located in the Extension Manager window. You can also submit an extension by visiting `http://dynamic.macromedia.com/bin/MM/ exchange/about_submission.jsp`. From this location you can start the submission process for your extension.

For more information on using Extensions, see the "Hands On 1: Using the Advanced Random Images Extension" section later in this chapter.

Creating Custom Shortcut Keys

There are two ways to modify your keyboard shortcut keys. The easiest, and the method discussed here, is to use the Keyboard Shortcuts editor. The alternative is to modify the `menus.xml` file, which will be discussed later in the section entitled "Creating Custom Menus."

To modify your keyboard shortcuts using the Keyboard Shortcuts editor, select Edit → Keyboard Shortcuts. This opens the Keyboard Shortcuts dialog box shown in Figure 32.4, which allows you to edit your keyboard shortcuts for Dreamweaver or select an alternative set of shortcuts.

Figure 32.4

Keyboard Shortcuts dialog box

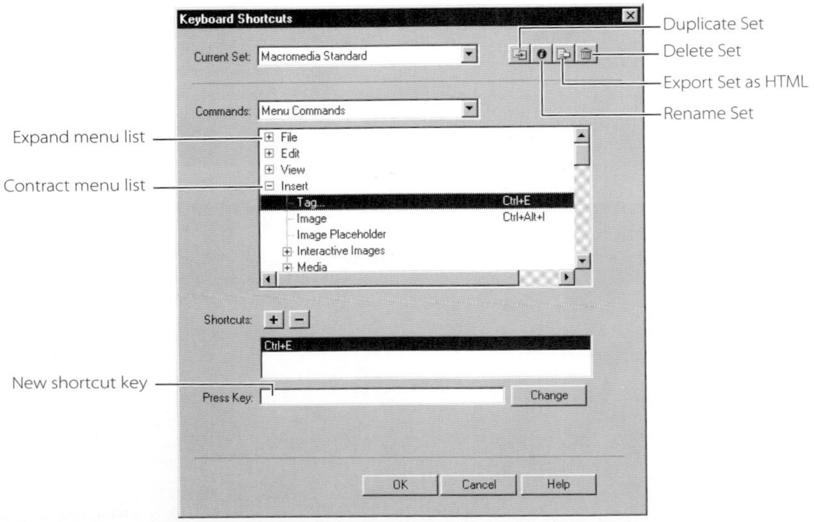

This editor allows you to customize sets of keyboard shortcuts. You can't directly edit the existing sets, but you can use the Duplicate Set button to create a copy of the set closest to your needs and then make your modifications to the copy. To duplicate a set, select the set from the Current Set list, and then click the Duplicate Set button to the right of the field. By default, the Macromedia Standard set is used for Dreamweaver 4.

Once you have duplicated a set of keyboard shortcuts, you are ready to start making your changes using these steps:

1. Select the set of keyboard shortcuts that you wish to modify.

2. If you wish to modify a menu item's shortcut key, select Menu Commands from the Commands list. Options on this list include the following:

   Code Editing Commands that function only in the Code view of the document window and the Code inspector.

   Document Editing Commands that function in the Design view of the document window.

   Menu Commands Commands that are found on the main menu bar in Dreamweaver.

   Site Menu Commands (Windows only) Commands that are found on the Site menu of the primary document window.

   Site Window (Windows only) Commands that are available when the Site panel is open.

3. From the Menu list, select the menu item you wish to modify. Use the plus (+) button and minus (–) button (Windows) or the triangle icons (Macintosh) to expand the contents of the menus when looking at them.

4. The list of current shortcuts for that command are shown in the Shortcuts field. To add an additional shortcut, press the plus (+) button. To remove one of the shortcuts press the minus (–) button.

5. When you are adding a shortcut, place your cursor in the Press Key field and press the key combination that you wish to use for this shortcut. If the shortcut is already assigned to a different command, you will be given the opportunity to change it.

> In Dreamweaver's Help system, search for "Keyboard Shortcut Matrix" to find a list of keyboard shortcut combinations that aren't, by default, used in Dreamweaver.

6. Click the Change button to add it to the list of shortcut keys.

7. Repeat steps 2 through 6 for every command, or menu option, that you wish to modify.

8. Once you are done modifying your keyboard shortcuts, click the OK button. Once you have altered your keyboard shortcuts, you will need to restart Dreamweaver before they become active.

When you are modifying your keyboard shortcuts, it's a good idea to use the Export to HTML button to create a printable list of your shortcuts. This way you always have a reference of your shortcuts in case of a computer crash, or if you take a long hiatus away from your Dreamweaver development tasks.

You can also modify your keyboard shortcuts in the `menu.xml` file located in your Dreamweaver Configuration/Menu folder. This document contains a series of tags that create sets of shortcuts. These shortcuts are modified in much the same way as the menu options, also contained in this file.

Changing the Default Document Template

Every time you open a new Dreamweaver document, you get the same page. This page is created from a default template located in the `Configuration/Templates/default.html` file. The contents of this file are used on every file that you create in Dreamweaver. So if you set this document to have a pink background, every new file that you create using Dreamweaver will have a pink background. The default document template is different from the site templates discussed in Chapter 4 that provide you with a customized layout for each site. If you work on multiple sites with Dreamweaver, you may prefer to do only minor modifications to the default document template, and you may otherwise rely on customized site templates.

The default document template does not have locked (non-editable) regions, as does a site template. A page based on the default document template can be modified at will. There are many ways you can adjust your default document template to save you time. Anything that appears on every page should be added, such as background and text color, copyright statements, comments, banner logos, footers, and so on.

No matter what you plan on doing with the default document template, you need to save a copy of the original template before you start making changes to it. To do this, open the `Configuration/Templates/default.html` document and save it as `original_default.html`. Also when you open this document use File → Open, not File → Open from Template, because although this document is a template, you don't want to open it to create a new document based on it. You want to modify the file itself.

Here is the code for the default document template.

```
<HTML>
<HEAD>
<TITLE>Untitled Document</TITLE>
<meta http-equiv="Content-Type"
      content="texL/html; charset-">
</HEAD>

<BODY BGCOLOR="#FFFFFF" TEXT="#000000">

</BODY>
</HTML>
```

As you can see from this code, the default document template is quite empty. It includes a title, background color, and a default text color. This code creates that blank white page that you see whenever you open a new document. To change that information, simply modify this page just as you would any other document. You can add tables, text, images, background colors, layers, behaviors, or any thing else that strikes your fancy.

If you are working on multiple sites, you may want to limit your modifications to simple changes, such as copyright notices, default page backgrounds, and text colors. But if you develop for only one site, you can make your default template as complex as you want, as shown in Figure 32.5.

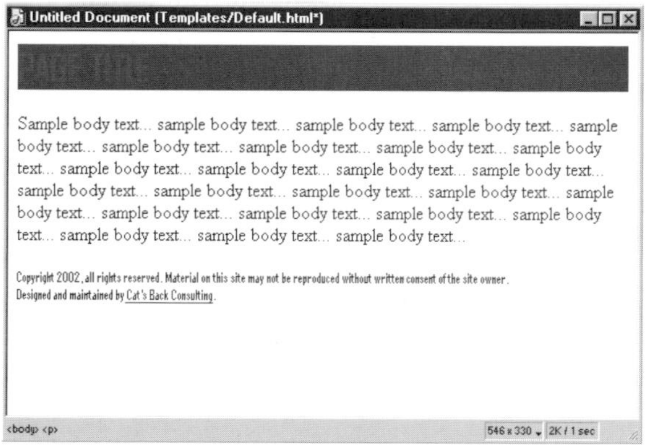

Once you have made your changes, be sure to save the file using File → Save As, rather than File → Save as Template. Remember, using the Save as Template option creates a site template, rather than modifying your document template. Now whenever you open a new document it will have the changes that you made.

Figure 32.5

Default document template with extensive modifications

Creating Dreamweaver Commands

If you ever find yourself repeating the same sequence of commands over and over, such as inserting navigation buttons at the bottom of each page, you might consider automating the task. Hey, doing stuff over and over is computer work, not people work!

There are actually a few ways to automate your tasks:

- Repeat single steps listed in the History panel.
- Record steps from the History panel (Window → History).
- Record a command as you perform the steps.

This History panel tracks all of the menus that you have opened, characters you have typed, and items that you have moved to the current document. It doesn't keep track of mouse movements per se; so if you wish to record a selection of complex menu selections, use your keyboard to open the menus. Remember, you can use the Tab and arrow keys to navigate through options in dialog boxes.

Replaying Steps from the History Panel

To repeat a series of steps, or a single step that you have already made in your document, you just need to select it from the History panel (shown in Figure 32.6). To replay steps, select the step you wish to repeat from the History list, and choose the Replay button located at the bottom of the panel.

Figure 32.6

The History panel

When you are replaying steps from the History panel, you don't have the option of changing their order, but you can selectively choose which steps to replay. By pressing Ctrl while you click steps in the History panel, you can select just the steps you want to repeat. For example, you could select the first five steps that you took, and then skip to step 10 and continue making your selections. Once you hit the Replay button, only the steps that you have selected will be played.

> If you see a step in your History panel with a red "X" in the lower-right corner of the icon, or one that is marked by a thin black line between steps, you won't be able to repeat that step. It will be skipped when the steps are replayed, and therefore it may cause your results to be skewed.

Creating Commands from the History Panel

You can save yourself a lot of work by recording the steps that you have already taken and saving them as a Dreamweaver command on the Commands menu.

To create a command from your History panel of precompleted steps, follow these instructions.

1. Select the steps you wish to save from the History panel. You can use the Ctrl key to select multiple discontinuous steps.

2. Click the Save Selected Steps as Command button in the lower-right corner of the History panel.

3. In the Command Name dialog box, type in a name for the new Dreamweaver command. When you are done, click the OK button.

4. Open the Command menu, and you will be able to see your new command, shown highlighted in Figure 32.7, at the bottom of this menu.

Recording Commands

Figure 32.7

New option on the Command menu

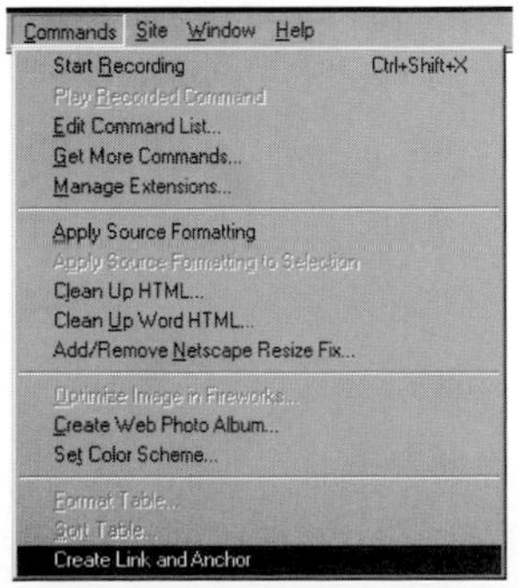

In addition to converting precompleted steps into a Dreamweaver command, you can also record the steps for these commands as you perform them. To start the command recorder, select Commands → Start Recording or press Ctrl + Shift + X (Cmd + Shift + X on the Macintosh).

With the recorder going, you will be able to see that your mouse pointer has a cassette tape attached to it, and you can perform all of the steps required for your command. When you are done recording your steps, press Ctrl + Shift + X (Cmd + Shift + X) again to stop the recorder. You won't be able to find the commands recorded in this fashion on your Commands menu because they are stored for immediate playback, and can be accessed by selecting Commands → Play Recorded Command or by pressing Ctrl + P (Cmd + P on the Macintosh).

If you wish to save your recorded command so that it can be used outside of this current document, you need to save the command from the History panel as addressed in the previous section.

Creating Custom Menus

It might seem drastic to be changing around the menus for Dreamweaver, but once you've worked with the program for a while, you'll realize that there are some features you (and your team) rely on heavily and some that just aren't part of your normal routine. You can create a custom configuration of the Dreamweaver menus to maximize your efficiency and put the most useful commands all together.

Dreamweaver menus are stored in Dreamweaver's `Configuration/Menus/menus.xml` file. The `menus.xml` file defines all of the menus, menu bars, menu options, and even the primary shortcut keys included in Dreamweaver. Despite the `.xml` extension, this file isn't true XML, and therefore, it can't be modified using an XML compliant editor. However, it can be modified in any text editor, such as Windows' WordPad (the file is too large for Notepad) or the Mac's BBEdit. But don't try to edit the menu files from within Dreamweaver! If Dreamweaver is running, then those files are in use.

Before you make any of these changes to your Dreamweaver installation, be sure you have made a backup copy of any of the Dreamweaver configuration files you plan to change. This way, if your changes don't work, then you still have a sure fire way to restore your Dreamweaver installation. If you create a file with invalid menu options, a variety of results could occur. You might simply have a few menu options that won't work, or you could end up with Dreamweaver not even being capable of loading correctly. Most of the time, you will end up with an entire menu, rather than just a menu option, that won't work, or even open.

Here is a segment of the `menus.xml` file. This file is used to specify the name, shortcut key, platform, command, and so on, that is used by Dreamweaver when the menu option is selected. The part of the file shown defines the menu item name and key for the New Window, Open, Close, Rename, and Delete commands.

```
<menubar name="Site Window" id="DWMainSite" platform="win">
    <menu name="_File" id="DWMenu_MainSite_File">
        <menuitem name="New _Window"
                key="Cmd+N" enabled="true"
                command="dw.createDocument()"
                id="DWMenu_MainSite_File_New" />
        <menuitem name="_Open..."
                key="Cmd+O" enabled="true"
                command="dw.openDocument()"
                id="DWMenu_MainSite_File_Open" />
        <menuitem name="_Close"
                key="Cmd+W" enabled="true"
```

```
                              command="dw.setFloaterVisibility(
                                  'site', false)"
                              id="DWMenu_MainSite_File_Close" />
              <separator />
              <menuitem name="_Rename"
                        key="F2" enabled="site.canRename()"
                        command="site.renameSelection()"
                        id="DWMenu_MainSite_File_Rename" />
              <menuitem name="_Delete"
                        key="Del"
                        enabled="dw.canDeleteSelection()"
                        command="dw.deleteSelection()"
                        id="DWMenu_MainSite_Edit_Clear" />
          </menu>
      </menubar>
```

If you are familiar with JavaScript, a quick read of this code shows you that many of the commands invoked to perform the menu options are based on JavaScript. As a result, once you learn JavaScript, you can easily modify your menus to add functionality. Simply create a JavaScript (`.js`) file containing all of the code for creating your function's interface, such as an HTML form, and then write the JavaScript code that will generate the appropriate HTML, and/or JavaScript, into your document.

If this sounds complicated, simply read through some of the existing Dreamweaver command files and study how they accomplish their given tasks. These files are all stored in the `/Configurations/Commands` directory or the `/Configurations/Shared/` directory.

Adding Menus and Menu Bars

Menus and menu bars can be added quite easily. Menu items, on the other hand, can be a bit more difficult because they have additional attributes and command requirements.

To add a menu bar to Dreamweaver, you simply need to type in the `<menubar></menubar>` code. As you can see from the previous code sample, the `<menubar>` code must precede, with `</menubar>` following, each set of menus you wish to appear on a single bar in your document.

The `<menubar>` element has the following attributes that can be set:

id (required) Defines the unique id of the menu bar or menu.

> Do not change the id's of existing menus because doing so prevents them from displaying properly in Dreamweaver.

name (required) Defines the name of the menu bar or menu that appears. If you are creating a shortcut menu, this would be left blank (`""`), but the attribute must be present.

app Defines whether the menu is available in `ultradev` (UltraDev) or `dreamweaver` (Dreamweaver). When this attribute is omitted, the menu is available in both applications.

platform Defines whether the menu is available on the `mac` (Macintosh), `win` (Windows), or both (attribute omitted).

Menu bars must contain at least one `<menu>` tag, which in turn must contain at least one `<menuitem>` or `<separator>` element. Individual menus are created by adding the tags `<menu>` `</menu>` between your `<menubar>` tags. So, imagine you want to create a menu bar called "Popup Menu" to let you quickly access a set of folders; your code might look like this:

```
<menubar name="Popup Menu"  id="DWSiteSpecific"
          app="Dreamweaver" platform="win">
   <menu name="_Folders"    id="DWFolders"
          app="Dreamweaver" platform="win">
   </menu>
</menubar>
```

As you can see from the previous example, both the `<menu>` and the `<menubar>` elements have the same attributes, so once you become familiar with one, you can implement the other. You can add submenus to your menus by inserting `<menu>` tags within other `<menu>` tags, as shown here:

```
<menu name="_Open Image" id="DWOpenImage"
          app="Dreamweaver" platform="win">
   <menu name="_Clipart" id="DWClipart"
          app="Dreamweaver" platform="win">
   </menu>
</menu>
```

> To create a menu name with a shortcut key, such as Ctrl + F (Command + F for the Mac), place the underscore character in front of the letter that should serve as the hot key. In the previous example, the Open Image menu could be opened by pressing Ctrl + O (Command + O on the Mac).

Adding Menu Items

Once you have created your menu bar and menus, you are ready to create individual menu items. Menu items can be created using the `<menuitem>` tag in conjunction with these attributes:

id (required) Defines the unique id of the menu item.

name (required) Defines the name of the menu item as it should appear in the menu. Place an underscore in front of the character that you wish to serve as the hot key to activate that menu in Windows.

app Defines whether the menu item is available in `ultradev` (UltraDev) or `dreamweaver` (Dreamweaver). When this attribute is omitted, the menu item is available in both applications.

arguments Allows you to specify a comma-separated list of arguments that should be passed to the file, specified by the `file` attribute. Each argument should be enclosed within single quotations (`'`) inside the attribute value's double quotations (`"`). For example, to pass the information that a table cell should get a background color and that the color should be yellow, you might use the following: `arguments="'true','yellow'"`.

checked Specifies a JavaScript function that will return a value of `true` if the menu item should have a check mark appearing next to it in your Dreamweaver menus when it's active.

command Specifies the JavaScript function that is executed whenever this menu item is selected.

domrequired Controls whether both the Design and Code views should be synchronized before the code specified by the menu item is executed. If set to `true`, then the document must be synchronized prior to running the code specified by this menu. When set to `false`, the document does not need to be synchronized.

dynamic Identifies a menu item that is configured dynamically by an HTML file. If you include this attribute, you must also include the `file` attribute.

enabled Specifies a JavaScript function that will return a value of `true` if this menu item should be currently enabled. For instance, this attribute causes a script to run to ensure that a table is selected before the Insert Row function is available in the Table menu.

file Specifies the file used to dynamically configure a menu item as specified by the `dynamic` attribute. The documents specified here are HTML documents that use JavaScript code to manipulate the Dreamweaver interface, such as opening a dialog box.

key Defines the shortcut key that can be used to activate this menu option. When you are specifying a key combination, use the plus (+) sign to separate each key, for instance Ctrl + Alt + F. Options for your keys include the following:

> **Alt or Opt** Indicates the Alt key in Windows or the Option key on a Macintosh.
>
> **Cmd** Indicates either the Ctrl key in Windows or the Cmd key on a Macintosh.
>
> **Ctrl** Indicates the Ctrl key for either Windows or Macintosh.
>
> **Shift** Indicates the Shift key for either Windows or Macintosh.
>
> **Special Keys** Such as F1 through F12, Home, End, Ins, Del, Tab, Esc, Backspace, Space, PgUp, and PgDn.

It is easier to use the Keyboard Shortcuts editor to modify these values than it is to modify them yourself in the `menus.xml` file. The Keyboard Shortcuts editor dialog box was discussed earlier in the chapter in the section entitled "Creating Custom Shortcut Keys."

platform Defines whether the menu is available on the `mac` (Macintosh), `win` (Windows), or both (attribute omitted).

If you add a new menu and menu items to your Dreamweaver interface, you could end up with a screen somewhat similar to Figure 32.8.

Figure 32.8

Customized Dreamweaver menu and menu items

The following code is used to create the sample menu shown in Figure 32.8.

```
<menu name="_New Addition" id="NewAddition">
    <menuitem name="Addition1" enabled="true"
              command="dw.add1('site files')"
              id="Addition1" />
    <menuitem name="Addition2" enabled="true"
              command="dw.add2('site map')"
              id="Addition2" />
    <menuitem name="Addition3" enabled="true"
              command="dw.add3('assets')"
          checked="dw.checkadd3('assets')"
          id="Addition3" />
    <separator />
    <menuitem name="Addition4" enabled="true"
              command="dw.add4(true)"
              platform="Win"
              id="Addition4" />
    <menuitem name="Addition5" enabled="true"
              command="dw.add5(false)"
              platform="Win"
              id="Addition5" />
</menu>
```

The `<separator>` tag is used to create a gray line in the middle of your menu to separate the menu contents into sections of more closely related options. This tag has no attributes.

Adding Objects to the Insert Bar

The Insert bar provides shortcuts for inserting all of the objects (images, horizontal rules, layers, and tables) that we used in earlier chapters to create our web pages. If you find that there are elements that you commonly need to insert that Dreamweaver may or may not use as you wish it to, such as `<fieldset>` (an HTML 4.0 tag used to group related information within a form, such as contact information), you can add them to the Insert bar. This may sound similar to what a Library object does, but the effect is much different. A Library item can only insert HTML code, while an object on the Insert bar can insert both HTML code and JavaScript into your document.

Most objects will use JavaScript to add the function itself into your document, as you can see by viewing the following. The JavaScript referenced here is also located in Dreamweaver's `Configuration/Objects/` folders. When creating your own object, you should always place all of the files related to a single object in the same folder. This will reduce confusion on your part and it will help you take advantage of Dreamweaver's built-in functionality, which automatically displays every icon and its associated HTML and JavaScript files in its Objects directories.

```
<HTML>
<HEAD>
<!-- Copyright 1999 Macromedia, Inc. All rights reserved. -->
<TITLE>Insert Form</TITLE>
<SCRIPT LANGUAGE="javascript"
SRC="../../Shared/MM/Scripts/CMN/docInfo.js"></SCRIPT>
<SCRIPT LANGUAGE="javascript">
function isDOMRequired() {
    // Return false, indicating that this object is //available in Code view.
    return false;
}
function objectTag() {
    return '<form name="'+ makeUniqueName('form','form') + '" method="post"
action=""></form>';
}
</SCRIPT>
</HEAD>
<BODY BGCOLOR="#FFFFFF">
</BODY>

</HTML>
```

One of the easiest ways to add a new object to the Insert bar is by starting with the code of an existing object of similar functionality. For instance, if you wanted the Insert bar to include a shortcut for inserting the `<fieldset>` element, then you may wish to start with the `Form.htm` file in your Dreamweaver's `Configuration/Objects/Forms` folder because a fieldset is a group of entry elements within a form. You can then modify this code to insert the `<fieldset>` object, rather than the form object.

In order to modify this existing code to add the `<fieldset>` element rather than the `<form>` object, you simply need to edit the following statement:

```
return '<form name="'+ makeUniqueName('form','form') + '" method="post"
action=""></form>';
```

Once edited to reference the `<fieldset>` object, this statement could look like this:

```
return '<fieldset name="'+ makeUniqueName('fieldset','fieldset') + '">
</fieldset>';
```

> You should also change the content of the `<title>` element if you wish to have your tool tip on the Insert bar say "Insert Fieldset" rather than "Insert Form."

After you make your changes, save the file as `fieldset.html`, or the name of the object for which you are modifying your document.

In addition to creating the HTML file, you need to create a GIF image to display on the Insert bar. This image must be 18×18 pixels and have the same name as the HTML file. For instance, if your modified object document is `myfieldset.html`, then the name of your GIF image should be `myfieldset.gif`. You can create this image in Fireworks. Both the GIF image and the HTML file should be saved back in the `Configuration/Objects/Forms` directory.

Once you have added the files to your Forms configuration directory, you need to modify the `Insertbar.xml` document. First you need to scroll through this file and find the statement:

```
<category id="DW_Insertbar_Forms" folder="Forms">
```

This denotes the start of the Forms category of your Insert bar. Now you simply need to copy and paste the existing fieldset information, shown at the beginning of the following example, and modify it so it reads like the second section of code.

```
<button id="DW_Forms_Fieldset"
    image="Forms\Fieldset.gif"
    enabled=""
    showIf=""
    file="Forms\Fieldset.htm"
    codeOnly="TRUE"/>

    <button id="DW_Forms_MyFieldset"
    image="Forms\MyFieldset.gif"
    enabled=""
    showIf=""
    file="Forms\MyFieldset.htm"
    codeOnly="TRUE"/>
```

Save the `Insertbar.xml` file. Now you are ready to restart Dreamweaver and view the additional icon on the Forms category of your Insert bar, as shown in Figure 32.9.

When the new Fieldset button, which you created, is clicked, you will add the following code into your HTML document, at the current cursor location:

```
<fieldset name="fieldset1"></fieldset>
```

You can modify your `menus.xml` file to add your `fieldset.html` objects. See "Creating Custom Menus" earlier in this chapter for directions on how this is done.

You can also create your own categories on the Insert bar by creating a new folder inside your Dreamweaver's `Configuration/Objects` folder. This is how most of the downloadable Dreamweaver extensions (discussed earlier in this chapter in the section entitled "Using the Extension Manager") create their own command objects.

Figure 32.9

New Fieldset icon located on the Forms category of the Insert bar

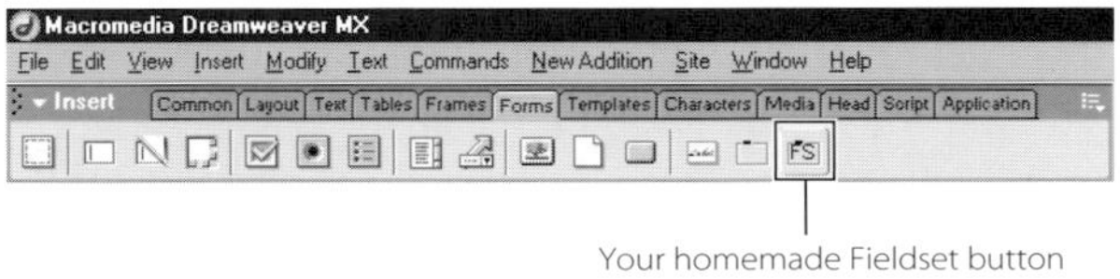

Your homemade Fieldset button

Updating Dreamweaver Dialog Boxes

Did you know that all of the dialog boxes you see when you open up a function in Dreamweaver are created from HTML forms? Because they are all HTML documents, you can make changes to a form and then have that change made active for all uses of Dreamweaver, not just the one site with which you may currently be working.

There are many reasons why you may wish to modify Dreamweaver's dialog boxes. You might simply want to add an additional comment to a dialog box so that you don't forget to do something that you have a tendency to forget. Or you might want to add a field to a dialog box in order to set the values for an option, or an attribute, that wasn't previously available through Dreamweaver but is available in your browser base.

The hardest part of modifying your dialog boxes' content is finding the code for the dialog boxes in the first place. Most of the documents that make up the Dreamweaver dialog boxes can be found in Dreamweaver's `Configuration/Commands` folder. There are a few dialog boxes that are stored in the `Configuration/Shared` folder also. (Their names are fairly self-explanatory, such as "Create Web Photo `Album.htm`," "Modify `NavBar.htm`," and so on.)

To modify the appearance of the dialog box, edit the HTML file. To modify the function of the dialog box's options, edit the JavaScript document(s) that is called from within the HTML document.

Take, for instance, the Flash Button dialog box. Figure 32.10 shows you what the dialog box looks like when it is opened in Dreamweaver. This dialog box, stored as `Configuration/Commands/Flash Button.html`, appears almost identical to the actual dialog box shown in Figure 32.11. A few things to note about these dialogs boxes include the following:

- The title of the HTML document is the title used for the dialog box.
- The buttons on the form might not show up the same as they do on the actual dialog box, or they might not be there at all. JavaScript generates most of those buttons.

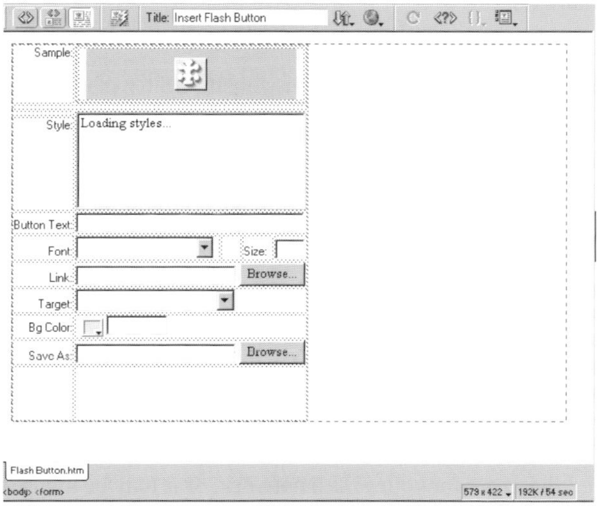

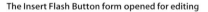

Figure 32.10

The Insert Flash Button form opened for editing

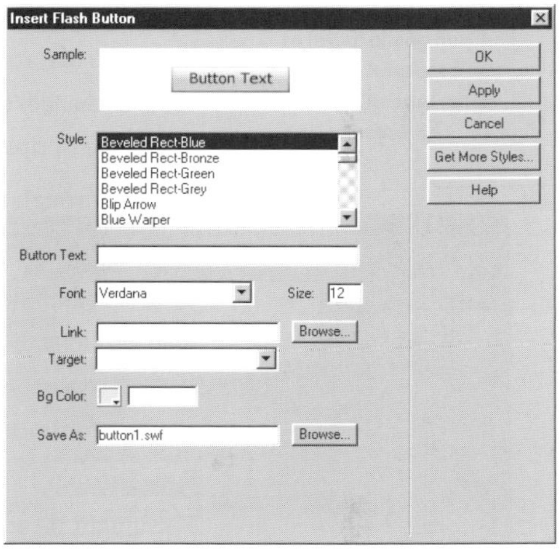

Figure 32.11

The Insert Flash Button dialog box as it is normally seen in Dreamweaver

To modify the Insert Flash Button dialog box, open the `Flash Button.html` file in Dreamweaver and modify it as you would any other document. Be sure not to remove any of the scripting code at the top of the document or you will lose part of your dialog box's functionality. In Figure 32.12, you can see the modified version of the dialog box made by adding the following code to the `Flash Button.html` document.

```
Be sure to save your Flash Button in a folder
that will be uploaded and accessible through your
templates.<br>
```

If you want to share these types of customizations with other users, simply copy the files you have modified and manually install them in each user's `Configuration/Commands` folder.

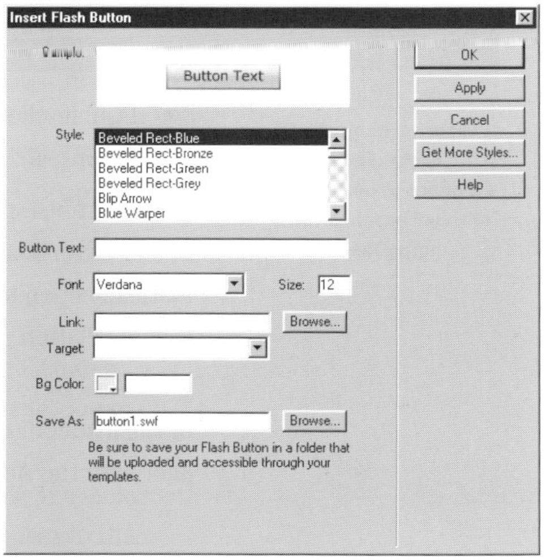

Figure 32.12

The modified Insert Flash Button dialog box.

Hands On 2: Add Custom Characters to the Insert Bar

The steps outlined in this tutorial allow you to create your own custom characters and add them to the Character tab of the Insert bar.

1. Open one of the HTML files in your /Macromedia/Dreamweaver MX/Configuration/ Objects/Characters directory in Dreamweaver. For instance, you can use the Trademark.html file shown in this example.

2. Change to Code view, by selecting View → Code. This opens the Trademark.html file shown below.

```
<HTML>
<HEAD>
<!-- Copyright 1999 Macromedia, Inc. All rights reserved. -->

<title>Trademark</TITLE>
<SCRIPT SRC="characters.js"></SCRIPT>
<SCRIPT LANGUAGE="javascript">

function isDOMRequired() {
        // Return false, indicating that this
        // object is available in Code view.
        return false;
}

function objectTag() {
  // Return the html tag that should be inserted
  // return "&trade;";
  // Supported only in the (4?-5 browsers).
        checkEncoding();
  return "&#153;";      // Generally supported.
}
</SCRIPT>
</HEAD>
<BODY BGCOLOR="#FFFFFF">

</BODY>
</HTML>
```

In this file, there are two JavaScript functions that insert a named entity—such as ¡, which inserts an inverted exclamation point—into your document. This entity is also referred to numerically by ¡.

3. Modify the `Trademark.html` file so that it inserts your entity item, `&iexcl;`. This is done by replacing the existing entity string on line 18 (you can view the line numbers in your document by selecting View → Code View Options → Line Numbers) with either the `&iexcl;` or the `&#161;` numerical entity.

The named entity `&iexcl;` is only supported by 4.0 and newer browsers such as Internet Explorer 4, Netscape Navigator 4, and Opera 4. For users of your site that are using other browsers or devices, you may want to consider using the numerical entity `&#161;` because it has more global support.

When you have finished completed, and as long as you are using the `&#161;` character, your document will appear as follows:

```
<HTML>
<HEAD>
<!-- Copyright 1999 Macromedia, Inc. All rights reserved. -->

<TITLE>Inverted Exclamation Point</TITLE>
<SCRIPT SRC="characters.js"></SCRIPT>
<SCRIPT LANGUAGE="javascript">

function isDOMRequired() {
// Return false, indicating that this object
// is available in code view.
        return false;
}

function objectTag() {
  // Return the html tag that should be inserted
  // return "&iexcl;";
  // Supported only in the (4?-5 browsers).
        checkEncoding();
  return "&#161;";  // Generally supported.
}
</SCRIPT>
</HEAD>
<BODY BGCOLOR="#FFFFFF">

</BODY>
</HTML>
```

4. Select File → Save As and save your new character description in the `/Macromedia/ Dreamweaver MX/Configuration/Objects/Characters` directory. Name the file `iexcl.html`.

5. Using your favorite graphics program, such as Fireworks, create an 18×18 pixel GIF image that contains the image you wish to serve as the button that will represent your new character in the Character category on the Insert bar. This graphic file also needs to be saved in your `/Macromedia/Dreamweaver4/Configuration/Objects/Characters` directory.

6. Restart Dreamweaver. When you restart Dreamweaver, your new icon will appear as the last icon in the Character category view of the Insert bar. You can add as many characters to your panel in this fashion as you want.

> Be careful that you only use valid named entities within your modified configuration files. If these entities are invalid, you will insert non-supported information into your document that may be viewed incorrectly, or not at all by web browsers.

Ready, Set, Go!

You're now some kind of cyclone ranger with these Dreamweaver and Fireworks apps! We think you're ready now to go where few dare to tread: into the fast paced world of developing applications with Dreamweaver. If you still have some questions, try the Online Resources listed in the appendices that follow.

## PART VII

Appendices

Dreamweaver inspires loyalty *and enthusiasm among its users, and you can see evidence of this in the many websites and discussion groups devoted to the software. The enjoyment that designers get from using the program encourages them to share what they've learned, discovered, or created. Going online is the best way to get the latest information about Dreamweaver, Fireworks, and other Macromedia products, and to contact other web designers if you have questions or problems you can't solve. The first appendix collects some websites, mailing lists, and other online resources that will help you continue to learn about Dreamweaver after you finish this book.*

In addition, the second appendix will help you get around in Dreamweaver. We hope that you will find this extensive list of keyboard shortcuts helpful and informative.

APPENDIX A ■ Online Resources

APPENDIX B ■ Dreamweaver MX Keyboard Shortcuts

Online Resources

Dreamweaver inspires loyalty and enthusiasm among its users, and you can see evidence of this in the many websites and discussion groups devoted to the software. The enjoyment that designers get from using the program encourages them to share what they've learned, discovered, or created.

Going online is the best way to get the latest information about Dreamweaver, Fireworks, and other Macromedia products, and to contact other web designers if you have questions or problems you can't solve. This appendix collects some websites, mailing lists, and other online resources that will help you continue to learn about Dreamweaver after you finish this book.

Starting Points

There are so many websites related to Dreamweaver that it can be helpful to begin with sites that collect links to other resources as well as providing their own software or instructional materials. The following websites are good starting points for finding out about Dreamweaver online.

Macromedia Resources

Dreamweaver Support Center (`http://www.macromedia.com/support/dreamweaver`) Any problems with Dreamweaver are reported here. You'll also find patches, how-tos, and tips.

Dreamweaver Templates (`http://www.macromedia.com/software/dreamweaver/download/templates`) Many of these templates are for professors or students. But some of the sites contain nice graphics for kids, members of a club, or musical groups.

Flash and Dreamweaver Tutorial Movies (`http://www.macromedia.com/software/flash/resources/integration/tutorials`) If you have QuickTime installed, you can watch movies that instruct you on how to integrate Flash with Dreamweaver. Download the Zip archives on this page, and you can follow the exercises yourself.

Dreamweaver Online Forums (`http://webforums.macromedia.com/dreamweaver`) Macromedia's own web-based discussion groups for Dreamweaver and Exchange users.

Other Starting Points

Massimo's Corner of the web (`http://www.massimocorner.com`) Team Macromedia member Massimo Forti contributes his own extensions to this site, but also includes links to commands and software created by others. Different parts of the site are devoted to Dreamweaver, UltraDev, and Fireworks.

About.com's Dreamweaver Tips and Tutorials page (`http://webdesign.about.com/cs/dreamweavertips`) It's good to get an unbiased look at Dreamweaver from outside Macromedia, and this page does include links to Dreamweaver-related news, FAQs, and tutorials by a variety of Dreamweaver enthusiasts and web designers.

Dreamweaver News and Information (`http://owlnet.net/dwnews`) A Dreamweaver enthusiast named Craig Foster provides tips, extensions, and a monthly Dreamweaver News newsletter to which you can subscribe.

Dreamweaver Software

Dreamweaver can do a lot, but some enterprising designers who have used the program in real-world situations have found ways to make it do more. They've come up with their own extensions, templates, commands, and other goodies that can be added to the program. Some are available for free, but don't expect the software to be updated or supported. Other extensions have to be purchased from their developers.

Third-Party Extensions

Macromedia Exchange for Dreamweaver (`http://www.macromedia.com/exchange/dreamweaver`) Macromedia makes a number of extensions available that add e-commerce, site productivity, and other categories. (There's a set of Fireworks extensions available, too.) Be sure to read the comments posted by individuals who have actually used (or tried to use) the extensions.

Dreamweaver Dabbling (`http://www.pawluk.com/public`) Self-proclaimed dabbler Hal Pawluk makes some nifty extensions available for download, including software that lets you create a pop-up menu and a jump menu.

Dreamweaver Fever (`http://dreamweaverfever.com/grow/`) Drew McLellan provides some unusual extensions, including one that automatically adds two paragraphs of "Greek" text, which designers use to mock up pages. (The "Pain" area of this site includes "pain relievers"— advanced-level tutorials, mostly relevant to UltraDev.)

Yaromat (`http://www.yaromat.com/dw`) Web designer Jaro von Flocken gives back to the Dreamweaver community by providing extensions, objects, behaviors, and other goodies on this site for free.

Project Seven Development (`http://www.projectseven.com`) One extension lets you scroll the contents of a layer. Others enable you to animate layers and create pop-up menus.

Website Templates

Templates2go.com (`http://www.templates2go.com`) Designer Linda Locke presents a package of 60 predesigned websites for business, publishing, personal, and e-commerce use. Cost is $79.

Dreamweaversites.com (`http://store.dreamweaverwebmaster.com/dwtemplates.asp`) Restrained, tasteful designs intended for business and e-commerce sites. You can buy one template at a time, typically for $15 to $25.

Heeha.com (`http://www.heeha.com`) A wide range of personal and business templates, many of which use a clean white page background. Some templates are available for free; others typically cost about $12.99.

Tutorials and Instruction

If this book's tutorials aren't enough, you can go online to get more step-by-step instructions. The following websites present free tips and tutorials for both Dreamweaver and Fireworks enthusiasts.

Dreamweaver Tutorials and Tips

Dreamweaver Tutorial (`http://www.intranetjournal.com/articles/200002/dream_index.html`) An article published in *Intranet Journal* focuses on the basics of using Dreamweaver. Although it's outdated—it only covers Dreamweaver 3—it's free, and it gives you an interactive look at some website design approaches, including frames, design notes, importing Word files, and using Java applets.

Dreamweaver Walk-Through (`http://hotwired.lycos.com/webmonkey/98/27/index1a.html`) A tutorial prepared by HotWired's Webmonkey department. Lesson 1 covers text, forms, and tables; Lesson 2 examines layers, style sheets, JavaScript, and timelines.

CNET's 12 Tips for Dreamweaver 4.0: (`http://home.cnet.com/webbuilding/0-3881-8-4363450-1.html`) Although this article covers Dreamweaver 4, the instructions on installing extensions, integrating with Flash, and customizing the program apply in general to Dreamweaver 5.

Creating Flash Buttons and Flash Text Effects (`http://webdesign.about.com/library/weekly/aa072501b.htm?terms=Dreamweaver+Tutorial`) A tutorial prepared by About.com that covers the topic quickly, with step-by-step instructions and graphics.

Fireworks Tutorials and Tips

Project Fireworks (`http://www.projectfireworks.com`) Web developer Kleanthis Economou has developed 30 separate tutorials based on requests received from Fireworks users. The instructions cover specific tools (such as the knife and eraser) and topics such as masks and slices.

Playing With Fire (`http://www.playingwithfire.com`) This is a companion site to a book by the same name. The authors provide instructions on drawing shapes, working with text, creating background tiles, and more.

Newsgroups and Mailing Lists

There's nothing like finding personal support when you run into a problem you can't solve or a question you can't answer immediately. Newsgroups and mailing lists not only give you a great place to get help, but you can also answer questions yourself and be part of the Dreamweaver community.

Macromedia_Dreamwvr (`http://groups.yahoo.com/group/Macromedia_Dreamwvr`) One of the Yahoo! discussion groups, it's for beginners as well as advanced users. You need a Yahoo! ID to subscribe, but you can obtain one for free from Yahoo!.

Dreamweaver Talk (`http://www.blueworld.com/blueworld/lists/dreamweaver.html`) An e-mail discussion group run by software developer Blue World Communications, Inc.

Dreamweaver MX Keyboard Shortcuts

This appendix lays out some essential keyboard shortcuts that will help you get around in Dreamweaver MX. If you keep this reference handy when you are working with the application, you will be able to save yourself (and your hand) a lot of mouse clicks.

CATEGORY/COMMAND	WINDOWS SHORTCUT	MACINTOSH SHORTCUT
Managing Files		
New document	Control + N	Command + N
Open an HTML file	Control + O	Command + O
Open in frame	Control + Shift + O	Command + Shift + O
Close	Control + W	Command + W
Save	Control + S	Command + S
Save as	Control + Shift + S	Command + Shift + S
Exit/Quit	Alt + F4 or Control + Q	Command + Q
General Editing		
Undo	Control + Z	Command + Z
Redo	Control + Y or Control + Shift + Z	Command + Y or Command + Shift + Z
Cut	Control + X or Shift + Delete	Command + X or Shift + Delete
Copy	Control + C	Command + C
Paste	Control + V or Shift + Insert	Command + V or Shift + Insert
Clear	Delete	Delete
Bold	Control + B	Command + B
Italic	Control + I	Command + I
Select All	Control + A	Command + A
Move to page up	Page Up	Page Up
Move to page down	Page Down	Page Down
Select to page up	Shift + Page Up	Shift + Page Up
Select to page down	Shift + Page Down	Shift + Page Down
Select line up/down	Shift + Up/Down	Shift + Up/Down
Move to start of line	Home	Home
Move to end of line	End	End
Select to start of line	Shift + Home	Shift + Home

continues

continued

CATEGORY/COMMAND	WINDOWS SHORTCUT	MACINTOSH SHORTCUT
General Editing		
Select to end of line	Shift + End	Shift + End
Go to previous/next Paragraph	Control + ↑/↓	Command + ↑/↓
Go to next/previous word	Control + →/←	Command + →/←
Select word left/right	Control + Shift + ←/→	Command + Shift + ←/→
Delete word left	Control + Backspace	Command + Backspace
Delete word right	Control + Delete	Command + Delete
Select character left/right	Shift + ←/→	Shift + ←/→
Find and Replace	Control + F	Command + F
Find next/find again	F3	Command + G
Replace	Control + H	Command + H
Copy HTML (in Design view)	Control + Shift + C	Command + Shift + C
Paste HTML (in Design view)	Control + Shift + V	Command + Shift + V
Preferences	Control + U	Command + U
Page Views		
Standard view	Control + Shift + F6	Command + Shift + F6
Layout view	Control + F6	Command + F6
Live Data mode	Control + R	Command + R
Live Data	Control + Shift + R	Command + Shift + R
Switch to next document	Control + Tab	Command + Tab
Switch to previous document	Control + Shift + Tab	Command + Shift + Tab
Switch between Design and Code views	Control + '	Command + '
Server debug	Control + Shift + G	Command + Shift + G
Refresh Design view	F5	F5
Viewing Page Elements		
Show/hide Visual Aids	Control + Shift + I	Command + Shift + I
Show/hide Rulers	Control + Alt + R	Command + Option + R
Show/hide Grid	Control + Alt + G	Command + Option + G
Snap to Grid	Control + Alt + Shift + G	Command + Option + Shift + G
Show/hide Head content	Control + Shift + W	Command + Shift + W
View page properties	Control + J	Command + J
View selection properties	Control + Shift + J	Command + Shift + J
Code Editing		
Switch to Design view	Control+'	Option + '
Print Code	Control + P	Command + P
Validate markup	Shift + F6	Shift + F6
Open Quick Tag Editor	Control + T	Command + T
Open Snippets panel	Shift + F9	Shift + F9
Show Code Hints	Control + Spacebar	Command + Spacebar

CATEGORY/COMMAND	WINDOWS SHORTCUT	MACINTOSH SHORTCUT
Code Editing		
Indent code	Control + Shift + >	Command + Shift + >
Outdent code	Control + Shift + <	Command + Shift + <
Insert tag	Control + E	Command + E
Edit tag (in Design view)	Control + F5	Command + F5
Select parent tag	Control + [	Command + [
Select child	Control +]	Command +]
Balance Braces	Control + '	Command + '
Toggle breakpoint	Control + Alt + B	Command + Option + B
Go to line	Control + G	Command + G
Move to top of code	Control + Home	Command + Home
Move to end of code	Control + End	Command + End
Select to top of code	Control + Shift + Home	Command + Shift + Home
Select to end of code	Control + Shift + End	Command + Shift + End
Text Editing		
Create a new paragraph	Enter	Return
Insert a line break 	Shift + Enter	Shift + Return
Insert a nonbreaking space	Control + Shift + Spacebar	Command + Shift + Spacebar
Move text or object	Drag item	Drag item
Copy text or object	Control-drag item	Control-drag item
Select a word	Double - click	Double-click
Add selected items to library	Control + Shift + B	Command + Shift + B
Open/close the Property Inspector	Control + Shift + J	Command + Shift + J
Switch between Design view and code editors	Alt + Tab	Option + Tab
Check spelling	Shift + F7	Shift + F7
Formatting Text		
Indent	Control + Alt +]	Command + Option +]
Outdent	Control + Alt + [	Command + Option + [
Remove formatting	Control + 0 (zero)	Command + 0 (zero)
Format paragraph	Control + Shift + P	Command + Shift + P
Apply Headings 1–6	Control + 1–6	Command + 1–6
Align Left/Center/Right/Justify	Control + Alt + Shift + L/C/R/J	Command + Alt + Shift + L/C/R/J
Edit Style Sheet	Control + Shift + E	Command + Shift + E
Working in Tables		
Select table (with cursor inside the table)	Control + A	Command + A
Move to the next cell	Tab	Tab

continues

continued

CATEGORY/COMMAND	WINDOWS SHORTCUT	MACINTOSH SHORTCUT
Working in Tables		
Move to the previous cell	Shift + Tab	Shift + Tab
Insert a row (before current)	Control + M	Command + M
Add a row at end of table	Tab (in the last cell)	Tab (in the last cell)
Delete current row	Control + Shift + M	Command + Shift + M
Insert a column	Control + Shift + A	Command + Shift + A
Delete a column	Control + Shift + - (hyphen)	Command + Shift + - (hyphen)
Merge selected table cells	Control + Alt + M	Command + Option + M
Split table cell	Control + Alt + S	Command + Option + S
Defer table update	Control + Spacebar	Command + Spacebar
Increase column span	Control + Shift +]	Command + Shift +]
Decrease column span	Control + Shift + [	Command + Shift + [
Working in Frames		
Select a frame	Alt-click (in frame)	Shift + Option-click (in frame)
Select next frame or frameset	Alt + →	Command + →
Select previous frame or frameset	Alt + ←	Command + ←
Select parent frameset	Alt + ↑	Command + ↑
Select first child frame or frameset	Alt + ↓	Command + ↓
Add a new frame to frameset	Select frame, then Alt-drag frame border	Select frame, then Option-drag frame border
Add a new frame to frameset using the push method	Select frame, then Alt + Control-drag frame border	Select frame, then Command + Option-drag frame border
Working with Layers		
Select a layer	Control + Shift-click	Command + Shift-click
Select and move layer	Shift + Control-drag	Command + Shift-drag
Add or remove layer from selection	Shift-click layer	Shift-click layer
Move selected layer by pixels	Arrow keys	Arrow keys
Move selected layer by snapping increment	Shift + Arrow keys	Shift + Arrow keys
Resize selected layer by pixels	Control + Arrow keys	Option + Arrow keys
Resize selected layer by snapping increment	Control + Shift + Arrow keys	Option + Shift + Arrow keys
Toggle the display of the grid	Control + Alt + G	Command + Option + G
Snap to grid	Control + Shift + Alt + G	Command + Shift + Option + G
Align layers left	Control + Shift + 1	Command + Shift + 1
Align layers right	Control + Shift + 3	Command + Shift + 3
Align layers top	Control + Shift + 4	Command + Shift + 4
Align layers bottom	Control + Shift + 6	Command + Shift + 6
Make same width	Control + Shift + 7	Command + Shift + 7
Make same height	Control + Shift + 9	Command + Shift + 9

CATEGORY/COMMAND	WINDOWS SHORTCUT	MACINTOSH SHORTCUT
Getting Help		
Using Dreamweaver Help topics	F1	F1
Using ColdFusion Help topics	Control + F1	Command + F1
Reference	Shift + F1	Shift + F1
Inserting Objects		
Any object (image, Shockwave movie, and so on)	Drag file from the Explorer or Site panel to the Document window	Drag file from the Explorer or Site panel to the Document window
Image	Control + Alt + I	Command + Option + I
Table	Control + Alt + T	Command + Option + T
Named anchor	Control + Alt + A	Command + Option + A
Managing Hyperlinks		
Check links sitewide	Control + F8	Command + F8
Check selected links	Shift + F8	Shift + F8
Create hyperlink (select text, image, or object)	Control + L	Command + L
Remove hyperlink	Control + Shift + L	Command + Shift + L
Drag and drop to create a hyperlink from a document	Select the text, image, or object, then Shift-drag the selection to a file in the Site panel	Select the text, image, or object, then Shift-drag the selection to a file in the Site panel
Drag and drop to create a hyperlink using the Property Inspector	Select the text, image, or object, then drag the Point-to-File icon in Property Inspector to a file in the Site panel	Select the text, image, or object, then drag the Point-to-File icon in Property Inspector to a file in the Site panel
Open the linked-to document in Dreamweaver	Control + double-click link	Command + double-click link
Previewing and Debugging in Browsers		
Preview in primary browser	F12	F12
Preview in secondary browser	Shift + F12	Shift + F12
Debug in primary browser	Alt + F12	Option + F12
Debug in secondary browser	Control + Alt + F12	Command + Option + F12
Managing a Site		
Connect/Disconnect	Control + Alt + Shift + F5	Command + Option + Shift + F5
Refresh	F5	F5
Create new file	Control + Shift + N	Command + Shift + F5
Create new folder	Control + Alt + Shift + N	Command + Option + Shift + N
Open selection	Control + Shift + Alt + O	Command + Option + Shift + O
Delete file	Control + X	Command + X
Copy file	Control + C	Command + C
Paste file	Control + V	Command + V
Duplicate file	Control + D	Command + D

continues

continued

CATEGORY/COMMAND	WINDOWS SHORTCUT	MACINTOSH SHORTCUT
Managing a Site		
Rename file	F2	F2
Get (selected files or folders from remote site)	Control + Shift + D	Command + Shift + D
Put (selected files or folders to remote site)	Control + Shift + U	Command + Shift + U
Check out	Control + Alt + Shift + D	Command + Option + Shift + D
Check in	Control + Alt + Shift + U	Command + Option + Shift + U
View site map	Alt + F8	Option + F8
Refresh Local pane	Shift + F5	Shift + F5
Refresh Remote pane	Alt + F5	Option + F5
Using a Site Map		
View site files	F8	F8
Refresh Local pane	Shift + F5	Shift + F5
View as root	Control + Shift + R	Command + Shift + R
Link to new file	Control + Shift + N	Command + Shift + N
Link to existing file	Control + Shift + K	Command + Shift + K
Change link	Control + L	Command + L
Remove link	Control + Shift + L	Command + Shift + L
Show/hide link	Control + Shift + Y	Command + Shift + Y
Show page titles	Control + Shift + T	Command + Shift + T
Zoom in site map	Control+ + (plus sign)	Command+ + (plus sign)
Zoom out site map	Control+ - (hyphen)	Command+ - (hyphen)
Opening and Closing Panels		
Insert bar	Control + F2	Command + F2
Properties	Control + F3	Command + F3
Answers	Alt + F1	Option + F1
CSS Styles	Shift + F11	Shift + F11
HTML Styles	Control + F11	Command + F11
Behaviors	Shift + F3	Shift + F3
Tag Inspector	F9	F9
Snippets	Shift + F9	Shift + F9
Reference	Shift + F1	Shift + F1
Databases	Control + Shift + F10	Command + Shift + F10
Bindings	Control + F10	Command + F10
Server Behaviors	Control + F9	Command + F9
Components	Control + F7	Command + F7
Site	F8	F8
Assets	F11	F11

CATEGORY/COMMAND	WINDOWS SHORTCUT	MACINTOSH SHORTCUT
Opening and Closing Panels		
Results → Search	Control + Shift + F	Command + Shift + F
Results → Validation	Control + Shift + F7	Command + Shift + F7
Results → Target Browser Check	Control + Shift + F8	Command + Shift + F8
Results → Link Checker	Control + Shift + F9	Command + Shift + F9
Results → Site Reports	Control + Shift + F11	Command + Shift + F11
Results → FTP Log	Control + Shift + F12	Command + Shift + F12
Results → Server Debug	Control + Shift + F5	Command + Shift + F5
Others → Code inspector	F10	F10
Others → Frames	Shift + F2	Shift + F2
Others → History	Shift + F10	Shift + F10
Others → Layers	F2	F2
Others → Sitespring	F7	F7
Others → Timelines	Alt + F9	Option + F9
Show/hide panels	F4	F4

Index

Note to the Reader: Throughout this index **boldfaced** page numbers indicate primary discussions of a topic. *Italicized* page numbers indicate illustrations.

absolute measurements, **236**

access
restrictions on, **552**
to web services, **532**

Access databases, 469

Access Denied Go To page, 552

accessibility
ensuring, 7
reminders for, **44**, *44*
standards for, **569–570**, *570*

Accessibility extension category, 595

ACO files, 109

Acrobat Reader, 350

ACT files, 109

action attribute, 400–401

Action field, 401

Action menu, 370

Action property, 408

actions, 370

active areas of button slices, 177

Active Server Pages (ASP), 442, 445, **468**

Active Server Pages.NET (ASP.NET), 442, **468**, **538–540**, *539–540*

ActiveX controls, **348–349**, *349*

Adaptive palette, 202

Add Arrowheads dialog box, **111**, *111*

Add Color to Transparency option, 206

Add Keyframe option, 392

Add Mask option, 158

Add Object to Timeline option, 392

Add Picture Frame dialog box, 74, **111**, *111–112*

Add Pop-Up Menu option, 182

Add Swatches option, 110

Add to Cart Button dialog box, 436

Add To Favorites option, 61, 428

A

Add Using WSDL panel, 535–536, *535*

administration, **545**, **575**
content. *See* content
journaling, **585–588**, *587–588*
login pages and processes, **550–552**, *551–552*
portals, **553–556**
restrictions, **552**
rolling back sites, **588**
updating sites, **589–591**, *589–591*
user, **546**
for privileges, **546–547**
for registration forms, **547–548**
for server behaviors, **548–550**, *548–549*
workflow, **582–585**, *583–584*

Adobe Acrobat Reader, 350

Advanced option, 390

Advanced Random Images extension, **614–615**, *615*

Advanced tab, 184, *184*

Aggressive Skate and Snowboard site, 423

AIFF (Audio Interchange File Format), 339

Align panel, 138, *138*

Align property, 408

Aligned option, 157

alignment
in CSS, 313
images, 280–281
objects, **137–138**, *138*
Rubber Stamp tool, 157
in tables, **239**
text, **267**

Alpha Transparency option, 205

alt attribute, 521

Alt property, 407

Alt tags and alternative text
for images, 280, 407

for slices, **194–195**
in XHTML, 521
Alternate Image Description option, 214
Amount of Texture setting, 86
anchors, link, **320–321**, **325**, *325*
Animate dialog box, 173
animation
creating, **396–398**, *396–397*
GIF, **207**, **350–351**
previewing, **398**
symbols for, **172–173**, *173*
Answers panel, **34**
Anti-Aliasing
exporting, 216
for fills, 97
for text, 139
AnyBrowser site, 368
Anything option, 389
app attribute
for menu items, 608
for menus, 607
App Servers extension category, 595
Appearance option, 390
Appearance tab, 183, *184*
applets, 31, **349–350**
Application panel, **35**
Apply Source Formatting option, 255
Apply Template to Page option, 57
applying
styles, **269**, **309**, **315**
templates, **56–57**, *57*
areas, exporting, **220**
arguments attribute, 524, 608
Arrowhead command, 74
arrowheads, 74, 111, *111*
ASP (Active Server Pages), 442, 445, **468**
ASP.NET (Active Server Pages.NET), 442, **468**,
538–540, *539–540*
assets, 13
inserting, **62**
templates. *See* templates
Assets Manager, **59–60**
Favorites tab, **61–62**
for templates, 49–50, *50*
Assets panel, 35

assigning
editable regions, **53**, *53*
privileges, **546–547**
Attach Style Sheet option, 316
attaching
CSS, **316**, *316*
JavaScript, 373
!ATTLIST element, 562–563
attributes
in XHTML, 520–521
in XML, 513
AU files, 339
audiences
considering, **7**
defining, **558**
audio files, **341–342**, *342*
formats for, **339**
playing clips, **379**, *379*
Audio Interchange File Format (AIFF), 339
Audio Video Interleave (AVI) format, 340
Authorizer program, 433
Auto option, 299
Auto Apply option, 269
Auto Indent option, 449, 454
Auto Levels option, **165**
automatic operations
HTML cleanup, **580–581**
image size placement, 278
Automatic Wrapping After Column option, 450
autonaming slices, 214
Autostretch columns, **237**
AVI (Audio Video Interleave) format, 340

B

b-trees, 481
background
in CSS, **313**, *313*
in Flash buttons, **360**
in frames, 295, *295*
in tables, 238
backups, **490**
Balance Braces option, 460
bandwidth, 338
Banner Generator, 428

Banner Network, 428
banners for marketing, **427–428**
BarinJar.com site, 310
BaseFont element, 561–562
Baseline Shift option, 139
Batch Process dialog box, 118, *118*
batch processing, **116–119**, *117–119*
bCentral merchant, 434
behaviors, 20, **369–370**
 built-in, **371**
 Call JavaScript, **373**, *373*
 Change Property, **373**, *374*
 Check Browser, **374**, *374*
 Check Plugin, **374–375**, *375*
 Control Shockwave or Flash, **375–376**, *376*
 Drag Layer, **376–377**, *377*
 and events, **370–372**
 for frames, **301**
 Go to Timeline Frame, **386–387**, *387*
 Go to URL, **377**, *377*
 Jump Menu, **378**, *378*
 Jump Menu Go, **378**, *378*
 with layers, **390–391**
 for multimedia, **351**
 Open Browser Window, **378–379**, *379*
 Play Sound, **379**, *379*
 Play Timeline, **387–388**, *388*
 Popup Message, **379**, *379*
 Preload Images, **380**, *380*
 rollover, **177–180**, *178–180*
 Set Nav Bar Image, **380–382**, *381–382*
 Set Text of Frame, **382–383**, *383*
 Set Text of Layer, **383**, *383*
 Set Text of Status Bar, **383–384**, *384*
 Set Text of Text Field, **384**, *385*
 Show-Hide Layers, **384–385**, *385*
 Show Pop-Up Menu, **389–390**, *390*
 Stop Timeline, **388**, *388*
 Swap Image and Swap Image Restore, **385–386**, *386*
 in templates, **52**, **58–59**
 in timelines, **386–388**, *387–388*, **391–393**, *391*, **397–398**, *397*
 Validate Form, **388–389**, *389*
Behaviors panel, 34, 78, 370, *370*

Berners-Lee, Tim, 18, 29
Bevel effect, **104**, *105*
Bezier curves, **126–128**, *127–128*
Bg Color feature, 360
BigNosedBird.com site, 417
binary tree indexes, 481
bindings
 for ColdFusion, **498**
 for databases, 471–472, **495**, 498
 in WSDL, 533
Bindings panel, 35
bitmap images, **147–148**
 borders for, **99–100**, *99–100*
 masking, **157**
  with bitmap masks, **157–161**, *158–160*
  with vector masks, **161–163**, *161–162*
 menus for
  Filters, **163–166**
  Select, **151–153**, *151–152*
 mode switching for, **148**
 plugins for, **166–169**, *167–169*
 tools for
  Blur, **153**, *153*
  Burn, **155**, *155*
  Dodge, **154–155**, *154–155*
  Rubber Stamp, **156–157**, *156*
  selection, **149–151**, *149–151*
  Sharpen, **153–154**, *154*
  Smudge, **156**, *156*
 Tools panel for, **149**, *149*
bitmap masks, **157**
 adding, **158–159**, *159*
 images as, **160–161**, *160*
 saving, **159**, *159*
 selections for, **158**, *158*
Black and White palette, 202
_blank target, 195, 300, 324
Blend Mode option, 150
block_model value, 518
block options for CSS, **313**, *313*
Blur effect, **104–105**
Blur filters, **163**
Blur tool, **153**, *153*
bold text, 264
Boolean logic, 479

borders
    for bitmaps, **99–100**, *99–100*
    in CSS, **314**, *314*
    for frames, **289–290**, *290*
    for images, 280–281
    for tables, 232, 235, 238–239
Box Lessons site, 311
box model, CSS, 309, 314
Box Model Hack site, 311
box options for CSS, **314**, *314*
braces ({}), balancing, **460**
branding, 422
breakpoints, 462
brick-and-mortar businesses, 424
Brightness and Contrast option, **165**
broadband connections, 338
broken links, **329–333**, *330–332*
Browser Compatibility Chart, 559
BrowserProfiles folder, 561
browsers
    checking, **374**
    compatibility, **14**, **557**
        designing for, **564–565**
        feature support in, **558–559**
        problems in, **564**
        resources for, **565–566**
        standards for, **565**
        target audiences in, **558**
        testing, **559–564**
    multiple, designing for, **30**
    opening windows in, **378–379**, *378*
    support for, 29–30
Browsers extension category, 595
Burn tool, **155**, *155*
Button editor, **174–177**, *175*, *177*
buttons and button symbols, 172
    creating, **175–177**, *175*, *177*
    editing, **177**
    Flash. *See* Flash objects
    in forms, **408**, *408*

C

Call JavaScript behavior, **373**, *373*
Canvas option, 73

Canvas Color option, 95
Canvas Size option, 95
Cardservice International, 434
Cascading Style Sheets. *See* CSS (Cascading Style
    Sheets)
case sensitivity in XML, 512
catalogs, online
    completeness of, **430**, *430*
    creating, **428–429**, *429*
    organizing, **430**
    updating, **429–430**
CDATA sections, 514–515
cell padding and spacing, 232
Centering option, 450
CFCs (ColdFusion Components), 496
CFML (ColdFusion Markup Language), 469, 493
cgi directory, **412–413**
CGI Resource Index site, 417
CGI scripts, **412**
    editing, **415–416**, *415*
    requirements, **412–413**
Change All Links To setting, 344
Change Link setting, 344
Change Link Sitewide dialog box, 331, *331*
Change Property behavior, **373**, *374*
Change Workspace option, 36
changes, tracking, 8
channels, 392
Char Width property
    for file fields, 406
    for forms, 402
Characters tab, 32
check boxes, **404–405**, *404*
Check Browser behavior, **374**, *374*
Check In/Check Out feature, 29, 41, **584–585**
Check Links option, 332
Check Links Sitewide option, 332
Check New Username behavior, 549–550, *549*
Check Plugin behavior, 351, **374–375**, *375*
Check Spelling dialog box, 259, *259*
Check Target Browsers feature, **560–561**
checked attribute, 608
Checked Value property, 404
CHMOD settings, **413**
Choose an Existing Spacer Image File option, 236

circles, 124
Citation option, 264
.class extension, 349
Clean Up CSS option, 254
Clean Up <font> Tags option, 254
Clean Up HTML/XHTML dialog box, 460, *460*,
  581, *581*
Clean Up Word HTML dialog box, 253–254,
  254, 580
cleaning up HTML, **460–461**, *460*, **580–582**, *581*
Clear Cell Heights/Widths option, 237
clickthroughs, 428
client-side image maps, 19, 327
Clip option, 243
Cloak Files Ending With setting, 572
cloaking
  Flash movies, **345–346**
  folders and files, **572–573**, *572*
Cloaking category, 42
Clone option, 140
cloning vs. duplicating, 136
closing
  paths, **128–129**
  templates, **55**
closing tags in XML, 512
code, 12, *12*, **447**
  color for, **450**
  debugging, **460–463**, *460–463*
  display options for, **449**, *449*
  editing, **457–458**, *457–458*
  editors for, **459**, *459*, **494**
  format options for, **449–450**
  hints for, **451**, **454–455**, **494**
  keyboard shortcuts for, **626–627**
  navigating, **458**
  printing, **459**
  rewriting, **450–451**
  shortcuts for, **454–456**, *455–456*
  snippets for, **455–456**, *456*
  structuring, **454**
  tags for
    custom, **453**, *453*
    libraries for, **451–453**, *451–453*
    Tag Chooser for, **455**, *455*

validating, **461**, *461*
  viewing, **448**, *448*
Code and Design view, 28, 54
Code Editing option, 601
Code Inspector, 448
Code Navigation menu, **31**
Code option, 264
Code panel, **34–35**
Code view, 28, **271**, 473
Code View Options option, 449
ColdFusion, **469**, **493**
  adding records in, **504–507**, *504*
  bindings for, **498**
  code editor in, **494**
  connecting to, **496–498**
  debugging, **463**
  main page for, **499–503**, *500*
  panels in, **494–496**
  Property Inspector in, **494**, 500–502
  server behaviors for, **499**
  setup for, **496**, *497*
ColdFusion Components (CFCs), 496
ColdFusion Markup Language (CFML), 469, 493
ColdFusion server model, 442, 445
collaboration, **41**
Collapse Empty Cells option, 246
color
  bitmaps, **165–166**
  code, **450**
  dithering, **107–108**, *108*, **204**, *204–205*
  for e-commerce sites, **423–425**, *423–425*
  Favorites view, 61
  Flash buttons, **360**
  frames, **295–296**, *295*
  in GIF images, 196, **203**, *203*
  gradient, **101–102**, *101*
  monitors, 14
  overlay, **193**
  strokes, 86–87, *87*
  in tables, **238–239**, *238*
  text, **265**, *265*
  in wireframes, 9
color images for bitmap masks, **160–161**, *160*
Color Mixer panel, 78
color table, **206**, *207*

Colors category, 60

columns

in framesets, **291**, *291*, **297–298**, *297*

in tables, 232, *232*

adding and removing, **237–238**

Autostretch, **237**

Combine Nested <font> Tags option, 582

command attribute, 524, 608

Command dialog box, 486–487

Command menu, 604, *604*

Command Name dialog box, 604

commands

Dreamweaver, creating, **603–605**, *603–604*

in Fireworks

creating, **114**

Creative menu, **111–113**, *111–113*

free, **115**

third party, **115**

Commands folder, 115, 612

Commands menu, **74**, *74*

comments

in browser profiles, 562

deleting, 581

common language runtime in .NET, 537

Common tab, 32

communication for e-commerce sites, 422

compatibility, browser. *See* browsers

Components panel, 35, **496**, 534–537, *534*, *536*

compression

GIF. *See* GIF (Graphics Interchange Format) files

JPEG

optimizing, **208–209**, *209*

options for, **207–208**, *207–208*

selective, **209–211**, *210–211*

confidence for e-commerce sites, 422

connection speed considerations, **15**

content, **13–14**, **576**

cleaning up HTML, **460–461**, *460*, **580–582**, *581*

creating files, **578**

deleting files, **578**

dynamic, **466–469**, *467–468*

adding, **474–476**, *475–476*

searching, **476–478**, *477*

for frames, **304**

for libraries, **63–64**, *63*

moving files, **577**

renaming files and folders, **578**

site maps and file list views for, **576–577**, *576*

synchronizing, **579–580**, *579–580*

in templates, **51**, **585**

updating, **590**, *590*

content_model attribute, 518

Contents option, 390

context sensitivity of Property Inspector, 33

continuing paths, **129**

control handles, **127–128**, *127–128*

Control Shockwave or Flash behavior, 351, **375–376**, *376*

Convert Frames to Layers option, 218

Convert Layers to Table dialog box, 246, *246*

Convert to Grayscale command, **112**

Convert to Sepia command, **112**

Convert to Symbol option, 172–173, *173*

Convert Widths to Pixels/Percent option, 237

converting

animation to symbols, 172–173, *173*

frames to layers, 218

to grayscale images, **112**

layers to tables, 246

objects to images, **283–284**, *284*

tables to layers, 247

text to paths, **139–140**, *140*

cookies, **551–552**

Copy option, 458

Copy Over Graphic option, 176

Copy Up Graphic option, 176

copying colors, 61

copyright law, 13

core classes in .NET, 537

corporate portals, 554

Costello, Eric, 310

Create a New Spacer Image option, 236

CREATE INDEX query, 481

Creating and Submitting Extensions option, 599

Creative menu, **111–113**, *111–113*

credit card payments, **432–435**, *433*

Crop tool, **137**, *137*

CSS (Cascading Style Sheets), **16**, *17*, **269**, **307**

attaching, **316**, *316*
background options for, **313**, *313*
benefits of, **308**
block options for, **313**, *313*
border options for, **314**, *314*
box options for, **314**, *314*
creating, **315–316**
for e-commerce sites, 425
editing, **317**, *317*
extensions options for, **314–315**
learning sources for, **310–311**
list options for, **314**
positioning options for, **314**
previewing, **317–318**, *318*
styles in
    applying, **309**, **315**
    creating, **312–313**, *312*
    editing, **315**, *315*
support for, 558
in templates, 52
tools for, **311**, *311*
types of, **310**
uses for, **308–309**
in XML, 513
"CSS in the Real World" lecture, 310
CSS Layers, exporting to, **218–219**
CSS master grid, 559
CSS Style Definition dialog box, 311, *311*,
  313, *313*
CSS Styles panel, 34, 311, *311*
curly braces ({}), balancing, **460**
curves, Bezier, **126 128**, *127 129*
Curves dialog box, 160, *161*, 165
Custom palette, 202
custom tags, **453**, *453*
customer taste, **423–425**, *423–425*
Cut option, 458

D

Daily option, 615
dashed lines, **91–93**, *92*
DashedLine command, 74
Data Bindings panel, 471–472, **495**, 498
Data Bindings/Server Behaviors window, **474**, *474*

Data-Driven Graphics Wizard, 110, *110*
Data Source Name Variable binding tool, 498
data types for databases, **479**
Database Definition Language (DDL), 480
Database Manipulation Language (DML), 480
databases, **465**, **469–470**
    connections to, **446**
    developmental models for, **468–469**
    drivers for, **470–471**
    filters for, **472**
    privileges for, **546–547**
    records in, **484–487**, *485*
    recordsets for, **487–488**, *488*
    schema, **478–480**
    sources for, **471–472**, *471*
    SQL for, **480–484**, *482*
    troubleshooting, **490**
    Web servers for, **467–468**, *467–468*
Databases panel, 35, **495**
dates, inserting, **258**, *258*
.dcr extension, 375
DDL (Database Definition Language), 480
Debug in Browser option, 462, 560
debugging
    code, **460–461**, *460–461*
    JavaScript, **462–463**, *462–463*
    keyboard shortcuts for, **629**
Default Attribute Case option, 450
default.html file, 602
Default option, 299
Default Proxy Generator dialog box, 535–536
Default Tag Case option, 450
default templates, **602–603**, *603*
Define HTML Style dialog box, 268, *269*
definition lists, 266
Definition option, 264
Delete Column option, 237
DELETE command, 483
Delete Record dialog box, 485, *485*
Delete Row option, 237
Delete Style option, 269
deleting
    breakpoints, 462
    columns, 237
    dynamic content, **476**

files, **578**
frames, 299, 392
gradient colors, 102
HTML styles, **269**
JPEG masks, 211
layers, **80**
library items, **65**
path points, **129–130**
records, **485–486**, *485*
rows
    database, **483–484**
    table, 237
Server Behaviors, 476
tag libraries, **452**
tags, 453
delimiters, 256
dependencies, 5–6
design considerations, **14–15**
CSS, **16**, *17*
layers, **18**
tables, **16–18**, *17*
text, **15–16**
Design Notes, **582**
creating, **583–584**, *583–584*
enabling, **583**
Design Notes category, 42
Design Notes dialog box, 29, 583, *583*
Design panel, **34**
Design Time Style Sheets dialog box, 318, *318*
Design view, 28, 473
Detach From Template option, 58
detaching templates, **58**
detect_in_attribute attribute, 518
developer tools in .NET, 537
DHTML/Layers extension category, 595
diagonal lines, 125
dialog boxes, updating, **612–613**, *613*
.dir extension, 375
directory lists, 266
discovery stage, 6
discussion boards, **555**
disjoint rollovers, **178–180**, *179–180*
display options for code, **449**, *449*
Distort tool, 124, 136, *137*

dithering
    in Fireworks, **107–108**, *108*
    in GIF compression, **204**, *204–205*
DML (Database Manipulation Language), 480
docked panel group area, 70
docking panels, **37**, *37*
DOCTYPE declarations, 520
Document Editing option, 601
Document Specific tab, **214**, *214*
document type definitions (DTDs), 513–514
Document window, **26–27**, *26*
documenting design, **51**
Dodge tool, **154–155**, *154–155*
domrequired attribute, 608
Down button state, 175
downloading extensions, **596–597**
Drag Layer behavior, **376–377**, *377*
dragging
    frames, **293**, *294*
    layers, **376–377**, *377*
Draw Layout Table option, 239
drawing layers, **240–241**, *240*
Dreamweaver HTML option, 213
drivers for databases, **470–471**
DROP INDEX command, 481
Drop Shadow option, 135, *135*
DTDs (document type definitions), 513–514
Duplicate CSS Style dialog box, 315
Duplicate Layer dialog box, 80, *80*
duplicate layers, **80**
Duplicate Set option, 601
duplicating vs. cloning, 136
.dwt extension, 52
dynamic attribute, 608
dynamic content, **466–469**, *467–468*
    adding, **474–476**, *475–476*
    searching, **476–478**, *477*
Dynamic List/Menu dialog box, 476, *476*
Dynamic Radio Buttons dialog box, 475, *475*

E

e-commerce sites, **421**
    color and type for, **423–425**, *423–425*
    identities for, **422**

logos for, **422–423**

marketing, **426–428**, *427*

transactions for

credit card payments, **432–435**, *433*

online catalogs for, **428–430**, *429–430*

shopping carts for, **431–432**, *431–432*, **435–137**

e-mail links, **325**, *325*

eCommerce extension category, 595

Edge Softness setting, 87

edges

feathered, **151–153**, *151–152*

for strokes 87

Edit Bitmap tool, 122

Edit Browser List option, 318, 536

Edit CSS Style option, 315

Edit Font List dialog box, 265, *265*, 313

Edit HTML Slice dialog box, 195, *195*

Edit menu, **72**, *72*

Edit NoFrames Content command, 301–302

Edit option

for Flash objects, 395

for images, 281

Edit Proxy Generator List, 535

Edit Sites dialog box

for Design Notes, 583

for Flash movies, 344–345

for testing servers, 445, 539

Edit Stroke dialog box, 87, *87*, 90–92, *90*, *92*

Edit Style Sheet dialog box, 315, *315*

Edit Tag mode, 271

Edit UDDI Site List option, 590

Edit with External Editor option, 317

editable regions in templates, 46–47

assigning, **53**, *53*

creating, **53**, *53*

tips for, **54**

editing

browser profiles, 563

button symbols, **177**

buttons, **177**, **361**, *361*

CGI scripts, **415–416**, *415*

code, **457–458**, *457–458*

CSS, **317**, *317*

effects, **105**

Flash movies, **344–345**, **352–353**, *352–353*

gradients, **101–103**, *101*, *103*

HTML, **269**, **271–272**, *271*

JPEG masks, 211

jump menus, **363–364**, *363–364*

keyboard shortcuts for, **625–626**

layers, 392

library items, **64–65**, *64–65*

links, **331**, **344**

SSIs, **66**

styles, **106**, **269**, **315**, *315*

tag libraries, **452**, *452*

templates, **58**

text, **259**

vectors

with control handles, **127–128**, *127–128*

with freeform editing tools, **130–133**, *130–133*

with Pen tool, **128–130**

editors

code, **459**, *459*, **494**

CSS, 317

image, 281

effects, **103–105**, *105*

!ELEMENT element, 562

Ellipse tool, **124**

Email Address option, 389

Email Link dialog box, 325, *325*

embed element, 343, 347, 349

embedding audio files, **342**, *342*

Emboss effect, **104**, *105*

Emphasis option, 264

Enable BBEdit Integration option, 459

Enable Cache option, 42

Enable Cloaking option, 572

enabled attribute, 524, 608

enabling Design Notes, **583**

end_string attribute, 518

enterprise portals, 554

Entire Site option, 579

!Error element, 562–563

error messages in browser profiles, 563

Evans, Joyce J., 67

events, **370–372**

Events menu, 371

Exact palette, 202

Exception category, 463

existing pages

    from templates, **56–57**, *57*

    templates from, **50–51**

Exit Bitmap mode, 77

Export Area tool, **220**

Export Current Frame Only option, 218

Export dialog box, 212, *212*, 217–219, *217*, *219*

Export File Format field, **200**, *201*

Export Preview feature, **199–200**, *200–201*, 220

Export Site dialog box, 571, *571*, 586

Export Slices option, 212

Export Styles as CSS File dialog box, 316, *316*

Export Symbols dialog box, 174

Export Template Data as XML dialog box,
    516, *517*

Export Wizard, 284, *284*

exporting

    with Fireworks, **211–213**, *212*

        areas, **220**

        to CSS Layers, **218–219**

        to Dreamweaver library, **218**

        to Flash, **215–216**, *216*

        HTML Setup for, **213–214**, *213–214*

        images, **215**

        layers and frames, **219**, *219*

        pages, **223–224**

        palettes, **109**

        to Photoshop, **216–217**

        styles, **107**

        as vectors, **217–218**, *217–218*

    pop-up menus, **185**, *185*

    sites as XML, **571**, *571*

    XML, **514–517**, *515–517*

Extending Dreamweaver manual, 598

extensibility, 510

Extensible Hypertext Markup Language (XHTML)

    support for, **520–522**

    validation in, **522–523**

Extensible Markup Language. *See* XML
    (Extensible Markup Language)

Extensible Style Language Transformations
    (XSLT) style sheets, 513

Extension Development extension category, 595

extensions and Extension Manager, 435, **594**

    creating, **598–600**

    in CSS, **314–315**

    installing, **597–598**, *597*

    Macromedia Exchange for Dreamweaver site
        for, **594–597**

    in templates, **52**

    third-party, **623**

    using, **598**, *598*

external editors

    code, **459**, *459*

    CSS, 317

eXtropia site, 417

Eyedropper tool, 122

F

Fade Image command, 74, **112–113**

Fairytale Brownies site, 423, *424*

Favorites tab, **61–62**

Feather option, 150, 158

feathered edges, **151–153**, *151–152*

federated portals, 554

FedEx site, 424

fieldset element, 610–611

fieldsets, **409–410**, *410*

file attribute, 524, 608

File Creation Date Range dialog box, 587

file fields, **405–406**, *406*

file list views, **576–577**, *576*

file management, keyboard shortcuts for, **625**

File Management menu, **29**

File menu, **72**, *72*

file permissions errors, 490

files

    cloaking, **572–573**, *572*

    creating and deleting, **578**

    formats for, 14

    moving, **577**

    renaming, **578**

Files panel, **35**

Fill Options option, 101

fills

    adding, **96–97**, *96–97*

    for borders, **99–100**, *99–100*

gradient, **100–103**, *100–103*
with patterns, **98**
with textures, **97–98**
Filters menu and filters
for bitmaps, **163–166**
for databases, **472**
in Fireworks, **74–75**, *75*
find and replace. *See also* searching
in Fireworks, 79
for HTML tags, **272**, *273*
for text, **260–262**, *260–261*
Find and Replace panel, 79
Fireworks, **69**
batch processing in, **116–119**, *117–119*
bitmaps with. *See* bitmap images
commands in
creating, **114**
Creative menu, **111–113**, *111–113*
free, **115**
third party, **115**
converting objects to images in, **283–284**, *284*
exporting with. *See* exporting
fills in. *See* fills
images in, **196–197**, *197*, **282–284**, *283–284*
importing Photoshop files in, **82–83**, *82–83*
layers in, **79–81**, *79–80*
Live Effects in, **103–105**, *105*
menu bar in, **71–75**, *72–75*
navigation objects for. *See* navigation
opening, **282**
opening and saving documents in, **82**
optimization in. *See* optimization methods
panels in, **77–79**, *77*
preferences in, **81**, *81*
Property Inspector in, **76**, *77*
rulers and grids in, **83–84**, *84*
slicing in. *See* slices
status bar in, **77**
strokes in. *See* strokes
Styles panel in, **106–107**, *106*
Swatches panel in, **109–110**, *109*
title bar in, **71**, *71*
toolbars in, **75**, *75*
Tools panel in, **76**
vectors in. *See* vectors

Web dithering in, **107–108**, *108*
workspace in, **70–71**, *70–71*
Fireworks extension category, 595
Fit Canvas option, 137
Fix Invalidly Nested Tags option, 254
Fixed option, 157
Fixed Ratio option, 149 150
Fixed Size option, 149
Flash Button dialog box, 361, 613, *613*
Flash Media extension category, 595
Flash objects, **393**
in Assets Manager, 60
behavior for, **375–376**, *376*
buttons
background for, **360**
benefits of, **358–359**
creating, **393–394**
resizing, **360–361**, *361*
rollover, **359–360**, *359*
saving and previewing, **360**
testing and editing, **361**, *361*
text for, **361–362**, *361*
exporting to, **215–216**, *216*
inserting, **393**, *393*
movies
adding, **343–344**, *343*
cloaking, **345–346**
editing links in, **344**
launch and edit features for, **344–345**, **352–353**, *352–353*
properties of, **395–396**, *395*
text, **394–395**, *394*
uses for, **5**
Flatten Selection option, 73
floating layout, **23–25**, *24–25*
folders
cloaking, **572–573**, *572*
creating, 578
local, **38–39**, **443–444**, *444*
Local Root, 42
names for, **38–39**, **578**
remote, **444–445**, *444*
fonts, 16
in CSS, 313
working with, **264–265**, *265*

Form.htm file, 610
format options for code, **449–450**
Format Table dialog box, 231, *231*
formats
  audio, **339**
  image, **196–197**, *197*
  table, **230–231**, *231*
  video, **340**
formatting
  CSS for. *See* CSS (Cascading Style Sheets)
  keyboard shortcuts for, **627**
  in templates, 54
  text, **262**
    alignment, **267**
    color, **265**, *265*
    with CSS, **269**
    fonts, **264–265**, *265*
    graphical, **269–270**
    with HTML styles, **268–269**, *268–269*
    indentation, **267–268**
    lists, **266–267**, *266*
    paragraphs, **266**
    phrase elements, **263–264**
    Property Inspector for, **263–268**
    size, **265**
    support for, **262–263**
    in templates, 54
forms, **399**
  buttons in, **408**, *408*
  CGI scripts for, **412–416**, *415*
  check boxes and radio buttons in, **404–405**, *404–405*
  elements of, **400**, *400*
  fieldsets and legends in, **409–410**, *410*
  file fields in, **405–406**, *406*
  hidden fields in, **408–409**
  hidden tags for, **410–411**
  images in, **407–408**, *407*
  with jump menus, **411–412**, *411*
  labels in, **409**, *409*
  List/Menu fields in, **406–407**, *406–407*
  search, **417–419**
  structure of, **400–401**, *400*
  target pages for, **416–417**, *417*

text fields in, **401–404**, *402–403*
  validating, **388–389**, *389*
Forms tab, 32
4-Up view, **199**, *200*
Frame dialog box, 167, *167*
frames, 18, **285**
  behaviors for, **301**
  borders for, **289–290**, *290*
  characteristics of, **289**
  color for, **295–296**, *295*
  content for, **304**
  creating, **292**
  deleting, 299, 392
  dragging, **293**, *294*
  exporting, **219**, *219*
  inserting, **293**
  keyboard shortcuts for, **628**
  margins for, **296**, *296*, **299**, *299*
  navigation elements in, **299–300**, *300*
  NoFrames content for, **301–302**
  saving, 289, **304–305**, *305*
  scrollbars in, **298–299**, *298*
  size of, **297–299**, *297*
  text of, **382–383**, *383*
  in timelines, **397**, *397*
  uses for, **287–288**
Frames options, 214
Frames panel, 78, 179, **291**, *291*
Frames tab, 32
frameset XHTML doctype, 520
framesets, **285**
  creating, **286**, *286–287*, **303**, *303*
  images for, **303–304**, *303*
  predefined, **292**, *292*
  rows and columns in, **291**, *291*, **297–298**, *297*
  saving, **294–295**
Free Transform option, 136
Freeform tool, **131–132**, *131–132*
FreeHand Compatible option, 218
Friends of Active Copyright Education site, 13
Frontpage HTML option, 213
FrontPage Migration Kit, 587, *587*
ftest_checkmousepos function, 366–367
ftest_getmousepos function, 367
ftest_hideall function, 366

ftest_hidedrop function, 366–367
ftest_showdown function, 365
ftest_showit function, 365–366
FTP
    connections for, 40–41
    for remote folders, 444
FTP Log panel, 35
functions, JavaScript, **365–367**

G

Gaussian Blur, 104–105, 163
General tab, **213**, *213*
Generator objects, **351**
Generic HTML option, 213
Get and Put Newer Files option, 579
GET command
    for forms, 401
    shortcuts for, 29
Get More Proxy Generators option, 535
Get More Styles option, 360
Get Newer Files from Remote option, 43, 579
GIF (Graphics Interchange Format) files, 14,
    196–197, *197*
    animated, **350–351**
    compression for, **200**
        animation in, **207**
        color table for, **206**, *207*
        colors for, **203**, *203*
        dithering for, **204**, *204–205*
        Export File Format field for, **200**, *201*
        indexed palette for, **201–202**
        interlacing in, **205**
        lossy, **205**
        Matte option for, **202–203**, *203*
        transparency in, **205–206**, *206*
    inserting, **276**
    size of, 282–283
    for swatches, 109
Glows effect, **104**, *105*
Go to Detail Page dialog box, 485, 488, *488*
Go to Timeline Frame behavior, **386–387**, *387*
Go to URL behavior, 301, **377**, *377*
GoLive HTML option, 213

gradients
    for fills
        colors in, **101–102**, *101*
        editing, **103**, *103*
        filling with, **100–101**, *100–101*
        transparency in, **102**
    for vector masks, **162–163**, *162*
graphical menus, **20**
graphical text, **269–270**
graphics. *See* images
Graphics Interchange Format. *See* GIF (Graphics
    Interchange Format) files
graphics symbols, 172
grayscale images, **112**
Grayscale palette, 202
Green pages, 534
grids
    in Fireworks, **83–84**, *84*
    in layers, 241
Gripper, 37
Group as Mask option, 160–163
groups, selection within, 135
guides for slicing, **190–191**

H

H property for images, 407
halo effect, 203
Hard Edge option, 97
Hard Line attribute, 89, *89*
head_model value, 518
Head tab, 33
<head> tag, 52
headings, text, 266
height of frames, **297–298**, *297*
Height property for List/Menu selections, 406
help, keyboard shortcuts for, **629**
hidden fields, **408–409**
hidden tags, **410–411**
Hide Panel command, 36
hiding
    layers, **80**, **384–385**, *385*
    panels, **36–37**, *36–37*
hierarchical menus, **20**
high-speed connections, 338

Highlight Invalid HTML option, 449
Highlights option, 154
hints for code, **451**, **454–455**, **494**
History list, 114
History Options menu, 93, 114
History panel, 35, 78, 93, **603–604**, *603–604*
Homesite/Coder style, **23**, *24*
Horizontal Scale option, 139
horizontal space setting, 280
Horizontal Text option, 139
hotspots, **19**, 79, 279
href attribute, 320
HSPACE attribute, 280
HTML, **270**
    cleaning up, **460–461**, *460*, **580–582**, *581*
    editing, 269, **271–272**, *271*
    limitations of, **246**
HTML Setup dialog box
    for autonaming, 194, *194*
    for exporting, **213–214**, *213–214*
HTML slices, 195
HTML styles, 34, **268–269**, *268–269*
HTML Styles panel, 34
!htmlmsg element, 562–563
HTTP (Hypertext Transfer Protocol), 18
Hue and Saturation option, **165**
Hue/Saturation dialog box, 168
Hyperlink dialog box, 324, *324*
hyperlinks. *See* links
hypertext, **18–19**
Hypertext Transfer Protocol (HTTP), 18

icon attribute, 519
icon_height attribute, 519
icon_width attribute, 519
id attribute
    for menu items, 607
    for menus, 606
    in XHTML, 520
identities for e-commerce sites, **422**
Ignore Whitespace Differences option, 260
IIS (Internet Information Server), **467**
Illustrator, exporting to, **217–218**, *217–218*

Image Align setting, 280–281
Image Alternate setting, 280
Image Link setting, 280
image maps, **181**, *181*, 279, 321
    building, **327–329**, *328–329*
    hotspots in, **19**, 79, 279
Image Placeholder dialog box, 281, *281*
Image Size dialog box, 283
Image Size setting, 279
Image Source (SRC) setting, 279
images, **13–14**, 148, **275**
    aligning, 280–281
    in Assets Manager, 60
    bitmap. *See* bitmap images
    borders for, 280–281
    converting objects to, **283–284**, *284*
    cutting text from, **141–142**, *141–142*
    dynamic, **476**
    exporting, **215**
    exporting layers and frames as, **219**, *219*
    in Fireworks, **196–197**, *197*, **282–284**,
        283–284
    in forms, **407–408**, *407*
    for framesets, **303–304**, *303*
    inserting, **276–278**, *277*
    in layers, **249**, **396**, *397*
    links to, 280–281, 321
    loading, **380**
    masking, **157**
        bitmap masks for, **157–161**, *158–160*
        vector masks for, **161–163**, *161–162*
    options for, **278–281**, *279*
    placeholders for, **281–282**, *281*
    random, **614–615**, *615*
    size of, **278–279**, **282–283**, *283*
    swapping, 178, **385–386**, *386*
Import dialog box, 82
Import Export Extension, **586–587**
Import Symbols dialog box, 174
Import Tabular Data dialog box, 256, *256*
Import Word HTML option, 253–254
Import XML dialog box, 515, *515*
Import XML DTD or Schema option, 453
importing
    CSS, 310

Photoshop files, **82–83**, *82–83*
sites, **43–44**, *43–44*
styles, **107**
tags, **519**
text and tables, **253–256**, *254–256*
XML, **514–517**, *515–517*
Include Areas without Slices option, 194, 212, 215
Inconsistent Region Names dialog box, 57, *57*
Indent Code option, 454
Indent Menu icon, 182, *183*
indenting
    code, 454
    text, **267–268**
index.html file, 38
Index Transparency option, 205
indexed palette, **201–202**
indexes in SQL, **481**
information architecture, **7–8**
    site maps, **8–9**, *9*
    wireframes, **9–10**, *10*
Init Val property, 402
Initial State property, 404
initializing site maps, **43**, *43*
Initially Selected property, 407
inline CSS, 310
Insert bar, **31–33**, *32*
    adding objects to, **610–612**, *612*
    custom characters for, **616–618**
    for extensions, 598, *598*
    for frames, 292, *292*
    for tables, 233
    for template regions, 54
Insert Column option, 237
INSERT command, 483
Insert Date dialog box, 258, *258*
Insert Flash button dialog box, 393, *393*
    for editing, 361, *361*
    modifying, 613, *613*
    for previewing, 360
    for rollovers, 359, *359*
Insert Flash Text dialog box, 361–362, *361*,
    394, *394*
Insert Go Button after Menu option, 363, 411
Insert HTML mode, 271
Insert Image option, 277

Insert Image Placeholder option, 281
Insert Jump Button dialog box, 362–363, *363*
Insert Jump Menu dialog box, 301, 363, 378, *378*,
    411, *411*
Insert Keywords dialog box, 427
Insert menu, 72, *72*
Insert Navigation Bar dialog box, 301, 357, *357*
Insert PayPal Add to Cart Button dialog box, 436
Insert Record dialog box, 504, *504*, **548–549**, *549*
Insert Records Server Behavior, 484
Insert Rollover Image dialog box, 356, *356*
Insert Row option, 237
Insert Rows or Columns dialog box, 237
Insert Slice option, 193
Insert Table dialog box, 232, *232*
Insert Tabular Data dialog box, 240
inserting
    assets, **62**
    dates, **258**, *258*
    dynamic content, **474–476**, *475–476*
    Flash objects, **393**, *393*
    frames, **293**
    graphics, **276–278**, *277*
    jump menus, **362–363**, *363*
    keyboard shortcuts for, **629**
    layers, **241–242**, *241*, **396**, *396*
    library items, **64**
    links, 322–325, *323–325*
    movies, **343–344**, *343*
    records, **484**, **504–507**, *504*
    rows, **483**
    snippets, **455–456**
    special characters, **257–258**, *259*
    tags, **455**, *455*
    text, **252**, *253*
Inset Emboss option, 176
Inset Path command, **140–141**, *140–141*
Inset Path dialog box, 141, *141*
instances, **173**
instruction, online resources for, **623–624**
integrated editors, **459**, *459*
integrated workspace, **22–23**, *22–23*
interlacing, **205**
Internet Explorer browser, 558
Internet Information Server (IIS), **467**

Intersect option, **134–135**, *134–135*
Invert option, **165–166**
Invisible Elements for grids, 241
isDOMRequired function, 616
italic text, 264

J

Java applets, **349–350**
Java Database Connectivity (JDBC), 468, 471
Java programming language, **31**
Java Server Pages (JSP), 442, 445, **469**
JavaScript alert boxes, 379
JavaScript programming language, **31**, **364–365**
    attaching, 373
    debugging, **462–463**, *462–463*
    functions in, **365–367**
    for menus, 606
    support for, 558
JavaScript server model, 445
JavaScript specifications for styles, 529
JDBC (Java Database Connectivity), 468, 471
Join option, **134**, *134*
joining paths, **129**, **134**, *134*
journaling
    purpose of, **585–586**
    report generation, **586–588**, *587–588*
JoyceJEvans.com site, 115
JPEG (Joint Photographic Experts Group) format
    files, 14, **197**
    compression for
        optimizing, **208–209**, *209*
        options for, **207–208**, *207–208*
        selective, **209–211**, *210–211*
    inserting, **276**
JSP (Java Server Pages), 442, 445, **469**
Jump Menu behavior, **378**, *378*
Jump Menu Go behavior, **378**, *378*
jump menus, **20**, **362**, *362*
    editing, **363–364**, *363–364*
    implementing, **411–412**, *411*
    inserting, **362–363**, *363*
    troubleshooting, **364**
JustAddCommerce shopping cart, 431–432

K

Kerning option, 139
key attribute, 524, 608
Keyboard option, 264
keyboard shortcuts
    creating, **600–602**, *600*
    for file management commands, 29
    list of, **625–631**
Keyboard Shortcuts editor, 600, *600*
keyframes, 392
keys for databases, **479**
keywords for marketing, **427**, *427*
Knife tool, **133**
knowledge transfer, **574**

L

L/T option, 243
Label property, 408
labels, **408–409**, *409*
launch features for Flash movies, **344–345**,
    352–353, *352–353*
Launcher, 27
Layer ID option, 243
layers, **18**, **227**, **240**, *240*
    adding, **249–250**
    behaviors with, **390–391**
    in browser compatibility, 565
    dragging, **376–377**, *377*
    drawing, **240–241**, *240*
    editing, 392
    exporting, **219**, *219*
    in Fireworks, **79–81**, *79–80*
    hiding, **80**, **384–385**, *385*
    images in, **249**, **396**, *397*
    inserting, **241–242**, *241*, **396**, *396*
    keyboard shortcuts for, **628**
    measurement units for, **244**
    Property Inspector for, **243–244**, 392
    with tables, **245–247**, *246*
    text of, **383**, *383*
    in timelines, **396**, *397*
    tracing images for, **242**, **247–248**, *247*
Layers Options menu, 77, *77*, 80
Layers panel, 70, *71*, 78, **243**, *243*

layout. *See also* layers; tables
   CSS for. *See* CSS (Cascading Style Sheets)
   templates for, **228–229**, *230*
layout mode, 28
Layout tab, 32
Layout View, tables in, **233–234**, *233–234*
.lbi extension, 63
.lck extension, 41
Leading option, 139
Learning extension category, 595
legends, **409–410**, *410*
levels of security, 547
Levels option for bitmap color, **166**
libraries, **45**, **62–63**
   in Assets Manager, 60
   content for, **63–64**, *63*
   exporting to, **218**
   items in
      deleting, **65**
      editing, **64–65**, *64–65*
      inserting, **64**
   for symbols, **173–174**
   tag, **451–453**, *451–453*
Library Editing window, 64
Library Inspector window, 64, *64*
Library panel, 79
Line Break Type option, 450
Line Numbers option, 449
Line tool, **125**
Link Checker panel, 35
Link External Style Sheet dialog box, 316
Link Management, **330**, *330*
link target setting for images, 280
links, **319**
   anchors for, **320–321**, **325**, *325*
   to audio files, **342**, *342*
   broken, **329–333**, *330–332*
   changing, **591**, *591*
   checking, **591**
   to CSS, 310
   design issues with, **321–322**
   editing, **331**, **344**
   in frames, **300**, *300*, **305**
   image maps for, **327–329**, *328–329*
   to images, 280–281, 321

   inserting, 322–325, *323–325*
   keyboard shortcuts for, **629**
   kinds of, **321**
   in movies, **344**
   paths to, **321**
   Property Inspector for, **322–324**, *323*
   from site maps, **325–327**, *326*, **331**
   to templates, **55**
   testing, **331–332**, *332*
   updating, **330–331**, *330–331*, **333**, *333*
List/Menu fields, **406–407**, *406–407*
list/menus, dynamic, **475**
List Values dialog box, 364, *364*
List Values property, 407
lists
   in CSS, **314**
   working with, **266–267**, *266*
Live Data mode, 473
Live Data Settings dialog box, 540, *540*
Live Data window, 540
Live Effects, **103–105**, *105*
Live Objects, **488**, *488*
Live Preview feature, 489
loading
   images, **380**
   palettes, **109–110**
local folders, **38–39**, **443–444**, *444*
Local/Network option, 444
Local Root folder, 42
local sites, synchronizing, **579–580**, *579–580*
Locate in Local Site option, 580
Locate in Remote Site option, 580
locked template regions, 46–47
locking
   layers, **81**
   regions, **54**
Log In User dialog box, 550–551, *551*
Log Out User server behavior, 552, *552*
logging users out, **552**, *552*
logins
   forms for, 548–549
   names for, 549–550, *549*
   processes for, **550–552**, *551–552*
logos, **422–423**
lossless compression, 196–197

lossy compression, 197, **205**, 207
low source setting for images, 280
LZW Lossless compression, 196–197

M

Macintosh palette, 202
Macromedia Exchange for Dreamweaver site, **594**
    downloading extensions in, **596–597**
    extension categories in, **595–596**
Macromedia Extension Installation (MXI) file, 599
Macromedia Flash. *See* Flash objects
Macromedia Flash SWF Export Options dialog
    box, 216, *216*
Magic Wand tool, **151**
mailing lists, **624**
main page, **499–503**, *500*
Main toolbar, **75**, *75*
main window, **473**, *473*
Maintain Appearance option, 216
Maintain Design Notes option, 583
Maintain Editability option, 216
Maintain Editability over Appearance option, 217
Maintain Fireworks Appearance option, 217
Maintain Paths option, 216
Make Column Autostretch option, 237
Make Custom Style (Class) option, 312
Make Document XHTML Compliant option,
    521–522
Make Link command, **325**
Make Nested Template option, 56
Manage Extensions option, 74, 115
Manage Saved Command dialog box, 110
Manage Saved Commands option, 74, 110
maps
    image, **181**, *181*, 279, 321
        building, **327–329**, *328–329*
        hotspots in, **19**, 79, 279
    site, **8–9**, *9*, **576–577**, *576*
        initializing, **43**, *43*
        keyboard shortcuts for, **630**
        links from, **325–327**, *326*, **331**
margins
    in browser compatibility, 565
    in CSS, 314

for frames, **296**, *296*, **299**, *299*
marker_model value, 518
marketing e-commerce sites, **426–428**, *427*
Marquee tool, **149–150**, *149–150*
mask objects, 157
masking images, **157**
    bitmap masks for, **157–161**, *158–160*
    vector masks for, **161–163**, *161–162*
Massimo Foti site, 115
master/detail pages
    creating, **488**, *488*
    rapid development of, **490–492**, *491–492*
Match Case option, 260
Matte option
    for GIF images, **202–203**, *203*
    for JPEG images, 207
mattes, 168, *168*
Matt's Script Archive site, 417
Max Chars property
    for file fields, 406
    for forms, 402
Maximum Number of Colors menu, 203
measurement units
    for frames, 297
    for layers, **244**
Media tab, 33
MegaCGI cgi scripts site, 417
Menu Commands option, 601
menu element, 523
menu lists, 266
menu.xml file, 602
menubar element, 523, 525
menuitem element, 523
menus and menu bars, **20**
    adding, **606–607**
    adding items to, **607–609**, *609*
    creating, **605–606**
    in Fireworks, **71–75**, *72–75*
    jump. *See* jump menus
    pop-up. *See* pop-up menus
    for XML, **523–528**, *528*
menus.xml file, 605
merchant accounts, 433
Merge Down option, 73
messages, popup, **379**, *379*

Meta dialog box, 52, *52*
meta tag information, **52**, *52*
method attribute, 400
Method field, 401
Microsoft UDDI Registry, 532
MIDI (Musical Instrument Digital Interface), 339
Midtones option, 154
.mno extension, 584
modes
　for bitmaps, **148**
　in HTML, 272
Modify menu, **73**, *73*
Modify toolbar, **75**, *75*
monitors
　differences in, **14**
　resolution of, 30
Most Accurate option, 246
Move to Record dialog box, 487
movies, **342–343**, *342–343*
　adding, **343–344**, *343*
　in Assets Manager, 60
　cloaking, **345–346**
　editing links in, **344**
　launch and edit features for, **344–345**,
　　352–353, *352–353*
moving
　files, **577**
　gradient colors, 102
MP3 files, 339
MPEG (Moving Picture Experts Group) format, 340
!msg element, 562–563
multiline text fields, **403**, *403*
multimedia, **337**
　ActiveX controls, **348–349**, *349*
　animated GIFs, **350–351**
　audio files, **341–342**, *342*
　audio formats, **339**
　behaviors for, **351**
　Java applets, **349–350**
　movies, **342–346**, *342–343*
　need for, **338**
　PDFs, **350**
　players, **340–341**
　plugins, **346–347**, *347*
　video formats, **340**

multiple browsers, designing for, **30**
Multiple Nav Bar HTML Pages option, 194, 214
munging, 4
Musical Instrument Digital Interface (MIDI), 339
MXI (Macromedia Extension Installation) file, 599
MXP files, 597, 600
MySQL databases, 445, 470

N

name attribute
　for forms, 400
　for menus, 606
Name field, 401
Name property
　for buttons, 408
　for check boxes, 404
　for forms, 402
　for hidden fields, 409
　for images, 407
　for List/Menu selections, 406
Named Anchor dialog box, 325, *325*
named anchors, 320, **325**, *325*
names
　browser profiles, 562
　commands, 604
　CSS, 316
　editable regions, 53
　events, 371
　files, **578**
　folders, **38–39**, **578**
　frames, 280
　layers, **81**
　login, 549–550, *549*
　slices, **194**, *194*, 214
　styles, 312
　templates, 49–50
　windows, 379
namespaces, XHTML, 520
narrowband connections, 338
Nav Bar Down State option, 176
navigation, 12
　code, **458**
　objects for, **171**
　　buttons, **174–177**, *175*, *177*

in frames, **299–300**, *300*, **305**
image maps, **181**, *181*
instances, **173**
libraries, **173–174**
menus, **181–185**, *182–185*, 321
Nav bars, **185–186**, *185–187*
rollover behaviors, **177–180**, *178–180*
symbols, **172–173**, *173*
recordsets, **487**
schemes for, **18–20**
updating, **591**, *591*
vectors for, **143–145**, *143–145*
navigation bars, **185–186**, *185–187*,
  357–358, *357*
creating, **249**
images for, **380–382**, *381–382*
Navigation extension category, 595
nested elements
frames, 287
tables, **239–240**, *239–240*
templates, **55–56**
in XML, 512
Nested Tables-No Spacers option, 213
.NET C# server model, 445
.NET platform, **537**
ASP.NET, **538–540**, *539–540*
framework for, **537–538**
.NET servers, 537
.NET VB server model, 445
Netscape Navigator browser, 558
Netscape plugins, **346–347**, *347*
New Attributes option, 452
New CSS Style dialog box, 312
New Document dialog box, 82, *82*, 429, 432
New/Duplicate Frame icon, 178
New Editable Region dialog box, 53, *53*
New from Template option, 56
New Layer option, 80
New Library Item option, 63
New Panel Group option, 71
New Snippet option, 456
New Style option, 93, 107, 268
New Tag Library option, 452
New Template option, 50
newsgroups, **624**

Nielsen, Jakob, 13
No Resize option, 299
No Transparency option, 205
NoFrames content, **301–302**
Non-Breaking Space option, 213
non-editable content, 585
Normal option, 615
notes, Design Notes, **582**
creating, **583–584**, *583–584*
enabling, **583**
_notes folder, 584
num items property, 403
Number option, 389
Number From option, 389
Numeric Transform dialog box, 137, *137*

O

object element, 343, 348–349
objects, 12, *12*
aligning, **137–138**, *138*
converting to images, **283–284**, *284*
cropping, **137**, *137*
slices from, **193**, *193*
objectTag function, 616
ODBC (Open Database Connectivity), 468, 470
ODBC Microsoft Access Setup window, 471, *471*
OLE DB standard, 470
onClick event, 370
1-Pixel Transparent Spacer option, 213
online catalogs
completeness of, **430**, *430*
creating, **428–429**, *429*
organizing, **430**
updating, **429–430**
online resources, **621**
Dreamweaver software, **622–623**
newsgroups and mailing lists, **624**
starting points, **622**
templates, **623**
third-party extensions, **623**
tutorials and instruction, **623–624**
online stores. *See* e-commerce sites
Online Style Guide, 310
onmouseout command, 366

onmouseover command, 366
opacity settings for layers, **80**
Open Attach Template option, 58
Open Browser Window behavior, **378–379**, *379*
Open Database Connectivity (ODBC), 468, 470
Open From Template option, 602
Open in Code View option, 448
Open URLs In menu, 363
opening
    browser windows, **378–379**, *378*
    documents, **82**
    Fireworks, **282**
    templates, **55**
Opera browser, 15
operating system considerations, **15**
optimization methods, **198**
    for GIF compression. *See* GIF (Graphics
        Interchange Format) files
    for JPEG compression
        optimizing, **208–209**, *209*
        options for, **207–208**, *207–208*
        selective, **209–211**, *210–211*
    Optimize panel for, **198–200**, *198–200*
    steps in, **221–222**
Optimize Options menu, 199, *199*
Optimize panel, 78, **198–200**, *198–200*
Optimize to Size dialog box, 200, *201*
optional template regions, 46–47, **53–54**
Options menu, 77, *77*
Oracle9i databases, 470
ordered lists, 266
Oval Marquee tool, **149**, **150**, *140*
Over button state, 174
Over While Down button state, 175
Overflow option, 243
overlay color, **193**

P

Package Extension option, 600
padding
    in cells, 232
    in CSS, 314
Page Properties dialog box
    for frames, 295, *295*
    for links, 322
    for tracing images, 242
pages, **11**
    content of, **13–14**
    design for. *See* design considerations
    elements of, **12**, *12*
    navigation schemes, **18–20**
    from templates, **56**
Paint Bucket/Gradient Fill tool, 122
palettes
    exporting, **109**
    indexed, **201–202**
    loading, **109–110**
panels, **34–35**, *34*
    in ColdFusion, **494–496**
    docking and undocking, **37**, *37*
    in Fireworks, **77–79**, *77*
    hiding, **36–37**, *36–37*
    keyboard shortcuts for, **630–631**
paragraphs
    formatting, **266**
    in templates, 54
parameters
    for ActiveX controls, 349, *349*
    for objects, 347, 395
    in templates, **51**
Parameters dialog box, 347, 349, *349*
Parameters option, 395
_parent target, 195, 300, 324
parse_attribute attribute, 518
password text fields, **403–404**
passwords, 549–551
Paste option, 458
Paste Inside option, 100
Path Scrubber tool, **132–133**, *132–133*
paths
    closing, **128–129**
    continuing, **129**
    converting text to, **139–140**, *140*
    in curves, 127
    joining, **129**, **134**, *134*
    to links, **321**
    points for, **129–130**
    reshaping, **133–135**, *134–135*
patterns, fills with, **98**

Paymentech service, 434
PayPal site, 435–436
PDAs (portable digital assistants), 14
PDF (Portable Document Format), **350**
Pen tool, **126**, **128–130**
percentages
    for frames, 297–298
    for tables, **236**
Perl Archive site, 417
Perl language, **412–414**
permissions errors, 490
persistent data, cookies for, **551–552**
Personal Web Server (PWS), **467**
photos, feathered edges for, **151–153**, *151–152*
Photoshop
    exporting to, **216–217**
    importing from, **82–83**, *82–83*
PHP, 442, **469**
PHP MySQL server model, 445
phrase elements, **263–264**
picture frames, 111, *111*
Pixel Radius setting, **164**
pixelated images, 148
pixels
    in bitmaps, 148
    for frames, 297
    for images, 278
placeholders
    for images, **281–282**, *281*
    in templates, 55
platform attribute
    for menu items, 609
    for menus, 607
Play Recorded Command option, 604
Play Sound behavior, 351, **379**, *379*
Play/Stop option, 395
Play Timeline behavior, **387–388**, *388*
plugins
    adding, **346–347**, *347*
    for bitmaps, **166–169**, *167–169*
    checking for, **374–375**
PNG (Portable Network Graphics) format,
    14, **197**
point-of-sale (POS) hardware, 433
Point to File icon, 323–324, *323*, 326, *326*

Pointer tool, 128–129
points for paths, **129–130**
Polygon tool, **125**
Polygon Lasso tool, **151**
Polygon Slice tool, **192**, *192*
Pop-Up Menu Editor dialog box, 181–184, *182*
pop-up menus, **181–185**, *182–185*
    Code Navigation, **31**
    displaying, **389–390**, *390*
    File Management, **29**
    Preview/Debug, **29–30**
    View Options, **31**
Popup Message behavior, **379**, *379*
portable digital assistants (PDAs), 14
Portable Document Format (PDF), **350**
Portable Network Graphics (PNG) format,
    14, **197**
portals, **553**
    discussion boards in, **555**
    meanings of, **554**
    personalization features for, **553**, **555**
    for reduced administration, **556**
ports in WSDL, 533
POS (point-of-sale) hardware, 433
Position dialog box, 184, *185*, 390
positioning
    CSS options for, **314**
    graphics, **276–278**, *277*
    pop-up menus, 184, *185*, 390
POST option, 401
posting board frameworks, 555
Powell, Adam, 340
predefined framesets, **292**, *292*
Preferences dialog box
    for accessibility, 44
    for code-only view, 448, *448*
    for color coding, 451, *451*
    for disconnects, 578
    for external editors, 459
    in Fireworks, **81**, *81*
    for HTML cleanup, 580
    for Launcher, 27
    for layers, 242
    for Link Management, 330, *330*
    for plugins, 166, *167*

for saving files, 577
for workspace, 36
for XHTML, 522
Preload Images behavior, **380**, *380*
presentation classes in .NET, 537
preset format for tables, **230–231**, *231*
preset strokes, **88–89**, *89*, **91**, *91*
Preview/Debug menu, **29–30**
Preview in Browser feature, **560**
previewing
    animation, **398**
    CSS, **317–318**, *318*
    Flash buttons, **360**
    keyboard shortcuts for, **629**
    slices, **199–200**, *200–201*
primary keys for databases, **479**
printing code, **459**
privileges, assigning, **546–547**
process flows, **8–9**, *9*
production environment, **570**
Productivity extension category, 596
profiles
    browser, **561–564**
    customer, **426**
Progressive option, 208–209
Project Fireworks site, 115
Project Log panel, 79
Project Seven Development site, 229
Properties window, **474**
Property Inspector, **33–34**, *33*
    for ActiveX controls, 348
    for applets, 349–350
    for audio, 342, *342*
    for button symbols, 177
    for ColdFusion, **494**, 500–502
    for CSS, 311–312, 315
    for fills, 96–97, *96*
    in Fireworks, **76**, *77*
    for Flash buttons, 361, *361*
    for formatting text, **263–268**
    for forms, 401–404, 406–409
    for frames, 290–291, *290*, 296–298, *297*
    for freeform tools, 131–133, *131–133*
    for image maps, 181, *181*, 327–329, *328–329*
    for images, 278–279, *279*

for jump menus, 363–364
for layers, **243–244**, 392
for library items, 64
for links, **322–324**, *323*
for movies, 343–345, *343*
for optimization, 198
for plugins, 347, *347*
for Rubber Stamp tool, 156
for selection tools, 149–150, *149–150*
for shape tools, 124–125, *125*
for slices, 193, *193*
for strokes, 86, *86*, 88
for tables, 234, **237–238**, *238*
Text tool with, **138–139**, *139*
for touch-up tools, 153–156, *153–156*
Proxy Generator dialog box, 535, *535*
pseudo-classes, 309, 312
Punch option, **135**, *135*
pure play companies, 424
Put command, shortcuts for, 29
Put Images in Subfolder option, 212, 219
Put Newer Files to Remote option, 333, 579
PWS (Personal Web Server), **467**

Q

quality assurance, **568–569**
Quality setting for JPEG images, 208
Quick Tag Editor, **271–272**, *271*, 452, 456
QuickTime format, 340
QuickTime player, **340–341**

R

radio buttons
    dynamic, **475–476**, *475*
    in forms, **404–405**, *405*
Radio Group dialog box, 405, *405*
random images, **614–615**, *615*
Random Images dialog box, 615
Range Kerning option, 139
raster images, 148
RDS option, 444
RealAudio files, 339
RealMedia format, 340

RealPlayer, **340**
Record Insertion Form window, 484
recording commands, **604–605**
records
    deleting, **485–486**, *485*
    inserting, **484**, **504–507**, *504*
    stored procedures for, **486–487**
Recordset dialog box, 482, *482*, 499, *500*
recordsets
    defining, **472**
    Live Objects in, **488**, *488*
    navigating, **487**
    repeated regions in, **487–488**
Rectangle tool, **123**, *123*
Rectangle Slice tool, **191–192**, *192*
recursive frames, 287
Redefine HTML Tag option, 312
Redraw Path tool, **130**, *130–131*
Reference panel, **31**, 35
Refresh Design View option, **31**, 454
regions in templates
    editable, **53**, *53*
    relocking, **54**
    repeating and optional, 46–47, **53–54**
registering sites, 427
registration forms, **547–548**
regular expressions, 261, 458
Relative option for frames, 297
relative paths to links, 321
Relative To: Site Root option, 277
Reload Modified Files option, 459
relocking regions, **54**
remote folders, **444–445**, *444*
Remote Info screen, 539, *539*
remote sites, 40
    servers for, **42**, *42*
    synchronizing, **573**, *573*, **579–580**, *579–580*
Remove All Breakpoints option, 462
Remove All Word Specific Markup option, 255
Remove Color from Transparency option, 206
Remove Dreamweaver Special Markup option, 581
Remove Empty Container Tags option, 581
Remove JPEG Mask option, 211
Remove Non-Dreamweaver HTML Comments
    option, 461, 581

Remove Redundant Nested Tags option, 581
Remove Specific Tag(s) option, 461, 581
Remove Template Markup option, 54
Remove Word Specific Markup option, 255
renaming files and folders, **578**
render_contents attribute, 518
reopening templates, **55**
Repeated Region dialog box, 487–488
repeating elements
    regions
        in recordsets, **487–488**
        in templates, 46–47, **53–54**
    SSIs for, **65–66**, *66*
    tables, 53
reports, **586**
    Site Import Export Extension for, **586–587**
    Site Summary Reports Extension for,
        587–588, *587–588*
Reports dialog box, 569, *570*, 584, 587, *587*
requirements gathering, **7**
Reset Size option, 395
Reshape Area tool, **132**, *132*
reshaping paths, **133–135**, *134–135*
resizing Flash buttons, **360–361**, *361*
resolution
    of bitmaps, 148
    of monitors, 30
resources
    for creating extensions, **598–599**
    online, **621–624**
Restore Bitmap Selection option, 158
Restrict Access behavior, 552
Restrict Access to Page dialog box, 547, 552, *552*
restrictions, **552**
result page sets, **476–478**, *477*
Results panel, **35**, 332, *332*
Retrospect packages, 588
rewriting code, **450–451**
Rich Media extension category, 596
RmiJdbc driver, 468
rolling back sites, **588**
Rollover Image option, 356
rollovers, 12, **177**, **355**
    creating, **356–357**, *356*
    disjoint, **178–180**, *179–180*

Flash buttons, **359–360**, *359*
simple, **178**, *178*
root elements
in XHTML, 520
in XML, 512
root folders, 38
in ASP.NET, 538
for web applications, **444–445**, *444*
rotating objects, 137, *137*
Rounded Rectangle tool, **123–124**, *124*
rows
database
deleting, **483–484**
inserting, **483**
selecting, **481–483**, *482*
in framesets, **291**, *291*, **297–298**, *297*
in tables, 232, *232*, **237–238**
Rubber Stamp tool, **156–157**, *156*
ruler guides, **190–191**
rulers, **83–84**, *84*

S

SalCentral registry, 532
Sample option, 264
sans-serif fonts, 264
Save All Frames option, 295
Save as Command option, 93, 114
Save As Template dialog box, 49, *49*, 51, 603
Save Bitmap Selection option, 158
Save Files Before Putting option, 577
Save Frame option, 294
Save Frame As option, 209, 294
Save Frame as Template option, 294
Save Frameset As option, 294
Save Frameset Page option, 294
Save on Launch option, 459
Save Selected Steps As Command option, 604
Save Selection as JPEG Mask option, 211
saved file status, 26
saving
bitmap masks, **159**, *159*
documents, **82**
Flash buttons, **360**
frames, 289, **304–305**, *305*

framesets, **294–295**
strokes, **93**
styles, **106–107**
schema, database, **478–480**
script_model value, 518
Scripting extension category, 596
scripts, CGI, **412**
editing, **415–416**, *415*
requirements, **412–413**
Scripts category in Assets Manager, 60
scrollbars, **298–299**, *298*
search engines, 52
search forms, **417–419**
Search panel, 35
search services for marketing, **426–427**
searching
for dynamic content, **476–478**, *477*
for editing code, **458**, *458*
in Fireworks, 79
for HTML tags, **272**, *273*
for text, **260–262**, *260–261*
Section 508 accessibility standards, **569–570**, *570*
Secure Sockets Layer (SSL) encryption, 433, 549
security
access restrictions, **552**
login pages and processes, **550–552**, *551–552*
privileges, **546–547**
registration forms, **547–548**
server behaviors, **548–550**, *548–549*
Security extension category, 596
segments in curves, 127
Select Behind tool, 136
SELECT command, 481–482
Select Destination for Exported Site dialog box, 586
Select External Editor dialog box, 459, *459*
Select File dialog box
for ActiveX controls, 348
for applets, 349
for audio, 342, *342*
for links, 300, 324–325, *324*
for SSIs, 66, *66*
Select First Item After URL Change option, 412
Select Host window, 166, *167*

Select Image Source dialog box, 242, 277, *277*, 351

Select Inverse option, 151–152

Select menu, **73**, *73*, **151–153**, *151–152*

Select Newer Local option, 579

Select Newer Remote option, 579

Select Parent Tag option, 457, 460

Select Table option, 232, 235

Select Transparent Color option, 206

Selected Files in Site option, 260

Selected Local Files Only option, 579

Selected Remote Files Only option, 579

Selected Slices Only option, 215

selecting
database rows, **481–483**, *482*
table parts, **235**

selection tools for bitmaps, **149–151**, *149–151*

Selections: Allow Multiple property, 407

selections for bitmap masks, **158**, *158*

selective JPEG compression, 198, **209–211**, *210–211*

Selective Quality option, 211

_self target, 195, 300, 324

separator element, 523

sepia, converting to, 112

Sequential option, 615

server behaviors, 466
adding, **548–550**, *548–549*
for ColdFusion, **499–503**, *500*

Server Behaviors panel, 35, 476, *477*, **495**

Server Debug panel, 35, 463

server-side image maps, 19, 327

server-side includes (SSIs), **65–66**, *66*, 258

servers
implementing, **467–468**, *467–468*
for multimedia content, 341
remote site, **42**, *42*
testing, **445–446**
troubleshooting, **489**
for web applications, **442–443**

Service Packs, 489

services. *See* web services

Set Background Color option, 254

Set Nav Bar Image behavior, **380–382**, *381–382*

Set/Remove Breakpoint option, 462

Set Text of Frame behavior, 301, **382–383**, *383*

Set Text of Layer behavior, **383**, *383*

Set Text of Status Bar behavior, **383–384**, *384*

Set Text of Text Field behavior, **384**, *385*

SGML (Standardized General Markup Language), 514

Shadows effect, **104**, *105*

Shadows option, 154

shape of Insert bar, 33

shape tools, **122**, *122*
Ellipse, **124**
Line, **125**
Polygon, **125**
Rectangle, **123**, *123*
Rounded Rectangle, **123–124**, *124*

Share a Selected Layer feature, **81**

Sharpen Amount setting, **164**

Sharpen filters, **164**

Sharpen JPEG Edges option, 207, 209

Sharpen tool, **153–154**, *154*

Shockwave
in Assets Manager, 60
behavior for, **375–376**, *376*
uses for, **5**

shopping carts, **431–432**, *431–432*, **435–437**

shortcuts
for code, **454–456**, *455–456*
keyboard
creating, **600–602**, *600*
for file management commands, 29
list of, **625–631**

Show Dependent Files option, 344

Show Down Image Initially option, 358

Show Events For menu, 370–371, 559

Show Grid option, 241

Show Guides option, 84, 190

Show-Hide Layers behavior, **384–385**, *385*

Show Icons in Panels and Launcher option, 27

Show Log On Completion option, 255, 461, 582

Show Pop-Up Menu behavior, 181, **389–390**, *390*

Show When File Is Opened option, 583–584

Silver Connection site, 431

Simple Object Access Protocol (SOAP), **532–534**

simple rollovers, **178**, *178*

Simplify dialog box, 130

Single Layer Editing, **81**
single-line text fields, **403**
Single Table-No Spacers option, 213
Site Definition dialog box, 39–41, *39–40*
 for ASP.NET, 539
 for cloaking, 572
 for Design Notes, 583
 for links, 344
 for local folders, 444, *444*
 for testing servers, 445, *445*
Site Definition Wizard, 345
Site editor, 496
Site Files window, **474**, *474*
Site Import Export Extension, **586–587**
Site Map Layout category, 43
site maps, **8–9**, *9*, **576–577**, *576*
 initializing, **43**, *43*
 keyboard shortcuts for, **630**
 links from, **325–327**, *326*, **331**
Site Menu Commands option, 601
Site panel, 35
Site Reports panel, 35
Site Summary Reports Extension, **587–588**,
 587–588
Site Window option, 601
Site Wizard, 13
SiteOwner.com site, 427
sites, **38**
 advanced setup for, **42–43**, *42–43*
 e-commerce. *See* e-commerce sites
 exporting, **571**, *571*
 importing, **13**, **11**, *43*, *44*
 keyboard shortcuts for, **629–630**
 local folders for, **38–39**
 rolling back, **588**
 Site Setup Wizard for, **39–41**, *39–40*
 synchronizing, **579–580**, *579–580*
 updating, **589–591**, *589–591*
size
 Flash buttons, **360–361**, *361*
 frames, **297–299**, *297*
 GIF files, 282–283
 images, **278–279**, **282–283**, *283*
 text, **265**
Skew tool, 136, *137*

Slice along Guides option, 212
Slice Guides option, 193
slices, 20, 79–80, **189**, **221**, *221*
 benefits of, **190**
 exporting, **220**
 names for, **194**, *194*, 214
 from objects, **193**, *193*
 overlay color for, **193**
 Polygon Slice tool for, **192**, *192*
 previewing, **199–200**, *200–201*
 Rectangle Slice tool for, **191–192**, *192*
 ruler guides for, **190–191**
 text, **195–196**, *195*
 URLs and Alt tags for, **194–195**
 viewing, **193**
Slideshow option, 615
Smaller Photoshop File option, 217
smart clients and devices in .NET, 537
Smoothing option, 207
Smudge tool, **156**, *156*
Snap to Grid option, 241
Snap to Guides option, 191
Snippet dialog box, 456, *456*
snippets, **455–456**, *456*
Snippets panel, 34
SOAP (Simple Object Access Protocol), **532–534**
Source Code mode, 272
Source Code option, 458
source paths to images, 279
sources for databases, **471–472**, *471*
SourceSafe Database option, 444
spacers in tables, **235–236**, *236*
spaces in names, 39
spacing in CSS, 313
special characters
 inserting, **257–258**, *259*
 in names, 39
Specific Tag mode, 272
Specified Tag option, 458
spell checking, 139, **259**, *259*
spiders, 301
.spl extension, 375
Splat! plugin, 75, **166–169**, *167–169*
Split option for paths, 134
Split Frame options, 293

SQL
    creating tables in, **480**
    indexes in, **481**
    rows in
        deleting, **483–484**
        inserting, **483**
        selecting, in, **481–483**, *482*
SQL Server databases, 469
Src property, 408
SSIs (server-side includes), **65–66**, *66*, 258
SSL (Secure Sockets Layer) encryption, 433, 549
standard mode, 28
Standard View, tables in, **231–232**, *232*
Standardized General Markup Language
    (SGML), 514
standards
    accessibility, **569–570**, *570*
    for browser compatibility, **565**
star shape, drawing, 125
Start Recording option, 604
start_string attribute, 518
starting points, online resources for, **622**
status bar, **27**
    in Fireworks, **77**
    text of, **383–384**, *384*
Step In option, 462
Step Out option, 462
Step Over option, 462
Stop Debugging option, 462
Stop Timeline behavior, **388**, *388*
stored procedures, **486–487**
storyboards, **9–10**, *10*
streamed files, 339
strict XHTML doctype, 520
strikethrough text, 263
string-delimited tags, 517
Stroke Category menu, 86–87, *86*
Stroke Options dialog box, 90
strokes, **85–86**
    adding, **87–88**
    for dashed lines, **91–93**, *92*
    options for, **86–87**, *86–87*
    preset, **88–89**, *89*, **91**, *91*
    saving as styles, **93**

texture for, **94–96**, *94–96*
    tip options for, **90**
Strong option, 264
structural tags, 263
Style Definition dialog box, 315
Style/Format extension category, 596
style sheets. *See* CSS (Cascading Style Sheets)
styles
    in Fireworks, **106–107**, *106*
    HTML, 34, **268–269**, *268–269*
    saving strokes as, **93**
    workspace, **36**
Styles Options menu, 93
Styles panel, 79, **106–107**, *106*
Submit Extension option, 600
Submit It! Free service, 427
Subselection tool, 123
Swap Image action, 357
Swap Image dialog box, 180, *180*, **385–386**, *386*
Swap Image Restore behavior, **385–386**
swapped images, 178
Swatches Options menu, 109–110
Swatches panel, 78, **109–110**, *109*
.swf extension, 375
Symbol Properties dialog box, 172, 175
symbols, **172–174**, *173*
    buttons, **174–177**, *175*, *177*
    instances, **173**
synchronization
    cloaking for, **572–573**, *572*
    for importing, 43, *44*
    for links, 333, *333*
    local and remote sites, **579–580**, *579–580*
    to remote server, **573**, *573*
Synchronize dialog box, 580, *580*
Synchronize Files dialog box, 43, *44*, 333, *333*,
    573, *573*, 579, *579*
Syntax Coloring option, 449

T

tab-delimited file, 256
Table Borders option, 235
Table tab, **213**, *214*

tables, **16–18**, *17*, **227**
    adding, **249**, *249*
    alignment in, **239**
    color in, **238–239**, *238*
    columns in, 232, *232*, **237–238**
    database. *See* databases
    importing, **253–256**, *254–256*
    keyboard shortcuts for, **627–628**
    with layers, **245–247**, *246*
    in Layout View, **233–234**, *233–234*
    nesting, **239–240**, *239–240*
    preset format for, **230–231**, *231*
    Property Inspector for, 234, **237–238**, *238*
    rows in, 232, *232*, **237–238**
    selecting parts of, **235**
    spacers in, **235–236**, *236*
    SQL, **480**
    in Standard View, **231–232**, *232*
Tables extension category, 596
Tables tab, 32
Tag Chooser, **455**, *455*
Tag Editors, 455, **457**, **494**
Tag Inspector, 34, **457–458**, *457–458*
Tag Library Editor dialog box, 452–453, *452–453*
tag_name attribute, 518
Tag option, 244
tag selectors, 27, 309
tag_type attribute, 518
tags
    balancing, **460**
    custom, **453**, *453*
    hidden, **410–411**
    inserting, **455**, *455*
    libraries for, **451–453**, *451–453*
    in XML, 512, **517–519**, *519*
target audiences, **558**
Target Browser Check panel, 35
target pages for forms, **416–417**, *417*
targets in frames, 195, **300**, *300*, **305**, 324
Teletype option, 264
templates, **45–47**, *46*
    applying, **56–57**, *57*
    in Assets Manager, 60
    based on templates, **55–56**
    behaviors for, **52**, **58–59**

    closing and reopening, **55**
    content in, **51**, **585**
    correcting, **589–590**, *589–590*
    creating, **48–50**, *49–50*
    default, **602–603**, *603*
    detaching, **58**
    in development process, **48**
    documenting design in, **51**
    Dreamweaver 4, **59**
    editing, **58**
    from existing pages, **50–51**
    extensions in, **52**
    for layout, **228–229**, *230*
    links to, **55**
    for maintenance, 574
    meta tag information in, **52**, *52*
    online resources for, **623**
    parameters in, **51**
    regions in
        editable, **53**, *53*
        relocking, **54**
        repeating and optional, 46–47, **53–54**
    saving frames as, 294
    updating pages linked to, **59**
    for XML, **514–517**, *515–517*
Templates folder, 55
Templates For setting, 56
Templates tab, 32
testing
    browser compatibility, **559–564**
    Flash buttons, **361**, *361*
    links, **331–332**, *332*
    QA, **568–569**
    usability, **568**
    user-acceptance, **569**
Testing Server category, 42
Testing Server screen, 539, *539*
testing servers, **445–446**, 539, *539*
text, **12–13**, *12*, **251**
    converting to paths, **139–140**, *140*
    cutting from images, **141–142**, *141–142*
    design considerations for, **15–16**
    dynamic, **475**
    editing, **259**
    entering, **256–258**, *257–258*

find and replace for, **260–262**, *260–261*
Flash, **394–395**, *394*
for Flash buttons, **361–362**, *361*
formatting. *See* formatting
of frames, **382–383**, *383*
HTML, **270–272**, *271*, *273*
importing, **253–256**, *254–256*
inserting, **252**, *253*
keyboard shortcuts for, **627**
of layers, **383**, *383*
for links, 321
organizing, **252**
in persistent page elements, **258–259**
slices, **195–196**, *195*
spell checking, 139, **259**, *259*
of status bar, **383–384**, *384*
of text fields, **384**, *385*
Text (Advanced) mode, 272, 458
Text Editor, 74
Text extension category, 596
text fields, **401–402**, *402*
multiline, **403**, *403*
password, **403–404**
single-line, **403**
text of, **384**, *385*
Text menu, **74**, *74*
Text tab, 32
Text tool, **138**
for converting text to paths, **139–140**, *140*
for cutting text from images, **141–142**, *141–142*
for inset paths, **140–141**, *140–141*
with Property Inspector, **138–139**, *139*
Texture Name setting, 86
textures
fills with, **97–98**
for strokes, 86, **94–96**, *94–96*
third-party items
bitmap plugins, **166–169**
extensions, **623**
XML tags, **517–519**, *519*
Threshold setting, **164**
thumbnails, **8–9**, *9*
timelines
behaviors in

adding, **397–398**, *397*
Go to Timeline Frame, **386–387**, *387*
Play Timeline, **387–388**, *388*
Stop Timeline, **388**, *388*
working with, **391–393**, *391*
frames in, **397**, *397*
layers in, **396**, *397*
Tip Size setting, 86
title bar
in Document window, **26–27**, *26*
in Fireworks, **71**, *71*
Title field, **28**
Toolbars, **27**
Code Navigation menu, **31**
File Management menu, **29**
in Fireworks, **75**, *75*
Preview/Debug menu, **29–30**
Refresh button, **31**
Title field, **28**
View Options menu, **31**
views, **28**
Tools panel, **76**, **149**, *149*
_top target, 195, 300, 324
tracing images, **242**, **247–248**, *247*
transactions
credit card payments, **432–435**, *433*
online catalogs for, **428–430**, *429–430*
shopping carts for, **431–432**, *431–432*,
435–437
transformations for vectors, **136–137**, *137*
transitional XHTML doctype, 520
transparency
in GIF compression, **205–206**, *206*
in gradient fills, **102**
in vector masks, **162–163**, *162*
Trim Canvas option, 111, 137
Trim Images option, 219
troubleshooting
backups for, **490**
databases, **490**
jump menus, **364**
servers, **489**
trust for e-commerce sites, 422
tutorials, **623–624**
Twist and Fade command, **113**, *113*

2-Up view, **199**
Type property
 for forms, 402
 for List/Menu selections, 406
type style for e-commerce sites, **423–425**, *423–425*

U

UAs (user agents), 309
UDDI (Universal Description, Discovery, and Integration Service), 532, **534**
Ultraweaver site, 115
Uncloak option, 346, 572
undocking panels, **37**, *37*
Ungroup option, 140, 162
unified core classes in .NET, 537
Uniform palette, 202
Union option for paths, **134**, *134*
unique strokes, **95–96**, *95–96*
unique usernames, **549–550**, *549*
units
 for frames, 297
 for layers, **244**
Universal Description, Discovery, and Integration Service (UDDI), 532, **534**
unordered lists, 266
Unsharp Mask dialog box, 164
Up button state, 174
Update All Images option, 615
Update Automatically on Save option, 258
Update Current Page option, 58, 65
Update Files dialog box, 330, *330*
Update Pages dialog box, 65, *65*
updating
 dialog boxes, **612–613**, *613*
 from library item changes, **65**
 links, **330–331**, *330–331*, **333**, *333*
 pages linked to templates, **59**
 sites, **589**
  content, **590**, *590*
  links, **591**, *591*
  navigation, **591**, *591*
 templates, **589–590**, *589–590*
Upload Design Notes for Sharing option, 583

uploaded files, 405
URL panel, 79
URL Prefix option, 446
URLs
 in Assets Manager, 60
 behavior for, **377**, *377*
 in Favorites view, 62
 for slices, **194–195**
usability testing, **568**
Use CSS Selector option, 312
Use Editable Region Names as XML Tags option, 516
Use Entire Document option, 156
Use Regular Expressions option, 261, 458
Use Standard Dreamweaver XML Tags option, 516
Use Transparent GIFs option, 246
user-acceptance testing, **569**
user administration, **546**
 for privileges, **546–547**
 for registration forms, **547–548**
 for server behaviors, **548–550**, *548–549*
user agents (UAs), 309
usernames, **549–551**, *549*
UTF-8 Coding option, 214

V

Validate Form behavior, **388–389**, *389*
Validate Markup option, 461
validating
 code, **461**, *461*
 forms, **388–389**, *389*
 XML and XHTML documents, **522–523**
Validation panel, 35
Validator Options dialog box, 522–523
Validator Preferences dialog box, 522–523
Value property, 409
variable list pane, 463
Variable option, 264
VBScript server model, 445
vector masks, **161–163**, *161–162*
Vector Path tool, **126**
vectors, **121**
 for aligning objects, **137–138**, *138*

Crop tool for, **137**, *137*
drawing tools for
   Pen, **126**
   Vector Path, **126**
  editing
    with control handles, **127–128**, *127–128*
    with freeform editing tools, **130–133**,
     130–133
    with Pen tool, **128–130**
  exporting objects as, **217–218**, *217–218*
  miscellaneous actions for, **135–136**
  for navigational elements, **143–145**, *143–145*
  path operations for, **133–135**, *134–135*
  shape tools for, **122**, *122*
    Ellipse, **124**
    Line, **125**
    Polygon, **125**
    Rectangle, **123**, *123*
    Rounded Rectangle, **123–124**, *124*
  Text tool for, **138–142**, *139–142*
  transformations for, **136–137**, *137*
versions, browser, 374, **564**
vertical portals, 554
vertical space setting for images, 280
Vertical Text option, 139
video formats, **340**
view area, **27**
View menu, **72**, *72*
View Options menu, **31**
viewing slices, **193**
views
  keyboard shortcuts for, **626**
  Toolbar for, **28**
Vis option, 243
VSPACE attribute, 280

W

W property for images, 407
WA PayPal eCommerce Toolkit extension, 435
WAI (Web Accessibility Initiative), 7
Warn When Fixing or removing Tags option, 581
WAV (Waveform) format, 339
Web 216 palette, 202
Web Accessibility In Mind (WebAIM) site, 7

Web Accessibility Initiative (WAI), 7
web applications, **441**
  code. *See* code
  database connections for, **446**
  local folders for, **443–444**, *444*
  remote folders for, **444–445**, *444*
  servers for, **442–443**
  supported server model for, **442**
  testing servers for, **445–446**
Web Design Group, 310
Web Dither dialog box, 108, *108*
Web dithering, **107–108**, *108*
Web Kitchen extension, 588
Web layers, **79–80**
Web-safe colors, 107, 196
Web servers. *See* servers
Web Service Chooser dialog box, 536
web services, **531–532**
  accessing, **532**
  adding, **534–537**, *534–536*
  SOAP, **533–534**
  UDDI, **534**
  WSDL, **533**
Web Services Description Language (WSDL),
  532–533
Web Standards Project site, 310
WebAIM (Web Accessibility In Mind) site, 7
WebDAV option, 444
WebMonkey site, 310
WebSnap Adaptive palette, 202
well-formed XML documents, 513
Wells Fargo Bank site, 433
WHERE clause, 482, 484
White pages, 534
width
  of frames, **297–298**, *297*
  in tables, 232
Window menu, **75**, *75*
windows, opening, **378–379**, *378*
Windows Media format, 340
Windows Media Player, **340–341**
Windows palette, 202
wireframes, **9–10**, *10*
Word documents, **253–256**, *254–256*
Word Wrap option, 449

workflow
Check In/Check Out for, **584–585**
Design Notes for, **582–584**, *583–584*
workspace, **21**, **36**
docking and undocking panels, **37**, *37*
in Fireworks, **70–71**, *70–71*
hiding panels, **36–37**, *36–37*
integrated, **22–23**, *22–23*
style of, **36**
Workspace Setup dialog box, 36
Wrap property, 402
Wrap Tag mode, 271
WSDL (Web Services Description Language),
532–533

X

XHTML (Extensible Hypertext Markup Language)
support for, **520–522**
validation in, **522–523**
XMethods registry, 532

XML (Extensible Markup Language), **509**
concepts in, **510–514**, *513*
custom tags in, **517–519**, *519*
exporting sites as, **571**, *571*
importance of, **529**
importing and exporting, **514–517**, *515–517*
menus for, **523–528**, *528*
support for, 558
validation in, **522–523**
XML Web Services, 537
XSLT (Extensible Style Language
Transformations) style sheets, 513

Y

Yahoo! Store, 434
Yellow pages, 534

Z

Z-Index option, 243
Zeldman, Jeffrey, 310

Final Cut Pro 3 and the Art of Filmmaking

by Jason Cranford Teague
and David Teague
ISBN: 0-7821- 4027-0
US $60

Despite its intuitive interface, Final Cut Pro still requires craft and skill to use well. This full-color book provides a hands-on, practical guide to all aspects of editing digital movies, with an emphasis on the kinds of tips, tricks, and shortcuts that professionals rely on to quickly get polished results.

In the course of this book, you'll learn shooting tips designed to help later in the edit room. You'll also hear from experienced editors on how they're using Final Cut Pro to capture the immediacy that digital video makes possible, while meeting the twin challenges of limited time and money.

Final Cut Pro 3 and the Art of Filmmaking gives you the insights, information, and lessons you'll need to complete tasks that film editors face every day, including:

- Mastering Final Cut Pro 3's new features, such as Voice Over, G4 Real-Time Effects, Titling, QuickView, and more

- Editing clips in the Timeline

- Creating transitions and complex overlays

- Adding effects, applying filters, and working with text

- Using the audio tools to make your film sound as good as it looks

- Readying your finished product for delivery–on the Internet, on videotape, or on DVD

www.sybex.com

TELL US WHAT YOU THINK!

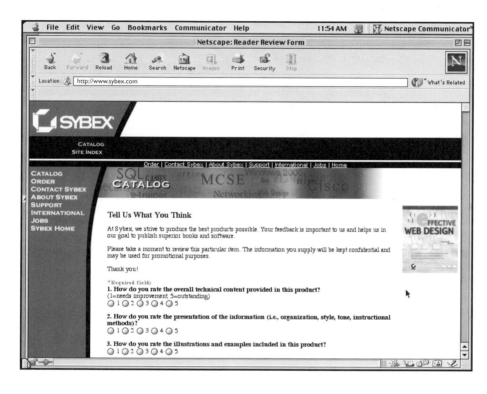

Your feedback is critical to our efforts to provide you with the best books and software on the market. Tell us what you think about the products you've purchased. It's simple:

1. Visit the Sybex website
2. Go to the product page
3. Click on **Submit a Review**
4. Fill out the questionnaire and comments
5. Click **Submit**

With your feedback, we can continue to publish the highest quality computer books and software products that today's busy IT professionals deserve.

www.sybex.com

SYBEX Inc. • 1151 Marina Village Parkway, Alameda, CA 94501 • 510-523-8233

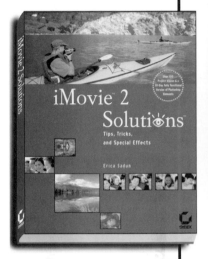
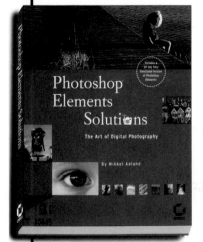

ABOUT SYBEX

Sybex has been part of the personal computer revolution from the very beginning. We were founded in 1976 by Dr. Rodnay Zaks, an early innovator of the microprocessor era and the company's president to this day. Dr. Zaks was involved in the ARPAnet and developed the first published industrial application of a microcomputer system: an urban traffic control system.

While lecturing on a variety of technical topics in the mid-1970s, Dr. Zaks realized there wasn't much available in the way of accessible documentation for engineers, programmers, and businesses. Starting with books based on his own lectures, he launched Sybex simultaneously in his adopted home of Berkeley, California, and in his original home of Paris, France.

Over the years, Sybex has been an innovator in many fields of computer publishing, documenting the first word processors in the early 1980s and the rise of the Internet in the early 1990s. In the late 1980s, Sybex began publishing our first desktop publishing and graphics books. As early adopters ourselves, we began desktop publishing our books in-house at the same time.

Now, in our third decade, we publish dozens of books each year on topics related to graphics, web design, digital photography, and digital video. We also continue to explore new technologies and over the last few years have been among the first to publish on topics like Maya and Photoshop Elements.

With each book, our goal remains the same: to provide clear, readable, skill-building information, written by the best authors in the field—experts who know their topics as well as they know their audience.

What's on the *Dreamweaver MX/Fireworks MX Savvy* CD

The CD that accompanies this book runs on all Windows and Macintosh operating systems and is chock-full o' digital freebies, samples, and projects.

To install the demos you want from the CD easily, just use the disc's interface. You can also access any of the folders and files directly through the Windows Explorer or Macintosh Finder interface.

Here are the types of useful material you will find on this CD:

Tutorials

Many of the tutorials in this book require the use of the files supplied on this CD (which are also available on the book's website at http://dreamweaverfireworkssavvy.com/ or http://dreamweaversavvy.com/). To try out a tutorial, copy the files from the appropriate chapter to a new folder on your own computer or network, and then follow the steps of the tutorial. (We'll point you to the CD in the text and with this CD icon when you need those files.)

Demo Software

The CD includes demo software for evaluation purposes. You will find a time-limited trial of the Macromedia Studio MX suite (including Dreamweaver MX, Fireworks MX, Flash MX and Freehand, as well as ColdFusion MX Server for Windows users), and Alien Skin Software's Splat! (which is referred to in the Fireworks section of this book).

Dreamweaver MX Extensions

In the final chapter of this book, you'll learn how to enrich the capabilities of Dreamweaver with extensions. Several members of the active extension developer community have contributed extensions to the CD. These include a drop-down menu builder, a DHTML slide show maker, conditional frameset content, a Macromedia-approved "close browser window" link, and more.

Web Resources

The CD also provides links to websites that offer useful Dreamweaver and Fireworks resources.